Data Science Programming

ALL-IN-ONE

by John Paul Mueller and
Luca Massaron

A Wiley Brand

Data Science Programming All-in-One For Dummies®

Published by: **John Wiley & Sons, Inc.**, 111 River Street, Hoboken, NJ 07030-5774, www.wiley.com

Copyright © 2020 by John Wiley & Sons, Inc., Hoboken, New Jersey

Published simultaneously in Canada

For general information on our other products and services, please contact our Customer Care Department within the U.S. at 877-762-2974, outside the U.S. at 317-572-3993, or fax 317-572-4002. For technical support, please visit https://hub.wiley.com/community/support/dummies.

Wiley publishes in a variety of print and electronic formats and by print-on-demand. Some material included with standard print versions of this book may not be included in e-books or in print-on-demand. If this book refers to media such as a CD or DVD that is not included in the version you purchased, you may download this material at http://booksupport.wiley.com. For more information about Wiley products, visit www.wiley.com.

Library of Congress Control Number: 2019954497

ISBN 978-1-119-62611-4; ISBN 978-1-119-62613-8 (ebk); ISBN 978-1-119-62614-5 (ebk)

Manufactured in the United States of America

SKY10075966_052424

Contents at a Glance

Table of Contents

Introduction

Data science is a term that the media has chosen to minimize, obfuscate, and sometimes misuse. It involves a lot more than just data and the science of working with data. Today, the world uses data science in all sorts of ways that you might not know about, which is why you need *Data Science Programming All-in-One For Dummies*.

In the book, you start with both the data and the science of manipulating it, but then you go much further. In addition to seeing how to perform a wide range of analysis, you also delve into making recommendations, classifying real-world objects, analyzing audio, and even creating art.

However, you don't just learn about amazing new technologies and how to perform common tasks. This book also dispels myths created by people who wish data science were something different than it really is or who don't understand it at all. A great deal of misinformation swirls around the world today as the media seeks to sensationalize, anthropomorphize, and emotionalize technologies that are, in fact, quite mundane. It's hard to know what to believe. You find reports that robots are on the cusp of becoming sentient and that the giant tech companies can discover your innermost thoughts simply by reviewing your record of purchases. With this book, you can replace disinformation with solid facts, and you can use those facts to create a strategy for performing data science development tasks.

About This Book

You might find that this book starts off a little slowly because most people don't have a good grasp on getting a system prepared for data science use. Book 1 helps you configure your system. The book uses Jupyter Notebook as an Integrated Development Environment (IDE) for both Python and R. That way, if you choose to view the examples in both languages, you use the same IDE to do it. Jupyter Notebook also relies on the literate programming strategy first proposed by Donald Knuth (see http://www.literateprogramming.com/) to make your coding efforts significantly easier and more focused on the data. In addition, in contrast to other environments, you don't actually write entire applications before you see something; you write code and focus on the results of just that code block as part of a whole application.

After you have a development environment installed and ready to use, you can start working with data in all its myriad forms in Book 2. This book covers a great many of these forms — everything from in-memory datasets to those found on large websites. In addition, you see a number of data formats ranging from flat files to Relational Database Management Systems (RDBMSs) and Not Only SQL (NoSQL) databases.

Of course, manipulating data is worthwhile only if you can do something useful with it. Book 3 discusses common sorts of analysis, such as linear and logistic regression, Bayes' Theorem, and K-Nearest Neighbors (KNN).

Most data science books stop at this point. In this book, however, you discover AI, machine learning, and deep learning techniques to get more out of your data than you might have thought possible. This exciting part of the book, Book 4, represents the cutting edge of analysis. You use huge datasets to discover important information about large groups of people that will help you improve their health or sell them products.

Performing analysis may be interesting, but analysis is only a step along the path. Book 5 shows you how to put your analysis to use in recommender systems, to classify objects, work with nontextual data like music and video, and display the results of an analysis in a form that everyone can appreciate.

The final minibook, Book 6, offers something you won't find in many places, not even online. You discover how to detect and fix problems with your data, the logic used to interpret the data, and the code used to perform tasks such as analysis. By the time you complete Book 6, you'll know much more about how to ensure that the results you get are actually the results you need and want.

To make absorbing the concepts easy, this book uses the following conventions:

» Text that you're meant to type just as it appears in the book is in **bold**. The exception is when you're working through a step list: Because each step is bold, the text to type is not bold.

» When you see words in *italics* as part of a typing sequence, you need to replace that value with something that works for you. For example, if you see "Type ***Your Name*** and press Enter," you need to replace *Your Name* with your actual name.

» Web addresses and programming code appear in monofont. If you're reading a digital version of this book on a device connected to the Internet, you can click or tap the web address to visit that website, like this: https://www.dummies.com.

» When you need to type command sequences, you see them separated by a special arrow, like this: File ⇨ New File. In this example, you go to the File menu first and then select the New File entry on that menu.

Foolish Assumptions

You might find it difficult to believe that we've assumed anything about you — after all; we haven't even met you yet! Although most assumptions are indeed foolish, we made these assumptions to provide a starting point for the book.

You need to be familiar with the platform you want to use because the book doesn't offer any guidance in this regard. (Book 1, Chapter 3 does, however, provide Anaconda installation instructions for both Python and R, and Book 1, Chapter 5 helps you install the TensorFlow and Keras frameworks used for this book.) To give you the maximum information about Python concerning how it applies to deep learning, this book doesn't discuss any platform-specific issues. You see the R version of the Python coding examples in the downloadable source, along with R-specific notes on usage and development. You really do need to know how to install applications, use applications, and generally work with your chosen platform before you begin working with this book.

You must know how to work with Python or R. You can find a wealth of Python tutorials online (see `https://www.w3schools.com/python/` and `https://www.tutorialspoint.com/python/` as examples). R, likewise, provides a wealth of online tutorials (see `https://www.tutorialspoint.com/r/index.htm`, `https://docs.anaconda.com/anaconda/navigator/tutorials/r-lang/`, and `https://www.statmethods.net/r-tutorial/index.html` as examples).

This book isn't a math primer. Yes, you see many examples of complex math, but the emphasis is on helping you use Python or R to perform data science development tasks rather than teaching math theory. We include some examples that also discuss the use of technologies such as data management (see Book 2), statistical analysis (see Book 3), AI, machine learning, deep learning (see Book 4), practical data science application (see Book 5), and troubleshooting both data and code (see Book 6). Book 1, Chapters 1 and 2 give you a better understanding of precisely what you need to know to use this book successfully. You also use a considerable number of libraries in writing code for this book. Book 1, Chapter 4 discusses library use and suggests other libraries that you might want to try.

This book also assumes that you can access items on the Internet. Sprinkled throughout are numerous references to online material that will enhance your learning experience. However, these added sources are useful only if you actually find and use them.

Icons Used in This Book

As you read this book, you see icons in the margins that indicate material of interest (or not, as the case may be). This section briefly describes each icon in this book.

TIP

Tips are nice because they help you save time or perform some task without a lot of extra work. The tips in this book are time-saving techniques or pointers to resources that you should try so that you can get the maximum benefit from Python or R, or from performing deep learning–related tasks. (Note that R developers will also find copious notes in the source code files for issues that differ significantly from Python.)

WARNING

We don't want to sound like angry parents or some kind of maniacs, but you should avoid doing anything that's marked with a Warning icon. Otherwise, you might find that your application fails to work as expected, you get incorrect answers from seemingly bulletproof algorithms, or (in the worst-case scenario) you lose data.

TECHNICAL STUFF

Whenever you see this icon, think advanced tip or technique. You might find these tidbits of useful information just too boring for words, or they could contain the solution you need to get a program running. Skip these bits of information whenever you like.

REMEMBER

If you don't get anything else out of a particular chapter or section, remember the material marked by this icon. This text usually contains an essential process or a bit of information that you must know to work with Python or R, or to perform deep learning–related tasks successfully. (Note that the R source code files contain a great deal of text that gives essential details for working with R when R differs considerably from Python.)

Beyond the Book

This book isn't the end of your Python or R data science development experience — it's really just the beginning. We provide online content to make this book more flexible and better able to meet your needs. That way, as we receive email from you, we can address questions and tell you how updates to Python, R, or their associated add-ons affect book content. In fact, you gain access to all these cool additions:

- » **Cheat sheet:** You remember using crib notes in school to make a better mark on a test, don't you? You do? Well, a cheat sheet is sort of like that. It provides you with some special notes about tasks that you can do with Python and R with regard to data science development that not every other person knows. You can find the cheat sheet by going to www.dummies.com, searching this book's title, and scrolling down the page that appears. The cheat sheet contains really neat information, such as the most common data errors that cause people problems with working in the data science field.

- » **Updates:** Sometimes changes happen. For example, we might not have seen an upcoming change when we looked into our crystal ball during the writing of this book. In the past, this possibility simply meant that the book became outdated and less useful, but you can now find updates to the book, if we have any, by searching this book's title at www.dummies.com.

  In addition to these updates, check out the blog posts with answers to reader questions and demonstrations of useful, book-related techniques at http://blog.johnmuellerbooks.com/.

- » **Companion files:** Hey! Who really wants to type all the code in the book and reconstruct all those neural networks manually? Most readers prefer to spend their time actually working with data and seeing the interesting things they can do, rather than typing. Fortunately for you, the examples used in the book are available for download, so all you need to do is read the book to learn Python or R data science programming techniques. You can find these files at www.dummies.com. Search this book's title, and on the page that appears, scroll down to the image of the book cover and click it. Then click the More about This Book button and on the page that opens, go to the Downloads tab.

Where to Go from Here

It's time to start your Python or R for data science programming adventure! If you're completely new to Python or R and its use for data science tasks, you should start with Book 1, Chapter 1. Progressing through the book at a pace that allows you to absorb as much of the material as possible makes it feasible for you to gain insights that you might not otherwise gain if you read the chapters in a random order. However, the book is designed to allow you to read the material in any order desired.

If you're a novice who's in an absolute rush to get going with Python or R for data science programming as quickly as possible, you can skip to Book 1, Chapter 3 with the understanding that you may find some topics a bit confusing later. Skipping to Book 1, Chapter 5 is okay if you already have Anaconda (the programming product used in the book) installed with the appropriate language (Python or R as you desire), but be sure to at least skim Chapter 3 so that you know what assumptions we made when writing this book.

This book relies on a combination of TensorFlow and Keras to perform deep learning tasks. Even if you're an advanced reader who wants to perform deep learning tasks, you need to go to Book 1, Chapter 5 to discover how to configure the environment used for this book. You must configure the environment according to instructions or you're likely to experience failures when you try to run the code. However, this issue applies only to deep learning. This book has a great deal to offer in other areas, such as data manipulation and statistical analysis.

1
Defining Data Science

Contents at a Glance

Chapter **1**

Considering the History and Uses of Data Science

The burgeoning uses for data in the world today, along with the explosion of data sources, create a demand for people who have special skills to obtain, manage, and analyze information for the benefit of everyone. The data scientist develops and hones these special skills to perform such tasks on multiple levels, as described in the first two sections of this chapter.

Data needs to be funneled into acceptable forms that allow data scientists to perform their tasks. Even though the precise data flow varies, you can generalize it to a degree. The third section of the chapter gives you an overview of how data flow occurs.

As with anyone engaged in computer work today, a data scientist employs various programming languages to express the manipulation of data in a repeatable manner. The languages that a data scientist uses, however, focus on outputs expected from given inputs, rather than on low-level control or a precise procedure, as a computer scientist would use. Because a data scientist may lack a formal programming education, the languages tend to focus on declarative strategies, with the data scientist expressing a desired outcome rather than devising a specific procedure. The fourth section of the chapter discusses various languages used by data scientists, with an emphasis on Python and R.

The final section of the chapter provides a very quick overview of getting tasks done quickly. Optimization without loss of precision is an incredibly difficult task and you see it covered a number of times in this book, but this introduction is enough to get you started. The overall goal of this first chapter is to describe data science and explain how a data scientist uses algorithms, statistics, data extraction, data manipulation, and a slew of other technologies to employ it as part of an analysis.

REMEMBER

You don't have to type the source code for this chapter manually (or, actually at all, given that you use it only to obtain an understanding of the data flow process). In fact, using the downloadable source is a lot easier. The source code for this chapter appears in the DSPD_0101_Quick_Overview.ipynb source code file for Python. See the Introduction for details on how to find these source files.

Considering the Elements of Data Science

At one point, the world viewed anyone working with statistics as a sort of accountant or perhaps a mad scientist. Many people consider statistics and the analysis of data boring. However, data science is one of those occupations in which the more you learn, the more you want to learn. Answering one question often spawns more questions that are even more interesting than the one you just answered. However, what makes data science so sexy is that you see it everywhere, used in an almost infinite number of ways. The following sections give you more details on why data science is such an amazing field of study.

Considering the emergence of data science

Data science is a relatively new term. William S. Cleveland coined the term in 2001 as part of a paper entitled "Data Science: An Action Plan for Expanding the Technical Areas of the Field of Statistics." It wasn't until a year later that the International Council for Science actually recognized data science and created a committee for it. Columbia University got into the act in 2003 by beginning publication of the *Journal of Data Science.*

REMEMBER

However, the mathematical basis behind data science is centuries old because data science is essentially a method of viewing and analyzing statistics and probability. The first essential use of statistics as a term comes in 1749, but statistics are certainly much older than that. People have used statistics to recognize patterns for thousands of years. For example, the historian Thucydides (in his History of the Peloponnesian War) describes how the Athenians calculated the height of the wall of Platea in fifth century BC by counting bricks in an unplastered section of the wall. Because the count needed to be accurate, the Athenians took the average of the count by several solders.

The process of quantifying and understanding statistics is relatively new, but the science itself is quite old. An early attempt to begin documenting the importance of statistics appears in the ninth century, when Al-Kindi wrote *Manuscript on Deciphering Cryptographic Messages.* In this paper, Al-Kindi describes how to use a combination of statistics and frequency analysis to decipher encrypted messages. Even in the beginning, statistics saw use in the practical application of science for tasks that seemed virtually impossible to complete. Data science continues this process, and to some people it might actually seem like magic.

Outlining the core competencies of a data scientist

As is true of anyone performing most complex trades today, the data scientist requires knowledge of a broad range of skills to perform the required tasks. In fact, so many different skills are required that data scientists often work in teams. Someone who is good at gathering data might team up with an analyst and someone gifted in presenting information. Finding a single person who possesses all the required skills would be hard. With this in mind, the following list describes areas in which a data scientist can excel (with more competencies being better):

>> **Data capture:** It doesn't matter what sort of math skills you have if you can't obtain data to analyze in the first place. The act of capturing data begins by managing a data source using database-management skills. However, raw data isn't particularly useful in many situations; you must also understand the data domain so that you can look at the data and begin formulating the sorts of questions to ask. Finally, you must have data-modeling skills so that you understand how the data is connected and whether the data is structured.

>> **Analysis:** After you have data to work with and understand the complexities of that data, you can begin to perform an analysis on it. You perform some analysis using basic statistical tool skills, much like those that just about everyone learns in college. However, the use of specialized math tricks and algorithms can make patterns in the data more obvious or help you draw conclusions that you can't draw by reviewing the data alone.

>> **Presentation:** Most people don't understand numbers well. They can't see the patterns that the data scientist sees. Providing a graphical presentation of these patterns is important to help others visualize what the numbers mean and how to apply them in a meaningful way. More important, the presentation must tell a specific story so that the impact of the data isn't lost.

Linking data science, big data, and AI

Interestingly enough, the act of moving data around so that someone can perform analysis on it is a specialty called Extract, Transform, and Load (ETL). The ETL specialist uses programming languages such as Python to extract the data from a number of sources. Corporations tend not to keep data in one easily accessed location, so finding the data required to perform analysis takes time. After the ETL specialist finds the data, a programming language or other tool transforms it into a common format for analysis purposes. The loading process takes many forms, but this book relies on Python to perform the task. In a large, real-world operation, you might find yourself using tools such as Informatica, MS SSIS, or Teradata to perform the task.

REMEMBER

Data science isn't necessarily a means to an end; it may instead be a step along the way. As a data scientist works through various datasets and finds interesting facts, these facts may act as input for other sorts of analysis and AI applications. For example, consider that your shopping habits often suggest what books you might like or where you might like to go for a vacation. Shopping or other habits can also help others understand other, sometimes less benign, activities as well. *Machine Learning For Dummies* and *Artificial Intelligence For Dummies*, both by John Paul Mueller and Luca Massaron (Wiley), help you understand these other uses of data science. For now, consider the fact that what you learn in this book can have a definite effect on a career path that will go many other places.

Understanding the role of programming

A data scientist may need to know several programming languages in order to achieve specific goals. For example, you may need SQL knowledge to extract data from relational databases. Python can help you perform data loading, transformation, and analysis tasks. However, you might choose a product such as MATLAB (which has its own programming language) or PowerPoint (which relies on VBA) to present the information to others. (If you're interested to see how MATLAB compares to the use of Python, you can get the book, *MATLAB For Dummies,* by John Paul Mueller [Wiley].) The immense datasets that data scientists rely on often require multiple levels of redundant processing to transform into useful processed data. Manually performing these tasks is time consuming and error prone, so programming presents the best method for achieving the goal of a coherent, usable data source.

Given the number of products that most data scientists use, sticking to just one programming language may not be possible. Yes, Python can load data, transform it, analyze it, and even present it to the end user, but the process works only when the language provides the required functionality. You may have to choose other languages to fill out your toolkit. The languages you choose depend on a number of criteria. Here are some criteria you should consider:

>> How you intend to use data science in your code (you have a number of tasks to consider, such as data analysis, classification, and regression)

>> Your familiarity with the language

>> The need to interact with other languages

>> The availability of tools to enhance the development environment

>> The availability of APIs and libraries to make performing tasks easier

Defining the Role of Data in the World

This section of the chapter is too short. It can't even begin to describe the ways in which data will affect you in the future. Consider the following subsections as offering tantalizing tidbits —appetizers that can whet your appetite for exploring the world of data and data science further. The applications listed in these sections are already common in some settings. You probably used at least one of them today, and quite likely more than just one. After reading the following sections, you might want to take the time to consider all the ways in which data currently affects your life. The use of data to perform amazing feats is really just the beginning. Humanity is at the cusp of an event that will rival the Industrial Revolution (see https://www.history.com/topics/industrial-revolution/industrial-revolution), and the use of data (and its associated technologies, such as AI, machine learning, and deep learning) is actually quite immature at this point.

Enticing people to buy products

Demographics, those vital or social statistics that group people by certain characteristics, have always been part art and part science. You can find any number of articles about getting your computer to generate demographics for clients (or potential clients). The use of demographics is wide ranging, but you see them used for things like predicting which product a particular group will buy (versus that of the competition). Demographics are an important means of categorizing people and then predicting some action on their part based on their group associations. Here are the methods that you often see cited for AIs when gathering demographics:

>> **Historical:** Based on previous actions, an AI generalizes which actions you might perform in the future.

>> **Current activity:** Based on the action you perform now and perhaps other characteristics, such as gender, a computer predicts your next action.

>> **Characteristics:** Based on the properties that define you, such as gender, age, and area where you live, a computer predicts the choices you are likely to make.

WARNING

You can find articles about AI's predictive capabilities that seem almost too good to be true. For example, the article at `https://medium.com/@ demografy/artificial-intelligence-can-now-predict-demographic- characteristics-knowing-only-your-name-6749436a6bd3` says that AI can now predict your demographics based solely on your name. The company in that article, Demografy (`https://demografy.com/`), claims to provide gender, age, and cultural affinity based solely on name. Even though the site claims that it's 90 to 95 percent accurate (see the Is Demografy Accurate answer at `https://demografy.com/faq` for details), this statistic is unlikely because some names are gender ambiguous, such as Renee, and others are assigned to one gender in some countries and another gender in others. In fact, the answer on the Demografy site seems to acknowledge this issue by saying the outcome "heavily depends on your particular list and may show considerably different results than these averages". Yes, demographic prediction can work, but exercise care before believing everything that these sites tell you.

If you want to experiment with demographic prediction, you can find a number of APIs online. For example, the DeepAI API at `https://deepai.org/machine- learning-model/demographic-recognition` promises to help you predict age, gender, and cultural background based on a person's appearance in a video. Each of the online APIs do specialize, so you need to choose the API with an eye toward the kind of input data you can provide.

Keeping people safer

You already have a good idea of how data might affect you in ways that keep you safer. For example, statistics help car designers create new designs that provide greater safety for the occupant and sometimes other parties as well. Data also figures into calculations for things like

>> Medications

>> Medical procedures

>> Safety equipment

>> Safety procedures

>> How long to keep the crosswalk signs lit

Safety goes much further, though. For example, people have been trying to predict natural disasters for as long as there have been people and natural disasters. No one wants to be part of an earthquake, tornado, volcanic eruption, or any other natural disaster. Being able to get away quickly is the prime consideration in such cases, given that humans can't control their environment well enough yet to prevent any natural disaster.

Data managed by deep learning provides the means to look for extremely subtle patterns that boggle the minds of humans. These patterns can help predict a natural catastrophe, according to the article on Google's solution at http://www.digitaljournal.com/tech-and-science/technology/google-to-use-ai-to-predict-natural-disasters/article/533026. The fact that the software can predict any disaster at all is simply amazing. However, the article at http://theconversation.com/ai-could-help-us-manage-natural-disasters-but-only-to-an-extent-90777 warns that relying on such software exclusively would be a mistake. Overreliance on technology is a constant theme throughout this book, so don't be surprised that deep learning is less than perfect in predicting natural catastrophes as well.

Creating new technologies

New technologies can cover a very wide range of applications. For example, you find new technologies for making factories safer and more efficient all the time. Space travel requires an inordinate number of new technologies. Just consider how the data collected in the past affects things like smart phone use and the manner in which you drive your car.

However, a new technology can take an interesting twist, and you should look for these applications as well. You probably have black-and-white videos or pictures of family members or special events that you'd love to see in color. Color consists of three elements: hue (the actual color); value (the darkness or lightness of the color); and saturation (the intensity of the color). You can read more about these elements at http://learn.leighcotnoir.com/artspeak/elements-color/hue-value-saturation/. Oddly enough, many artists are color-blind and make strong use of color value in their creations (read https://www.nytimes.com/2017/12/23/books/a-colorblind-artist-illustrator-childrens-books.html as one of many examples). So having hue missing (the element that black-and-white art lacks) isn't the end of the world. Quite the contrary: Some artists view it as an advantage (see https://www.artsy.net/article/artsy-editorial-the-advantages-of-being-a-colorblind-artist for details).

When viewing something in black and white, you see value and saturation but not hue. *Colorization* is the process of adding the hue back in. Artists generally perform this process using a painstaking selection of individual colors, as described at https://fstoppers.com/video/how-amazing-colorization-black-and-white-photos-are-done-5384 and https://www.diyphotography.net/know-colors-add-colorizing-black-white-photos/. However, AI has automated this process using Convolutional Neural Networks (CNNs), as described at https://emerj.com/ai-future-outlook/ai-is-colorizing-and-beautifying-the-world/.

REMEMBER

The easiest way to use CNN for colorization is to find a library to help you. The Algorithmia site at https://demos.algorithmia.com/colorize-photos/ offers such a library and shows some example code. You can also try the application by pasting a URL into the supplied field. The article at https://petapixel.com/2016/07/14/app-magically-turns-bw-photos-color-ones/ describes just how well this application works. It's absolutely amazing!

Performing analysis for research

Most people think that research focuses only on issues like health, consumerism, or improving efficiency. However, research takes a great many other forms as well, many of which you'll never even hear about, such as figuring out how people move in order to keep them safer. Think about a manikin for a moment. You can pose the manikin in various ways to see how that pose affects an environment, such as in car crash research. However, manikins are simply snapshots in a process that happens in real time. In order to see how people interact with their environment, you must pose the people in a fluid, real time, manner using a strategy called *person poses*.

Person poses don't tell you who is in a video stream, but rather what elements of a person are in the video stream. For example, using a person pose can tell you whether the person's elbow appears in the video and where it appears. The article at https://medium.com/tensorflow/real-time-human-pose-estimation-in-the-browser-with-tensorflow-js-7dd0bc881cd5 tells you more about how this whole visualization technique works. In fact, you can see how the system works through a short animation of one person in the first case and three people in the second case.

Person poses can have all sorts of useful purposes. For example, you might use a person pose to help people improve their form for various kinds of sports — everything from golf to bowling. A person pose could also make new sorts of video games possible. Imagine being able to track a person's position for a game without the usual assortment of cumbersome gear. Theoretically, you could use person poses to perform crime-scene analysis or to determine the possibility of a person committing a crime.

Another interesting application of pose detection is for medical and rehabilitation purposes. Software powered by data managed by deep learning techniques could tell you whether you're doing your exercises correctly and track your improvements. An application of this sort could support the work of a professional rehabilitator by taking care of you when you aren't in a medical facility (an activity called telerehabilitation; see https://matrc.org/telerehabilitation-telepractice for details).

REMEMBER

Fortunately, you can at least start working with person poses today using the tfjs-models (PoseNet) library at https://github.com/tensorflow/tfjs-models/tree/master/posenet. You can see it in action with a webcam, complete with source code, at https://ml5js.org/docs/posenet-webcam. The example takes a while to load, so you need to be patient.

Providing art and entertainment

Book 5, Chapter 4 provides you with some good ideas on how deep learning can use the content of a real-world picture and an existing master painter (live or dead) for style to create a combination of the two. In fact, some pieces of art generated using this approach are commanding high prices on the auction block. You can find all sorts of articles on this particular kind of art generation, such as the *Wired* article at https://www.wired.com/story/we-made-artificial-intelligence-art-so-can-you/.

However, even though pictures are nice for hanging on the wall, you might want to produce other kinds of art. For example, you can create a 3-D version of your picture using products like Smoothie 3-D. The articles at https://styly.cc/tips/smoothie-3d/ and https://3dprint.com/38467/smoothie-3d-software/ describe how this software works. It's not the same as creating a sculpture; rather, you use a 3-D printer to build a 3-D version of your picture. The article at https://thenextweb.com/artificial-intelligence/2018/03/08/try-this-ai-experiment-that-converts-2d-images-to-3d/ offers an experiment that you can perform to see how the process works.

REMEMBER

The output of an AI doesn't need to consist of something visual, either. For example, deep learning enables you to create music based on the content of a picture, as described at https://www.cnet.com/news/baidu-ai-creates-original-music-by-looking-at-pictures-china-google/. This form of art makes the method used by AI clearer. The AI transforms content that it doesn't understand from one form to another. As humans, we see and understand the transformation, but all the computer sees are numbers to process using clever algorithms created by other humans.

Making life more interesting in other ways

Data is part of your life. You really can't perform too many activities anymore that don't have data attached to them in some way. For example, consider gardening. You might think that digging in the earth, planting seeds, watering, and harvesting fruit has nothing to do with data, yet the seeds you use likely rely on research conducted as the result of gathering data. The tools you use to dig are now ergonomically designed based on human research studies. The weather reports you use to determine whether to water or not rely on data. The clothes you wear, the shoes you employ to work safely, and even the manner in which you work are all influenced by data. Now, consider that gardening is a relatively nontechnical task that people have performed for thousands of years, and you get a good feel for just how much data affects your daily life.

Creating the Data Science Pipeline

Data science is partly art and partly engineering. Recognizing patterns in data, considering what questions to ask, and determining which algorithms work best are all part of the art side of data science. However, to make the art part of data science realizable, the engineering part relies on a specific process to achieve specific goals. This process is the data science pipeline, which requires the data scientist to follow particular steps in the preparation, analysis, and presentation of the data. The following sections help you understand the data science pipeline better so that you can understand how the book employs it during the presentation of examples.

Preparing the data

The data that you access from various sources doesn't come in an easily packaged form, ready for analysis — quite the contrary. The raw data not only may vary substantially in format, but you may also need to transform it to make all the data sources cohesive and amenable to analysis. Transformation may require changing data types, the order in which data appears, and even the creation of data entries based on the information provided by existing entries.

Performing exploratory data analysis

The math behind data analysis relies on engineering principles in that the results are provable and consistent. However, data science provides access to a wealth of statistical methods and algorithms that help you discover patterns in the data. A single approach doesn't ordinarily do the trick. You typically use an iterative process to rework the data from a number of perspectives. The use of trial and error is part of the data science art.

Learning from data

As you iterate through various statistical analysis methods and apply algorithms to detect patterns, you begin learning from the data. The data might not tell the story that you originally thought it would, or it might have many stories to tell. Discovery is part of being a data scientist. In fact, it's the fun part of data science because you can't ever know in advance precisely what the data will reveal to you.

REMEMBER

Of course, the imprecise nature of data and the finding of seemingly random patterns in it means keeping an open mind. If you have preconceived ideas of what the data contains, you won't find the information it actually does contain. You miss the discovery phase of the process, which translates into lost opportunities for both you and the people who depend on you.

Visualizing

Visualization means seeing the patterns in the data and then being able to react to those patterns. It also means being able to see when data is not part of the pattern. Think of yourself as a data sculptor — removing the data that lies outside the patterns (the outliers) so that others can see the masterpiece of information beneath. Yes, you can see the masterpiece, but until others can see it, too, it remains in your vision alone.

Obtaining insights and data products

The data scientist may seem to simply be looking for unique methods of viewing data. However, the process doesn't end until you have a clear understanding of what the data means. The insights you obtain from manipulating and analyzing the data help you to perform real-world tasks. For example, you can use the results of an analysis to make a business decision.

In some cases, the result of an analysis creates an automated response. For example, when a robot views a series of pixels obtained from a camera, the pixels that form an object have special meaning, and the robot's programming may dictate some sort of interaction with that object. However, until the data scientist builds an application that can load, analyze, and visualize the pixels from the camera, the robot doesn't see anything at all.

Comparing Different Languages Used for Data Science

None of the existing programming languages in the world can do everything. One such language endeavor, Ada, has received limited success because the language is incredibly difficult to learn (see https://www.nap.edu/read/5463/chapter/3 and https://news.ycombinator.com/item?id=7824570 for details). The problem is that if you make a language robust enough to do everything, it's too complex to do anything. Consequently, as a data scientist, you likely need exposure to a number of languages, each of which has a forte in a particular aspect of data science development. The following sections help you to better understand the languages used for data science, with a special emphasis on Python and R, the languages supported by this book.

Obtaining an overview of data science languages

Many different programming languages exist, and most were designed to perform tasks in a certain way or even make a particular profession's work easier to do. Choosing the correct tool makes your life easier. It's akin to using a hammer instead of a screwdriver to drive a screw. Yes, the hammer works, but the screwdriver is much easier to use and definitely does a better job. Data scientists usually use only a few languages because they make working with data easier. With this idea in mind, here are the top languages for data science work in order of preference:

>> **Python (general purpose):** Many data scientists prefer to use Python because it provides a wealth of libraries, such as NumPy, SciPy, MatPlotLib, pandas, and Scikit-learn, to make data science tasks significantly easier. Python is also a precise language that makes using multiprocessing on large datasets easier, thereby reducing the time required to analyze them. The data science community has also stepped up with specialized IDEs, such as Anaconda, that implement the Jupyter Notebook concept, which makes working with data science calculations significantly easier. (Chapter 3 of this minibook demonstrates how to use Jupyter Notebook, so don't worry about it in this chapter.) In addition to all these aspects in Python's favor, it's also an excellent language for creating *glue code* (code that is used to connect various existing code elements together into a cohesive whole) with languages such as C/C++ and Fortran. The Python documentation actually shows how to create the required extensions. Most Python users rely on the language to see patterns, such as allowing a robot to see a group of pixels as an object. It also sees use for all sorts of scientific tasks.

>> **R (special purpose statistical):** In many respects, Python and R share the same sorts of functionality but implement it in different ways. Depending on which source you view, Python and R have about the same number of proponents, and some people use Python and R interchangeably (or sometimes in tandem). Unlike Python, R provides its own environment, so you don't need a third-party product such as Anaconda. However, Chapter 3 of this minibook shows how you can use R in Jupyter Notebook so that you can use a single IDE for all your needs. Unfortunately, R doesn't appear to mix with other languages with the ease that Python provides.

>> **SQL (database management):** The most important thing to remember about Structured Query Language (SQL) is that it focuses on data rather than tasks. (This distinction makes it a full-fledged language for a data scientist, but only part of a solution for a computer scientist.) Businesses can't operate without good data management — the data is the business. Large organizations use some sort of relational database, which is normally accessible with SQL, to store their data. Most Database Management System (DBMS) products rely on SQL as their main language, and DBMS usually has a large number of data analysis and other data science features built in. Because you're accessing the data natively, you often experience a significant speed gain in performing data science tasks this way. Database Administrators (DBAs) generally use SQL to manage or manipulate the data rather than necessarily perform detailed analysis of it. However, the data scientist can also use SQL for various data science tasks and make the resulting scripts available to the DBAs for their needs.

>> **Java (general purpose):** Some data scientists perform other kinds of programming that require a general-purpose, widely adapted, and popular language. In addition to providing access to a large number of libraries (most of which aren't actually all that useful for data science, but do work for other needs), Java supports object orientation better than any of the other languages in this list. In addition, it's strongly typed and tends to run quite quickly. Consequently, some people prefer it for finalized code. Java isn't a good choice for experimentation or ad hoc queries. Oddly enough, an implementation of Java exists for Jupyter Notebook, but it isn't refined and is not usable for data science work at this time. (You can find helpful information about the Jupyter Java implementation at https://blog.frankel.ch/teaching-java-jupyter-notebooks/, https://github.com/scijava/scijava-jupyter-kernel, and https://github.com/jupyter/jupyter/wiki/Jupyter-kernels.)

>> **Scala (general purpose):** Because Scala uses the Java Virtual Machine (JVM), it does have some of the advantages and disadvantages of Java. However, like Python, Scala provides strong support for the functional programming paradigm, which uses lambda calculus as its basis (see *Functional Programmming For Dummies,* by John Paul Mueller [Wiley] for details). In addition, Apache Spark is written in Scala, which means that you have good support for cluster computing

when using this language. Think huge dataset support. Some of the pitfalls of using Scala are that it's hard to set up correctly, it has a steep learning curve, and it lacks a comprehensive set of data science–specific libraries.

Defining the pros and cons of using Python

Given the right data sources, analysis requirements, and presentation needs, you can use Python for every part of the data science pipeline. In fact, that's precisely what you do in this book. Every example uses Python to help you understand another part of the data science equation. Of all the languages you could choose for performing data science tasks, Python is the most flexible and capable because it supports so many third-party libraries devoted to the task. The following sections help you better understand why Python is such a good choice for many (if not most) data science needs.

Considering the shifting profile of data scientists

Some people view the data scientist as an unapproachable nerd who performs miracles on data with math. The data scientist is the person behind the curtain in an Oz-like experience. However, this perspective is changing. In many respects, the world now views the data scientist as either an adjunct to a developer or as a new type of developer. The ascendance of applications of all sorts that can learn is the essence of this change. For an application to learn, it has to be able to manipulate large databases and discover new patterns in them. In addition, the application must be able to create new data based on the old data — making an informed prediction of sorts. The new kinds of applications affect people in ways that would have seemed like science fiction just a few years ago. Of course, the most noticeable of these applications define the behaviors of robots that will interact far more closely with people tomorrow than they do today.

From a business perspective, the necessity of fusing data science and application development is obvious: Businesses must perform various sorts of analysis on the huge databases they have collected — to make sense of the information and use it to predict the future. In truth, however, the far greater impact of the melding of these two branches of science — data science and application development — will be felt in terms of creating altogether new kinds of applications, some of which aren't even possible to imagine with clarity today. For example, new applications could help students learn with greater precision by analyzing their learning trends and creating new instructional methods that work for that particular student. This combination of sciences might also solve a host of medical problems that seem impossible to solve today — not only in keeping disease at bay, but also by solving problems, such as how to create truly usable prosthetic devices that look and act like the real thing.

Working with a multipurpose, simple, and efficient language

Many different ways are available for accomplishing data science tasks. This book covers only one of the myriad methods at your disposal. However, Python represents one of the few single-stop solutions that you can use to solve complex data science problems. Instead of having to use a number of tools to perform a task, you can simply use a single language, Python, to get the job done. The Python difference is the large number scientific and math libraries created for it by third parties. Plugging in these libraries greatly extends Python and allows it to easily perform tasks that other languages could perform, but with great difficulty.

TIP

Python's libraries are its main selling point; however, Python offers more than reusable code. The most important thing to consider with Python is that it supports four different coding styles:

>> **Functional:** Treats every statement as a mathematical equation and avoids any form of state or mutable data. The main advantage of this approach is having no side effects to consider. In addition, this coding style lends itself better than the others to parallel processing because you have no state to consider. Many developers prefer this coding style for recursion and for lambda calculus.

>> **Imperative:** Performs computations as a direct change to program state. This style is especially useful when manipulating data structures and produces elegant, but simple, code.

>> **Object-oriented:** Relies on data fields that are treated as objects and manipulated only through prescribed methods. Python doesn't fully support this coding form because it can't implement features such as data hiding. However, this is a useful coding style for complex applications because it supports encapsulation and polymorphism. This coding style also favors code reuse.

>> **Procedural:** Treats tasks as step-by-step iterations in which common tasks are placed in functions that are called as needed. This coding style favors iteration, sequencing, selection, and modularization.

Defining the pros and cons of using R

The standard download of R is a combination of an environment and a language. It's a form of the S programming language, which John Chambers originally created at Bell Laboratories to make working with statistics easier. Rick Becker and Allan Wilks eventually added to the S programming language as well. The goal of the R language is to turn ideas into software quickly and easily. In other words, R is a language designed to help someone who doesn't have much programming experience create code without a huge learning curve.

This book uses R instead of S because R is a free, downloadable product that can run most S code without modification; in contrast, you have to pay for S. Given the examples used in the book, R is a great choice. You can read more about R in general at https://www.r-project.org/about.html.

WARNING

You don't want to make sweeping generalizations about the languages used for data science because you must also consider how the languages are used within the field (such as performing machine learning or deep learning tasks). Both R and Python are popular languages for different reasons. Articles such as "In data science, the R language is swallowing Python" (http://www.infoworld.com/article/2951779/application-development/in-data-science-the-r-language-is-swallowing-python.html) initially seem to say that R is becoming more popular for some reason, which isn't clearly articulated. The author wisely backs away from this statement by pointing out that R is best used for statistical purposes and Python is a better general-purpose language. The best developers always have an assortment of programming tools in their tool belts to make performing tasks easier. Languages address developer needs, so you need to use the right language for the job. After all, all languages ultimately become machine code that a processor understands — an extremely low-level, processor-specific language that few developers understand any longer because high-level programming languages make development easier.

You can get a basic copy of R from the Comprehensive R Archive Network (CRAN) site at https://cran.r-project.org/. The site provides both source code versions and compiled versions of the R distribution for various platforms. Unless you plan to make your own changes to the basic R support or want to delve into how R works, getting the compiled version is always better. If you use RStudio, you must also download and install a copy of R.

REMEMBER

This book uses a version of R specially designed for use in Jupyter Notebook (as described in Chapter 3 of this minibook). Because you can work with Python and R using the same IDE, you save time and effort because now you don't have to learn a separate IDE for R. However, you might ultimately choose to work with a specialized R environment to obtain language help features that Jupyter Notebook doesn't provide. If you use a different IDE, the screenshots in the book won't match what you see onscreen, and the downloadable source code files may not load without error (but should still work with minor touchups).

The RStudio Desktop version (https://www.rstudio.com/products/rstudio/#Desktop) can make the task of working with R even easier. This product is a free download, and you can get it in Linux (Debian/Ubuntu, RedHat/CentOS, and SUSE Linux), Mac, and Windows versions. The book doesn't use the advanced features found in the paid version of the product, nor will you require the RStudio Server features for the examples.

You can try other R distributions if you find that you don't like Jupyter Notebook or RStudio. The most common alternative distributions are StatET (`http://www.walware.de/goto/statet`), Red-R (`https://decisionstats.com/2010/09/28/red-r-1-8-groovy-gui/` or `http://www.red-r.org/`), and Rattle (`http://rattle.togaware.com/`). All of them are good products, but RStudio appears to have the strongest following and is the simplest product to use outside Jupyter Notebook. You can read discussions about the various choices online at places such as `https://www.quora.com/What-are-the-best-choices-for-an-R-IDE`.

Learning to Perform Data Science Tasks Fast

It's time to see the data science pipeline in action. Even though the following sections use Python to provide a brief overview of the process you explore in detail in the rest of the book, they also apply to using R. Throughout the book, you see Python used directly in the text for every example, with some R additions. The downloadable source contains R versions of the examples that reflect the capabilities that R provides.

You won't actually perform the tasks in the following sections. In fact, you don't find installation instructions for Python until Chapter 3, so in this chapter, you can just follow along in the text. This book uses a specific version of Python and an IDE called Jupyter Notebook, so please wait until Chapter 3 to install these features (or skip ahead, if you insist, and install them now). Don't worry about understanding every aspect of the process at this point. The purpose of these sections is to help you gain an understanding of the flow of using Python to perform data science tasks. Many of the details may seem difficult to understand at this point, but the rest of the book will help you understand them.

REMEMBER

The examples in this book rely on a web-based application named Jupyter Notebook. The screenshots you see in this and other chapters reflect how Jupyter Notebook looks in Firefox on a Windows 7 system. The view you see will contain the same data, but the actual interface may differ a little depending on platform (such as using a notebook instead of a desktop system), operating system, and browser. Don't worry if you see some slight differences between your display and the screenshots in the book.

Loading data

Before you can do anything, you need to load some data. The book shows you all sorts of methods for performing this task. In this case, Figure 1-1 shows how to load a dataset called Boston that contains housing prices and other facts about houses in the Boston area. The code places the entire dataset in the boston variable and then places parts of that data in variables named X and y. Think of variables as you would storage boxes. The variables are important because they enable you to work with the data.

FIGURE 1-1:
Loading data into
variables so
that you can
manipulate it.

Loading data

```
In [1]:  from sklearn.datasets import load_boston
         boston = load_boston()
         X, y = boston.data,boston.target
```

Training a model

Now that you have some data to work with, you can do something with it. All sorts of algorithms are built into Python. Figure 1-2 shows a linear regression model. Again, don't worry precisely how this works; later chapters discuss linear regression in detail. The important thing to note in Figure 1-2 is that Python lets you perform the linear regression using just two statements and to place the result in a variable named hypothesis.

FIGURE 1-2:
Using the variable
content to train a
linear regression
model.

Training a model

```
In [2]:  from sklearn.linear_model import LinearRegression
         hypothesis = LinearRegression(normalize=True)
         hypothesis.fit(X,y)

Out[2]:  LinearRegression(copy_X=True, fit_intercept=True, n_jobs=None, normalize
         =True)
```

Viewing a result

Performing any sort of analysis doesn't pay unless you obtain some benefit from it in the form of a result. This book shows all sorts of ways to view output, but Figure 1-3 starts with something simple. In this case, you see the coefficient output from the linear regression analysis.

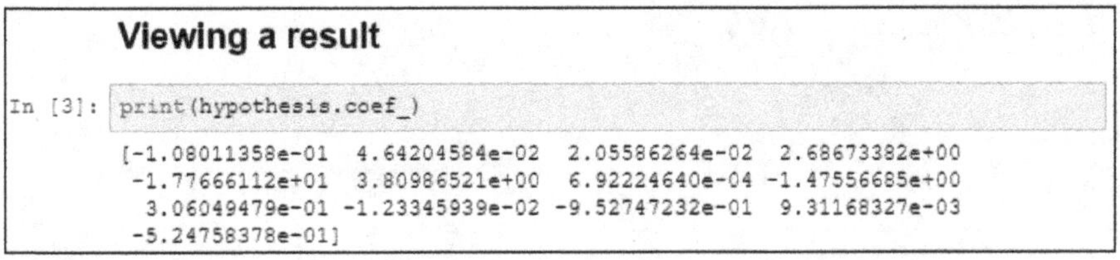

FIGURE 1-3:
Outputting
a result as a
response to the
model.

Viewing a result

```
In [3]: print(hypothesis.coef_)

[-1.08011358e-01  4.64204584e-02  2.05586264e-02  2.68673382e+00
 -1.77666112e+01  3.80986521e+00  6.92224640e-04 -1.47556685e+00
  3.06049479e-01 -1.23345939e-02 -9.52747232e-01  9.31168327e-03
 -5.24758378e-01]
```

TIP

One of the reasons that this book uses Jupyter Notebook is that the product helps you to create nicely formatted output as part of creating the application. Look again at Figure 1-3 and you see a report that you could simply print and offer to a colleague. The output isn't suitable for many people, but those experienced with Python and data science will find it quite usable and informative.

Chapter **2**

Placing Data Science within the Realm of AI

S ome people perceive data science as simply a method of managing data for use with an AI discipline, but you can use your data science skills for a great many tasks other than AI. You use data science skills for various types of statistical analysis that don't rely on an AI, such as to perform analytics, manage data in various ways, and locate information that you use directly rather than as an input into anything. However, the data science to AI connection does exist as well, so you need to know about it as a data scientist, which is the focus of the first part of this chapter.

Many terms used in data science become muddled because people misuse them. When you hear the term *AI*, you might think about all sorts of technologies that are either distinct AI subcategories or have nothing to do with AI at all. The second part of the chapter defines AI and then clarifies its connection to machine learning, which is a subcategory of AI, and finally to deep learning, which is actually a subcategory of machine learning. Understanding this hierarchy is important in understanding the role data science plays in making these technologies work.

The first two sections define the endpoints of a data pipeline. The third section describes the pipeline between data science and AI (and its subcategories). This data pipeline is a particular implementation of data science skills, so you need to know about it. You also need to consider that this data pipeline isn't the only one you need to create and use as a data scientist. For example, you might be involved in a type of data mining that doesn't rely on AI but rather on specific sorts of filtering, sorting, and the use of statistical analysis. The articles at https://www.innoarchitech.com/blog/data-science-big-data-explained-non-data-scientist and https://www.northeastern.edu/graduate/blog/what-does-a-data-scientist-do/ give you some other ideas about how data scientists create and use data pipelines.

Seeing the Data to Data Science Relationship

Obviously, to become a data scientist, you must have data to work with. What isn't obvious is the kind of data, the data sources, and the uses of the data. Data is the requirement for analysis, but that analysis can take many forms. For example, the article at https://blog.allpsych.com/spending-habits-can-reveal-personality-traits/ talks about data used to guess your psychological profile, which can then be used for all sorts of purposes — many positive; others not. The issue is that these analyses often help others know more about you than you know yourself, which is a scary thought when you consider how someone might use the information.

The following sections discuss data, not the moral or ethical complications of gathering it. In general, you find that some analyses work fine with just a little data, but others require huge amounts of it. For example, later sections discuss AI, machine learning, and deep learning, which require ascending amounts of data to perform well.

Considering the data architecture

A data architecture consists of a number of elements. Although you may not always have to deal with these elements as a data scientist, you should know about them to create robust solutions:

» Format

» Speed of access

» Cost of access

» Industry

» Use

Data comes in many forms. Book 2 discusses all sorts of architectures in detail — everything from in-memory databases to those found in huge corporate databases. The form of the data differs as well. A Relational Database Management System (RDBMS) provides a highly structured dataset that's easy to interact with, but it places restrictions on the data form. On the other hand, a Not Only SQL (NoSQL) database is freeform, so it's flexible in a way that an RDBMS isn't. The form of the data determines what you need to do to manicure it for your particular need, because raw data rarely comes in precisely the format you require.

The data architecture also considers how you access the data. Even though online data sources are convenient and accessible from just about everywhere, they come with a speed penalty that you must consider when using them. Localized databases are faster, but now you have to deal with data that might be stale or not as pertinent to a particular need. You also risk losing the true world view as you focus on data that comes from your organization.

Some people are under the assumption that the quality of data is the same no matter what the source. Quality does vary, however, and you need to consider how the quality of your data affects your analysis. When data appears in the public domain, it may not be very high quality because no one has vetted it. This isn't to say that you can't find high-quality, public-domain data — just that the likelihood is less. Likewise, data you pay to access isn't always guaranteed to meet your specific needs even if it is high quality. The cost of access affects your analysis because the tendency is to reduce costs by taking the penalty in quality.

The industry generating or using the data also matters. You can become blindsided by the biases of your particular industry. The data you need to perform a financial analysis may actually reside in the data generated by the energy industry. Yet, if you don't look in that particular industry's offerings, you won't ever find this hidden data, and your analysis will fail or at least produce less robust results.

WARNING

Perhaps the most problematic component of data architecture, however, is how you use the data you obtain. Logic errors occur all the time, and having a list of best practices might seem as though it could provide a solution to the problem, but it can't. Intuition and strong logical analysis often form a part of the most successful data usage. This means that if you perform a survey and obtain results that seem ludicrous, they probably are, and you need to review the data again, rather than publish the sensational results you think you might have obtained from a flawed analysis.

Acquiring data from various sources

A data source need not come in the form of a huge corporate database. Some of the more interesting forms of analysis use mundane and tiny datasets derived from sources such as Point-of-Sale (POS) systems. The article at https://blog.magestore.com/pos-data/ makes a strong case for analyzing POS data for more than simply knowing when to reorder certain items and determining sales on a given day. Some datasets are public domain and free (often used for testing and training a deep learning application) and others require a purchase. Some sites actually sell data as a commodity, such as Data World (https://data.world/datasets/wildlife). The point is that you're drowning in a sea of data and may not even know it.

The source of the data also determines a great many details about what you can expect. For example, POS data can prove hard to analyze because the terminals lack standardization for the most part, and you can't be sure precisely what form the data will take. If you have terminals from various vendors, each of whom uses a different data format, the problem is compounded because you now need custom cleaning solutions for each of the data sources.

REMEMBER

A data source may be unreliable because it is accessible only during certain hours of the day or might experience unexpected down times. For example, consider getting data from a rover on Mars. All sorts of issues can occur, as described in the article at https://www.theatlantic.com/science/archive/2018/09/curiosity-opportunity-nasa-rover-problems/570769/. Of course, most people aren't working with a rover on Mars, but corporate databases can go offline as well. Lest you think that the cloud fixes reliability, check out the article at https://www.networkworld.com/article/3394341/when-it-comes-to-uptime-not-all-cloud-providers-are-created-equal.html. In short, you always need a Plan B when it comes to data, and having a Plan C is likely a good idea as well.

Performing data analysis

At some point, every data scientist performs an analysis, which means working with the data to produce a usable result. The analysis could be anything. You might simply want to know the average of sales for March over the last ten years. Whatever the reason for the analysis, the results you achieve depend on these issues:

>> The reliability of the data

>> The quality of the data

>> The quantity of the data

>> Selection of the right algorithm

>> Presentation of the result in the correct manner

>> Interpretation of the result

>> Tuning of the result

TIP

As you proceed through the book, starting with Book 2, you find that all these issues come under discussion for various data sources, algorithms, and analysis techniques. However, always keep in mind that automation never trumps human insight and intuition. As you go through the book, remember that you must ultimately decide whether a result is correct (at least, correct enough) and useful.

Archiving the data

Archiving data is important for historical reasons. You want to have the data available to repeat a particular analysis. A new algorithm might reveal something different about the data, or you may have to subject your analysis method to peer review. Only when the data becomes outdated do you consider getting rid of it. Unlike a shirt that you accidentally send to a resale store but may still be able to buy back, you can't retrieve your data after it's gone.

Most people will find it easy to argue that static data, the type you collect once or at specific intervals, requires archiving. Part of the reason is that static data is controllable. You won't suddenly find all your storage devices cluttered with it.

REMEMBER

Some sections of this book deal with live data — the sort that changes minute by minute. Archiving such data might seem to be useless. You might argue that no one will actually need the data you collected five minutes ago. However, just as police use recordings of live camera feeds to find the culprit in a burglary or a carjacking, you need to archive live data to locate the source of issues in your organization. Always archive all your data even if the archive lasts only a short time.

Defining the Levels of AI

AI is a broad term for a set of technologies that use data in a particular way to perform specific kinds of analysis. The underlying assumption is that a computer will automate the process of performing this analysis through algorithms that manipulate the data in distinctive ways. When you look at AI, you see a high-level technology that leads to refined technologies such as machine learning. Machine learning isn't AI; instead, it's a subset of AI, and keeping the distinction clear is important. Likewise, one refinement of machine learning is deep learning. Again, deep learning isn't machine learning, and you need to keep them separate. The following sections offer definitions for these three terms and help you understand them.

Beginning with AI

Before you can use a term in any meaningful and useful way, you must have a definition for it. After all, if nobody agrees on a meaning, the term has none; it's just a collection of characters. Defining the idiom (which is a term whose meaning isn't clear from the meanings of its constituent elements) is especially important with technical terms that have received more than a little press coverage at various times and in various ways.

REMEMBER

Saying that AI is an artificial intelligence doesn't really tell you anything meaningful, which is why so many discussions and disagreements arise over this term. Yes, you can argue that what occurs is artificial, not having come from a natural source. However, the intelligence part is, at best, ambiguous. Even if you don't necessarily agree with the definition of AI as it appears in the sections that follow, this book uses AI according to that definition, and knowing it will help you follow the rest of the text more easily.

Discerning intelligence

People define intelligence in many different ways. However, you can say that intelligence involves certain mental activities composed of the following actions:

- » **Learning:** Having the ability to obtain and process new information

- » **Reasoning:** Being able to manipulate information in various ways

- » **Understanding:** Considering the result of information manipulation

- » **Grasping truths:** Determining the validity of the manipulated information

- » **Seeing relationships:** Divining how validated data interacts with other data

- » **Considering meanings:** Applying truths to particular situations in a manner consistent with their relationship

- » **Separating fact from belief:** Determining whether the data is adequately supported by provable sources that can be demonstrated to be consistently valid

The list could easily get quite long, but even this list is relatively prone to interpretation by anyone who accepts it as viable. As you can see from the list, however, intelligence often follows a process that a computer system can mimic as part of a simulation:

1. Set a goal based on needs or wants.

2. Assess the value of any currently known information in support of the goal.

3. Gather additional information that could support the goal.

4. Manipulate the data such that it achieves a form consistent with existing information.

5. Define the relationships and truth values between existing and new information.

6. Determine whether the goal is achieved.

7. Modify the goal in light of the new data and its effect on the probability of success.

8. Repeat Steps 2 through 7 as needed until the goal is achieved (found true) or the possibilities for achieving it are exhausted (found false).

Even though you can create algorithms and provide access to data in support of this process within a computer, a computer's capability to achieve intelligence is severely limited. For example, a computer is incapable of understanding anything because it relies on machine processes to manipulate data using pure math in a strictly mechanical fashion. Likewise, computers can't easily separate truth from mistruth (as described in Book 6, Chapter 2). In fact, no computer can fully implement any of the mental activities described in the list that describes intelligence.

As part of deciding what intelligence actually involves, categorizing intelligence is also helpful. Humans don't use just one type of intelligence, but rather rely on multiple intelligences to perform tasks. Howard Gardner of Harvard has defined a number of these types of intelligence (see http://www.pz.harvard.edu/projects/multiple-intelligences for details), and knowing them helps you to relate them to the kinds of tasks that a computer can simulate as intelligence. Here is a modified version of these intelligences with additional description:

>> **Visual-spatial:** Physical environment intelligence used by people like sailors and architects (among many others). To move at all, humans need to understand their physical environment — that is, its dimensions and characteristics. Every robot or portable computer intelligence requires this capability, but the capability is often difficult to simulate (as with self-driving cars) or less than accurate (as with vacuums that rely as much on bumping as they do on moving intelligently).

>> **Bodily-kinesthetic:** Body movements, such as those used by a surgeon or a dancer, require precision and body awareness. Robots commonly use this kind of intelligence to perform repetitive tasks, often with higher precision than humans, but sometimes with less grace. It's essential to differentiate between human augmentation, such as a surgical device that provides a surgeon with enhanced physical ability, and true independent movement. The former is simply a demonstration of mathematical ability in that it depends on the surgeon for input.

>> **Creative:** Creativity is the act of developing a new pattern of thought that results in unique output in the form of art, music, and writing. A truly new kind of product is the result of creativity. An AI can simulate existing patterns of thought and even combine them to create what appears to be a unique presentation but is really just a mathematically based version of an existing pattern. In order to create, an AI would need to possess self-awareness, which would require intrapersonal intelligence.

>> **Interpersonal:** Interacting with others occurs at several levels. The goal of this form of intelligence is to obtain, exchange, give, and manipulate information based on the experiences of others. Computers can answer basic questions because of keyword input, not understanding. The intelligence occurs while obtaining information, locating suitable keywords, and then giving information based on those keywords. Cross-referencing terms in a lookup table and then acting upon the instructions provided by the table demonstrates logical intelligence, not interpersonal intelligence.

>> **Intrapersonal:** Looking inward to understand one's own interests and then setting goals based on those interests is currently a human-only kind of intelligence. As machines, computers have no desires, interests, wants, or creative abilities. An AI processes numeric input using a set of algorithms and provides an output — it isn't aware of anything that it does, nor does it understand anything that it does.

>> **Linguistic:** Working with words is an essential tool for communication because spoken and written information exchange is far faster than any other form. This form of intelligence includes understanding spoken and written input, managing the input to develop an answer, and providing an understandable answer as output. In many cases, computers can barely parse input into keywords, can't actually understand the request at all, and output responses that may not be understandable at all. In humans, spoken and written linguistic intelligence come from different areas of the brain (https://releases.jhu.edu/2015/05/05/say-what-how-the-brain-separates-our-ability-to-talk-and-write/), which means that even with humans, someone who has high written linguistic intelligence may not have similarly high spoken linguistic intelligence. Computers don't currently separate written and spoken linguistic ability.

>> **Logical-mathematical:** Calculating a result, performing comparisons, exploring patterns, and considering relationships are all areas in which computers currently excel. When you see a computer beat a human on a game show, this is the only form of intelligence, out of seven, that you're actually seeing. Yes, you might see small bits of other kinds of intelligence, but this one is the focus. Basing an assessment of human versus computer intelligence on just one area isn't a good idea.

Discovering four ways to define AI

As described in the previous section, the first concept that's important to understand is that AI doesn't really have anything to do with human intelligence. Yes, some AI is modeled to simulate human intelligence, but that's what it is: a simulation. When thinking about AI, notice an interplay between goal seeking, data processing used to achieve that goal, and data acquisition used to better understand the goal. AI relies on algorithms to achieve a result that may or may not have anything to do with human goals or methods of achieving those goals. With this understanding in mind, you can categorize AI in four ways:

>> **Acting humanly:** When a computer acts like a human, it best reflects the Turing test, in which the computer succeeds when differentiation between the computer and a human isn't possible (see https://www.turing.org. uk/scrapbook/test.html for details). This category also reflects what the media would have you believe AI is all about. You see it employed for technologies such as natural language processing, knowledge representation, automated reasoning, and machine learning (all four of which must be present to pass the test).

>> **Thinking humanly:** When a computer thinks as a human, it performs tasks that require intelligence (as contrasted with rote procedures) from a human to succeed, such as driving a car. To determine whether a program thinks like a human, you must have some method of determining how humans think, which the cognitive modeling approach defines. This model relies on three techniques that are used to create a model, which forms the basis for a simulation:

- **Introspection:** Detecting and documenting the techniques used to achieve goals by monitoring one's own thought processes.

- **Psychological testing:** Observing a person's behavior and adding it to a database of similar behaviors from other persons given a similar set of circumstances, goals, resources, and environmental conditions (among other things).

- **Brain imaging:** Monitoring brain activity directly through various mechanical means, such as Computerized Axial Tomography (CAT), Positron Emission Tomography (PET), Magnetic Resonance Imaging (MRI), and Magnetoencephalography (MEG).

>> **Thinking rationally:** Applying some type of standard to studying how humans think enables the creation of guidelines that describe typical human behaviors. A person is considered rational when following these behaviors within certain levels of deviation. A computer that thinks rationally relies on the recorded behaviors to create a guide as to how to interact with an environment based on the data at hand. The goal of this approach is to solve

problems logically, when possible. In many cases, this approach would enable the creation of a baseline technique for solving a problem, which would then be modified to actually solve the problem. In other words, the solving of a problem in principle is often different from solving it in practice, but you still need a starting point.

>> **Acting rationally:** Studying how humans act in given situations under specific constraints enables you to determine which techniques are both efficient and effective. A computer that acts rationally relies on the recorded actions to interact with an environment based on conditions, environmental factors, and existing data. As with rational thought, rational acts depend on a solution in principle, which may not prove useful in practice. However, rational acts do provide a baseline upon which a computer can begin negotiating the successful completion of a goal.

Using categories to define kinds of AI

The categories used to define AI offer a way to consider various uses for or ways to apply AI. Some of the systems used to classify AI by type are arbitrary and not distinct. For example, some groups view AI as either strong (generalized intelligence that can adapt to a variety of situations) or weak (specific intelligence designed to perform a particular task well). The problem with strong AI is that it doesn't perform any task well, while weak AI is too specific to perform tasks independently. Even so, having just two type classifications won't do the job even in a general sense. The four classification types promoted by Arend Hintze (see http://theconversation.com/understanding-the-four-types-of-ai-from-reactive-robots-to-self-aware-beings-67616 for details) form a better basis for understanding AI:

>> **Reactive machines:** The machines you see beating humans at chess or playing on game shows are examples of reactive machines. A reactive machine has no memory or experience upon which to base a decision. Instead, it relies on pure computational power and smart algorithms to re-create every decision every time. This is an example of a weak AI used for a specific purpose.

>> **Limited memory:** A self-driving car or autonomous robot can't afford the time to make every decision from scratch. These machines rely on a small amount of memory to provide experiential knowledge of various situations. When the machine sees the same situation, it can rely on experience to reduce reaction time and to provide more resources for making new decisions that haven't yet been made. This is an example of the current level of strong AI.

>> **Theory of mind:** A machine that can assess both its required goals and the potential goals of other entities in the same environment has a kind of understanding that is feasible to some extent today, but not in any commercial form. However, for self-driving cars to become truly autonomous, this level of AI must be fully developed. A self-driving car would not only need to know that it must go from one point to another, but also intuit the potentially conflicting goals of drivers around it and react accordingly.

>> **Self-awareness:** This is the sort of AI that you see in movies. However, it requires technologies that aren't even remotely possible now because such a machine would have a sense of both self and consciousness. In addition, instead of merely intuiting the goals of others based on environment and other entity reactions, this type of machine would be able to infer the intent of others based on experiential knowledge.

Advancing to machine learning

Machine learning is a specific application of AI used to simulate human learning through algorithms developed using various techniques, such as matching a series of inputs to a desired set of outputs. The following sections explore machine learning as it applies to this book.

Exploring what machine learning can do for AI

Machine learning relies on algorithms to analyze huge datasets. Currently, machine learning can't provide the sort of AI that the movies present. Even the best algorithms can't think, feel, present any form of self-awareness, or exercise free will. What machine learning can do is perform predictive analytics far faster than any human can. As a result, machine learning can help humans work more efficiently. The current state of AI, then, is one of performing analysis, but humans must still consider the implications of that analysis — making the required moral and ethical decisions. The essence of the matter is that machine learning provides just the learning part of AI, and that part is nowhere near ready to create an AI of the sort you see in films.

REMEMBER

The main point of confusion between learning and intelligence is that people assume that simply because a machine gets better at its job (learning), it's also aware (intelligence). Nothing supports this view of machine learning. The same phenomenon occurs when people assume that a computer is purposely causing problems for them. The computer can't assign emotions and therefore acts only upon the input provided and the instruction contained within an application to process that input. A true AI will eventually occur when computers can finally emulate the clever combination used by nature:

- **>> Genetics:** Slow learning from one generation to the next
- **>> Teaching:** Fast learning from organized sources
- **>> Exploration:** Spontaneous learning through media and interactions with others

Considering the goals of machine learning

At present, AI is based on machine learning, and machine learning is essentially different from statistics. Yes, machine learning has a statistical basis, but it makes some different assumptions than statistics do because the goals are different. Table 2-1 lists some features to consider when comparing AI and machine learning to statistics.

TABLE 2-1:   **Comparing Machine Learning to Statistics**

Technique	Machine Learning	Statistics
Data handling	Works with big data in the form of networks and graphs; raw data from sensors or web text is split into training and test data.	Models are used to create predictive power on small samples.
Data input	The data is sampled, randomized, and transformed to maximize accuracy scoring in the prediction of out-of-sample (or completely new) examples.	Parameters interpret real-world phenomena and focus on magnitude.
Result	Probability is taken into account for comparing what could be the best guess or decision.	The output captures the variability and uncertainty of parameters.
Assumptions	The scientist learns from the data.	The scientist assumes a certain output and tries to prove it.
Distribution	The distribution is unknown or ignored before learning from data.	The scientist assumes a well-defined distribution.
Fitting	The scientist creates a best-fit, but generalizable, model.	The result is fit to the present data distribution.

Defining machine learning limits based on hardware

Huge datasets require huge amounts of memory. Unfortunately, the requirements don't end there. When you have huge amounts of data and memory, you must also have processors with multiple cores and high speeds. One of the problems that scientists are striving to solve is how to use existing hardware more efficiently. In some cases, waiting for days to obtain a result to a machine learning problem simply isn't possible. The scientists who want to know the answer need it quickly, even if the result isn't quite right. In addition, investments in better hardware also require investments in better science. This book considers some of the following issues as part of making your machine learning experience better:

>> **Obtaining a useful result:** As you work through the book, you discover that you need to obtain a useful result first, before you can refine it. In addition, sometimes tuning an algorithm goes too far and the result becomes quite fragile (and possibly useless outside a specific dataset).

>> **Asking the right question:** Many people get frustrated in trying to obtain an answer from machine learning because they keep tuning their algorithm without asking a different question. To use hardware efficiently, sometimes you must step back and review the question you're asking. The question might be wrong, which means that even the best hardware will never find the answer.

>> **Relying on intuition too heavily:** All machine learning questions begin as a hypothesis. A scientist uses intuition to create a starting point for discovering the answer to a question. Failure is more common than success when working through a machine learning experience. Your intuition adds the art to the machine learning experience, but sometimes intuition is wrong, and you have to revisit your assumptions.

Considering the true uses of AI and machine learning

You find AI and machine learning used in a great many applications today. The only problem is that the technology works so well that you don't know that it even exists. In fact, you might be surprised to find that many devices in your home already make use of both technologies. Both technologies definitely appear in your car and most especially in the workplace. In fact, the uses for both AI and machine learning number in the millions — all safely out of sight even when they're quite dramatic in nature. Here are just a few of the ways in which you might see AI and machine learning used together:

>> **Fraud detection:** You get a call from your credit card company asking whether you made a particular purchase. The credit card company isn't being nosy; it's simply alerting you to the fact that someone else could be making a purchase using your card. The AI embedded within the credit card company's code detected an unfamiliar spending pattern and alerted someone to it.

>> **Resource scheduling:** Many organizations need to schedule the use of resources efficiently. For example, a hospital may have to determine where to put a patient based on the patient's needs, availability of skilled experts, and the amount of time the doctor expects the patient to be in the hospital.

>> **Complex analysis:** Humans often need help with complex analysis because there are literally too many factors to consider. For example, the same set of symptoms could indicate more than one problem. A doctor or other expert might need help making a diagnosis in a timely manner to save a patient's life.

>> **Automation:** Any form of automation can benefit from the addition of AI to handle unexpected changes or events. A problem with some types of automation today is that an unexpected event, such as an object in the wrong place, can actually cause the automation to stop. Adding AI to the automation can allow the automation to handle unexpected events and continue as if nothing happened.

>> **Customer service:** The customer service line you call today may not even have a human behind it. The automation is good enough to follow scripts and use various resources to handle the vast majority of your questions. With good voice inflection (provided by AI as well), you may not even be able to tell that you're talking with a computer.

>> **Safety systems:** Many of the safety systems found in machines of various sorts today rely on AI to take over the vehicle in a time of crisis. For example, many automatic braking systems rely on AI to stop the car based on all the inputs that a vehicle can provide, such as the direction of a skid.

>> **Machine efficiency:** AI can help control a machine in such a manner as to obtain maximum efficiency. The AI controls the use of resources so that the system doesn't overshoot speed or other goals. Every ounce of power is used precisely as needed to provide the desired services.

This list doesn't even begin to scratch the surface. You can find AI and machine learning combined in many other ways. However, it's also useful to view uses of machine learning outside the normal realm that many consider the domain of AI. Here are a few uses for machine learning that you might not associate with AI:

>> **Access control:** In many cases, access control is a yes-or-no proposition. An employee smartcard grants access to a resource in much the same way that people have used keys for centuries. Some locks do offer the capability to set times and dates that access is allowed, but the coarse-grained control doesn't really answer every need. By using machine learning, you can determine whether an employee should gain access to a resource based on role and need. For example, an employee can gain access to a training room when the training reflects an employee role.

>> **Animal protection:** The ocean might seem large enough to allow animals and ships to cohabitate without problems. Unfortunately, many animals get hit by ships each year. A machine learning algorithm could allow ships to avoid animals by learning the sounds and characteristics of both the animal and the ship.

>> **Predicting wait times:** Most people don't like waiting when they have no idea of how long the wait will be. Machine learning allows an application to determine waiting times based on staffing levels, staffing load, complexity of the problems the staff is trying to solve, availability of resources, and so on.

Getting detailed with deep learning

An understanding of deep learning begins with a precise definition of terms. Otherwise, you have a hard time separating the media hype from the realities of what deep learning can actually provide. Deep learning is part of both AI and machine learning, as shown in Figure 2-1. To understand deep learning, you must begin at the outside — that is, you start with AI, and then work your way through machine learning, and then finally define deep learning. The following sections help you through this process.

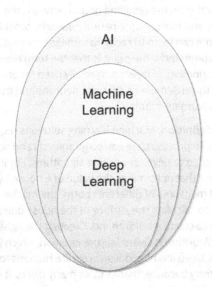

FIGURE 2-1:
Deep learning
is a subset of
machine learning
which is a
subset of AI.

Moving from machine learning to deep learning

Deep learning is a subset of machine learning, as previously mentioned. In both cases, algorithms appear to learn by analyzing huge amounts of data, although learning can occur even with tiny datasets in some cases. However, deep learning varies in the depth of its analysis and the kind of automation it provides. You can summarize the differences between the two like this:

» **A completely different paradigm:** Machine learning consists of a set of many different techniques that enable a computer to learn from data and to use what it learns to provide an answer, often in the form of a prediction. Machine learning relies on different paradigms, such as using statistical analysis, finding analogies in data, using logic, and working with symbols. Contrast the myriad techniques used by machine learning with the single technique used by deep learning, which mimics human brain functionality. It processes data using computing units, called *neurons*, arranged into ordered sections, called *layers*. The technique at the foundation of deep learning is the *neural network*.

» **Flexible architectures:** Machine learning solutions offer many knobs (adjustments) called *hyperparameters* that you tune to optimize algorithm learning from data. Deep learning solutions use hyperparameters, too, but they also use multiple user-configured layers (with the user specifying number and type). In fact, depending on the resulting neural network, the number of layers can be quite large and form unique neural networks capable of specialized learning: Some can learn to recognize images, while others can detect and parse voice commands. The point is that the term *deep* is appropriate; it refers to the large number of layers potentially used for analysis. The architecture consists of the ensemble of different neurons and their arrangement in layers in a deep learning solution.

» **Autonomous feature definition:** Machine learning solutions require human intervention to succeed. To process data correctly, analysts and scientists use a lot of their own knowledge to develop working algorithms. For instance, in a machine learning solution that determines the value of a house by relying on data containing the wall measures of different rooms, the machine learning algorithm won't be able to calculate the surface of the house unless the analyst specifies how to calculate it beforehand. Creating the right information for a machine learning algorithm is called feature creation, which is a time-consuming activity. Deep learning doesn't require humans to perform any feature-creation activity because, thanks to its many layers, it defines its own best features. That's also why deep learning outperforms machine learning in otherwise very difficult tasks such as recognizing voice and images, understanding text, or beating a human champion at the Go game (the digital form of the board game in which you capture your opponent's territory).

You need to understand a number of issues with regard to deep learning solutions, the most important of which is that the computer still doesn't understand anything and isn't aware of the solution it has provided. It simply provides a form of feedback loop and automation conjoined to produce desirable outputs in less time than a human could manually produce precisely the same result by manipulating a machine learning solution.

The second issue is that some benighted people have insisted that the deep learning layers are hidden and not accessible to analysis. This isn't the case. Anything a computer can build is ultimately traceable by a human. In fact, the General Data Protection Regulation (GDPR) (https://eugdpr.org/) requires that humans perform such an analysis (see the article at https://www.pcmag.com/commentary/361258/how-gdpr-will-impact-the-ai-industry for details). The requirement to perform this analysis is controversial, but current law says that someone must do it.

The third issue is that self-adjustment goes only so far. Deep learning doesn't always ensure a reliable or correct result. In fact, deep learning solutions can go horribly wrong (see the article at https://www.theverge.com/2016/3/24/11297050/tay-microsoft-chatbot-racist for details). Even when the application code doesn't go wrong, the devices used to support the deep learning can (see the article at https://www.pcmag.com/commentary/361918/learning-from-alexas-mistakes?source=SectionArticles for details). Despite these problems, you can see deep learning being used for a number of extremely popular applications, as described at https://medium.com/@vratulmittal/top-15-deep-learning-applications-that-will-rule-the-world-in-2018-and-beyond-7c6130c43b01.

Performing deep learning tasks

Humans and computers are best at different tasks. Humans are best at reasoning, thinking through ethical solutions, and being emotional. A computer is meant to process data — lots of data — really fast. You commonly use deep learning to solve problems that require looking for patterns in huge amounts of data — problems whose solution is nonintuitive and not immediately noticeable. The article at http://www.yaronhadad.com/deep-learning-most-amazing-applications/ tells you about 30 different ways in which people are currently using deep learning to perform tasks. In just about every case, you can sum up the problem and its solution as processing huge amounts of data quickly, looking for patterns, and then relying on those patterns to discover something new or to create a particular kind of output.

Employing deep learning in applications

Deep learning can be a stand-alone solution, as illustrated in this book, but it's often used as part of a much larger solution and mixed with other technologies. For example, mixing deep learning with expert systems is not uncommon. The article at https://www.sciencedirect.com/science/article/pii/0167923694900213 describes this mixture to some degree. However, real applications are more than just numbers generated from some nebulous source. When working in the real world, you must also consider various kinds of data sources and understand how those data sources work. A camera may require a different sort of deep learning solution to obtain information from it, while a thermometer or proximity detector may output simple numbers (or analog data that requires some sort of processing to use). Real-world solutions are messy, so you need to be prepared with more than one solution to problems in your toolkit.

Knowing when not to use deep learning

Deep learning is only one way to perform analysis, and it's not always the best way. For example, even though expert systems are considered old technology, you can't really create a self-driving car without one for the reasons described at https://aitrends.com/ai-insider/expert-systems-ai-self-driving-cars-crucial-innovative-techniques/. A deep learning solution turns out to be way too slow for this particular need. Your car will likely contain a deep learning solution, but you're more likely to use it as part of the voice interface.

REMEMBER

AI in general and deep learning in particular can make the headlines when the technology fails to live up to expectations. For example, the article at https://www.techrepublic.com/article/top-10-ai-failures-of-2016/ provides a list of AI failures, some of which relied on deep learning as well. It's a mistake to think that deep learning can somehow make ethical decisions or that it will choose the right course of action based on feelings (which no machine has). Anthropomorphizing the use of deep learning will always be a mistake. Some tasks simply require a human.

Speed and the capability to think like a human are the top issues for deep learning, but there are many more. For example, you can't use deep learning if you don't have sufficient data to train it. In fact, the article at https://www.sas.com/en_us/insights/articles/big-data/5-machine-learning-mistakes.html offers a list of five common mistakes that people make when getting into machine learning and deep learning environments. If you don't have the right resources, deep learning will never work.

Creating a Pipeline from Data to AI

The previous two sections reveal the need for high-quality and reliable data for any analysis need, especially when it comes to AI, machine learning, and deep learning. In some cases, you need huge quantities of data to make these technologies work correctly. However, before you can do anything, you need a pipeline from the clean source of data you create to the technology used to analyze it. The following sections help you understand these requirements.

Considering the desired output

The point of performing any sort of analysis is to obtain a result that reflects certain characteristics. For example, you may want a probability in one case and a categorization in another. The result might have to be numeric in one case, a string in another, a category in another, or a voice output in another. The output determines all other characteristics of the analysis.

Book 2 tells you about data and how to condition it in various ways. In Book 3, you discover basic analysis techniques that are more machine learning–oriented in nature (or are even basic statistics). Book 4 engages you in simple deep learning. However, the real-world look at output comes in Book 5, in which you see data used in interesting ways, such as working with images and analyzing music and video. In other words, most of this book looks at output first and the input and algorithms to obtain it second.

Defining a data architecture

The emphasis of an analysis model is the data used to feed it. In Book 4, Chapter 1, you begin combining algorithms to obtain various effects. This sort of analysis requires that you supply data in a particular form or else the analysis model you create won't work. So, what you really need is a definition of the data architecture — which is the form in which the data must appear in order to work with the analysis model — before you can massage the raw data. The data architecture reflects the requirements of the pipe through which the data flows to an output.

Combining various data sources

When working in a real-world environment, you seldom find the data you need in one place. The main reason for this issue is that databases store information in a form that reflects the needs of its users — those people who rely on the database for informational needs rather than analysis needs. Another reason is that a data scientist must often look to the results of surveys, generated data, and other analyses for the particulars needed to provide probabilities or perform categorization. Book 2, Chapter 1 helps you understand the need to combine data from various sources into a form that you can use to perform a required analysis.

REMEMBER

The use of multiple data sources does mean that you spend a great deal more time ensuring that the data isn't only in the required form, but also that it meshes correctly. You may find that concatenating the datasets won't work — you might have to perform a join, merge, or a cross-tabulation instead. Unless you can visualize how the data should mesh to provide a desired output, the analysis will be flawed, even if you do choose the correct algorithms.

Checking for errors and fixing them

Data errors may not actually appear as errors when you first look at them. In fact, in another situation, the data might not have an error at all. Whether the data is erroneous or not depends on how you use the data and what outcome you need from it. It's not the same as locating an error in code or finding a misplaced symbol in an equation — data errors are grayer, meaning less concrete, than other errors you experience. The grayness of data errors is why Book 6 spends so much time looking at them in multiple ways.

WARNING

Never assume that the data does contain an error unless you prove there is an error. The data may simply not perform as you want it to because of errors in format or conditioning. Book 6, Chapter 1 gives you some clues geared toward what you might call *absolute errors* — those that you can possibly prove in some way. Of course, if you decide that the original data is erroneous, fix the perceived error in the original data file, and then later discover that the use or analysis technique is flawed instead, you have damaged your data without any sort of gain. Always work on a copy of your data and make fixes only when you have proven to yourself that the data is truly flawed.

Performing the analysis

Your data pipeline has to remain functional during the analysis if you expect to get the right result. At a minimum, this requirement means that the data remains accessible. Most of the analyses performed in this book rely on static datasets because they're easier to use for example code. However, when you perform real-time analysis, your data pipeline must continue to stream data to the algorithm. In addition, the data pipeline must deliver the data in a timely manner so that the analysis reflects the real-time nature of the application.

Validating the result

To ensure that you get the correct result, you must actually validate the result in some way, which means creating measurable criteria that defines success. Of course, most data scientists know that they have to meet this requirement during the testing phase. A problem can arise, however, when the data, conditions, requirements, or even algorithmic specifications change over time. The changes can occur slowly, but generally you find that the results are marginal on one day and incorrect on the next. Consequently, the need to validate the result isn't a one-time process, but rather is something you continue to do during the life of the application.

Enhancing application performance

When you say that an analysis performs well, the term may mean something different to the listener than it does to you. As with many areas of communication, the meaning of *performance* depends on the biases of the listener and changes in society as a whole (among other things). When looking at analysis performance, you need to consider these issues:

>> **Speed:** The analysis is useful only when delivered in a timely manner.

>> **Accuracy:** How fast you deliver incorrect information doesn't matter — it's still incorrect.

>> **Reliability:** The data pipeline, analysis model, and output mechanisms should perform correctly every time.

>> **Predictability:** The result should appear within a defined tolerance unless you find a good reason for a change (such as a difference in conditions).

Chapter **3**

Creating a Data Science Lab of Your Own

This book helps you gain an understanding of data science using two different languages: Python and R. Of course, not everyone will want to learn both languages, and you're not required to do so. Still, you need to choose one of them and create a data science lab of your own so that you can follow along with the examples. Consequently, this chapter begins by examining various options you have for creating your lab — they're extensive because data science has become so popular, and so many people with different skill sets need data science to perform tasks. After you choose the options you want, you usually need to perform some amount of setup to create your lab. This chapter also helps you toward that end.

As part of performing some data science tasks, you also use a framework. In most cases, your language will require that you import either *libraries* or *packages* containing add-on code that makes performing data science tasks easier. The add-ons reside within your application and become part of it. A *framework* is different because it controls your application environment, and your application resides within it. Frameworks and libraries aren't mutually exclusive, and you generally use them together to perform specific tasks. This chapter provides you with additional details about frameworks and helps you understand what they can provide.

An *Integrated Development Environment (IDE)* also makes the task of performing data science tasks easier by providing you with an editor and associated tools to write code, compile it as needed, and perform tasks such as testing and debugging. This book relies on Anaconda, which is a suite of various tools used to create data science code, including the Jupyter Notebook IDE. This chapter doesn't provide you with a complete Anaconda tutorial; that task might require an entire book by itself. However, you do gain enough knowledge to perform essential tasks to make your learning experience better.

The final part of this chapter discusses the downloadable source code for this book. You don't have to manually type all the source code you see, and in fact it can be detrimental to do so because you might have to deal with issues like typos. Using the downloadable source makes your job a lot easier and helps you spend your time learning about data science rather than debugging faulty code. Of course, after you learn a particular topic, it's a good idea to practice what you learn by typing the code manually. You can find instructions for obtaining the downloadable source in the book's Introduction. This chapter helps you work with the code after you have it downloaded.

REMEMBER

You don't have to type the source code for this chapter manually. In fact, it's a lot easier if you use the downloadable source. The source code for this chapter appears in the DSPD_0103_Sample.ipynb source code file for Python and the DSPD_R_0103_Sample.ipynb source code file for R. See the Introduction for details on how to find these source files.

Considering the Analysis Platform Options

Your analysis platform defines how you interact with the various tools used to perform analysis with data science. It also determines any limitations or requirements needed to implement the platform successfully. The two common approaches today are to set up a desktop PC with the required tools or to rely on an online IDE instead. Both options come with issues that you must consider. For example, the PC option provides environmental flexibility and reliability, but at a cost. Meanwhile, an online IDE provides locational flexibility, often at a greatly reduced cost, if not free.

REMEMBER

The chapter also considers the use of the Graphics Processing Unit (GPU), which may seem confusing because most people associate a GPU with drawing objects onscreen. Using one or more GPUs can greatly speed your analysis. The final section helps you understand why a GPU can be so important, especially when performing complex analysis or using techniques such as deep learning.

Using a desktop system

Desktop systems offer significant flexibility in configuring a data-analysis environment specifically suited to your needs. You have control over every aspect of a desktop system, which means that if you don't like how a system performs, you can change it so that the performance becomes acceptable. For example, you can often make a desktop system fly by adding a GPU, additional memory, a faster processor, or even a faster hard drive. However, all this flexibility costs something. You need to buy the various pieces of hardware you want to make the system happen. So, you might have to balance cost against needs and consider how much performance you can afford.

Along with system control, you must also consider issues like data control. A desktop system can maintain data on the local system, which can help you meet privacy, governmental, and other requirements. The consistent access provided by a local system can also make a difference. Of course, when using a desktop system, you must consider backup and data redundancy needs. You don't want a local lightning storm to wipe out all your hard work.

TIP

A desktop system also comes with various human environment benefits. You don't have to deal with using a small screen for seeing output from a complex analysis as you might when working with a tablet. In fact, you can spread the output across as many screens as your system will support — two, in most cases, even with a low-end system. You also have aspects like better keyboard support and so on to consider. These comfort features may not seem important when performing analysis, but they can become essential when dealing with a huge amount of data over the long hours needed to work with it.

The most important consideration when working with desktop systems is consistency. After you create and set up your environment, you can count on the desktop setup to perform in a certain way each time you use it, barring some sort of hardware or other error. When you're in a rush, you don't want to find that the resources you were counting on to get the job done suddenly become unavailable.

Working with an online IDE

Online IDEs have become popular for two reasons: They often cost nothing to use, and you can use them just about anywhere you have an Internet connection. This chapter discusses the use of Google Colaboratory (often shortened to Colab) later, but you need to be aware that online IDEs exist in a lot of places and in many forms. Choosing the online IDE that you prefer based on your personal needs can require time, but after you've determined which one you want, you can load it up into any device that supports a browser and has a keyboard (even if that keyboard exists only on a screen).

REMEMBER

Even though online IDEs are normally associated with tablets and other smaller devices because of their connectivity flexibility, you can also use one with a desktop system. Of course, you use it within a browser, so you may not have the level of flexibility that you get with a dedicated system. In addition, you likely won't make use of any special features possessed by your desktop system. This said, you can also get by with a much less expensive desktop system should you decide to go the online IDE route.

Considering the need for a GPU

A *CPU* is a general-purpose processor that can perform a wide assortment of tasks. The designers might not even have a clue about just what sorts of tasks the CPU design will perform. However, this general processing orientation takes space, so a CPU usually contains just a few cores — each of which can perform a single instruction at a time. An 8-core CPU can perform up to eight general tasks at a time.

GPUs perform a significantly more defined and less flexible array of tasks than CPUs, but this specialization has an advantage in size. Consequently, a GPU can perform a significantly greater number of tasks simultaneously because it typically has far more cores than a CPU does. The trade-off is that you can't build a complete application using a GPU. A GPU still requires input from a CPU to know what to do and when to do it. The following sections discuss GPUs in greater detail.

Using NVidia products for desktop systems

The reason NVidia appears so often in GPU discussions is that the company is at the forefront of making GPUs useful for tasks other than mere graphics display. Data science relies heavily on matrix manipulation (see Book 2, Chapter 3 for details about matrix manipulation), which is something a GPU does quite well. The company created the Compute Unified Device Architecture (CUDA), which makes it possible to use GPUs to perform data analysis. You can read a detailed discussion of precisely why CUDA is important at https://www.datascience.com/blog/cpu-gpu-machine-learning. The point is that you can't use just any GPU for data science; you need a GPU with CUDA cores, in most cases.

REMEMBER

Don't think that you get GPU support without a lot of effort. To use a GPU, you must install the required libraries and learn new programming techniques. Consequently, even though the processing speed is faster, you partly pay for it with greater development and testing time. Plus, applications that require a GPU to perform adequately limit the number of platforms on which they'll run.

TECHNICAL STUFF

A GPU is more than just one order of magnitude more powerful than a CPU when it comes to performing specific math operations. Currently, the most powerful GPU in the world is the NVidia Titan V (https://www.nvidia.com/en-us/titan/titan-v/), which comes with 5,120 CUDA cores. That's 640 times the processing power of a CPU when you consider just the physical processing capacity. A GPU also optimizes math tasks, so the actual impact is significantly larger. The article at https://www.anandtech.com/show/12673/titan-v-deep-learning-deep-dive provides specifics on just how much more powerful a GPU is. However, to put this scenario into easily understood terms, a test application that required more than nine hours to run using just a standard PC with eight cores required only five minutes to run on a system sporting a Titan V GPU.

WARNING

Note that adding a large GPU like the Titan V to your system will increase power and cooling requirements. You'll likely need additional cooling fans (which are noisy) to keep your system cool. Something that many people don't consider is that the addition could make your office considerably warmer as well. If you don't address these additional requirements, you might find that your system can't complete processing tasks without overheating.

Defining framework needs

A framework, such as TensorFlow, which is used to perform deep learning tasks, creates an environment in which to run applications under controlled conditions. The "Presenting Frameworks" section, later in this chapter, describes precisely what a framework is and why you want to use one. However, the important thing to consider about frameworks and GPUs is that most frameworks provide some level of built-in GPU support. Consequently, you have all the advantages of using a GPU, with far fewer of the disadvantages.

Creating a Data Science
Lab of Your Own

Understanding the limits of online GPUs

When working with an online IDE, you may see an option to use a GPU with it, which is optimal when you can get it. However, you need to be aware that the GPU may not always be available, even if you check the option to request one. In addition, you can't be sure of what sort of GPU support you get, especially considering that the online IDE is likely free. The lack of GPU support is one of the things that makes using an online IDE risky if you need to process a lot of data and get the results quickly.

Choosing a Development Language

You might be amazed at the number of ways that people use computers and the tasks that computers perform without your knowledge. Computers come in all sorts of form factors — not just the smart phone, tablet, laptop, or desktop system you use. If you have newer appliances in your home, you might find that they contain computers. Even thermostats now sport computers that do everything from maintain complex operating schedules to report the efficiency of your system in an email sent directly to your Inbox. So, it shouldn't surprise you that no single best computer language exists to express the myriad ideas that people have for using them in both mundane and interesting ways. In fact, it shouldn't even surprise you that people rely on a number of different languages to perform data analysis using data science techniques.

REMEMBER

When contemplating the development language you want to use to write your data science application, you must consider the needs of your project and your personal needs first. A computer speaks only one language: machine code. In fact, the computer doesn't actually understand machine code; the machine code simply flips switches inside the processor to cause it to perform certain actions. The computer language you use always ends up translated into machine code at some point, so the language you use should meet your needs. The computer doesn't know or care about which language you use. With the goal of meeting your needs in mind, this book uses these two languages to help you perform data science tasks with greater ease:

>> **Python:** Many data scientists choose Python because it's easy to learn, has strong community support, supports multiple programming paradigms, and provides access to a long list of useful packages. According to the article at https://www.datanami.com/2018/07/19/python-gains-traction-among-data-scientists/, a whopping 48 percent of younger data scientists prefer Python to any other language. These numbers go down for older data scientists.

>> **R:** At one time, data scientists favored R over Python, but Python has caught up over the years, enough that you might wonder whether learning R is still a good idea. Statisticians originally created R to perform statistical analysis, and it's still the favored language for that purpose today because you can create incredibly complex models with it. Some developers also prefer the manner in which R helps you create presentations. In fact, the Shiny add-on (http://shiny.rstudio.com/) lets you create interactive applications directly from your R analysis. Yes, you have access to MatPlotLib in Python, but R has built-in functionality that tends to work better for certain tasks. Like Python, R also supports a strong developer community that continually pumps out more packages to help you get work done faster. In some cases, developers choose R over Python simply because of the growing pains Python has suffered, as expressed by the article at https://www.r-bloggers.com/why-r-for-data-science-and-not-python/.

USING OTHER PROGRAMMING LANGUAGES FOR DATA SCIENCE

The reason this book uses these languages is that they represent popular choices for common data science and general application development needs, but you must remember that other languages support data science, too. One way to help you decide which language to choose when you have several in mind and they all seem equally good at the task you want to perform is to look at language popularity on sites such as Tiobe (https://www.tiobe.com/tiobe-index/). The Tiobe Index is one of the most cited language- popularity lists because it proves to be correct so often. (Alternatives include paid sites like IEEE Spectrum, where Python currently appears as the most used language.) However, make sure that you also consider factors such as your personal knowledge, availability of resources, cost, and so on when making a choice.

The article at https://bigdata-madesimple.com/top-8-programming-languages-every-data-scientist-should-master-in-2019/ provides you with other language choices such as Java, SQL, and Julia. All these languages have benefits and potential problems. Choose your language carefully because many of them currently come with hidden issues and you may find that you can't make things work in the middle of a project because of a lack of library support. Most especially, make sure you look at issues such as plotting your data because some languages are weak in this area.

Obtaining and Using Python

If you choose to use Python to follow the book examples, you need to install a copy of Python on your system. The following sections provide detailed information for installing Python as part of Anaconda on a Windows system, with an overview for both Mac and Linux systems. If you don't plan to install Python on your system, you can skip this section.

Working with Python in this book

The Python environment changes constantly. As the Python community continues to improve Python, the language experiences *breaking changes* — those that create new behaviors while reducing backward compatibility. These changes might not be major, but they're a distraction that will reduce your ability to discover data science programming techniques. Obviously, you want to discover data science with as few distractions as possible, so having the correct environment is essential. Here is what you need to use Python with this book:

>> Jupyter Notebook version 5.5.0

>> Anaconda 3 environment version 5.2.0

>> Python version 3.7.3

TIP

If you don't have this setup, you may find that the examples don't work as intended. The screenshots will most likely differ and the procedures may not work as planned.

WARNING

As you go through the book, you need to install various Python packages to make the code work. Like the Python environment you configure in this chapter, these packages have specific version numbers. If you use a different version of a package, the examples may not execute at all. In addition, you may become frustrated trying to work through error messages that have nothing to do with the book's code but instead result from using the wrong version number. Make sure to exercise care when installing Anaconda, Jupyter Notebook, Python, and all the packages needed to make your deep learning experience as smooth as possible.

USE OF NOTEBOOK IN THE BOOK

This book shortens Jupyter Notebook to just Notebook in the interest of brevity. Whenever you see Notebook in a chapter, think of the Jupyter Notebook IDE.

Obtaining and installing Anaconda for Python

Before you can move forward, you need to obtain and install a copy of Anaconda. Yes, you can obtain and install Notebook separately, but then you lack various other applications that come with Anaconda, such as the Anaconda Prompt, which appears in various parts of the book. The best idea is to install Anaconda using the instructions that appear in the following sections for your particular platform (Linux, MacOS, or Windows).

Getting Continuum Analytics Anaconda

The basic Anaconda package is a free download from `https://repo.anaconda.com/archive/` to obtain the 5.2.0 version used in this book. Simply click one of the Python 3.6 Version links to obtain access to the free product. The filename you want begins with `Anaconda3-5.2.0-` followed by the platform and 32-bit or 64-bit version, such as `Anaconda3-5.2.0-Windows-x86_64.exe` for the Windows 64-bit version. Anaconda supports the following platforms:

>> Windows 32-bit and 64-bit (The installer may offer you only the 64-bit or 32-bit version, depending on which version of Windows it detects.)

>> Linux 32-bit and 64-bit

>> macOS 64-bit

The free product is all you need for this book. However, when you look on the site, you see that many other add-on products are available. These products can help you create robust applications. For example, when you add Accelerate to the mix, you obtain the capability to perform multicore and GPU-enabled operations. The use of these add-on products is outside the scope of this book, but the Anaconda site provides details on using them.

Installing Anaconda for Windows

Anaconda comes with a graphical installation application for Windows, so getting a good install means using a wizard, much as you would for any other installation. Of course, you need a copy of the installation file before you begin, and you can find the required download information in the "Getting Continuum Analytics Anaconda" section, earlier in this chapter. The following procedure should work fine on any Windows system, whether you use the 32-bit or the 64-bit version of Anaconda:

1. **Locate the downloaded copy of Anaconda on your system.**

    The name of this file varies, but normally it appears as Anaconda3-5.2.0-Windows-x86.exe for 32-bit systems and Anaconda3-5.2.0-Windows-x86_64.exe for 64-bit systems. The version number is embedded as part of the filename. In this case, the filename refers to version 5.2.0, which is the version used for this book. If you use some other version, you may experience problems with the source code and need to make adjustments when working with it.

2. **Double-click the installation file.**

    (You may see an Open File – Security Warning dialog box that asks whether you want to run this file. Click Run if you see this dialog box pop up.) You see an Anaconda 5.2.0 Setup dialog box similar to the one shown in Figure 3-1. The exact dialog box you see depends on which version of the Anaconda installation program you download. If you have a 64-bit operating system, using the 64-bit version of Anaconda is always best for obtaining the best possible performance. This first dialog box tells you when you have the 64-bit version of the product.

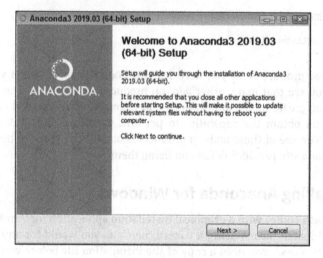

FIGURE 3-1:
The setup process begins by telling you whether you have the 64-bit version.

3. **Click Next.**

    The wizard displays a licensing agreement. Be sure to read through the licensing agreement so that you know the terms of usage.

4. **Click I Agree if you agree to the licensing agreement.**

You're asked what sort of installation type to perform, as shown in Figure 3-2. In most cases, you want to install the product just for yourself. The exception is if you have multiple people using your system and they all need access to Anaconda. The selection of Just Me or All Users will affect the installation destination folder in the next step.

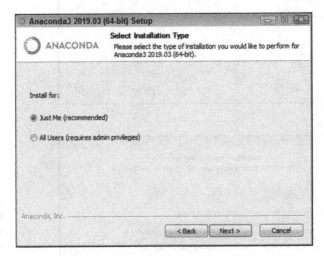

FIGURE 3-2: Tell the wizard how to install Anaconda on your system.

5. **Choose one of the installation types and then click Next.**

The wizard asks where to install Anaconda on disk, as shown in Figure 3-3. The book assumes that you use the default location, which will generally install the product in your C:\Users\<User Name>\Anaconda3 folder. If you choose some other location, you may have to modify some procedures later in the book to work with your setup. You may be asked whether you want to create the destination folder. If so, simply allow the folder creation.

6. **Choose an installation location (if necessary) and then click Next.**

You see the Advanced Installation Options, shown in Figure 3-4. These options are selected by default and you have no good reason to change them in most cases. You might need to change them if Anaconda won't provide your default Python 3.6 setup. However, the book assumes that you've set up Anaconda using the default options.

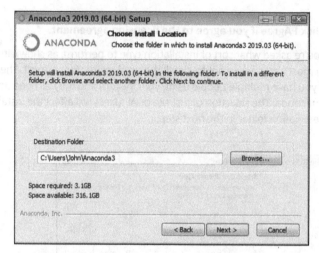

FIGURE 3-3:
Specify an
installation
location.

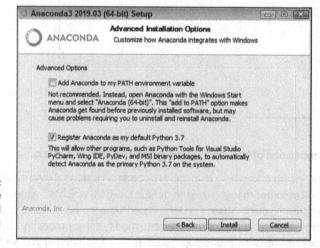

FIGURE 3-4:
Configure
the advanced
installation
options.

TIP

The Add Anaconda to My PATH Environment Variable option is deselected by default, and you should leave it deselected. Adding it to the PATH environment variable does offer the ability to locate the Anaconda files when using a standard command prompt, but if you have multiple versions of Anaconda installed, only the first version that you installed is accessible. Opening an Anaconda Prompt instead is far better so that you gain access to the version you expect.

7. **Change the advanced installation options (if necessary) and then click Install.**

You see an Installing dialog box with a progress bar. The installation process can take a few minutes, so get yourself a cup of coffee and read the comics for a while. When the installation process is over, you see a Next button enabled.

8. **Click Next.**

The wizard tells you that the installation is complete.

9. **Click Next.**

Anaconda offers you the chance to integrate Visual Studio code support. You don't need this support for this book, and adding it might change the way that the Anaconda tools work. Unless you absolutely need Visual Studio support, you want to keep the Anaconda environment pure.

10. **Click Skip.**

You see a completion screen. This screen contains options to discover more about Anaconda Cloud and to obtain information about starting your first Anaconda project. Selecting these options (or deselecting them) depends on what you want to do next, and the options don't affect your Anaconda setup.

11. **Select any required options. Click Finish.**

You're ready to begin using Anaconda.

Creating an Anaconda for Mac setup

As with the Windows installation, you must download a copy of Anaconda 5.2.0 for your Mac system. However, you can use a number of methods to perform this task based on the precise version of macOS that you own. The instructions at https://mas-dse.github.io/startup/anaconda-macosx-install/ provide a terminal-based installation where you don't have to work through extra steps to get the task done. This version relies on using curl to perform the download. The instructions at https://docs.anaconda.com/anaconda/install/mac-os/ provide both a graphical installation and a terminal installation that works for other users. Choose the installation method that works best for your particular setup.

Creating an Anaconda for Linux setup

As with the Windows installation, you need a copy of Anaconda 5.2.0 to make the examples in this book execute properly. However, each version of Linux seems to come with slightly different installation instructions. Most Linux users will find that the instructions at https://docs.anaconda.com/anaconda/install/linux/ or https://docs.anaconda.com/anaconda/install/linux-power8/ work best. However, owners of an Ubuntu setup may find that they prefer the instructions at https://www.osetc.com/en/how-to-install-anaconda-on-ubuntu-16-04-17-04-18-04.html or https://www.digitalocean.com/community/tutorials/how-to-install-anaconda-on-ubuntu-18-04-quickstart better.

Defining a Python code repository

The code you create and use in this book will reside in a repository on your hard drive. Think of a *repository* as a kind of filing cabinet where you put your code. Notebook opens a drawer, takes out the folder, and shows the code to you. You can modify it, run individual examples within the folder, add new examples, and simply interact with your code in a natural manner. The following sections get you started with Notebook so that you can see how this whole repository concept works.

Defining the book's folder

You use folders to hold your code files for a particular project. The project for this book is DSPD (which stands for *Data Science Programming All-in-One For Dummies*). The following steps help you create a new folder for this book:

1. **Choose New⇨Folder.**

    Notebook creates a new folder for you. The name of the folder can vary, but for Windows users, it's simply listed as Untitled Folder. You may have to scroll down the list of available folders to find the folder in question.

2. **Select the box next to Untitled Folder.**

3. **Click Rename at the top of the page.**

    You see the Rename Directory dialog box, shown in Figure 3-5.

4. **Type DSPD and press Enter.**

    Notebook renames the folder for you.

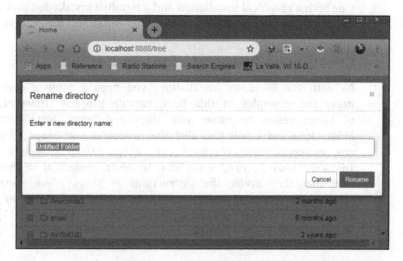

FIGURE 3-5:
Create a folder to use to hold the book's code.

Creating a new notebook

Every new notebook is like a file folder. You can place individual examples within the file folder, just as you would sheets of paper into a physical file folder. Each example appears in a cell. You can put other sorts of data in the file folder, too, but you see how to perform these tasks as the book progresses. Use these steps to create a new notebook:

1. **Click the DSPD entry on the home page.**

    You see the contents of the project folder for this book, which will be blank if you're performing this exercise from scratch.

2. **Choose New⇨Python 3.**

    A new tab opens in the browser with the new notebook, as shown in Figure 3-6. Notice that the notebook contains a cell and that Notebook has highlighted the cell so that you can begin typing code in it. The title of the notebook is Untitled right now. That's not a particularly helpful title, so you need to change it.

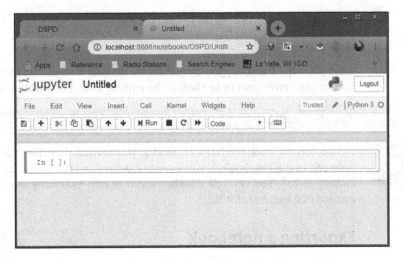

FIGURE 3-6: Provide a new name for your notebook.

3. **Click Untitled on the page.**

    Notebook asks what you want to use as a new name, as shown in Figure 3-7.

4. **Type** DSPD_0103_Sample **and press Enter.**

    The new name tells you that this is a file for *Data Science Programming All-in-One For Dummies*, Book 1, Chapter 3, Sample.ipynb. Using this naming convention helps you to easily differentiate these files from other files in your repository.

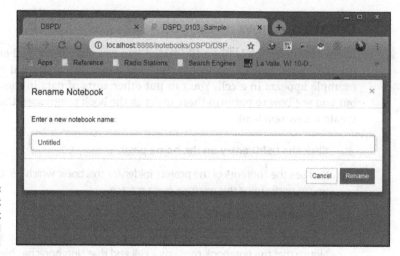

FIGURE 3-7:
A notebook
contains cells that
you use to hold
code.

After you create a new notebook, you see a cell that is ready to receive code. Simply type:

```
myString = "Hello, World!"
print(myString)
```

After you type the code, you can test it by clicking Run on the toolbar. Here is the output you can expect to see below the editing area, but within the same cell:

```
Hello, World!
```

TIP

Notice that the code cell has a [1] next to it, showing that this is the first executed code cell in the Notebook. If you were to execute this cell again, the number would change to [2]. You can tell whether a cell is still executing because you see [*] instead of a number if it is.

Exporting a notebook

Creating notebooks and keeping them all to yourself isn't much fun. At some point, you want to share them with other people. To perform this task, you must export your notebook from the repository to a file. You can then send the file to someone else, who will import it into his or her repository.

The previous section, "Creating a new notebook," shows how to create a notebook named DSPD_0103_Sample. You can open this notebook by clicking its entry in the repository list. The file reopens so that you can see your code again. To export this code, choose File⇨ Download As ⇨ Notebook (.ipynb). What you see next depends on your browser, but you generally see some sort of dialog box for saving the notebook as a file. Use the same method for saving the Notebook file as you use for any other file you save using your browser.

Saving a notebook

You eventually want to save your notebook so that you can review the code later and impress your friends by running it after you ensure that it doesn't contain any errors. Notebook periodically saves your notebook for you automatically. However, to save it manually, you choose File⇨Save and Checkpoint.

Closing a notebook

You definitely shouldn't just close the browser window when you finish working with your notebook. Doing so will likely cause data loss. You must perform an orderly closing of your file, which includes stopping the kernel used to run the code in the background. After you save your notebook, you can close it by choosing File⇨Close and Halt. You see your notebook entered in the list of notebooks for your project folder, as shown in Figure 3-8.

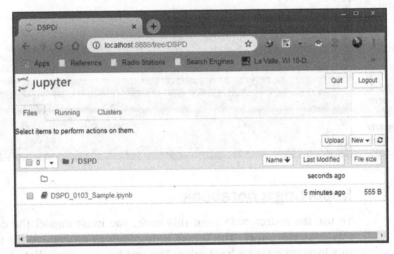

FIGURE 3-8:
Your saved notebooks appear in a list in the project folder.

Removing a notebook

Sometimes notebooks get outdated or you simply don't need to work with them any longer. Rather than allow your repository to get clogged with files you don't need, you can remove these unwanted notebooks from the list. Use these steps to remove the file:

1. **Select the check box next to the DSPD_0103_Sample.ipynb entry.**

2. **Click the Delete (trash can) icon.**

   A Delete notebook warning message appears, like the one shown in Figure 3-9.

3. **Click Delete.**

   Notebook removes the notebook file from the list.

WARNING

Exercise care when deleting notebook files. Notebook lacks any form of Undo for files, so trying to recover a deleted file can prove difficult.

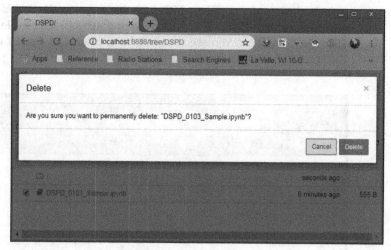

FIGURE 3-9:
Notebook warns you before removing any files from the repository.

Importing a notebook

To use the source code from this book, you must import the downloaded files into your repository. The source code comes in an archive file that you extract to a location on your hard drive. The archive contains a list of .ipynb (IPython Notebook) files containing the source code for this book (see the Introduction for details on downloading the source code). The following steps tell how to import these files into your repository:

1. **Click the Upload on the Notebook DSPD page.**

   What you see depends on your browser. In most cases, you see some type of File Upload dialog box that provides access to the files on your hard drive.

2. **Navigate to the directory containing the files that you want to import into Notebook.**

3. **Highlight one or more files to import and then click the Open (or other, similar) button to begin the upload process.**

   You see the file added to an upload list, as shown in Figure 3-10. The file isn't part of the repository yet — you've simply selected it for upload.

4. **Click Upload.**

   Notebook places the file in the repository so that you can begin using it.

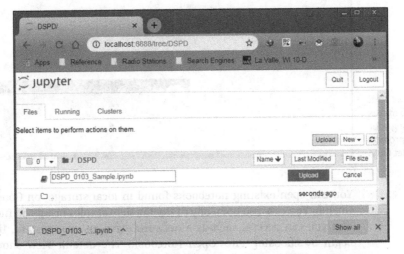

FIGURE 3-10:
The files you
want to add to
the repository
appear as part of
an upload list.

Working with Python using Google Colaboratory

Colaboratory (https://colab.research.google.com/notebooks/welcome.ipynb), or Colab for short, is a Google cloud-based service that replicates Notebook in the cloud. This is a custom implementation, so you may find Colab and Notebook to be out of sync at times — meaning that features in one may not always work in the other. You don't have to install anything on your system to use Colab. In most respects, you use Colab as you would a desktop installation of Notebook. The main reason to learn more about Colab is if you want to use a device other than a standard desktop setup to work through the examples in this book. If you want a fuller tutorial of Colab, you can find one in Chapter 4 of *Python For Data Science For Dummies*, 2nd Edition, by John Paul Mueller and Luca Massaron (Wiley). For now, this section gives you the basics of using existing files. Figure 3-11 shows the opening Colab display.

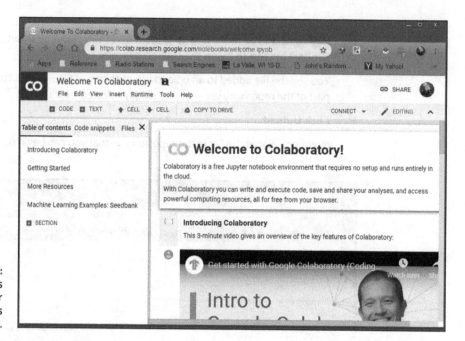

FIGURE 3-11:
Colab makes
using your
Python projects
on a tablet easy.

You can open existing notebooks found in local storage, on Google Drive, or on GitHub. You can also open any of the Colab examples or upload files from sources that you can access, such as a network drive on your system. In all cases, you begin by choosing File⇨Open Notebook. The default view shows all the files you opened recently, regardless of location. The files appear in alphabetical order. You can filter the number of items displayed by typing a string into Filter Notebooks. Across the top are other options for opening notebooks.

TIP

Even if you're not logged in, you can still access the Colab example projects. These projects help you understand Colab but don't allow you to do anything with your own projects. Even so, you can still experiment with Colab without logging into Google first. Here is a quick list of the ways to use files with Colab:

>> **Using Drive for existing notebooks:** Google Drive is the default location for many operations in Colab, and you can always choose it as a destination. When working with Drive, you see a listing of files. To open a particular file, you click its link in the dialog box. The file opens in the current tab of your browser.

>> **Using GitHub for existing notebooks:** When working with GitHub, you initially need to provide the location of the source code online. The location must point to a public project; you can't use Colab to access your private projects. After you make the connection to GitHub, you see a list of repositories (which are containers for code related to a particular project) and branches (which

represent particular implementations of the code). Selecting a repository and branch displays a list of notebook files that you can load into Colab. Simply click the required link and it loads as if you were using Google Drive.

>> **Using local storage for existing notebooks:** If you want to use the downloadable source for this book, or any local source, for that matter, you select the Upload tab of the dialog box. In the center, you see a single button called Choose File. Clicking this button opens the File Open dialog box for your browser. You locate the file you want to upload, just as you normally would for any file you want to open. Selecting a file and clicking Open uploads the file to Google Drive. If you make changes to the file, those changes appear on Google Drive, not on your local drive.

TIP

Google is aware that people want to use Colab for their R projects (along with other languages; see the "Using other programming languages for data science" sidebar, earlier in this chapter, for details). However, Colab doesn't currently support these languages and no date set exists for implementing the required support. Consequently, if you choose to use Colab for the book's projects, you must work with Python.

Defining the limits of using Azure Notebooks with Python and R

As with Colab, you can use Azure Notebooks (see Figure 3-12) (https://notebooks.azure.com/) to run your Python code. Fortunately, in this case, an R kernel available, as described at https://notebooks.azure.com/help/jupyter-notebooks/available-kernels. You can also install R packages and use them in your code, as described at https://notebooks.azure.com/help/jupyter-notebooks/package-installation/r. One of the most important issues that differentiate Colab and Azure Notebooks is that Google released Colab in 2014, so it has become a mature product, while Azure Notebooks is still in preview mode. Here are some other issues to consider:

>> Colab supports 20GB of memory; Azure Notebooks is limited to 4GB.

>> Azure Notebooks doesn't provide any GPU support.

>> Azure Notebooks does provide better file support than Colab using the Libraries feature.

>> Azure Notebooks provides configuration support using YAML files.

>> Azure Notebooks provides an integrated bash terminal, but you can run bash commands directly in your Colab code using the ! command.

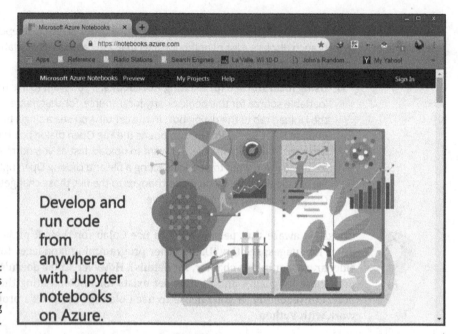

FIGURE 3-12:
Azure Notebooks provides another means of running Python code.

Obtaining and Using R

This book relies on Anaconda for demonstrating the data science code. You must begin by installing Anaconda, as described in the "Obtaining and installing Anaconda for Python" section, earlier in this chapter. After you have an Anaconda installation in place, you can use the instructions in the following sections to create an R environment in which you can execute the book's R code.

Obtaining and installing Anaconda for R

To install R, you must open the Anaconda Prompt. For Windows users, this means choosing Start⇨All Programs⇨Anaconda3⇨Anaconda Prompt. You see the Anaconda Prompt, shown in Figure 3-13. Notice the word *(base)* at the beginning of the prompt. This is the current environment — the base environment.

At the Anaconda Prompt, type **conda create -n R_env r-essentials r-base** and press Enter. This command creates a new Anaconda environment called R_env. Whenever you want to work with R code, you use the R_env environment. Within this environment, conda, the Anaconda command-line utility, installs R essentials and base packages. This set of packages is enough to get you started. However, you can install other packages later as needed for specific kinds of analysis. The installation process displays a series of messages that ends with a listing of packages that conda will install, like those shown in Figure 3-14.

FIGURE 3-13:
Open an
Anaconda Prompt
to install R.

FIGURE 3-14:
The conda utility
tells you which
packages it will
install.

You can begin the installation process by typing **y** and pressing Enter. At this point, conda begins to download and extract packages. When the downloads complete, conda performs various transactional processes that can include compiling some of the packages it downloaded into executables (or other forms). This process can take a while, so you might want to have a good book ready or some coffee to drink.

REMEMBER

After the installation process completes, you're still in the (base) environment. To work with the (R_env), you must type **conda activate R_env** at the Anaconda Prompt. You can how use whatever directory command your platform supports to see a list of the files that conda installed. To leave the (R_env) environment and go back to the (base) environment, you type **conda deactivate** and press Enter.

Starting the R environment

Fortunately, you won't work at the Anaconda Prompt when you want to work with R code. However, you won't start Notebook directly, either, because doing so

Creating a Data Science
Lab of Your Own

starts the (base) environment and you want the (R_env) environment. Instead, you start Anaconda Navigator, which appears in Figure 3-15. Notice that this utility provides you with access to all the GUI tools that Anaconda supports (and if you don't see what you need, you can always install more).

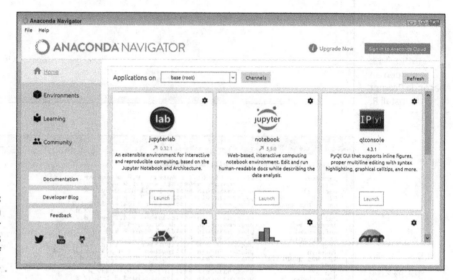

FIGURE 3-15:
Anaconda
Navigator
provides access
to a number of
useful tools.

To start R, you must first select R_env in the Applications On drop-down list box, as shown in Figure 3-16. The tools you see will change to reflect what you can do with this environment. The important tool for this book is Notebook. Note the gear icon in the upper-right corner of the square. If you need to change the version of Notebook, click the icon and choose Install Specific Version from the list.

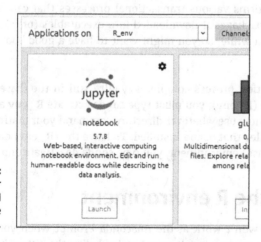

FIGURE 3-16:
Changing your
environment will
often change the
available tool list.

Click Launch in the Notebook square to start the application. You see Notebook start in a browser, just as you do when working with Python, but now you're working with R instead.

Defining an R code repository

Because you're using Notebook, everything with R works precisely the same as it does for Python, as described in the "Defining a Python code repository" section, earlier in this chapter. The name of the R repository for this book is DSPD_R. Use the instructions in the "Defining a Python code repository" section to create an R repository and experiment with an R file. However, instead of choosing Python 3 from the New drop-down list, you choose R instead. Otherwise, everything works as it would for Python. The test file for this section is DSPD_R_0103_Sample.ipynb.

TIP

Something important to note when using R is that you can download your code as an .r file, as shown in Figure 3-17. In fact, you have not only the Notebook formats to choose from, but a number of R-specific formats as well. To keep things simple, the downloadable source for this book relies on .ipynb files for all source code to ensure that you get the required comments with the file.

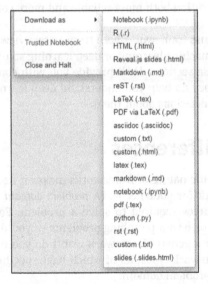

Download as	▸	Notebook (.ipynb)
Trusted Notebook		R (.r)
		HTML (.html)
Close and Halt		Reveal.js slides (.html)
		Markdown (.md)
		reST (.rst)
		LaTeX (.tex)
		PDF via LaTeX (.pdf)
		asciidoc (.asciidoc)
		custom (.txt)
		custom (.html)
		latex (.tex)
		markdown (.md)
		notebook (.ipynb)
		pdf (.tex)
		python (.py)
		rst (.rst)
		custom (.txt)
		slides (.slides.html)

FIGURE 3-17:
You can save R code in .r files, but the .r files lack Notebook comments.

You can perform a quick test of your R environment using the following code:

```
myString <- "Hello, World!"
print(myString)
```

After you click Run, you see the following output:

```
[1] "Hello, World!"
```

Presenting Frameworks

Sometimes you use a framework to work with an application, especially as you move from data science–specific analysis into other areas, such as machine learning and deep learning. Consequently, an overview of frameworks is helpful. You may find that you need to move from the environment provided for the majority of the examples in this book to something better suited for complex applications.

In a framework environment, your code makes requests of the framework, which then fulfills the request for you. Consequently, frameworks provide a kind of structure for application development. Because of this structure, frameworks are domain specific, answering specific kinds of application development needs. By taking care of some of the details for you and controlling the manner in which your application executes, a framework reduces the amount of coding you perform and makes your application both more reliable and more consistent.

The following sections discuss frameworks both from an overview perspective and in more detail as part of a machine learning or deep learning solution. It's important to remember that these sections don't provide you with complete information on frameworks, but they do help you understand deep learning frameworks well enough to make good decisions about them.

Defining the differences

The problem domain–specific nature of frameworks makes it necessary to locate the right sort of framework for your needs. (A *problem domain* is a description of the expertise and resources required to solve a problem. For example, you wouldn't go to a doctor to solve your plumbing problems — you'd go to a plumber instead.) Simply asking for a general framework won't do you much good. Here are some examples of framework types, all of which have specific characteristics to meet the needs of their problem domain:

>> Application framework (of the sort used to create end-user applications)

>> Artistic (drawing, music, and other creative forms)

>> Cactus framework (high-performance scientific computing)

>> Decision support system

>> Earth system modeling

>> Financial modeling

>> Web framework (including language-specific frameworks for languages like such as AJAX and JavaScript)

REMEMBER

The diversity of software frameworks is amazing, and you're unlikely to ever need them all. They do have two important features in common. In each case, the framework defines a series of *frozen spots* that define the characteristics of the application and that the developer can't change. In addition, the framework defines *hot spots* that a developer does use to define the specifics to the target software. For example, a frozen spot in a web application might define the interface on which a user relies to make requests, while a hot spot might define how to fulfill that request. Someone designing a book search application would focus on the specifics of book searches while disregarding the requirements of state management and request handling.

Explaining the popularity of frameworks

In thinking about software, you can easily see the progression of tools used to create it. At one time, developers had to input their code using keypunch cards, which was extremely time consuming and error prone. Editors made the job easier, allowing you to type what you want to get done. Next came the Integrated Development Environment (IDE). Using an IDE allows modeling, compilation, and testing of the code in a single environment, along with other things. The use of libraries enables you to create large, complex applications quickly. So, a framework — which is an environment in which a developer needs to consider only the specifies of a particular application — is simply the next step in making developers more productive while also making applications more robust and less error prone. Hence the popularity of frameworks with developers.

REMEMBER

However, a framework is much more than simply a means of creating code faster, with less effort and fewer errors. A framework lets you create a standardized environment in which everyone uses the same libraries, tools, Application Programming Interfaces (APIs), and other programs. The use of a standardized environment enables you to transfer code between systems without fear of introducing odd application issues because of environmental inconsistencies. In addition, team development issues are fewer because the collaboration environment is simplified.

Because a framework handles all the low-level details, you must also consider the makeup of an application team. In the past, the team might need people who were adept at interacting with the hardware or creating user interface basics. The use of a framework means that all these tasks are already completed, so a team is made up of subject-matter experts who can communicate effectively with each other, making a coherent approach to application development possible.

The most important reason that frameworks are so popular now relates to how coding is done today. At one time, developers needed to know how to interact with the hardware and software at an extremely low level. Today, frameworks make coding easy in an environment in which

>> Most applications consist mainly of API calls strung together to achieve a specific purpose.

>> People need to understand how APIs perform, rather than what they do or how they do it. A developer needs to consider what data structures the API accepts and how well it processes data under pressure.

>> The immense installed base of existing software means keeping that code in place and finding fast, efficient methods to interact with it.

>> The focus is on architecture rather than details. Because most new applications rely heavily on existing code accessed through libraries or APIs, developers don't spend as much time learning the idiosyncrasies of a language; it's better to discover which pile of code can do the work without having to write any of the code yourself.

>> Getting the algorithm correct is what matters most.

>> Tools have become so smart that they often correct minor coding errors and interpret ambiguities in developer code correctly, so the emphasis is on getting ideas down rather than writing perfect code.

>> Visual languages, in which you drag and drop objects in a graphical environment, are becoming more common. At some point, code could actually disappear (at least, for most application developers).

>> Knowing a single platform isn't enough. Most applications today must execute flawlessly on Windows, Linux, macOS, Android, most smart phones, and myriad other platforms because users want software in a form they understand.

CONSIDERING FRAMEWORK NEGATIVES

Depending on whom you talk to, a framework solution isn't always the panacea that supporters would make it out to be. One of the bigger issues when using a framework is that the framework becomes its own application. A development team needs to learn both the framework and all the tools used to write the application. Consequently, if most of the team members on a development effort haven't used the framework before, they'll need additional time to overcome the framework's learning curve. However, after they learn how to use a framework, they'll easily gain back part of this initial investment in time through higher productivity overall.

Another problem with frameworks is their tendency to use resources inefficiently. The size of a framework application, framework included, is generally larger than an application developed using libraries. Of course, monolithic applications are generally the most efficient because they can use only the resources required for that application. All the code bloat found in frameworks comes from trying to create a one-size-fits-all solution.

The frameworks discussed in this book are all public offerings. In fact, most of them are open source as well. However, some proponents of frameworks feel that every enterprise should have its own framework that is developed using the common code from applications in that enterprise. With that approach, the resulting framework has a consistent look and feel that matches the pre-framework applications that the enterprise has to maintain. However, developing a custom framework for a particular enterprise is time consuming. Therefore, many people point out that a framework-based solution isn't as useful or easy to learn as nonframework solutions.

Choosing a particular library

The previous sections in this chapter discuss the appeal of frameworks in general and trace how frameworks can create a significantly better work environment for developers. Also covered are features that make a framework used for machine learning or deep learning special. Of course, the amount of automation that a framework supplies and the number of typical features it supports are the starting point for finding a framework that meets your needs. You also need to consider issues such as learning curve with regard to the ease of using the framework.

TIP

One of the more important considerations when choosing a framework is to remember that frameworks are domain specific, which means that if you need to create an application that spans domains, such as a deep learning application that includes a web interface, you need multiple frameworks. Getting frameworks that work well with each other can be critical. If you also host your application in the cloud, you need to consider which frameworks work with the cloud vendor's offering, too. For example, if you choose to use TensorFlow as your framework, you can also rely on Amazon Web Services (AWS) to host your application (see https://aws.amazon.com/tensorflow/ for details).

REMEMBER

As another option when using TensorFlow, you can go directly to Google Cloud (see https://cloud.google.com/tpu/ for details), where you can train your deep learning solution using GPUs or Tensor Processing Units (TPUs). The TPUs were developed by Google specifically for neural network machine learning use TensorFlow. TPUs are Application-Specific Integrated Circuits (ASICs) optimized for a particular use. In this case, they're for neural network processing using TensorFlow.

Application size and complexity also play a role in deep learning framework choice because you often need a higher-end framework to interact properly with large applications. The need to deal with applications of various sorts is offset by the usual cost and availability concerns. Many of the low-end deep learning frameworks in this chapter cost you nothing to try and could provide everything needed to get started.

Accessing the Downloadable Code

The "Importing a notebook" section of this chapter discusses the mechanics of importing an .ipynb file into the Notebook environment. Each of the languages used for this book has its own separate folder in the downloadable source: Python and R. To access the downloadable code for a particular example, you first locate the correct language file. Inside the folder, you find the source code files that you can then import into Notebook.

REMEMBER

Some of the book examples come with prerequisites. You might have to load a new library or perform a configuration change. The downloadable code won't work properly without these changes. As part of performing any setups, you need to ensure that you install the correct versions of any libraries or packages. Otherwise, breaking changes in older or newer versions of these elements will cause the code to fail in some extremely odd ways. Trying to figure out just why a particular piece of code is failing in this circumstance, especially through email, can prove nearly impossible.

Even though this chapter discusses the use of online products to execute the code, these options come without any sort of guarantee, and you need to know how to upload the downloadable source to the online product you want to use. In some cases, all you really need to do is drag and drop the file from where you downloaded it to the online product.

IN THIS CHAPTER

» **Using packages and libraries to your benefit**

» **Working with Python packages**

» **Working with R libraries**

Chapter **4**

Considering Additional Packages and Libraries You Might Want

The terms *package* and *library* refer to code written not by the original developers but rather by a third party. Such code doesn't necessarily appear as part of a language's default installation; in fact, none of the packages and libraries in this chapter comes along with a default installation. You must obtain and install each one in some way to use it.

Third-party code alleviates the need for you to write something yourself. In most cases, you find that such code contains essential features in an easy-to-use and consistent manner. The code's developers perform required updates and ensure that the code is as bug free as possible for you. You may find that the code is compiled in binary form or provided as source that is interpreted with the rest of your application. Some packages and libraries cost money to use, but none of the packages in this chapter cost anything unless you obtain a special high-end version that provides some level of additional support or functionality.

REMEMBER

The terms *package* and *library* prove confusing for many people, which isn't surprising. Different languages and different developers use the terms in various ways. For the purposes of this book, a *Python package* is equivalent to an *R library* in that it contains a collection of functions you download as a group.

Packages and libraries consist of smaller units to make working with the package or library easier and to reduce resource usage. For the purposes of this book, Python packages contain individual *modules* of like functionality. You work with a module to obtain a specific level of functionality after obtaining a package containing the module. Likewise, R libraries contain *packages*. The nuances among all these various packaging methods won't matter for this book.

With these naming differences in mind, this chapter begins by discussing how you use third-party code in a generic way to perform data science tasks. If you were to write a data science application completely from scratch, without the use of third-party packages or libraries, it would take an incredibly long time. However, you need to know that you could do it should you want to do so. Packages and libraries aren't magic — they're simply code.

The last two parts of the chapter discuss specific packages and libraries for each of the book's languages: Python and R. You use some of these packages and libraries in the book, but others answer specific needs that you won't have until you have spent more time working with data science. In fact, you may not use all the packages and libraries listed in this chapter, even if you learn how to perform data science tasks using all three languages.

Considering the Uses for Third-Party Code

As with languages, third-party code exists to fulfill the needs of the user. A computer understands only machine language — the essential language used to flip the switches within its processor. As with any code, an interpreter or compiler serves to translate the third-party code into machine language. Consequently, the computer doesn't care whether you use one scientific package or another. So your first concern is to choose a package or library that makes sense to you — one that makes tasks easier and reduces the amount of code you must write.

REMEMBER

Developers who write third-party code used in packages and libraries are just like you: They possess various skill levels and sometimes make mistakes. Consequently, when you do find a package or library that you like, you need to consider how the developer wrote its code. You should consider these questions:

- » Is the code relatively error free? (The bug-free anything is a myth.)
- » Does the code enjoy community support?
- » Will the developer (or development team) continue to support the code?
- » Do independent benchmark tests exist that show that the code executes quickly?
- » Has anyone validated the code's resource usage levels?
- » Have tests shown correct outputs even when working with less than perfect inputs?

Even if you happen to find a high-quality package or library that has a superior feature set, you must still use it correctly. If you get a science package that specializes in data analysis, the lesser elements of the package may not perform well when attempting a machine learning task. Sometimes you must mix packages and libraries together in a smart manner to obtain a desired result for your particular application. The package or library developer has no way to know anything about your application in advance, so the burden of choosing the correct features falls on you, which is where experimentation comes into play.

TIP

The smart developer doesn't rely on just one or two packages or libraries. It's akin to creating a perfume. Using just one flower is nice, but it's hardly going to produce a spectacular result. Instead, the perfumer visits the garden and chooses just the right flowers with which to create the exquisite oils used in a perfume that dazzles. Likewise, a masterful developer will have an entire garden of packages and libraries from which to choose, mixing those features that specifically answer a particular application's needs.

Another important consideration is that many packages and libraries provide the means for addressing the disparity between language features. For example, you find that some Python packages help Python to address the statistical analysis disparity between Python and R. A package or library can address the concern where using a particular language almost meets a particular application need, but not quite.

Obtaining Useful Python Packages

Many developers use Python as a language of choice for general analysis needs in scenarios in which an application needs to perform a wide range of data science tasks rather than specialize in a particular area. However, Python isn't a general-purpose language like Java. You wouldn't use it to create a user interface for a refrigerator, even if that refrigerator is smart. Python's popularity stems from having just enough specialization to make it easy for someone who has to perform detailed analysis to learn, but it's not so specialized as to make some general tasks undoable. With this level of specialization in mind, the following sections discuss various Python packages used for certain kinds of analysis, but you should know that Python can do more. You can find a significantly longer list of packages at https://wiki.python.org/moin/UsefulModules.

Accessing scientific tools using SciPy

The SciPy stack (http://www.scipy.org/) contains a host of other packages that you can also download separately. These packages provide support for mathematics, science, and engineering. When you obtain SciPy, you get a set of packages designed to work together to create applications of various sorts. These packages are

- » NumPy
- » SciPy
- » matplotlib
- » Jupyter
- » SymPy
- » pandas

Of course, these are just the packages listed on the SciPy main page. If you dig further into the details found at https://www.scipy.org/about.html, you discover other packages, called the SciPy ecosystem, that are built upon or around SciPy. For example, when it comes to data and computation, you find these packages:

- » Scikit-image
- » Scikit-learn
- » h5py
- » PyTables

The SciPy package itself focuses on numerical routines, such as routines for numerical integration and optimization. SciPy is a general-purpose package that provides functionality for multiple problem domains. It also provides support for domain-specific packages, such as Scikit-learn, Scikit-image, and statsmodels.

TECHNICAL STUFF

R intrinsically provides much of the SciPy functionality as part of the language. You can find discussions comparing R to SciPy functionality online. For example, you can find a comparison of R optim to SciPy optimize at `https://stackoverflow.com/questions/51813317/r-optim-vs-scipy-optimize`. Even though the functionality isn't precisely the same, you find that R and Python with SciPy can produce equivalent results.

Performing fundamental scientific computing using NumPy

The NumPy library (`https://numpy.org/`) provides the means for performing n-dimensional array manipulation, which is critical for data science work. NumPy functions also include support for linear algebra, Fourier transform, and random-number generation (see the listing of functions at `https://docs.scipy.org/doc/numpy/reference/routines.html`).

TECHNICAL STUFF

Many discussions online talk about how NumPy helps Python developers bridge the statistical processing gap with R (see `https://stackoverflow.com/questions/3545057/numpy-for-r-user` as an example). You also find that pandas is important in helping bridge this gap. However, when you use a package to overcome an apparent language deficiency, the only true way to determine which language is better is to perform tests. In addition, it's important to understand that you won't find a one-for-one correlation between the features that a package provides and the deficiencies that it helps to overcome. Complicating matters further, some R libraries, such as reticulate (see the "Using your Python code in R with reticulate" section, later in this chapter, for details), let you load certain Python packages within R (see `https://cran.r-project.org/web/packages/reticulate/vignettes/python_packages.html` for details). Consequently, even if a Python package offers advantages over another language, the other language may still be able to use the Python package.

Performing data analysis using pandas

The pandas library (`http://pandas.pydata.org/`) provides support for data structures and data analysis tools. The library is optimized to perform data science tasks especially fast and efficiently.

The basic principle behind pandas is to provide data analysis and modeling support for Python that is similar to other languages, such as R. The focus of this modeling is the `dataframe`. You can find a comparison of pandas and R functionality on the site at `https://pandas.pydata.org/pandas-docs/stable/getting_started/comparison/comparison_with_r.html` (complete with some coding examples).

Considering Additional Packages and Libraries You Might Want

Implementing machine learning using Scikit-learn

The Scikit-learn library (http://scikit-learn.org/stable/) is one of a number of Scikit libraries that build on the capabilities provided by NumPy and SciPy to allow Python developers to perform domain-specific tasks. In this case, the library focuses on data mining and data analysis. It provides access to the following sorts of functionality:

» Classification

» Regression

» Clustering

» Dimensionality reduction

» Model selection

» Preprocessing

A number of these functions appear as chapter headings in the book. As a result, you can assume that Scikit-learn is the most important library for the book (even though it relies on other libraries to perform its work).

R doesn't offer a single library that precisely matches Scikit-learn. However, it does provide the caret library, which gives you similar functionality. You can find a comparison of the two at https://www.analyticsvidhya.com/blog/2016/12/cheatsheet-scikit-learn-caret-package-for-python-r-respectively/. The "Conducting advanced training using caret" section, later in this chapter, provides additional information. Another popular R library for machine learning is Mlr (https://cran.r-project.org/web/packages/mlr/index.html). Again, it offers some of what you find in Scikit-learn, but the two aren't a complete match (see the "Performing machine learning tasks using Mlr" section, later in this chapter, for more details).

TIP

If you need a single-source solution for machine learning needs and don't mind jumping through a few hoops to get it, H2O (https://www.h2o.ai/products/h2o/) provides a solution for R, Python, and Scala developers.

Going for deep learning with Keras and TensorFlow

Keras (https://keras.io/) is an application programming interface (API) that is used to train deep learning models. An *API* often specifies a model for doing something, but it doesn't provide an implementation. Consequently, you need an implementation of Keras to perform useful work, which is where TensorFlow (`https://www.tensorflow.org/`) comes into play.

TIP

You can also use Microsoft's Cognitive Toolkit, CNTK (`https://www.microsoft.com/en-us/cognitive-toolkit/`), or Theano (`https://github.com/Theano`) to implement Keras, but this book focuses on TensorFlow. A good reason to focus on TensorFlow is that you can find a version of it for R (`https://tensorflow.rstudio.com/`). Even though you find language differences in the three implementations, by using a single product, you significantly reduce your learning curve.

When working with an API, you're looking for ways to simplify your approach to tasks. Keras makes things easy in the following ways:

>> **Consistent interface:** The Keras interface is optimized for common use cases with an emphasis on actionable feedback for fixing user errors.

>> **Lego approach:** Using a black-box approach makes it easy to create models by connecting configurable building blocks together with only a few restrictions on how you can connect them.

>> **Extendable:** You can easily add custom building blocks to express new ideas for research that include new layers, loss functions, and models.

>> **Parallel processing:** To run applications fast today, you need good parallel processing support. Keras runs on both CPUs and GPUs.

>> **Direct Python support:** You don't have to do anything special to make the TensorFlow implementation of Keras work with Python, which can be a major stumbling block when working with other sorts of APIs.

Plotting the data using matplotlib

The matplotlib library (`http://matplotlib.org/`) gives you a MATLAB-like interface for creating data presentations of the analysis you perform. The library is currently limited to 2-D output, but it still provides you with the means to express graphically the data patterns you see in the data you analyze. Without this library, you couldn't create output that people outside the data science community could easily understand.

TECHNICAL STUFF

R doesn't provide a matplotlib equivalent. Yes, you can still output plots, but Python appears to have a clear advantage in this case. The best libraries to use with R for output are ggplot2 (see the "Visualizing data using ggplot2" section of the chapter for details) and Esquisse (see the "Enhancing ggplot2 using esquisse" section of the chapter for details).

When working with R, you can also use reticulate to import matplotlib into your R configuration. The article at https://rstudio.github.io/reticulate/articles/r_markdown.html shows you how to perform this task. However, the implementation is less than perfect; you may need to use workarounds, as described in the article at https://community.rstudio.com/t/matplotlib-inline-plots-with-reticulate-on-rstudio-server/16357.

Creating graphs with NetworkX

To properly study the relationships between complex data in a networked system (such as that used by your GPS setup to discover routes through city streets), you need a library to create, manipulate, and study the structure of network data in various ways. In addition, the library must provide the means to output the resulting analysis in a form that humans understand, such as graphical data. NetworkX (https://networkx.github.io/) enables you to perform this sort of analysis. The advantage of NetworkX is that nodes can be anything (including images) and edges can hold arbitrary data. These features allow you to perform a much broader range of analysis with NetworkX than using custom code would (and such code would be time consuming to create).

TECHNICAL STUFF

Even though the preferred package for Python is NetworkX, some developers use igraph (https://igraph.org/redirect.html) because it supports both R and Python (https://igraph.org/python/) directly. If you already have some code that relies on NetworkX, the discussion at https://stackoverflow.com/questions/23235964/interface-between-networkx-and-igraph tells you have to interface one with the other. The "Creating graphs with igraph" section of the chapter discusses the igraph in more detail.

Parsing HTML documents using Beautiful Soup

The Beautiful Soup library (http://www.crummy.com/software/BeautifulSoup/) download is actually found at https://pypi.python.org/pypi/beautifulsoup4/4.3.2. This library provides the means for parsing HTML or XML data in a manner that Python understands. It allows you to work with tree-based data.

Besides giving you a means for working with tree-based data, Beautiful Soup takes a lot of the work out of working with HTML documents. For example, it automatically converts the *encoding* (the manner in which characters are stored in a document) of HTML documents from UTF-8 to Unicode. A Python developer would normally need to worry about things like encoding, but with Beautiful Soup, you can focus on your code instead.

TECHNICAL STUFF

R uses the rvest (`https://cran.r-project.org/web/packages/rvest/index.html`) library to obtain similar (but not precisely the same) parsing results as Beautiful Soup. The article at `https://www.dataquest.io/blog/python-vs-r/` gives an objective comparison of R and Python, including a segment on HTML document parsing. Even using rvest, R requires more code, which says a lot because R is normally quite frugal when it comes to code. The "Parsing HTML documents using rvest" section, later in this chapter, provides more insights into using rvest.

Locating Useful R Libraries

R supplies a wealth of built-in functionality for its core proficiency of statistical analysis, so you frequently find that you don't need to use libraries with it as often as if you were to use Python. However, you do need libraries at times, especially if you have certain goals that fall outside the normal range of R proficiencies. The following sections discuss some R libraries that you might want to add to your collection to perform data science tasks with greater ease. Be sure to also read through the "Obtaining Useful Python Packages" section, earlier in this chapter, if you want to understand how R and Python packages compare.

Using your Python code in R with reticulate

If you already work with Python and have a substantial investment in Python code, you can continue to use that investment in many cases by adding reticulate (`https://rstudio.github.io/reticulate/`) to your R toolbox. You use reticulate to access your Python code from R in a nearly seamless manner. In fact, you have access to four techniques for accomplishing this task:

>> R Markdown

>> Sourcing Python scripts

>> Importing Python modules

>> Using Python interactively within an R session

REMEMBER

The reticulate library automatically marshals your data between languages. For example, it can translate between R and pandas `dataframes`, among other objects. In addition, you gain access to your Python environment, such as the one you configure in Chapter 3 of this minibook.

Considering Additional Packages and Libraries You Might Want

There are limits to what the reticulate library can do for you. For example, it won't suddenly force R to allow passing of data by reference rather than value. So, you can't use it to solve certain R graphics plotting issues. However, you can find it invaluable in overcoming other R deficiencies, such as performing some types of data fitting tasks. The downloadable source (as described in the Introduction) contains examples of using reticulate to overcome learning issues discussed in Book 4, Chapter 3; Book 5, Chapter 2; and Book 5, Chapter 5. In addition, you find it called in as a separate library in Book 5, Chapter 3 and Book 6, Chapter 3.

Conducting advanced training using caret

The Classification and Regression Training (CARET) library (normally written as *caret*) (`http://topepo.github.io/caret/index.html`) originally started as a method to provide consistent access to the built-in R functions. It does more than simply provide access now; you use this library to perform the following:

» Visualizations

» Data splitting

» Preprocessing

» Feature selection

» Model tuning using resampling

» Variable importance estimation

The documentation provided on the host site is extensive but can be a little hard to follow, and it doesn't always contain the complete code needed for an example to work. The Cran site at `https://cran.r-project.org/web/packages/caret/vignettes/caret.html` provides additional information that makes using this library easier.

Performing machine learning tasks using mlr

Machine Learning in R (MLR) (`https://mlr.mlr-org.com/`) standardizes the interface provided for the built-in R machine learning functions, making them significantly easier to use. In addition, you write less code when you use the mlr library because it consolidates some functionality. The site page offers a host of features that this library supports, but here is a quick overview of the supervised and unsupervised learning functionality:

>> Classification

>> Regression

>> Survival analysis

>> Evaluation and optimization methods

>> Clustering

Visualizing data using ggplot2

When working declaratively, you tell a library what you want done, but you let the library decide how to do it. The ggplot2 library (https://ggplot2.tidyverse.org/) relies on the Grammar of Graphics (GG) system to declare how to present information onscreen so that others can easily understand it. As with matplotlib, you might have to put in some effort to discover precisely how to perform every task in ggplot2, which is why the site page tells you about places to find tutorials. However, one of the more helpful aids with this library is the cheat sheet found at https://github.com/rstudio/cheatsheets/blob/master/data-visualization-2.1.pdf.

Enhancing ggplot2 using esquisse

When working with complex products that help you display data in graphic form, trying to get started can prove difficult. The ggplot2 library gives you significant flexibility, but the learning curve can be steep. The esquisse add-on (https://github.com/dreamRs/esquisse), which isn't a library, reduces the complexity of using ggplot2 by helping you create a starting point interactively.

REMEMBER

You use a GUI to design the output you want to present, but in a simple manner. The add-on doesn't provide access to advanced ggplot2 features — it focuses on making things simple so that you can see what to do at the outset and then add to the result you get to obtain the refinements you need.

Creating graphs with igraph

Network graphs help you present complex data in a visual manner. For example, you might want to create an application that shows how to get from one place in a city to another. To create such a presentation, you need a network graph. The igraph library (https://igraph.org/redirect.html) enables you to add network graphing functionality directly to both Python and R. (The R-specific details appear at https://igraph.org/r/.) This library focuses on efficiency,

Considering Additional Packages and Libraries You Might Want

portability, and ease of use, so you might find that it doesn't contain all the functionality offered by NetworkX (described earlier in the chapter). You use igraph to

>> Generate graphs

>> Compute centrality measures

>> Compute path length based properties

Parsing HTML documents using rvest

HTML documents contain all sorts of formatting in the form of tags that make working with the data nearly impossible in any significant way without parsing. The rvest library (https://github.com/tidyverse/rvest) focuses on performing simple forms of parsing for elements such as HTML tables, as described in the article at https://blog.rstudio.com/2014/11/24/rvest-easy-web-scraping-with-r/. The point is to get the data into a form that you can use to create a dataframe for additional processing.

TIP

Getting started with rvest may take a little time because of the complexity of formatting used by most web pages. The tutorial at https://www.analyticsvidhya.com/blog/2017/03/beginners-guide-on-web-scraping-in-r-using-rvest-with-hands-on-knowledge/ offers a quick hands-on tutorial that makes working with rvest easier.

Wrangling dates using lubridate

To obtain correct analysis output in most cases, you need to deal with dates and times. However, dates and times come in many forms, so interpreting them can prove problematic. For example, you must ask yourself when looking at 02/03/19 whether the date represents 3 February 2019 or 2 March 2019. In fact, it could represent something completely different, such as 19 March 2002. You just don't know unless you have some means for interpreting the date, such as through lubridate (https://lubridate.tidyverse.org/). By knowing the point of origin for the date, you can interpret it correctly.

Times can be even harder. Now you must also consider issues other than simply format. Two times might be in the same format, but reflect different time zones.

You must also consider the issue of dissection. For example, you might need to know what day of the week 3 February 2019 happened on. Unfortunately, the information doesn't appear as part of the date; you must dissect the date and then use the information to look up the day of the week. You can also use lubridate to perform date and time math to determine things like intervals.

Making big data simpler using dplyr and purrr

Often, a language comes with functionality that helps you perform a wealth of useful tasks, but accessing that functionality can prove difficult. R enables you to manage huge datasets in various ways so that you can make hard problems simple. However, accessing that functionality can prove difficult, and a library like dplyr (`https://dplyr.tidyverse.org/`) reduces your workload. Using dplyr, you can

>> Fit a specific model to subsets of a data frame

>> Calculate summary statistics for each data group

>> Perform group-wise transformations, such scaling or standardizing

The way in which dplyr performs its task is to

>> Make calling conventions more consistent

>> Use the `foreach` package to make parallelism easier to manage

>> Improve the input and output functionality for `dataframes`

>> Monitor processes with enhanced error handling

Unfortunately, dplyr works only with `dataframes`. When working with lists, you want to use purrr (`https://purrr.tidyverse.org/`) instead. When working with purrr, you rely on functional programming techniques to map data in various ways, such as by splitting large pieces into small ones. The first argument for all purrr functions is the data, so this library makes working with pipes incredibly easy.

IN THIS CHAPTER

» **Understanding frameworks**

» **Using a basic framework**

» **Working with TensorFlow**

Chapter **5**

Leveraging a Deep Learning Framework

U sing a deep learning framework can greatly reduce the time, cost, and complexity of developing a deep learning solution. Even though deep learning frameworks have many characteristics of frameworks in general, they also provide specific functionality. This chapter explores some aspects of that functionality.

Not everyone uses the same ideas and concepts for running deep learning applications. In addition, not every organization wants to invest in a complex deep learning framework when a less expensive and simpler framework will do. Consequently, you find a lot of deep learning frameworks that can provide you with basic functionality that you can use for experimentation and for simpler applications. This chapter explores some of these basic frameworks and compares them so that you have a better idea of what is available.

To provide the best possible learning environment, this book relies on the TensorFlow framework for the examples. The final sections of the chapter describe TensorFlow and tell you how to install it. TensorFlow works better for the situations presented in this book than the other solutions covered earlier in the chapter, and these final sections explain why. The discussion also tells you precisely why TensorFlow is a good general solution to many deep learning scenarios.

Understanding Deep Learning Framework Usage

Book 1, Chapter 3 offers a basic overview of frameworks in the "Presenting Frameworks" section. Some of the examples in this book, most notably those in minibooks 4 and 5, rely on TensorFlow to achieve their goal. If you want to move on to more advanced examples, you need a deep learning framework.

A *framework* is an abstraction that provides generic functionality, which your application code modifies to serve its own purposes. Unlike a library that runs within your application, when you're using a framework, your application runs within it. You can't modify basic framework functionality, which means that you have a stable environment in which to work, but most frameworks offer some level of extensibility. Frameworks are generally specific to a particular need, such as the web frameworks used to create online applications.

When thinking about a deep learning framework, what you're really considering is how the framework manages the frozen spots and the hot spots used by the application. In most cases, a deep learning framework provides frozen spots and hot spots in these areas:

>> Hardware access (such as using a GPU with ease)

>> Standard neural network layer access

>> Deep learning primitive access

>> Computational graph management

>> Model training

>> Model deployment

>> Model testing

>> Graph building and presentation

>> Inference (forward propagation)

>> Automatic differentiation (backpropagation)

A good deep learning framework also exhibits specific characteristics that you may not find in other framework types. These characteristics help create an environment in which the deep learning framework enables you to create intelligent applications that learn and process data quickly. Here are some of the characteristics to consider when looking at a deep learning framework:

>> Optimizes for performance rather than resource usage or some other consideration

>> Performs tasks using parallel operations to reduce the time spent creating a model and associated neural network

>> Computes gradients automatically

>> Makes coding easy because many of the people using deep learning frameworks aren't developers, but rather subject matter experts

>> Interacts well with standard libraries used for plotting, machine learning, and statistics

Frameworks address other issues, such as providing good community support for specific problem domains, and the focus on specific issues determines the viability of a particular framework for a particular purpose. As with many forms of software development aid, you need to choose the framework you use carefully.

Working with Low-End Frameworks

Low-end deep learning frameworks often come with a built-in trade-off. You must choose between cost and usage complexity, as well as the need to support large applications in challenging environments. The trade-offs you're willing to endure will generally reflect what you can use to complete your project. With this caveat in mind, the following sections discuss a number of low-end frameworks that are incredibly useful and work well with small to medium-size projects, but that come with trade-offs for you to consider as well.

Chainer

Chainer (https://chainer.org/) is a library written purely in Python that relies on the NumPy (http://www.numpy.org/) and CuPy (https://cupy.chainer.org/) libraries. Preferred Networks (https://www.preferred-networks.jp/en/) leads the development of this library, but IBM, Intel, Microsoft, and NVidia also play a role. The main point with this library is that helps you use the CUDA capabilities of your GPU by adding only a few lines of code. In other words, this library gives you a simple way to greatly enhance the speed of your code when working with huge datasets.

Many deep learning libraries today, such as Theano and TensorFlow (discussed later in this chapter), use a static deep learning approach called define and run, in which you define the math operations and then perform training based on those operations. Unlike Theano and TensorFlow, Chainer uses a define-by-run approach, which relies on a dynamic deep learning approach in which the code defines math operations as the training occurs. Here are the two main advantages to this approach:

>> **Intuitive and flexible approach:** A define-by-run approach can rely on a language's native capabilities rather than require you to create special operations to perform analysis.

>> **Debugging:** Because the define-by-run approach defines the operations during training, you can rely on the internal debugging features to locate the source of errors in a dataset or the application code.

TIP

TensorFlow 2.0 can also use define-by-run by relying on Chainer to provide eager execution.

PyTorch

PyTorch (https://pytorch.org/) is the successor to Torch (http://torch.ch/) written in the Lua (https://www.lua.org/) language. A core one of the Torch libraries (the PyTorch autograd library) started as a fork of Chainer, which is described in the previous section. Facebook initially developed PyTorch, but many other organizations use it today, including Twitter, Salesforce, and the University of Oxford. Here are the features that make PyTorch special:

>> Extremely user friendly

>> Efficient memory usage

>> Relatively fast

>> Commonly used for research

Some people like PyTorch because it's easy to read like Keras, but the scientist doesn't lose the ability to use complicated neural networks. In addition, PyTorch supports dynamic computational model graphing directly (see the "Grasping why TensorFlow is so good" section, later in the chapter, for more details on this issue), which makes it more flexible than TensorFlow without the addition of TensorFlow Fold.

MXNet

The biggest reason to use MXNet is speed. It might be hard to figure out whether MXNet (https://mxnet.apache.org/) or CNTK (https://www.microsoft.com/en-us/cognitive-toolkit/) is faster, but both products are quite fast and are often used as a contrast to the slowness that some people experience when working with TensorFlow. (The white paper at https://arxiv.org/pdf/1608.07249v7.pdf provides some details on benchmarking of deep learning code.)

MXNet is an Apache product that supports a host of languages, including Python, Julia, C++, R, and JavaScript. Numerous large organizations use it, including Microsoft, Intel, and Amazon Web Services. Here are the aspects that make MXNet special:

» Features advanced GPU support

» Can be run on any device

» Provides a high-performance imperative API

» Offers easy model serving

» Provides high scalability

It may sound like the perfect product for your needs, but MXNet does come with at least one serious failing: It lacks the level of community support that TensorFlow offers. In addition, most researchers don't look at MXNet favorably because it can become complex, and a researcher isn't dealing with a stable model in most cases.

Microsoft Cognitive Toolkit/CNTK

As mentioned in the previous section, its speed is one of the reasons to use the Microsoft Cognitive Toolkit (CNTK). Microsoft uses CNTK for big datasets — really big ones. As a product, it supports the Python, C++, C#, and Java programming languages. Consequently, if you're a researcher who relies on R, this isn't the product for you. Microsoft has used this product in Skype, Xbox, and Cortana. This product's special features are

» Great performance

» High scalability

» Highly optimized components

» Apache Spark support

» Azure Cloud support

As with MXNet, CNTK has a distinct problem in its lack of adequate community support. In addition, it tends not to provide much in the way of third-party support, either, so if the package doesn't contain the features you need, you might not get them at all.

Understanding TensorFlow

At the moment, TensorFlow is at the top of the heap with regard to deep learning frameworks (see the chart at https://towardsdatascience.com/deep-learning-framework-power-scores-2018-23607ddf297a for details). TensorFlow's success stems from many reasons, but mainly it comes from providing a robust environment in a relatively easy-to-use package. The following sections help you understand why this book uses TensorFlow. You discover what makes TensorFlow so exciting and how add-ons make it even easier to use.

TensorFlow SUPPORT ON COLAB

Many developers today rely on online environments, such as Colab, to perform tasks because installing and configuring TensorFlow on a desktop machine can prove difficult, and you must have a GPU that TensorFlow supports (https://developer.nvidia.com/cuda-gpus) if you want accelerated processing. In addition, you have all sorts of other issues to consider (https://www.tensorflow.org/install/gpu).

Colab appears to make things easy. To get CPU support, all you do is select a configuration box. To ensure that you have the proper support, you simply run a little extra Colab-specific code (https://colab.research.google.com/notebooks/gpu.ipynb). However, reality seldom works the same as theory. For one thing, you have to reinstall everything every time you start a new Colab session because the library support isn't persistent (https://www.kdnuggets.com/2018/02/essential-google-colaboratory-tips-tricks.html). Of course, you may not have access to a GPU at all (it's at Google's discretion) or the GPU support may have limits (https://stackoverflow.com/questions/48750199/google-colaboratory-misleading-information-about-its-gpu-only-5-ram-available).

To ensure that you have the best possible learning experience, this book uses an extremely simplified TensorFlow setup that avoids many of the pitfalls that other environments experience. This environment will work for the book, any learning experience you're likely to have in school, small experimental projects, and even projects for small to medium-sized businesses that use small to medium-sized datasets. You could never use this setup to run a Facebook-type project.

Grasping why TensorFlow is so good

A product has to offer quite a bit in terms of functionality, ease-of-use, and reliability to make much of a dent in the market when people have many choices. Part of the reason for TensorFlow's success is that it supports a number of the most popular languages: Python, Java, Go, and JavaScript. In addition, it's quite extensible. Each extension is an *op* (as in operation), which you can read about at https://www.tensorflow.org/guide/extend/op. The point is that when a product has great support for multiple languages and allows for significant extensibility, the product becomes popular because people can perform tasks in a manner that best suits them, rather than what the vendor thinks the user needs.

The manner in which TensorFlow evaluates and executes code is important as well. Natively, TensorFlow supports only static computational graphs. However, the TensorFlow Fold extension (https://github.com/tensorflow/fold) supports dynamic graphs as well. A *dynamic graph* is one in which the structure of the computational graph varies as a function of the input data structure and changes dynamically as the application runs. Using dynamic batching, TensorFlow Fold can create a static graph from the dynamic graphs, which it can then feed into TensorFlow. This static graph represents the transformation of one or more dynamic graphs modeling uncertain data. Of course, you might not even need to build a computational graph because TensorFlow also supports *eager execution* (evaluating operations immediately without building a computational graph) so that it can evaluate Python code immediately (called *dynamic execution*). The inclusion of this dynamic functionality makes TensorFlow extremely flexible in the data it can accommodate.

REMEMBER

In addition to various kinds of dynamic support, TensorFlow also enables you to use a GPU to speed calculations. You can actually use multiple GPUs and spread the computational model over several machines in a cluster. The capability to bring so much computing power to solving a problem makes TensorFlow faster than much of the competition. Speed is important because answers to questions often have a short life expectancy; getting an answer tomorrow for a question you have today won't work in many scenarios. For example, a doctor who relies on the services of an AI to provide alternatives during a surgery needs answers immediately or the patient could die.

Computational features only help you obtain a solution to a problem. TensorFlow also helps you visualize the solution in various ways using the TensorBoard extension (https://www.tensorflow.org/guide/summaries_and_tensorboard). This extension helps you to

>> Visualize the computational graph

>> Plot graph execution metrics

>> Show additional data as needed

As with many products that include a lot of functionality, TensorFlow comes with a steep learning curve. However, it also enjoys considerable community support, provides access to a wealth of hands-on tutorials, has great third-party support for online courses, and offers many other aids to reduce the learning curve. You'll want to start with the tutorial at https://www.tensorflow.org/tutorials/ and peruse the guide of offerings at https://www.tensorflow.org/guide/.

Making TensorFlow easier by using TFLearn

One of the major complaints people have about using TensorFlow directly is that the coding is both low level and difficult at times. The trade-off that you make with TensorFlow is that you gain additional flexibility and control by writing more code. However, not everyone needs the depth that TensorFlow can provide, which is why packages such as TFLearn (http://tflearn.org/), which stands for TensorFlow Learn, are so important. (You can find a number of packages on the market that attempt to reduce the complexity; TFLearn is just one of them.)

REMEMBER

TFLearn does make working with TensorFlow easier, but in specific ways:

>> A high-level Application Programming Interface (API) helps you to produce results with less code and reduce the amount of standardized (boilerplate) code you write.

>> Prototyping is faster, akin to the functionality found in PyTorch (described earlier in this chapter).

>> Transparency with TensorFlow means that you can see how the functions work and use them directly without relying on TFLearn.

>> The use of helper functions automates many tasks that you normally need to perform manually.

>> The use of great visualization helps you see the various aspects of your application, including the computational model, with greater ease.

You get all this functionality, and more, without giving up the aspects that make TensorFlow such a great product. For example, you still have full access to TensorFlow's capability to use CPUs, GPUs, and even multiple systems to bring more computing power to task on any problem.

Using Keras as the best simplifier

Keras is less of a framework and more of an API (a set of interface specifications that you can use with multiple frameworks as backends). It's generally lumped in as a deep learning framework, though, because that's how people use it. To use Keras, you must also have a deep learning framework, such as TensorFlow, Theano, MXNet, or CNTK. Keras is actually bundled with TensorFlow, which also makes it the easy solution for reducing TensorFlow complexity.

TIP

This book assumes that you use Keras with TensorFlow, but knowing that you can use Keras with other deep learning frameworks is an advantage. That's why this book doesn't use the Keras version incorporated into TensorFlow, but instead installs it separately (see `https://medium.com/tensorflow/standardizing-on-keras-guidance-on-high-level-apis-in-tensorflow-2-0-bad2b04c819a` for details). You can use the same interface with multiple frameworks, enabling you to use the framework that you need without having to deal with yet another learning curve. The biggest selling point of Keras is that it puts the process of creating applications using a deep learning framework into a paradigm that most people can understand well.

You can't develop an application of any kind that is both easy to use and able to handle truly complex situations — all while being flexible as well. So Keras doesn't necessarily handle all situations well. For example, it's a good product to use when your needs are simple, but not a good choice if you plan to develop a new kind of neural network.

The strength of Keras is that it lets you perform fast prototyping with little hassle. The API doesn't get in your way while it tries to provide flexibility that you might not need in the current project. In addition, because Keras simplifies how you perform tasks, you can't extend it as you can with other products, which limits your ability to add functionality to an existing environment.

WARNING

More than a few people have complained about the sometimes ambiguous error reporting provided by Keras. However, Keras partially offsets this issue by providing strong community support. In addition, many of the people complaining about the error messages are also apparently trying to do something complex. Keeping the fast prototyping nature of Keras in mind could prevent you from trying projects that might be too much for the product to handle.

Getting your copy of TensorFlow and Keras

Your copy of Python that comes with Anaconda doesn't include a copy of Tensor-Flow or Keras; you must install these products separately. To avoid problems with integrating TensorFlow with the Anaconda tools, don't follow the instructions found at `https://www.tensorflow.org/install/pip` for installing the product using pip. Likewise, avoid using the Keras installation instructions at `https://keras.io/#installation`.

REDUCING CONDA AND PIP ERRORS

Before you do too much with your Anaconda installation, it helps to update both Conda and Package Installer for Python (PIP) — the two applications you use to install new features in the Python environment. Using an outdated version of either package manager could cause you considerable pain in trying to get anything to install correctly. In fact, as you install various packages, they tell you when your copy of the package manager you use is outdated in many cases. To update Conda and PIP, you use these commands:

```
conda update conda
python -m pip install --upgrade pip
```

Whenever you're in doubt about the status of either package manager, perform an update before you try to install a new package. The process takes only a few minutes and will save you considerable time later.

To ensure that your copies of TensorFlow and Keras are available with Notebook, you must open an Anaconda prompt, not a standard command prompt or a terminal window. Otherwise, you can't ensure that you have the appropriate paths set up. The following steps will get you started with your installation.

1. At the Anaconda prompt, type python --version **and press Enter.**

You see the currently installed Python version, which should be version 3.7.3 for this book, as shown in Figure 5-1. The path you see in the window is a function of your operating system, which is Windows in this case, but you may see a different path when using the Anaconda prompt.

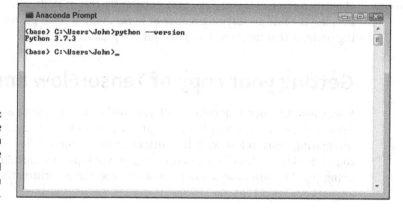

FIGURE 5-1:
Be sure to use the Anaconda prompt for the installation and check the Python version.

2. **Type** conda update --all **and press Enter.**

Before you attempt to install TensorFlow and Keras, make sure that the conda environment is up to date. Otherwise, you might find that some dependencies are outdated and that your installation won't work. Conda will perform an analysis of your system and then provide a list of steps to take. When asked whether you should proceed, type **Y** and press Enter. This step will take a while — time to refill your coffee cup.

TECHNICAL STUFF

The next step is to create an environment in which to execute code that relies on TensorFlow and Keras. The advantage of using an environment is that you maintain a pristine environment for later use with other libraries. You use Conda, rather than another environment product such as virtualenv, to ensure that the software integrates with the Anaconda tools. If you use a product such as virtualenv, the resulting installation will work, but you'll have to perform a lot of other steps to access it, and these steps don't appear in the book. The name of the environment for this book is TF_env.

3. **Type** conda create -n TF_env python=3.6 anaconda=2019.03 tensorflow=1.11.0 keras=2.2.4 nb_conda **and press Enter.**

WARNING

You may see a warning message about the availability of a newer version of Conda. Ignoring this message generally isn't safe, especially when working with a Windows 10 system. When asked whether you should proceed, exit the installation process by typing **N** and pressing Enter. Update your copy of Conda using the information in the "Reducing Conda and PIP errors" sidebar, and then restart the installation process. If you don't see an error message, type **Y** and press Enter when asked to proceed.

Notice that this installation is actually using Python 3.6. The Python 3.7.3 version used for the other examples in the book is incompatible with the current version of TensorFlow.

This step can require some time to execute because your system will have to download TensorFlow 1.11.0 and Keras 2.2.4 from an online source. After the download is complete, the setup needs to create a complete installation for you. You see the Anaconda prompt return after all the required steps are complete. In the meantime, reading a good technical article or getting coffee can help pass the time.

4. **Type** conda activate TF_env **and press Enter.**

The prompt changes to show the TF_env environment rather than the base or root environment. Any tasks you perform now will affect the TensorFlow environment rather than the original base environment.

Leveraging a Deep Learning Framework

5. **Type** python -m pip install --upgrade pip **and press Enter.**

Note that this step upgrades the copy of pip used for TF_env, rather than the base environment. This step requires a little time, but not nearly as long as creating the environment. The purpose of this step is to ensure that you have the most current version of pip installed so that later commands (some of which appear in the book's code) don't fail.

6. **Type** conda deactivate **and press Enter.**

Deactivating an environment returns you to the base environment. You perform this step to ensure that you always end a session in the base environment.

7. **Close the Anaconda Prompt.**

Your TensorFlow and Keras installations are now ready for use.

Fixing the C++ build tools error in Windows

Many Python features require C++ build tools for compilation because the developers wrote the code in C++, rather than Python, to obtain the best speed in performing certain kinds of processing. Fortunately, Linux and macOS both come with C++ build tools installed. So, you don't have to do anything special to make Python build commands work.

Windows users, however, need to install a copy of the C++ 14 or higher build tools if they don't already have them installed. In fact, the Notebook environment is actually quite picky — you need Visual C++ 14 or higher, rather than just any version of C++ (such as GCC, https://www.gnu.org/software/gcc/). If you recently installed Visual Studio or another Microsoft development product, you may have the build tools installed and won't need to install a second copy.

This book uses the most current tools available as of this writing, which are found in C++ 17. Getting just the build tools won't cost you anything. The following steps show a short and easy method for getting your required build tools if you don't already have C++ 14 or above installed:

1. **Download the offline build tools installer from** https://aka.ms/vs/15/release/vs_buildtools.exe.

Your download application downloads a copy of vs_buildtools.exe. Trying to use the online build tools often comes with too many options, and Microsoft, naturally, wants you to buy its product.

2. **Locate the downloaded file on your hard drive and double-click** vs_ buildtools.exe.

   You see a Visual Studio Installer dialog box. Before you can install the build tools, you need to tell the installer what you want to install.

3. **Click Continue.**

   The Visual Studio Installer downloads and installs some additional support files. After this installation is complete, it asks which Workload to install, as shown in Figure 5-2.

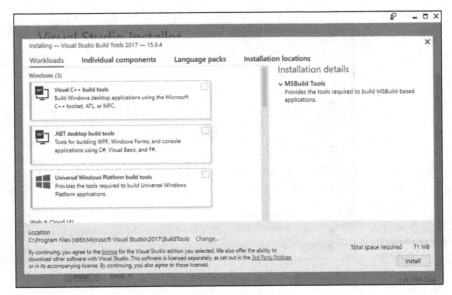

FIGURE 5-2:
Choose the Visual
C++ Build Tools
workload to
support your
Python setup.

4. **Select the Visual C++ Build Tools option and then click Install.**

   You don't need to install anything more than the default features. The Installation Details pane on the right side of the Visual Studio Installer window contains a confusing array of options that you won't need for this book. The download process of approximately 1.1GB begins immediately. You can get a cup of coffee while you wait. The Visual Studio Installer window displays the progress of the download and installation. At some point, you see a message saying that the installation succeeded.

5. **Close the Visual Studio Installer window.**

   Your copy of the Visual C++ Build Tools is ready for use. You may need to restart your system after performing the installation, especially if you had Visual Studio installed previously.

Accessing your new environment in Notebook

When you open Notebook, it automatically selects the base or root environment — the default environment for the Anaconda tools. However, you need to access the TF_env environment to work with the code in this book. To make this happen, open Anaconda Navigator, rather than Jupyter Notebook as usual. In the resulting window, shown in Figure 5-3, you see an Applications On drop-down list. Choose the TF_env option from the drop-down list. You can then click Launch in the Jupypter Notebook panel to start Notebook using the TF_env environment.

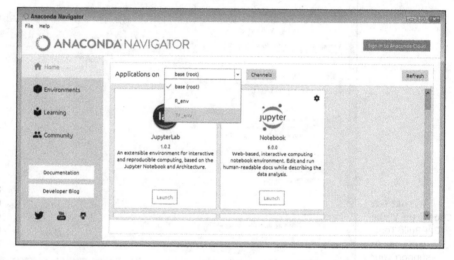

FIGURE 5-3: Select an environment to use in Anaconda Navigator.

2

Interacting with Data Storage

Contents at a Glance

Chapter **1**

Manipulating Raw Data

D ata scientists not only work with data but also spend considerable time pursuing data from various sources. Sometimes this pursuit resembles that of a detective ferreting out clues from arcane sources. Consequently, any in-depth conversation about data, as you see it in later chapters of this mini-book, must begin with the simple idea of obtaining data in a manner that will prove useful for analysis later. The acquisition of raw data in various forms is the focus of this chapter.

If you find it surprising that a data scientist doesn't automatically know where to find a particular piece of information, consider the vastness of data today. Looking for a needle in a haystack is easy compared to locating that much-needed piece of data from all the sources that a data scientist has available. In some cases, you find that you must generate data with specific characteristics to perform tests that validate assumptions about raw data, so the data you need may not even exist until you create it. The first section of this chapter looks at raw data sources.

Recognizing the forms of data is also important because you rarely find data in the form you need. For example, you can find a great deal of raw textual data in various places and lightly formatted data in others. After a while, you recognize the patterns of data and the processes used to obtain it in a specific form. The second section of this chapter views data formats from a raw data perspective, which may not represent the final data format used for an analysis.

Because you rarely perform an analysis once, the data you obtain must be reliable in that you can be certain that the data will appear from a particular source, in an expected form, and with the characteristics that you need. The final section of this chapter describes reliability as it applies to raw data.

Defining the Data Sources

To perform an analysis, you must have data. However, data must have a source, and the source you rely on affects all sorts of factors that also affect your analysis. Even though you can categorize data sources in a wide variety of ways, the following sections look at data as coming from the following:

» **Locally:** On a hard drive attached to your system or your network. The main advantages of this data source are speed and reliability.

» **Web or other online sources:** The data is located somewhere other than a system that you control directly in most cases. The main advantages of this data source are diversity and freshness (how current the data is).

» **Dynamically generated:** The application creates the data in some manner. The main advantages of this data source are consistency and completeness (meaning that you won't find any missing data unless you specifically add it).

» **Synthetically generated**: You create the data you use according to criteria defined by a software script. (An example is the make_classification function from Scikit-learn: https://scikit-learn.org/stable/modules/generated/sklearn.datasets.make_classification.html.) Synthetically generating data can help you test your algorithms or prove a theory. The main advantage is that you have full control of the data and its characteristics.

Obtaining data locally

In many cases, the data you need to work with won't appear within a library, as the toy datasets do, for example, in the Scikit-learn library. Real-world data usually appears in a file of some type. A flat file presents the easiest kind of file to work with. The data appears as a simple list of entries that you can read one at a time, if desired, into memory. Depending on the requirements for your project, you can read all or part of the file.

A problem with using native Python techniques is that the input isn't intelligent. For example, when a file contains a header, Python simply reads it as yet more data to process, rather than as a header. You can't easily select a particular column of data. The pandas library used in the sections that follow makes it much easier to read and understand flat-file data. Classes and methods in the pandas library interpret (parse) the flat-file data to make it easier to manipulate.

REMEMBER

The least formatted and therefore easiest-to-read flat-file format is the text file. However, a text file also treats all data as strings, so you often have to convert numeric data into other forms. A comma-separated value (CSV) file provides more formatting and more information, but it requires a little more effort to read. At the high end of flat-file formatting are custom data formats, such as an Excel file, which contains extensive formatting and could include multiple datasets in a single file.

The following sections describe these three levels of flat-file dataset. (Chapter 4 of this minibook contains examples of how to access them.) These sections assume that the file structures the data in some way. For example, the CSV file uses commas to separate data fields. A text file might rely on tabs to separate data fields. An Excel file uses a complex method to separate data fields and to provide a wealth of information about each field. You can work with unstructured data as well, but working with structured data is much easier because you know where each field begins and ends.

Working with flat files

A flat file is simply a file that contains data in some form, normally as text. The overriding characteristic of a flat file is that it contains a single data entry, normally a table. You commonly see flat files with these characteristics:

» Each data row is separated by a carriage return, line feed, or combination of the two.

» Each column is separated by a tab or other control character that isn't used for rows.

» The data isn't formatted in any way, so strings aren't normally quoted.

» The file may or may not contain a header row to identify the columns.

» The file normally relies on pure text, such as ASCII or UTF-8 formatted characters.

A flat file represents the simplest available method of transferring data between any two entities, even when they're different platforms or if the devices would normally prove incompatible. The problems for the data scientist using flat files are numerous, especially when the flat file comes within documentation:

>> The flat file may not rely on control characters to define rows and columns; it may use some sort of positional format instead.

>> Interpreting some data proves impossible, such as whether 1 represents a numeric value or a string.

>> Missing data is nearly impossible to locate and add in.

>> Parsing the file can be difficult or impossible when the original file contains mistakes.

You use flat files when simplicity and ease of data transfer override other considerations. The ability to generally view the data in a form that humans can recognize and understand directly is also a big plus. However, you also need to consider the additional time required to process this type of file.

Using organized databases

Databases come in many forms. You also get different interpretations of the term depending on the experiences of the person describing a database. For some people, a CSV file is an example of a database, rather than a flat file, because of the organization and formatting that a CSV file provides. However, other people consider a CSV a kind of flat file because it doesn't go far enough in formatting the data and in providing some sort of standardized access method. At the other end of the spectrum are relational databases that include their own programming language, diagramming, and extensive control over data format. The point is that databases are organized methods of storing data that have these characteristics:

>> Rows and columns are distinctly identified using a specific methodology.

>> Some form of data formatting is employed so that it becomes possible to separate the string form of 1 from the integer form of 1.

>> Some form of column identification is provided so that it becomes possible to perform tasks like comparing files of the same type.

>> The file may contain metadata to characterize the file content and parsing requirements.

>> Because the files are organized, finding and fixing many data issues, such as missing data, become easier.

TIP

The preceding isn't a complete list of the characteristics found in all organized data sources, but it's a good start. You might find all sorts of additional features that include security and other management needs. However, a general rule of thumb is that as the number of database features increase, so does complexity and the need for specific parsing mechanisms. You can parse a CSV using a general text processor if necessary, but you can't say the same for an Excel file or a file used by a SQL database. In fact, in some cases, you need a specific parser for each version of a database product.

Complexity isn't the only potential issue when using organized databases. You can also encounter the following issues, which make using an organized database significantly more difficult:

>> The file sizes are usually larger than a corresponding flat file, which means using more resources to manage them.

>> Some databases only work on a specific operating system platform, which means you can't use them on all the devices in your organization.

>> The appearance of multiple tables and other objects within a single file complicates parsing.

>> The data isn't understandable by a human in its raw form.

>> Creating bridges between various files can prove difficult, necessitating the use of transformations and other coding tricks.

Relational and NoSQL databases

The vast majority of data used by organizations rely on relational databases because these databases provide the means for organizing massive amounts of complex data in a manner that makes the data easy to manipulate. The goal of a database manager is to make data easy to manipulate; the focus of most data storage is to make data easy to retrieve.

Relational databases accomplish both the manipulation and data retrieval objectives with relative ease. However, because data storage needs come in all shapes and sizes for a wide range of computing platforms, many different relational database products exist. In fact, for the data scientist, the proliferation of different Database Management Systems (DBMSs) using various data layouts is one of the main problems you encounter with creating a comprehensive dataset for analysis.

The one common denominator among many relational databases is that they all rely on a form of the same language to perform data manipulation, which does make the data scientist's job easier. The Structured Query Language (SQL) lets you perform all sorts of management tasks in a relational database, retrieve data as needed, and even shape it in a particular way so that the need to perform additional shaping is unnecessary.

In addition to standard relational databases that rely on SQL, you find a wealth of databases of all sorts that don't have to rely on SQL. These Not Only Structured Query Language (NoSQL) databases are used in large data storage scenarios in which the relational model can become overly complex or can break down in other ways. The databases generally don't use the relational model. Of course, you find fewer of these DBMSes used in the corporate environment because they require special handling and training. Still, some common DBMSes are used because they provide special functionality or meet unique requirements. The process is essentially the same for using NoSQL databases as it is for relational databases:

1. Import required database engine functionality.

2. Create a database engine.

3. Make any required queries using the database engine and the functionality supported by the DBMS.

The details vary quite a bit, and you need to know which library to use with your particular database product. For example, when working with MongoDB (https://www.mongodb.org/), you must obtain a copy of the PyMongo library (https://api.mongodb.org/python/current/) and use the MongoClient class to create the required engine.

Consuming freeform databases

Freeform databases can contain multiple tables, each of which has a different format. In addition, the data within a table need not necessarily following a specific format. Because you can't gauge the format by using a header, these databases require a great deal more formatting. Products such as askSam (https://asksam.software.informer.com/) commonly see use for freeform informational databases. Accessing askSam would require a special parser. (You can likely use the same technique applied to relational databases as described at https://www.dummies.com/programming/big-data/data-science/data-science-how-to-use-python-to-manage-data-from-relational-databases/.)

Unlike other forms of data storage, a freeform database may not even use the table convention for storing information. You may find that it uses a hierarchical format instead, which means relying on special coding to move from record to record. The simple need to know what data the file contains and in the order in which it appears can prove difficult to meet. However, freeform storage can also prove to be incredibly space efficient, and you can use it to customize the data store so that the database becomes more flexible than just about any other means of storing data.

REMEMBER

Most people would categorize eXtensible Markup Language (XML) and JavaScript Object Notation (JSON) as types of freeform databases. Both use hierarchical storage techniques and provide extreme flexibility. As long as you don't violate the few rules that each of these formats requires you to observe, the systems generally work as you might think they should. However, the flexibility these file formats provides can become a problem because the files can literally contain anything. To combat this issue, XML files can rely on an XML Schema Definition (XSD) file (https://www.tutorialspoint.com/xsd/index.htm) and JSON can rely on a JSON Schema file (https://www.tutorialspoint.com/json/json_schema.htm).

Another important consideration is that some freeform databases rely on a different disk storage format than their in-memory presentation; the hierarchy or other in-memory form is built from data as it appears on disk. The use of this approach means that you can create a robust in-memory presentation that requires less disk storage space than conventional databases require. Because freeform databases have significantly fewer rules than other data storage techniques, presenting a solid list of characteristics, pros, and cons is impossible.

Using online data sources

The amount of data available online defies conception. In fact, you can't even visualize it because it boggles the imagination. The fact that each day sees more data added to online sources than many people could consume in a lifetime says much about online data. At some point, you use online data or you find yourself hopelessly outmatched by others who do. With this reality in mind, the following sections discuss online sources of raw data — some of which needs considerable manipulation before it provides any sort of useful information.

Accessing publicly available datasets

Governments, universities, nonprofit organizations, and other entities often maintain publicly available databases that you can use alone or combined with other databases to create big data for machine learning. For example, you can combine several Geographic Information Systems (GIS) to help create the big data required to make decisions such as where to put new stores or factories. The machine learning algorithm can take all sorts of information into account — everything from the amount of taxes you have to pay to the elevation of the land your store sits on (which can contribute to making your store easier to see).

FINDING YET MORE DATA ON DATA SCIENCE CENTRAL

A data scientist must have resources for locating data because no one person can possibly know about every source. Many of the resources you find online cover mainstream topics that you might find helpful in enabling your data service, but that might fall short of affording an ultimate resource. Data Science Central (https://www.datasciencecentral.com/) provides access to a relatively large number of data science experts who tell you about the most obscure facts of data science. One of the more interesting blog posts appears at https://www.datasciencecentral.com/profiles/blogs/huge-trello-list-of-great-data-science-resources.

Data Science Central points you to a Trello list (https://trello.com/) of some truly amazing resources. Navigating the huge list can be a bit difficult, but the process is aided by the treelike structure that Trello provides for organizing information. You want to meander through this sort of list when you have time and simply want to see what is available. The categories include the following (with possibly more by the time you read this book):

- Data news
- Data business people track
- Data journalist track
- Data padawan track
- Data scientist track
- Statistics
- R
- Python
- Big data and other tools
- Data
- Others

The best part about using public data is that it's usually free, even for commercial use (or you pay a nominal fee for it). In addition, many of the organizations that created them maintain these sources in nearly perfect condition because the organization has a mandate, uses the data to attract income, or uses the data internally. When obtaining public source data, you need to consider a number of issues to ensure that you actually get something useful. Here are some of the criteria you should think about when making a decision:

>> The cost, if any, of using the data source

>> The formatting of the data source

>> Access to the data source (which means having the proper infrastructure in place, such as an Internet connection when using Twitter data)

>> Permission to use the data source (some data sources are copyrighted)

>> Potential issues in cleaning the data to make it useful for machine learning

Scraping data from websites

It's important to understand that many of the data sources you use come from online content in the form of web pages and other web sources. *Scraping data* is the process of extracting useful data from a web page, while removing the non-data elements, such as tags. One of the better products for performing this task is BeautifulSoup (https://www.crummy.com/software/BeautifulSoup/). The example in the "Scraping Textual Datasets from the Web" section of Book 4, Chapter 4 tells you how to use this library in a practical way.

Relying on data from APIs

An Application Programming Interface (API) relies on a system of requests and responses to serve data. A client makes a request and a server provides a response. The specifics of each API vary, and you find that the strategies can become quite complex. The underlying technology for various APIs also differs. However, from a data perspective, you can expect to see the information sent and retrieved in a standards-oriented manner using technologies such as

>> XML

>> JSON

>> Binary (generally only for private APIs)

TECHNICAL STUFF

Pure text messaging is uncommon and perhaps even nonexistent today. The XML formats can become quite specialized. For example, when using the Simple Object Access Protocol (SOAP) to interact with an API, you use a specially format-ted XML document that follows the SOAP messaging format (see https://www.w3schools.com/xml/xml:soap.asp for details). When working with an API, you must fully understand the techniques for interacting with it, in addition to later transforming the data to meet your needs.

Binary formats such as the Common Object Request Broker Architecture (CORBA) may seem outdated, but you see them used for private APIs for a number of reasons, including security and performance. You can often transmit binary data at significantly higher speeds than text data of the same content. The article at `https://www.guru99.com/comparison-between-web-services.html` discusses the whole alphabet soup of technologies used for web services, including:

>> Representation State Transfer (REST)

>> SOAP

>> CORBA

>> Distributed Common Object Model (DCOM)

>> Java Remote Method Invocation (RMI)

Of the binary formats, CORBA seems to be the most popular given that Microsoft fully embraces SOAP for its web offerings today. You can get a better overview of CORBA at `https://www.sciencedirect.com/topics/computer-science/common-object-request-broker-architecture`. The article at `http://wwwconference.org/proceedings/www2002/alternate/395/index.html` provides a more detailed view of why CORBA might be a good choice when working with certain kinds of APIs.

No matter which kind of API you use and the type of data it serves, you generally need to do the following:

1. Transform the data from its transmitted form to a form suitable for processing.

2. Remove any extraneous information used as part of the transmission process.

3. Clean the data to remove undesirable elements.

4. Validate that the data is complete and hasn't suffered transmission errors.

5. Translate the data into a form that matches the other data used for your analysis.

Gaining access to private data

You can obtain data from private organizations such as Amazon and Google, both of which maintain immense databases that contain all sorts of useful information. In this case, you should expect to pay for access to the data, especially when used in a commercial setting. You may not be allowed to download the data to your personal servers, so that restriction may affect how you use the data in a machine learning environment. For example, some algorithms work slower with data that they must access in small pieces.

The biggest advantage of using data from a private source is that you can expect better consistency. The data is likely cleaner than from a public source. In addition, you usually have access to a larger database with a greater variety of data types. Of course, it all depends on where you get the data.

Employing dynamic data sources

Dynamic data sources are those that change over time. For example, the weather doesn't remain static — it may rain today and not tomorrow. The probability of rain changes, which affects how you plan outside activities. The current weather predictions are always dynamic because they're always changing. However, once the weather occurs and becomes historical in nature, it also becomes a static data source. The weather, once past, doesn't change. If there was a tornado on a certain day, the tornado doesn't somehow go away in the future — there is always a tornado for that day.

REMEMBER

As with the weather, many data sources start as dynamic data sources and become static data sources in the future. Consequently, when viewing data for use within an application, you must always consider whether the data is dynamic or static. Static data is easier to handle because it never changes. Dynamic data requires that you perform updates on a specific schedule and then perform your analysis again if you are to get any benefit from the analysis. With these differences between dynamic and static in mind, the following sections discuss various forms of raw dynamic data and consider how you might handle them as part of an analysis.

Monitoring the user

Users receive a large share of the monitoring associated with dynamic data. Because this monitoring is usually surreptitious to avoid biasing the data, it's more akin to spying. People spy on each other for all sorts of reasons — everything from performing marketing studies to conducting efficiency analysis. Much of this spying is benign; some of it is even helpful to the user. For example, sleep studies spy on the sleeper to determine whether modern technology can assist in reducing harmful sleep habits. The reason for monitoring (spying on) the user varies, but the result is normally data that reflects habits of some sort that prove helpful in predicting future actions. Even recommender systems, those aids that tell you that one item goes with another item or that people who purchased a particular item also bought another, rely on the study of buying habits.

REMEMBER

When it comes to users, you need to consider issues beyond simple monitoring and analysis. The article "AI is finding out when the person using your account isn't you" (see https://thenextweb.com/problem-solvers/2018/07/13/authentication-cybersecurity/) points out a particular problem with current thinking. It discusses the use of behavioral analytics as a means for discovering the fraudulent use of an ID, but behavioral analytics don't consider that human behaviors can change suddenly because of catastrophic events, such as the loss of a loved one. Fortunately, the article also discusses other approaches, such as the use of facial recognition and biometrics. However, no matter how you perform monitoring (or spying, as the case might be), the data received is apt to contain flaws that you must ferret out as part of the analysis.

For the most part, humans do change slowly (see "Change Doesn't Happen Overnight: It Happens in These Five Stages" at https://www.forbes.com/sites/amymorin/2014/03/17/change-doesnt-happen-overnight-it-happens-in-these-five-stages/ for details), so behavioral analytics work much of the time. However, you want to maintain the outlook that human behavior is quite dynamic and you need to constantly look for those changes that signal a major life event if your job is to predict the future.

Obtaining generated data

Your existing data may not work well for some data analysis scenarios, but that doesn't keep you from creating a new data source using the old data as a starting point. For example, you might find that you have a customer database that contains all the customer orders, but the data isn't useful for your particular analysis because it lacks tags required to group the data into specific types. One of the new job types that you can expect to create is people who massage data to make it better suited for a particular analysis type, including the addition of specific information types such as tags.

REMEMBER

Data analysis of all sorts has a significant effect on your business. The article at https://www.computerworld.com/article/3007053/how-machine-learning-will-affect-your-business.html describes some of the ways in which you can expect machine learning to change how you do business. One of the points in this article is that machine learning typically works on 80 percent of the data. In 20 percent of the cases, you still need humans to take over the job of deciding just how to react to the data and then act upon it. The point is that using machine learning to manipulate your data saves money by taking over repetitious tasks that humans don't really want to do in the first place (making them inefficient). However, machine learning doesn't get rid of the need for humans completely, and it creates the need for new types of jobs that are a bit more interesting than the ones that machine learning has taken over. Also important to consider is that you need more humans at the outset until the modifications they make train the algorithm to understand what sorts of changes to make to the data.

Whether you work with AI, machine learning, deep learning, or perform some sort of other data analysis, as a data scientist, you may also need to generate test data. Some packages and libraries include data generators for this purpose. You can also find data generators online that perform *mocking*, which is the simulation of a data source using fake data that reflects the data you expect from the actual source. The Mockaroo (https://mockaroo.com/) and Generate Data (https://www.generatedata.com/) sites are examples of this sort of data generation.

Considering other kinds of data sources

Your organization has data hidden in all kinds of places. Recognizing the data as data can be a problem, though. For example, you may have sensors on an assembly line that track how products move through the assembly process and ensure that the assembly line remains efficient. Those same sensors can potentially feed information into an algorithm because they could provide inputs on how product movement affects customer satisfaction or the price you pay for postage. The idea is to discover how to create mashups that present existing data as a new kind of data that lets you do more to make your organization work well.

REMEMBER

Big data can come from any source, even your email. A recent article discusses how Google uses your email to create a list of potential responses for new emails. (See the article at https://www.semrush.com/blog/deep-learning-an-upcoming-gmail-feature-that-will-answer-your-emails-for-you/.) Instead of having to respond to every email individually, you can simply select a canned response at the bottom of the page. This sort of automation isn't possible without the original email data source. Looking for big data in specific locations will blind you to the big data sitting in common places that most people don't think about as data sources. Tomorrow's applications will rely on these alternative data sources, but to create these applications, you must begin seeing the data hidden in plain view today.

Some of these applications already exist, and you're completely unaware of them. The article at https://www.microsoft.com/en-us/research/video/the-master-algorithm-how-the-quest-for-the-ultimate-learning-machine-will-remake-our-world/ makes the presence of these kinds of applications more apparent. (You can watch just the video at https://www.youtube.com/watch?v=8Ppqep-KAYI&feature=youtu.be.) By the time you complete the video, you begin to understand that many uses of machine learning are already in place and users already take them for granted (or have no idea that the application is even present).

Considering the Data Forms

Previous sections of the chapter have discussed the forms data appears in from an overview perspective. The form of data you receive affects the following:

>> How you interact with it

>> The level of information you can expect to derive from it

>> Issues related to data complexity

>> Time required to process and manicure it

>> Biases that could appear within it

The following sections provide a detailed view of the various data forms that you can expect to encounter. They break these forms into three main groups: pure text, formatted text, and binary. You might see data in other forms, but not often and usually not in a meaningful form.

Working with pure text

Pure text consists of the alphanumeric characters in the character set you use, such as American Standard Code for Information Interchange (ASCII) or Unicode Transformation Format 8-bit (UTF-8), and specific control characters, such as tab, linefeed, and carriage return. The reason for this extreme limit is to make the data created with pure text universally acceptable by the greatest number of devices and operating systems in existence.

With compatibility in mind, standard ASCII (http://www.asciitable.com/) is perhaps the most universal character set of all. However, even with these limits, ASCII isn't universal because some very old systems use Extended Binary Coded Decimal Interchange Code (EBCDIC) (see https://pediaa.com/difference-between-ascii-and-ebcdic/ for details). When you compare an ASCII table to an EBCDIC table (http://www.astrodigital.org/digital/ebcdic.html), you see that the two encodings are incompatible.

TIP

About now, you may be wondering why this whole encoding issue is important given that most modern computers can use extended ASCII (a 256-character version of original ASCII) and UTF-8 without any problem at all. The problem is that the data you need might not be from a modern machine, especially if your analysis has a historical basis to it. Consequently, you need to know that pure text, even with its extreme limitations, is hardly the universal transfer media that you might think it would be. When working with data, even pure text, you must be ready to deal with the unexpected.

Pure text doesn't necessarily come in a specific format, either. You can order data in a file using a number of approaches. Therefore, you need to know how the data is organized before you can process it. Here are a few of the most common approaches to data organization:

>> **Freeform:** This text appears in a semiformatted state using control characters to separate fields and another set of control characters to separate rows.

>> **Text-based freeform:** This form is similar to freeform but relies on special text combinations instead of control characters to separate fields and rows. For example, a ZZ pair could signal the end of a field, while a ZZZ triplet could signal the end of a row. In most cases, you find this form used only with specialized applications or in-house uses.

>> **Positional:** This text doesn't rely on any control characters to separate fields, but instead relies on the size of each field to determine the beginning and ending of a field. Rows are separated using control characters, normally the carriage return, line feed, or a combination of the two.

>> **Continuous:** This text that doesn't use control characters for any purpose, but simply relies on field size to determine every aspect of data format.

TECHNICAL STUFF

Lest you think that this list is complete, it's not. Point-of-Sale (POS) terminals are notorious for using truly unconventional data formats, for example. The article at https://www.acceleratedanalytics.com/blog/2010/01/15/top-questions-about-point-of-sale-data-analysis/ offers some clues as to just how convoluted the supposedly pure text data provided by POS terminals can become. As the article reveals, you can't simply import the data into your Windows system and view it in Excel.

Of course, the biggest problem with pure text is that you get just the data — no context, no description, and especially no metadata. To use pure text formats, you must know about the source used to create the data, which means intimate knowledge of the originator as well. In some cases, pure text simply can't provide what you need to perform a complete data analysis.

Accessing formatted text

Formatted text can take on a number of forms. You begin with pure text, but then add clues as to the formatting of the data. Here are some things that you find in a formatted text file that you won't fine in a pure text file:

>> Contains headers to describe the fields

>> Contains metadata to tell you about the data source and other data features

- **»** Uses quoting to make strings and numbers different
- **»** Treats numbers with decimal points as floating point, even when the number lacks a decimal portion or the decimal portion is 0
- **»** Uses True and False (or some variant) to define Boolean values
- **»** Uses keywords to denote data categories
- **»** Specifies field boundaries by using delimiters
- **»** Specifies rows by using carriage return, linefeed, or both

Not every formatted text file contains all these features, and some formatted text files rely on other characteristics to amplify the information you need. The point is that the underlying data is supported by additional, nondata information that tells you about the data so that you can interpret it with greater precision.

When you begin working with highly formatted text files, such as XML, JSON, and HTML, you start to see patterns and hierarchies. For example, the tags and other organizational aids used with these kinds of file aren't part of the data; instead, they're part of the metadata. You use them to see the construction and texture of the data. Automated processing designed to interpret these organizational aids can create datasets of extreme complexity that allow you to perform advanced analysis with a higher degree of confidence.

The use of stylesheets and other data input aids also increases the consistency of highly formatted text files by imposing rules for validating new data. Ensuring the absolute integrity of any data resource is impossible, but the use of validation tools does reduce the incidence of incorrect data and make the data more reliable.

REMEMBER

The positive aspects of formatting come at a price, unfortunately. As the data format becomes more complex and the tools for working with it become more useful, the ability to transfer the data anywhere you want diminishes. In addition, the processing requirements for such data increases, increasing the likelihood that you need a more capable device to even see the data correctly, much less process it. There is no free lunch. The increased use of formatting conveys more information but also requires more resources to handle and reduces flexibility.

Deciphering binary data

Binary data comes in many forms and it doesn't just pertain to older technologies such as CORBA. Graphics are binary, as is music and many other forms of non-textual information.

Nontextual data generally comes only as binary data, but you find exceptions. For example, Scalable Vector Graphics (SVG) come as XML files (https://www.w3schools.com/graphics/svg_intro.asp) that describe what to draw rather than the drawing itself. Theoretically, you can use the same techniques with SVG that you use with any XML file to perform an analysis of the graphic image it describes, rather than rely on deciphering binary data. All graphics files that fall into this category are vector graphics (based on math) rather than raster graphics (based on individual pixels) (see https://vector-conversions.com/vectorizing/raster_vs_vector.html for details).

Things get more complicated when you want to analyze the rendering of a vector graphic because now you have a raster graphic rendering to deal with. For example, you might want to know why a vector graphic produces a moiré pattern (http://mathworld.wolfram.com/MoirePattern.html) at one resolution and not another. The point is that you may find that you started with text, but now are working with binary data despite your desire to avoid doing so by using a textual data format.

REMEMBER

When working with text, binary formats often became popular for a number of reasons:

>> Transmitting the data is more efficient than pure text.

>> The data can contain formatting information inline, so the formatting doesn't get lost.

>> Securing the data from prying eyes is quite easy.

>> The use of checksums and other binary strategies can increase reliability and make the data self-repairing.

>> You can include information that isn't possible with text formats, such as placing graphics and text together (as in a PDF).

Binary data became unpopular for a number of reasons that include complexity, difficulty of processing, and platform specificity. However, you see binary data of this sort today and you'll likely continue to see it in the future. In some cases, you really do need to use a binary format.

When working with binary data, you need to consider all sorts of features that you may not find in other file types, such as a signature identifying the kind of binary data. The file may contain structural information and processing hints. You may find data in several formats residing in the same file. In short, binary data simply requires more processing than normal data because it doesn't appear in a form that humans understand. Consequently, when working with binary data, you must know something about the application that generated the data and have specifications available that describe the data format.

Understanding the Need for Data Reliability

Data, like everything else, has a certain reliability. The problem is determining what reliability means when it concerns data. In most cases, to ensure that you have reliable data, you must consider these issues:

>> The data source remains available.

>> Static data doesn't change.

>> Dynamic data is updated as often as needed to ensure that it doesn't get stale.

>> Errant data is corrected, but with a change in dataset version number so that you know it has changed.

>> The data files aren't corrupted in some manner (and not just from a virus or adware, but also from natural and unnatural sources).

>> Alternative sites provide data access when a host site becomes unavailable.

>> Someone is actually maintaining the data (it isn't orphaned in some way).

>> The creator of the data source is fully identified.

>> A third party has vetted the data to ensure its integrity.

REMEMBER

When your data meets all these criteria, you have data that is reasonably reliable. To summarize, the data must remain accessible in a form that you expect and without any outside tampering to be useful. Otherwise, you can't be sure that any analysis you perform using the data has meaning. It's hard to hit the bull's-eye when the target constantly changes position.

Of course, these criteria talk about only the actual data file and its raw content, to an extent. The data itself must meet certain characteristics to be reliable. What you want in this case is data that has been

>> Examined thoroughly during a peer review

>> Validated to meet appropriate standards

>> Collected with good scientific principles and statistical means in mind

>> Relies on best practices for meeting a particular need

>> Reflects reality with regard to specific conditions

In most cases, simply knowing that you have data is not enough. You need to know that the data targets something specifically oriented toward your analysis needs. Collecting emails from various people is useful only when those people are part of a target group for your analysis. Otherwise, you begin drawing incorrect conclusions from the data, and your analysis is no longer valid. One of the most important aspects of reliable data, then, is peer review, which can help ensure that bias and other issues don't cloud the judgment of those collecting the data. The "Considering the Five Mistruths in Data" section of Book 6, Chapter 2 discusses the sorts of issues that can make reasonable-looking data unacceptable.

Chapter **2**

Using Functional Programming Techniques

This chapter isn't about a specific programming language (even though it uses Python to present examples); it's about a programming paradigm. A *paradigm* is a framework that expresses a particular set of assumptions, relies on particular ways of thinking through problems, and uses particular methodologies to solve those problems. Other paradigms you may use are imperative, procedural, object-oriented, and declarative. Consequently, this chapter is different because it focuses on the problems you need to solve. The first part of this chapter discusses how the functional programming paradigm accomplishes this problem solving, and the second part points out how functional programming differs from other paradigms you may have used.

Throughout this chapter, you consider why you'd want to use functional programming at all. The math orientation of functional programming means that you might not create an application using it; you might instead solve straightforward math problems or devise *what if* scenarios to test. Because functional programming is unique in its approach to solving problems, you might wonder how it actually accomplishes its goals. The third part looks at essential functional programming methods. Finally, the fourth part considers how you use functional programming for data manipulation, which is, of course, the topic of this book.

REMEMBER

You don't have to type the source code for this chapter manually. In fact, using the downloadable source is a lot easier. The source code for this chapter appears in the DSPD_0202_Functional.ipynb source code file for Python source code file for Python and the DSPD_R_0202_Functional.ipynb source code file for R. See the Introduction for details on how to find these source files.

Defining Functional Programming

Functional programming has somewhat different goals and approaches than other paradigms use. Goals define what the functional programming paradigm is trying to do in forging the approaches used by languages that support it. However, the goals don't specify a particular implementation; doing that is within the purview of the individual languages. The following sections give you additional information on how the functional programming paradigm differs.

Differences with other programming paradigms

The main difference between the functional programming paradigm and other paradigms is that functional programs use math functions rather than statements to express ideas. This difference means that rather than write a precise set of steps to solve a problem, you use math functions, and you don't worry about how the language performs the task. In some respects, this approach makes languages that support the functional programming paradigm similar to applications such as MATLAB. Of course, with MATLAB, you get a user interface, which reduces the learning curve. However, you pay for the convenience of the user interface with a loss of power and flexibility, which functional languages do offer. Using this approach to defining a problem relies on the *declarative programming* style, which you see used with other paradigms and languages, such as Structured Query Language (SQL) for database management.

In contrast to other paradigms, the functional programming paradigm doesn't maintain state. The use of *state* enables you to track values between function calls. Other paradigms use state to produce variant results based on environment, such as determining the number of existing objects and doing something different when the number of objects is zero. As a result, calling a functional program function always produces the same result given a particular set of inputs, thereby making functional programs more predictable than those that support state.

Because functional programs don't maintain state, the data they work with is also *immutable*, which means that you can't change it. To change a variable's value, you must create a new variable. Again, this makes functional programs more predictable than other approaches and could make functional programs easier to run on multiple processors.

Understanding its goals

Imperative programming, the kind of programming that most developers have done until now, is akin to an assembly line, where data moves through a series of steps in a specific order to produce a particular result. The process is fixed and rigid, and the person implementing the process must build a new assembly line every time an application requires a new result. Object-oriented programming (OOP) simply modularizes and hides the steps, but the underlying paradigm is the same. Even with modularization, OOP often doesn't allow rearrangement of the object code in unanticipated ways because of the underlying interdependencies of the code.

REMEMBER

Functional programming gets rid of the interdependencies by replacing procedures with pure functions, which requires the use of immutable state. Consequently, the assembly line no longer exists; an application can manipulate data using the same methodologies as those used in pure math. The seeming restriction of immutable state provides the means to allow anyone who understands the math of a situation to also create an application to perform the math.

Using pure functions creates a flexible environment in which code order depends on the underlying math. That math models a real-world environment, and as our understanding of that environment changes and evolves, the math model and functional code can change with it — without the usual problems of brittleness that cause imperative code to fail. Modifying functional code is faster and less error prone because the person implementing the change must understand only the math and doesn't need to know how the underlying code works. In addition, learning how to create functional code can be faster as long as the person understands the math model and its relationship to the real world.

Functional programming also embraces a number of unique coding approaches, such as the capability to pass a function to another function as input. This capability enables you to change application behavior in a predictable manner that isn't possible using other programming paradigms.

Using Functional
Programming Techniques

Understanding Pure and Impure Languages

Languages that support functional programming fall into two categories: pure and impure. A *pure language* allows only functional programming techniques and fully implements the functional programming paradigm. An *impure language* allows the use of other programming techniques and may only mostly implement the functional programming paradigm. Both pure and impure languages have specific advantages and disadvantages, as described in the sections that follow.

Using the pure approach

Programming languages that use the pure approach to the functional programming paradigm rely on lambda calculus principles, for the most part. In addition, a pure-approach language allows the use of functional programming techniques only, so the result is always a functional program. Haskell is probably the most popular pure language because it provides the purest implementation, according to articles such as the one found on Quora at https://www.quora.com/What-are-the-most-popular-and-powerful-functional-programming-languages. Haskell is also a relatively popular language, according to the TIOBE index (https://www.tiobe.com/tiobe-index/). Other pure-approach languages include Lisp, Racket, Erlang, and OCaml.

WARNING

As with many elements of programming, opinions run strongly regarding whether a particular programming language qualifies for pure status. For example, many people would consider JavaScript to be a pure language, even though it's untyped. Others feel that domain-specific declarative languages such as SQL and Lex/Yacc qualify for pure status even though they aren't general programming languages. Simply having functional programming elements doesn't qualify a language as adhering to the pure approach.

Using the impure approach

Many developers have come to see the benefits of functional programming. However, they also don't want to give up the benefits of their existing language, so they use a language that mixes functional features with one of the other programming paradigms (as described in the "Comparing the Functional Paradigm" section that follows). For example, you can find functional programming features in languages such as C++, C#, and Java. When working with an impure language, you need to exercise care because your code won't work in a purely functional manner, and the features that you might think will work in one way actually work in another. For example, you can't pass a function to another function in some languages.

TIP

At least one language, Python, is designed from the outset to support multiple programming paradigms (see `https://blog.newrelic.com/2015/04/01/python-programming-styles/` for details). In fact, some online courses make a point of teaching this particular aspect of Python as a special benefit (see `https://www.coursehero.com/file/p1hkiub/Python-supports-multiple-programming-paradigms-including-object-oriented/`). The use of multiple programming paradigms makes Python quite flexible but also leads to complaints and apologists. This chapter relies on Python to demonstrate the impure approach to functional programming because it's both popular and flexible, plus it's easy to learn.

Comparing the Functional Paradigm

You might think that only a few programming paradigms exist besides the functional programming paradigm explored in this chapter, but the world of development is literally packed with them. That's because no two people truly think completely alike. Each paradigm represents a different approach to the puzzle of conveying a solution to problems by using a particular methodology while making assumptions about things like developer expertise and execution environment. In fact, you can find entire sites that discuss the issue, such as the one at `https://cs.lmu.edu/~ray/notes/paradigms/`. Oddly enough, some languages (such as Python) mix and match compatible paradigms to create an entirely new way to perform tasks based on what has happened in the past.

REMEMBER

The following sections discuss just four of these other paradigms. These paradigms are neither better nor worse than any other paradigm, but they represent common schools of thought. Many languages in the world today use just these four paradigms, so your chances of encountering them are quite high.

Imperative

Imperative programming takes a step-by-step approach to performing a task. The developer provides commands that describe precisely how to perform the task from beginning to end. During the process of executing the commands, the code also modifies application state, which includes the application data. The code runs from beginning to end. An imperative application closely mimics the computer hardware, which executes machine code. *Machine code* is the lowest set of instructions that you can create and is mimicked in early languages, such as assembler.

Procedural

Procedural programming implements imperative programming, but adds functionality such as code blocks and procedures for breaking up the code. The compiler or interpreter still ends up producing machine code that runs step by step, but the use of procedures makes it easier for a developer to follow the code and understand how it works. Many procedural languages provide a disassembly mode in which you can see the correspondence between the higher-level language and the underlying assembler. Examples of languages that implement the procedural paradigm are C and Pascal.

TECHNICAL STUFF

Early languages, such as Basic, used the imperative model because developers creating the languages worked closely with the computer hardware. However, Basic users often faced a problem called *spaghetti code*, which made large applications appear to be one monolithic piece. Unless you were the application's developer, following the application's logic was often hard. Consequently, languages that follow the procedural paradigm are a step up from languages that follow the imperative paradigm alone.

Object-oriented

The procedural paradigm does make reading code easier. However, the relationship between the code and the underlying hardware still makes it hard to relate what the code is doing to the real world. The object-oriented paradigm uses the concept of objects to hide the code, but the more important aim is to make modeling the real world easier. A developer creates code objects that mimic the real-world objects they emulate. These objects include properties, methods, and events to allow the object to behave in a particular manner. Examples of languages that implement the object-oriented paradigm are C++ and Java.

REMEMBER

Languages that implement the object-oriented paradigms also implement both the procedural and imperative paradigms. The fact that objects hide the use of these other paradigms doesn't mean that a developer hasn't written code to create the object using these older paradigms. Consequently, the object-oriented paradigm still relies on code that modifies application state, but could also allow for modifying variable data.

Declarative

Functional programming actually implements the declarative programming paradigm, but the two paradigms are separate. Other paradigms, such as logic programming, implemented by the Prolog language, also support the declarative programming paradigm. The short view of declarative programming is that it does the following:

>> Describes what the code should do, rather than how to do it

>> Defines functions that are referentially transparent (without side effects)

>> Provides a clear correspondence to mathematical logic

Using Python for Functional Programming Needs

Remember that functional programming is a paradigm, which means that it doesn't have an implementation. The basis of functional programming is lambda calculus (https://brilliant.org/wiki/lambda-calculus/), which is actually a math abstraction. Consequently, when you want to perform tasks by using the functional programming paradigm, you're really looking for a programming language that implements functional programming in a manner that meets your needs. In fact, you may even be performing functional programming tasks in your current language without realizing it. Every time you create and use a lambda function, you're likely using functional programming techniques (in an impure way, at least).

In addition to using lambda functions, languages like Python that implement the functional programming paradigm have some other features in common. Here is a quick overview of these features:

>> **First-class and higher-order functions:** Both first-class and higher-order functions allow you to provide a function as an input, as you would when using a higher-order function in calculus.

>> **Pure functions:** A pure function has no side effects. When working with a pure function, you can

- Remove the function if no other functions rely on its output

- Obtain the same results every time you call the function with a given set of inputs

- Reverse the order of calls to different functions without any change to application functionality

- Process the function calls in parallel without any consequence

- Evaluate the function calls in any order, assuming that the entire language doesn't allow side effects

>> **Recursion:** Functional language implementations rely on recursion to implement looping. In general, recursion works differently in functional languages because no change in application state occurs.

>> **Referential transparency:** The value of a variable (a bit of a misnomer because you can't change the value) never changes in a functional language implementation because functional languages lack an assignment operator.

REMEMBER

You often find a number of other considerations for performing tasks in functional programming language implementations, but these issues aren't consistent across languages. For example, some languages use strict (eager) evaluation, while other languages use non-strict (lazy) evaluation. Under strict evaluation, the language fully checks the function before evaluating it. Even when a term within the function isn't used, a failing term will cause the function as a whole to fail. However, under non-strict evaluation, the function fails only if the failing term is used to create an output. The Miranda, Clean, and Haskell languages all implement non-strict evaluation.

Various functional language implementations also use different type systems, so the manner in which the underlying computer detects the type of a value changes from language to language. In addition, each language supports its own set of data structures. These kinds of issues aren't well defined as part of the functional programming paradigm, yet they're important to creating an application, so you must rely on the language you use to define them for you. Assuming a particular implementation in any given language is a bad idea because it isn't well defined as part of the paradigm.

Understanding How Functional Data Works

Data is a representation of something — perhaps a value. However, it can just as easily represent a real-world object. The data itself is always abstract, and existing computer technology represents it as a number. Even a character is a number: The letter *A* is actually represented as the number 65. The letter is a value, and the number is the representation of that value: the data. The following sections discuss data with regard to how it functions within the functional programming paradigm.

Working with immutable data

Being able to change the content of a variable is problematic in many languages. The memory location used by the variable is important. If the data in a particular memory location changes, the value of the variable pointing to that memory location changes as well. The concept of immutable data requires that specific memory locations remain untainted.

REMEMBER

Python data isn't immutable in all cases. The "Passing by reference versus by value" section that appears later in the chapter gives you an example of this issue. When working with Python code, you can rely on the id function to help you determine when changes have occurred to variables. For example, in the following code, the output of the comparison between id(x) and oldID will be false:

```
x = 1
oldID = id(x)
x = x + 1
id(x) == oldID
```

WARNING

Every scenario has some caveats, and doing this with Python does as well. The id of a variable is always guaranteed unique except in certain circumstances:

>> One variable goes out of scope and another is created in the same location.

>> The application is using multiprocessing and the two variables exist on different processors.

>> The interpreter in use doesn't follow the CPython approach to handling variables.

When working with other languages, you need to consider whether the data supported by that language is actually immutable and what set of events occurs when code tries to modify that data. When working with Python, you can detect changes, but not all languages support the functionality required to ensure that immutability is maintained.

Considering the role of state

Application *state* is a condition that occurs when the application performs tasks that modify global data. An application doesn't have state when using functional programming. The lack of state has the positive effect of ensuring that any call to a function will produce the same results for a given input every time, regardless of when the application calls the function. However, the lack of state has a negative effect as well: The application now has no memory. When you think about state, think about the capability to remember what occurred in the past, which, in the case of an application, is stored as global data.

Eliminating side effects

The term *declaration* has a number of meanings in computer science, and different people use the term in different ways at different times. For example, in the context of a language such as C, a declaration is a language construct that defines the properties associated with an identifier. You see declarations used for defining all sorts of language constructs, such as types and enumerations. However, that's not how the functional paradigm uses the term *declaration*. When making a functional declaration, you're telling the underlying language to do something. The declaration "Make me a cup of tea!" has only one output: the cup of tea. The declaration doesn't describe how to make the tea; the assumption is that the recipient of the declaration knows how to perform the task.

A *procedure* details what to do, when to do it, and how to do it. Nothing is left to chance and no knowledge is assumed on the part of the recipient. The steps appear in a specific order, and performing a step out of order will cause problems. For example, given the procedure for making a cup of tea, imagine pouring the hot water over the teabag before placing the teabag in the cup. Procedures are often error prone and inflexible, but they do allow for precise control over the execution of a task. Even though making a declaration might seem to be superior to a procedure, using procedures does have advantages that you must consider when designing an application.

The procedure has a *side effect* instead of a value. After making a cup of tea, the procedure indicates that the recipient of the request should take the cup of tea to the requestor. However, the procedure must successfully conclude for this event to occur. The procedure isn't returning the tea; the recipient of the request is performing that task. Consequently, the procedure isn't returning a value.

Side effects also occur in data. When you pass a variable to a function, the expectation in functional programming is that the variable's data will remain untouched — immutable. A side effect occurs when the function modifies the variable data so that upon return from the function call, the variable changes in some manner.

Passing by reference versus by value

The point at which Python shows itself to be an impure language is the use of passing by reference. When you pass a variable by reference, it means that any change to the variable within the function results in global change to the variable's value. In short, using passing by reference produces a side effect, which isn't allowed when using the functional programming paradigm.

Normally, you can write functions in Python that don't cause the passing by reference problem. For example, the following code doesn't modify x, even though you might expect it to:

```python
def DoChange(x, y):
    x = x.__add__(y)
    return x
x = 1
print(x)
print(DoChange(x, 2))
print(x)
```

The value of x outside the function remains unchanged:

```
1
3
1
```

However, you need to exercise care when creating functions using some objects and built-in methods. For example, the following code will modify the output:

```python
def DoChange(aList):
    aList.append(4)
    return aList
aList = [1, 2, 3]
print(aList)
print(DoChange(aList))
print(aList)
```

The following output shows that aList doesn't remain the same:

```
[1, 2, 3]
[1, 2, 3, 4]
[1, 2, 3, 4]
```

REMEMBER

The appended version will become permanent in this case because the built-in function, append, performs the modification. To avoid this problem, you must create a new variable within the function, change its value, and then return the new variable, as shown in the following code:

```python
def DoChange(aList):
    newList = aList.copy()
    newList.append(4)
    return newList
```

Using Functional Programming Techniques

```
aList = [1, 2, 3]
print(aList)
print(DoChange(aList))
print(aList)
```

Here are the new results:

```
[1, 2, 3]
[1, 2, 3, 4]
[1, 2, 3]
```

TIP

In the first case, you see the changed list, but the second case keeps the list intact. Whether you encounter a problem with particular Python objects depends on their mutability. An int isn't mutable, so you don't need to worry about having problems with functions changing its value. On the other hand, a list is mutable, which is the source of the problems with the examples that use a list in this section. The article at https://medium.com/@meghamohan/mutable-and-immutable-side-of-python-c2145cf72747 offers insights into the mutability of various Python objects.

Working with Lists and Strings

After you have used lists, you might be tempted to ask what a list can't do. The list data structure is the most versatile offering for most languages. In most cases, lists are simply a sequence of values that need not be of the same type. You access the elements in a list using an index that begins at 0 for most languages, but could start at 1 for some. The indexing method varies among languages, but accessing specific values using an index is common. Besides storing a sequence of values, you sometimes see lists used in these coding contexts:

>> Stack

>> Queue

>> Deque

>> Sets

Generally, lists offer more manipulation methods than other kinds of data structures simply because the rules for using them are so relaxed. Many of these manipulation methods give lists a bit more structure for use in meeting specialized needs. Lists are also easy to search and to perform various kinds of analysis. The point is that lists often offer significant flexibility at the cost of absolute reliability and dependability. (You can easily use lists incorrectly, or create scenarios in which lists can actually cause an application to crash, such as when you add an element of the wrong type.)

TIP

Depending on the language you use, lists can provide an impressive array of features and make conversions between types easier. For example, using an iterator in Python lets you perform tasks such as outputting the list as a tuple, processing the content one element at a time, and unpacking the list into separate variables. The list features you obtain with a particular language depend on the functions the language provides and your own creativity in applying them.

LIST AND ARRAY DIFFERENCE

At first, lists may simply seem to be another kind of array. Many people wonder how lists and arrays differ. After all, from a programming perspective, the two can sound like the same thing. It's true that lists and arrays both store data sequentially, and you can often store any sort of data you want in either structure (although arrays tend to be more restrictive).

The main difference comes in how arrays and lists store the data. An array always stores data in sequential memory locations, which gives an array faster access times in some situations but also slows the creation of arrays. In addition, because an array must appear in sequential memory, updating arrays is often hard, and some languages don't allow you to modify arrays in the same ways as you can lists.

A list stores data using a linked data structure in which a list element consists of the data value and one or two pointers. Lists take more memory because you must now allocate memory for pointers to the next data location (and to the previous location as well in doubly-linked lists, which is the kind used by most languages today). Lists are often faster to create and add data to because of the linking mechanism, but they provide slower read access than arrays.

Creating lists

Python, like most programming languages, makes creating lists easy. You use the following code to create a list:

```
a = [1, 2, 3, 4]
```

The variable a now contains a list of four values from 1 to 4. You can also create a list in Python based on a range. Here is one method for creating a list in Python based on a range:

```
b = list(range(1, 13))
```

This example combines the list function with the range function to create the list. Notice that the range function accepts a starting value, 1, and a stop value, 13. The resulting list will contain the values 1 through 12 because the stop value is always one more than the actual output value, as shown by this code:

```
print(b)
```

Here is the result you see:

```
[1, 2, 3, 4, 5, 6, 7, 8, 9, 10, 11, 12]
```

Python supports list comprehensions, but again, the code for creating a list in this manner is different. Here's an example of how you could create the list, c, using list comprehensions:

```
c = [a * 2 for a in range(1,5)]
print(c)
```

TIP

This example shows the impure nature of Python because you rely on a statement rather than lambda calculus to get the job done. As an alternative, you can define the range function stop value by specifying len(a)+1. (The alternative approach makes it easier to create a list based on comprehensions because you don't have to remember the source list length.) Here is the output from this example:

```
[2, 4, 6, 8]
```

Evaluating lists

Python provides a lot of different ways to evaluate lists. To start with, you can obtain a particular element using an index enclosed in square brackets. For example, assuming that you have a list defined as a = [1, 2, 3, 4, 5, 6], typing **a[0]** and pressing Enter will produce an output of 1. To interact with lists in Python, you use modifications of an index, as shown here:

- » a[0]: Obtains the head of the list, which is 1 in this case

- » a[1:]: Obtains the tail of the list, which is [2,3,4,5,6] in this case

- » a[:-1]: Obtains all but the last element, which is [1,2,3,4,5] in this case

- » a[-1:]: Obtains just the last element, which is 6 in this case

- » a[:-3]: Requires the number of elements you want to see as input and then shows that number from the beginning of the list, which is [1,2,3] in this case

- » a[-3:]: Requires the number of elements you don't want to see as input and then shows the remainder of the list after dropping the required elements, which is [4,5,6] in this case

Python probably provides more ways to slice and dice lists than you'll ever need or want. You can also perform similar levels of basic analysis using Python, as shown here:

- » len(a): Returns the number of elements in a list.

- » not a: Checks for an empty list. This check is different from a is None, which checks for an actual null value — a not being defined.

- » min(a): Returns the smallest list element.

- » max(a): Returns the largest list element.

- » sum(a): Adds the numbers of the list together.

Interestingly enough, Python has no single method call to obtain the product of a list — that is, all the numbers multiplied together. Python relies heavily on third-party libraries such as NumPy (https://numpy.org/) to perform this task. One of the easiest ways to obtain a product without resorting to a third-party library is shown here:

```
from functools import reduce
print(reduce(lambda x, y: x * y, a))
```

Using a, the output is 720 in this case. The reduce method found in the functools library (see https://docs.python.org/3/library/functools.html for details) is incredibly flexible in that you can define almost any operation that works on every element in a list. In this case, the lambda function multiplies the current list element, y, by the accumulated value, x. If you wanted to encapsulate this technique into a function, you could do so using the following code:

```
prod = lambda z: reduce(lambda x, y: x * y, z)
print(prod(a))
```

As before, you obtain an output of 720. Python does provide you with a number of statistical calculations in the statistics library (see https://pythonprogramming.net/statistics-python-3-module-mean-standard-deviation/ for details). However, you may find that you want to create your own functions to determine things like the average value of the entries in a list. The following code shows the Python version:

```
avg = lambda x: sum(x) // len(x)
print(avg(a))
```

As before, the output is 3. Note the use of the // operator to perform integer division. If you were to use the standard division operator, you would receive a floating-point value as output.

Performing common list manipulations

List manipulation means changing the list. However, in the functional programming paradigm, you can't change anything. For all intents and purposes, every variable points to a list that is a constant — one that can't change for any reason whatsoever. So when you work with lists in functional code, you need to consider the performance aspects of such a requirement. Every change you make to any list will require the creation of an entirely new list, and you have to point the variable to the new structure. To the developer, the list may appear to have changed, but underneath, it hasn't; in fact, it can't, or the underlying reason to use the functional programming paradigm fails. With this caveat in mind, here are the common list manipulations you want to consider (which are in addition to the evaluations described earlier):

>> **Concatenation:** Adding two lists together to create a new list with all the elements of both

>> **Repetition:** Creating a specific number of duplicates of a source list

>> **Membership:** Determining whether an element exists within a list and potentially extracting it

>> **Iteration:** Interacting with each element of a list individually

>> **Editing:** Removing specific elements, reversing the list in whole or in part, inserting new elements in a particular location, sorting, or in any other way modifying a part of the list while retaining the remainder

When working with Python, you have access to a whole array of list manipulation functions. Many of them are dot functions that you append to a list. Of course, using the dot functions is fine if you want to modify your original list, but in many situations, modifying the original idea is simply a bad idea, so you need another way to accomplish the task. In this case, you can use the following code to reverse a list and place the result in another list without modifying the original:

```
reverse = lambda x: x[::-1]
b = reverse(a)
print(b)
```

Using a from the previous sections, you see an output of

```
[6, 5, 4, 3, 2, 1]
```

TIP

Python provides an amazing array of list functions — too many to cover in this chapter (but you do see more as the book progresses). One of the best places to find a comprehensive list of Python list functions is at https://likegeeks.com/python-list-functions/.

Understanding the Dict and Set alternatives

Python supports both dictionaries and sets. To create a dictionary, you provide name value pairs, as shown here:

```
myDict = {"First": 1, "Second": 2, "Third": 3}
```

The first value, the name, is also a key. The keys are separated from the values by a colon; individual entries are separated by commas. You can access any value in the dictionary using the key, such as print(myDict["First"]), which outputs a value of 1.

Sets in Python are either mutable (the set object) or immutable (the frozenset object). The immutability of the frozenset allows you to use it as a subset within another set or make it hashable for use in a dictionary. (The set object doesn't offer these features.) Python has other kinds of sets, too, but for now, the focus is on immutable sets for functional programming uses. Be aware, however, that other set types exist that may work better for your particular application. The following code creates a frozenset:

```
myFSet = frozenset([1, 2, 3, 4, 5, 6])
```

You use the frozenset to perform math operations or to act as a list of items. For example, you could create a set consisting of the days of the week. You can't locate individual values in a frozenset but rather must interact with the object as a whole. However, the object is iterable, so the following code tells you whether myFSet contains the value 1:

```
for entry in myFSet:
    if entry == 1:
        print(True)
```

Considering the use of strings

Strings convey thoughts in human terms. Humans don't typically speak numbers or math; they use strings of words made up of individual letters to convey thoughts and feelings. Unfortunately, computers don't know what a letter is, much less strings of letters used to create words or groups of words used to create sentences. None of it makes sense to computers. So, as foreign as numbers and math might be to most humans, strings are just as foreign to the computer (if not more so).

Humans see several kinds of objects as strings, but computer languages usually treat them as separate entities. Two of them are important for programming tasks in this book: characters and strings. A *character* is a single element from a character set, such as the letter *A*. Character sets can contain nonletter components, such as the carriage return control character. Extended character sets can provide access to letters used in languages other than English. However, no matter how someone structures a character set, a character is always a single entity within that character set. Depending on how the originator structures the character set, an individual character can consume 7, 8, 16, or even 32 bits.

A *string* is a sequential grouping of zero or more characters from a character set. When a string contains zero elements, it appears as an empty string. Most strings contain at least one character, however. The representation of a character in memory is relatively standard across languages; it consumes just one memory location for the specific size of that character. Strings, however, appear in various forms depending on the language. So computer languages treat strings differently from characters because of how each of them uses memory.

Strings don't just see use as user output in applications. Yes, you do use strings to communicate with the user, but you can also use strings for other purposes such as labeling numeric data within a dataset. Strings are also central to certain data formats, such as XML. In addition, strings appear as a kind of data. For example, HTML relies on the agent string to identify the characteristics of the client system. Consequently, even if your application doesn't ever interact with the user, you're likely to use strings in some capacity.

Python, as an impure language, also comes with a full list of string functions — too many to go into in this chapter. Creating a string is exceptionally easy:

```
myString = "Hello There!"
```

Strings are first-class citizens in Python, and you have access to all the usual manipulation features found in other languages, including special formatting and escape characters. (The tutorial at `https://www.tutorialspoint.com/python/python_strings.htm` doesn't even begin to show you everything, but it's a good start.)

REMEMBER

An important issue for Python developers is that strings are immutable. Of course, that leads to all sorts of questions relating to how someone can seemingly change the value of a string in a variable. However, what really happens is that when you change the contents of a variable, Python actually creates a new string and points the variable to that string rather than the existing string.

TIP

One of the more interesting aspects of Python is that you can also treat strings sort of like lists. The "Evaluating lists" section, later in this chapter, talks about how to evaluate lists, and many of the same features work with strings. You have access to all the indexing features to start with, but you can also do things like the following:

>> `min(myString)`: Returns the space in the example string

>> `max(myString)`: Returns the letter *r* in the example string

Obviously, you can't use `sum(myString)` because there is nothing to sum. In fact, you get a `TypeError` exception if you try. With Python, if you're not quite sure whether something will work on a string, give it a try.

Employing Pattern Matching

Patterns consist of a set of qualities, properties, or tendencies that form a characteristic or consistent arrangement — a repetitive model. Humans are good at seeing strong patterns everywhere and in everything. In fact, we purposely place patterns in everyday things, such as wallpaper or fabric. However, computers are better than humans are at seeing weak or extremely complex patterns because computers have the memory capacity and processing speed to do so. The capability to see a pattern is *pattern matching*. Pattern matching is an essential component in the usefulness of computer systems and has been from the outset, so this chapter is hardly about something radical or new. Even so, understanding how computers find patterns is incredibly important in defining how this seemingly old technology plays such an important part in new applications such as AI, machine learning, deep learning, and data analysis of all sorts.

The most useful patterns are those that we can share with others. To share a pattern with someone else, you must create a language to define it — an *expression.* This chapter also discusses regular expressions, a particular kind of pattern language, and their use in performing tasks such as data analysis. The creation of a regular expression helps you describe to an application what sort of pattern it should find, and then the computer, with its faster processing power, can locate the precise data you need in a minimum amount of time. This basic information helps you understand more complex pattern matching of the sort that occurs within the realms of AI and advanced data analysis.

Of course, working with patterns using pattern matching through expressions of various sorts works a little differently in the functional programming paradigm. The final sections of this chapter look at how to perform pattern matching using the two languages for this book: Haskell and Python. These examples aren't earth shattering, but they do give you an idea of just how pattern matching works within functional programs so that you can apply pattern matching to other uses.

Looking for patterns in data

When you look at the world around you, you see patterns of all sorts. The same holds true for data that you work with, even if you aren't fully aware of seeing the pattern at all. For example, telephone numbers and social security numbers are examples of data that follows one sort of pattern — that of a positional pattern. A telephone number in the United States consists of an area code of three digits, an exchange of three digits (even though the exchange number is no longer held by a specific exchange), and an actual number within that exchange of four digits.

The positions of these three entities is important to the formation of the telephone number, so you often see a telephone number pattern expressed as (999) 999-9999 (or some variant), where the value 9 is representative of a number. The other characters provide separation between the pattern elements to help humans see the pattern.

Other sorts of patterns exist in data, even if you don't think of them as such. For example, the arrangement of letters from A to Z is a pattern. This statement may not seem like a revelation, but the use of this particular pattern occurs almost constantly in applications when the application presents data in ordered form to make it easier for humans to understand and interact with the data. Organizational patterns are essential to the proper functioning of applications today, yet humans take them for granted, for the most part.

Another sort of pattern is the progression. One of the easiest and most often applied patterns in this category is the exponential progression expressed as N^x, where a number N is raised to the x power. For example, an exponential progression of 2 starting with 0 and ending with 4 would be: 1, 2, 4, 8, and 16. The language used to express a pattern of this sort is the algorithm, and you often use programming language features, such as recursion, to express it in code.

Some patterns are abstractions of real-world experiences. Consider color, for example. To express color in terms that a computer can understand requires the use of three or four three-digit variables, where the first three are always some value of red, blue, and green. The fourth entry can be an alpha value, which expresses opacity, or a gamma value, which expresses a correction used to define a particular color with the display capabilities of a device in mind. These abstract patterns help humans model the real world in the computer environment so that still other forms of pattern matching can occur (along with other tasks, such as image augmentation or color correction).

Transitional patterns help humans make sense of other data. For example, referencing all data to a known base value enables you to compare data from different sources, collected at different times and in different ways, using the same scale. Knowing how various entities collect the required data provides the means for determining which transition to apply to the data so that it can become useful as part of a data analysis.

Data can even have patterns when missing or damaged. The pattern of unusable data could signal a device malfunction, a lack of understanding of how the data collection process should occur, or even human behavioral tendencies. The point is that patterns occur in all sorts of places and in all sorts of ways, which is why having a computer recognize them can be important. Humans may see only part of the picture, but a properly trained computer can potentially see them all.

REMEMBER

So many kinds of patterns exist that documenting them all fully would easily take an entire book. Just keep in mind that you can train computers to recognize and react to data patterns automatically in such a manner that the data becomes useful to humans in various endeavors. The automation of data patterns is perhaps one of the most useful applications of computer technology today, yet very few people even know that the act is taking place. What they see instead is an organized list of product recommendations on their favorite site or a map containing instructions on how to get from one point to another — both of which require the recognition of various sorts of patterns and the transition of data to meet human needs.

Understanding regular expressions

Regular expressions are special strings that describe a data pattern. The use of these special strings is so consistent across programming languages that knowing how to use regular expressions in one language makes it significantly easier to use them in all other languages that support regular expressions. As with all reasonably flexible and feature-complete syntaxes, regular expressions can become quite complex, which is why you'll likely spend more than a little time working out the precise manner by which to represent a particular pattern to use in pattern matching.

REMEMBER

You use regular expressions to refer to the technique of performing pattern matching using specially formatted strings in applications. However, the actual code class used to perform the technique appears as Regex, regex, or even RegEx, depending on the language you use. Some languages use a different term entirely, but they're in the minority. Consequently, when referring to the code class rather than the technique, use Regex (or one of its other capitalizations).

TIP

The following sections constitute a brief overview of regular expressions. You can find the more detailed Python documentation at https://docs.python.org/3.6/library/re.html. This source of additional help can become quite dense and hard to follow, though, so you might also want to review the tutorial at https://www.regular-expressions.info/ for further insights.

CAPITALIZATION MATTERS!

When working with regular expressions, you must exercise extreme care in capitalizing the pattern correctly. For example, telling the regular expression compiler to look for a lowercase *a* excludes an uppercase *A*. To look for both, you must specify both.

The same holds true when defining control characters, anchors, and other regular expression pattern elements. Some elements may have both lowercase and uppercase equivalents. For example, \w may specify any word character, while \W specifies any nonword character. The difference in capitalization is important.

Defining special characters using escapes

Character escapes usually define a special character of some sort, very often a control character. You escape a character using the backslash (\), which means that if you want to search for a backslash, you must use two backslashes in a row (\\). The character in question follows the escape. Consequently, \b signals that you want to look for a backspace character. Programming languages standardize these characters in several ways:

» **Control character:** Provides access to control characters such as tab (\t), newline (\n), and carriage return (\r). Note that the \n character (which has a value of \u000D) is different from the \r character (which has a value of \u000A).

» **Numeric character:** Defines a character based on numeric value. The common types include octal (\nnn), hexadecimal (\xnn), and Unicode (\unnnn). In each case, you replace the *n* with the numeric value of the character, such as \u0041 for a capital letter *A* in Unicode. Note that you must supply the correct number of digits and use 0s to fill out the code.

» **Escaped special character:** Specifies that the regular expression compiler should view a special character, such as (or [, as a literal character rather than as a special character. For example, \(would specify an opening parenthesis rather than the start of a subexpression.

Defining wildcard characters

A wildcard character can define a kind of character, but never a specific character. You use wildcard characters to specify any digit or any character at all. The following list tells you about the common wildcard characters. Your language may not support all these characters, or it may define characters in addition to those listed. Here's what the following characters match with:

Character	Matches With
.	Any character (with the possible exception of the newline character or other control characters)
\w	Any word character
\W	Any nonword character
\s	Any whitespace character
\S	Any non-whitespace character
\d	Any decimal digit
\D	Any nondecimal digit

Working with anchors

Anchors define how to interact with a regular expression. For example, you may want to work with only the start or end of the target data. Each programming language appears to implement some special conditions with regard to anchors, but they all adhere to the basic syntax (when the language supports the anchor). The following table defines the commonly used anchors:

Anchor	What It Does
^	Looks at the start of the string.
$	Looks at the end of the string.
*	Matches zero or more occurrences of the specified character.
+	Matches one or more occurrences of the specified character. The character must appear at least once.
?	Matches zero or one occurrences of the specified character.
{m}	Specifies *m* number of the preceding characters required for a match.
{m,n}	Specifies the range from *m* to *n*, which is the number of the preceding characters required for a match.
expression | *expression*	Performs or searches where the regular expression compiler will locate either one expression or the other expression and count it as a match.

REMEMBER

You may find figuring out some of these anchors difficult. The idea of matching means to define a particular condition that meets a demand. For example, consider this pattern: h?t, which would match *hit* and *hot*, but not *hoot* or *heat*, because the ? anchor matches just one character. If you instead wanted to match *hoot* and *heat* as well, then you'd use h*t, because the * anchor can match multiple characters. Using the right anchor is essential to obtaining a desired result.

Delineating subexpressions using grouping constructs

A grouping construct tells the regular expression compiler to treat a series of characters as a group. For example, the grouping construct [a-z] tells the regular expression compiler to look for all lowercase characters between *a* and *z*. However, the grouping construct [az] (without the dash between *a* and *z*) tells the regular expression compiler to look for just the letters *a* and *z*, but nothing in between, and the grouping construct [^a-z] tells the regular expression compiler to look for everything but the lowercase letters *a* through *z*. The following list describes the commonly used grouping constructs. The italicized letters and words in this list are placeholders.

Construct	What It Means
[*x*]	Look for a single character from the characters specified by *x*.
[*x-y*]	Search for a single character from the range of characters specified by *x* and *y*.
[^*expression*]	Locate any single character not found in the *character expression*.
(*expression*)	Define a regular *expression* group. For example, ab{3} would match the letter *a* and then three copies of the letter *b*, that is, abbb. However, (ab){3} would match three copies of the expression ab: ababab.

Using pattern matching in analysis

Pattern matching in computers is as old as the computers themselves. In looking at various sources, you can find different starting points for pattern matching, such as editors. However, the fact is that you can't really do much with a computer system without having some sort of pattern matching occur. For example, the mere act of stopping certain kinds of loops requires that a computer match a pattern between the existing state of a variable and the desired state. Likewise, user input requires that the application match the user's input to a set of acceptable inputs.

Using Functional
Programming Techniques

Developers recognize that function declarations also form a kind of pattern and that to call the function successfully, the caller must match the pattern. Sending the wrong number or types of variables as part of the function call causes the call to fail. Data structures also form a kind of pattern because the data must appear in a certain order and be of a specific type.

Where you choose to set the beginning for pattern matching depends on how you interpret the act. Certainly, pattern matching isn't the same as counting, as in a for loop in an application. However, someone could argue that testing for a condition in a while loop matches the definition of pattern matching to some extent. Many people look at editors as the first use of pattern matching because editors were the first kinds of applications to use pattern matching to perform a search, such as to locate a name in a document. Searching is most definitely part of the act of analysis because you must find the data before you can do anything with it.

The act of searching is just one aspect, however, of a broader application of pattern matching in analysis. The act of filtering data also requires pattern matching. A search is a singular approach to pattern matching in that the search succeeds the moment that the application locates a match. Filtering is a batch process that accepts all the matches in a document and discards anything that doesn't match, enabling you to see all the matches without doing anything else. Filtering can also vary from searching in that searching generally employs static conditions, while filtering can employ some level of dynamic condition, such as locating the members of a set or finding a value within a given range.

Filtering is the basis for many of the analysis features in declarative languages, such as SQL, when you want to locate all the instances of a particular data structure (a record) in a large data store (the database). The level of filtering in SQL is much more dynamic than in mere filtering because you can now apply conditional sets and limited algorithms to the process of locating particular data elements.

Regular expressions, although not the most advanced of modern pattern-matching techniques, offer a good view of how pattern matching works in modern applications. You can check for ranges and conditional situations, and you can even apply a certain level of dynamic control. Even so, the current master of pattern matching is the algorithm, which can be fully dynamic and incredibly responsive to particular conditions.

Working with pattern matching

Pattern matching in Python closely matches the functionality found in many other languages. Python provides robust pattern-matching capabilities using the regular expression (re) library (https://docs.python.org/3.6/library/re.html). The resource at https://www.regular-expressions.info/python.

html provides a good overview of the Python capabilities. The following sections detail Python functionality using a number of examples.

Performing simple Python matches

All the functionality you need for employing Python in basic RegEx tasks appears in the re library. The following code shows how to use this library:

```
import re
vowels = "[aeiou]"
print(re.search(vowels,
            "This is a test sentence.").group())
```

The search() function locates only the first match, so you see the letter i as output because it's the first item in vowels. You need the group() function call to output an actual value because search() returns a match object, as described at https://docs.python.org/3.6/library/re.html#match-objects.

When you look at the Python documentation, you find quite a few functions devoted to working with regular expressions, some of them not entirely clear in their purpose. For example, you have a choice between performing a search or a match. A match works only at the beginning of a string. Consequently, this code:

```
print(re.match(vowels, "This is a test sentence."))
```

returns a value of None because none of the vowels appears at the beginning of the sentence. However, this code:

```
print(re.match("a", "abcde").group())
```

returns a value of a because the letter *a* appears at the beginning of the test string.

REMEMBER

Neither search nor match will locate all occurrences of the pattern in the target string. To locate all the matches, you use findall or finditer instead. For example, this code:

```
print(re.findall(vowels, "This is a test sentence."))
```

returns a list like this:

```
['i', 'i', 'a', 'e', 'e', 'e', 'e']
```

Because this is a list, you can manipulate it as you would any other list.

Match objects are useful in other ways. For example, you can create a more complete search by using the `start()` and `end()` functions, as shown in the following code:

```
testSentence = "This is a test sentence."
m = re.search(vowels, testSentence)
while m:
    print(testSentence[m.start():m.end()])
    testSentence = testSentence[m.end():]
    m = re.search(vowels, testSentence)
```

This code keeps performing searches on the remainder of the sentence after each search until it no longer finds a match, as shown here:

```
i
i
a
e
e
e
e
```

Using the `finditer()` function would be easier, but this code points out that Python does provide everything needed to create relatively complex pattern-matching code.

Doing more than matching

Python's regular expression library makes it quite easy to perform a wide variety of tasks that don't strictly fall into the category of pattern matching. This chapter discusses only a few of the more interesting capabilities. One of the most commonly used is splitting strings. For example, you might use the following code to split a test string using a number of whitespace characters:

```
testString = "This is\ta test string.\nYippee!"
whiteSpace = "[\s]"
print(re.split(whiteSpace, testString))
```

The escaped character, \s, stands for all space characters, which includes the set of [\t\n\r\f\v]. The `split()` function can split any content using any of the accepted regular expression characters, so it's an extremely powerful data manipulation function. The output from this example looks like this:

```
['This', 'is', 'a', 'test', 'string.', 'Yippee!']
```

Performing substitutions using the sub() function is another forte of Python. Rather than perform common substitutions one at a time, you can perform them all simultaneously, as long as the replacement value is the same in all cases. Consider the following code:

```
testString = "Stan says hello to Margot from Estoria."
pattern = "Stan|hello|Margot|Estoria"
replace = "Unknown"
re.sub(pattern, replace, testString)
```

The output of this example is

```
Unknown says Unknown to Unknown from Unknown.
```

You can create a pattern of any complexity and use a single replacement value to represent each match. This is handy when performing certain kinds of data manipulation for tasks such as dataset cleanup prior to analysis.

Working with Recursion

Some people confuse recursion with a kind of looping. The two are completely different sorts of programming and wouldn't even look the same if you could view them at a low level. In *recursion,* a function calls itself repetitively and keeps track of each call through stack entries, rather than an application state, until a condition used to determine the need to make the function call meets some requirement. At this point, the list of stack entries unwinds with the function passing the results of its part of the calculation to the caller until the stack is empty and the initiating function has the required output of the call. Although this sounds mind-numbingly complex, in practice, recursion is an extremely elegant method of solving certain computing problems and may be the only solution in some situations. The following sections introduce you to the basics of recursion using Python, so don't worry if this initial definition leaves you in doubt as to what recursion means.

Performing tasks more than once

One of the main advantages of using a computer is its capability to perform tasks repetitively — often far faster and with greater accuracy than a human can. Even a language that relies on the functional programming paradigms requires some method of performing tasks more than once; otherwise, creating the language wouldn't make sense. Because the conditions under which functional languages repeat tasks differ from those of other languages using other paradigms, thinking about the whole concept of repetition again is worthwhile, even if you've worked with these other languages. The following sections give you a brief overview.

Defining the need for repetition

The act of repeating an action seems simple enough to understand. However, repetition in applications occurs more often than you might think. Here are just a few uses of repetition to consider:

>> Performing a task a set number of times

>> Performing a task a variable number of times until a condition is met

>> Performing a task a variable number of times until an event occurs

>> Polling for input

>> Creating a message pump

>> Breaking a large task into smaller pieces and then executing the pieces

>> Obtaining data in chunks from a source other than the application

>> Automating data processing using various data structures as input

In fact, you could easily create an incredibly long list of repeated code elements in most applications. The point of repetition is to keep from writing the same code more than once. Any application that contains repeated code becomes a maintenance nightmare. Each routine must appear only once to make its maintenance easy, which means using repetition to allow execution more than one time.

Using recursion instead of looping

The functional programming paradigm doesn't allow the use of loops for two simple reasons. First, a loop requires the maintenance of state, and the functional programming paradigm doesn't allow state. Second, loops generally require mutable variables so that the variable can receive the latest data updates as the loop continues to perform its task. As mentioned previously, you can't use mutable variables in functional programming. These two reasons would seem to sum up the entirety of why to avoid loops, but there is yet another.

One of the reasons that functional programming is so amazing is that you can use it on multiple processors without concern for the usual issues found with other programming paradigms. Because each function call is guaranteed to produce precisely the same result, every time, given the same inputs, you can execute a function on any processor without regard to the processor use for the previous call. This feature also affects recursion because recursion lacks state.

When a function calls itself, it doesn't matter where the next function call occurs; it can occur on any processor in any location. The lack of state and mutable variables makes recursion the perfect tool for using as many processors as a system has to speed applications as much as possible.

Understanding recursion

Recursion, in its essence, is a method of performing tasks repetitively, wherein the original function calls itself. Various methods are available for accomplishing this task, as described in the following sections. The important aspect to keep in mind, though, is the repetition. Whether you use a list, dictionary, set, or collection as the mechanism to input data is less important than the concept of a function's calling itself until an event occurs or it fulfills a specific requirement. Basic recursion is the kind that you normally see demonstrated for most languages. In this case, the doRep function creates a list containing a specific number, n, of a value, x, as shown here for Python:

```
def doRep(x, n):
    y = []
    if n == 0:
        return []
    else:
        y = doRep(x, n - 1)
        y.append(x)
        return y

print(doRep(4, 5))
```

To understand this code, you must think about the process in reverse. The code begins with a call to doRep() with x = 4 and n = 5. Before it does anything else, the code actually calls doRep() repeatedly until n == 0. So, when n == 0, the first actual step in the recursion process is to create an empty list, which is what the code does.

At this point, the call returns and the first actual step concludes, even though you have called doRep() six times before it gets to this point. The next actual step, when n == 1, is to make y equal to the first actual step, an empty list, and then append x to the empty list by calling y.append(x). At this point, the second actual step concludes by returning [4] to the previous step, which has been waiting in limbo all this time. The recursion continues to unwind until n == 5, at which point it performs the final append and returns [4, 4, 4, 4, 4] to the caller.

TIP

Sometimes it's incredibly hard to wrap your head around what happens with recursion, so putting a `print` statement in the right place can help. Here's a modified version of the Python code with the `print` statement inserted. Note that the `print` statement goes after the recursive call so that you can see the result of making it.

```python
def doRep(x, n):
    y = []
    if n == 0:
        return []
    else:
        y = doRep(x, n - 1)
        print(y)
        y.append(x)
        return y

print(doRep(4, 5))
```

This version of the code returns the following:

```
[]
[4]
[4, 4]
[4, 4, 4]
[4, 4, 4, 4]
[4, 4, 4, 4, 4]
```

Using recursion on lists

Lists represent multiple inputs to the same call during the same execution. A list can contain any data type in any order. You use a list when a function requires more than one value to calculate an output. For example, consider the following Python list:

```python
myList = [1, 2, 3, 4, 5]
```

If you wanted to use standard recursion to sum the values in the list and provide an output, you could use the following code:

```python
def lSum(list):
    if not list:
        return 0
    else:
        return list[0] + lSum(list[1:])

print(lSum(myList))
```

You see an output of 15 in this case. The function relies on slicing to remove one value at a time from the list and add it to the sum. The *base case* (principle, simplest, or foundation) is that all the values are gone and now list contains the empty set, ([]), which means that it has a value of 0.

Using lambda functions in Python recursion isn't always easy, but this particular example lends itself using a lambda function quite easily. The advantage is that you can create the entire function in a single line, as shown in the following code (with two lines, but using a line-continuation character):

```
lSum2 = lambda list: 0 if not list \
    else list[0] + lSum2(list[1:])

print(lSum2(myList))
```

As before, the result is 15. The code works precisely the same as the longer example, relying on slicing to get the job done.

Considering advanced recursive tasks

You have full access to the various data structures in Python when using functional programming techniques. For example, a *dictionary* takes the exclusivity of sets one step further by creating key/value pairs, in which the key is unique but the value need not be. Using keys makes searches faster because the keys are usually short and you need only to look at the keys to find a particular value. Python places the key first, followed by the value. Here's a dictionary definition in Python:

```
myDic = {"a": 1, "b": 2, "c": 3, "d": 4}
```

You can access the individual values by using the key. Python uses a form of index to access individual values, such as myDic["b"], which also accesses the value 2. You can use recursion with dictionaries in the same manner as you do lists. However, recursion really begins to shine when it comes to complex data structures. Consider this Python nested dictionary:

```
myDic = {"A":{"A": 1, "B":{"B": 2, "C":{"C": 3}}}, "D": 4}
```

In this case, you have a dictionary nested within other dictionaries down to four levels, creating a complex dataset. In addition, the nested dictionary contains the same "A" key value as the first-level dictionary (which is allowed), the same "B" key value as the second level, and the "C" key on the third level. You might need to look for the repetitious keys, and recursion is a great way to do that, as shown here:

```python
def findKey(obj, key):
    for k, v in obj.items():
        if isinstance(v, dict):
            findKey(v, key)
        else:
            if key in obj:
                print(obj[key])

print(findKey(myDic, "B"))
```

This code looks at all the entries by using a `for` loop. Notice that the loop unpacks the entries into key, `k`, and value, `v`. When the value is another dictionary, the code recursively calls `findKey` with the value and the key as input. Otherwise, if the instance isn't a dictionary, the code checks to verify that the key appears in the input object and prints just the value of that object. In this case, an object can be a single entry or a sub-dictionary. Here is the output from this example:

```
{'B': 2, 'C': {'C': 3}}
2
None
```

Passing functions instead of variables

Being able to pass a function to another function provides much needed flexibility. The passed function can modify the receiving function's response without modifying that receiving function's execution. The two functions work in tandem to create output that's an amalgamation of both.

TIP

Normally, when you use this function-within-a-function technique, one function determines the process used to produce an output, while the second function determines how the output is achieved. This isn't always the case, but when creating a function that receives another function as input, you need to have a particular goal in mind that actually requires that function as input. Given the complexity of debugging this sort of code, you need to achieve a specific level of flexibility by using a function rather than some other input.

Also tempting is to pass a function to another function to mask how a process works, but this approach can become a trap. Try to execute the function externally when possible and input the result instead. Otherwise, you might find yourself trying to discover the precise location of a problem rather than processing data.

For the example in this section, you can't use a lambda function to perform the required tasks with Python, so the following code relies on standard functions instead:

```python
def doAdd(x, y):
    return x + y

def doSub(x, y):
    return x - y

def compareWithHundred(function, x, y):
    z = function(x, y)
    out = lambda x: "GT" if 100 > x \
        else "EQ" if 100 == x else "LT"
    return out(z)

print(compareWithHundred(doAdd, 99, 2))
print(compareWithHundred(doSub, 99, 2))
print(compareWithHundred(doAdd, 99, 1))
```

This example outputs one of three strings: GT when 100 > x; EQ when 100 == x; and LT when 100 < x. To use compareWithHundred(), you pass either doAdd() or doSub(), which simply adds to or subtracts from the second argument, x, the third argument, y. To make the comparison, compareWithHundred() uses a lambda function, which appears on two lines in this case. The output from this example shows how the comparisons work:

```
LT
GT
EQ
```

Performing Functional Data Manipulation

The act of manipulating data means to modify it in some controlled way. You want some of the data, but not all of it. Data analysis often hinges on manipulating data in specific ways. The rest of the book does show various sorts of data manipulation, but the following sections provide you with a quick start.

Slicing and dicing

In some respects, slicing and dicing is considerably easier in Python than in some other languages. For one thing, you use indexes to perform the task. Also, Python offers more built-in functionality. Consequently, the one-dimensional list example looks like this:

```
myList = [1, 2, 3, 4, 5]

print(myList[:2])
print(myList[2:])
print(myList[2:3])
```

The use of indexes enables you to write the code succinctly and without using special functions. The output is as you would expect:

```
[1, 2]
[3, 4, 5]
[3]
```

Slicing a two-dimensional list is every bit as easy as working with a one-dimensional list. Here's the code and output for the two-dimensional part of the example:

```
myList2 = [[1,2],[3,4],[5,6],[7,8],[9,10]]

print(myList2[:2])
print(myList2[2:])
print(myList2[2:3])
```

Here's the output:

```
[[1, 2], [3, 4]]
[[5, 6], [7, 8], [9, 10]]
[[5, 6]]
```

Dicing does require using a special function, but the function is concise in this case and doesn't require multiple steps:

```
def dice(lst, rb, re, cb, ce):
    lstr = lst[rb:re]
    lstc = []
    for i in lstr:
        lstc.append(i[cb:ce])
    return lstc
```

To call dice(), you need to provide a two-dimensional list (lst), the beginning row (rb), ending row (re), beginning column (cb), and the ending column (ce). In this case, you can't really use a lambda function — or not easily, at least. The code slices the incoming list first and then dices it, but everything occurs within a single function. Notice that Python requires the use of looping, but this function uses a standard for loop instead of relying on recursion. The disadvantage of this approach is that the loop relies on state, which means that you can't really use it in a fully functional setting. Here's the test code for the dicing part of the example:

```
myList3 = [[1,2,3],[4,5,6],[7,8,9],[10,11,12],[13,14,15]]

print(dice(myList3, 1, 4, 1, 2))
```

Here's the output:

```
[[5], [8], [11]]
```

Mapping your data

You can find a number of extremely confusing references to the term *map* in computer science. For example, a map is associated with database management (see https://en.wikipedia.org/wiki/Data_mapping), in which data elements are mapped between two distinct data models. However, for this chapter, *mapping* refers to a process of applying a high-order function to each member of a list. Because the function is applied to every member of the list, the relationships among list members is unchanged. Many reasons exist to perform mapping, such as ensuring that the range of the data falls within certain limits. The following code provides an example of mapping:

```
square = lambda x: x**2
double = lambda x: x + x
items = [0, 1, 2, 3, 4]

print(list(map(square, items)))
print(list(map(double, items)))
```

The output shows that you get a square or double of each value in the list, as shown here:

```
[0, 1, 4, 9, 16]
[0, 2, 4, 6, 8]
```

Note that you must convert the map object to a list object before printing it. Given that Python is an impure language, creating code that processes a list of inputs against two or more functions is relatively easy, as shown in this code:

```
funcs = [square, double]

for i in items:
    value = list(map(lambda items: items(i), funcs))
    print(value)
```

Here is the output from this example:

```
[0, 0]
[1, 2]
[4, 4]
[9, 6]
[16, 8]
```

Filtering data

Python doesn't provide the niceties of other languages when it comes to filtering. For example, you don't have access to special keywords, such as odd or even. In fact, all the filtering in Python requires the use of lambda functions. To perform filtering, you use code like this:

```
items = [0, 1, 2, 3, 4, 5]

print(list(filter(lambda x: x % 2 == 1, items)))
print(list(filter(lambda x: x > 3, items)))
print(list(filter(lambda x: x % 3 == 0, items)))
```

which results in the following output:

```
[1, 3, 5]
[4, 5]
[0, 3]
```

Notice that you must convert the filter output using a function such as list. You don't have to use list; you could use any data structure, including set and tuple. The lambda function you create must evaluate to True or False.

Organizing data

Placing data in a particular order makes it easier to perform tasks like seeing patterns. A computer can often use unsorted data, but humans need sorted data to make sense of it. The examples in this section use the following list:

```
original = [(1, "Hello"), (4, "Yellow"), (5, "Goodbye"),
            (2, "Yes"), (3, "No")]
```

To understand these examples, you need to know how to use the sort() method versus the sorted() function. When you use the sort() method, Python changes the original list, which may not be what you want. In addition, sort() works only with lists, while sorted() works with any iterable. The sorted() function produces output that doesn't change the original list. Consequently, if you want to maintain your original list form, you use the following call:

```
sorted(original)
```

The output is sorted by the first member of the tuple: [(1, 'Hello'), (2, 'Yes'), (3, 'No'), (4, 'Yellow'), (5, 'Goodbye')], but the original list remains intact. Reversing a list requires the use of the reverse keyword, as shown here:

```
sorted(original, reverse=True)
```

Python can make use of lambda functions to perform special sorts. For example, to sort by the second element of the tuple, you use the following code:

```
sorted(original, key=lambda x: x[1])
```

TIP

The key keyword is extremely flexible. You can use it in several ways. For example, key=str.lower would perform a case-insensitive sort. Some of the common lambda functions appear in the operator module. For example, you could also sort by the second element of the tuple using this code:

```
from operator import itemgetter
sorted(original, key=itemgetter(1))
```

You can also create complex sorts. For example, you can sort by the length of the second tuple element by using this code:

```
sorted(original, key=lambda x: len(x[1]))
```

Notice that you must use a lambda function when performing a custom sort. For example, trying this code will result in an error:

```
sorted(original, key=len(itemgetter(1)))
```

Even though itemgetter is obtaining the key from the second element of the tuple, it doesn't possess a length. To use the second tuple's length, you must work with the tuple directly.

Chapter **3**

Working with Scalars, Vectors, and Matrices

In Book 2, Chapter 1, you discover techniques for locating the data you need and use it for data science needs (Book 2, Chapter 4 continues this discussion). Simply knowing how to control a language by using its constructs to perform tasks isn't enough, though. The goal of mathematical algorithms is to turn one kind of data into another kind of data. *Manipulating data* means taking raw input and doing something with it to achieve a desired result. For example, until you do something with traffic data, you can't see the patterns that emerge that tell you where to spend additional money in improvements. The traffic data in its raw form does nothing to inform you; you must manipulate it to see the pattern in a useful manner. Therefore, those arcane mathematical symbols are useful after all. You use them as a sort of machine to turn raw data into something helpful, which is what you discover in this chapter.

In times past, people actually had to perform the various manipulations to make data useful by hand, which required advanced knowledge of math. Fortunately, you can find Python and R libraries to perform most of these manipulations using a little code. (In fact, both languages provide a great deal of native capability in this regard, with R being superior in this instance.) You don't have to memorize arcane manipulations anymore — just know which language features to use. That's what this chapter helps you achieve. You discover the means to perform various kinds of data manipulations using easily accessed language libraries designed especially for the purpose.

The chapter begins with scalar, vector, and matrix manipulations (see Chapter 2 of this minibook for the functional version of some of these techniques). You also discover how to speed up the calculations so that you spend less time manipulating the data and more time doing something really interesting with it, such as discovering just how to keep quite so many traffic jams from occurring.

REMEMBER

You don't have to type the source code for this chapter manually. In fact, using the downloadable source is a lot easier. The source code for this chapter appears in the DSPD_0203_Data_Forms.ipynb source code file for Python and the DSPD_R_0203_Data_Forms.ipynb source code file for R. See the Introduction for details on how to find these source files.

Considering the Data Forms

To perform useful data science analysis, you often need to work with larger amounts of data that comes in specific forms. These forms have odd-sounding names, but the names are quite important. The three terms you need to know for this chapter are as follows:

>> **Scalar:** A single base data item. For example, the number 2 shown by itself is a scalar.

>> **Vector:** A one-dimensional array (essentially a list) of data items. For example, an array containing the numbers 2, 3, 4, and 5 would be a vector. You access items in a vector using a zero-based *index,* a pointer to the item you want. The item at index 0 is the first item in the vector, which is 2 in this case.

>> **Matrix:** A two-or-more-dimensional array (essentially a table) of data items. For example, an array containing the numbers 2, 3, 4, and 5 in the first row and 6, 7, 8, and 9 in the second row is a matrix. You access items in a matrix using a zero-based row-and-column index. The item at row 0, column 0 is the first item in the matrix, which is 2 in this case.

Both Python and R provide substantial native capability to work with scalars, vectors, and matrices, but you still have to do considerable work to perform some tasks. To reduce the amount of work you do, you can rely on code written by other people and found in libraries. The following sections describe how to use the NumPy library to perform various tasks on scalars, vectors, and matrixes in Python. The downloadable source provides the same techniques for R developers.

Defining Data Type through Scalars

Every data form in Python and R begins with a *scalar* — a single item of a particular type. Precisely how you define a scalar depends on how you want to view objects within your code and the definitions of scalars for your language. For example, R provides these native, simple data types:

>> Character

>> Numeric (real or decimal)

>> Integer

>> Logical

>> Complex

In many respects, R views strings as vectors of characters; the scalar element is a character, not a string. The difference is important when thinking about how R works with scalars. R also provides a character vector, which is different from an R string. You can read about the difference at https://www.gastonsanchez.com/r4strings/chars.html.

Python provides these native, simple data types:

>> Boolean

>> Integer

>> Float

>> Complex

>> String

Note that Python doesn't include a character data type because it works with strings, not with characters. Yes, you can create a string containing a single character and you can interact with individual characters in a string, but there isn't an actual character type. To see this fact for yourself, try this code:

```
anA = chr(65)
print(type(anA))
```

REMEMBER

The output will be <class 'str'>, rather than <class 'char'>, which is what most languages would provide. Consequently, a string is a scalar in Python but a vector in R. Keeping language differences in mind will help as you perform analysis on your data.

Most languages also support what you might term as semi-native data types. For example, Python supports a `Fraction` data type that you create by using code like this:

```
from fractions import Fraction
x = Fraction(2, 3)
print(x)
print(type(x))
```

The fact that you must import `Fraction` means that it's not available all the time, as something like `complex` or `int` is. The tip-off that this is not a built-in class is the class output of `<class 'fractions.Fraction'>`. However, you get `Fraction` with your Python installation, which means that it's actually a part of the language (hence, semi-native).

TIP

External libraries that define additional scalar data types are available for most languages. Access to these additional scalar types is important in some cases. Python provides access to just one data type in any particular category. For example, if you need to create a variable that represents a number without a decimal portion, you use the integer data type. Using a generic designation like this is useful because it simplifies code and gives the developer a lot less to worry about. However, in scientific calculations, you often need better control over how data appears in memory, which means having more data types — something that `numpy` provides for you. For example, you might need to define a particular scalar as a `short` (a value that is 16 bits long). Using `numpy`, you could define it as `myShort = np.short(15)`. You could define a variable of precisely the same size using the `np.int16` function. You can discover more about the scalars provided by the NumPy library for Python at `https://www.numpy.org/devdocs/reference/arrays.scalars.html`. You also find that most languages provide means of extending the native types (see the articles at `https://docs.python.org/3/extending/newtypes.html` and `http://greenteapress.com/thinkpython/thinkCSpy/html/app02.html` for additional details).

Creating Organized Data with Vectors

A vector is essentially a list or array of scalars that are grouped together to allow access using a single name. The underlying type is a scalar of some sort, but vectors act as a means of organizing the individual scalars and making them easier to work with. The following sections describe working with vectors from an overview perspective.

Defining a vector

The NumPy library provides essential functionality for scientific computing in Python. To use numpy, you import it using the following:

```
import numpy as np
```

Now you can access numpy using the common two-letter abbreviation np.

Use the numpy functions to create a vector. Here are some examples to try:

```
myVect1 = np.array([1, 2, 3, 4])
print(myVect1)
myVect2 = np.arange(1, 10, 2)
print(myVect2)
```

The array() function creates a vector using explicit numbers, while the arange() function creates a vector by defining a range. When using arange(), the first input tells the starting point, the second the stopping point, and the third the step between each number. A fourth argument lets you define the data type for the vector. You can also create a vector with a specific data type. All you need to do is specify the data type like this:

```
myVect3 = np.array(np.int16([1, 2, 3, 4]))
print(myVect3)
print(type(myVect3))
print(type(myVect3[0]))
```

The output tells you the facts about this particular array, including that the vector type is different from the scalar type of the items it contains:

```
[1 2 3 4]
<class 'numpy.ndarray'>
<class 'numpy.int16'>
```

Creating vectors of a specific type

In some cases, you need special numpy functions to create a vector (or a matrix) of a specific type. For example, some math tasks require that you fill the vector with ones. In this case, you use the ones function like this:

```
myVect4 = np.ones(4, dtype=np.int16)
print(myVect4)
```

The output shows that you do have a vector filled with a series of ones:

```
[1 1 1 1]
```

You can also use a `zeros()` function to fill a vector with zeros.

Performing math on vectors

You can perform basic math functions on vectors as a whole, which makes this incredibly useful and less prone to errors that can occur when using programming constructs such as loops to perform the same task. For example, `print(myVect1 + 1)` produces an output of [2, 3, 4, 5] when working with standard Python integers. As you might expect, `print(myVect1 - 1)` produces an output of [0, 1, 2, 3]. You can even use vectors in more complex math scenarios, such as `print(2 ** myVect1)`, where the output is [2, 4, 8, 16].

WARNING

When you want to use NumPy functions and techniques on a standard Python list, you need to perform a conversion. Consider the following code:

```
myVect5 = [1, 2, 3, 4]
print(type(myVect5[0]))
print(type((2 ** np.array(myVect5))[0]))
```

The output shows that the type changes during the transition:

```
<class 'int'>
<class 'numpy.int32'>
```

Performing logical and comparison tasks on vectors

As a final thought on scalar and vector operations, you can also perform both logical and comparison tasks. For example, the following code performs comparison operations on two arrays:

```
a = np.array([1, 2, 3, 4])
b = np.array([2, 2, 4, 4])

print(a == b)
print(a < b)
```

The output tells you about the relationships between the two arrays:

```
[False  True False  True]
[ True False  True False]
```

Starting with two vectors, a and b, the code checks whether the individual elements in a equal those in b. In this case, a[0] doesn't equal b[0]. However, a[1] does equal b[1]. The output is a vector of type bool that contains true or false values based on the individual comparisons. Likewise, you can check for instances when a < b and produce another vector containing the truth-values in this instance.

Logical operations rely on special functions. You check the logical output of the Boolean operators AND, OR, XOR, and NOT. Here is an example of the logical functions:

```
a = np.array([True, False, True, False])
b = np.array([True, True, False, False])

print(np.logical_or(a, b))
print(np.logical_and(a, b))
print(np.logical_not(a))
print(np.logical_xor(a, b))
```

The output tells you about the logical relationship between the two vectors:

```
[ True  True  True False]
[ True False False False]
[False  True False  True]
[False  True  True False]
```

You can also use numeric input to these functions. When using numeric input, a 0 is false and a 1 is true. As with comparisons, the functions work on an element-by-element basis even though you make just one call. You can read more about the logic functions at https://docs.scipy.org/doc/numpy-1.10.0/reference/routines.logic.html.

Multiplying vectors

Adding, subtracting, or dividing vectors occurs on an element-by-element basis, as described in the "Performing math on vectors" section, earlier in this chapter. However, when it comes to multiplication, things get a little odd. In fact, depending on what you really want to do, things can become quite odd indeed. First, consider the element-by-element multiplications below:

```
myVect = np.array([1, 2, 3, 4])
print(myVect * myVect)
print(np.multiply(myVect, myVect))
```

The following output shows that both approaches produce the same result.

```
[ 1,  4,  9, 16]
[ 1,  4,  9, 16]
```

WARNING

Unfortunately, an element-by-element multiplication can produce incorrect results when working with algorithms. In many cases, what you really need is a *dot product*, which is the sum of the products of two number sequences. When working with vectors, the dot product is always the sum of the individual element-by-element multiplications and results in a single number. For example, myVect.dot(myVect) results in an output of 30. If you sum the values from the element-by-element multiplication, you find that they do indeed add up to 30. The discussion at https://www.mathsisfun.com/algebra/vectors-dot-product.html tells you about dot products and helps you understand where they might fit in with algorithms. You can learn more about the linear algebra manipulation functions for numpy at https://docs.scipy.org/doc/numpy/reference/routines.linalg.html.

Creating and Using Matrices

A matrix is simply an extension of the vertex in that you now have a tabular structure consisting of multiple vertexes in multiple rows, all addressed by a single variable name. The table structure is at least two dimensions, but you find matrices of many more dimensions than two. The following sections give you an overview of using matrices.

Creating a matrix

Many of the same techniques you use with vectors also work with matrixes. To create a basic matrix, you simply use the array function as you would with a vector, but you define additional dimensions. A *dimension* is a direction in the matrix. For example, a two-dimensional matrix contains rows (one direction) and columns (a second direction). The following array call:

```
myMatrix1 = np.array([[1,2,3], [4,5,6], [7,8,9]])
print(myMatrix1)
```

produces a matrix containing three rows and three columns, like this:

```
[[1 2 3]
 [4 5 6]
 [7 8 9]]
```

Note how you embed three lists within a container list to create the two dimensions. To access a particular array element, you provide a row and column index value, such as myMatrix1[0, 0] to access the first value of 1.

You can produce matrixes with any number of dimensions using a similar technique, like this:

```
myMatrix2 = np.array([[[1,2], [3,4]], [[5,6], [7,8]]])
print(myMatrix2)
```

This code produces a three-dimensional matrix with x, y, and z axes that looks like this:

```
[[[1 2]
  [3 4]]

 [[5 6]
  [7 8]]]
```

In this case, you embed two lists, within two container lists, within a single container list that holds everything together. To access individual values, you must provide an x, y, and z index value. For example, myMatrix2[0, 1, 1] accesses the value 4.

Creating matrices of a specific type

In some cases, you need to create a matrix that has certain start values. For example, if you need a matrix filled with ones at the outset, you can use the ones function like this:

```
myMatrix3 = np.ones([4,4], dtype=np.int32)
print(myMatrix3)
```

The output shows a matrix containing four rows and four columns filled with int32 values, like this:

```
[[1 1 1 1]
 [1 1 1 1]
 [1 1 1 1]
 [1 1 1 1]]
```

Likewise, a call to

```
myMatrix4 = np.ones([4,4,4], dtype=np.bool)
print(myMatrix4)
```

creates a three-dimensional array, like this:

```
[[[ True  True  True  True]
  [ True  True  True  True]
  [ True  True  True  True]
  [ True  True  True  True]]

 [[ True  True  True  True]
  [ True  True  True  True]
  [ True  True  True  True]
  [ True  True  True  True]]

 [[ True  True  True  True]
  [ True  True  True  True]
  [ True  True  True  True]
  [ True  True  True  True]]

 [[ True  True  True  True]
  [ True  True  True  True]
  [ True  True  True  True]
  [ True  True  True  True]]]
```

This time, the matrix contains Boolean values of True. There are also functions for creating a matrix filled with zeros, the identity matrix, and for meeting other needs. You can find a full listing of vector and matrix array-creation functions at https://docs.scipy.org/doc/numpy/reference/routines.array-creation.html.

Using the matrix class

The NumPy library supports an actual matrix class. The matrix class supports special features that make performing matrix-specific tasks easier. The easiest method to create a NumPy matrix is to make a call similar to the one you use for the array function but to use the mat function instead, such as:

```
myMatrix5 = np.mat([[1,2,3], [4,5,6], [7,8,9]])
print(myMatrix5)
```

which produces the following matrix:

```
[[1 2 3]
 [4 5 6]
 [7 8 9]]
```

You can also convert an existing array to a matrix using the asmatrix function, such as print(np.asmatrix(myMatrix3)). Use the asarray function to convert a matrix object back to an array form.

WARNING

The only problem with the matrix class is that it works on only two-dimensional matrixes. If you attempt to convert a three-dimensional matrix to the matrix class, you see an error message telling you that the shape is too large to be a matrix.

Performing matrix multiplication

Multiplying two matrixes involves the same concerns as multiplying two vectors (as discussed in the "Multiplying vectors" section, earlier in this chapter). The following code produces an element-by-element multiplication of two matrixes:

```
a = np.array([[1,2,3],[4,5,6]])
b = np.array([[1,2,3],[4,5,6]])

print(a*b)
```

The output shows that each element in one matrix is multiplied directly by the same element in the second matrix:

```
[[ 1  4  9]
 [16 25 36]]
```

Working with Scalars, Vectors, and Matrices

WARNING

Note that a and b are the same shape: two rows and three columns. To perform an element-by-element multiplication, the two matrixes must be the same shape. Otherwise, you see an error message telling you that the shapes are wrong. As with vectors, the `multiply` function also produces an element-by-element result.

Dot products work completely differently with matrixes. In this case, the number of columns in matrix a must match the number of rows in matrix b. However, the number of rows in matrix a can be any number, and the number of columns in matrix b can be any number as long as you multiply a by b. For example, the following code produces a correct dot product:

```
a = np.array([[1,2,3],[4,5,6]])
b = np.array([[1,2,3,4],[3,4,5,6],[5,6,7,8]])

print(a.dot(b))
```

Note that the output contains the number of rows found in matrix a and the number of columns found in matrix b:

```
[[22 28 34 40]
 [49 64 79 94]]
```

So how does all this work? To obtain the value found in the output array at index [0,0] of 22, you sum the values of a[0,0]*b[0,0] (which is 1), a[0,1]*b[1,0] (which is 6), and a[0,2]*b[2,0] (which is 15) to obtain the value of 22. The other entries work precisely the same way.

TIP

An advantage of using the `numpy matrix` class is that some tasks become more straightforward. For example, multiplication works precisely as you expect it should. The following code produces a dot product using the `matrix` class:

```
a = np.mat([[1,2,3],[4,5,6]])
b = np.mat([[1,2,3,4],[3,4,5,6],[5,6,7,8]])

print(a*b)
```

The output with the * operator is the same as using the `dot` function with an array.

```
[[22 28 34 40]
 [49 64 79 94]]
```

This example also points out that you must know whether you're using an array or a matrix object when performing tasks such as multiplying two matrixes.

TIP

To perform an element-by-element multiplication using two `matrix` objects, you must use the numpy `multiply` function.

Executing advanced matrix operations

This book takes you through all sorts of interesting matrix operations, but you use some of them commonly, which is why they appear in this chapter. When working with arrays, you sometimes get data in a shape that doesn't work with the algorithm. Fortunately, numpy comes with a special `reshape` function that lets you put the data into any shape needed. In fact, you can use it to reshape a vector into a matrix, as shown in the following code:

```
changeIt = np.array([1,2,3,4,5,6,7,8])

print(changeIt)
print()
print(changeIt.reshape(2,4))
print()
print(changeIt.reshape(2,2,2))
```

REMEMBER

The starting shape of `changeIt` is a vector, but using the `reshape` function turns it into a matrix. In addition, you can shape the matrix into any number of dimensions that work with the data, as shown here:

```
[1 2 3 4 5 6 7 8]

[[1 2 3 4]
 [5 6 7 8]]

[[[1 2]
  [3 4]]

 [[5 6]
  [7 8]]]
```

WARNING

You must provide a shape that fits with the required number of elements. For example, calling `changeIt.reshape(2,3,2)` will fail because there aren't enough elements to provide a matrix of that size.

You may encounter two important matrix operations in some algorithm formulations. They are the transpose and inverse of a matrix. *Transposition* occurs when a matrix of shape n x m is transformed into a matrix m x n by exchanging the rows with the columns. Most texts indicate this operation by using the superscript T, as in A^T. You see this operation used most often for multiplication in order to obtain

Working with Scalars, Vectors, and Matrices

the right dimensions. When working with numpy, you use the transpose function to perform the required work. For example, when starting with a matrix that has two rows and four columns, you can transpose it to contain four rows with two columns each, as shown in this example:

```
changeIt2 = np.array([[1, 2, 3, 4], [5, 6, 7, 8]])
print(np.transpose(changeIt2))
```

The output shows the expected transformation:

```
[[1 5]
 [2 6]
 [3 7]
 [4 8]]
```

You apply *matrix inversion* to matrixes of shape m x m, which are square matrixes that have the same number of rows and columns. This operation is quite important because it allows the immediate resolution of equations involving matrix multiplication, such as y=bX, in which you have to discover the values in the vector b. Because most scalar numbers (exceptions include zero) have a number whose multiplication results in a value of 1, the idea is to find a matrix inverse whose multiplication will result in a special matrix called the identity matrix. To see an identity matrix in numpy, use the identity function, like this:

```
print(np.identity(4))
```

Note that an identity matrix contains all ones on the diagonal.

```
[[1. 0. 0. 0.]
 [0. 1. 0. 0.]
 [0. 0. 1. 0.]
 [0. 0. 0. 1.]]
```

Finding the inverse of a scalar is quite easy (the scalar number n has an inverse of n^{-1} that is 1/n). It's a different story for a matrix. Matrix inversion involves quite a large number of computations. The inverse of a matrix A is indicated as A^{-1}. When working with numpy, you use the linalg.inv function to create an inverse. The following example shows how to create an inverse, use it to obtain a dot product, and then compare that dot product to the identity matrix by using the allclose function.

```
a = np.array([[1,2], [3,4]])
b = np.linalg.inv(a)

print(np.allclose(np.dot(a,b), np.identity(2)))
```

In this case, you get an output of True, which means that you have successfully found the inverse matrix.

REMEMBER

Sometimes, finding the inverse of a matrix is impossible. When a matrix cannot be inverted, it is referred to as a *singular matrix* or a *degenerate matrix*. Singular matrixes aren't the norm; they're quite rare.

Extending Analysis to Tensors

A simple way of starting to look at tensors is that they begin as a generalized matrix that can be any number of dimensions. They can be 0-D (scalar), 1-D (a vector), or 2-D (a matrix). In fact, tensors can have more dimensions than imaginable. Tensors have the number of dimensions needed to convey the meaning behind some object using data. Even though most humans view data as a 2-D matrix that has rows containing individual objects and columns that have individual data elements that define those objects, in many cases a 2-D matrix won't be enough. For instance, you may need to process data that has a time element, creating a 2-D matrix for every observed instant. All these sequences of 2-D matrixes require a 3-D structure to store because the third dimension is time.

REMEMBER

However, tensors are more than simply a fancy sort of matrix. They represent a mathematical entity that lives in a structure filled with other mathematical entities. All these entities interact with each other such that transforming the entities as a whole means that individual tensors must follow a particular transformation rule. This fact makes tensors handy in various kinds of analysis and most especially for deep learning. The dynamic nature of tensors distinguishes them from standard matrixes. Every tensor within a structure responds to changes in every other tensor that occurs as part of a transformation.

To think about how tensors work with regard to deep learning, consider that an algorithm could require three inputs to function, as expressed by this vector:

```
inputs = np.array([5, 10, 15])
```

These are single values based on a single event. Perhaps they represent a query about which detergent is best on Amazon. However, before you can feed these values into the algorithm, you must weight their values based on the training performed on the model. In other words, given the detergents bought by a large group of people, the matrix represents which one is actually best given specific inputs. It's not that the detergent is best in every situation, just that it represents the best option given certain inputs.

The act of weighting the values helps reflect what the deep learning application has learned from analyzing huge datasets. For the sake of argument, you could see the weights in the matrix that follows as learned values:

```
weights = np.array([[.5,.2,-1], [.3,.4,.1], [-.2,.1,.3]])
```

Now that weighting is available for the inputs, you can transform the inputs based on the learning the algorithm performed in the past:

```
result = np.dot(inputs, weights)
print(result)
```

The output of

```
[2.5 6.5 0.5]
```

transforms the original inputs so that they now reflect the effects of learning. The vector, inputs, is a hidden layer in a neural network, and the output, result, is the next hidden layer in the same neural network. The transformations or other actions that occur at each layer determine how each hidden layer contributes to the whole neural network, which was weighting, in this case. Later chapters help you understand the concepts of layers, weighting, and other activities within a neural network. For now, simply consider that each tensor interacts with the structure based on the activities of every other tensor.

Using Vectorization Effectively

Vectorization is a process in which an application processes multiple scalar values simultaneously, rather than one at a time. The main reason to use vectorization is to save time. In many cases, a processor will include a special instruction related to vectorization, such as the SSE instruction in x86 systems (https://docs.oracle.com/cd/E26502_01/html/E28388/eojde.html). Instead of performing single instructions within a loop, a vectorization approach will perform them as a group, making the process considerably faster.

When working with huge amounts of data, vectorization becomes important because you perform the same operation many different times. Anything you can do to keep the process out of a loop will make the code as a whole execute faster. Here is an example of a simple vectorization:

```
def doAdd(a, b):
    return a + b

vectAdd = np.vectorize(doAdd)

print(vectAdd([1, 2, 3, 4], [1, 2, 3, 4]))
```

When you execute this code, you get the following output:

```
[2 4 6 8]
```

The vectAdd function worked on all the values at one time, in a single call. Consequently, the doAdd function, which allows only two scalar inputs, was extended to allow four inputs at one time. In general, vectorization offers these benefits:

>> Code that is concise and easier to read

>> Reduced debugging time because of fewer lines of code

>> The means to represent mathematical expressions more closely in code

>> A reduced number of inefficient loops

Selecting and Shaping Data

You may not need to work with all the data in a dataset. In fact, looking at just one particular column might be beneficial, such as age, or a set of rows with a significant amount of information. You perform two steps to obtain just the data you need to perform a particular task:

1. Filter rows to create a subset of the data that meets the criterion you select (such as all the people between the ages of 5 and 10).

2. Select data columns that contain the data you need to analyze. For example, you probably don't need the individuals' names unless you want to perform some analysis based on name.

The act of slicing and dicing data gives you a subset of the data suitable for analysis. The following sections describe various ways to obtain specific pieces of data to meet particular needs.

Slicing rows

Slicing can occur in multiple ways when working with data, but the technique of interest in this section is to slice data from a row of 2-D or 3-D data. A 2-D array may contain temperatures (x axis) over a specific time frame (y axis). Slicing a row would mean seeing the temperatures at a specific time. In some cases, you might associate rows with cases in a dataset.

A 3-D array might include an axis for place (x axis), product (y axis), and time (z axis) so that you can see sales for items over time. Perhaps you want to track whether sales of an item are increasing, and specifically where they are increasing. Slicing a row would mean seeing all the sales for one specific product for all locations at any time. The following example demonstrates how to perform this task:

```
x = np.array([[[1, 2, 3], [4, 5, 6], [7, 8, 9],],
              [[11,12,13], [14,15,16], [17,18,19],],
              [[21,22,23], [24,25,26], [27,28,29]]])
print(x[1])
```

In this case, the example builds a 3-D array. It then slices row 1 of that array to produce the following output:

```
[[11 12 13]
 [14 15 16]
 [17 18 19]]
```

Slicing columns

Using the examples from the previous section, slicing columns would obtain data at a 90-degree angle from rows. In other words, when working with the 2-D array, you would want to see the times at which specific temperatures occurred. Likewise, you might want to see the sales of all products for a specific location at any time when working with the 3-D array. In some cases, you might associate columns with features in a dataset. The following example demonstrates how to perform this task using the same array as in the previous section:

```
x = np.array([[[1, 2, 3], [4, 5, 6], [7, 8, 9],],
              [[11,12,13], [14,15,16], [17,18,19],],
              [[21,22,23], [24,25,26], [27,28,29]]])
print(x[:,1])
```

Note that the indexing now occurs at two levels. The first index refers to the row. Using the colon (:) for the row means to use all the rows. The second index refers to a column. In this case, the output will contain column 1. Here's the output you see:

```
[[ 4  5  6]
 [14 15 16]
 [24 25 26]]
```

REMEMBER

This is a 3-D array. Therefore, each of the columns contains all the z axis elements. What you see is every row — 0 through 2 for column 1 with every z axis element 0 through 2 for that column.

Dicing

The act of dicing a dataset means to perform both row and column slicing such that you end up with a data wedge. For example, when working with the 3-D array, you might want to see the sales of a specific product in a specific location at any time. The following example demonstrates how to perform this task using the same array as in the previous two sections:

```
x = np.array([[[1, 2, 3], [4, 5, 6], [7, 8, 9],],
              [[11,12,13], [14,15,16], [17,18,19],],
              [[21,22,23], [24,25,26], [27,28,29]]])
print(x[1,1])
print(x[:,1,1])
print(x[1,:,1])
print()
print(x[1:2, 1:2])
```

This example dices the array in four different ways. First, you get row 1, column 1. Of course, what you may actually want is column 1, z axis 1. If that's not quite right, you could always request row 1, z axis 1 instead. Then again, you may want rows 1 and 2 of columns 1 and 2. Here's the output of all four requests:

```
[14 15 16]
[ 5 15 25]
[12 15 18]

[[[14 15 16]]]
```

Concatenating

Data used for data science purposes seldom comes in a neat package. You may need to work with multiple databases in various locations, each of which has its own data format. Performing analysis on such disparate sources of information with any accuracy is impossible. To make the data useful, you must create a single dataset (by *concatenating*, or combining, the data from various sources).

Part of the process is to ensure that each field you create for the combined dataset has the same characteristics. For example, an age field in one database might appear as a string, but another database could use an integer for the same field. For the fields to work together, they must appear as the same type of information.

The following sections help you understand the process involved in concatenating and transforming data from various sources to create a single dataset. After you have a single dataset from these sources, you can begin to perform tasks such as analysis on the data. Of course, the trick is to create a single dataset that truly represents the data in all those disparate datasets; modifying the data would result in skewed results.

Adding new cases and variables

You often find a need to combine datasets in various ways or even to add new information for the sake of analysis purposes. The result is a combined dataset that includes either new cases or variables. The following example shows techniques for performing both tasks:

```
import pandas as pd

df = pd.DataFrame({'A': [2,3,1],
                   'B': [1,2,3],
                   'C': [5,3,4]})

df1 = pd.DataFrame({'A': [4],
                    'B': [4],
                    'C': [4]})

df = df.append(df1)
df = df.reset_index(drop=True)
print(df)

df.loc[df.last_valid_index() + 1] = [5, 5, 5]
print()
print(df)

df2 = pd.DataFrame({'D': [1, 2, 3, 4, 5]})

df = pd.DataFrame.join(df, df2)
print()
print(df)
```

The easiest way to add more data to an existing DataFrame is to rely on the append() method. You can also use the concat() method. In this case, the three cases found in df are added to the single case found in df1. To ensure that the data is appended as anticipated, the columns in df and df1 must match. When you append two DataFrame objects in this manner, the new DataFrame contains the old index values. Use the reset_index() method to create a new index to make accessing cases easier.

You can also add another case to an existing DataFrame by creating the new case directly. Any time you add a new entry at a position that is one greater than the last_valid_index(), you get a new case as a result.

Sometimes you need to add a new variable (column) to the DataFrame. In this case, you rely on join() to perform the task. The resulting DataFrame will match cases with the same index value, so indexing is important. In addition, unless you want blank values, the number of cases in both DataFrame objects must match. Here's the output from this example:

```
   A  B  C
0  2  1  5
1  3  2  3
2  1  3  4
3  4  4  4

   A  B  C
0  2  1  5
1  3  2  3
2  1  3  4
3  4  4  4
4  5  5  5

   A  B  C  D
0  2  1  5  1
1  3  2  3  2
2  1  3  4  3
3  4  4  4  4
4  5  5  5  5
```

Removing data

At some point, you may need to remove cases or variables from a dataset because they aren't required for your analysis. In both cases, you rely on the drop()

method to perform the task. The difference in removing cases or variables is in how you describe what to remove, as shown in the following example:

```
import pandas as pd

df = pd.DataFrame({'A': [2,3,1],
                   'B': [1,2,3],
                   'C': [5,3,4]})

df = df.drop(df.index[[1]])
print(df)

df = df.drop('B', 1)
print()
print(df)
```

The example begins by removing a case from df. Notice how the code relies on an index to describe what to remove. You can remove just one case (as shown), ranges of cases, or individual cases separated by commas. The main concern is to ensure that you have the correct index numbers for the cases you want to remove.

Removing a column is different. This example shows how to remove a column using a column name. You can also remove a column by using an index. In both cases, you must specify an axis as part of the removal process (normally 1). Here's the output from this example:

```
   A  B  C
0  2  1  5
2  1  3  4

   A  C
0  2  5
2  1  4
```

Sorting and shuffling

Sorting and shuffling are two ends of the same goal — to manage data order. In the first case, you put the data into order, while in the second, you remove any systematic patterning from the order. In general, you don't sort datasets for the purpose of analysis because doing so can cause you to get incorrect results. However, you might want to sort data for presentation purposes. The following example shows both sorting and shuffling:

```
import pandas as pd
import numpy as np
```

```
df = pd.DataFrame({'A': [2,1,2,3,3,5,4],
                   'B': [1,2,3,5,4,2,5],
                   'C': [5,3,4,1,1,2,3]})

df = df.sort_values(by=['A', 'B'], ascending=[True, True])
df = df.reset_index(drop=True)
print(df)

index = df.index.tolist()
np.random.shuffle(index)
df = df.loc[df.index[index]]
df = df.reset_index(drop=True)
print()
print(df)
```

It turns out that sorting the data is a bit easier than shuffling it. To sort the data, you use the sort_values() method and define which columns to use for indexing purposes. You can also determine whether the index is in ascending or descending order. Make sure to always call reset_index() when you're done so that the index appears in order for analysis or other purposes.

To shuffle the data, you first acquire the current index using df.index.tolist() and place it in index. A call to random.shuffle() creates a new order for the index. You then apply the new order to df using loc[]. As always, you call reset_index() to finalize the new order. Here's the output from this example (but note that the second output may not match your output because it has been shuffled):

```
   A  B  C
0  1  2  3
1  2  1  5
2  2  3  4
3  3  4  1
4  3  5  1
5  4  5  3
6  5  2  2

   A  B  C
0  2  1  5
1  2  3  4
2  3  4  1
3  1  2  3
4  3  5  1
5  4  5  3
6  5  2  2
```

Working with Scalars, Vectors, and Matrices

Aggregating

Aggregation is the process of combining or grouping data together into a set, bag, or list. The data may or may not be alike. However, in most cases, an aggregation function combines several rows together statistically using algorithms such as average, count, maximum, median, minimum, mode, or sum. You have several reasons to aggregate data:

>> Make it easier to analyze

>> Reduce the ability of anyone to deduce the data of an individual from the dataset for privacy or other reasons

>> Create a combined data element from one data source that matches a combined data element in another source

The most important use of data aggregation is to promote anonymity in order to meet legal or other concerns. Sometimes even data that should be anonymous turns out to provide identification of an individual using the proper analysis techniques. For example, researchers have found that it's possible to identify individuals based on just three credit card purchases (see https://www.computerworld.com/article/2877935/how-three-small-credit-card-transactions-could-reveal-your-identity.html for details). Here's an example that shows how to perform aggregation tasks:

```
import pandas as pd

df = pd.DataFrame({'Map': [0,0,0,1,1,2,2],
                   'Values': [1,2,3,5,4,2,5]})

df['S'] = df.groupby('Map')['Values'].transform(np.sum)
df['M'] = df.groupby('Map')['Values'].transform(np.mean)
df['V'] = df.groupby('Map')['Values'].transform(np.var)

print(df)
```

In this case, you have two initial features for this DataFrame. The values in Map define which elements in Values belong together. For example, when calculating a sum for Map index 0, you use the Values 1, 2, and 3.

To perform the aggregation, you must first call groupby() to group the Map values. You then index into Values and rely on transform() to create the aggregated data using one of several algorithms found in NumPy, such as np.sum. Here are the results of this calculation:

```
    Map  Values  S    M    V
0    0         1  6  2.0  1.0
1    0         2  6  2.0  1.0
2    0         3  6  2.0  1.0
3    1         5  9  4.5  0.5
4    1         4  9  4.5  0.5
5    2         2  7  3.5  4.5
6    2         5  7  3.5  4.5
```

Working with Trees

A tree structure looks much like the physical object in the natural world. Using trees helps you organize data quickly and find it in a shorter time than using other data-storage techniques. You commonly find trees used for search and sort routines, but they have many other purposes as well. The following sections help you understand trees at a basic level.

Understanding the basics of trees

Building a tree is similar to how a tree grows in the physical world. Each item you add to the tree is a *node*. Nodes connect to each other using *links*. The combination of nodes and links forms a structure that looks much like a tree, as shown in Figure 3-1.

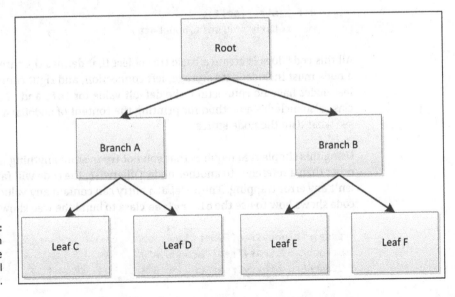

FIGURE 3-1:
A tree in Python looks much like the physical alternative.

Note that the tree has just one root node — just as with a physical tree. The *root node* provides the starting point for the various kinds of processing you perform. Connected to the root node are either branches or leaves. A *leaf node* is always an ending point for the tree. *Branch nodes* support either other branches or leaves. The type of tree shown in Figure 3-1 is a binary tree because each node has, at most, two connections.

In looking at the tree, you see that Branch B is the child of the Root node. That's because the Root node appears first in the list. Leaf E and Leaf F are both children of Branch B, making Branch B the parent of Leaf E and Leaf F. The relationship between nodes is important because discussions about trees often consider the child/parent relationship between nodes. Without these terms, discussions of trees could become quite confusing.

Building a tree

Python doesn't come with a built-in tree object. You must either create your own implementation or use a tree supplied with a library. A basic tree implementation requires that you create a class to hold the tree data object. The following code shows how you can create a basic tree class:

```python
class binaryTree:
    def __init__(self, nodeData, left=None, right=None):
        self.nodeData = nodeData
        self.left  = left
        self.right = right

    def __str__(self):
        return str(self.nodeData)
```

All this code does is create a basic tree object that defines the three elements that a node must include: data storage; left connection; and right connection. Because leaf nodes have no connection, the default value for left and right is None. The class also includes a method for printing the content of nodeData so that you can see what data the node stores.

Using this simple tree requires that you not try to store anything in left or right other than a reference to another node. Otherwise, the code will fail because there isn't any error trapping. The nodeData entry can contain any value. The following code shows how to use the binaryTree class to build the tree shown in Figure 3-1:

```python
tree = binaryTree("Root")
BranchA = binaryTree("Branch A")
BranchB = binaryTree("Branch B")
```

```
tree.left = BranchA
tree.right = BranchB

LeafC = binaryTree("Leaf C")
LeafD = binaryTree("Leaf D")
LeafE = binaryTree("Leaf E")
LeafF = binaryTree("Leaf F")
BranchA.left = LeafC
BranchA.right = LeafD
BranchB.left = LeafE
BranchB.right = LeafF
```

You have many options when building a tree, but building it from the top down (as shown in this code) or the bottom up (in which you build the leaves first) are two common methods. Of course, you don't really know whether the tree actually works at this point. *Traversing the tree* means checking the links and verifying that they actually do connect as you think they should. The following code shows how to use recursion (as described in Book 2, Chapter 2) to traverse the tree you just built.

```
def traverse(tree):
    if tree.left != None:
        traverse(tree.left)
    if tree.right != None:
        traverse(tree.right)
    print(tree.nodeData)

traverse(tree)
```

As the output shows, the traverse function doesn't print anything until it gets to the first leaf:

```
Leaf C
Leaf D
Branch A
Leaf E
Leaf F
Branch B
Root
```

The traverse function then prints both leaves and the parent of those leaves. The traversal follows the left branch first, and then the right branch. The root node comes last.

Trees have different kinds of data storage structures. Here is a quick list of the kinds of structures you commonly find:

>> **Balanced trees:** A kind of tree that maintains a balanced structure through reorganization so that it can provide reduced access times. The number of elements on the left side differs from the number on the right side by at most one.

>> **Unbalanced trees:** A tree that places new data items wherever necessary in the tree without regard to balance. This method of adding items makes building the tree faster but reduces access speed when searching or sorting.

>> **Heaps:** A sophisticated tree that allows data insertions into the tree structure. The use of data insertion makes sorting faster. You can further classify these trees as max heaps and min heaps, depending on the tree's capability to immediately provide the maximum or minimum value present in the tree.

Representing Relations in a Graph

Graphs are another form of common data structure used in algorithms. You see graphs used in places like maps for GPS and all sorts of other places where the top-down approach of a tree won't work. The following sections describe graphs in more detail.

Going beyond trees

A graph is a sort of tree extension. As with trees, you have nodes that connect to each other to create relationships. However, unlike binary trees, a graph can have more than one or two connections. In fact, graph nodes often have a multitude of connections. To keep things simple, though, consider the graph shown in Figure 3-2.

In this case, the graph creates a ring where A connects to both B and F. However, it need not be that way. Node A could be a disconnected node or could also connect to C. A graph shows connectivity between nodes in a way that is useful for defining complex relationships.

Graphs also add a few new twists that you might not have thought about before. For example, a graph can include the concept of directionality. Unlike a tree, which has parent/child relationships, a graph node can connect to any other node with a specific direction in mind. Think about streets in a city. Most streets are bidirectional, but some are one-way streets that allow movement in only one direction.

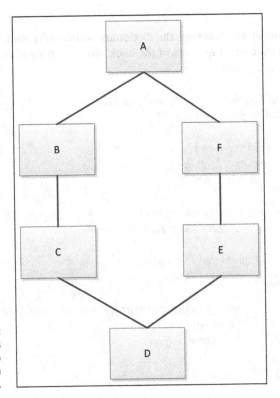

FIGURE 3-2:
Graph nodes
can connect to
each other in
myriad ways.

The presentation of a graph connection might not actually reflect the realities of the graph. A graph can designate a weight to a particular connection. The weight could define the distance between two points, define the time required to traverse the route, or provide other sorts of information.

Arranging graphs

Most developers use dictionaries (or sometimes lists) to build graphs. Using a dictionary makes building the graph easy because the key is the node name and the values are the connections for that node. For example, here is a dictionary that creates the graph shown in Figure 3-2:

```
graph = {'A': ['B', 'F'],
         'B': ['A', 'C'],
         'C': ['B', 'D'],
         'D': ['C', 'E'],
         'E': ['D', 'F'],
         'F': ['E', 'A']}
```

This dictionary reflects the bidirectional nature of the graph in Figure 3-2. It could just as easily define unidirectional connections or provide nodes without any connections at all. However, the dictionary works quite well for this purpose, and you see it used in other areas of the book. Now it's time to traverse the graph using the following code:

```python
def find_path(graph, start, end, path=[]):
        path = path + [start]

        if start == end:
            print("Ending")
            return path

        for node in graph[start]:
            print("Checking Node ", node)

            if node not in path:
                print("Path so far ", path)

                newp = find_path(graph, node, end, path)
                if newp:
                    return newp

find_path(graph, 'B', 'E')
```

This simple code does find the path, as shown in the output:

```
Checking Node  A
Path so far  ['B']
Checking Node  B
Checking Node  F
Path so far  ['B', 'A']
Checking Node  E
Path so far  ['B', 'A', 'F']
Ending

['B', 'A', 'F', 'E']
```

Other strategies help you find the shortest path (see *Algorithms For Dummies*, by John Paul Mueller and Luca Massaron [Wiley] for details on these techniques). For now, the code finds only a path. It begins by building the path node by node. As with all recursive routines, this one requires an exit strategy, which is that when the start value matches the end value, the path ends.

Because each node in the graph can connect to multiple nodes, you need a for loop to check each of the potential connections. When the node in question already appears in the path, the code skips it. Otherwise, the code tracks the current path and recursively calls find_path to locate the next node in the path.

Chapter **4**

Accessing Data in Files

nless the data you use is a live feed or is generated in some manner, it likely comes from a file. In fact, files provide the means to preserve the majority of data used for analysis purposes. So the use of files for storage isn't the issue; instead, the question is what sort of file you might expect to see. The format of the data in the file says a lot about the kind of information you can expect from it. Chapter 1 of this minibook describes the format of files from an overview perspective. This chapter demonstrates how to access data found in files of various formats.

Major divisions appear in the complexity of file storage as well. The files described in this chapter are flat file in nature, which means that they contain just one table. However, the chapter also discusses both textual and binary storage in both local and online sources. Chapter 5 of this minibook looks at relational databases, and Chapter 6 discusses NoSQL databases. Each form of data storage has pros and cons.

REMEMBER

You don't have to type the source code for this chapter manually. In fact, using the downloadable source is a lot easier. The source code for this chapter appears in the DSPD_0204_Data.ipynb source code file for Python and the DSPD_R_0204_Data.ipynb source code file for R. See the Introduction for details on how to find these source files. In addition to the source code files, you must also have access to the Colors.txt, FixedWidth.txt, FixedWidth2.txt, Titanic.csv, Colors.csv, XMLData.xml, and Values.xls files.

Understanding Flat File Data Sources

The most commonly used flat file is a pure text file because you can send it nearly anywhere. Text files can use a variety of storage formats. However, a common format is to have a header line that documents the purpose of each field, followed by another line for each record in the file. The file separates the fields using tabs. See Figure 4-1 for an example of the Colors.txt file used for the example in this section.

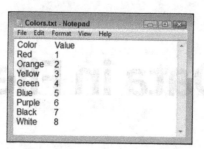

Native Python provides a wide variety of methods that you can use to read such a file. However, letting someone else do the work is far easier. In this case, you can use the pandas library to perform the task. Within the pandas library, you find a set of *parsers*, code used to read individual bits of data and determine the purpose of each bit according to the format of the entire file. Using the correct parser is essential if you want to make sense of file content. In this case, you use the read_csv() method to accomplish the task (older versions of pandas use the read_table() method instead), as shown in the following code:

```
import pandas as pd
color_table = pd.io.parsers.read_csv("Colors.txt",
                                      sep='\t')
print(color_table)
```

The code imports the pandas library, uses the read_csv() method to read Colors.txt into a variable named color_table, and then displays the resulting memory data onscreen using the print function. Note that you must use the sep='\t' argument because the text file uses tabs to separate field entries. Here's the output you can expect to see from this example:

```
   Color Value
0     Red     1
1  Orange     2
2  Yellow     3
3   Green     4
```

```
4      Blue      5
5      Purple    6
6      Black     7
7      White     8
```

Notice that the parser correctly interprets the first row as consisting of field names. It numbers the records from 0 through 7. Using read_csv() method arguments, you can adjust how the parser interprets the input file, but the default settings usually work best. You can read more about the read_csv() arguments at https://pandas.pydata.org/pandas-docs/version/0.25.0/reference/api/pandas.read_csv.html.

Working with Positional Data Files

Positional data files, those in which each field takes up a specific amount of space, see use in various technologies, such as Point-of-Sale (POS) systems. These files also go by the names fixed width-field and fixed-length files. No matter what you call them, an advantage of this file format is that you can read the data as a record or a structure in most programming languages. Processing is simplified because you don't have to worry about any (or very few) control characters. The downside is that these files consume more space than flat files that rely on tabs, but even the space requirement is easier to calculate because each record will always consume the same amount of space.

You usually find positional data files in two forms. The first eschews any sort of control characters at all, and the second relies on a carriage return, linefeed, or both to separate records. The files lack other control characters and you generally see them limited to the standard (7-bit) or extended (8-bit) ASCII character set. At least one vendor relied on a custom 6-bit (64-character) setup to save space (by using uppercase alpha characters, ten digits, and a number of punctuation marks such as period, question mark, space, and comma). With these constraints in mind, Figure 4-2 shows the FixedWidth.txt file used for the first example in this section.

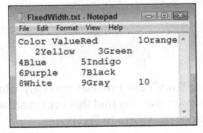

FIGURE 4-2: Each field in this file consumes precisely the same space.

Notice that no formatting is provided, as shown in Figure 4-1. All the data simply runs together. You use a different technique to process this file than you do with a flat file, as shown here:

```
row = 0

with open("FixedWidth.txt", "r") as FW:
    while True:
        Color = FW.read(6)
        if not Color:
            break
        Value = FW.read(5)
        if row == 0:
            color_table2 = pd.DataFrame(
                columns=[Color, Value])
        else:
            color_table2 = color_table2.append(
                [{'Color ': Color, 'Value': Value}],
                ignore_index=True, sort=False)
        row=row+1

print(color_table2)
```

The lack of any sort of row marker means that you must process this file record by record rather than line by line. The first entry is the column header, so the code produces a DataFrame containing the columns it finds. The code assumes that it's reading a particular file. You could modify the code to make it more generic and use it for any file. Each of the rows that follow is appended to the DataFrame, as shown. Here's what you see as output:

```
    Color  Value
0   Red        1
1   Orange     2
2   Yellow     3
3   Green      4
4   Blue       5
5   Indigo     6
6   Purple     7
7   Black      8
8   White      9
9   Gray      10
```

As you can see, the resulting DataFrame provides precisely what you expect in terms of formatted data. However, you may find that your positional data file does provide some sort of row marker, as shown in Figure 4-3.

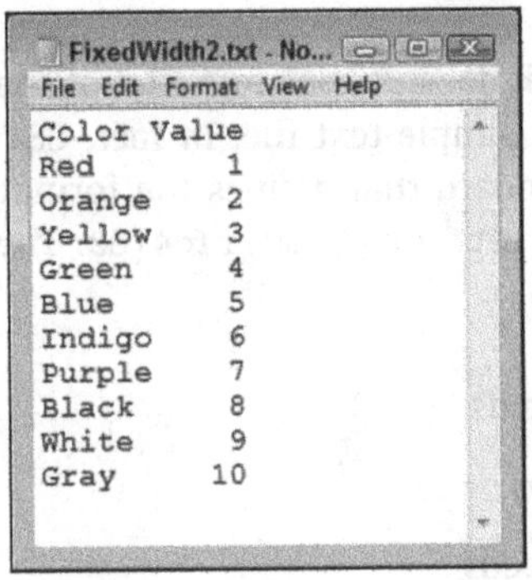

FIGURE 4-3:
This file
includes carriage
returns for row
indicators.

In this case, processing the file becomes infinitely easier, as shown here:

```
color_table3 = pd.read_fwf("FixedWidth2.txt",
                           widths=[6, 5])
print(color_table3)
```

The output is the same as before, but the amount of processing you need to perform is significantly less. The read_fwf() function assumes that the first row is a header, as described at https://pandas.pydata.org/pandas-docs/stable/reference/api/pandas.read_fwf.html. If your file lacks a header, you simply add the header=None argument. You can use the other arguments defined for a TextFileWriter at https://tedboy.github.io/pandas/io/io2.html as well.

Accessing Data in CSV Files

The Comma-Separated Value (CSV) format predates the PC by a number of years. In fact, IBM originally used it with the Formula Translation (FORTRAN) language, as described at https://blog.sqlizer.io/posts/csv-history/. The fact that CSV is so obvious and useful at the same time explains why it has remained one of the better methods to transfer data from anyplace to anywhere. The following sections tell you more about CSV and explain how you can use it in your data science endeavors.

Working with a simple CSV file

One of the things that differentiates a database from a pure text file is formatting, which enables you to discover more about the data simply by the manner in which it's organized. Of the simple database files, CSV is the most common because you can send it almost anywhere and it doesn't consume a lot of space. A CSV file also provides more formatting than a simple text file. In fact, CSV files can become quite complicated. There is a standard that defines the format of CSV files, and you can see it at https://tools.ietf.org/html/rfc4180. The CSV file used for this example is quite simple:

>> A header defines each of the fields

>> Fields are separated by commas

>> Records are separated by linefeeds

>> Strings are enclosed in double quotes

>> Integers and real numbers appear without double quotes

Figure 4-4 shows the raw format for the Titanic.csv file used for this example. You can see the raw format using any text editor.

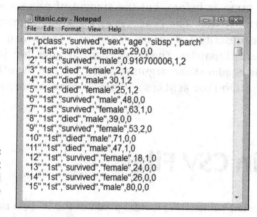

FIGURE 4-4:
The raw format of a CSV file is still text and quite readable.

Applications such as Excel can import and format CSV files so that they become easier to read. Figure 4-5 shows the same file in Excel.

Excel actually recognizes the header as a header. If you were to use features such as data sorting, you could select header columns to obtain the desired result. Fortunately, pandas also enables you to work with the CSV file as formatted data, as shown in the following example:

```
import pandas as pd
titanic = pd.read_csv("Titanic.csv")
X = titanic[['age']]
print(X)
```

FIGURE 4-5:
Use an
application such
as Excel to create
a formatted CSV
presentation.

As with the previous example, this example uses the read_csv() parser. However, because a CSV file provides more formatting information, you don't need to add the sep='\t' argument. Selecting a specific field is quite easy — you just supply the field name as shown. The output from this example looks like this (although some values are omitted for the sake of space):

```
            age
0        29.0000
1         0.9167
2         2.0000
3        30.0000
4        25.0000
5        48.0000
...
1304     14.5000
1305   9999.0000
1306     26.5000
1307     27.0000
1308     29.0000
[1309 rows x 1 columns]
```

A human-readable output like this one is nice when working through an example, but you might also need the output as a list. To create the output as a list, you simply change the third line of code to read X = titanic[['age']].values. Notice the addition of the values property. The output changes to something like this (with some values omitted for the sake of space):

```
[[ 29. ]
 [  0.91670001]
 [  2. ]
 ...,
```

```
[ 26.5 ]
[ 27.  ]
[ 29.  ]]
```

Making use of header information

The previous section makes use of a standards-based CSV file, which doesn't offer much in the way of data format information. If you know the file well through examination, you can always guess about its content, but that's not the same as actually knowing the data types. Some CSV users extend the standard by adding header information as described at https://support.spatialkey.com/providing-data-types-in-csv-headers/ and https://support.symantec.com/us/en/article.HOWTO41097.html. Figure 4-6 shows a CSV file that employs some of these concepts to provide type information.

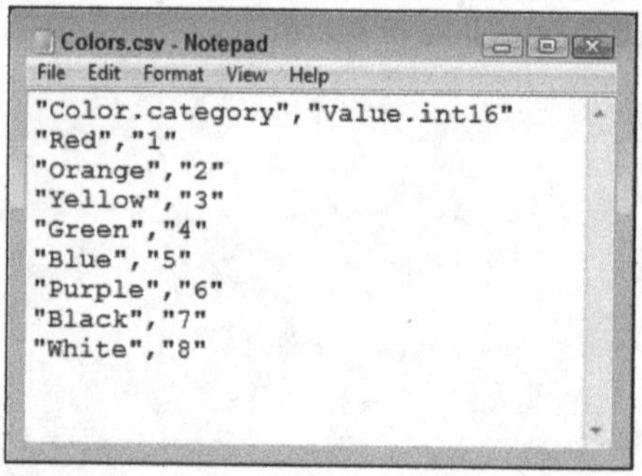

FIGURE 4-6: CSV headers can contain data type information, among other clues.

Obviously, processing this file requires a little extra code, as shown here:

```
color_table4 = pd.read_csv("Colors.csv")
print("Original types:\n", color_table4.dtypes, "\n")

for col in color_table4.columns:
    col_split = col.split('.')
    color_table4 = color_table4.rename(
        columns={col: col_split[0]})
    color_table4 = color_table4.astype(
        {col_split[0]: col_split[1]})

print("New types:\n", color_table4.dtypes, "\n")
print(color_table4)
```

The header information now contains both a header name and a data type. The first `print` statement shows you the original header state, including the data types it uses. The `for` loop removes the type information from the header and uses it to change the data type of each column. Here is the output from this example:

```
Original types:
  Color.category    object
Value.int16          int64
dtype: object

New types:
  Color     category
Value          int16
dtype: object

        Color  Value
0         Red      1
1      Orange      2
2      Yellow      3
3       Green      4
4        Blue      5
5      Purple      6
6       Black      7
7       White      8
```

Moving On to XML Files

Markup languages as a whole have been around for a number of years. The XML file format started as a means to transfer formatted data when scientists found that HTML just wasn't up to the task. You can read a brief history about XML at `https://ccollins.wordpress.com/2008/03/03/a-brief-history-of-xml/`. XML provides metadata that you won't find with a flat file. This metadata helps preserve the format and context of data. The following sections tell you more about XML and describe how to use it.

Working with a simple XML file

One of the most beneficial data access techniques to know when working with web data is accessing XML. All sorts of content types, and even some web pages, rely on XML. Working with web services and microservices means working with XML (in most cases). With this idea in mind, the example in this section works with

XML data found in the `XMLData.xml` file, shown in Figure 4-7. In this case, the file is simple and uses only a couple of levels. XML is hierarchical and can become quite a few levels deep.

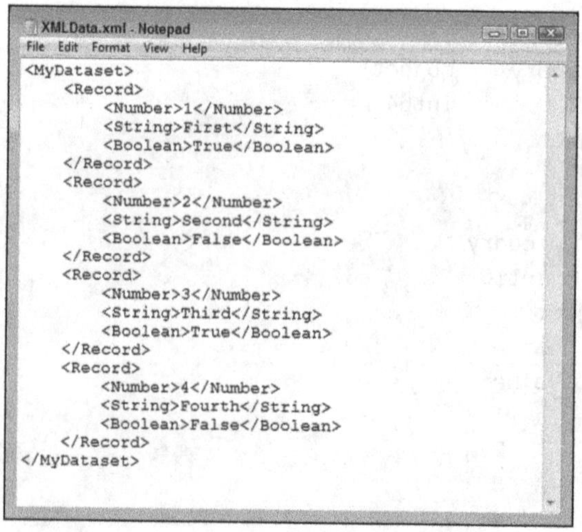


```
<MyDataset>
    <Record>
        <Number>1</Number>
        <String>First</String>
        <Boolean>True</Boolean>
    </Record>
    <Record>
        <Number>2</Number>
        <String>Second</String>
        <Boolean>False</Boolean>
    </Record>
    <Record>
        <Number>3</Number>
        <String>Third</String>
        <Boolean>True</Boolean>
    </Record>
    <Record>
        <Number>4</Number>
        <String>Fourth</String>
        <Boolean>False</Boolean>
    </Record>
</MyDataset>
```

FIGURE 4-7: XML is a hierarchical format that can become quite complex.

The technique for working with XML, even simple XML, can be a bit harder than anything else you've worked with so far. Here's the code for this example:

```
from lxml import objectify
import pandas as pd

xml = objectify.parse(open('XMLData.xml'))
root = xml.getroot()

df = pd.DataFrame(columns=('Number', 'String', 'Boolean'))

for i in range(0,4):
    obj = root.getchildren()[i].getchildren()
    row = dict(zip(['Number', 'String', 'Boolean'],
                   [obj[0].text, obj[1].text,
                    obj[2].text]))
    row_s = pd.Series(row)
    row_s.name = i
    df = df.append(row_s)

print(df)
```

The example begins by importing libraries and parsing the data file using the `objectify.parse()` method. Every XML document must contain a root node, which is `<MyDataset>` in this case. The root node encapsulates the rest of the content, and every node under it is a child. To do anything practical with the document, you must obtain access to the root node using the `getroot()` method.

The next step is to create an empty `DataFrame` object that contains the correct column names for each record entry: `Number`, `String`, and `Boolean`. As with all other pandas data handling, XML data handling relies on a `DataFrame`. The for loop fills the `DataFrame` with the four records from the XML file (each in a `<Record>` node).

The process looks complex but follows a logical order. The `obj` variable contains all the children for one `<Record>` node. These children are loaded into a dictionary object in which the keys are `Number`, `String`, and `Boolean` to match the `DataFrame` columns.

Now the code has a dictionary object that contains the row data. The code creates an actual row for the `DataFrame` next. It gives the row the value of the current for loop iteration. It then appends the row to the `DataFrame`. To see that everything worked as expected, the code prints the result, which looks like this:

```
   Number String Boolean
0       1  First    True
1       2 Second   False
2       3  Third    True
3       4 Fourth   False
```

Parsing XML

XML files provide additional information about the content of a dataset, but they aren't perfect. Simply extracting data from an XML file may not be enough to use it because the data may not be in the correct format. You could end up with a dataset containing only strings. Obviously, you can't perform much data manipulation with strings. The following example reads an XML file into memory and shapes the XML data to create a new `DataFrame` containing just the `<Number>` and `<Boolean>` elements in the correct format:

```
from lxml import objectify
import pandas as pd
from distutils import util

xml = objectify.parse(open('XMLData.xml'))
root = xml.getroot()
df = pd.DataFrame(columns=('Number', 'Boolean'))
```

```
for i in range(0, 4):
    obj = root.getchildren()[i].getchildren()
    row = dict(zip(['Number', 'Boolean'],
                    [obj[0].pyval,
                     bool(util.strtobool(obj[2].text))]))
    row_s = pd.Series(row)
    row_s.name = obj[1].text
    df = df.append(row_s)

print(type(df.loc['First']['Number']))
print(type(df.loc['First']['Boolean']))
```

The DataFrame df is initially instantiated as empty, but as the code loops through the root node's children, it extracts a list containing the following:

» A <Number> element (expressed as an int)

» An ordinal element (a string)

» A <Boolean> element (expressed as a string)

that the code uses to increment df. In fact, the code relies on the ordinal number element as the index label and constructs a new individual row to append to the existing DataFrame. This operation programmatically converts the information contained in the XML tree into the right data type to place into the existing variables in df. The number elements are already available as int type; the conversion of the <Boolean> element is a little harder. You must convert the string to a numeric value using the strtobool() function in distutils.util. The output is a 0 for False values and a 1 for True values. However, that's still not a Boolean value. To create a Boolean value, you must convert the 0 or 1 using bool().

TIP

This example also shows how to access individual values in the DataFrame. Notice that the name property now uses the <String> element value for easy access. You provide an index value using loc and then access the individual feature using a second index. The output from this example is

```
<class 'int'>
<class 'bool'>
```

Using XPath for data extraction

Using XPath to extract data from your dataset can greatly reduce the complexity of your code and potentially make it faster as well. The following example shows an XPath version of the example in the previous section. Notice that this version is shorter and doesn't require the use of a for loop.

```
from lxml import objectify
import pandas as pd
from distutils import util

xml = objectify.parse(open('XMLData.xml'))
root = xml.getroot()


map_number = map(int, root.xpath('Record/Number'))
map_bool = map(str, root.xpath('Record/Boolean'))
map_bool = map(util.strtobool, map_bool)
map_bool = map(bool, map_bool)
map_string = map(str, root.xpath('Record/String'))


data = list(zip(map_number, map_bool))


df = pd.DataFrame(data,
                  columns=('Number', 'Boolean'),
                  index = list(map_string))


print(df)
print(type(df.loc['First']['Number']))
print(type(df.loc['First']['Boolean']))
```

The example begins just like the previous example, with the importing of data and obtaining of the root node. At this point, the example creates a data object that contains record number and Boolean value pairs. Because the XML file entries are all strings, you must use the map() function to convert the strings to the appropriate values. Working with the record number is straightforward: You just map it to an int. The xpath() function accepts a path from the root node to the data you need, which is 'Record/Number' in this case.

Mapping the Boolean value is a little more difficult. As in the previous section, you must use the util.strtobool() function to convert the string Boolean values to a number that bool() can convert to a Boolean equivalent. However, if you try to perform just a double mapping, you'll encounter an error message saying that lists don't include a required function, tolower().To overcome this obstacle, you perform a triple mapping and convert the data to a string using the str() function first.

Creating the DataFrame is different, too. Instead of adding individual rows, you add all the rows at one time by using data. Setting up the column names is the same as before. However, now you need some way of adding the row names, as in the previous example. This task is accomplished by setting the index parameter to a mapped version of the xpath( ) output for the 'Record/String' path. Here's the output you can expect:

```
        Number Boolean
First       1     True
Second      2    False
Third       3     True
Fourth      4    False
<type 'numpy.int64'>
<type 'numpy.bool_'>
```

Considering Other Flat-File Data Sources

You have many other flat-file data sources at your disposal, all of which likely require specialized processing. This chapter uses Excel, an application that you might have on your system. If you don't have the application on your system, you can interact with an Internet version of the application. Excel and other Microsoft Office applications provide highly formatted content that you can use in a freeform database manner. You can specify every aspect of the information these files contain. The Values.xls file used for this example provides a listing of sine, cosine, and tangent values for a random list of angles. You can see this file in Figure 4-8.

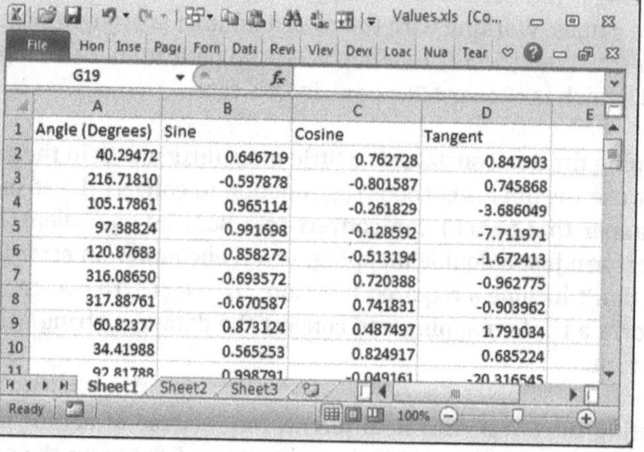

FIGURE 4-8:
An Excel file is highly formatted and might contain information of various types.

When you work with Excel or other Microsoft Office products, you begin to experience some complexity. For example, an Excel file can contain more than one worksheet, so you need to tell pandas which worksheet to process. In fact, you can choose to process multiple worksheets, if desired. When working with other Office products, you have to be specific about what to process. Just telling pandas to process something isn't good enough. Here's an example of working with the Values.xls file.

```
import pandas as pd
xls = pd.ExcelFile("Values.xls")
trig_values = xls.parse('Sheet1', index_col=None,
                        na_values=['NA'])
print(trig_values)
```

The code begins by importing the pandas library as normal. It then creates a pointer to the Excel file using the ExcelFile() constructor. This pointer, xls, lets you access a worksheet, define an index column, and specify how to present empty values. The index column is the one that the worksheet uses to index the records. Using a value of None means that pandas should generate an index for you. The parse() method obtains the values you request. You can read more about the Excel parser options at https://pandas.pydata.org/pandas-docs/stable/generated/pandas.ExcelFile.parse.html.

TIP

You don't absolutely have to use the two-step process of obtaining a file pointer and then parsing the content. You can also perform the task using a single step, like this: trig_values = pd.read_excel("Values.xls", 'Sheet1', index_col= None, na_values=['NA']). Because Excel files are more complex, using the two-step process is often more convenient and efficient because you don't have to reopen the file for each read of the data.

Working with Nontext Data

Nontext data files consist of a series of bits. The file doesn't separate the bits from each other in any way. You can't simply look into the file and see any structure because there isn't any to see. Unstructured file formats rely on the file user to know how to interpret the data. For example, each pixel of a picture file could consist of three 32-bit fields. Knowing that each field is 32-bits is up to you. A header at the beginning of the file may provide clues about interpreting the file, but even so, it's up to you to know how to interact with the file.

The example in this section shows how to work with a picture as an unstructured file. The example image is a public domain offering from https://commons.wikimedia.org/wiki/Main_Page. To work with images, you need to access the Scikit-image library (https://scikit-image.org), which is a free-of-charge collection of algorithms used for image processing. You can find a tutorial for this library at `http://scipy-lectures.github.io/packages/scikit-image/`. The first task is to be able to display the image onscreen using the following code. (This code can require a little time to run. The image is ready when the busy indicator disappears from the Notebook tab. You'll also see a `YAMLLoadWarning` message, which is a function of the library and not the book code.)

```
from skimage.io import imread
from skimage.transform import resize
from matplotlib import pyplot as plt
import matplotlib.cm as cm

example_file = ("http://upload.wikimedia.org/" +
    "wikipedia/commons/7/7d/Dog_face.png")
image = imread(example_file, as_gray=True)
plt.imshow(image, cmap=cm.gray)
plt.show()
```

The code begins by importing a number of libraries. It then creates a string that points to the example file online and places it in `example_file`. This string is part of the `imread()` method call, along with `as_gray`, which is set to `True`. The `as_gray` argument tells Python to turn any color images into gray scale. Any images that are already in gray scale remain that way.

Now that you have an image loaded, it's time to render it (make it ready to display onscreen. The `imshow()` function performs the rendering and uses a gray-scale color map. The `show()` function actually displays `image` for you, as shown in Figure 4-9.

FIGURE 4-9:
The image appears onscreen after you render and show it.

You now have an image in memory, and you may want to find out more about it. When you run the following code, you discover the image type and size:

```
print("data type: %s, shape: %s" %
      (type(image), image.shape))
```

The output from this call tells you that the image type is a numpy.ndarray and the image size is 90 pixels by 90 pixels. The image is actually an array of pixels that you can manipulate in various ways. For example, if you want to crop the image, you can use the following code to manipulate the image array:

```
image2 = image[5:70,0:70]
plt.imshow(image2, cmap=cm.gray)
plt.show()
```

The numpy.ndarray in image2 is smaller than the one in image, so the output is smaller as well. Figure 4-10 shows typical results. The purpose of cropping the image is to make it a specific size. Both images must be the same size for you to analyze them. Cropping is one way to ensure that the images are the correct size for analysis.

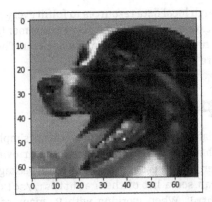

FIGURE 4-10:
Cropping the image makes it smaller.

Another method that you can use to change the image size is to resize it. The following code resizes the image to a specific size for analysis (you can safely ignore the UserWarning message that displays when you run this code):

```
image3 = resize(image2, (30, 30), mode='symmetric')
plt.imshow(image3, cmap=cm.gray)
print("data type: %s, shape: %s" %
      (type(image3), image3.shape))
```

The output from the print() function tells you that the image is now 30 pixels by 30 pixels in size. You can compare it to any image with the same dimensions.

After you have all the images the right size, you need to flatten them. A dataset row is always a single dimension, not two dimensions. The image is currently an array of 30 pixels by 30 pixels, so you can't make it part of a dataset. The following code flattens image3 so that it becomes an array of 900 elements that is stored in image_row.

```
image_row = image3.flatten()
print("data type: %s, shape: %s" %
      (type(image_row), image_row.shape))
```

Notice that the type is still a numpy.ndarray. You can add this array to a dataset and then use the dataset for analysis purposes. The size is 900 elements, as anticipated.

Downloading Online Datasets

You're unlikely to find enough local data resources to fulfill every analysis need. At some point, you need to locate data online to perform experimentation or develop new analysis methods. Fortunately, you don't have to look far. The following sections discuss how to acquire and use online datasets.

Working with package datasets

Most languages support datasets you can use to perform simple data tasks or experimentation without having to create a dataset of your own. For example, Python supports a number of these datasets in Python packages such as the Scikit-learn library. You can see a list of them at https://scikit-learn.org/stable/datasets/index.html. When working with R, many of these datasets are included directly with the language, as shown at https://stat.ethz.ch/R-manual/R-devel/library/datasets/html/00Index.html. These datasets demonstrate various ways in which you can interact with data, and you use them in the examples to perform a variety of tasks. The following list provides a quick overview of the functions used to import the datasets from Scikit-learn into your Python code:

» load_boston(): Regression analysis with the Boston house prices dataset

» load_iris(): Classification with the Iris dataset

» `load_digits([n_class])`: Classification with the digits dataset

» `fetch_20newsgroups(subset='train')`: Data from 20 newsgroups

The technique for loading each of these datasets is the same across examples. The following example shows how to load the Boston house prices dataset:

```
from sklearn.datasets import load_boston
Boston = load_boston()
print(Boston.data.shape)
```

The output from the `print()` call is (506, 13).

TIP

Package datasets need not necessarily be contrived. Keras offers a download-able wrapper for IMDb data. This dataset appears among other useful datasets at `https://keras.io/datasets/`. In particular, the IMDb textual data offered by Keras is cleansed of punctuation, normalized into lowercase, and transformed into numeric values. Each word is coded into a number representing its ranking in frequency. Most frequent words have low numbers; less frequent words have higher numbers. Using the Keras datasets is similar to using other packages, as shown here:

```
from keras.datasets import imdb

top_words = 10000
((x_train, y_train),
 (x_test, y_test)) = imdb.load_data(num_words=top_words,
                                    seed=21)
print("Training examples: %i" % len(x_train))
print("Test examples: %i" % len(x_test))
```

Using public domain datasets

Public domain datasets enable you to expand the number of datasets at your disposal without having to generate the data yourself. In many cases, these public domain datasets are more complex than their package counterparts, but they also model the real world better. The following sections discuss how you can work with public domain datasets.

Downloading the file

Before you can use a public domain dataset, you need to locate the one that best matches your analysis scenario, which can take time (albeit less time than creating a dataset of your own unless the dataset you need is quite simple).

Fortunately, you can find repositories and compilations of datasets online, such as the ones found at Awesome Public Datasets (`https://github.com/awesomedata/awesome-public-datasets`) and Data.gov (`https://catalog.data.gov/dataset?q=public+domain`). You should also spend time looking at articles for potential dataset sources, such as this one at *Forbes* (`https://www.forbes.com/sites/bernardmarr/2016/02/12/big-data-35-brilliant-and-free-data-sources-for-2016/#54573865b54d`).

Some of these datasets come from the scientific community. For example, Kaggle (`https://www.kaggle.com/`) is a huge community of data scientists and others who need to work with large datasets to obtain the information needed to meet various goals. You can create new projects on Kaggle, view the work done by others on completed projects, or participate in one of its ongoing competitions. However, Kaggle is more than simply a community of really smart people who like to play with data; it's also a place where you can obtain resources needed to learn all about deep learning and to create projects of your own.

TIP

The best place to find out how Kaggle can help you discover more about deep learning is at `https://www.kaggle.com/m2skills/datasets-and-tutorial-kernels-for-beginners`. This site lists the various datasets and tutorial kernels that Kaggle provides. A *tutorial kernel* is a kind of project you use to learn how to analyze data in various ways. For example, you can find a tutorial kernel about mushroom classification at `https://www.kaggle.com/uciml/mushroom-classification`.

Opening and using an archive

Seeing an example of how to work with public domain data is useful. This section relies on an example of a public domain downloadable file — the German Traffic Sign Recognition Benchmark (GTSRB) found at this Institute für NeuroInformatik at Ruhr-Universität Bochum page: `http://benchmark.ini.rub.de/?section=gtsrb`. The following code snippet downloads it to the same directory as the Python code. Note that the download process can take a little time to complete, so now might be a good time to refill your teacup.

```
import urllib.request
url = "https://sid.erda.dk/public/archives/\
daaeac0d7ce1152aea9b61d9f1e19370/\
GTSRB_Final_Training_Images.zip"
filename = "./GTSRB_Final_Training_Images.zip"
urllib.request.urlretrieve(url, filename)
```

After retrieving the dataset as a `.zip` file from the Internet, the code sets an image size. (All images are resized to square images, so the size represents the sides in pixels.) The code also sets the portion of data to keep for testing purposes, which means excluding certain images from training to have a more reliable measure of how the neural network works.

A loop through the files stored in the downloaded .zip file retrieves individual images, resizes them, stores the class labels, and appends the images to two separate lists: one for the training and one for testing purposes. The sorting uses a hash function, which translates the image name into a number and, based on that number, decides where to append the image.

```python
import zipfile
from imageio import imread
from skimage.transform import resize

IMG_SIZE = 32
TEST_SIZE = 0.2
X, Xt, y, yt = list(), list(), list(), list()

archive = zipfile.ZipFile(
                './GTSRB_Final_Training_Images.zip', 'r')
file_paths = [file for file in archive.namelist()
              if '.ppm' in file]

for filename in file_paths:
    with archive.open(filename) as img_file:
        img = imread(img_file.read())
    img = resize(img,
                 output_shape=(IMG_SIZE, IMG_SIZE),
                 mode='reflect', anti_aliasing=True)
    img_class = int(filename.split('/')[-2])

    if (hash(filename) % 1000) / 1000 > TEST_SIZE:
        X.append(img)
        y.append(img_class)
    else:
        Xt.append(img)
        yt.append(img_class)

archive.close()
```

At this point, you could use the data for analysis purposes of some sort. That is, you didn't have to generate the data yourself; someone else obtained it for you. So you can focus on your code without having to consider a data source until your code is ready for use in the real world.

Chapter **5**

Working with a Relational DBMS

Relational databases accomplish both the manipulation and data retrieval objectives with relative ease. However, because data storage needs come in all shapes and sizes for a wide range of computing platforms, many different relational database products exist. In fact, for the data scientist, the proliferation of different Relational Database Management Systems (RDBMSs) using various data layouts is one of the main problems you encounter with creating a comprehensive dataset for analysis. The first part of this chapter focuses on common characteristics of RDBMS so that you have a better idea of what commonality you can expect when working with them.

The second part of the chapter discusses the mechanics of working with an RDBMS. However, in contrast to how code is done in many other chapters in this book, writing functional code is nearly impossible in this case because of variations between RDBMS and the fact that we, as the authors, can't be sure what RDBMS you have at your disposal. Trying to create a functional example can't be done in these circumstances, but you do receive enough information to work with your product to create your own RDBMS-specific applications.

Interacting with an RDBMS is complex, but it's only the first step in a longer process. The third part of the chapter discusses what you need to know to move the data from the RDBMS into an environment in which you can perform analysis on it. The fact that RDBMSs vary in characteristics is exacerbated by the significant differences in relational design that have plagued Database Administrators (DBAs) for years. You can't even be sure at the outset about table design differences between data sources, which is a considerable problem given that you must combine tables to obtain a complete picture of the data.

Finally, RDBMS vendors do make a huge effort to differentiate their products. Yes, standards exist, but vendors also have a strong incentive to add functionality that makes their product better than the competition in some way, which is a problem for the data scientist because now you have to deal with those differences when making various products work together. The final part of the chapter discusses a few of these issues.

Considering RDBMS Issues

Chapter 4 of this minibook discusses various sorts of flat-file databases. In most cases, these databases contain just one table, and you rely on just one file for the entire database. An exception might be a specialty database of the sort used by point-of-sale (POS) systems, but generally, you have only one thing to worry about.

REMEMBER

An RDBMS can handle extremely complex data because it relies on Edgar (Ted) Frank Codd's (https://history-computer.com/ModernComputer/Software/Codd.html) relational rules, as described at https://www.w3resource.com/sql/sql-basic/codd-12-rule-relation.php. An RDBMS, by definition, relates data in multiple tables together so that you can store a great deal of information in an incredibly small space while still making that data accessible with less effort than you might normally require.

JUST HOW COMPLEX IS COMPLEX?

To give you some idea of just how complex an RDBMS can become, consider Microsoft's AdventureWorks database (http://merc.tv/img/fig/AdventureWorks2008.gif), which is designed to mimic the real world. The diagram shows all the tables that this database contains. This database requires a great deal of commentary to even start to understand (see one such commentary at http://www.wilsonmar.com/sql_adventureworks.htm), and there are databases that are considerably more complex than this one. Unlike most forms of data storage discussed in this book, the RDBMS gives you the best idea of what you might be facing when developing a truly complex real-world analysis.

The following sections offer an extremely brief overview of RDBMS characteristics as they apply to data science. If you were to perform an analysis based on information from a complex RDBMS, you would probably require the services of a skilled DBA to help you. Yes, the data can become that complicated.

Defining the use of tables

A single table contains just one sort of information, much as a flat-file database does. However, unlike a flat-file database, the single table may be part of a much larger picture. For example, consider an employee entry in a database. The employee information table may contain just *one-off information* (those entries that consume just one record), such as name and employee number. To locate the employee's contact information, you may need to look at another table that records just contact information.

An employee could have multiple contacts — such as multiple addresses, multiple phone numbers, and so on — so a one-to-many relationship exists between the employee information table and the contacts table. The relation between the single employee entry and the multiple contact information records is what an RDBMS is all about. You enter each piece of information only once. To obtain a complete record for analysis purposes, you need both tables (and often a great many more).

REMEMBER

When you're a DBA, you need to understand the relationships between all the tables. Even a manager might need to understand the fact that multiple tables constitute a single employee record. A data scientist may not be interested in all the tables and may not even want all of them. In fact, if your sole purpose is to create an analysis of where employees live (to help city planners develop travel patterns, for example, as part of an infrastructure upgrade), you don't even need the entire contacts table. Perhaps all you really need is the locality, city, and state for each of the employees. You don't want the information to be personally identifiable, so you don't even want the employee number that would normally be part of that table (to create the relationship between the employee and the contact).

Unfortunately, as a data scientist, the contacts table may not actually contain everything you need. What you need is a locality, not a precise address. The contacts table contains a precise address that you would then need to cross-reference to a locality, say the Port View area of town. The resolution of the information depends on the purpose to which you put it. A fine-grained resolution of precise address may actually make the analysis harder than it needs to be and provide less useful information. Now you need:

>> Part of the contacts table

>> Nothing from the employee information table (except to create the initial data request)

>> An external database that provides localities based on the precise address

TIP

Often, when you start looking at data for analysis, what you find is that it's presenting a view of something that satisfies someone else's needs, not yours. Before you make an initial data request and start cleaning the data, you need to work through how you plan to use the data in your analysis, which may mean spending considerable time looking at a diagram of the database schema. The database schema will show things like:

>> How one table is linked to another

>> Which fields link to other fields to create the relationship

>> The type of relationship (such as one-to-many, one-to-one, or many-to-many)

>> Fields used for indexing

>> Fields used as a key for searching

Understanding keys and indexes

For data scientists, keys and indexes take on a different meaning than they might for other RDBMS users. However, the use of these two elements is the same. Multiple kinds of keys exist, as described here:

>> **Primary key:** One or more table columns that uniquely identify each row in the table. Unlike other kinds of databases, an RDBMS contains code that ensures that each primary key is unique. For data scientists, the use of a primary key means that you can count on the uniqueness of each record. In addition, primary keys can't contain missing elements, so you can be sure that the information you receive from a primary key is always complete, but not necessarily correct.

>> **Foreign key:** An entry in a secondary table that points to a primary key in another table. For example, a contacts table will contain a foreign key containing the employee ID of an employee in an employee information table. The key is unique in the employee information table, but you may see multiple copies of the key in the contacts table — each of which points at a particular employee.

>> **Other keys:** Depending on the resource you use, you may see terms such as super key, composite key, alternate key, and so on. For the most part, as a data scientist, you really don't care about these other keys unless they somehow affect how you retrieve information from the RDBMS.

As you can see from the list, a *key* is part of a mechanism to uniquely identify records. Because the keys are unique, you can generally use the indexes created from them to search for a single result in the table when working with a primary key, to search for or a group of related entries when working with a foreign key.

An *index* is part of a mechanism to make searching for data efficient, regardless of whether the data is unique. For example, you can create an index that views telephone numbers based on area code. The area code isn't unique, but you can search on the area code to locate all the numbers that use it. The goal is to find information groups rather than unique information.

TECHNICAL STUFF

For purists, a key is part of the database's logical structure, not an entity. When you create a key, the RDBMS also creates an index for you based on that key. You can also create indexes that aren't based on a key. So, you always search using an index, even you appear to be using a key to do it. This can become a confusing issue for some, and for a data scientist, it doesn't really matter. All that matters is locating all the records in the RDBMS that meet certain criteria.

Using local versus online databases

In general, an RDBMS works the same whether you access it locally or remotely. You still obtain data based on a query in the form that the RDBMS is designed to provide and within the constraints that you specify. However, some mechanics of working with online databases differ from those experienced when working locally:

>> The method of access will likely differ, and you may need to configure elements like firewalls to work with the RDBMS.

>> Access times will increase when working remotely, and response times may be longer still.

>> An RDBMS may limit the forms of response data to those that work well with a remote connection, meaning that you may need to perform additional data transformations.

>> A remote connection may experience limits in data access for security reasons.

You may find additional differences between local and online access, but these are the most common. The point is that, when working with large amounts of sensitive data, a local connection may prove more useful. Even if you make the request, place the data on a hard drive, and move it to the remote location, you may still find that you save time and effort. Oddly enough, this is a common practice even with large online services such as AWS (see https://aws.amazon.com/blogs/aws/send-us-that-data/ for details).

Working in read-only mode

An RDBMS devotes considerable resources to keeping data safe, as described by Codd's 12 rules. However, you can reduce the overhead of interacting with data simply by telling the RDBMS that you have no desire to modify anything. In fact, as a data scientist, you really don't want to modify anything most of the time, so opening the database in full read/write mode makes no sense whatsoever. Consequently, by opening your database in read-only mode, you can gain a speed advantage in performing various tasks.

TIP

A second level of read-only is to create a database snapshot. A snapshot takes a picture of the database at a specific time so that you have static data. Chapter 1 of this minibook discusses the use of static and dynamic data sources. However, in this case, the choice has significant consequences. When you choose to access an RDBMS database in read-only mode, you still have the database engine performing updates in the background, costing you time. If you use a snapshot, no updates take place and you can access data much faster.

Of course, read-only mode and the use of snapshots increase data access speed at the cost of interactivity. You must first consider how you need to interact with the database (normally you don't want to change anything; you just want to acquire data for analysis). Then you must consider whether the data changes quickly enough to warrant using a dynamic setup.

Accessing the RDBMS Data

Understanding how an RDBMS works from the data science perspective enables you to access the database in an efficient manner. However, depending on the data you need, you may need to rely on several techniques to access it. An RDBMS doesn't simply spit out a file with the information you need; you need to understand how to request the data in a manner that reduces the number of requests while increasing the number of records you receive that actually match your requirements. The following sections discuss a few of the most common data access methods.

KEEPING REQUESTS UNDER CONTROL

The temptation exists to request every possible record with every possible field to reduce the number of requests that an application makes from an RDBMS. However, this trap increases resource usage, reduces response speed, and makes manicuring the data later painful. In a perfect world, you would tailor a request in a manner that retrieves just the records you need and only the fields you actually require for analysis. The world isn't perfect, though, so you normally end up with extra data. However, you can reduce the waste and make your applications run considerably faster by reducing the amount of data you request.

In addition, you must also choose the correct request technique. The more work you can perform on the server, the less you have to transport across the network (no matter what kind of network you use). However, you need to keep in mind that working on the server keeps you from seeing the entire dataset, so this approach involves a trade-off. You may actually end up missing data that would make your analysis better by putting too many restrictions on the request. In the end, making requests is more art than science, and you gain a good understanding of what to do only through practice.

Using the SQL language

The one common denominator among many relational databases is that they all rely on a form of the same language to perform data manipulation, which does make the data scientist's job easier. The Structured Query Language (SQL) lets you perform all sorts of management tasks in a relational database, retrieve data as needed, and even shape it in a particular way so that the need to perform additional shaping is unnecessary.

Creating a connection to a database can be a complex undertaking. For one thing, you need to know how to connect to that particular database. However, you can divide the process into smaller pieces. The first step is to gain access to the database engine using a product like SQLAlchemy (https://www.sqlalchemy.org/). You use two lines of code similar to the following code. (Note, however, that the code presented here is not meant to execute and perform a task; the examples at https://docs.sqlalchemy.org/en/13/core/engines.html will help you in this regard.)

```
from sqlalchemy import create_engine
engine = create_engine('sqlite:///:memory:')
```

After you have access to an engine, you can use the engine to perform tasks specific to that DBMS. The output of a read method is always a `DataFrame` object that contains the requested data. To write data, you must create a `DataFrame` object or use an existing `DataFrame` object. You normally use these methods to perform most tasks:

>> `read_sql_table()`: Reads data from a SQL table to a `DataFrame` object

>> `read_sql_query()`: Reads data from a database using a SQL query to a `DataFrame` object

>> `read_sql()`: Reads data from either a SQL table or query to a `DataFrame` object

>> `DataFrame.to_sql()`: Writes the content of a `DataFrame` object to the specified tables in the database

The `sqlalchemy` library provides support for a broad range of SQL databases. The following list contains just a few of them:

>> SQLite

>> MySQL

>> PostgreSQL

>> SQL Server

>> Other relational databases, such as those you can connect to using Open Database Connectivity (ODBC)

You can discover more about working with databases using SQLAlchemy at `https://docs.sqlalchemy.org/en/13/core/tutorial.html`. This tutorial helps you through some of the unique elements of different vendor offerings with regard to accessing data. The techniques that you discover in this book for using the toy databases also work with RDBMSs. However, these principles apply only to retrieving and manicuring the data. If you want to start creating database objects, updating tables, and performing other database tasks, you must follow the SQLAlchemy techniques for doing so because they don't quite match what you would do within the database manager. In addition, you also need to know about differences between vendor SQL implementations to make the code work properly. If you need to expand your knowledge of the SQL language, check out *SQL All-in-One For Dummies* by Allen G Taylor (Wiley).

OPENING A FIREWALL PORT

One of the issues you may have to consider when working with an RDBMS is that the request port differs from the standard port 80 or 443 (for SSL) used for many requests. These special ports often vary by vendor and product. For example, the default SQL Server port is 1433, which means reconfiguring your firewall to make an exception (https://docs.microsoft.com/en-us/sql/sql-server/install/configure-the-windows-firewall-to-allow-sql-server-access?view=sql-server-2017). Even when using a local network setup, you must make the change in the firewall configuration, which can become a sticking point in some cases when opening a port is an issue for support staff.

Relying on scripts

A *script* (sometimes called a stored procedure) is like a mini-application that exists within the RDBMS environment. For many RDBMSs, a script is merely a series of SQL statements bound together by a little glue code. The advantage of working with scripts is that you can obtain relatively precise results because the script will perform a substantial amount of data manipulation for you. In addition, with the use of the right arguments, you can make the script quite flexible so that it can answer a wide variety of needs.

Using a script means that you can perform at least some of the processing needed to obtain useful data on the server rather than on the client. The problem is figuring out how to create a script that provides a generic enough response, yet delivers the data you need. The tutorial at https://www.w3schools.com/sql/ gives the basics of creating SQL statements, and the tutorial at https://docs.microsoft.com/en-us/sql/ssms/tutorials/scripting-ssms?view=sql-server-2017 helps you understand the tool used to create and manage scripts, SQL Server Management Studio (SSMS), for Microsoft's product.

REMEMBER

Unfortunately, scripting is an area in which the RDBMS characteristics tend to vary by vendor. The script you create for SQL Server is unlikely to run on MySQL. Consequently, you need to know each RDBMS or work with a DBA for that RDBMS to create the custom script you require. The disadvantage of using scripts is complexity. This is a platform-specific solution that requires substantial time to hone in many cases.

Relying on views

You can frequently use views to obtain a particular piece of data you need on a regular basis. A *view* is the stored result of a SQL query. As a result, it represents a static dataset, but you can rerun the view to update the information. A view differs from a *snapshot* in that a snapshot isn't updateable and a snapshot is a static image of the database as a whole. (Depending on which resource you use, you may find conflicting definitions of *view* and *snapshot*, but these are the definitions used for this book.) When you download a view, you see just the piece of the database reflected by the SQL query, while a snapshot would provide raw information that you could query locally in ways that you hadn't originally intended with the view.

Using views is very efficient because you transfer only the data you need. Unlike scripts, views tend to be generic across platforms because most platforms use a standard set of SQL commands (with some small modifications as the commands become more complex). You require less intimate knowledge of the platform to use a view, and a DBA who is reluctant to let you create a script (because they are more powerful and flexible) may let you create a view, which can't modify the database content.

REMEMBER

The negative part of using views is that they're single use: The same query means the same result unless the underlying data changes. In addition, views are significantly less powerful than scripts, so using one means that you spend more time manicuring the data locally after you receive it. What you gain with views is ease of use, but that gain comes with a loss of flexibility and efficiency.

Relying on functions

A *function* in an RDBMS works like a function in functional programming (see Chapter 2 of this minibook) because SQL is a declarative programming environment. Functions differ from scripts in a number of important ways. Functions

- » Can't modify state (including database records)
- » Can be used to calculate values
- » Must return a value (scripts can simply perform tasks without returning a value)
- » Can appear as part of SQL statements when they return a scalar value
- » Can't call scripts (but scripts can call functions)

Other differences likely exist between scripts and functions depending on the RDBMS vendor, but these are the important differences from a data science perspective. The two most important of these differences are that a function won't modify state (which is good because you don't usually want to modify state, even accidentally) and you can use a function to calculate values.

TIP

The ability to calculate values and then use that calculation as part of a request is extremely important. For example, you could perform part of your statistical analysis on the server using a function and then use the result to make another request without ever passing information back to the client. This means that you gain a significant advantage in analysis efficiency.

Creating a Dataset

When working with a product such as SQLAlchemy (see the "Using the SQL language" section of the chapter), you use standard Python structures, along with those provided by libraries such as NumPy and pandas. For example, when you make a query, you retrieve a `DataFrame` that looks like any other `DataFrame` you might use with the toy databases used in this book. Consequently, much of what you do with SQLAlchemy output is the same as what you do with any `DataFrame` you have already used. However, the following sections point out some complexities that you need to consider when interacting with an RDBMS that you may not have to deal with otherwise.

Working with a Relational DBMS

Combining data from multiple tables

No matter how hard you try to complete queries on the server, you often have to combine data from queries on the client to create a complete dataset. The important thing is to try to get the database server to do as much of the work for you as possible by creating SQL queries that retrieve precisely what you need. Otherwise, you can spend considerable time trying to determine how to perform the task locally using two `DataFrame` objects in a manner that you might not otherwise use.

WARNING

If you do end up having to combine tables locally, you must do so with a database style merge or join, as described at `https://pandas.pydata.org/pandas-docs/stable/user_guide/merging.html#database-style-dataframe-or-named-series-joining-merging`. If you simply concatenate the two tables, you won't end up with the correct result and your analysis will be tainted.

Unfortunately, you can only join two `DataFrame` objects at a time. If you were to perform the same task on the database server, you could perform one single large join across multiple tables. So, performing the task locally means performing multiple small tasks rather than one big task. To guarantee success, you need to work through a small subset of the data to ensure that you see the correct result before working on the huge datasets normally contained within an RDBMS.

Ensuring data completeness

An RDBMS is a specialized engine that contains all sorts of safeguards not found with your local setup. As you go through the pandas documentation for performing database style merges and joins, note the topics on looking for duplicate keys. When you work with an RDBMS, the RDBMS would automatically detect the duplicate keys and ask how to handle them. This lack of data automation means that you must now perform additional work to manicure your data properly.

Along with duplicate keys, you must consider that you could have to deal with missing keys and missing data. This wouldn't mean that the software is inept, but rather that it lacks the functionality that an RDBMS can provide. In working through a data importation procedure, you must validate attributes such as the data types of the various fields and determine whether the fields are consistent. You perform this kind of work manually because automatic validation is likely to produce inexact results.

TIP

At this point, you may wonder why you'd even attempt to import data into one or more DataFrame objects and then perform the work locally. The answer goes back to some of the original assumptions at the start of the chapter. The data in the RDBMS may simply not reflect what you need to perform an analysis. For example, if you have precise addresses in the RDBMS, but what you need is localities, you may not have the option of performing all the work in the RDBMS because it simply doesn't have the data you need. Now you find yourself working with multiple data sources, some of which may not even appear in an RDBMS — perhaps the locality information is found in a flat-file database or is the result of an API query.

Slicing and dicing the data as needed

Slicing and dicing the data works much as it does for any Python object (see the "Selecting and Shaping Data" section of Book 2, Chapter 3), except that you must now consider how the data is put together before you do anything. The DataFrame you create as the result of various database requests and manipulations may contain complexities that would make normal slicing and dicing strategies inappropriate. For example, cutting off the keys can save space but might also result in an unusable DataFrame.

Mixing RDBMS Products

The DBA at your organization is likely using a single product at a complex and detailed level far beyond what you need. The managers are accessing this data in a manner that helps them perform tasks such as evaluating employees and seeing the latest sales figures. Your RDBMS use will differ from anyone else's at the organization, in many cases, because you need outside data to perform analysis correctly. For example, knowing the sales figures from your organization isn't enough; you may need to know how the compare to other organizations so that you can determine how you're performing against the competition with greater confidence. This difference means that you're quite likely to use more than one RDBMS, each with its own rules.

To determine how best to mix and match the RDBMS products you need, you should review feature comparisons like the one found at `https://medium.com/@mindfiresolutions.usa/a-comparison-between-mysql-vs-ms-sql-server-58b537e474be` for MySQL and SQL Server. Knowing what to expect from each RDBMS will reduce the errors you make when creating queries on each system to retrieve the data you need. In addition, you can start to determine how to deal with RDBMS-specific differences in things like data type handling. One of the more critical issues is how the products handle dates when you perform time-related analysis.

The complexities mount as you begin adding other data sources. If RDBMS isn't complex enough already, you need to consider what happens when you start dealing with flat-file, API, and generated sources. Perhaps some of these sources provide dynamic data when you have a static view or snapshot of the RDBMS data. If so, you need to consider how best to handle that issue. Unfortunately, no best practices exist in this regard. The best approach is probably to experiment to see whether you get what you expected, or if you can explain differences you didn't expect.

Chapter **6**

Working with a NoSQL DMBS

The previous chapter talks about the inordinate amount of organization surrounding Relational Database Management Systems (RDBMSs). In fact, authors write huge tomes about the topic, yet no one resource manages to communicate just how organized these databases are. The hierarchical database is quite the opposite in terms of organization. It isn't untidy by any means; it always knows which pile contains the data it has on hand. Still, sometimes the viewer wonders about it all at first glance. Yet, you often need a hierarchical form of data storage, such as the Not Only SQL (NoSQL) database, to store the chaotic information of the real world in a manner that would elude the RDBMS. That type of storage capability is what this chapter considers.

Books 3 and 4 of this minibook give you the underpinnings and simplified techniques of hierarchical data storage in the form of trees, graphs, and XML. You could add JavaScript Object Notation (JSON) (see Chapter 1 of this minibook for an overview of JSON as a raw data storage methodology) into the mix of technologies that allow hierarchical storage as well. The first part of this chapter takes a more detailed look at the various strategies used to store data in a hierarchical form.

The next part of the chapter discusses how data access occurs. You spend some time looking at a NoSQL implementation and discover how you access it as a database engine using techniques similar to those used with an RDBMS. Even though the underlying storage strategies differ greatly from an RDBMS, any useful hierarchical data storage methodology must provide a way to manage records in a consistent manner.

The final part of this chapter discusses some of the alternative forms of hierarchical data storage. All the straightforward methods of data storage might seem to be taken already, but that's not the case. As long as humans have a need to store data, someone will come up with another method of doing so that provides some benefit not offered by the other methods.

Considering the Ramifications of Hierarchical Data

You can use hierarchies to store data of various types. A hierarchy has the advantage of providing a searchable method of locating disorganized data. Each data element may differ in size and content, but the hierarchy will provide a means of searching it anyway. This ability to locate what you might not otherwise find in an RDBMS is a significant difference between the RDBMS and the hierarchy, as explained in the following sections.

Understanding hierarchical organization

Hierarchies appear all over the place. The organizational chart used to describe the responsibilities, status, and interrelationships in a company is a hierarchy. Deep learning requires the use of hierarchies of neurons to perform tasks. Trees and graphs are programming structures that rely on hierarchies. In fact, if you really think about it, you can't get around the hierarchy. Even looking outside your window, you see plants, shrubs, bushes, and yes, even trees that form hierarchies. Hierarchies of animals also exist when it comes to the food chain, with the most capable predators at the top and the least aware microscopic organisms at the bottom. Sometimes the linkage in a hierarchy seems to defy imagination, such as with the whale that eats massive quantities of krill and plankton. A hierarchy can happen anywhere, even in completely unexpected places and in the most difficult to understand ways.

For all the complexities that hierarchies represent, however, they're actually quite simple in construction. A hierarchy normally consists of these elements:

>> Object nodes, whether real, imagined, or abstract in nature

>> Linkages between nodes

- **»** Directionality, whether top to bottom, one-way, two-way, cyclic, or any other direction you can imagine

- **»** Attributes that describe node, linkage, and directionality as needed (or are absent when not)

REMEMBER

In some minds, a hierarchy denotes a system of ranking objects, as in an organizational chart. However, you can use the hierarchical structure without ranking anything. For example, when you use a hierarchy to define the content of a warehouse, the hierarchy doesn't rank the various items; rather, it might simply group like items together under the root node of the warehouse as a whole.

Developing strategies for freeform data

You can easily assign strategies that are normally employed by RDBMS to hierarchical databases when the only experience a person has is with the RDBMS. For example, when working with a warehouse, the automatic response to linkage is to attach a part number to everything. Unfortunately, although a part number works fine in an RDBMS, it doesn't work at all with a hierarchy.

CHOOSING HIERARCHIES OVER RDBMS

An RDBMS works best when data is consistent, records have approximately the same size, and you have a unique method of identifying each item. For example, if your goal is to catalog a warehouse strictly according to part number, product name, location, and so on, then an RDBMS will work best because each item is formatted precisely the same. The problem is that this form might not serve well when you have a warehouse containing a large group of unlike items.

Another way to view the warehouse is as a group of objects with unique characteristics, such as whether the item is frozen or refrigerated when such a designation works. Some items may have colors; others may employ specific metals. In this case, you work with items based on individual attributes rather than rely on some other strategy. A hierarchical organization works best in this case because you need to group like items together. For example, you wouldn't put metal working equipment and food items in the same group; they're different sorts of items based on how you interact with them. Likewise, you might put the blue metal working equipment into one group and the red metal working equipment into another group, with the difference being the color in this case.

REMEMBER

What you really want is something that describes the item, such as the item name. For example, item number 1234–5678JX isn't descriptive, but `Radial Tires (P 225/70R14 98S SL RWL)` is. Making the name descriptive is helpful in differentiating like items. You may have many different radial tire sizes, so providing a descriptive part number will help.

Of course, using a consistent numbering strategy is relatively easy to search, as long as you know the item number. Searching a hierarchy of names is harder unless you use techniques such as those found in Book 4, Chapter 4 to perform natural language processing. By using the correct search techniques, you can get around issues like

>> Misspellings

>> Word order

>> Nomenclature consistency

>> Missing terms

>> Punctuation

>> Diacritical marks

>> Language inconsistencies (think *colour* versus *color*)

In addition, you may find performing tasks such as displaying the item data more difficult because each item can contain unique information. Creating flexible forms is an essential element of making freeform data stored in a hierarchy manageable. The form will need to construct its content based on the actual item data available.

The point is that freeform data requires a different kind of handling than the rows and columns found in an RDBMS table. You may even find it necessary to create methods for restructuring the hierarchy at times. Perhaps you normally link items together using the item name, but you find a sudden need to link items by physical location instead.

Performing an analysis

Most data scientists don't have a problem figuring out how to perform an analysis using RDBMS data because the data is already in tabular form, which is compatible with programming structures like a pandas `DataFrame`. Freeform data presents certain challenges based on the need to describe an item, rather than simply document it (as is done in an RDBMS). You may need to squint at the data a little and choose a different means of obtaining analysis information based on the following:

>> **Consistent attributes:** Even if the attributes vary greatly among items, some attributes may remain consistent, such as size, value, weight, and so on. You can use these consistent elements as a basis for comparison, such as value and size versus storage cost.

>> **Item inconsistencies:** Given enough items in a particular group, you may be able to perform an analysis of items in that group (rather than the warehouse as a whole) based on item inconsistencies.

>> **Promised versus realized attributes:** The value of an item description is that you can determine whether the promised item composition matches the item as it actually appears in the real world.

>> **Missingness:** Items in one group may have attributes or attribute values that are missing in another, similar, group.

TIP

Generally, you can't use every part of an item description in an analysis, just as you wouldn't use the information in the real world. For example, when shopping at the store, the cost and perceived value of an item are more important than the color of the packaging, even though the color of the packaging may ultimately affect whether you buy the item. Packaging can also affect issues such as how many items you buy. However, when you view two like items and one is significantly more expensive than the other, you're more likely to let price decide which item you get.

Freeform data arranged in a hierarchy focuses on description, so your analysis must focus on description, too. You must think through the process of determining which attributes are consistent enough to allow for the particular analysis you need to perform. You need to consider how a descriptive entry can make your analysis more efficient or correct than using the abstractions of an RDBMS.

Working around dangling data

The one area in which an RDBMS and a hierarchical data source have an equal set of problems is with dangling data — the orphaned record or object that simply doesn't connect to anything. With an RDBMS, the problem generally occurs as the result of code that deletes a parent record without also removing all the child records. Because of the nature of an RDBMS, locating such records or eliminating them from happening at all is relatively easy using rules. Dangling freeform data in a hierarchical form isn't nearly so easy to locate.

The problem is one of linkages. It's hard to tell sometimes whether every object in the database connects to something else (ending with the root item that connects to everything else). The only way to locate dangling data is to traverse the tree as you would a graph, binary search tree (BST), or binary heap. For example, consider Figure 6-1. If Leaf F is disconnected from the rest of the tree, you need to

1. Determine that Leaf F exists.

2. Traverse the entire tree to know what is and isn't connected (creating a list of nodes in the process).

3. Search for Leaf F in the connection list.

4. Define Leaf F as disconnected when it doesn't appear in the list.

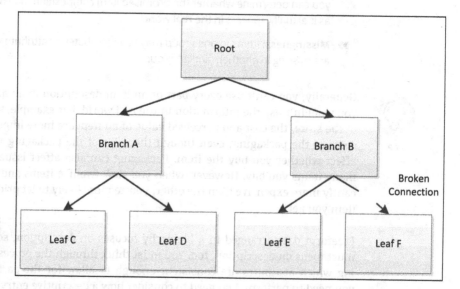

FIGURE 6-1:
A hierarchical construction relies on links to each item.

The process of knowing that Leaf F exists is problematic. You could create a historical database to track which items should appear in the database at any given time. The process is incredibly time consuming and error prone, yet you must have a procedure in place for locating these dangling data items or database corruption will quickly create issues for any analysis you want to perform. Unfortunately, the tree support for Python is lacking, and you sometimes can't locate a library to perform the task, either, so some of these error-handling techniques require custom code. Chapters 5 through 7 of *Algorithms For Dummies*, by John Paul Mueller and Luca Massaron (Wiley), provide code and extensive details about how to manage various kinds of tree structures.

Different kinds of data storage structures are available. Here is a quick list of the kinds of structures you commonly find:

- **Balanced trees:** A kind of tree that maintains a balanced structure through reorganization so that it can provide reduced access times. The number of elements on the left size differs from the number on the right side by one at most.

- **Unbalanced trees:** A tree that places new data items wherever necessary in the tree without regard to balance. This method of adding items makes building the tree faster but reduces access speed when searching or sorting.

- **Heaps:** A sophisticated tree that allows data insertions into the tree structure. The use of data insertion makes sorting faster. You can further classify these trees as max heaps and min heaps, depending on the tree's capability to immediately provide the maximum or minimum value present in the tree.

Accessing the Data

Any data you store is useless unless you can obtain access to it. How this access occurs depends on the data storage strategy:

>> Flat-file storage such as XML requires a search of the tree.

>> In-memory structures, such as dictionaries, rely on keys that you can locate using a single search.

>> NoSQL databases rely on keys as well, but you can also sort and index them in various ways.

You need to be aware of the kind of data storage that you're using, including its limits and advantages. The following sections provide an overview of data access in a general way, discussing some of the ways in which hierarchical data storage methods can differ.

Creating a picture of the data form

Figure 6-1 shows a basic hierarchy and how you start at the root node to find any particular leaf. The picture shows a basic binary tree. Not every form of hierarchical storage works this way, though. You may find that the data storage you use relies on any of these structures:

>> **Ternary tree:** Uses up to three links for each data node.

>> **Binary Search Tree (BST):** The left and right subtrees must also be BST.

>> **Adelson-Velsky and Landis (AVL) tree:** A kind of self-balancing BST, which improves tree performance.

Many other kinds of trees exist as well, and sometimes a data storage technique will rely on a graph instead. Without a picture of what the data looks like, you have no hope of truly understanding how to access any particular node. Consequently, one of the first issues you must deal with is determining how the data storage is laid out, and the best way to do this is in graphic form. The article at https://www.freecodecamp.org/news/all-you-need-to-know-about-tree-data-structures-bceacb85490c/ tells how someone actually draws the tree structure to better understand it.

Employing the correct transiting strategy

Of all the tasks that applications do, searching is the more time consuming and also the one required most. Even though adding data (and sorting it later) does require some amount of time, the benefit of creating and maintaining a dataset comes from using it to perform useful work, which means searching it for important information. Consequently, you can sometimes get by with less efficient Create, Read, Update, and Delete (CRUD) functionality and even a less-than-optimal sort routine, but searches must proceed as efficiently as possible. The only problem is that no one search performs every task with absolute efficiency, so you must weigh your options based on what you expect to do as part of the search routines.

Two of the more efficient methods of searching involve the use of the binary search tree (BST) and binary heap. Both of the search techniques rely on a tree-like structure to hold the keys used to access data elements. However, the arrangement of the two methods is different, which is why one has advantages over the other when performing certain tasks. Figure 6-2 shows the arrangement for a BST.

Note how the keys follow an order in which lesser numbers appear to the left and greater numbers appear to the right. The root node contains a value that is in the middle of the range of keys, giving the BST an easily understood balanced approach to storing the keys. Contrast this arrangement to the binary heap shown in Figure 6-3.

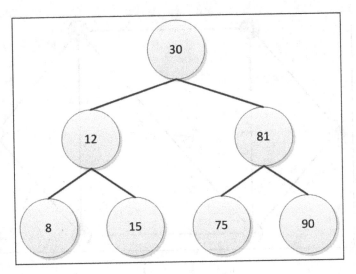

FIGURE 6-2:
The arrangement
of keys when
using a BST.

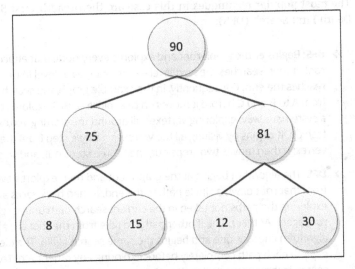

FIGURE 6-3:
The arrangement
of keys when
using a binary
heap.

Each level contains values that are less than the previous level, and the root contains the maximum key value for the tree. In addition, in this particular case, the lesser values appear on the left and the greater on the right (although this order isn't strictly enforced). The figure actually depicts a *binary max heap*. You can also create a *binary min heap*, in which the root contains the lowest key value and each level builds to higher values, with the highest values appearing as part of the leaves.

The manner you use to traverse a tree or graph is important. Consider the graph shown in Figure 6-4 as the starting point for discussion in this case.

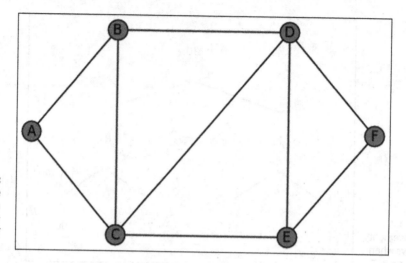

FIGURE 6-4:
An example
graph that you
can use for
certain types of
data storage.

The most popular techniques in this case are the Breadth First Search (BFS) and Depth First Search (DFS):

» **BFS:** Begins at the graph root and explores every node that attaches to the root. It then searches the next level — exploring each level in turn until it reaches the end. Consequently, in the example graph, the search explores from A to B and C before it moves on to explore D. BFS explores the graph in a systematic way, exploring vertexes all around the starting vertex in a circular fashion. It begins by visiting all the vertexes a single step from the starting vertex; it then moves two steps out, then three steps out, and so on.

» **DFS:** The algorithm begins at the graph root and then explores every node from that root down a single path to the end. It then backtracks and begins exploring the paths not taken in the current search path until it reaches the root again. At that point, if other paths to take from the root are available, the algorithm chooses one and begins the same search again. The idea is to explore each path completely before exploring any other path. To make this search technique work, the algorithm must mark each vertex it visits. In this way, it knows which vertexes require a visit and can determine which path to take next.

Even though Figure 6-4 shows a graph, the same techniques work with trees. The article at https://www.geeksforgeeks.org/bfs-vs-dfs-binary-tree/ describes the same process using a tree rather than a graph. Using BFS or DFS can make a difference according to the way in which you need to traverse a graph.

From a programming point of view, the difference between the two algorithms is how each one stores the vertexes to explore the following:

>> A queue for BFS, a list that works according to the FIFO principle. Newly discovered vertexes don't wait long for processing.

>> A stack for DFS, a list that works according to the last in/first out (LIFO) principle.

The choice between BFS and DFS depends on how you plan to apply the output from the search. Developers often employ BFS to locate the shortest route between two points as quickly as possible. This means that you commonly find BFS used in applications such as GPS, where finding the shortest route is paramount. For the purposes of this book, you also see BFS used for spanning tree, shortest path, and many other minimization algorithms.

A DFS focuses on finding an entire path before exploring any other path. You use it when you need to search in detail rather than generally. For this reason, you often see DFS used in games, in which finding a complete path is important. It's also an optimal approach to performing tasks such as finding a solution to a maze.

REMEMBER

Sometimes you have to decide between BFS and DFS based on the limitations of each technique. BFS needs lots of memory because it systematically stores all the paths before finding a solution. On the other hand, DFS needs less memory, but you have no guarantee that it'll find the shortest and most direct solution.

Ordering the data

You have essentially two methods of ordering your hierarchical data: sorting and indexing. When sorting the data, you create a new version of the dataset in a specific order depending on the storage strategy you use. You use sorting only on small datasets. Indexing is the method of choice when working with large datasets. Even though you have a lot of options when it comes to indexing, here are the most popular:

>> **B-Tree:** This is one of the most common indexing methods for DBMSs. When working with a B-tree, the internal nodes can have a variable number of child nodes depending on a predefined range. The advantage of this approach is that the code has to balance the tree less often. The disadvantage is that the tree has more unused space.

>> **B+-Tree:** This is a variation of the B-tree in which all the keys reside in the leaf nodes, providing a boost in speed.

>> **T-Tree:** This is a mix of AVL-trees (see https://www.geeksforgeeks.org/avl-tree-set-1-insertion/ for details) and B-trees in which the resulting tree is balanced but each node can have a different number of children. A T-Tree tends to have better overall performance than a corresponding AVL-Tree. The nodes each contain one key/value pair and a pointer tuple. A T-Tree provides three kinds of nodes:

- **T-Node:** Has both a right and left child
- **Half-leaf node:** Has just one child
- **Leaf node:** Has no children

>> **O2-Tree:** This is an evolution of Red-Black trees (see https://www.geeksforgeeks.org/red-black-tree-set-1-introduction-2/ for details), which is a form of Binary-Search tree in which the leaf nodes contain a tuple with the key/value pairs and a pointer to the next node. The basic reason to use this kind of indexing is that it enhances overall indexing performance. As with Red-Black trees, every node is either red or black, with a black root. When a node is red, both of its children are black. Leaf nodes are double linked both forward and backward, making this index incredibly easy to traverse.

Interacting with Data from NoSQL Databases

Hierarchical data formats can take many forms. For example, XML and JSON files are a type of hierarchical storage. However, these flat file formats are relatively limited in scope, so you need something with additional functionality, such as the databases described in the slide show at https://www.computerworld.com/article/3412345/the-best-nosql-database-options-for-the-enterprise.html. Many of these offerings are in the cloud, so you don't even have to worry about creating a localized implementation. All these NoSQL databases are designed to handle the complexities of corporate data in a manner consistent with hierarchical storage.

NoSQL databases are used in large data storage scenarios in which the relational model can become overly complex or can break down in other ways. The databases generally don't use the relational model. Of course, you find fewer of these DBMSs used in the corporate environment because they require special handling and training. Still, some common DBMSs are used because they provide special functionality or meet unique requirements. The process is essentially the same for using NoSQL databases as it is for relational databases:

1. Import required database engine functionality.

2. Create a database engine.

3. Make any required queries using the database engine and the functionality supported by the DBMS.

The details vary quite a bit, and you need to know which library to use with your particular database product. For example, when working with MongoDB (https://www.mongodb.org/), you must obtain a copy of the PyMongo library (https://api.mongodb.org/python/current/) and use the MongoClient class to create the required engine. The MongoDB engine relies heavily on the find() function to locate data. Following is a pseudo-code example of a MongoDB session. (You won't be able to execute this code in Notebook; it's shown only as an example.)

```
import pymongo
import pandas as pd
from pymongo import Connection
connection = Connection()
db = connection.database_name
input_data = db.collection_name
data = pd.DataFrame(list(input_data.find()))
```

Working with Dictionaries

Chapter 2 of this minibook describes how to create and use dictionaries. In that chapter, you use scalar values as the value portion of the key/value pair. However, you don't have to use a scalar value. You can use other standard data types as the value, or you can even create a class to hold custom data. The point is that you use the key to locate the data and the value to hold the data.

Here's an example of using a list. You can create a dictionary containing a series of lists like this:

```
X = {'a': [1, 2, 3], 'b': [4, 5, 6]}
```

To access a particular key, you use code like this:

```
print(X['a'])
```

The output in this instance is a list: [1, 2, 3]. To access a given list element, you use code like this:

```
print(X['a'][1])
```

What you see is the value 2 as output. The point of this example is that you could easily implement a hierarchical data storage setup using a dictionary by providing a pointer to the next key as one of the value elements, like this:

```
X = {'a': ['b', 1, 2, 3], 'b': ['a', 4, 5, 6]}
```

To move to the next node, you simply index it as you would a value:

```
print("Next element is: ", X['a'][0])
```

You see Next element is: b as the output. You can create a B-tree or any other hierarchical structure using this approach if desired. Using a custom class is similar to working with a list, but you have to design the class. The article at https://code.tutsplus.com/tutorials/how-to-implement-your-own-data-structure-in-python--cms-28723 offers a discussion of this approach.

Developing Datasets from Hierarchical Data

You can work with hierarchical data directly in your applications. It means using various traversal techniques and writing a lot of code to deal with the various nodes. Unfortunately, it also means that you have to reinvent the wheel in performing many common tasks that libraries like pandas make extremely easy. Still, sometimes you have no other choice but to work with the data in hierarchical form.

Sometimes, you may find that your hierarchical data is amenable to being stuffed into a pandas DataFrame by using smart coding techniques and looking for patterns. For example, the discussion at https://stackoverflow.com/questions/48374823/parsing-hierarchical-data-from-xml-to-pandas talks about moving a particular XML dataset (which is hierarchical) into a DataFrame. In looking at the data for this example, you see that it's already in a somewhat tabular format. If the data were completely freeform, the example wouldn't work because creating the required rows and columns wouldn't be possible. Even so, this XML example is somewhat typical of certain kinds of data, such as log entries.

WARNING

You can find some examples of complex data imports online, but generally the code for these examples is extremely brittle, which means that it'll break the moment anything unexpected happens with your data source. In many cases, unless the data you want to use as part of a DataFrame is already in a form that lends itself to tabular display, the better bet is to simply work with it as a hierarchical data source.

Processing Hierarchical Data into Other Forms

You eventually need to consider how to work with forms of data that you require for your analysis that simply defy easy storage using existing methods. Because you can find nearly constant development in this area, you can safely assume that other data scientists face the same issues as you do.

One of the more interesting newer entries into this field is object storage of the sort provided by Amazon Web Services (AWS) Simple Storage Service (S3) (https://aws.amazon.com/what-is-cloud-object-storage/). The methodology seems incredibly messy at first because you simply throw objects into what amounts to an electronic bucket. The data doesn't even appear neatly stacked on shelves. Yet, this storage method offers fast and easy storage of items that just don't fit anywhere else and seemingly defy organization.

TIP

Image files can prove especially difficult to deal with because not only are they stored in a hierarchical manner but the images themselves can present problems. The article at https://realpython.com/storing-images-in-python/ offers some interesting ways to work with image files that you want to use as part of an analysis. Besides the usual disk storage technique (using the Pillow library), this article tells you about these techniques:

» Lightning Memory-Mapped Databases (LMDB)

» Hierarchical Data Format (HDF5)

3

Manipulating Data Using Basic Algorithms

Contents at a Glance

Chapter **1**

Working with Linear Regression

S ome people find linear regression a confusing topic, so the first part of this chapter helps you understand it and what makes it special. Instead of assuming that you can simply look at a linear regression and figure it out, the first section gives you a more detailed understanding of both simple and multiple linear regressions.

Data science is based on data, and you store data in variables. A *variable* is a kind box where you stuff data. The second part of this chapter tells you how variables used for linear regression can vary from other sorts of variables that you might have used in the past. Just as you need the right box to use for a given purpose, so is getting the right variable for your data important.

The third part of this chapter looks at both simple and complex uses of linear regression. You begin by using linear regression to make predictions, which can help you envision the future in many respects. A more complex example discusses a way to use linear regression as a starting point for more complex tasks, such as machine learning.

REMEMBER

You don't have to type the source code for this chapter manually. In fact, using the downloadable source is a lot easier. The source code for this chapter appears in the DSPD_0301_Linear_Regression.ipynb source code file for Python and the DSPD_R_0301_Linear_Regression.ipynb source code file for R. See the Introduction for details on how to find these source files.

Considering the History of Linear Regression

Sometimes data scientists seem to talk in circles or use terms in a way that most people don't. When you think about data, what you're really thinking about is what the data means; that is, you're thinking about answers. In other words, having data is like the game show *Jeopardy!*: You have the answer to a question, but you have to come up with the correct question. A *regression* defines the question so that you can use it to work with other data. In this case, the question is the same one you answered in math class — the equation you must solve. A regression provides an equation. Now that you have the equation, you can plug other numbers into it.

Now that you know what a regression is, you need to know what sort of equation it provides. A *linear regression* provides an equation for a straight line. You create an equation that will draw a straight line through a series of data points. By knowing the equation that best suits the data points you have, you can predict other data points along the same line. So, the history of linear regression begins not with an answer, but with the search for a question in the form of an equation.

It may seem odd that the math came before the name, but in this case it did. Carl Friedrich Gauss first discovered the least squares method in 1795 (see https://priceonomics.com/the-discovery-of-statistical-regression/ for details) as a means for improving navigation based on the movement of planets and stars. Given that this was the age of discovery, people in power would pay quite a lot to improve navigation. The use of least squares seemed so obvious to Gauss, however, that he thought someone else must have invented it earlier. That's why Adrien-Marie Legendre published the first work on least squares in 1805. Gauss would eventually get most of the credit for the work, but only after a long fight.

The least squares technique didn't actually have a name as a generalized method until 1894, when Sir Francis Galton wrote a paper on the correlation between the size of parent sweet pea seeds and their progeny (see https://www.tandfonline.com/doi/full/10.1080/10691898.2001.11910537 for details). He found that, as generations progressed, the seeds produced by the progeny of parents that produce large seeds tended to get smaller — toward the mean size of the seeds as a whole. The seeds regressed toward the mean rather than continuing to get larger, which is where the name regression comes from.

REMEMBER

One of the important things to take away from regression history is that it presents itself as an answer to a practical problem. In every case, the user starts with data, such as the location of planets or the size of sweet pea seeds, and needs to answer a question by using an equation that expresses the correlation between the data. By understanding this correlation, you can make a prediction of how the data will change in the future, which has practical uses in navigation and botany, in these cases.

Combining Variables

The previous section gives you a history of regression that discusses why you want to use it. If you already have data that correlates in some manner, but lack an equation to express it, then you need to use regression. Some data lends itself to expression as an equation of a straight line, which is how you use linear regression in particular. With this in mind, the following sections guide you through a basic examination of linear regression as it applies to specific variable configurations.

Working through simple linear regression

Think about a problem in which two variables correlate, such as the size of parent sweet pea seeds compared to the size of child sweet pea seeds. However, in this case, the problem is something that many people are either experiencing now or have experienced in the past — dealing with grades and studying. Before you move forward, though, you need to consider the following equation model:

```
y = a + bx
```

All equations look daunting at first. When thinking about grades, y is the grade.

The grade you expect to get if you don't study at all is a, which is also called the y-intercept (or constant term). Some people actually view this constant in terms of probability. A multiple choice test containing four answers for each question would give you a 25 percent chance of success. So, for the purposes of this example, you use a value for a of 25. None of the y data points will be less than 25 because you should get at least that amount.

Now you have half of the equation, and you don't have to do anything more than consider the probabilities of guessing correctly. The bx part is a little more difficult to determine. The value x defines the number of hours you study. Given that 0 hours of study is the least you can do (there is no anti-study in the universe), the first x value is 0 with a y value of 25. This example is looking at the data simply, so it will express x in whole hours. Say that you have only eight hours of available study time, so x will go from 0 through 8. The x value is called an explanatory or independent variable because it determines the value of y, which is the dependent variable.

The final piece, b, is the slope variable. It determines how much your grade will increase for each hour of study. You have data from previous tests that show how your grade increased for each hour of study. This increase is expressed as b, but you really don't know what it is until you perform analysis on your data. Consequently, this example begins by importing some libraries you need to perform the analysis and defining some data:

```
%matplotlib inline
import numpy as np
import matplotlib.pyplot as plt

x = range(0,9)
y = (25, 33, 41, 53, 59, 70, 78, 86, 98)
```

The purpose of the %matplotlib inline line is to allow you to see your data results within your Notebook. This is a magic function and you see a number of them in the book. As previously mentioned, the x values range from 0 through 8 and the y values reflect grades for each additional hour of study. The analysis portion of the code comes next:

```
plt.scatter(x, y)

z = np.polyfit(x, y, 1)
p = np.poly1d(z)

plt.plot(x, p(x), 'g-')
plt.show()
```

This example relies on graphics to show you how the data appears, so the first task is to plot the x and y data as a scatterplot so that you can see the individual data points. The analysis comes from the polyfit() function, which fits a linear model, z, to the data points. The poly1d() function call creates the actual function used to display the data points. After you have this function, p, you can use it to plot the regression line onscreen, as shown in Figure 1-1.

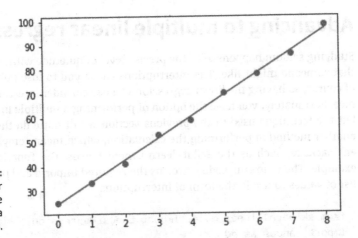

FIGURE 1-1:
Drawing a linear regression line through the data points.

Creating a graph of your data and the line that goes through the data points is nice, but it still doesn't provide you with a question. To get the question, which is an equation, you must use this line of code:

```
print(np.poly1d(p))
```

This line of code simply extracts the equation from p using poly1d(). The result is shown here:

```
9.033 x + 24.2
```

The data suggests that you'll likely not get all of those no-study-time questions correct, but you'll get a little over 24 percent of them. Then, for each hour of study, you get an additional 9 points. From a practical perspective, say that you want to go to a movie with a friend and it'll consume 2 of your 8 hours of study time. The grade you can expect is

```
9.033 * 6 + 24.2 = 78.398
```

TIP

Of course, you have a computer, so let it do the math for you. This line of code will provide you with the grade you can expect (rounded to one decimal place):

```
print(np.poly1d(p(6)))
```

REMEMBER

The values for the intercept and the slope are actually decided by the linear regression algorithm in order to create an equation that has specific characteristics. In fact, an equation can fit a cloud of points in infinite ways, but only one whose resulting squared errors are minimal (hence the least squares name). You discover more about this issue later, in the "Defining the family of linear models" section of the chapter.

Working with Linear Regression

Advancing to multiple linear regression

Studying seldom happens with the precise level of quietude without interruptions that someone might like. The interruptions cause you to lose points on the test, of course, so having the linear regression you use consider interruptions might be nice. Fortunately, you have the option of performing a multiple linear regression, but the technique used in the previous section won't quite do the job. You need another method of performing the calculation, which means employing a different package, such as the Scikit-learn LinearRegression function used in this example. The following code performs the required imports and provides another list of values to use in the form of interruptions:

```
from sklearn.linear_model import LinearRegression
import pandas as pd

i = (0, -1, -3, -4, -5, -7, -8, -9, -11)
```

The pandas package helps you create a DataFrame to store the two individual independent variables. The equation model found in the previous section now changes to look like this:

```
y = a + b₁x₁ + b₂x₂
```

The model is also turned on its head a little. The two independent variables now represent the grade obtained for a certain number of hours of study (b_1x_1) and the points lost on average due to interruptions (b_2x_2) for each hour of study. If this seems confusing, keep following the example and you'll see how things work out in the end. The following code performs the analysis and displays it onscreen:

```
studyData = pd.DataFrame({'Grades': y, 'Interrupt': i})

plt.scatter(x, y)
plt.scatter(x, i)
plt.legend(['Grades', 'Interruptions'])

regress = LinearRegression()
model = regress.fit(studyData, x)
studyData_pred = model.predict(studyData)

plt.plot(studyData_pred, studyData, 'g-')
plt.show()
```

The code begins by creating a DataFrame that contains the grades and the interruptions. The regression comes next. However, this time you're using a LinearRegression object instead of calling polyfit() as the previous section does. You then fit the model to each of the independent variables and use the resulting model to perform a prediction. Figure 1-2 shows the results so far.

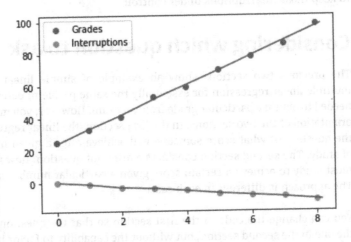

FIGURE 1-2: Developing a multiple regression model.

At this point, you have two sets of data points and two lines going through them, none of which seems particularly useful. However, what you have is actually quite useful. Say that you hope to get a 95, but you think that you might lose up to 7 points because of interruptions. Given what you know, you can plug the numbers into your model to determine how long to study using the following code:

```
print(model.predict([[95, -7]]).round(2).item(0))
```

REMEMBER

To use the prediction, you must provide a two-dimensional array with the data. The output in this case is

```
7.47
```

You must study at least seven and a half hours to achieve your goal. Now you begin to wonder what would happen if you could control the interruptions, but you want to be sure that you get at least a 90. What if you think that the worst-case scenario is losing eight points and the best-case scenario is that you don't lose any as a result of interruptions. The following code shows how to check both values at the same time:

```
print(model.predict([[90, 0], [98, -8]]).round(2))
```

Working with Linear Regression

This time, you get two responses in an ndarray:

```
[6.29 7.86]
```

In the best-case scenario, you can get by with a little over six hours of study, but in the worst-case scenario, you need almost eight hours of study. It's a good idea to keep those interruptions under control!

Considering which question to ask

The previous two sections show an example of simple linear regression and multiple linear regression for essentially the same problem: determining what is needed to obtain a particular grade from an exam. However, you must consider the orientation of the two sections. In the first section, the linear regression considers the question of what score someone will achieve after a given number of hours of study. The second section considers a different question: how many hours one must study to achieve a certain score given a particular number of interruptions. The approach is different in each case.

TIP

You can change the code in the first section so that the question is the same as the one in the second section, but without the capability to factor in interruptions. Essentially, the variables x and y will simply switch roles. Here is the code to use in this situation:

```
plt.scatter(y, x)

z = np.polyfit(y, x, 1)
p = np.poly1d(z)

plt.plot(y, p(y), 'g-')
plt.show()

print(np.poly1d(p(95)))
```

Figure 1-3 shows the new graphic for this part of the example. Note that you can now ask the model how many hours of study are needed to achieve a 95, rather than obtain the score for a certain number of hours of study. In this case, you must study 7.828 hours to obtain the 95.

Although you can change the question for a simple linear regression, the same can't be said of the multiple linear regression in the second section. To create a correct model, you must ask the question as shown in the example because the two independent variables require it. Discovering which question to ask is important.

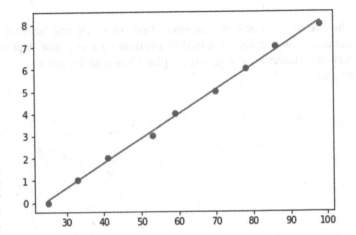

FIGURE 1-3:
Changing the
simple linear
regression
question.

Reducing independent variable complexity

In some situations, you must ask a question in a particular way, but the variables seem to get in the way. When that happens, you need to decide whether you can make certain assumptions. For example, you might ask whether the conditions in your dorm are stable enough that you can count on a certain number of lost points for each hour of study. If so, you can reduce the number of independent variables from two to one by combining the grades with the interruptions during your analysis, like this:

```
plt.scatter(x, y)
plt.scatter(x, i)
plt.legend(['Grades', 'Interruptions'])

y2 = np.array(y) + np.array(i)
print(y2)

z = np.polyfit(x, y2, 1)
p = np.poly1d(z)

plt.plot(x, p(x), 'g-')
plt.show()
```

This code looks similar to the code used for simple linear regression, but it combines the two independent variables into a single independent variable. When you print y2, you see that the values originally found in y are now reduced by the values originally found in i:

```
[25 32 38 49 54 63 70 77 87]
```

The assumption now is that every hour of study will have the same baseline number of lost points due to interruptions; y and i now depend on each other directly. However, the resulting plot shown in Figure 1-4 displays the effect of i on y.

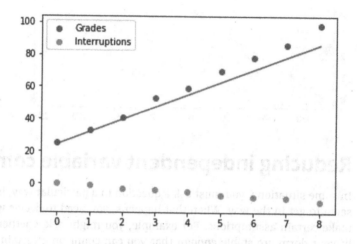

FIGURE 1-4:
Seeing the effect
of i on y.

You haven't ignored the data; you've simplified it by making an assumption that may or may not be correct. (Only time will tell.) The following code performs the same test on the model as before:

```
print(np.poly1d(p))
print(np.poly1d(p(6)))
```

Because of the change in the model, the output is different. (Compare this output with the output shown in the "Working through simple linear regression" section, earlier in this chapter.)

```
7.683 x + 24.27
70.37
```

REMEMBER

Even though the y-intercept hasn't changed much, the number of points you receive for each hour of study has, which means that you must study harder now to overcome the expected interruptions. The point of this example is that you can reduce complexity as long as you're willing to live with the consequences of doing so.

Manipulating Categorical Variables

In data science, a *categorical variable* is one that has a specific value from a limited selection of values. The number of values is usually fixed. Many developers know categorical variables by the moniker *enumerations*. Each of the potential values that a categorical variable can assume is a *level*.

To understand how categorical variables work, say that you have a variable expressing the color of an object, such as a car, and that the user can select blue, red, or green. To express the car's color in a way that computers can represent and effectively compute, an application assigns each color a numeric value, so blue is 1, red is 2, and green is 3. Normally when you print each color, you see the value rather than the color.

TIP

If you use `pandas.DataFrame` (https://pandas.pydata.org/pandas-docs/stable/reference/api/pandas.DataFrame.html), you can still see the symbolic value (blue, red, and green), even though the computer stores it as a numeric value. Sometimes you need to rename and combine these named values to create new symbols. Symbolic variables are just a convenient way of representing and storing qualitative data.

CHECKING YOUR VERSION OF PANDAS

The categorical variable examples in this section depend on your having a minimum version of pandas 0.23.0 installed on your system. However, your version of Anaconda may have a previous pandas version installed instead. Use the following code to check your version of pandas:

```
import pandas as pd
print(pd.__version__)
```

You see the version number of pandas you have installed. Another way to check the version is to open the Anaconda Prompt, type **pip show pandas**, and press Enter. If you have an older version, open the Anaconda Prompt, type **pip install pandas –upgrade**, and press Enter. The update process will occur automatically, along with a check of associated packages. When working with Windows, you may need to open the Anaconda prompt using the Administrator option. (Right-click the Anaconda prompt entry in the Start menu and choose Run as Administrator from the context menu.)

When using categorical variables for data science, you need to consider the algorithm used to manipulate the variables. Some algorithms, such as trees and ensembles of three, can work directly with the numeric variables behind the symbols. Other algorithms, such as linear and logistic regression and SVM, require that you encode the categorical values into binary variables. For example, if you have three levels for a color variable (blue, red, and green), you have to create three binary variables:

» One for blue (1 when the value is blue; 0 when it is not)

» One for red (1 when the value is red; 0 when it is not)

» One for green (1 when the value is green; 0 when it is not)

Creating categorical variables

Categorical variables have a specific number of values, which makes them incredibly valuable in performing a number of data science tasks. For example, imagine trying to find values that are out of range in a huge dataset. In this example, you see one method for creating a categorical variable and then using it to check whether some data falls within the specified limits:

```
import pandas as pd

car_colors = pd.Series(['Blue', 'Red', 'Green'],
                        dtype='category')

car_data = pd.Series(
    pd.Categorical(
        ['Yellow', 'Green', 'Red', 'Blue', 'Purple'],
                categories=car_colors, ordered=False))

find_entries = pd.isnull(car_data)

print(car_colors)
print()
print(car_data)
print()
print(find_entries[find_entries == True])
```

The example begins by creating a categorical variable, `car_colors`. The variable contains the values `Blue`, `Red`, and `Green` as colors that are acceptable for a car. Note that you must specify a `dtype` property value of `category`.

The next step is to create another series. This one uses a list of actual car colors, named `car_data`, as input. Not all the car colors match the predefined acceptable values. When this problem occurs, pandas outputs Not a Number (NaN) instead of the car color.

Of course, you could search the list manually for the nonconforming cars, but the easiest method is to have pandas do the work for you. In this case, you ask pandas which entries are null using isnull() and place them in find_entries. You can then output just those entries that are actually null. Here's the output you see from the example:

```
0       Blue
1       Red
2       Green
dtype: category
Categories (3, object): [Blue, Green, Red]

0       NaN
1       Green
2       Red
3       Blue
4       NaN
dtype: category
Categories (3, object): [Blue, Green, Red]

0       True
4       True
dtype: bool
```

Looking at the list of car_data outputs, you can see that entries 0 and 4 equal NaN. The output from find_entries verifies this fact for you. If this were a large dataset, you could quickly locate and correct errant entries in the dataset before performing an analysis on it.

Renaming levels

Sometimes, the naming of the categories you use is inconvenient or otherwise wrong for a particular need. Fortunately, you can rename the categories as needed using the technique shown in the following example:

```
import pandas as pd

car_colors = pd.Series(['Blue', 'Red', 'Green'],
                        dtype='category')
car_data = pd.Series(
    pd.Categorical(
```

```
            ['Blue', 'Green', 'Red', 'Blue', 'Red'],
        categories=car_colors, ordered=False))

car_colors.cat.categories = ["Purple", "Yellow", "Mauve"]
car_data.cat.categories = car_colors

print(car_data)
```

All you really need to do is set the cat.categories property to a new value, as shown. Here is the output from this example:

```
0       Purple
1       Yellow
2        Mauve
3       Purple
4        Mauve
dtype: category
Categories (3, object): [Purple, Yellow, Mauve]
```

Combining levels

A particular categorical level might be too small to offer significant data for analysis. Perhaps only a few of the values exist, which may not be enough to create a statistical difference. In this case, combining several small categories might offer better analysis results. The following example shows how to combine categories:

```
import pandas as pd

car_colors = pd.Series(['Blue', 'Red', 'Green'],
    dtype='category')
car_data = pd.Series(
    pd.Categorical(
        ['Blue', 'Green', 'Red', 'Green', 'Red', 'Green'],
        categories=car_colors, ordered=False))

car_data = car_data.cat.set_categories(
    ["Blue", "Red", "Green", "Blue_Red"])
print(car_data.loc[car_data.isin(['Red'])])
car_data.loc[car_data.isin(['Red'])] = 'Blue_Red'
car_data.loc[car_data.isin(['Blue'])] = 'Blue_Red'

car_data = car_data.cat.set_categories(
    ["Green", "Blue_Red"])
```

```
print()
print(car_data)
```

What this example shows you is that you have only one `Blue` item and only two `Red` items, but you have three `Green` items, which places `Green` in the majority. Combining `Blue` and `Red` together is a two-step process. First, you add the `Blue_Red` category to `car_data`. Then you change the `Red` and `Blue` entries to `Blue_Red`, which creates the combined category. As a final step, you can remove the unneeded categories.

However, before you can change the `Red` entries to `Blue_Red` entries, you must find them. This is where a combination of calls to `isin()`, which locates the `Red` entries, and `loc[]`, which obtains their index, provides precisely what you need. The first `print` statement shows the result of using this combination. Here's the output from this example.

```
2       Red
4       Red
dtype: category
Categories (4, object): [Blue, Red, Green, Blue_Red]

0       Blue_Red
1          Green
2       Blue_Red
3          Green
4       Blue_Red
5          Green
dtype: category
Categories (2, object): [Green, Blue_Red]
```

Notice that you now have three `Blue_Red` entries and three `Green` entries. The `Blue` and `Red` categories are no longer in use. The result is that the levels are now combined as expected.

Using Linear Regression to Guess Numbers

Regression has a long history in statistics, from building simple but effective linear models of economic, psychological, social, or political data, to hypothesis testing for understanding group differences, to modeling more complex problems with ordinal values, binary and multiple classes, count data, and hierarchical relationships. It's also a common tool in data science, a Swiss Army knife of machine learning that you can use for every problem. Stripped of most of its statistical properties, data science practitioners perceive linear regression as a simple, understandable, yet effective algorithm for estimations, and, in its logistic regression version, for classification as well.

Defining the family of linear models

As mentioned in the "Working through simple linear regression" section, earlier in this chapter, linear regression is a statistical model that defines the relationship between a target variable and a set of predictive *features* (the columns in a table that define entries of the same type, such as grades and interruptions in the earlier examples). It does so by using a formula of the following type:

```
y = a + bx
```

As shown in earlier examples, a (alpha) and b (beta coefficient) are estimated on the basis of the data, and they are found using the linear regression algorithm so that the difference between all the real y target values and all the y values derived from the linear regression formula are the minimum possible.

CONSIDERING SIMPLE AND COMPLEX

Simple and *complex* aren't absolute terms in data science; their meaning is relative to the data problem you're facing. Some algorithms are simple summations; others require complex calculations and data manipulations (and Python deals with both the simple and complex algorithms for you). The data makes the difference. As a good practice, test multiple models, starting with the basic ones. You may discover that a simple solution performs better in many cases. For example, you may want to keep things simple and use a linear model instead of a more sophisticated approach and get more solid results. This is in essence what is implied by the "no free lunch" theorem: No one approach suits all problems, and even the most simple solution may hold the key to solving an important problem.

REMEMBER

The "no free lunch" theorem by David Wolpert and William Macready states that "any two optimization algorithms are equivalent when their performance is averaged across all possible problems." If the algorithms are equivalent in the abstract, no one is superior to the other unless proved in a specific, practical problem. See the discussion at http://www.no-free-lunch.org/ for more details about no-free-lunch theorems; two of them are actually used for machine learning.

You can express this relationship graphically as the sum of the square of all the vertical distances between all the data points and the regression line. Such a sum is always the minimum possible when you calculate the regression line correctly using an estimation called ordinary least squares, which is derived from statistics or the equivalent gradient descent, a machine learning method. The differences between the real y values and the regression line (the predicted y values) are defined as residuals (because they are what are left after a regression: the errors). The following code shows how to display the residuals:

```
import seaborn

x = range(0,9)
y = (15, 33, 41, 69, 59, 40, 78, 86, 98)

plt.scatter(x, y, color='purple', marker='*')
plt.grid()

z = np.polyfit(x, y, 1)
p = np.poly1d(z)

plt.plot(x, p(x), 'g-')

seaborn.residplot(np.array(x), np.array(y), color='red')
plt.show()
```

The Seaborn package (https://seaborn.pydata.org/) provides some visualizations not found in other packages, including the ability to calculate and display the residuals. The actual linear regression looks much like the one earlier in the chapter, with just a few changes to the data values to make the errors more prominent. Figure 1-5 shows the output with the original data as purple stars, the regression as a green line, and the residuals as red dots.

Using more variables in a larger dataset

The "Advancing to multiple linear regression" section, earlier in this chapter, provides a simple demonstration of multiple linear regression with an incredibly small dataset. The problem is that if the dataset is as small as that one, the practical value of performing an analysis is extremely limited. This section moves on to a larger dataset, one that still isn't the size of what you see in the real world, but that's large enough to make analysis worthwhile. The following sections consider issues that the previous parts of the chapter haven't.

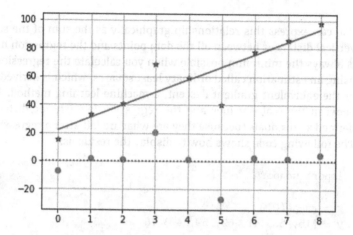

FIGURE 1-5:
Using a residual
plot to see errant
data.

Using the Boston dataset

When you have many variables, their scale isn't important in creating precise linear regression predictions. But a good habit is to standardize x because the scale of the variables is quite important for some variants of regression (that you see later on) and it's insightful for your understanding of data to compare coefficients according to their impact on y.

The following example relies on the Boston dataset from Scikit-learn. It tries to guess Boston housing prices using a linear regression. The example also tries to determine which variables influence the result more, so the example standardizes the *predictors* (the features used to predict a particular outcome).

```
from sklearn.datasets import load_boston
from sklearn.preprocessing import scale
boston = load_boston()
X = scale(boston.data)
y = boston.target
```

The regression class in Scikit-learn is part of the linear_model module. To obtain a good regression, you need to make the various variables the same scale so that one independent variable doesn't play a larger role than the others. Having previously scaled the X variable using scale(), you have no other preparations or special parameters to decide when using this algorithm.

```
from sklearn.linear_model import LinearRegression
regression = LinearRegression(normalize=True)
regression.fit(X, y)
```

TIP

You can find out more detail about the meaning of the variables present in the Boston dataset by issuing the following command: `print(boston.DESCR)`. You see the output of this command in the downloadable source code.

Checking the fit using R^2

The previous section contains code that fits a line to the data points. The `regression.fit(X, y)` call performs this task. The act of *fitting* creates a line or curve that best matches the data points provided by the data; you fit the line or curve to the data points in order to perform various tasks, such as predictions, based on the trends or patterns produced by the data. The fit of an analysis is important.

>> When the line follows the data points too closely, it's *overfitted*.

>> When the line doesn't follow the data points closely enough, it's *underfitted*.

REMEMBER

Overfitting and underfitting can cause your model to perform poorly and make inaccurate predictions, so knowing how well the model fits the data points is essential.

Now that the algorithm is fitted, you can use the `score` method to report the R^2 measure, which is a measure that ranges from 0 to 1 and points out how using a particular regression model is better in predicting y than using a simple mean would be. You can also see R^2 as being the quantity of target information explained by the model (the same as the squared correlation), so getting near 1 means being able to explain most of the y variable using the model.

```
print(regression.score(X, y))
```

Here is the resulting score:

```
0.740607742865
```

In this case, R^2 on the previously fitted data is about 0.74, a good result for a simple model. You can interpret the R^2 score as the percentage of information present in the target variable that has been explained by the model using the predictors. A score of 0.74, therefore, means that the model has fit the larger part of the information you wanted to predict and that only 26 percent of it remains unexplained.

REMEMBER

Calculating R^2 on the same set of data used for the training is considered reasonable in statistics when using linear models. In data science and machine learning, it's always the correct practice to test scores on data that has not been used for training. Algorithms of greater complexity can memorize the data better than they learn from it, but this statement can be also true sometimes for simpler models, such as linear regression.

CHAPTER 1 **Working with Linear Regression** 273

Working with Linear Regression

Considering the coefficients

To understand what drives the estimates in the multiple regression model, you have to look at the `coefficients_` attribute, which is an array containing the regression beta coefficients (the b part of the y = a + bx equation). The coefficients are the numbers estimated by the linear regression model in order to effectively transform the input variables in the formula into the target y prediction. The `zip` function will generate an iterable of both attributes, and you can print it for reporting:

```
print([a + ':' + str(round(b, 2)) for a, b in zip(
    boston.feature_names, regression.coef_,)])
```

The reported variables and their rounded coefficients (b values, or slopes, as described in the "Defining the family of linear models" section, earlier in this chapter) are

```
['CRIM:-0.92', 'ZN:1.08', 'INDUS:0.14', 'CHAS:0.68',
 'NOX:-2.06', 'RM:2.67', 'AGE:0.02', 'DIS:-3.1',
 'RAD:2.66', 'TAX:-2.08', 'PTRATIO:-2.06', 'B:0.86',
 'LSTAT:-3.75']
```

DIS is the weighted distances to five employment centers. It shows the major absolute unit change. For example, in real estate, a house that's too far from people's interests (such as work) lowers the value. As a contrast, AGE and INDUS, with both proportions describing building age and showing whether nonretail activities are available in the area, don't influence the result as much because the absolute value of their beta coefficients is lower than DIS.

Understanding variable transformations

Linear models, such as linear and logistic regression, are actually linear combinations that sum your features (weighted by learned coefficients) and provide a simple but effective model. In most situations, they offer a good approximation of the complex reality they represent. Even though they're characterized by a high *bias* (deviations from expected values for any number of reasons), using a large number of observations can improve their coefficients and make them more competitive when compared to complex algorithms.

However, they can perform better when solving certain problems if you pre-analyze the data using the Exploratory Data Analysis (EDA) approach. After performing the analysis, you can transform and enrich the existing features by

» Linearizing the relationships between features and the target variable using transformations that increase their correlation and make their cloud of points in the scatterplot more similar to a line.

» Making variables interact by multiplying them so that you can better represent their conjoint behavior.

» Expanding the existing variables using the polynomial expansion in order to represent relationships more realistically. In a polynomial expansion, you create a more complex equation after multiplying variables together and after raising variables to higher powers. In this way, you can represent more complex curves with your equation, such as ideal point curves, when you have a peak in the variable representing a maximum, akin to a parabola.

Doing variable transformations

An example is the best way to explain the kind of transformations you can successfully apply to data to improve a linear model. This example uses the Boston dataset, which originally had ten variables to explain the different housing prices in Boston during the 1970s. The current dataset has twelve variables, along with a target variable containing the median value of the houses. The following sections use this dataset to demonstrate how to perform certain linear regression-related tasks.

Considering the effect of ordering

The Boston dataset has implicit ordering. Fortunately, order doesn't influence most algorithms because they learn the data as a whole. When an algorithm learns in a progressive manner, ordering can interfere with effective model building. By using seed (to create a consistent sequence of random numbers) and shuffle from the random package (to shuffle the index), you can reindex the dataset:

```
from sklearn.datasets import load_boston
import random
from random import shuffle

boston = load_boston()
random.seed(0) # Creates a replicable shuffling
new_index = list(range(boston.data.shape[0]))
shuffle(new_index) # shuffling the index
X, y = boston.data[new_index], boston.target[new_index]
print(X.shape, y.shape, boston.feature_names)
```

In the code, random.seed(0) creates a replicable shuffling operation, and shuffle(new_index) creates the new shuffled index used to reorder the data. After that, the code prints the X and y shapes as well as the list of dataset variable names:

```
(506, 13) (506,) ['CRIM' 'ZN' 'INDUS' 'CHAS' 'NOX' 'RM'
 'AGE' 'DIS' 'RAD' 'TAX' 'PTRATIO'  'B' 'LSTAT']
```

Storing the Boston database in a DataFrame

Converting the array of predictors and the target variable into a pandas DataFrame helps support the series of explorations and operations on data. Moreover, although Scikit-learn requires an ndarray as input, it will also accept DataFrame objects:

```
import pandas as pd
df = pd.DataFrame(X,columns=boston.feature_names)
df['target'] = y
```

Looking for transformations

The best way to spot possible transformations is by graphical exploration, and using a scatterplot can tell you a lot about two variables. You need to make the relationship between the predictors and the target outcome as linear as possible, so you should try various combinations, such as the following:

```
ax = df.plot(kind='scatter', x='LSTAT', y='target', c='b')
```

In Figure 1-6, you see a representation of the resulting scatterplot. Notice that you can approximate the cloud of points by using a curved line rather than a straight line. In particular, when LSTAT is around 5, the target seems to vary between values of 20 to 50. As LSTAT increases, the target decreases to 10, reducing the variation.

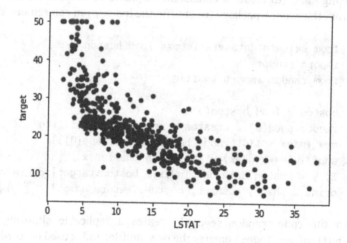

FIGURE 1-6:
Nonlinear relationship between variable LSTAT and target prices.

Logarithmic transformation can help in such conditions. However, your values should range from zero to one, such as percentages, as demonstrated in this example. In other cases, other useful transformations for your x variable could include x**2, x**3, 1/x, 1/x**2, 1/x**3, and sqrt(x). The key is to try them and test the result. As for testing, you can use the following script as an example:

```
import numpy as np
from sklearn.feature_selection import f_regression
single_variable = df['LSTAT'].values.reshape(-1, 1)
F, pval = f_regression(single_variable, y)
print('F score for the original feature %.1f' % F)
F, pval = f_regression(np.log(single_variable),y)
print('F score for the transformed feature %.1f' % F)
```

The code prints the F score, a measure to evaluate how predictive a feature is in a machine learning problem, both the original and the transformed feature. The score for the transformed feature is a great improvement over the untransformed one:

```
F score for the original feature 601.6
F score for the transformed feature 1000.2
```

The F score is useful for variable selection. You can also use it to assess the usefulness of a transformation because both f_regression and f_classif are themselves based on linear models, and are therefore sensitive to every effective transformation used to make variable relationships more linear.

Creating interactions between variables

In a linear combination, the model reacts to how a variable changes in an independent way with respect to changes in the other variables. In statistics, this kind of model is a *main effects model*.

The Naïve Bayes classifier (discussed in Book 3, Chapter 3) makes a similar assumption for probabilities, and it also works well with complex text problems. The following sections discuss and demonstrate variable interactions.

Understanding the need to see interactions

Even though machine learning works by using approximations, and a set of independent variables can make your predictions work well in most situations, sometimes you may miss an important part of the picture. You can easily catch this problem by depicting the variation in your target associated with the conjoint variation of two or more variables in two simple and straightforward ways:

» **Existing domain knowledge of the problem:** For instance, in the car market, having a noisy engine is a nuisance in a family car but considered a plus for sports cars (car aficionados want to hear that you have an ultra-cool and expensive car). By knowing a consumer preference, you can model a noise-level variable and a car-type variable together to obtain exact predictions using a predictive analytic model that guesses the car's value based on its features.

» **Testing combinations of different variables:** By performing group tests, you can see the effect that certain variables have on your target variable. Therefore, even without knowing about noisy engines and sports cars, you can catch a different average of preference level when analyzing your dataset split by type of cars and noise level.

Detecting interactions

The following example shows how to test and detect interactions in the Boston dataset. The first task is to load a few helper classes, as shown here:

```
from sklearn.linear_model import LinearRegression
from sklearn.model_selection import cross_val_score, KFold
regression = LinearRegression(normalize=True)
crossvalidation = KFold(n_splits=10, shuffle=True,
                        random_state=1)
```

The code reinitializes the pandas DataFrame using only the predictor variables. A for loop matches the different predictors and creates a new variable containing each interaction. The mathematical formulation of an interaction is simply a multiplication:

```
df = pd.DataFrame(X,columns=boston.feature_names)
baseline = np.mean(cross_val_score(regression, df, y,
                                   scoring='r2',
                                   cv=crossvalidation))
interactions = list()
for var_A in boston.feature_names:
    for var_B in boston.feature_names:
        if var_A > var_B:
            df['interaction'] = df[var_A] * df[var_B]
            cv = cross_val_score(regression, df, y,
```

```
                                    scoring='r2',
                                    cv=crossvalidation)
            score = round(np.mean(cv), 3)
            if score > baseline:
                interactions.append((var_A, var_B, score))
print('Baseline R2: %.3f' % baseline)
print('Top 10 interactions: %s' % sorted(interactions,
                                    key=lambda x :x[2],
                                    reverse=True)[:10])
```

The code starts by printing the baseline R² score for the regression; then it reports the top ten interactions whose addition to the mode increase the score:

```
Baseline R2: 0.716
Top 10 interactions: [('RM', 'LSTAT', 0.79),
('TAX', 'RM', 0.782), ('RM', 'RAD', 0.778),
('RM', 'PTRATIO', 0.766), ('RM', 'INDUS', 0.76),
('RM', 'NOX', 0.747), ('RM', 'AGE', 0.742),
('RM', 'B', 0.738), ('RM', 'DIS', 0.736),
('ZN', 'RM', 0.73)]
```

The code tests the specific addition of each interaction to the model using a 10 folds cross-validation. The code records the change in the R² measure into a stack (a simple list) that an application can order and explore later.

The baseline score is 0.699, so a reported improvement of the stack of interactions to 0.782 looks quite impressive. Knowing how this improvement is made possible is important. The two variables involved are RM (the average number of rooms) and LSTAT (the percentage of lower-status population). A plot will disclose the case about these two variables:

```
colors = ['b' if v > np.mean(y) else 'r' for v in y]
scatter = df.plot(kind='scatter', x='RM', y='LSTAT',
                c=colors)
```

The scatterplot in Figure 1-7 clarifies the improvement. In a portion of houses at the center of the plot, you need to know both LSTAT and RM to correctly separate the high-value houses from the low-value houses; therefore, an interaction is indispensable in this case.

Working with Linear Regression

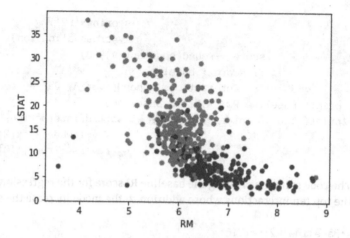

FIGURE 1-7:
Combined
variables LSTAT
and RM help to
separate high
from low prices.

Putting the interaction data to use

Adding interactions and transformed variables leads to an extended linear regression model, a *polynomial regression*. Data scientists rely on testing and experimenting to validate an approach to solving a problem, so the following code slightly modifies the previous code to redefine the set of predictors using interactions and quadratic terms by squaring the variables:

```
polyX = pd.DataFrame(X,columns=boston.feature_names)
cv = cross_val_score(regression, polyX, y,
                     scoring='neg_mean_squared_error',
                     cv=crossvalidation)
baseline = np.mean(cv)
improvements = [baseline]
for var_A in boston.feature_names:
    polyX[var_A+'^2'] = polyX[var_A]**2
    cv = cross_val_score(regression, polyX, y,
                         scoring='neg_mean_squared_error',
                         cv=crossvalidation)
    improvements.append(np.mean(cv))
    for var_B in boston.feature_names:
        if var_A > var_B:
            poly_var = var_A + '*' + var_B
            polyX[poly_var] = polyX[var_A] * polyX[var_B]
            cv = cross_val_score(regression, polyX, y,
                                 scoring='neg_mean_squared_error',
                                 cv=crossvalidation)
            improvements.append(np.mean(cv))
import matplotlib.pyplot as plt
plt.figure()
```

```
plt.plot(range(0,92),np.abs(improvements),'-')
plt.xlabel('Added polynomial features')
plt.ylabel('Mean squared error')
plt.show()
```

To track improvements as the code adds new, complex terms, the example places values in the improvements list. Figure 1-8 shows a graph of the results that demonstrates that some additions are great because the squared error decreases, and other additions are terrible because they increase the error instead.

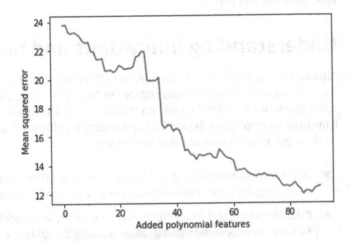

FIGURE 1-8:
Adding
polynomial
features
increases the
predictive power.

Of course, instead of unconditionally adding all the generated variables, you could perform an ongoing test before deciding to add a quadratic term or an interaction, checking by cross-validation to see whether each addition is really useful for your predictive purposes. This example is a good foundation for checking other ways of controlling the existing complexity of your datasets or the complexity that you have to induce with transformation and feature creation in the course of data exploration efforts. Before moving on, you check both the shape of the actual dataset and its cross-validated mean squared error:

```
print('New shape of X:', np.shape(polyX))
crossvalidation = KFold(n_splits=10, shuffle=True,
                        random_state=1)
cv = cross_val_score(regression, polyX, y,
                     scoring='neg_mean_squared_error',
                     cv=crossvalidation)
print('Mean squared error: %.3f' % abs(np.mean(cv)))
```

Even though the mean squared error is good, the ratio between 506 observations and 104 features isn't all that good because the number of observations may not be enough for a correct estimate of the coefficients.

```
New shape of X: (506, 104)
Mean squared error: 12.514
```

TIP

As a rule of thumb, divide the number of observations by the number of coefficients. The code should have at least 10 to 20 observations for every coefficient you want to estimate in linear models. However, experience shows that having at least 30 of them is better.

Understanding limitations and problems

Although linear regression is a simple yet effective estimation tool, it has quite a few problems. The problems can reduce the benefit of using linear regressions in some cases, but it really depends on the data. You determine whether any problems exist by employing the method and testing its efficacy. Unless you work hard on data, you may encounter these limitations:

>> Linear regression can model only quantitative data. When modeling categories as response, you need to modify the data into a logistic regression.

>> If data is missing and you don't deal with it properly, the model stops working. You need to impute the missing values or, using the value of zero for the variable, create an additional binary variable pointing out that a value is missing.

>> Outliers are quite disruptive for a linear regression because linear regression tries to minimize the square value of the residuals, and outliers have big residuals, forcing the algorithm to focus more on them than on the mass of regular points.

>> The relation between the target and each predictor variable is based on a single coefficient; no automatic way exists to represent complex relations like a parabola (there is a unique value of x maximizing y) or exponential growth. The only way you can manage to model such relations is to use mathematical transformations of x (and sometimes y) or add new variables.

>> The greatest limitation is that linear regression provides a summation of terms, which can vary independently of each other. It's hard to figure out how to represent the effect of certain variables that affect the result in very different ways according to their value. A solution is to create *interaction terms*, that is, to multiply two or more variables to create a new variable; however, doing so requires that you know what variables to multiply and that you

create the new variable before running the linear regression. In short, you can't easily represent complex situations with your data, just simple ones.

Learning One Example at a Time

Finding the right coefficients for a linear model is just a matter of time and memory. However, sometimes a system won't have enough memory to store a huge dataset. In this case, you must resort to other means, such as learning from one example at a time rather than having all of them loaded into memory. The following sections demonstrate the one-example-at-a-time approach to learning.

Using Gradient Descent

The gradient descent finds the right way to minimize the cost function one iteration at a time. After each step, it checks all the model's summed errors and updates the coefficients to make the error even smaller during the next data iteration. The efficiency of this approach derives from considering all the examples in the sample. The drawback of this approach is that you must load all the data into memory.

Unfortunately, you can't always store all the data in memory because some datasets are huge. In addition, learning using simple learners requires large amounts of data to build effective models (more data helps to correctly disambiguate multicollinearity). Getting and storing chunks of data on your hard disk is always possible, but it's not feasible because of the need to perform matrix multiplication, which requires data swapping from disk to select rows and columns. Scientists who have worked on the problem have found an effective solution. Instead of learning from all the data after having it all (which is called an *iteration*), the algorithm learns from one example at a time, as picked from storage using sequential access, and then goes on to learn from the next example. When the algorithm has learned all the examples, it starts from the beginning unless it meets some stopping criterion (such as completing a predefined number of iterations).

Implementing Stochastic Gradient Descent

When you have too much data, you can use the Stochastic Gradient Descent Regressor (SGDRegressor) or Stochastic Gradient Descent Classifier (SGDClassifier) as a linear predictor. The only difference with other methods described earlier in the chapter is that they actually optimize their coefficients using only one observation at a time. It therefore takes more iterations before the code reaches comparable results using a simple or multiple regression, but it requires much less memory and time.

DETERMINING WHEN YOU HAVE TOO MUCH DATA

Up to this point, the book has dealt with small example databases. Real data, apart from being messy, can also be quite big — sometimes so big that it can't fit in memory, no matter what the memory specifications of your machine are. In a data science project, data can be deemed big when one of these two situations occur:

- It can't fit in the available computer memory.

- Even if the system has enough memory to hold the data, the application can't elaborate the data using machine learning algorithms in a reasonable amount of time.

The increase in efficiency occurs because both predictors rely on Stochastic Gradient Descent (SGD) optimization — a kind of optimization in which the parameter adjustment occurs after the input of every observation, leading to a longer and a bit more erratic journey toward minimizing the error function. Of course, optimizing based on single observations, and not on huge data matrices, can have a tremendous beneficial impact on the algorithm's training time and the amount of memory resources.

Using the `fit()` method

When using SGDs, you'll always have to deal with chunks of data unless you can stretch all the training data into memory. To make the training effective, you should standardize by having the StandardScaler infer the mean and standard deviation from the first available data. The mean and standard deviation of the entire dataset is most likely different, but the transformation by an initial estimate will suffice to develop a working learning procedure:

```
from sklearn.linear_model import SGDRegressor
from sklearn.preprocessing import StandardScaler

SGD = SGDRegressor(loss='squared_loss',
                   penalty='l2',
                   alpha=0.0001,
                   l1_ratio=0.15,
                   max_iter=2000,
                   random_state=1)
scaling = StandardScaler()
scaling.fit(polyX)
scaled_X = scaling.transform(polyX)
```

```
cv = cross_val_score(SGD, scaled_X, y,
        scoring='neg_mean_squared_error',
        cv=crossvalidation)
score = abs(np.mean(cv))
print('CV MSE: %.3f' % score)
```

The resulting mean squared error after running the SGDRegressor is

```
CV MSE: 12.179
```

Using the `partial_fit()` method

In the preceding example, you used the `fit` method, which requires that you preload all the training data into memory. You can train the model in successive steps by using the `partial_fit` method instead, which runs a single iteration on the provided data and then keeps it in memory and adjusts it when receiving new data. This time, the code uses a higher number of iterations:

```
from sklearn.metrics import mean_squared_error
from sklearn.model_selection import train_test_split

X_tr, X_t, y_tr, y_t = train_test_split(scaled_X, y,
                                        test_size=0.20,
                                        random_state=2)
SGD = SGDRegressor(loss='squared_loss',
                   penalty='l2',
                   alpha=0.0001,
                   l1_ratio=0.15,
                   max_iter=2000,
                   random_state=1)
improvements = list()
for z in range(10000):
    SGD.partial_fit(X_tr, y_tr)
    score = mean_squared_error(y_t, SGD.predict(X_t))
    improvements.append(score)
```

Having kept track of the algorithm's partial improvements during 10000 iterations over the same data, you can produce a graph and understand how the improvements work, as shown in the following code. Note that you could have used different data at each step.

```
import matplotlib.pyplot as plt
plt.figure(figsize=(8, 4))
plt.subplot(1,2,1)
```

```
range_1 = range(1,101,10)
score_1 = np.abs(improvements[:100:10])
plt.plot(range_1, score_1,'o--')
plt.xlabel('Iterations up to 100')
plt.ylabel('Test mean squared error')
plt.subplot(1,2,2)
range_2 = range(100,10000,500)
score_2 = np.abs(improvements[100:10000:500])
plt.plot(range_2, score_2,'o--')
plt.xlabel('Iterations from 101 to 5000')
plt.show()
```

As shown in the first of the two panes in Figure 1-9, the algorithm initially starts with a high error rate, but it manages to reduce it in just a few iterations, usually 5–10. After that, the error rate slowly improves by a smaller amount at each iteration. In the second pane, you can see that after 1,500 iterations, the error rate reaches a minimum and starts increasing. At that point, you're starting to overfit because data already understands the rules and you're actually forcing the SGD to learn more when nothing is left in the data other than noise. Consequently, it starts learning noise and erratic rules.

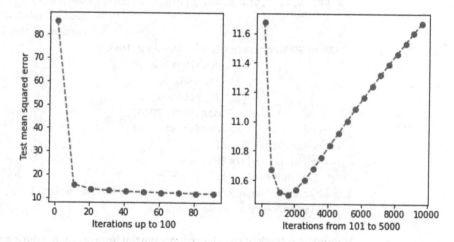

FIGURE 1-9:
A slow descent optimizing squared error.

TIP

Unless you're working with all the data in memory, grid-searching and cross-validating the best number of iterations will be difficult. A good trick is to keep a chunk of training data to use for validation apart in memory or storage. By checking your performance on that untouched part, you can see when SGD learning performance starts decreasing. At that point, you can interrupt data iteration (a method known as early stopping).

Considering the effects of regularization

Regularization is the act of applying a penalty to certain coefficients to ensure that they don't cause overfitting or underfitting. When using the SGDs, apart from different cost functions that you have to test for their performance, you can also try using regularizations like the following to obtain better predictions:

- » **L1 (Lasso):** This form of regularization adds a penalty equal to the sum of the absolute value of the coefficients. This form of regularization can shrink some of the coefficients to zero, which means that they don't contribute toward the model. Look at this form of regularization as a kind of input data (feature) selection.

- » **L2 (Ridge):** This form of regularization adds a penalty equal to the sum of the squared value of the coefficients. Unlike L1, none of the features will shrink to zero in this case. You use this form of regularization when you want to be sure that all the features play a role in creating the model, but also that all the features have the same opportunity to influence the model.

- » **Elasticnet:** This is a combination of L1 and L2. You use it when you want to ensure that important features have a little more say in the resulting model, but that all the features have at least a little say.

To use these regularizations, you set the `penalty` parameter and the corresponding controlling `alpha` and `l1_ratio` parameters. Some of the SGDs are more resistant to outliers, such as `modified_huber` for classification or `huber` for regression.

REMEMBER

SGD is sensitive to the scale of variables, and that's not just because of regularization but is also because of the way it works internally. Consequently, you must always standardize your features (for instance, by using `StandardScaler`) or you force them in the range [0,+1] or [-1,+1]. Failing to do so will lead to poor results.

Chapter **2**

Moving Forward with Logistic Regression

inear regression, as described in the previous chapter, has limits. It helps you find only certain kinds of equations based on you data. To move forward in your ability to analyze data, you need logistic regression because it can help you model data with greater complexity. Of course, the modeling process itself is more complex as a result. The first part of this chapter helps you understand the origins of logistic regression and consider how it differs from linear regression so that you know which kind of regression to apply to particular datasets.

The second part of this chapter considers two uses for logistic regression: guessing the class of a particular object and the probability of something like an event. You find that these two uses are actually two sides of the same coin, in a way. In some respects, it comes down to how you view the analysis you perform and how you employ it against new data.

Even though a single chapter can't possibly exhaust the topic of logistic regression, the third part of the chapter takes you a little deeper by exploring multiclass logistic regression. Instead of simply telling you that an object is of one class or another, multiclass logistic regression can help you determine which of multiple classes reflects the nature of an object.

REMEMBER

You don't have to type the source code for this chapter manually. In fact, using the downloadable source is a lot easier. The source code for this chapter appears in the DSPD_0302_Logistic_Regression.ipynb source code file for Python and the DSPD_R_0302_Logistic_Regression.ipynb source code file for R. See the Introduction for details on how to find these source files.

Considering the History of Logistic Regression

Some kinds of data don't neatly fit in a straight line. In the previous chapter of this minibook, you read about the history of linear regression, which is also the start of the history for logistic regression. In that history, you discover that data represents the answer to a question that comes in the form of an equation, and that linear regression helps you locate the question, the equation, itself. You're still looking for an equation with logistic regression, but now you're looking for a more flexible equation, one that can handle data that doesn't express itself in the form of a straight line.

The original use for logistic regression was determining population growth. In 1789, Thomas Robert Malthus published a book entitled *An Essay on the Principle of Population,* in which he postulated that uncontained human population growth would represent a geometric progression. More than 200 years later, this principle is still used in many settings for things like economic analysis (see the article at https://www.intelligenteconomist.com/malthusian-theory/ for details). However, the key word here is *uncontained.* Population growth is seldom left to itself, without outside influence. The result would be impossibly high numbers that could never model how population growth actually works over the long term.

REMEMBER

Consequently, in a series of three papers from 1838 to 1847, Pierre François Verhulst, under guidance from his mentor Adolphe Quetelet, created a better model to describe population growth using the logistic function. Some contention exists as to where the name *logistic* comes from, but it apparently strives to create a contrast with a logarithmic function. When working with a logistic function, the curve follows these steps:

1. The curve begins with exponential growth because the object being modeled has both unlimited resources and unlimited area in which to grow.

2. As saturation of the environment and depletion of resources occurs, growth takes on a linear form.

3. At maturity, when there is little room to grow and fewer resources to use, growth tends toward stopping and possibly does stop.

The logistic function model didn't happen in a vacuum. Verhulst modeled it on French, Belgian, Essex, and Russian population growth. In other words, he started with the data and created an equation to act as a question for the data.

Oddly enough, the logistic function didn't take off immediately; instead, it languished until someone else discovered a need for it. In 1920, Raymond Pearl (who had just been appointed Director of Biometry and Vital Statistics at Johns Hopkins University) and Lowell J. Reed published a paper on the food needs of a growing population, entitled *On the Rate of Growth of the Population of the United States since 1790 and Its Mathematical Representation*. This is actually just the first of a whole series of papers that would investigate issues like longevity, fertility, contraception, and the effects of smoking and alcohol. The history of the logistic function and logistic regression associated with it is long and complex, but you can find a relatively complete treatment of the topic at `https://papers.tinbergen.nl/02119.pdf`.

Differentiating between Linear and Logistic Regression

Both linear and logistic regression see a lot of use in data science but are commonly used for different kinds of problems. You need to know and understand both types of regression to perform a full range of data science tasks. Of the two, logistic regression is harder to understand in many respects because it necessarily uses a more complex equation model. The following sections give you a basic overview of how linear and logistic regression differ so that you can better understand the information in the rest of the chapter.

Considering the model

Any discussion of the difference between linear and logistic regression must start with the underlying equation model. The equation for linear regression is straightforward, as discussed in Book 3, Chapter 1:

```
y = a + bx
```

You may see this equation in other forms and you may see it called ordinary least-squares regression, but the essential concept is always the same. Depending on the source you use, some of the equations used to express logistic regression can become downright terrifying unless you're a math major. However, the start of this discussion can use one of the simplest views of logistic regression:

```
p = f(a + bx)
```

This equation model says that the probability of an occurrence, p, is equal to the logistic function, f, applied to two model parameters, a and b, and one explanatory variable, x. When you look at this particular model, you see that it really isn't all that different from the linear regression model, except that you now feed the result of the linear regression through the logistic function to obtain the required curve. The output (dependent variable) is a probability ranging from 0 (not going to happen) to 1 (definitely will happen), or a categorization that says something is either part of the category or not part of the category. (You can also perform multiclass categorization, as described later in this chapter, but focus on the binary response for now.) The best way to view the difference between linear regression output and logistic regression output is to say the following:

>> **Linear regression is continuous.** A continuous value can take any value within a specified interval (range) of values. For example, no matter how closely the height of two individuals matches, you can always find someone whose height fits between those two individuals. Examples of continuous values include:

- Height

- Weight

- Waist size

>> **Logistic regression is discrete.** A discrete value has specific values that it can assume. For example, a hospital can admit only a specific number of patients in a given day. You can't admit half a patient (at least, not alive). Examples of discrete values include:

- Number of people at the fair

- Number of jellybeans in the jar

- Colors of automobiles produced by a vendor

Defining the logistic function

Of course, now you need to know about the logistic function. You can find a variety of forms of this function as well, but here's the easiest one to understand:

```
f(x) = eˣ / eˣ + 1
```

You already know about f, which is the logistic function, and x equals the algorithm you want to use, which is a + bx in this case. That leaves e, which is the natural logarithm and has an irrational value of 2.718, for the sake of

discussion (you can see a better approximation of the whole value at https://
www.intmath.com/exponential-logarithmic-functions/5-logs-base-e-ln.
php). Another way you see this function expressed is

```
f(x) = 1 / (1 + e⁻ˣ)
```

REMEMBER

Both forms are correct, but the first form is easier to use. Consider a simple problem in which a, the y-intercept, is 0, and b, the slope, is 1. The example uses x values from –6 to 6. Consequently, the first $f(x)$ value would look like this when calculated (all values are rounded):

```
(1) e⁻⁶ / (1 + e⁻⁶)
(2) 0.00248 / 1 + 0.00248
(3) 0.002474
```

As you might expect, an x value of 0 would result in an $f(x)$ value of 0.5, and an x value of 6 would result in an $f(x)$ value of 0.9975. Obviously, a linear regression would show different results for precisely the same x values. If you calculate and plot all the results from both logistic and linear regression using the following code, you receive a plot like the one shown in Figure 2-1.

```
import matplotlib.pyplot as plt
%matplotlib inline
from math import exp

x_values = range(-6, 7)
lin_values = [(0 + 1*x) / 13 for x in range(0, 13)]
log_values = [exp(0 + 1*x) / (1 + exp(0 + 1*x))
              for x in x_values]

plt.plot(x_values, lin_values, 'b-^')
plt.plot(x_values, log_values, 'g-*')
plt.legend(['Linear', 'Logistic'])
plt.show()
```

This example relies on list comprehension (https://www.pythonforbeginners.
com/basics/list-comprehensions-in-python) to calculate the values because it makes the calculations clearer. The linear regression uses a different numeric range because you must normalize the values to appear in the 0 to 1 range for comparison. This is also why you divide the calculated values by 13. The exp(x) call used for the logistic regression raises e to the power of x, e^x, as needed for the logistic function.

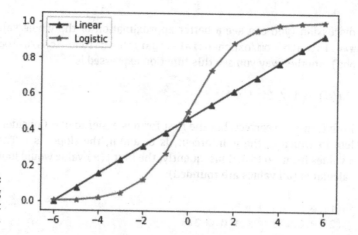

FIGURE 2-1:
Contrasting
linear to logistic
regression.

WARNING

The model discussed here is simplified, and some math majors out there are probably throwing a temper tantrum of the most profound proportions right now. The Python or R package you use will actually take care of the math in the background, so really, what you need to know is how the math works at a basic level so that you can understand how to use the packages. This section provides what you need to use the packages. However, if you insist on carrying out the calculations the old way, chalk to chalkboard, you'll likely need a lot more information.

Understanding the problems that logistic regression solves

You can separate logistic regression into several categories. The first is simple logistic regression, in which you have one dependent variable and one independent variable, much as you see in simple linear regression. However, because of how you calculate the logistic regression, you can expect only two kinds of output:

» **Classification:** Decides between two available outcomes, such as male or female, yes or no, or high or low. The outcome is dependent on which side of the line a particular data point falls.

» **Probability:** Determines the probability that something is true or false. The values true and false can have specific meanings. For example, you might want to know the probability that a particular apple will be yellow or red based on the presence of yellow and red apples in a bin.

Fitting the curve

As part of understanding the difference between linear and logistic regression, consider the grade prediction problem from the previous chapter, which lends itself well to linear regression. In the following code, you see the effect of trying to use logistic regression with that data:

```
x1 = range(0,9)
y1 = (0.25, 0.33, 0.41, 0.53, 0.59,
      0.70, 0.78, 0.86, 0.98)
plt.scatter(x1, y1, c='r')

lin_values = [0.242 + 0.0933*x for x in x1]
log_values = [exp(0.242 + .9033*x) /
             (1 + exp(0.242 + .9033*x))
             for x in range(-4, 5)]

plt.plot(x1, lin_values, 'b-^')
plt.plot(x1, log_values, 'g-*')
plt.legend(['Linear', 'Logistic', 'Org Data'])
plt.show()
```

The example has undergone a few changes to make it easier to see precisely what is happening. It relies on the same data that was converted from questions answered correctly on the exam to a percentage. If you have 100 questions and you answer 25 of them correctly, you have answered 25 percent (0.25) of them correctly. Instead of performing the actual analysis, the code uses the equation found in the "Working through simple linear regression" section of Book 3, Chapter 1. The values are normalized to produce values between 0 and 1 percent. Figure 2-2 shows the output of this experiment.

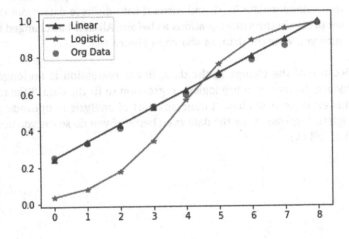

FIGURE 2-2:
Considering the approach to fitting the data.

As you can see from the figure, the linear regression follows the data points closely. The logistic regression doesn't. However, logistic regression often is the correct choice when the data points naturally follow the logistic curve, which happens far more often than you might think. You must use the technique that fits your data best, which means using linear regression in this case.

Considering a pass/fail example

An essential point to remember is that logistic regression works best for probability and classification. Consider that points on an exam ultimately predict passing or failing the course. If you get a certain percentage of the answers correct, you pass, but you fail otherwise. The following code considers the same data used for the example in the previous section, but converts it to a pass/fail list. When a student gets at least 70 percent of the questions correct, success is assured.

```
y2 = [0 if x < 0.70 else 1 for x in y1]
plt.scatter(x1, y2, c='r')

lin_values = [0.242 + 0.0933*x for x in x1]
log_values = [exp(0.242 + .9033*x) /
              (1 + exp(0.242 + .9033*x))
              for x in range(-4, 5)]

plt.plot(x1, lin_values, 'b-^')
plt.plot(x1, log_values, 'g-*')
plt.legend(['Linear', 'Logistic', 'Org Data'])
plt.show()
```

This is an example of how you can use list comprehensions in Python to obtain a required dataset or data transformation. The list comprehension for y2 starts with the continuous data in y1 and turns it into discrete data. Note that the example uses precisely the same equations as before. All that has changed is the manner in which you view the data, as shown in Figure 2-3.

Because of the change in the data, linear regression is no longer the option to choose. Instead, you use logistic regression to fit the data. Take into account that this example really hasn't done any sort of analysis to optimize the results. The logistic regression fits the data even better if you do so (as you see in the sections that follow).

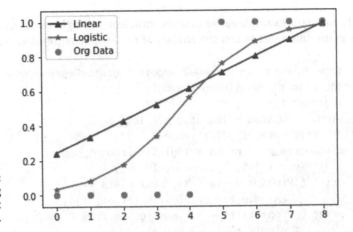

FIGURE 2-3:
Contrasting
linear to logistic
regression.

Using Logistic Regression to Guess Classes

As noted earlier in the chapter, linear regression is well suited for estimating values, but it isn't the best tool for predicting the class of an observation. The previous sections focus on helping you understand the difference between linear and logistic regression. However, the examples use an exceptionally simple dataset to get the job done, which isn't what you encounter in the real world. The following sections use a larger dataset to help you better understand the nuances of working with logistic regression. Even though this dataset is still smaller than real-world counterparts, it provides enough data for you to begin understanding how to use logistic regression in a real-world setting.

Applying logistic regression

Logistic regression is similar to linear regression, with the only difference being the y data, which should contain integer values indicating the class relative to the observation. Using the Iris dataset from the Scikit-learn `datasets` module, you can use the values 0, 1, and 2 to denote three classes that correspond to three species:

```
from sklearn.datasets import load_iris
iris = load_iris()
X = iris.data[:-1,:]
y = iris.target[:-1]
```

To make the example easier to work with, leave a single value out so that later you can use this value to test the efficacy of the logistic regression model on it:

```
from sklearn.linear_model import LogisticRegression
logistic = LogisticRegression()
logistic.fit(X, y)
single_row_pred = logistic.predict(
    iris.data[-1, :].reshape(1, -1))
single_row_pred_proba = logistic.predict_proba(
    iris.data[-1, :].reshape(1, -1))
print ('Predicted class %s, real class %s'
        % (single_row_pred, iris.target[-1]))
print ('Probabilities for each class from 0 to 2: %s'
        % single_row_pred_proba)
```

The preceding code snippet outputs the following:

```
Predicted class [2], real class 2
Probabilities for each class from 0 to 2:
  [[ 0.00168787  0.28720074  0.71111138]]
```

In contrast to linear regression, logistic regression doesn't just output the resulting class (in this case, the class 2) but also estimates the probability of the observation's being part of all three classes. Based on the observation used for prediction, logistic regression estimates a probability of 71 percent of its being from class 2 — a high probability, but not a perfect score, therefore leaving a margin of uncertainty.

TIP

Using probabilities lets you guess the most probable class, but you can also order the predictions with respect to being part of that class. This is especially useful for medical purposes: Ranking a prediction in terms of likelihood with respect to others can reveal what patients are at most risk of getting or already having a disease.

Considering when classes are more

The problem considered in the previous section concerning logistic regression automatically handles a multiple class problem (it started with three iris species to guess). Most algorithms provided by Scikit-learn that predict probabilities or a score for class can automatically handle multiclass problems using two different strategies:

>> **One-Versus-Rest (OVR):** The algorithm compares every class with all the remaining classes, building a model for every class. If you have ten classes to

guess, you have ten models. This approach relies on the OneVsRestClassifier class from Scikit-learn. You might also see this strategy referred to as One-Versus-All (OVA).

>> **One-Versus-One (OVO):** The algorithm compares every class against every individual remaining class, building a number of models equivalent to n * (n–1) / 2, where n is the number of classes. If you have ten classes, you have 45 models, 10 * (10 – 1) / 2. This approach relies on the OneVsOneClassifier class from Scikit-learn.

In the case of logistic regression, the default multiclass strategy is the one versus the rest. The example in this section shows how to use both strategies with the handwritten digit dataset, containing a class for numbers from 0 to 9. The following code loads the data and places it into variables:

```
from sklearn.datasets import load_digits
digits = load_digits()
train = range(0, 1700)
test = range(1700, len(digits.data))
X = digits.data[train]
y = digits.target[train]
tX = digits.data[test]
ty = digits.target[test]
```

The observations are actually a grid of pixel values. The grid's dimensions are 8 pixels by 8 pixels. To make the data easier to learn by machine learning algorithms, the code aligns them into a list of 64 elements. The example reserves a part of the available examples for a test:

```
from sklearn.multiclass import OneVsRestClassifier
from sklearn.multiclass import OneVsOneClassifier
OVR = OneVsRestClassifier(LogisticRegression()).fit(X, y)
OVO = OneVsOneClassifier(LogisticRegression()).fit(X, y)
print('One vs rest accuracy: %.3f' % OVR.score(tX, ty))
print('One vs one accuracy: %.3f' % OVO.score(tX, ty))
```

The performances of the two multiclass strategies are

```
One vs rest accuracy: 0.938
One vs one accuracy: 0.969
```

The two multiclass classes OneVsRestClassifier and OneVsOneClassifier operate by incorporating the estimator (in this case, LogisticRegression). After incorporation, they usually work just like any other learning algorithm in Scikit-learn. Interestingly, the one-versus-one strategy obtained the highest accuracy thanks to its high number of models in competition.

Defining logistic regression performance

A logistic regression model will perform in a certain way. You split the data into two parts: training and testing. During training, the model will fine-tune the weights used to determine the classification or probability of like data. During testing, you verify the accuracy of the model. By using data from other datasets, you can further refine your estimation of the accuracy of the model in detecting the class of a particular object or of determining the probability of an object belonging to a certain class. Accuracy determines three things:

» The number of correct guesses, which includes both true positives (something is part of the class) and true negatives (something is not part of the class)

» The number of false positives, with a guess saying that an object is part of a class, but it isn't

» The number of false negatives, with a guess saying that an object isn't part of a class, but it really is

To determine the *accuracy* of a model, you divide the number of correct guesses by the total number of objects. For example, an application might say that 80 objects are part of the class, but only 70 of these objects actually are. It might also say that 20 objects aren't part of the class, yet 30 of the objects actually are. The total number of objects is 100, so the accuracy is as follows: 70 true positives + 20 true negatives / 100 object total, or 90 percent.

However, you often see different measures used to define performance because accuracy is too inclusive. When you see the term *precision*, what it really means is the number of true positives divided by the number of total positives, and it doesn't account for true negatives or false negatives. For example, if an application says that 80 out of 100 objects are part of the class, yet it has guessed incorrectly in 10 of those cases, the precision is 70 true positives / 70 true positives + 10 false positives, or 87.5 percent. What this measure really asks is how many of the selected items are relevant to the analysis.

You also see the term *recall* used, which is the measure of the relevance of the selected items. In this case, you begin with the number of true positives, which is 70 in the example, and divide it by a combination of the true positives and the false negatives. In this case, the recall is 70 / 70 + 0, or 100 percent. An inverse relationship exists between recall and precision; to get better recall, you must normally trade precision. (The article at https://towardsdatascience.com/precision-vs-recall-386cf9f89488 describes the relationships between accuracy, precision, and recall.) The examples at https://www.kaggle.com/pablovargas/comparing-logistic-regression-performance help you see how these three measures are used in real-world situations.

Remember that you don't ever get any form of analysis without cost. As you train with more examples and perform additional verification, the time required to create a model and maintain it for changing conditions increases. At some point, your model becomes incredibly accurate, but the cost in time is so great that the answer you receive is no longer relevant. So, another indicator of performance is timeliness; the task must proceed fast enough to ensure that the answer is still useful.

Switching to Probabilities

Up to now, the chapter has considered only regression models, which express numeric values as outputs from data learning. Most problems, however, also require classification. The following sections talk about how you can address both numeric and classification output.

Specifying a binary response

A solution to a problem involving a binary response (the model has to choose from between two possible classes) would be to code a response vector as a sequence of ones and zeros (or positive and negative values). The following Python code proves both the feasibility and limits of using a binary response:

```
import numpy as np

a = np.array([0, 0, 0, 0, 1, 1, 1, 1])
b = np.array([1, 2, 3, 4, 5, 6, 7, 8]).reshape(8,1)
from sklearn.linear_model import LinearRegression
regression = LinearRegression()
regression.fit(b,a)
print (regression.predict(b)>0.5)
```

When you run this code, you see the following output:

```
[False False False False  True  True  True  True]
```

In statistics, linear regression can't solve classification problems because doing so would create a series of violated statistical assumptions. So, for statistics, using regression models for classification purposes is mainly a theoretical problem, not a practical one. When performing tasks such as deep learning, the problem with linear regression is that it serves as a linear function that's trying to minimize prediction errors; therefore, depending on the slope of the computed line, it may not be able to solve the data problem.

When a linear regression is given the task of predicting two values, such as 0 and +1, which represent two classes, it tries to compute a line that provides results close to the target values. In some cases, even though the results are precise, the output is too far from the target values, which forces the regression line to adjust in order to minimize the summed errors. The change results in fewer summed deviance errors but more misclassified cases.

Linear regression doesn't produce acceptable results when the priority is classification accuracy, as shown in Figure 2-4 on the left. Therefore, it won't work satisfactorily in many classification tasks. Linear regression works best on a continuum of numeric estimates. However, for classification tasks, you need a more suitable measure, such as the probability of class ownership.

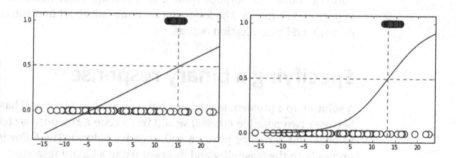

FIGURE 2-4: Probabilities do not work as well with a straight line as they do with a sigmoid curve.

Transforming numeric estimates into probabilities

The "Defining the logistic function" section, earlier in this chapter, describes how logistic regression differs from linear regression using the logistic function. In this function, the target is the probability that the response f(x = 1) will correspond to the class 1. The letter x is the *regression result,* the sum of the variables weighted by their coefficients. The exponential function, exp(x), corresponds to Euler's number e elevated to the power of x. A linear regression using this transformation formula (also called a *link function*) for changing its results into probabilities is a logistic regression.

Logistic regression (shown on the right in Figure 2-4) is the same as a linear regression except that the y data contains integer numbers indicating the class that's relative to the observation. So, using the Boston dataset from the Scikit-learn datasets module, you can try to guess what makes houses in an area overly expensive (median values >= 40). The first step is to load the Boston dataset, t as shown here:

```
from sklearn.datasets import load_boston
from sklearn.preprocessing import scale
boston = load_boston()
X, y = scale(boston.data), boston.target
```

Now that you have the dataset loaded, you can perform the analysis:

```
from sklearn.linear_model import LogisticRegression
from sklearn.model_selection import train_test_split

binary_y = np.array(y >= 40).astype(int)
X_train, X_test, y_train, y_test = train_test_split(X,
            binary_y, test_size=0.33, random_state=5)
logistic = LogisticRegression()
logistic.fit(X_train,y_train)
from sklearn.metrics import accuracy_score
print('In-sample accuracy: %0.3f' %
        accuracy_score(y_train, logistic.predict(X_train)))
print('Out-of-sample accuracy: %0.3f' %
        accuracy_score(y_test, logistic.predict(X_test)))
```

Here's the output from this example:

```
In-sample accuracy: 0.973
Out-of-sample accuracy: 0.958
```

The example splits the data into training and test sets, enabling you to check the efficacy of the logistic regression model on data that the model hasn't used for learning. The resulting coefficients tell you the probability of a particular class's being in the target class (which is any class encoded using a value of 1). If a coefficient increases the likelihood, it will have a positive coefficient; otherwise, the coefficient is negative.

```
for var,coef in zip(boston.feature_names,
                    logistic.coef_[0]):
        print ("%7s : %7.3f" %(var, coef))
```

The output shows the effect of each coefficient (not necessarily in order):

```
  CRIM :  -0.006
    ZN :   0.197
 INDUS :   0.580
```

```
    CHAS :    -0.023
     NOX :    -0.236
      RM :     1.426
     AGE :    -0.048
     DIS :    -0.365
     RAD :     0.645
     TAX :    -0.220
 PTRATIO :    -0.554
       B :     0.049
   LSTAT :    -0.803
```

Reading the results on your screen, you can see that in Boston, criminality (CRIM) has some effect on prices. However, the level of poverty (LSTAT), distance from work (DIS), and pollution (NOX) all have much greater effects. Moreover, contrary to linear regression, logistic regression doesn't simply output the resulting class (in this case a 1 or a 0) but also estimates the probability of the observation's being part of one of the two classes:

```
print('\nclasses:',logistic.classes_)
print('\nProbs:\n',logistic.predict_proba(X_test)[:3,:])
```

The point is that you get a great deal more information based on the data you provide, as shown here:

```
classes: [0 1]

Probs:
 [[ 0.39022779  0.60977221]
 [ 0.93856655  0.06143345]
 [ 0.98425623  0.01574377]]
```

In this small sample, only the first case has a 61 percent probability of being an expensive housing area. When you perform predictions using this approach, you also know the probability that your forecast is accurate and can act accordingly, choosing only predictions with the right level of accuracy. (For instance, you might pick only predictions that exceed an 80 percent likelihood.)

Working through Multiclass Regression

In some situations, you must consider more than a simple binary outcome or work with more than just one class. In fact, the world is full of such situations, such as the following:

>> Selecting the color of an object from a list of colors

>> Identifying an object shape from a list of shapes

>> Choosing a particular action from a list of potential actions

>> Determining an object type from a list of types

However, when you work through a multiclass regression, what you really do is allow the package to break the multiple classes into multiple binary decisions. The task occurs in the background, where you really don't need to worry about the details, but you could also perform this task manually if necessary. With these understandings in mind, the following sections discuss multiclass regression and various affiliated multiclass and multi-output strategies.

Understanding multiclass regression

All regression eventually breaks down into a binary decision, but your package will hide this fact from view to help you simplify any problem you're trying to solve. In fact, you usually receive support for these kinds of multiclass problems:

>> **Multiclass classification:** In this case, you have an object and must decide between multiple classes. For example, when examining a car's color, you must decide whether it's blue, green, brown, or red. The assumption is that the object is assigned to just one class, meaning that the car can't be both blue and green but must appear as blue or green.

>> **Multilabel classification:** This problem concerns an object that can have more than one class. For example, a car might have a blue upper half and a contrasting brown lower half. In this case, the car color is both blue and brown. You often see this sort of classification used to tag text. A book might contain humor but also talk about politics and its effects on medicine.

>> **Multi-output regression:** In this case, you perform a detailed analysis of complex objects and assign the object more than one target class. The classifications are binary, but the object has multiple properties. For example, you might say that a piece of fruit is an apple or a pear and that its exterior color is either yellow or green. The kind of fruit and its color are two separate target classes that you must handle individually.

>> **Multi-output/multiclass classification:** In this case, an object can have multiple values assigned to multiple target classes. For example, you might consider the exterior and interior colors of a car, which you would assign as separate target classes. Another example is weather, when you assign the current weather conditions properties such as temperature range (cold, cool, warm, or hot), humidity (dry, moderate, or humid), wind speed (calm, pleasant, brisk, or hurricane), wind direction (cardinal points of the compass), and so on.

>> **Multitask classification:** With enough care, you can perform multiple classifications for each of multiple targets, with each being able to include multiple classes. Obviously, the more complexity you create for a classification and its outputs, the longer the classification takes.

REMEMBER

Along with the kind of classification you want to perform, you must also consider the strategy used to perform it. The "Considering when classes are more" section, earlier in this chapter, discusses strategies in more detail.

Developing a multiclass regression implementation

In the "Considering when classes are more" section, earlier in this chapter, you see a comparison of strategies. In the following example, you see the OVR strategy used with the Iris dataset, in which a flower can appear as part of the Setosa, Versicolour, or Virginica class (see https://archive.ics.uci.edu/ml/datasets/iris for details). The first step is to import the data, as shown here:

```
from sklearn import datasets
iris = datasets.load_iris()
X, y = iris.data, iris.target
```

The X data includes columns for sepal length, sepal width, petal length, and petal width, and the y data contains the iris class. The next step is to perform the multiclass classification, as shown here:

```
from sklearn.multiclass import OneVsRestClassifier
from sklearn.svm import LinearSVC
irisClass = OneVsRestClassifier(LinearSVC(
    random_state=0)).fit(X, y).predict(X)
```

You can now plot the results based on sepal length and sepal width, using the
irisClass regression results to provide the colors for the various entries, as
shown here:

```
plt.scatter(X[:,0], X[:,1], c=irisClass)
plt.show()
```

REMEMBER

Notice how you use X[:,0] and X[:,1] to separate out the sepal length (x-axis)
and sepal width (y-axis) for the scatterplot. The result is the plot shown in
Figure 2-5.

FIGURE 2-5:
The plot shows
the result of
a multiclass
regression among
three classes.

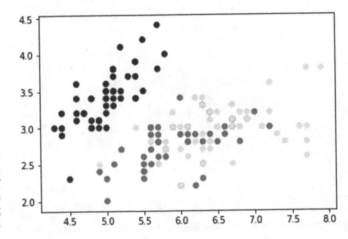

Chapter **3**

Predicting Outcomes Using Bayes

S ometimes, a method of doing something seems less complicated than it actually is, which is how things went with Bayes' Theorem. The theorem receives its name from the Reverend Thomas Bayes, who discovered it in the 1740s and promptly discarded it. Later, Pierre Simon Laplace worked on it to give it its modern form, and then he discarded it as well. According to Sharon McGrayne's book, *The Theory That Would Not Die*, many people used Bayes' Theorem for all sorts of purposes, from mounting a defense for Captain Dreyfus (see https://www.business-standard.com/article/markets/the-bayesian-curse-112011300083_1.html for details) to breaking the German Enigma code (see https://www.investsmart.com.au/investment-news/the-theory-that-cracked-the-enigma-code/138342 for details), but they generally used it in secret. Not until the twenty-first century would anyone actually admit to using it for all the practical things it can do. So, this chapter is your introduction to a widely kept secret that can perform amazing practical tasks in statistics, and when you see it in its original form, you'll declare Bayes' Theorem to be surprisingly simple.

Of course, things never stay simple. The second part of this chapter moves into detailed uses of Bayes' Theorem by employing the networked version. The networked version uses the same basic form of the original version, but now you consider the complexity of evidence and the places that evidence can take you. Unsurprisingly, tracking down and employing all the evidence in an analysis can take time and sometimes become error prone. Court trials follow the same path. Yet, using Bayes helps you clear the muddy waters and make sense of difficult issues.

Book 3, Chapters 1 and 2 help you discover both linear and logistic regression. The third part of this chapter helps you combine this knowledge with your newly acquired knowledge of Bayes' Theorem to create a powerful method of performing data analysis by uniting two simpler methods.

REMEMBER

You don't have to type the source code for this chapter manually. In fact, using the downloadable source is a lot easier. The source code for this chapter appears in the DSPD_0303_Bayes.ipynb source code file for Python and the DSPD_R_0303_Bayes.ipynb source code file for R. See the Introduction for details on how to find these source files.

Understanding Bayes' Theorem

Before you begin using Bayes' Theorem to perform practical tasks, knowing a little about its history is helpful. The reason this knowledge is so useful is because the theorem doesn't seem to be able to do everything it purports to do when you first see it, which is why many statisticians rejected it outright. After you do have a basic knowledge of how the theorem came into being, you need to look at the theorem itself. The following sections provide you with a history of Bayes' Theorem that then moves into the theorem itself. These sections discuss the theorem from a practical perspective.

Delving into Bayes history

You might wonder why anyone would name an algorithm Naïve Bayes (yet you find this algorithm among the most effective machine learning algorithms in packages such as Scikit-learn). The *naïve* part comes from its formulation; it makes some extreme simplifications to standard probability calculations. The reference to Bayes in its name relates to the Reverend Bayes and his theorem on probability.

The Reverend Thomas Bayes (1701–1761) was an English statistician and a philosopher who formulated his theorem during the first half of the eighteenth century. The theorem is based on a thought experiment and then a demonstration using the simplest of means. Reverend Bayes wanted to determine the probability of a future event based on the number of times it occurred in the past. It's hard to contemplate how to accomplish this task with any accuracy.

The demonstration relied on the use of two balls. An assistant would drop the first ball on a table where the end position of this ball was equally possible in any location, but not tell Bayes its location. The assistant would then drop a second ball, tell Bayes the position of the second ball, and then provide the position of the first ball relative to the location of this second ball. The assistant would then drop the second ball a number of additional times — each time telling Bayes the location of the second ball and the position of the first ball relative to the second. After each toss of the second ball, Bayes would attempt to guess the position of the first. Eventually, he was to guess the position of the first ball based on the evidence provided by the second ball.

The theorem was never published while Bayes was alive. His friend Richard Price found Bayes' notes after his death in 1761 and published the material for Bayes, but no one seemed to read it at first. The theorem has deeply revolutionized the theory of probability by introducing the idea of conditional probability — that is, probability conditioned by evidence. The critics saw problems with Bayes' Theorem that you can summarize as follows:

>> Guessing has no place in rigorous mathematics.

>> If Bayes didn't know what to guess, he would simply assign all possible outcomes an equal probability of occurring.

>> Using the prior calculations to make a new guess presented an insurmountable problem.

Often, it takes a problem to illuminate the need for a previously defined solution, which is what happened with Bayes' Theorem. By the late eighteenth century, the need to study astronomy and make sense of the observations made by the

>> Chinese in 1100 BC

>> Greeks in 200 BC

>> Romans in AD 100

>> Arabs in AD 1000

became essential. The readings made by these other civilizations not only reflected social and other biases but also were unreliable because of the differing methods of observation and the technology use. You might wonder why the study of astronomy suddenly became essential, and the short answer is money. Navigation of the late eighteenth century relied heavily on accurate celestial observations (https://penobscotmarinemuseum.org/pbho-1/history-of-navigation/navigation-18th-century), so anyone who could make the readings more accurate could reduce the time required to ship goods from one part of the world to another.

Pierre-Simon Laplace wanted to solve the problem, but he couldn't just dive into the astronomy data without first having a means to dig through all that data to find out which was correct and which wasn't. He encountered Richard Price, who told him about Bayes' Theorem. Laplace used the theorem to solve an easier problem, that of the births of males and females. Some people had noticed that more boys than girls were born each year, but no proof existed for this observation. Laplace used Bayes' Theorem to prove that more boys are born each year than girls based on birth records. Other statisticians took notice and started using the theorem, often secretly, for a host of other calculations, such as the calculation of the masses of Jupiter and Saturn from a wide variety of observations by Alexis Bouvard (see https://www.revolvy.com/page/Alexis-Bouvard for details).

Considering the basic theorem

When thinking about Bayes' Theorem, it helps to start from the beginning — that is, probability itself. *Probability* tells you the likelihood of an event and is expressed in a numeric form. The probability of an event is measured in the range from 0 to 1 (from 0 percent to 100 percent) and it's empirically derived from counting the number of times a specific event happens with respect to all the events. You can calculate it from data!

When you observe events (for example, when a feature has a certain characteristic) and you want to estimate the probability associated with the event, you count the number of times the characteristic appears in the data and divide that figure by the total number of observations available. The result is a number ranging from 0 to 1, which expresses the probability.

When you estimate the probability of an event, you tend to believe that you can apply the probability in each situation. The term for this belief is *a priori* because it constitutes the first estimate of probability with regard to an event (the one that comes to mind first). For example, if you estimate the probability of an unknown person's being a female, you might say, after some counting, that it's 50 percent, which is the prior, or the first, probability that you will stick with.

The prior probability can change in the face of evidence, that is, something that can radically modify your expectations. For example, the evidence of whether a person is male or female could be that the person's hair is long or short. You can estimate having long hair as an event with 35 percent probability for the general population, but within the female population, it's 60 percent. If the percentage is higher in the female population, contrary to the general probability (the prior for having long hair), that's useful information for making a prediction.

Imagine that you have to guess whether a person is male or female and the evidence is that the person has long hair. This sounds like a predictive problem, and in the end, this situation is similar to predicting a categorical variable from data: We have a target variable with different categories and you have to guess the probability of each category based on evidence, the data. Reverend Bayes provided a useful formula:

```
P(B|E) = P(E|B)*P(B) / P(E)
```

The formula looks like statistical jargon and is a bit counterintuitive, so it needs to be explained in depth. Reading the formula using the previous example as input makes the meaning behind the formula quite a bit clearer:

>> **P(B|E):** The probability of being a female (the belief B) given long hair (the evidence E). This part of the formula defines what you want to predict. In short, it says to predict y given x where y is an outcome (male or female) and x is the evidence (long or short hair).

>> **P(E|B):** The probability of having long hair, the evidence of when a person is female. In this case, you already know that it's 60 percent. In every data problem, you can obtain this figure easily by simple cross-tabulation of the features against the target outcome.

>> **P(B):** The probability of being a female, which has a 50 percent general chance (a prior).

>> **P(E):** The probability of having long hair in general, which is 35 percent (another prior).

TIP

When reading parts of the formula such as P(B|E), you should read them as follows: probability of B given E. The | symbol translates as *given*. A probability expressed in this way is a conditional probability, because it's the probability of a belief, B, conditioned by the evidence presented by E. In this example, plugging the numbers into the formula translates into

```
60% * 50% / 35% = 85.7%
```

Therefore, getting back to the previous example, even if being a female is a 50 percent probability, just knowing evidence like long hair takes it up to 85.7 percent, which is a more favorable chance for the guess. You can be more confident in guessing that the person with long hair is a female because you have a bit less than a 15 percent chance of being wrong.

Using Naïve Bayes for Predictions

Even though Bayes' Theorem looks relatively simple compared to some of the other calculations you have already performed in this book, it really can do amazing things. The following sections discuss the basic theorem before you do anything fancy with it.

Finding out that Naïve Bayes isn't so naïve

Naïve Bayes, leveraging the simple Bayes' Theorem, takes advantage of all the evidence available in order to modify the prior base probability of your predictions. Because your data contains so much evidence — that is, it has many features — the data makes a big sum of all the probabilities derived from a simplified Naïve Bayes formula.

REMEMBER

As discussed in the "Using Linear Regression to Guess Numbers" section of Book 3, Chapter 1, summing variables implies that the model takes them as separate and unique pieces of information. But this implication doesn't hold true in reality, because applications exist in a world of interconnections, with every piece of information connecting to many other pieces. Using one piece of information more than once means giving more emphasis to that particular piece.

Because you don't know (or you simply ignore) the relationships among each piece of evidence, you probably just plug all of them in to Naïve Bayes. The simple and naïve move of throwing everything that you know at the formula works well indeed, and many studies report good performance despite the fact that you make a naïve assumption. Using everything for prediction is okay, even though it seemingly shouldn't be given the strong association between variables. Here are some of the ways in which you commonly see Naïve Bayes used:

>> Building spam detectors (catching all annoying emails in your inbox)

>> Sentiment analysis (guessing whether a text contains positive or negative attitudes with respect to a topic, and detecting the mood of the speaker)

>> Text-processing tasks such as spell correction, or guessing the language used to write or classify the text into a larger category

TIP

Naïve Bayes is also popular because it doesn't need as much data to work. It can naturally handle multiple classes. With some slight variable modifications (transforming them into classes), it can also handle numeric variables. Scikit-learn provides three Naïve Bayes classes in the `sklearn.naive_bayes` module:

>> `MultinomialNB`: Uses the probabilities derived from a feature's presence. When a feature is present, it assigns a certain probability to the outcome, which the textual data indicates for the prediction.

>> `BernoulliNB`: Provides the multinomial functionality of Naïve Bayes, but it penalizes the absence of a feature. This class assigns a different probability when the feature is present than when it's absent. In fact, it treats all features as dichotomous variables. (The distribution of a dichotomous variable is a Bernoulli distribution.) You can also use it with textual data.

>> GaussianNB: Defines a version of Naïve Bayes that expects a normal distribution of all the features. Hence, this class is suboptimal for textual data in which words are sparse (use the multinomial or Bernoulli distributions instead). If your variables have positive and negative values, this is the best choice.

Predicting text classifications

Naïve Bayes is particularly popular for document classification. In textual problems, you often have millions of features involved, one for each word spelled correctly or incorrectly. Sometimes the text is associated with other nearby words in *n-grams*, that is, sequences of consecutive words. Naïve Bayes can learn the textual features quickly and provide fast predictions based on the input.

UNDERSTANDING ANACONDA NOTIFICATIONS

Newer versions of Anaconda display various notifications to help you understand why a particular process is taking longer than expected. For example, when you download the 20newsgroups dataset, you may see the following message:

```
Downloading 20news dataset. This may take a few minutes.
Downloading dataset from
https://ndownloader.figshare.com/files/5975967 (14 MB)
```

The message will often appear in the same background color and the same text characteristics as an error message. This message isn't an error; it simply gives you additional information about the progress of a task. If you don't see the message, it may simply mean that you have already downloaded the dataset at some point or that you're using an older version of Anaconda that doesn't support the message.

You could see other notifications for other needs. For example, when a package installation requires additional time to complete, you may see a notification message even if you have a copy of the package on your local system. All these messages help you understand what Anaconda is doing in the background.

This section tests text classifications using the binomial and multinomial Naïve Bayes models offered by Scikit-learn. The examples rely on the 20newsgroups dataset, which contains a large number of posts from 20 kinds of newsgroups. The dataset is divided into a training set, for building your textual models, and a test set, which is comprised of posts that temporally follow the training set. You use the test set to test the accuracy of your predictions:

```
from sklearn.datasets import fetch_20newsgroups
newsgroups_train = fetch_20newsgroups(
            subset='train', remove=('headers', 'footers',
                                    'quotes'))
newsgroups_test = fetch_20newsgroups(
            subset='test', remove=('headers', 'footers',
                                   'quotes'))
```

After loading the two sets into memory, you import the two Naïve Bayes models and instantiate them. At this point, you set alpha values, which are useful for avoiding a zero probability for rare features (a zero probability would exclude these features from the analysis). You typically use a small value for alpha, as shown in the following code:

```
from sklearn.naive_bayes import BernoulliNB, MultinomialNB
Bernoulli = BernoulliNB(alpha=0.01)
Multinomial = MultinomialNB(alpha=0.01)
```

REMEMBER

In some cases, you use what is known as the hashing trick to model textual data without fear of encountering new words when using the model after the training phase. (You can find the details of this technique in the "Performing the Hashing Trick" in Chapter 12 of *Python For Data Science For Dummies*, 2nd Edition, by John Paul Mueller and Luca Massaron [Wiley].) You can use two different hashing tricks, one counting the words (for the multinomial approach) and one recording whether a word appeared in a binary variable (the binomial approach). You can also remove *stop words*, that is, common words found in the English language, such as "a," "the," "in," and so on.

```
import sklearn.feature_extraction.text as txt
multinomial = txt.HashingVectorizer(stop_words='english',
                              binary=False, norm=None)
binary = txt.HashingVectorizer(stop_words='english',
                        binary=True, norm=None)
```

At this point, you can train the two classifiers and test them on the test set, which is a set of posts that temporally appear after the training set. The test measure is accuracy, which is the percentage of right guesses that the algorithm makes:

```
import numpy as np
target = newsgroups_train.target
target_test = newsgroups_test.target
multi_X = np.abs(
    multinomial.transform(newsgroups_train.data))
multi_Xt = np.abs(
    multinomial.transform(newsgroups_test.data))
bin_X = binary.transform(newsgroups_train.data)
bin_Xt = binary.transform(newsgroups_test.data)

Multinomial.fit(multi_X, target)
Bernoulli.fit(bin_X, target)

from sklearn.metrics import accuracy_score
for name, model, data in [('BernoulliNB', Bernoulli,
                             bin_Xt),
                  ('MultinomialNB', Multinomial,
                   multi_Xt)]:
    accuracy = accuracy_score(y_true=target_test,
                        y_pred=model.predict(data))
    print ('Accuracy for %s: %.3f' % (name, accuracy))
```

The reported accuracies for the two Naïve Bayes models are

```
Accuracy for BernoulliNB: 0.570
Accuracy for MultinomialNB: 0.651
```

You might notice that both models don't take long to train and report their predictions on the test set. Consider that the training set is made up of more than 11,000 posts containing more than 300,000 words, and the test set contains about 7,500 other posts.

```
print('number of posts in training: %i'
      % len(newsgroups_train.data))
D={word:True for post in newsgroups_train.data
   for word in post.split(' ')}
print('number of distinct words in training: %i'
      % len(D))
print('number of posts in test: %i'
      % len(newsgroups_test.data))
```

Running the code returns all these useful text statistics:

```
number of posts in training: 11314
```

```
number of distinct words in training: 300972
number of posts in test: 7532
```

Getting an overview of Bayesian inference

In reading about the thought experiment that Bayes originally used to create his theorem in the "Delving into Bayes history" section of the chapter, you discover the dynamic nature of the underlying technique. Each previous estimate acts as the basis for the next estimate — it's a refinement. Essentially, dropping the second ball enables you to create a better estimate of the actual location of the first ball through the process of inference. Each piece of new data further improves the overall estimate so that the estimate begins to match real-world results. The following sections offer an overview of how inference can work to refine a Bayes probability.

Coming to the wrong conclusion

Often, people make assumptions about data that aren't true. By making a single observation of the relationship between data elements under dubious conditions that could change, many people conclude that something is true when it isn't. A single observation of the moon when it's full may lead one to believe that the moon is always full, yet it isn't. You need more observations to determine that the moon sometimes disappears altogether. To determine the current state of the moon, you then need enough observations to determine the moon's cycle and then consider the progress of that cycle to properly conclude that the moon is currently at the first quarter — neither full nor new. Bayesian inference assumes the following:

>> Data is limited to the observations made, which may not represent actual conditions.

>> When modeling the data, you can easily fit the curve to the known observations a little too closely (overfitting) so that any conclusions about future data using the model are flawed.

>> Some facts are more important than other facts, but the model often doesn't contain this information, so making accurate predictions is impossible without knowing more about the facts.

>> Conclusions are accurate only when you consider all the facts, rather than only the most likely fact.

Getting the required inference packages

Performing Bayesian inference requires the use of the PyMC3 (https://pypi.org/project/pymc3/) package, which relies on Markov chain Monte Carlo (MCMC) sampling to allow inference on increasingly complex models. You use this package for Bayesian statistical modeling in this book. To install the package, you begin by opening an Anaconda Prompt (don't use a standard command prompt or terminal window because they won't have the required environmental setup). At the prompt, you type the following (all on one line):

```
conda create -n PYMC3_env python=3.7.3 anaconda=2019.03
  pymc3 nb_conda
```

and press Enter. The command will run for a while, seemingly doing nothing. However, at some point you see a description of what conda will do. Simply type **y** and press Enter to install the package.

To perform plotting using PyMC3, you also need the ArviZ package (https://arviz-devs.github.io/arviz/). Type these entries at the prompt to install this package:

```
activate PYMC3_env
conda install arviz
deactivate
```

As before, you need to type **y** and press Enter when prompted to perform the installation.

Developing a simple inference example

The "Coming to the wrong conclusion" section, earlier in this chapter, tells you about some assumptions for Bayesian inference that could seem mind boggling, so it's time for an example. Consider that your company tasks you with determining how many of each car color to produce to ensure that your company doesn't have an overstock. So, you go out to the parking lot and count 3 red cars, 2 black cars, and 1 tan car. (The example uses smaller numbers to make things simpler.) A simple solution would be to make 50 percent of the cars red, 33 percent of the cars black, and 17 percent of the cars tan, but the simple solution is probably wrong for these reasons (among others):

» You may not see all the cars driven by every employee.

» The numbers in your parking lot may not reflect reality.

To work through this problem, you need to make some assumptions and use some additional data. For example, you know that your company is interested in making only red, black, and tan cars, so you don't need to consider other car colors in your analysis. You also discover that marketing has survey numbers that you can use to form a prior belief about the actual numbers. In this case, the survey shows that people actually prefer red cars in this ratio: for every 4 red car voters, 3 people voted for tan cars, and 1 person voted for a black car.

The technique used to create the initial (the prior) belief relies on the Dirichlet-multinomial distribution. You can read about it at https://ixkael.github.io/dirichlet-multinomial-conjugate-priors/, but this example seeks to simplify these ideas for those who really want to get some work done and don't have a degree in statistics. The important aspects to consider are as follows:

» **Number of trials (observations):** Represented by n, which contains 6 in this case (3 red, 2 black, and 1 tan cars).

» **Number of outcomes:** Represented by k, which totals 3 in this case: one each for red, black, and tan.

» **A vector of probabilities for each outcome:** Represented by p in this case, this vector represents the output of the analysis.

The Dirichlet-multinomial distribution also relies on a special hyperparameter, α, which is a parameter of the prior. It contains the starting point information that exists before you make any observations, which would be the survey results of 4 red, 1 black, and 3 tan cars in this case. The survey simply represents an expectation — a guess. Because this is a survey, it's an educated guess, but it's still a guess. The code will contain two distributions: multinomial (parameters—event probabilities) and Dirichlet (prior distribution), as described here:

```
multinomial: (n=20, p_red=?, p_black=?, p_tan=?)
Dirichlet: (k=3, α_red, α_black, α_tan)
```

You must also account for the support data, represented by c, which is an array containing the three observed values of 7 red cars (4 survey and 3 observed); 3 black cars (1 survey and 2 observed); and 4 tan cars (3 survey and 1 observed). The final model looks like this:

```
(p | c, α)
```

Use the following code to calculate the probabilities for each outcome:

```
import numpy as np

colors = ['Red', 'Black', 'Tan']
c = np.array([3, 2, 1])
alphas = np.array([4, 1, 3])

expected_p = (alphas + c) / (c.sum() + alphas.sum())

new_values = dict(zip(colors, expected_p))
for x in new_values:
    print("{}:\t{:2.2%}".format(x, new_values[x]))
```

Based on the combination of the survey and the parking lot observation, you can now see that the percentages of colors to paint the cars has changed, like this:

```
Red:    50.00%
Black:  21.43%
Tan:    28.57%
```

As you continue to gather data, you can further refine the estimates, just as described for the original experiment. You must first create a model using the following code (which may generate deprecation notices depending on your setup):

```
import pymc3 as pm

with pm.Model() as model:
    parameters = pm.Dirichlet('parameters', a=alphas,
                                shape=3)
    observed_data = pm.Multinomial(
        'observed_data', n=6, p=parameters, shape=3,
        observed=c)
```

Note that `model` contains the two previously discussed distributions: `Dirichlet` and `Multinomial`. You can now train the model using this code:

```
with model:
    trace = pm.sample(draws=1000, chains=2, tune=500,
                        discard_tuned_samples=True)
```

The process samples data based on the No-U-Turn Sampler (NUTS), which is useful on models that have many continuous parameters. Basically, it searches for areas in the model where higher probabilities occur. The output you see explains how the sampling process occurs:

```
Auto-assigning NUTS sampler...
Initializing NUTS using jitter+adapt_diag...
Multiprocess sampling (2 chains in 4 jobs)
NUTS: [parameters]
Sampling 2 chains: 100%|████████████| 3000/3000
    [00:11<00:00, 253.26draws/s]
```

NUTS uses `parameters`, which you previously defined as part of the model — the previously collected survey information. The progress bar shows the sampling process. If you're interested in the whole jitter+adapt_diag methodology, you can read about it at https://discourse.pymc.io/t/what-exactly-is-jitter-adapt-diag-and-why-is-it-the-default-now/451. Essentially, it's a sliding-window approach to interacting with the data.

At this point, you have a model that can predict with some level of precision how many cars to create in each of the colors. Of course, seeing the predictions is always nice, and you can do so with the following code:

```
dataPlot1 = pm.plots.traceplot(trace, combined=True)
dataPlot1[0][0].set_title(
    "Red Posterior Probability Distribution")
dataPlot1[0][1].set_title("Red Trace Samples")
dataPlot1[1][0].set_title(
    "Black Posterior Probability Distribution")
dataPlot1[1][1].set_title("Black Trace Samples")
dataPlot1[2][0].set_title(
    "Tan Posterior Probability Distribution")
dataPlot1[2][1].set_title("Tan Trace Samples")
```

The output from this code appears in Figure 3-1. The graphs on the left show the probability distribution for each color, and the graphs on the right show the sample process used for each of the colors.

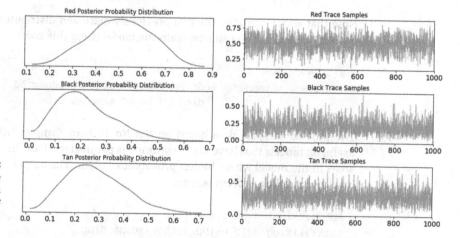

FIGURE 3-1: Seeing the probabilities for each of the colors.

All that remains is to determine the values to use and consider the probability that these values are correct by estimating the Highest Posterior Density (HPD) (you can read more about this estimation at https://support.sas.com/documentation/cdl/en/statug/63033/HTML/default/viewer.htm#statug_introbayes_sect005.htm). The following code shows how to create the required plots:

```
dataPlot2 = pm.plots.plot_posterior(trace, figsize=(20,6))
dataPlot2[0].set_title('Red', fontsize=20)
dataPlot2[1].set_title('Black', fontsize=20)
dataPlot2[2].set_title('Tan', fontsize=20)
```

Figure 3-2 shows how the plots appear. Note that Red has a mean of 0.5 (50 percent), Black a mean of 0.2 (20 percent), and Tan a mean of 0.3 (30 percent). Each of these percentages reflects the number of cars to paint a certain color. The 94% HPD says that 94 percent of the estimates lie in the region shown, which is a high level of confidence that the calculation is correct.

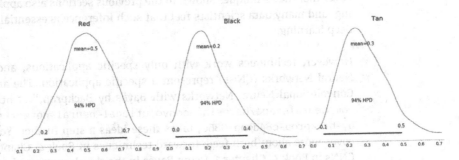

FIGURE 3-2:
Determining
how many cars
to paint specific
colors.

Moving forward with Bayes inference and deep learning

When performing data science tasks, you are often tasked with making algorithms work within specific fields such as AI learning, which relies on algorithms to define how and what to learn. In this environment, an *algorithm* is a kind of container. It provides a box for storing a method to solve a particular kind of a problem. Algorithms process data through a series of well-defined states. The states need not be deterministic, but the states are defined nonetheless. The goal is to create an output that solves a problem. In some cases, the algorithm receives inputs that help define the output, but the focus is always on the output.

Algorithms must express the transitions between states using a well-defined and formal language that the computer can understand. In processing the data and solving the problem, the algorithm defines, refines, and executes a function. The function is always specific to the kind of problem being addressed by the algorithm.

A group of scientists, called Bayesians, perceived that uncertainty was the key aspect to keep an eye on and that learning wasn't assured, but rather took place as a continuous updating of previous beliefs that grew more and more accurate. This perception led the Bayesians to adopt statistical methods and, in particular, derivations from Bayes' Theorem, which helps you calculate probabilities under specific conditions (for instance, seeing a card of a certain *seed*, the starting value for a pseudo-random sequence, drawn from a deck after three other cards of same seed).

An application that relies on deep learning techniques uses Bayesian inference in a method called forward propagation (also called a feed-forward neural network) to help the neural network learn from the data you provide. In the article "Probabilistic Deep Learning: Bayes by Backprop," at https://medium.com/neuralspace/probabilistic-deep-learning-bayes-by-backprop-c4a3de0d9743, you discover that the techniques shown in the previous sections also apply to deep learning, and many data scientists feel that such inference is essential to the future of deep learning.

However, techniques work with only specific applications, and Convolutional Neural Networks (CNNs) represent a specific application. The article "Bayesian Convolutional Neural Networks with Bayes by Backprop," at https://medium.com/neuralspace/bayesian-convolutional-neural-networks-with-bayes-by-backprop-c84dcaaf086e, takes these ideas a step further. You can also discover more about both feed-forward techniques in Book 4, Chapter 2, and about CNNs in Book 4, Chapter 3. Using Bayes in the simple manner shown so far is just the starting point for significantly more complex techniques.

Working with Networked Bayes

Not all decisions come in neat packages that rely on just one prediction. Sometimes, you must consider multiple levels of decision making to better model a situation. Networked Bayes is a type of Probabilistic Graphical Model (PGM), which also includes the Markov Network. The difference between these two PGMs is that Bayes relies on a directed acyclic graph, while the Markov version is both undirected and cyclic. Both of these models model certain kinds of dependencies, but you use them in different ways and for different purposes. The following sections help you better understand networked Bayes and explain how you can use it to make predictions.

Considering the network types and uses

You use networked Bayes for a number of purposes that include prediction, anomaly detection, diagnostics, automated insight, reasoning, time series prediction, and decision making under uncertainty. However, you don't use just one form of networked Bayes to perform all these tasks. Four different types or disciplines of networked Bayes exist, as described in the following list:

>> **Descriptive:** Considers how to describe or categorize data based on the probability that it is one thing or another. This discipline has these characteristics and uses:

- Automated insight

- Large patterns

- Anomalous patterns

- Multivariate

>> **Diagnostic:** Specifies the cause of an error or determines whether something is useful based on the probability that the underlying assumptions about it are correct. This discipline has these characteristics and uses:

- Value of information

- Reasoning

- Troubleshooting

- Tracing anomalies

>> **Predictive:** Defines a future value based on current information (as was done in the original experiment). This discipline has these characteristics and uses:

- Supervised or unsupervised learning

- Anomaly detection

- Time series

- Latent variables

>> **Prescriptive:** Performs decision-making based on the truth-values of the underlying data and outputs these decisions with levels of confidence (based on probabilities). This discipline has these characteristics and uses:

- Decision automation

- Cost based decision-making

- Decision support

- Decision-making under uncertainty

One of the best ways to explore how you might use a networked Bayes setup is to play with it. You find an interactive version of the Asia Bayesian network (see Figure 3-3) at https://www.bayesserver.com/examples/networks/asia. By selecting the various boxes, you can see how each node of the network affects the overall probability of a particular disease to be detected in a person who visits a clinic. When you select a box, that particular condition becomes known and the probability is now 100 percent. If you leave the box deselected, the network uses an assumed set of percentages for true and false. Notice that the network has a definite hierarchy and a definite direction between decision-making steps.

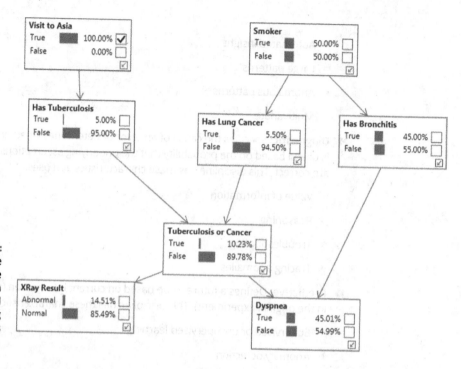

FIGURE 3-3:
The interactive version of the Asia Bayesian network is helpful in understanding how networks work.

When using graphs to represent a prediction model, you have a number of options from which to choose. As specified in the next section, networked Bayes relies on the directed acyclic graph. However, you need to know that graphs have a number of different characteristics, as specified in the following list:

» **Cyclic:** The edges forms a cycle that take you back to the initial vertex after having visited the intermediary vertexes.

» **A-cyclic:** This graph lacks cycles.

» **Directed:** Edges connect vertexes in a single direction, with an arrow or other indicator specifying the direction.

» **Undirected:** Edges connect vertexes in both directions (typically without arrows or other indicators).

» **Weighted:** Each edge has a cost associated with it, such as time, money, or energy, which you must pay to pass through it.

» **Unweighted:** All the edges have no cost or the same cost.

» **Dense:** This type of graph has a large number of edges when compared to the number of vertexes.

» **Sparse:** This type of graph has a small number of edges when compared to the number of vertexes.

Understanding Directed Acyclic Graphs (DAGs)

A *Directed Acyclic Graph (DAG)* is a finite directed graph that doesn't have any loops in it. In other words, you start from a particular location and follow a specific route to an ending location without ever going back to the starting location. When using topological sorting, a DAG always directs earlier vertexes to later vertexes. This kind of graph has all sorts of practical uses, such as schedules, with each milestone representing a particular milestone.

DAGs are one of the most important kinds of graphs because they see so many practical uses. The basic principles of DAGs are that they

>> Follow a particular order so that you can't get from one vertex to another and back to the beginning vertex using any route.

>> Provide a specific path from one vertex to another so that you can create a predictable set of routes.

You see DAGs used for many organizational needs. For example, a family tree is an example of a DAG. Even when the activity doesn't follow a chronological or other overriding order, the DAG enables you to create predictable routes, which makes DAGs easier to process than many other kinds of graphs you work with.

However, DAGs can use optional routes. Imagine that you're building a burger. The menu system starts with a bun bottom. You can optionally add condiments to the bun bottom, or you can move directly to the burger on the bun. The route always ends up with a burger, but you have multiple paths for getting to the burger. After you have the burger in place, you can choose to add cheese or bacon before adding the bun top. The point is that you take a specific path, but each path can connect to the next level in several different ways.

REMEMBER

The DAG is commonly used with the evidence portion of a Bayes calculation. You use an evidentiary tree to decide various probabilities of evidence. For example, when deciding whether to play tennis, you might consider this tree of evidence:

1. Rain
2. Wind
3. Temperature
4. Humidity

If it isn't raining, the wind isn't too high, and the temperature is just right, it's a good day to play tennis. However, you must also consider all the other probabilities, which means calculating them for each branch of the tree. You don't need to consider any item more than once. When the prediction considers rain, it need not consider rain again. The tree also has an order, so you consider the chance of rain first. You see this particular tree in action in the "Employing networked Bayes in predictions" section, later in this chapter.

TIP

When working with DAGs, you often see the nomenclature, p(A, B), which means the probability of A and B. In other words, you no longer seek to find just the probability of A, but you want instead the probability of A and B occurring together, which means that they must both be true. You can see a conditional form of this nomenclature as well, p(A, B | C), which means the probability of A and B both occurring given the evidence presented by C. To put this in a real-world context, you might want to consider the probability that it's both raining and windy given that you can see that the trees are bending an abnormal amount.

Sometimes you see this process extended further still by *instantiation*. In this case, you already know whether one of the items in the prediction is true or false. For example, you might see p(A = True, B | C), which means the probability of B given that A is True and the evidence presented by C.

Employing networked Bayes in predictions

Bayes' Theorem can help you deduce how likely something is to happen in a certain context, based on the general probabilities of the fact itself and the evidence you examine, and combined with the probability of the evidence given the fact. Seldom will a single piece of evidence diminish doubts and provide enough certainty in a prediction to ensure that it will happen. As a true detective, to reach certainty, you have to collect more evidence and make the individual pieces work together in your investigation. Noticing that a person has long hair isn't enough to determine whether person is female or a male. Adding data about height and weight could help increase confidence.

The Naïve Bayes algorithm helps you arrange all the evidence you gather and reach a more solid prediction with a higher likelihood of being correct. Gathered evidence considered singularly couldn't save you from the risk of predicting incorrectly, but all evidence summed together can reach a more definitive resolution. The following example shows how things work in a Naïve Bayes classification. This is an old, renowned problem, but it represents the kind of capability that you can expect from an AI. The dataset is from the paper "Induction of Decision Trees," by John Ross Quinlan (https://dl.acm.org/citation.cfm?id=637969). Quinlan is a computer scientist who contributed to the development of a machine learning algorithm called decision trees in a fundamental way, but his example works well with any kind of learning algorithm. The problem requires that the AI guess the best conditions to play tennis given the weather conditions. The set of features described by Quinlan is as follows:

>> **Outlook:** Sunny, overcast, or rainy

>> **Temperature:** Cool, mild, hot

>> **Humidity:** High or normal

>> **Windy:** True or false

The following table contains the database entries used for the example:

Outlook	Temperature	Humidity	Windy	PlayTennis
Sunny	Hot	High	False	No
Sunny	Hot	High	True	No
Overcast	Hot	High	False	Yes
Rainy	Mild	High	False	Yes
Rainy	Cool	Normal	False	Yes
Rainy	Cool	Normal	True	No
Overcast	Cool	Normal	True	Yes
Sunny	Mild	High	False	No
Sunny	Cool	Normal	False	Yes
Rainy	Mild	Normal	False	Yes
Sunny	Mild	Normal	True	Yes
Overcast	Mild	High	True	Yes
Overcast	Hot	Normal	False	Yes
Rainy	Mild	High	True	No

The option of playing tennis depends on the four arguments shown in Figure 3-4.

The result of this AI learning example is a decision as to whether to play tennis, given the weather conditions (the evidence). Using just the outlook (sunny, overcast, or rainy) won't be enough, because the temperature and humidity could be too high or the wind might be strong. These arguments represent real conditions that have multiple causes, or causes that are interconnected. The Naïve Bayes algorithm is skilled at guessing correctly when multiple causes exist.

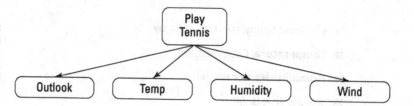

FIGURE 3-4:
A Naïve Bayes
model can
retrace evidence
to the right
outcome.

The algorithm computes a score, based on the probability of making a particular decision and multiplied by the probabilities of the evidence connected to that decision. For instance, to determine whether to play tennis when the outlook is sunny but the wind is strong, the algorithm computes the score for a positive answer by multiplying the general probability of playing (9 played games out of 14 occurrences) by the probability of the day's being sunny (2 out of 9 played games) and of having windy conditions when playing tennis (3 out of 9 played games). The same rules apply for the negative case (which has different probabilities for not playing given certain conditions):

```
likelihood of playing: 9/14 * 2/9 * 3/9 = 0.05
likelihood of not playing: 5/14 * 3/5 *  3/5 = 0.13
```

Because the score for the likelihood is higher, the algorithm decides that it's safer not to play under such conditions. It computes such likelihood by summing the two scores and dividing both scores by their sum:

```
probability of playing : 0.05 / (0.05 + 0.13) = 0.278
probability of not playing :  0.13 / (0.05 + 0.13) = 0.722
```

Look at this example in a little more detail. The dataset is quite simple, consisting of only 14 observations relative to the weather conditions, with results that say whether playing tennis is appropriate.

The example contains four features: outlook, temperature, humidity, and wind, all expressed using qualitative classes instead of measurements (you could express temperature, humidity, and wind strength numerically) to convey a more intuitive understanding of how the weather features relate to the outcome. After these features are processed by the algorithm, you can represent the dataset using a tree-like schema, as shown in Figure 3-5. As the figure shows, you can inspect and read a set of rules by splitting the dataset to create parts in which the predictions are easier by looking at the most frequent class (in this case, the outcome, which is whether to play tennis).

To read the nodes of the tree, just start from the topmost node, which corresponds to the original training data; next, start reading the rules. Note that each node has two derivations: The left branch means that the upper rule is true (stated as yes in a square box), and the right one means that it is false (stated as no in a square box).

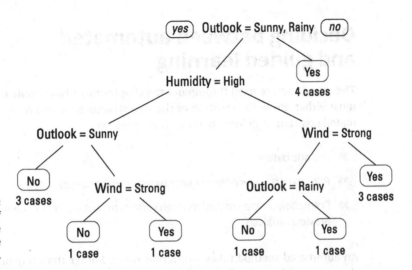

FIGURE 3-5:
A visualization of
the decision tree
built from the
play-tennis data.

On the right of the first rule, you see an important terminal rule (a terminal leaf), in a circle, stating a positive result, Yes, that you can read as play tennis=True. According to this node, when the outlook isn't sunny (Sun) or rainy (Rain), it's possible to play. (The numbers under the terminal leaf show four examples affirming this rule and zero denying it.) Note that you could understand the rule better if the output simply stated that when the outlook is overcast, play is possible. Frequently, decision tree rules aren't immediately usable, and you need to interpret them before use. However, they are clearly intelligible (and much better than a coefficient vector of values).

On the left, the tree proceeds with other rules related to Humidity. Again, on the left, when humidity is high and outlook is sunny, most terminal leaves are negative, except when the wind isn't strong. When you explore the branches on the right, you see that the tree reveals that play is always possible when the wind isn't strong, or when the wind is strong but it doesn't rain.

Bayesian networks, though intuitive, have complex math behind them, and they're more powerful than a simple Naïve Bayes algorithm because they mimic the world as a sequence of causes and effects based on probability. Bayesian networks are so effective that you can use them to represent any situation. They have varied applications, such as medical diagnoses, the fusing of uncertain data arriving from multiple sensors, economic modeling, and the monitoring of complex systems such as a car. For instance, because driving in highway traffic may involve complex situations with many vehicles, the Analysis of MassIve Data STreams (AMIDST) consortium, in collaboration with the automaker Daimler, devised a Bayesian network that can recognize maneuvers by other vehicles and increase driving safety. You can read more about this project and see the complex Bayesian network at `http://project.amidsttoolbox.com/use-cases/identification-and-interpretation-of-maneuvers-in-traffic.html`.

Deciding between automated and guided learning

The tree structure used throughout the chapter must have some sort of start. You must either guide the creation of the tree structure, or you must allow for automated creation. A guided method often relies on

>> Historic data

>> Prior expert knowledge (a guess based on experience)

>> Premodeled data created through various means, such as experimentation or previous analysis

An automated method takes a different route. Rather than rely on human input, this route reviews the data and automatically generates the tree. You can divide this approach into two tasks:

>> **Structure learning:** Create a tree structure based on the connectivity expressed in the data.

>> **Parameter learning:** Given a particular kind of tree structure, calculate the parameters used to create it.

These kinds of learning see use when working with extremely complex data. You can read about two significant uses of these learning approaches:

>> Comparison of automatic and guided learning for Bayesian networks to analyze pipe failures in the water distribution system (https://www.sciencedirect.com/science/article/pii/S0951832017309377)

>> Construction and application of Bayesian networks in flood decision supporting system (https://ieeexplore.ieee.org/abstract/document/1174468)

Considering the Use of Bayesian Linear Regression

Linear regression used on its own is a simple prediction methodology that relies on the use of data points, as described in Chapter 1 of this minibook. The problem is that the technique doesn't work well when you have insufficient data or suffer from a poor data distribution. Bayesian linear regression can overcome these problems by using the priors on the coefficients and noise so that in the absence of data, the priors can take over. More important, you can now use Bayes to determine the confidence level of the data in the following ways:

>> Calculate the confidence level of the estimated linear relation

>> Determine the full posterior distribution

>> Assess the estimated noise level

>> Assess the estimated gradient

>> Determine the direction of steepest ascent

>> Discover the location of an optimum or saddle-point

TIP

This particular technique enables you to fill in missing data. You can see the effect of this strategy demonstrated in the articles found at `https://towardsdatascience.com/bayesian-linear-regression-in-python-using-machine-learning-to-predict-student-grades-part-1-7d0ad817fca5` and `https://towardsdatascience.com/bayesian-linear-regression-in-python-using-machine-learning-to-predict-student-grades-part-2-b72059a8ac7e`.

Considering the Use of Bayesian Logistic Regression

Logistic regression helps you make predictions based on one or more inputs, as described in Chapter 2 of this minibook. For example, it could predict whether a person will get cancer based on weight and smoking habits. It works on discrete values, versus the continuous values used by linear regression. Adding Bayes to the mix helps ascertain the confidence level of a particular analysis. For example, it's now possible to say that if someone smokes and is overweight, they will get cancer with a confidence factor of so many percent. However, it goes further than that by assigning a prior to each of the independent values, giving them a weight of a sort in the calculation. With this in mind, here are the benefits of using Bayesian logistic regression:

>> The output consists of a range of inferential solutions, rather than a point estimate.

>> Starts with prior information, rather than just a belief in the calculation.

>> Updating the prediction becomes possible based on changing evidence.

» Reduces potential bias in a prediction based on features that may not significantly contribute to an outcome.

» Potentially improves the overall accuracy of a prediction.

REMEMBER

It's important to know that these advantages are crucial in certain fields, such as medicine. The article at https://academic.oup.com/aje/article/153/12/1222/124010 discusses the use of Bayesian logistic regression in improving the accuracy of disease predictions for situations in which some features have a small probability (such as the effect of smoking on fetus health). You can see an example of building a Bayesian logistic regression using Python and PyMC3 at https://towardsdatascience.com/building-a-bayesian-logistic-regression-with-python-and-pymc3-4dd463bbb16.

Chapter **4**

Learning with K-Nearest Neighbors

P revious chapters in this minibook demonstrate that you have multiple options when it comes to performing regression and classification tasks. The K-Nearest Neighbors (KNN) algorithm is another way to perform these tasks (along with others) and it has its own sets of pros and cons. The chapter begins by introducing you to KNN and showing you some of the more basic tasks you can perform with it. Along the way, you discover how KNN differs from other methods of performing both regression and classification.

The next part of the chapter discusses tuning. The k parameter provides the means to tune your algorithm. The need for tuning is high with KNN because of the way it works. This part of the chapter helps you understand, through demonstration, why the k parameter is so important and how to choose one correctly.

The final sections of this chapter look at regression and classification. You use regression to predict future values and classification to determine the type of something. Both tasks are essential in machine learning and deep learning. However, you can employ regression and classification in a substantial number of other ways.

REMEMBER

You don't have to type the source code for this chapter manually. In fact, using the downloadable source is a lot easier. The source code for this chapter appears in the DSPD_0304_KNN.ipynb source code file for Python and the DSPD_R_0304_KNN.ipynb source code file for R. See the Introduction for details on how to find these source files.

Considering the History of K-Nearest Neighbors

Some confusion surrounds the history of KNN, partly because it's the work of so many people. In many cases, articles ascribe the initial idea to Evelyn Fix and J. L. Hodges, as described in an unpublished U.S. Air Force School of Aviation Medicine report in 1951 (http://www.scholarpedia.org/article/K-nearest_neighbor).

The paper must have gotten lost, because it wasn't until 1967 that Thomas M. Cover and Peter E. Hart worked out some of the formal KNN properties. The history of KNN shows that the methodology relies on incremental innovations:

>> **1970:** M. E. Hellman added new rejection approaches.

>> **1975:** Keinosuke Fukunaga and Larry D. Hostetler refined density estimates (with respect to the Bayes error rate).

>> **1976:** Sahibsingh A. Dudani introduced a distance-weighted KNN rule (WKNN).

>> **1978:** T. Bailey and A. K. Jain reexamined the relationship between unweighted KNN and WKNN, showing that WKNN can achieve a lower error rate in some cases.

>> **1983:** A. Jozwik developed a fuzzy KNN classification method.

>> **1985:** James M. Keller, Michael R. Gray, and James A. Givens presented three methods for using the fuzzy KNN classification method.

>> **2000:** Sergio Bermejo and Joan Cabestany presented adaptive soft learning KNN classifiers.

Probably a great many other people have contributed to KNN, so it's hard to say that KNN as it appears today is the result of any one person's work. However, the idea for KNN didn't come out of the blue, nor was it some late-night inspiration. Some references say that KNN has much older sources (see http://37steps.com/4370/nn-rule-invention/ for details).

One of these inspirational sources is Occam's razor (http://math.ucr.edu/home/baez/physics/General/occam.html), which essentially says that the hypothesis with the fewest assumptions is probably the correct one. You can actually find this rule stated in so many ways that it boggles the mind, but the basic idea is always the same: Simple is better.

Even though Occam performed his work in the fourteenth century, some sources assert that Occam's work relied heavily on the still older work of Ibn al-Haytham (965 to 1040) (http://www.ibnalhaytham.com/). This scientist used a precursor of the modern scientific method to explain many things about how the eye acts as a light sensor, and he demonstrated that the brain actually sees the light. In short, KNN is one of the few algorithms that you really can't pin down as having been invented at any particular time. As with many good scientific methods, it has been in development for a long time.

Learning Lazily with K-Nearest Neighbors

This section talks about the basics of KNN: how and why they work. You begin by considering the basis of KNN and work through several examples in the sections that follow.

Understanding the basis of KNN

KNN isn't about building rules from data based on coefficients or probability. Rather, KNN works on the basis of similarities. When you have to predict something like a class, you may do best by finding the most similar observations to the one you want to classify or estimate. You can then derive the answer you need from the similar cases.

Observing how many observations are similar doesn't imply learning something, but rather measuring. Because KNN isn't learning anything, it's considered lazy, and you'll hear it referenced as a lazy learner or an instance-based learner. The idea is that similar premises usually provide similar results, and you don't want to forget to get such low-hanging fruit before trying to climb the tree!

The algorithm is fast during training because it only has to memorize data about the observations. It actually calculates more during predictions. When it encounters too many observations, the algorithm can become slow and memory consuming. You're best advised not to use it with big data, or predicting anything may take almost forever! Moreover, this simple and effective algorithm works better when you have distinct data groups without too many variables involved because the algorithm is also sensitive to the dimensionality curse.

The curse of dimensionality happens as the number of variables increases. Consider a situation in which you're measuring the distance between observations and, as the space becomes larger and larger, it becomes difficult to find real neighbors — a problem for KNN, which sometimes mistakes a far observation for a near one. Rendering the idea is just like playing chess on a multidimensional chessboard. When playing on the classic 2-D board, most pieces are near, and you can more easily spot opportunities and menaces for your pawns when you have 32 pieces and 64 positions. However, when you start playing on a 3-D board, such as those found in some sci-fi films, your 32 pieces can become lost in 512 possible positions. Now just imagine playing with a 12-D chessboard. You can easily misunderstand what is near and what is far, which is what happens with KNN.

TIP

You can still make KNN smart in detecting similarities between observations by removing redundant information and simplifying the data dimensionality using data-reduction techniques.

Predicting after observing neighbors

For an example showing how to use KNN, you can start with the following digits dataset, also used in the "Considering when classes are more" section of Book 3, Chapter 2, which relies on logistic regression to perform classification. KNN is particularly useful, just like Naïve Bayes, when you have to predict many classes, or in situations that require you to build too many models or rely on a complex model.

```
from sklearn.datasets import load_digits
from sklearn.decomposition import PCA
digits = load_digits()
train = range(0, 1700)
test = range(1700, len(digits.data))
pca = PCA(n_components = 25)
pca.fit(digits.data[train])
X = pca.transform(digits.data[train])
y = digits.target[train]
tX = pca.transform(digits.data[test])
ty = digits.target[test]
```

The KNN algorithm is quite sensitive to outliers. Moreover, you have to rescale your variables and remove some redundant information. In this example, you use Principle Component Analysis (PCA) (see https://towardsdatascience.com/a-one-stop-shop-for-principal-component-analysis-5582fb7e0a9c for a discussion of PCA when used alone) to perform the analysis.

REAL-WORLD USE OF PCA AND KNN

The techniques you see in this chapter also see use in the real world. For example, look at the article at https://www.ncbi.nlm.nih.gov/pubmed/19514813, which describes using PCA-based KNN to locate diseased tissue in the colon. The use of this technique in a real-world setting enables the medical community to diagnose problems earlier and with greater accuracy, saving lives in the process.

TIP

Rescaling is not necessary because the data represents pixels, which means that it's already scaled. You can avoid the problem with outliers by keeping the neighborhood small, that is, by not looking too far for similar examples.

TIP

Knowing the data type can save you a lot of time and many mistakes. For example, in this case, you know that the data represents pixel values. Doing Exploratory Data Analysis (EDA) (as described in the "Understanding variable transformations" section of Book 3, Chapter 1) is always the first step and can provide you with useful insights, but getting additional information about how the data was obtained and what the data represents is also a good practice and can be just as useful. To see this task in action, you reserve cases in tX and try a few cases that KNN won't look up when looking for neighbors:

```
from sklearn.neighbors import KNeighborsClassifier
kNN = KNeighborsClassifier(n_neighbors=5, p=2,
                           metric='euclidean')
kNN.fit(X, y)
```

The output shows the actual classifier configuration:

```
KNeighborsClassifier(algorithm='auto', leaf_size=30,
        metric='euclidean', metric_params=None,
        n_jobs=None, n_neighbors=5, p=2,
        weights='uniform')
```

KNN uses a distance measure to determine which observations to consider as possible neighbors for the target case. The discussion of the DistanceMetric class at https://scikit-learn.org/stable/modules/generated/sklearn.neighbors.DistanceMetric.html tells about the available options. You can easily change the predefined distance using the p parameter:

>> When p is 2, use the Euclidean distance, which is the distance between two points on a plane (a concept that you likely studied at school). In a K-means

application, each data point is a vector of features, so when comparing the distance of two points, you do the following:

1. Create a list containing the differences of the elements in the two vectors.

2. Square all the elements of the difference vector.

3. Calculate the square root of the summed elements.

In the end, the Euclidean distance is really just a big sum. When the variables making up the difference vector are significantly different in scale from each other, you end up with a distance dominated by the elements with the largest scale. Rescaling the variables is important so that they use a similar scale before applying the K-means algorithm. You can use a fixed range or a statistical normalization with zero mean and unit variance to achieve this goal.

» When p is 1, use the Manhattan distance metric, which is the absolute distance between observations. In a 2-D square, when you go from one corner to the opposite one, the Manhattan distance is the same as walking the perimeter, whereas Euclidean is like walking on the diagonal. Although the Manhattan distance isn't the shortest route, it's a more realistic measure than Euclidean distance, and it's less sensitive to noise and high dimensionality.

Usually, the Euclidean distance is the right measure, even though the KNeighborsClassifier default is the Minkowski distance (https://people.revoledu.com/kardi/tutorial/Similarity/MinkowskiDistance.html). Sometimes the Euclidean distance can give you worse results, especially when the analysis involves many correlated variables. The following code shows that the analysis seems fine using the Euclidean distance in this case:

```
print('Accuracy: %.3f' % kNN.score(tX,ty) )
print('Prediction: %s Actual: %s'
    % (kNN.predict(tX[-15:,:]),ty[-15:]))
```

The code returns the accuracy of 99 percent for this example and a sample of the predictions you can compare with the actual values in order to spot differences:

```
Accuracy: 0.990
Prediction: [2 2 5 7 9 5 4 8 1 4 9 0 8 9 8]
    Actual: [2 2 5 7 9 5 4 8 8 4 9 0 8 9 8]
```

TIP

Even though this example does well with the Euclidean distance, you may need to try other distance measures to get accurate results with your data. Verifying the results is always the best idea.

Choosing the k parameter wisely

A critical parameter that you have to define in KNN is k. As k increases, KNN considers more points for its predictions, and the decisions are less influenced by noisy instances that could exercise an undue influence. Your decisions are based on an average of more observations, and they become more solid. When the k value you use is too large, you start considering neighbors that are too far, sharing less and less with the case you have to predict.

It's an important trade-off. When the value of k is less, you consider a more homogeneous pool of neighbors but can more easily make an error by taking the few similar cases for granted. When the value of k is more, you consider more cases at a higher risk of observing neighbors that are too far or that are outliers. Getting back to the previous example with handwritten digit data, you can experiment with changing the k value, as shown in the following code:

```
for k in [1, 5, 10, 50, 100, 200]:
    kNN = KNeighborsClassifier(n_neighbors=k, p=2,
                                metric='euclidean')
    kNN.fit(X, y)
    print('for k = %3i accuracy is %.3f'
          % (k, kNN.score(tX, ty))
```

After running this code, you get an overview of what happens when k changes and determine the value of k that best fits the data:

```
for k =    1 accuracy is 0.979
for k =    5 accuracy is 0.990
for k =   10 accuracy is 0.969
for k =   50 accuracy is 0.959
for k =  100 accuracy is 0.959
for k =  200 accuracy is 0.907
```

Through experimentation, you find that setting n_neighbors (the parameter representing k) to 5 is the optimum choice, resulting in the highest accuracy. Using just the nearest neighbor (n_neighbors =1) isn't a bad choice, but setting the value above 5 instead brings decreasing results in the classification task.

TIP

As a rule of thumb, when your dataset doesn't have many observations, set k as a number near the squared number of available observations. However, no general rule exists, and trying different k values is always a good way to optimize your KNN performance. Always start from low values and work toward higher values.

Leveraging the Correct k Parameter

The k parameter is the one you can work on tuning to make a KNN algorithm perform well in prediction and regression. The following sections describe how to use the k parameter to tune the KNN algorithm.

Understanding the k parameter

The k value, an integer number, is the number of neighbors that the algorithm has to consider in order to figure out an answer. The smaller the k parameter, the more the algorithm will adapt to the data you are presenting, risking overfitting but nicely fitting complex separating boundaries between classes. The larger the k parameter, the more it abstracts from the ups and downs of real data, which derives nicely smoothed curves between classes in data but does so at the expense of accounting for irrelevant examples.

TIP

As a rule of thumb, first try the nearest integer of the square root of the number of examples available as a k parameter in KNN. For instance, if you have 1,000 examples, start with k = 31 (or k = 32 because the actual square root is 31.62277660168379) and then decrease the value in a grid search backed up by cross-validation.

Using irrelevant or unsuitable examples is a risk that a KNN algorithm takes as the number of examples it uses for its distance function increases. The previous illustration of the problem of data dimensions shows how to compute a well-ordered data space as a library in which you could look for similar books in the same bookshelf, bookcase, and section. However, things won't look so easy when the library has more than one floor. At that point, books upstairs and downstairs are not necessarily similar, therefore being near but on a different floor won't assure that the books are similar. Adding more dimensions weakens the role of useful ones, but that is just the beginning of your trouble.

Now imagine having more than the three dimensions in daily life (four if you consider time). The more dimensions, the more space you gain in your library. (As in geometry, you multiply dimensions to get an idea of the volume.) At a certain point, you will have so much space that your books will fit easily with space left over. For instance, you could have 20 binary variables, with each representing a dimension — but think of the dimensions as providing separation, as with a category. Books on space-based science fiction that include dolphins could appear on one bookshelf, in a particular bookcase, in a particular section, on a particular floor, at a particular time (and so on, until you come up with 20 levels of separation). You could have 2 raised to the 20th power combinations; that is, 1,048,576 possible different dimensions — places to put books. It's great to have a million book locations, but if you don't have a million books to fill them (so there is at least one book in each location), most of your library will be empty. So you obtain a book and then look for similar books to place in the same bookcase (those that fulfill all the requirements for all 20 dimensions). The chances of finding two books that are so alike that they meet the same precise values for 20 dimensions are slim, so you end up putting the next book in an empty location, but still, your library is relatively empty. Think about it: You start with *The Hitchhiker's Guide to the Galaxy* and end up having a book on gardening as its nearest neighbor. This is the curse of dimensionality. The more dimensions, the more likely you are to experience some false similarity, misunderstanding far for near.

Using the right-sized k parameters alleviates the problem because the more neighbors you have to find, the further KNN has to look — but you have other remedies. PCA can compress the space, making it denser and removing noise and irrelevant, redundant information. In addition, feature selection can do the trick, selecting only the features that can really help KNN find the right neighbors.

KNN is an algorithm that's sensitive to outliers. Neighbors on the boundaries of your data cloud in the data space could be outlying examples, causing your predictions to become erratic. You need to clean your data before using it. Running a K-means first can help you identify outliers gathered into groups of their own. (Outliers love to stay in separate groups; you can view them as the hermit types in your data.) Also, keeping your neighborhood large can help you minimize (but sometimes not avoid completely) the problem at the expense of a lower fit to the data (more bias than overfitting).

Experimenting with a flexible algorithm

The KNN algorithm has slightly different implementations in R and Python. In R, the algorithm is found in the library named class. The function is just for classification and uses only the Euclidean distance for locating neighbors. It does offer a convenient version with automatic cross-validation for discovering the best k value. There's also another R library, FNN (https://cran.r-project.org/web/packages/FNN/index.html), which contains one KNN variant for classification and another for regression problems. The peculiarity of the FFN functions is that they can deal with the complexity of distance computations using different algorithms, but the Euclidean distance is the only distance available. (See the R downloadable source for additional details.)

The Python experiment with KNN uses the Python class from Scikit-learn and demonstrates how such a simple algorithm is quite adept at learning shapes and nonlinear arrangements of examples in the data space. The block of code prepares a tricky dataset: In two dimensions, two classes are arranged in bull's-eye concentric circles, as shown in Figure 4-1.

```
import numpy as np
from sklearn.datasets import make_circles, make_blobs
strange_data  = make_circles(n_samples=500, shuffle=True,
                             noise=0.15, random_state=101,
                             factor=0.5)
center = make_blobs(n_samples=100, n_features=2,
                    centers=1, cluster_std=0.1,
                    center_box=(0, 0))
first_half    = np.row_stack((strange_data[0][:250,:],
                  center[0][:50,:]))
first_labels  = np.append(strange_data[1][:250],
                  np.array([0]*50))
second_half   = np.row_stack((strange_data[0][250:,:],
                  center[0][50:,:]))
second_labels = np.append(strange_data[1][250:],
                  np.array([0]*50))

%matplotlib inline
import matplotlib.pyplot as plt
plt.scatter(first_half[:,0], first_half[:,1], s=2**7,
    c=first_labels, edgecolors='white',
            alpha=0.85, cmap='winter')
plt.grid() # adds a grid
plt.show() # Showing the result
```

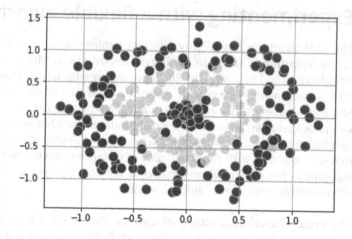

FIGURE 4-1:
The bull's-eye
dataset, a
nonlinear cloud
of points that is
difficult to learn.

After having built the dataset, you can test the experiment by setting the classification algorithm to learn the patterns in data after fixing a neighborhood of 3 and
setting the weights to be uniform (Scikit-learn allows you to weight less distant

observations when it's time to average them or pick the most frequent observations), and the Euclidean distance as metric. Scikit-learn algorithms, in fact, allow you to both regress and classify using different metrics, such as Euclidean, Manhattan, or Chebyshev, as shown in this Python code:

```
from sklearn.neighbors import KNeighborsClassifier
from sklearn.metrics import accuracy_score

for metric in ['euclidean', 'manhattan', 'chebyshev']:
    kNN = KNeighborsClassifier(n_neighbors=3,
                               weights='uniform',
                               algorithm='auto',
                               metric=metric)
    kNN.fit(first_half,first_labels)
    score = accuracy_score(y_true=second_labels,
                           y_pred=kNN.predict(second_half))
    print ("%(metric)s learning accuracy\
score:%(value)0.3f" %
           {'metric':metric, 'value':score})
```

When you run this example, you see the outputs from each of the metrics, as shown here:

```
euclidean learning accuracy    score:0.930
manhattan learning accuracy    score:0.940
chebyshev learning accuracy    score:0.930
```

Implementing KNN Regression

Book 3, Chapter 1 introduces you to the grade prediction regression. The purpose of the regression is to determine what grade you receive after a certain number of hours of study. The "Advancing to multiple linear regression" section of that chapter even considers the effects of interruptions on your grade. The KNN version of that example uses the same data, but the number of hours (x in the original example) must appear as a 2-D array instead of a simple range, as shown here:

```
hours = np.array(range(0,9)).reshape(-1, 1)
print(hours)
answers = (25, 33, 41, 53, 59, 70, 78, 86, 98)
interrupt = (0, -1, -3, -4, -5, -7, -8, -9, -11)
```

The variables use names that are more readable in this case so that you can follow the code with greater ease. To create a model, you must combine the two features: answers and interrupt, into a single variable, features, using this code:

```
features = list(zip(answers, interrupt))
print(features)
```

The output is a list of tuples that match the number of answers that are correct to the effect of interruptions on those correct answers, like this:

```
[(25, 0), (33, -1), (41, -3), (53, -4), (59, -5),
 (70, -7), (78, -8), (86, -9), (98, -11)]
```

At this point, the data is ready to use. The process that the example uses is to fit the model, make a prediction, and then use the prediction to calculate a result. When working with KNN, what you actually receive as a prediction is the number of correct answers and the effect of the interruptions as separate answers. You must then calculate the actual result as a separate step. Here is the code needed to perform the required tasks:

```
from sklearn.neighbors import KNeighborsRegressor

gradeModel = KNeighborsRegressor(n_neighbors=2)
gradeModel.fit(hours, features)

prediction = gradeModel.predict([[6]])
print(prediction)

correct = prediction[0][0] + prediction[0][1]
print('You will answer {0} questions correctly.'.format(
    correct))
```

The outputs show the result of the regression and the calculated result:

```
[[74.  -7.5]]
You will answer 66.5 questions correctly.
```

In comparing the example in this chapter with the one found in Book 3, Chapter 1, you should note that the answer in that chapter is 78.4 for the number of correct answers, while this example predicts 74 correct answers. There is a difference between analysis methods, so you always need to consider which one provides you with the best results. The following code replicates the plot shown in Book 3, Chapter 1, Figure 1-2:

```
plt.scatter(hours, answers)
plt.scatter(hours, interrupt)
plt.legend(['Grades', 'Interruptions'])

studyData_pred = gradeModel.predict(hours)
plt.plot(hours, studyData_pred)
plt.show()
```

The output shown in Figure 4-2 tells you that the KNN approach models the data points differently than multiple linear regression does.

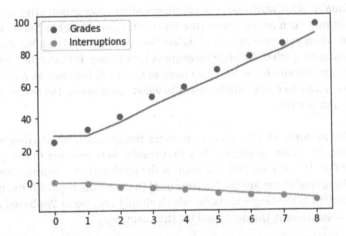

FIGURE 4-2:
The KNN approach models the data differently than multiple linear regression.

Implementing KNN Classification

No matter if the problem is to guess a number or a class, the idea behind the learning strategy of the K-Nearest Neighbors (KNN) algorithm is always the same. The algorithm finds the most similar observations to the one you have to predict and from which you derive a good intuition of the possible answer by averaging the neighboring values, or by picking the most frequent answer class among them.

The learning strategy in a KNN is more like memorization. It's just like remembering what the answer should be when the question has certain characteristics (based on circumstances or past examples) rather than really knowing the answer, because you understand the question by means of specific classification rules. In a sense, KNN is often defined as a lazy algorithm because no real learning is done at the training time — just data recording.

Being a lazy algorithm implies that KNN is quite fast at training but very slow at predicting. (Most of the searching activities and calculations on the neighbors is done at that time.) It also implies that the algorithm is quite memory intensive because you have to store your dataset in memory (which means that the number of possible applications is limited when dealing with big data). Ideally, KNN can make the difference when you're working on classification and you have many labels to deal with (for instance, when a software agent posts a tag on a social network or when proposing a product-selling recommendation). KNN can easily deal with hundreds of labels, whereas other learning algorithms have to specify a different model for each label.

Usually, KNN works out the neighbors of an observation after using a measure of distance such as Euclidean (the most common choice) or Manhattan (works better when you have many redundant features in your data). No absolute rules exist concerning what distance measure is best to use. It really depends on the implementation you have. You also have to test each distance as a distinct hypothesis and verify by cross-validation as to which measure works better with the problem you're solving.

The example in this section answers the question of whether someone should drive based on conditions. The first condition is pertains to the road: Dry, Damp, or Flooded. The second condition is the environment: Sunny, Cloudy, or Raining. These conditions are the features used to create the input for the model. The third element is the target variable, which simply says No or Yes based on the two conditions. Here is the data used for the example:

```
road = ['Dry', 'Dry', 'Dry', 'Damp', 'Damp', 'Damp',
        'Flooded', 'Flooded', 'Flooded']
weather = ['Sunny', 'Cloudy', 'Raining', 'Sunny',
           'Cloudy', 'Raining', 'Sunny', 'Cloudy',
           'Raining']
drive = ['Yes', 'Yes', 'Yes', 'Yes', 'Maybe', 'No', 'No',
         'No', 'No']
```

Obviously, the computer would have difficulty using the labels provided, so you need to encode them in some way. For example, you could encode Damp as 0, Dry as 1, and Flooded as 2. Fortunately, Scikit-learn performs this task for you, as shown here:

```
from sklearn import preprocessing
encoder = preprocessing.LabelEncoder()

roadEnc = encoder.fit_transform(road)
print(roadEnc)
```

```
weatherEnc = encoder.fit_transform(weather)
print(weatherEnc)
driveEnc = encoder.fit_transform(drive)
print(driveEnc)
```

The output shows that the encoder automatically encodes the data in alphabetical order so that even though Sunny comes first in the weather list, it appears as a 2 in the encoding:

```
[1 1 1 0 0 0 2 2 2]
[2 0 1 2 0 1 2 0 1]
[1 1 1 1 1 0 0 0 0]
```

Before you go further, you must combine the features into a single list, like this:

```
features = list(zip(roadEnc, weatherEnc))
print(features)
```

You end up with a series of tuples that match every road condition with a weather condition, like this:

```
[(1, 2), (1, 0), (1, 1), (0, 2), (0, 0), (0, 1), (2, 2),
 (2, 0), (2, 1)]
```

At this point, you can fit the model, ask a question, and get a result. The following code shows how the model performs this task for damp and cloudy conditions:

```
answers = ['Maybe', 'No', 'Yes']

driveModel = KNeighborsClassifier(n_neighbors=3,
                                  metric='manhattan')
driveModel.fit(features, driveEnc)

prediction = driveModel.predict([[0, 0]])
print('Should I drive? {0}'.format(
    answers[prediction[0]]))
```

The output shows that the model is undecided in this particular case:

```
Should I drive? Maybe
```

4

Performing Advanced Data Manipulation

Contents at a Glance

IN THIS CHAPTER

» **Considering decision trees**

» **Performing predictions**

» **Using gradient descent**

» **Working with multiple predictors**

Chapter **1**

Leveraging Ensembles of Learners

After discovering so many complex and powerful algorithms, you might be surprised to discover that a summation of simpler machine learning algorithms can often outperform the most sophisticated solutions. Such is the power of *ensembles*, which are groups of models made to work together to produce better predictions. The amazing thing about ensembles is that they are made up of groups of singularly nonperforming algorithms.

Ensembles don't work much differently from the collective intelligence of crowds, through which a set of wrong answers, if averaged, provides the right answer. Sir Francis Galton, the British, Victorian-era statistician known for having formulated the idea of correlation, narrated the anecdote of a crowd in a county fair that could guess correctly the weight of an ox after all the people's previous answers were averaged. You can find similar examples everywhere and easily re-create the experiment by asking friends to guess the number of sweets in a jar and averaging their answers. The more friends who participate in the game, the more precise the averaged answer.

Luck isn't what's behind the result; it's simply the *law of large numbers* in action (see more at https://www.britannica.com/science/law-of-large-numbers).

Even though an individual has a slim chance of getting the right answer, the guess is better than a random value. By accumulating guesses, the wrong answers tend to distribute themselves around the right one. Opposite wrong answers cancel each other when averaging, leaving the pivotal value around which all answers are distributed, which is the right answer. You can employ such an incredible fact in many practical ways (consensus forecasts in economics and political sciences are examples) and in machine learning.

REMEMBER

You don't have to type the source code for this chapter manually. In fact, using the downloadable source is a lot easier. The source code for this chapter appears in the DSPD_0401_Random_Forests.ipynb source code file for Python and DSPD_R_0401_Random_Forests.ipynb source code file for R. See the Introduction for details on how to find these source files.

Leveraging Decision Trees

Ensembles are based on a recent idea (formulated around 1990), but they leverage older tools, such as decision trees, which have been part of machine learning since 1950. Texts such as *Machine Learning For Dummies,* by John Paul Mueller and Luca Massaron (Wiley), cover decision trees as simple learners. You can also find an overview of them at https://towardsdatascience.com/decision-trees-in-machine-learning-641b9c4e8052. Decision trees at first looked quite promising and appealing to practitioners because of their ease of use and understanding. After all, a decision tree can easily do the following:

>> Handle mixed types of target variables and predictors, with very little or no feature preprocessing (missing values are handled almost automatically)

>> Ignore redundant variables and select only the relevant features

>> Work out-of-the box, with no complex hyperparameters to fix and tune

>> Visualize the prediction process as a set of recursive rules arranged in a tree with branches and leaves, thus offering ease of interpretation

Given the range of positive characteristics, you may wonder why practitioners slowly started distrusting decision trees after a few years. The main reason is that the resulting models often have high variance in the estimates.

To grasp the critical problem of decision trees better, you can consider the problem visually. Think of the tricky situation of the bull's-eye problem that requires a machine learning algorithm to approximate nonlinear functions (as neural networks do) or to transform the feature space (as when using a linear model with polynomial expansion or kernel functions in support vector machines). Figure 1-1 shows the squared decision boundary of a single decision tree (on the left) as compared to an ensemble of decision trees (on the right).

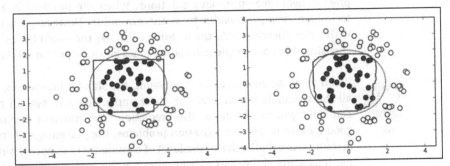

FIGURE 1-1:
Comparing a single decision tree output to an ensemble of decision trees.

Decision trees partition the feature space into boxes and then use the boxes for classification or regression purposes. When the decision boundary that separates classes in a bull's-eye problem is an ellipse, decision trees can approximate it by using a certain number of boxes.

The visual example seems to make sense and might give you confidence when you see the examples placed far from the decision boundary. However, in proximity of the boundary, things are quite different from how they appear. The decision boundary of the decision tree is very imprecise, and its shape is extremely rough and squared. The issue is visible on bidimensional problems. It decisively worsens both as feature dimensions increase and when in the presence of noisy observations (observations that are somehow randomly scattered around the feature space). You can improve decision trees using some interesting heuristics that stabilize results from trees:

>> Keep only the correctly predicted cases to retrain the algorithm.

>> Build separate trees for misclassified examples.

>> Simplify trees by pruning the less decisive rules.

Apart from these heuristics, the best trick is to build multiple trees using different samples and then compare and average their results. The example in Figure 1-1, shown previously, indicates that the benefit is immediately visible. As you build more trees, the decision boundary gets smoother, slowly resembling the hypothetical target shape.

Growing a forest of trees

Improving a decision tree by replicating it many times and averaging results to get a more general solution sounded like such a good idea that it spread, and practitioners created various solutions. When the problem is a regression, the technique averages results from the ensemble. However, when the trees deal with a classification task, the technique can use the ensemble as a voting system, choosing the most frequent response class as an output for all its replications.

TIP

When using an ensemble for regression, the standard deviation, calculated from all the ensemble's estimates for an example, can give you an estimate of how confident you can be about the prediction. The standard deviation shows how good a mean is. For classification problems, the percentage of trees predicting a certain class is indicative of the level of confidence in the prediction, but you can't use it as a probability estimate because it's the outcome of a voting system.

Deciding on how to compute the solution of an ensemble happened quickly; finding the best way to replicate the trees in an ensemble required more research and reflection. The first solution is *pasting*, that is, sampling a portion of your training set. Initially proposed by Leo Breiman, pasting reduces the number of training examples, which can become a problem for learning from complex data. It shows its usefulness by reducing the learning sample noise (sampling fewer examples reduces the number of outliers and anomalous cases). After pasting, Professor Breiman also tested the effects of bootstrap sampling (sampling with replacement), which not only leaves out some noise (when you bootstrap, on average you leave out 37 percent of your initial example set) but also, thanks to sampling repetition, creates more variation in the ensembles, improving the results. This technique is called *bagging* (also known as *bootstrap aggregation*).

REMEMBER

Bootstrapping is one of the validation alternatives. It's a method long used to estimate the sampling distribution of statistics, which are presumed not to follow a previously assumed distribution. Bootstrapping works by building a number (the more the better) of samples of size n (the original in-sample size) drawn with repetition. To *draw with repetition* means that the process could draw an example multiple times to use it as part of the bootstrapping resampling. Bootstrapping has the advantage of offering a simple and effective way to estimate the true error measure. In fact, bootstrapped error measurements usually have much less variance than cross-validation ones. On the other hand, validation becomes more complicated because of the sampling with replacement, so your validation sample comes from the out-of-bootstrap examples. Moreover, using some training samples repeatedly can lead to a certain bias in the models built with bootstrapping.

Breiman noticed that results of an ensemble of trees improved when the trees differ significantly from each other (statistically, they're *uncorrelated*), which leads to the last technique transformation: sampling from the training features. This technique allows for the creation of mostly uncorrelated ensembles of trees. The approach performs predictions better than bagging. The transformation tweak samples both features and examples. Breiman, in collaboration with Adele Cutler, named the new ensemble Random Forests (RF).

REMEMBER

Random Forests is a trademark of Leo Breiman and Adele Cutler (see `https://www.stat.berkeley.edu/~breiman/RandomForests/`). For this reason, open source implementations often have different names, such as randomForest in R (see `https://www.rdocumentation.org/packages/randomForest/versions/4.6-14/topics/randomForest`) or RandomForestClassifier in Python's Scikit-learn (see `https://scikit-learn.org/stable/modules/generated/sklearn.ensemble.RandomForestClassifier.html`).

RF is a classification (naturally multiclass) and regression algorithm that uses a large number of decision tree models built on different sets of bootstrapped examples and subsampled features. Its creator strove to make the algorithm easy to use (little preprocessing and few hyperparameters to try) and understandable (the decision tree basis) that can democratize the access of machine learning to nonexperts. In other words, because of its simplicity and immediate usage, RF can allow anyone to apply machine learning successfully. The algorithm works through a few repeated steps:

1. Bootstrap the training set multiple times. The algorithm obtains a new set to use to build a single tree in the ensemble during each bootstrap.

2. Randomly pick a partial feature selection in the training set to use for finding the best split variable every time you split the sample in a tree.

3. Create a complete tree using the bootstrapped examples. Evaluate new subsampled features at each split. Don't limit the full tree expansion to allow the algorithm to work better.

4. Compute the performance of each tree using examples you didn't choose in the bootstrap phase (out-of-bag estimates, or OOB). OOB examples provide performance metrics without cross-validation or using a test set (equivalent to out-of-sample).

5. Produce feature importance statistics and compute how examples associate in the tree's terminal nodes.

6. Compute an average or a vote on new examples when you complete all the trees in the ensemble. Declare for each of them the average estimate or the winning class as a prediction.

All these steps reduce both the bias and the variance of the final solution because the solution limits the bias. The solution builds each tree to its maximum possible extension, thus allowing a fine fitting of even complex target functions, which

Leveraging Ensembles of Learners

means that each tree is different from the others. It's not just a matter of building on different bootstrapped example sets: Each split taken by a tree is strongly randomized, meaning that the solution considers only a random feature selection. Consequently, even if an important feature dominates the others in terms of predictive power, the times a tree doesn't contain the selection allows the tree to find different ways of developing its branches and terminal leaves.

The main difference with bagging is this opportunity to limit the number of features to consider when splitting the tree branches. If the number of selected features is small, the complete tree will differ from others, thus adding uncorrelated trees to the ensemble. On the other hand, if the selection is small, the bias increases because the fitting power of the tree is limited. As always, determining the right number of features to consider for splitting requires that you use cross-validation or OOB estimate results.

No problem arises in growing a high number of trees in the ensemble. You do need to consider the cost of the computational effort because completing a large ensemble takes a long time. A simple demonstration conveys how an RF algorithm can solve a simple problem using a growing number of trees. Python and R offer good implementations of the algorithm:

>> The Python implementation is easier to parallelize.

>> The R implementation has more parameters.

Seeing Random Forests in action

Because the test is computationally expensive, the example starts with the Python implementation. This example uses the digits dataset that you use in the previous chapter when challenging a support vector classifier:

```
import numpy as np
from sklearn import datasets
from sklearn.model_selection import validation_curve
from sklearn.ensemble import RandomForestClassifier

digits = datasets.load_digits()
X,y = digits.data, digits.target
series = [10, 25, 50, 100, 150, 200, 250, 300]
RF = RandomForestClassifier(random_state=101)
train_scores, test_scores = validation_curve(RF,
        X, y, 'n_estimators', param_range=series,
            cv=10, scoring='accuracy',n_jobs=-1)
```

The example begins by importing functions and classes from Scikit-learn: numpy, the datasets module, the validation_curve function, and RandomForest Classifier. The last item is Scikit-learn's implementation of RF for classification problems. The validation_curve function is particularly useful for the tests because it returns the cross-validated results of multiple tests performed on ensembles made of differing numbers of trees (similar to learning curves).

TIP

The example will build almost 11,000 decision trees. To make the example run faster, the code sets the n_jobs parameter to –1, allowing the algorithm to use all available CPU resources. This setting may not work on some computer configurations, which means setting n_jobs to 1. Everything will work, but the process takes longer.

After completing the computations, the code outputs a plot that reveals how the RF algorithm converges to a good accuracy after building a few trees, as shown in Figure 1-2. It also shows that adding more trees isn't detrimental to the results, although you may see some oscillations in accuracy because of estimate variances that even the ensemble can't control fully.

```
import matplotlib.pyplot as plt
%matplotlib inline
plt.figure()
plt.plot(series, np.mean(test_scores,axis=1), '-o')
plt.xlabel('number of trees')
plt.ylabel('accuracy')
plt.grid()
plt.show()
```

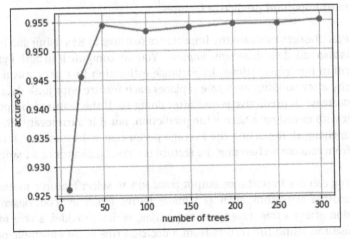

FIGURE 1-2:
Seeing the
accuracy of
ensembles of
different sizes.

Understanding the importance measures

Random Forests algorithms have these benefits:

>> They fit complex target functions, but have little risk in overfitting.

>> They select the features they need automatically (although the random subsampling of features in branch splitting influences the process).

>> They are easy to tune up because they have few hyperparameters, and the most important one you should care is often just the number of subsampled features.

>> They offer OOB error estimation, saving you from setting up verification by cross-validation or test set.

Note that each tree in the ensemble is independent from the others (after all, they should be uncorrelated), which means that you can build each tree in parallel to the others. Given that all modern computers have multiprocessor and multithread functionality, they can perform computations of many trees at the same time, which is a real advantage of RF over other machine learning algorithms.

An RF ensemble can also provide additional output that could be helpful when learning from data. For example, it can tell you which features are more important than others. You can build trees by optimizing a purity measure (entropy or gini index) so that each split chooses the feature that improves the measure the most. When the tree is complete, you check which features the algorithm uses at each split and sum the improvement when the algorithm uses a feature more than once. When working with an ensemble of trees, simply average the improvements that each feature provides in all the trees. The result shows you the ranking of the most important predictive features.

Practitioners evaluate the importance features in RFs using *gini importance*, which is also called *mean decrease impurity*. You can compute it in both Python and R algorithm implementations. Importance estimation that uses mean decrease impurity after building each tree replaces each feature with junk data and records the decrease in predictive power after doing so. If the feature is important, crowding it with casual data harms the prediction, but if it's irrelevant, the predictions are unchanged. Reporting the average performance decrease in all trees that results from randomly changing the feature is a good indicator of a feature's importance.

TIP

You can use importance output from RFs to select features to use in the RF or in another algorithm, such as a linear regression. The Scikit-learn algorithm version offers a *tree-based feature selection*, which provides a way to select relevant features using the results from a decision tree or an ensemble of decision trees. You can use this kind of feature selection by employing the `SelectFromModel` function found in the `feature_selection` module (see `https://scikit-learn.org/stable/modules/generated/sklearn.feature_selection.SelectFromModel.html`).

Configuring your system for importance measures with Python

To make the example code work for checking importance measures in Python, you need to install the rfpimp (`https://pypi.org/project/rfpimp/`) package. The article at `https://explained.ai/rf-importance/index.html` tells why this particular package is so important. To install the package, you begin by opening an Anaconda Prompt (don't use a standard command prompt or terminal window because neither has the required environmental setup). At the prompt, you type

```
conda install -c conda-forge rfpimp
```

and press Enter. The command runs for a while, seemingly doing nothing. However, at some point you see a description of what conda will do, as shown in Figure 1-3. Simply type **y** and press Enter to install the package.

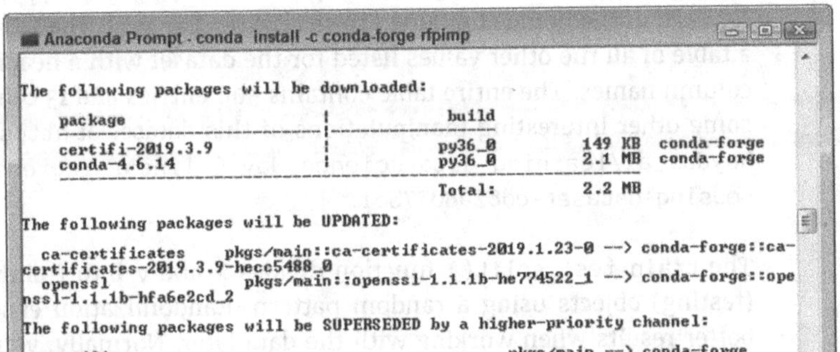

FIGURE 1-3:
Installing the rfpimp package in Python.

Seeing importance measures in action

To provide an interpretation of importance measures derived from RFs, this example relies on the Boston Housing dataset (`https://www.cs.toronto.edu/~delve/data/boston/bostonDetail.html`), which is easily accessible in both of the languages used for this book. The goal of this particular example is to determine which dataset features affect the price of a home the most.

The approach used for each of the languages is similar, as is the output. You can find the R implementation of this code in the downloadable source files mentioned at the beginning of the chapter. Here is the beginning Python code used for this example:

```python
import pandas as pd
from sklearn.datasets import load_boston
from sklearn.model_selection import train_test_split

boston = load_boston()

y = boston.target
X = pd.DataFrame(boston.data, columns =
                    boston.feature_names)
X_train, X_valid, y_train, y_valid = train_test_split(
    X, y, test_size = 0.8, random_state = 123)
```

The code begins by obtaining a copy of the Boston Housing dataset. Your language will determine precisely how the code performs this task, but the data is the same in all cases.

The task that this code is performing uses a `numpy.ndarray`, y, to hold the prices for each of the homes (obtained from `boston.target`). The X DataFrame contains a table of all the other values listed for the dataset with a heading containing the column names. The entire table contains 506 entries and 13 columns. You can see some other interesting manipulations of this dataset at https://medium.com/@haydar_ai/learning-data-science-day-9-linear-regression-on-boston-housing-dataset-cd62a80775ef.

The `train_test_split()` function divides X and y into training and validation (testing) objects using a random pattern. Randomization ensures that you get better results when working with the data later. Normally, you'd make the randomization completely random, but this example uses a random seed value of 123 so that the results are repeatable. The splitting process uses 20 percent of the original dataset for training and 80 percent for validation, so X_train contains 101 entries and X_valid contains 405. With the four datasets ready to go, it's time to perform the regression using the following code:

```python
from sklearn.ensemble import RandomForestRegressor

rf = RandomForestRegressor(n_estimators = 100,
                           n_jobs = -1,
                           oob_score = True,
```

```
                          bootstrap = True,
                          random_state = 123)
rf.fit(X_train, y_train)

print('R^2 Training Score: ', rf.score(X_train, y_train))
print('OOB Score: ', rf.oob_score_)
print('R^2 Validation Score: ', rf.score(X_valid,
                                          y_valid))
```

The regression begins by creating an RF estimator that uses 100 trees (n_estimators) to do its work. You want this task to complete as quickly as possible, so setting n_jobs to –1 tells the estimator to use all available CPUs. The estimator will rely on boostrap samples rather than use the entire dataset to begin building the trees. It will also output an OOB score. The results of fitting the model using rf.fit() follow.

```
R^2 Training Score:  0.9620949187819494
OOB Score:  0.7093667260280889
R^2 Validation Score:  0.8239084223508335
```

The training score tells you how well the model worked with the training data — the data that the model has already seen. The validation score tells you how the model performs with data that it hasn't seen before. To get great results, the two numbers should be quite near 1.0 and similar as well. The OOB score tends to be lower than the validation score because it relies on data that is more fully randomized. The discussion at https://forums.fast.ai/t/oob-score-vs-validation-score/7859/2 tells you more about the differences.

Now that you have a model to use, you can calculate the importance measures. The following code shows one method for performing this task:

```
from sklearn.metrics import r2_score
from rfpimp import permutation_importances

def r2(rf, X_train, y_train):
    return r2_score(y_train, rf.predict(X_train))

perm_imp = permutation_importances(
    rf, X_train, y_train, r2)
print(perm_imp)
```

The code begins by creating the r2 function. This function accepts the RF estimator, the X training, and the y training data as input. The output is a score that specifies the coefficient of determination, which is a fancy way of saying that it tells you how well the model can predict an outcome — that is, whether the data points stay close to the regression line or stray far away from it. Obviously, the model is more accurate when the data points stay close to the line.

The actual calculation of which measure is most important takes place with the permutation_importances() function. The rfpimp package actually contains a number of importance functions, but the discussion at https://explained.ai/rf-importance/index.html tells you that permutation importance (which avoids model parameter interpretation issues) provides the best result when working with Python. On the other hand, when working with R, you need to use the basic importance measure instead. After performing the calculation, you get the importance measures shown here:

```
          Importance
Feature
RM          0.788692
LSTAT       0.472561
DIS         0.059678
CRIM        0.054513
NOX         0.018895
AGE         0.015089
TAX         0.011688
B           0.009622
PTRATIO     0.008837
RAD         0.007896
INDUS       0.002389
ZN          0.000766
CHAS        0.000213
```

In looking at the data, you see that the number of rooms is most important in determining price, while the fact that the home borders the Charles River matters least. It makes sense that the number of rooms would have a heavy emphasis on the price, as would the economic status of the surrounding neighborhood.

Working with Almost Random Guesses

Thanks to bootstrapping, bagging produces variance reduction by inducing some variations in otherwise similar predictors. Bagging is most effective when the models created are different from each other and, though it can work with different kinds of models, it mostly performs with decision trees. Bagging and its evolution, the RFs, aren't the only ways to leverage an ensemble. The following sections discuss another technique that relies on a process of guessing based on using the output of multiple weak learners to discover the answer to a part of the problem, and then put the pieces together to create the whole answer.

Understanding the premise

Instead of striving for ensemble elements' independence, a totally contrarian strategy is to create interrelated ensembles of simple machine learning algorithms to solve complex target functions. This approach is called *boosting*, which works by building models sequentially and training each model using information from the previous one. Numerous boosting algorithms exist, but these seem to be the most popular:

>> AdaBoost

>> GBM

>> XGBoost

Contrary to bagging, which prefers to work with fully grown trees, boosting uses *biased* models, which are models that can predict simple target functions well. Simpler models include decision trees with a single split branch (called stumps), linear models, perceptrons, and Naïve Bayes algorithms. These models may not perform well when the target function to guess is complex (they're weak learners), but they can be trained fast and perform at least slightly better than a random lucky guess (which means that they can model a part of the target function).

Each of the algorithms in the ensemble guesses a part of the function well, so when summed together, they can guess the entire function. It's a situation not too different from the story of the blind men and the elephant (https://americanliterature.com/author/james-baldwin/short-story/the-blind-men-and-the-elephant).

In the story, a group of blind men needs to discover the shape of an elephant, but each man can feel only a part of the whole animal. One man touches the tusk, one the ears, one the proboscides, one the body, and one the tail, which are different parts of the entire elephant. Only when they put what each one learned separately together can they figure out the elephant's shape. The information for the target function to guess is transmitted from one model to the other by modifying the original dataset so that the ensemble can concentrate on the parts of the dataset that have yet to be learned.

Bagging predictors with AdaBoost

The first boosting algorithm formulated in 1995 is AdaBoost (short for Adaptive Boosting) by Yoav Freund and Robert Schapire. Most people use this particular algorithm for classification problems. It seeks to turn a series of poor learners into a single strong one. The math behind this algorithm can be a bit daunting, but you can read about it at https://towardsdatascience.com/boosting-algorithm-adaboost-b6737a9ee60c. Here's a quick summary of what the algorithm actually does for you:

1. Transform each of the features in a dataset into predictions. Each prediction is actually a summary of the output of a number of weak learning models. You perform the transformation using this process:

    a. Fit the classifiers to the dataset and choose the one with the lowest classification error.

    b. Calculate the weight for each classifier in the ensemble. When a classifier's output is better than a random guess, provide it with a positive value. Likewise, when a classifier's output is worse than a random guess, provide it with a negative value. Consequently, each classifier adds to the output, even if it isn't a good guesser.

2. Output the results as a vector of signs that show which class is most likely for a particular prediction. AdaBoost is a binary prediction algorithm, so you would see results that say a particular dataset entry is part of a particular class or not part of a particular class.

Both of the languages found in this book can perform analysis using AdaBoost, as described at the following:

>> **Python:** https://scikit-learn.org/stable/modules/ensemble.html#adaboost

>> **R:** https://cran.r-project.org/web/packages/adabag/index.html

Getting the details about AdaBoost weighting

Note that the algorithm multiplies each model by an alpha value, which differs for each model. This is the weight of the model in the ensemble, and alpha is devised in a smart way because its value is related to the capacity of the model to produce the fewest prediction errors possible.

Alpha gets a larger value as the error of the model gets smaller. The algorithm multiplies models with fewer errors by larger alpha values, thus such models play a more important role in the summation at the core of the AdaBoost algorithm. Models that produce more prediction errors are weighted less.

The role of the coefficient alpha doesn't end with model weighting. Errors output by a model in the ensemble don't simply dictate the importance of the model in the ensemble itself but also modify the relevance of the training examples used for learning. AdaBoost learns the data structure by using a simple algorithm a little at a time; the only way to focus the ensemble on different parts of the data is to assign weights. Assigning weights tells the algorithm to count an example according to its weight; therefore, a single example can count the same as two, three, or even more examples. You can also make an example disappear from the learning process by making it count less and less. When considering weights, reducing the cost function of the learning function becomes easier by working on the examples that weigh more (more weight = more cost function reduction). Using weights effectively guides the learning process.

Initially, the examples have the same contribution in the construction of the model. The optimization happens as usual. After creating the first model and estimating a total error, the algorithm checks each example to determine whether the prediction is correct. If correctly predicted, nothing happens; each example's weight remains the same as before. If misclassfied, each example has its weight increased and in the next iteration, examples with larger weight influence the model, placing a greater emphasis on finding a solution for the larger example.

At each iteration, the AdaBoost algorithm is guided by weights to work on the part of data that's less predictable. In fact, you don't need to work on data that the algorithm can predict well. Weighting is a smart solution for conditioning learning, and gradient boosting machines refine and improve the process. Notice that the strategy here is different from RF. In RF, the goal is to create independent predictions; here, the predictors are chained together because earlier predictors determine how later predictors work. Because boosting algorithms rely on a chain of calculations, you can't easily parallelize the computations, so they're slower.

REMEMBER

Consider the kinds of learning algorithms that work well with AdaBoost. Usually they are weak learners, which means that they don't have much predictive power. Because AdaBoost approximates complex functions using an ensemble of its parts, using machine learning algorithms that train quickly and have a certain bias makes sense, so the parts are simple. Performing the task using weak learners with AdaBoost is like drawing a circle using a series of lines (where each weak learner is a line): Even though the line is straight, all you have to do is draw a polygon with as many sides as possible to approximate the circle. Commonly, decision stumps are the favored weak learner for an AdaBoost ensemble, but you can also successfully use linear models or Naïve Bayes algorithms.

Seeing AdaBoost in action

The following example leverages the bagging function provided by Scikit-learn to determine whether decision trees, perceptron, or the K-Nearest Neighbors (KNN) algorithm is best for handwritten digits recognition. You previously saw this dataset used for the example in the "Seeing Random Forests in action" section, earlier in this chapter.

```
import numpy as np
from sklearn.ensemble import AdaBoostClassifier
from sklearn.tree import DecisionTreeClassifier
from sklearn.linear_model import Perceptron
from sklearn.naive_bayes import BernoulliNB
from sklearn.model_selection import cross_val_score
from sklearn import datasets

digits = datasets.load_digits()
X,y = digits.data, digits.target
```

The first step is to obtain the required data. This means loading the data into memory and then extracting the necessary information. The `data` attribute contains the information that the algorithm needs to learn, and the `target` attribute contains the label associated with each of the data elements. Now that the data is loaded, you can perform analysis on it, as shown here:

```
DT = cross_val_score(AdaBoostClassifier(
        DecisionTreeClassifier(),
        random_state=101) ,X, y,
        scoring='accuracy',cv=10)
P = cross_val_score(AdaBoostClassifier(
        Perceptron(max_iter=5), random_state=101,
        algorithm='SAMME') ,X, y,
        scoring='accuracy',cv=10)
NB = cross_val_score(AdaBoostClassifier(
        BernoulliNB(), random_state=101)
        ,X,y,scoring='accuracy',cv=10)

print ("Decision trees: %0.3f\nPerceptron: %0.3f\n"
        "Naive Bayes: %0.3f" %
        (np.mean(DT),np.mean(P), np.mean(NB)))
```

In this case, you see three different weak classifiers: decision tree, perceptron, and multivariate Bernoulli Naïve Bayes (BernoulliNB) combined into an ensemble. When working with the Perceptron() classifier, you need to set max_iter to define how long you want the classifier to keep working. Each of these classifiers has a different level of success in classifying the digits, as shown here:

```
Decision trees: 0.826
Perceptron: 0.909
Naive Bayes: 0.802
```

TIP

You can improve the performance of AdaBoost by increasing the number of elements in the ensemble until the cross-validation doesn't report worsening results. The parameter you can increase is n_estimators, and it's currently set to 50. The weaker your predictor is, the larger your ensemble should be in order to perform the prediction well.

Meeting Again with Gradient Descent

You don't have to rely strictly on erroneous output to determine which algorithm works best, as with AdaBoost. The gradient boosting machines (GBM) algorithm uses the gradient descent optimization to determine the right weights for learning in the ensemble. The resulting performance is impressive, making GBM one of the most powerful predictive tools that you can learn to use in machine learning. The following sections help you work with GBM.

Understanding the GBM difference

As in AdaBoost, you start with a formulation that defines how to obtain a correct result using a boosting strategy. The GBM formulation requires that the algorithm make a weighted sum of multiple models. In fact, what changes the most is not the principle of how boosting works but rather the optimization process for getting the weight and power of the summed functions, which weak learners can't determine.

Up to this point, things aren't all that different from AdaBoost. However, note that the algorithm weights each model by a constant factor, v, the shrinkage factor. This is where you start noticing the first difference between AdaBoost and GBM. The fact is that v is just like alpha. However, here it's fixed and forces the

Leveraging Ensembles of Learners

algorithm to learn in any case, no matter the performance of the previously added learning function. Considering this weighting difference, the algorithm builds the chain by reiterating the following sequence of operations:

1. After each iteration, the algorithm sums the result of the previous models with a new model that is built on the same features but uses a differently weighted series of examples.

2. From a gradient descent optimization, derives the weights with respect to a cost function, optionally of different kinds. This approach differs from AdaBoost, which relies on the misclassified errors from the previous model.

GBM can take on different problems: regression, classification, and ranking (for ordering examples), with each problem using a particular cost function. Gradient Descent helps discover the set of values that reduces the cost function. This calculation is equivalent to selecting the best examples to use to obtain a better prediction. The secret of GBM's performance lies in weights optimized by Gradient Descent, as well as in these three smart tricks:

» **Shrinkage:** Acts as a learning rate in the ensemble. As in Gradient Descent, you must fix an adequate learning rate to avoid jumping too far from the solution, which is the same as in GBM. Small shrinkage values lead to better predictions.

» **Subsampling:** Emulates the pasting approach. If each subsequent tree builds on a subsample of the training data, the result is a Stochastic Gradient Descent. For many problems, the pasting approach helps reduce noise and influence by outliers, thus improving the results.

» **Trees of fixed size:** Fixing the tree depth used in boosting is like fixing a complexity limit to learning functions that you put into the ensemble, yet relying on more sophisticated trees than the stumps used in AdaBoost. Depth acts like power in a polynomial expansion: The deeper the tree, the larger the expansion, thus increasing both the ability to intercept complex target functions and the risk of overfitting.

You can create GBM applications using both of the languages found in this book, as described at the following sites:

» **Python:** https://scikit-learn.org/stable/modules/ensemble. html#gradient-boosting

» **R:** https://cran.r-project.org/web/packages/gbm/index.html

REMEMBER

XGBoost is a variant of GBM created by Tianqi Chen from Washington University, XGBoost is available for Python, R, Java, Scala, Julia, and C++, and it can work both on your local computer as well as on cloud clusters (made of hundreds of machines). Many practitioners consider it better performing than any standard GBM implementation because of the technical choices of its creator. You can find it at https://github.com/dmlc/xgboost.

Seeing GBM in action

The following example continues the test found in the "Seeing AdaBoost in action" section, earlier in this chapter. In this case, you create a GBM classifier for the handwritten digits dataset and test its performance. (Note that this example may run for a long time.)

```
import numpy as np
from sklearn.ensemble import GradientBoostingClassifier
from sklearn.model_selection import cross_val_score
from sklearn import datasets

digits = datasets.load_digits()
X,y = digits.data, digits.target
```

As before, you begin by obtaining the appropriate dataset and processing its content. The analysis part of the example appears here:

```
GBM = cross_val_score(
    GradientBoostingClassifier(n_estimators=300,
        subsample=0.8, max_depth=2, learning_rate=0.1,
        random_state=101), X, y, scoring='accuracy',cv=10)

print ("GBM: %0.3f" % (np.mean(GBM)))
```

The output tells you what you need to know about accuracy. Even though this example requires more time to run, the accuracy is also much higher than the three weak learners used with AdaBoost.

```
GBM: 0.950
```

Leveraging Ensembles
of Learners

Averaging Different Predictors

Up to this section, the chapter discusses ensembles made of the same kind of machine learning algorithms, but both averaging and voting systems can also work fine when you use a mix of different machine learning algorithms. This is the *averaging* approach, and it's widely used when you can't reduce the estimate variance.

As you try to learn from data, you have to try different solutions, thus modeling your data using different machine learning solutions. It's good practice to check whether you can put some of them successfully into ensembles using prediction averages or by counting the predicted classes. The principle is the same as in bagging noncorrelated predictions, when models mixed together can produce less variance–affected predictions. To achieve effective averaging, you have to

1. Divide your data into training and test sets.

2. Use the training data with different machine learning algorithms.

3. Record predictions from each algorithm and evaluate the viability of the result using the test set.

4. Correlate all the predictions available with each other.

5. Pick the predictions that least correlate and average their result. Or, if you're classifying, pick a group of least correlated predictions and, for each example, pick as a new class prediction the class that the majority of them predicted.

6. Test the newly averaged or voted-by-majority prediction against the test data. If successful, you create your final model by averaging the results of the models part of the successful ensemble.

TIP To understand which models correlate the least, take the predictions one by one, correlate each one against the others, and average the correlations to obtain an averaged correlation. Use the averaged correlation to rank the selected predictions that are most suitable for averaging.

Chapter **2**

Building Deep Learning Models

The idea of ensembles of learners appears in the previous chapter of this minibook. To make the computer better able to model complex real-world problems, you combine algorithms in different ways. Each algorithm adds to the whole. The computer doesn't actually understand anything. You rely on math to create a model that approximates learning. Creating models that approximate learning is what this chapter is about, too, but now you move to another level of learning called deep learning. In deep learning, a computer builds a complex structure called a *neural network* that is able to delve into datasets at an incredibly low level and model the data more precisely than any ensemble. The whole principle relies on mimicking the human brain using a mathematical neuron.

The first part of the chapter discusses the nature of a computer neuron and tells why it's important. However, it starts with an historical view of the impact on data science by the perceptron, a device that was amazing in its time, but also oversold.

After you understand the mathematical neuron, you move on to how a computer models a neuron. The second part of the chapter discusses what must occur to make a computer appear to learn. Obviously, a computer doesn't learn in the same manner as a human does, despite the use of language that makes this learning appear to be the case. A computer requires huge amounts of data to build a neural network; it can't make the leaps that humans do in understanding very complex ideas using just a few examples.

The final part of the chapter moves from neural networks into deep learning. Although neural networks use lots of layers, deep learning uses even more layers of neurons to perform various tasks. In addition, the manner in which a deep learning neural network activates neurons is different. Each of these sections builds upon the other to help you see the flow of neurons used to make it appear that computers can think like humans, even though a computer has no concept of thought or understanding. The entire process relies on math.

REMEMBER

You don't have to type the source code for this chapter manually. In fact, using the downloadable source is a lot easier. The source code for this chapter appears in the DSPD_0402_Deep_Learning.ipynb source code file for Python and the DSPD_R_0402_Deep_Learning.ipynb source code file for R. See the Introduction for details on how to find these source files.

Discovering the Incredible Perceptron

Data science programming involves working with computers in many different ways, most of which involve some sort of intense math. You might think that all these endeavors are new, but they're not. Some of the math has been around for hundreds of years. (really, Bayes Theorem, https://www.mathsisfun.com/data/bayes-theorem.html, originally appeared in 1763). Looking at history is helpful to gain an idea of how things are progressing and how we currently use this older information.

The perceptron, which isn't hundreds of years old, is actually a type (implementation) of machine learning for most people who are discovering AI, but other sources will tell you that it's a true form of deep learning. You can start the journey toward discovering how machine learning algorithms work by looking at models that figure out their answers using lines and surfaces to divide examples into classes or to estimate value predictions. These are *linear models*, and this chapter presents one of the earliest linear algorithms used in machine learning: the perceptron. Later chapters help you discover other sorts of modeling that are significantly more advanced than the perceptron. However, before you can advance to these other topics, you should understand the interesting history of the perceptron.

Understanding perceptron functionality

Frank Rosenblatt, of the Cornell Aeronautical Laboratory, devised the perceptron in 1957 under the sponsorship of the United States Naval Research. Rosenblatt was a psychologist and pioneer in the field of artificial intelligence. Proficient in cognitive science, his idea was to create a computer that could learn by trial and error, just as a human does.

The idea was successfully developed, and at the beginning, the perceptron wasn't conceived as just a piece of software; it was created as software running on dedicated hardware. You can see it at https://blogs.umass.edu/comphon/2017/06/15/did-frank-rosenblatt-invent-deep-learning-in-1962/. Using that combination allowed faster and more precise recognition of complex images than any other computer could do at the time. The new technology raised great expectations and caused a huge controversy when Rosenblatt affirmed that the perceptron was the embryo of a new kind of computer that would be able to walk, talk, see, write, and even reproduce itself and be conscious of its existence. If true, it would have been a powerful tool, and it introduced the world to AI.

Needless to say, the perceptron didn't realize the expectations of its creator. It soon displayed a limited capacity, even in its image-recognition specialization. The general disappointment ignited the first *AI winter* (a period of reduced funding and interest resulting from overhyping, for the most part) and the temporary abandonment of connectionism until the 1980s.

REMEMBER

Connectionism is the approach to machine learning that is based on neuroscience as well as the example of biologically interconnected networks. You can retrace the root of connectionism to the perceptron. The perceptron is an iterative algorithm that strives to determine, by successive and reiterative approximations, the best set of values for a vector, w, which is also called the *coefficient vector*. The creation of vector w is the learning process, but the computer really isn't learning anything; instead, it's creating a set of weights that match a particular model.

When the perceptron has achieved a suitable coefficient vector, it can predict whether an example is part of a class. For instance, one of the tasks the perceptron initially performed was to determine whether an image received from visual sensors resembled a boat (an image-recognition example required by the United States Office of Naval Research, the sponsor of the research on the perceptron). When the perceptron saw the image as part of the boat class, this meant that it classified the image as a boat.

Vector w can help predict the class of an example when you multiply it by the matrix of *features*. These features are the attributes or properties that describe the object or other entity in question, X. The entity X contains the entity information as numeric values expressed relative to your example. The algorithm adds the result of the multiplication to a constant term, called the bias, b. What X really contains are the properties (features) of the objects that you want classified, such as a boat. A boat can be a certain color, have a particular length, require masts, and so on. If the result of the sum is zero or positive, the perceptron classifies the example as part of the class. When the sum is negative, the example isn't part of the class. Here's the perceptron formula, where the sign function outputs 1 (when the example is part of the class) when the value inside the parentheses is equal or above zero; otherwise, it outputs 0:

```
y = sign(Xw + b)
```

Note that this algorithm contains all the elements that characterize a deep neural network, meaning that all the building blocks enabling the technology were present since the beginning:

1. **Numeric processing of the input:** X contains numbers, and no symbolic values are used as input until you process it as a number. For instance, you can't input symbolic information such as red, green, or blue until you convert these color values to numbers. You might choose, as an example, to represent red as the value 1, but it must appear as a number.

2. **Weights and bias:** The perceptron transforms X by multiplying it by the weights in vector w and adding the bias, b.

3. **Summation of results:** Using matrix multiplication when multiplying X by the w vector (an aspect of matrix multiplication covered in Book 2, Chapter 3).

4. **Activation function:** The perceptron activates a result of the input being part of the class when the summation exceeds a threshold — which, in this case, occurs when the resulting sum is zero or more.

5. **Iterative learning of the best set of values for the vector w:** The solution relies on successive approximations based on the comparison between the perceptron output and the expected result. When the output doesn't match the expected result, the values in vector w change.

Touching the nonseparability limit

The secret to perceptron calculations is in how the algorithm updates the vector w values. Such updates happen by randomly picking one of the misclassified examples. You have a misclassified example when the perceptron determines that an example is part of the class, but it isn't, or when the perceptron determines that an example isn't part of the class, but it is. The perceptron handles one misclassified example at a time (call it x_t) and operates by changing the w vector using a simple weighted addition:

$$w = w + \eta(x_t * y_t)$$

This formula is called the update strategy of the perceptron, and the letters stand for different numerical elements:

1. The letter w is the *coefficient vectors*, which is updated to correctly show whether the misclassified example t is part of the class.

2. The Greek letter eta (η) is the *learning rate*. It's a floating number between 0 and 1. When you set this value near zero, it can limit the capability of the formula to update the vector w almost completely, whereas setting the value near one makes the update process fully impact the w vector values. Setting different learning rates can speed up or slow down the learning process. Many other algorithms use this strategy, and lower eta is used to improve the optimization process by reducing the number of sudden w value jumps after an update. The trade-off is that you have to wait longer before getting the concluding results.

3. The x_t variable refers to the vector of numeric features for the example t.

4. The y_t variable refers to the ground truth of whether the example t is part of the class. For the perceptron, algorithm y_t is numerically expressed with +1 when the example is part of the class and with -1 when the example is not part of the class.

The update strategy provides intuition about what happens when using a perceptron to learn the classes. If you imagine the examples projected on a Cartesian plane, the perceptron is nothing more than a line trying to separate the positive class from the negative one. As you may recall from linear algebra, everything expressed in the form of y = xb+a is actually a line in a plane. The perceptron uses a formula of y = xw + b, which uses different letters but expresses the same form, that is, the line in a Cartesian plane.

Initially, when w is set to zero or to random values, the separating line is just one of the infinite possible lines found on a plane, as shown in Figure 2-1. The updating phase defines it by forcing it to become nearer to the misclassified point. As the algorithm passes through the misclassified examples, it applies a series of corrections. In the end, using multiple iterations to define the errors, the algorithm places the separating line at the exact border between the two classes.

In spite of being such a smart algorithm, the perceptron showed its limits quite soon. Apart from being capable of guessing two classes using only quantitative features, it had an important limit: If two classes had no border because of mixing, the algorithm couldn't find a solution and kept updating itself infinitely.

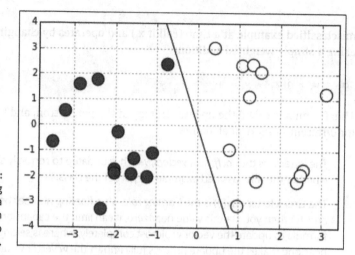

REMEMBER

If you can't divide two classes spread on two or more dimensions by any line or plane, they're *nonlinearly separable.* Overcoming data's being nonlinearly separable is one of the challenges that machine learning has to overcome in order to become effective against complex problems based on real data, not just on artificial data created for academic purposes.

When the nonlinearly separability matter came under scrutiny and practitioners started losing interest in the perceptron, experts quickly theorized that they could fix the problem by creating a new feature space in which previously inseparable classes are tuned to become separable. Thus, the perceptron would be as fine as before. Unfortunately, creating new feature spaces is a challenge because it requires computational power that's only partially available to the public today.

In recent years, the algorithm has had a revival thanks to big data. The perceptron, in fact, doesn't need to work with all the data in memory, but it can do fine using single examples (updating its coefficient vector only when a misclassified case makes it necessary). It's therefore a perfect algorithm for online learning, such as learning from big data an example at a time.

Hitting Complexity with Neural Networks

The previous section of the chapter helped you discover the neural network from the perspective of the perceptron. Of course, there is more to neural networks than that simple beginning. The capacity and other issues that plague the perceptron see at least partial resolution in newer algorithms. The following sections help you understand neural networks as they exist today.

Considering the neuron

The core neural network component is the *neuron* (also called a *unit*). Many neurons arranged in an interconnected structure make up a neural network, with each neuron linking to the inputs and outputs of other neurons. Thus, a neuron has two forms of input depending on its location in the neural network:

>> Features from examples

>> The results of other neurons

When the psychologist Rosenblatt conceived the perceptron (see the "Understanding perceptron functionality" section, earlier in this chapter), he thought of it as a simplified mathematical version of a brain neuron. A perceptron takes values as inputs from the nearby environment (the dataset or other neurons), weights them (as brain cells do, based on the strength of the in-bound connections), sums all the weighted values, and activates when the sum exceeds a threshold. This threshold outputs a value of 1 (a prediction that the inputs belong to a certain class, for example); otherwise, the output is 0.

Unfortunately, a perceptron can't learn when the classes it tries to process aren't linearly separable. To perform this task, the perceptron would need to know how to perform an XOR operation to separate different classes even when mixed, rather than just draw a line between them. However, scholars discovered that even though a single perceptron couldn't learn the logical operation XOR shown in Figure 2-2 (the exclusive OR, which is true only when the inputs are dissimilar), two perceptrons working together could.

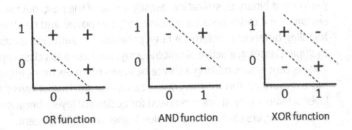

FIGURE 2-2:
Learning logical
XOR using a
single separating
line isn't possible.

OR function   AND function   XOR function

Neurons in a neural network are a further evolution of the perceptron: They take many weighted values as inputs, sum them, and provide the summation as the result, just as a perceptron does. However, they also provide a more sophisticated transformation of the summation, something that the perceptron can't do. In observing nature, scientists noticed that neurons receive signals but don't always release a signal of their own. It depends on the amount of signal received. When a neuron acquires enough stimuli, it fires an answer; otherwise, it remains silent. In a similar fashion, algorithmic neurons, after receiving weighted values, sum them and use an *activation function* to evaluate the result, which transforms it in a nonlinear way. For instance, the activation function can release a zero value unless the input achieves a certain threshold, or it can dampen or enhance a value by nonlinearly rescaling it, thus transmitting a rescaled signal.

A neural network has different activation functions, as shown in Figure 2-3.

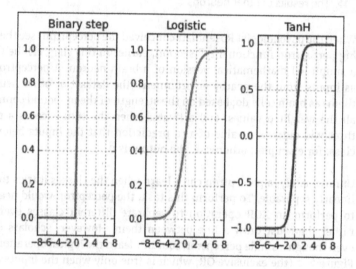

FIGURE 2-3:
Plots of different
activation
functions.

» **Binary step:** This function doesn't apply any transformation; it simply performs a binary classification. Mostly a relic of the past, data scientists seldom use it today because it lacks predictive power and flexibility in handling different problems. A huge potential for confusion exists when multiple classes are active simultaneously. Because each class reports being 100 percent active, making a choice between them becomes impossible. Even more important, this function doesn't allow for stacking of layers. If the first layer activates fully, there is no need for additional layers because the additional layers can't make the value higher than 100 percent.

» **Logistic:** Neural networks commonly use the sigmoid function because it provides a steep gradient around the zero point. A small change in X produces a large change in Y. Each layer can do its part to bring a signal to full activation because an output from the previous layer may not be fully activated; it might be only 50 percent activated. However, this function produces a problem called vanishing gradients in which the network refuses to learn because the values of X must be truly huge to create even a small change in Y.

» **Hyperbolic Tangent (TanH):** This is really a scaled sigmoid function, which means that it has more gradient strength. Essentially, the curve is steeper, so decisions are made more quickly.

The figure shows how an input (expressed on the horizontal axis) can transform an output into something else (expressed on the vertical axis). The point is that different activation functions produce different plots and work in different ways. There are other activation functions not shown in Figure 2-3 (this section provides only an introduction). For example, the Rectified Linear Units (ReLU) is by far the most commonly used activation function today. The "Choosing the right activation function" section, later in this chapter, describes activation functions in more detail.

TIP

You learn more about activation functions later in the chapter, but note for now that activation functions clearly work well in certain ranges of x values. For this reason, you should always rescale inputs to a neural network using statistical standardization (zero mean and unit variance) or normalize the input in the range from 0 to 1 or from −1 to 1.

REMEMBER

Activation functions are what make a neural network perform in a classification or regression; yet, the initial choice of the sigmoid or tanh activations for most networks pose a critical limit when using networks that are more complex, because both activations work optimally for a very restricted range of values.

Pushing data with feed-forward

In a neural network, you must consider the architecture, which is how the neural network components are arranged. Contrary to other algorithms, which have a fixed pipeline that determines how algorithms receive and process data, neural networks require you to decide how information flows by fixing the number of units (the neurons) and their distribution in layers, as shown in Figure 2-4.

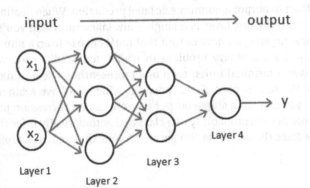

FIGURE 2-4:
An example of the architecture of a neural network.

input → output

x_1

x_2

y

Layer 1

Layer 2

Layer 3

Layer 4

The figure shows a simple neural architecture. Note how the layers filter information in a progressive way. This is a feed-forward input because data feeds in one direction, forward, into the network. Only Layer 1 receives input from the original dataset; the other layers feed each other. Connections exclusively link the units in one layer with the units in the following layer (information flow from left to right). No connections exist between units in the same layer or with units outside the next layer. Moreover, the information pushes forward (from the left to the right). Processed data never returns to previous neuron layers.

Using a neural network is like using a stratified filtering system for water: You pour the water from above and the water is filtered at the bottom. The water has no way to go back; it just goes forward and straight down, and never laterally. In the same way, neural networks force data features to flow through the network and mix with each other only according to the network's architecture. By using the best architecture to mix features, the neural network creates new composed features at every layer and helps achieve better predictions. Unfortunately, you have no way to determine the best architecture without empirically trying different solutions and testing whether the output data helps predict your target values after flowing through the network.

The first and last layers play an important role. The first layer, called the *input layer*, picks ups the features from each data example processed by the network. The last layer, called the *output layer*, releases the results.

A neural network can process only numeric, continuous information; it can't be constrained to work with qualitative variables (for example, labels indicating a quality such as red, blue, or green in an image). You can process qualitative variables by transforming them into a continuous numeric value, such as a series of binary values. When a neural network processes a binary variable, the neuron treats the variable as a generic number and turns the binary values into other values, even negative ones, by processing across units.

Note the limitation of dealing only with numeric values because you can't expect the last layer to output a nonnumeric label prediction. When dealing with a regression problem, the last layer is a single unit. Likewise, when you're working with a classification and you have output that must choose from a number *n* of classes, unless you have a binary problem in which you predict only two classes, you should have *n* terminal units, each one representing a score linked to the probability of the represented class. However, when you have a binary classification problem, you can use a single output neuron, as in a regression problem, because you just predict the probability of a class and automatically infer the probability of the other class (because it is 100 percent minus the predicted probability).

To put the need for multiple input and terminal units into perspective, when classifying a multiclass problem such as an iris species, think about the famous Iris classification example, created by R. A. Fisher (https://archive.ics.uci.edu/ml/datasets/iris). In this case, the input layer has enough units for each of the attributes:

>> Sepal length in cm

>> Sepal width in cm

>> Petal length in cm

>> Petal width in cm

The output layer has as many units as species. In a neural network based on the Iris dataset, you therefore have three units representing one of the three Iris species:

>> Setosa

>> Versicolor

>> Virginica

The predicted class is the one that gets the higher score at the end based on four input attributes.

TECHNICAL STUFF

Some neural networks have special final layers, collectively called softmax, which can adjust the probability of each class based on the values received from a previous layer. In classification, the final layer may represent both a partition of probabilities thanks to softmax (a multiclass problem in which total probabilities sum to 100 percent) or an independent score prediction (because an example can have more classes, which is a multilabel problem in which summed probabilities can be more than 100 percent). When the classification problem is a binary classification, a single output suffices. Also, in regression, you can have multiple output units, each one representing a different regression problem. (For instance, in forecasting, you can have different predictions for the next day, week, month, and so on.)

Defining hidden layers

Neural networks have different layers, each one having its own weights and using its own activation function. Because the neural network segregates computations by layers, knowing the reference layer is important because you can account for certain units and connections. You can refer to every layer using a specific number and generically talk about each layer using the letter *l*.

HIDDEN LAYERS

Outside this book, the layers between the input and the output are sometimes called *hidden layers*, and the layer count starts from the first hidden layer. This is just a different convention from the one used in this book. The examples in the book always start counting from the input layer, so the first hidden layer is layer number 2.

Each layer can have a different number of units, and the number of units located between two layers dictates the number of connections. By multiplying the number of units in the starting layer with the number in the following layer, you can determine the total number of connections between the two: *number of connections*$^{(l)}$ = *units*$^{(l)}$ * *units*$^{(l+1)}$.

A matrix of weights, usually named with the uppercase Greek letter Theta (Θ), represents the connections. For ease of reading, the book uses the capital letter W, which is a fine choice because it is a matrix or a multidimensional array. Thus, you can use W^1 to refer to the connection weights from layer 1 to layer 2, W^2 for the connections from layer 2 to layer 3, and so on.

Weights represent the strength of the connection between neurons in the network. When the weight of the connection between two layers is small, it means that the network dumps values flowing between them and signals that taking this route won't likely influence the final prediction. Alternatively, a large positive or negative value affects the values that the next layer receives, thus changing certain predictions. This approach is analogous to brain cells, which don't stand alone but connect with other cells. As a person grows in experience, connections between neurons tend to weaken or strengthen to activate or deactivate certain brain network cell regions, causing other processing or an activity (a reaction to a danger, for instance, if the processed information signals a life-threatening situation).

Executing operations

Now that you know some conventions regarding layers, units, and connections, you can start examining the operations that neural networks execute in detail. To begin, you can call inputs and outputs in different ways:

>> **a:** The result stored in a unit in the neural network after being processed by the activation function (called *g*). This is the final output that is sent further along the network.

>> **z:** The multiplication between a and the weights from the W matrix. z represents the signal going through the connections, analogous to water in pipes that flows at a higher or lower pressure depending on the pipe diameter. In the same way, the values received from the previous layer become higher or lower because of the connection weights used to transmit them.

Each successive layer of units in a neural network progressively processes the values taken from the features. (Picture a conveyor belt.) As data transmits in the network, it arrives at each unit as a value produced by the summation of the values present in the previous layer and weighted by connections represented in the matrix W. When the data with added bias exceeds a certain threshold, the activation function increases the value stored in the unit; otherwise, it extinguishes the signal by reducing it. After processing by the activation function, the result is ready to push forward to the connection linked to the next layer. These steps repeat for each layer until the values reach the end and you have a result, as shown in Figure 2-5.

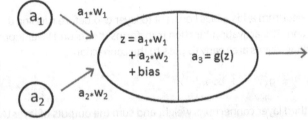

FIGURE 2-5: A detail of the feed-forward process in a neural network.

The figure shows a detail of the process that involves two units pushing their results to another unit. This series of events happens in every part of the network:

1. The input A1 is multiplied by its weighting factor W1.

2. The input A2 is multiplied by its weighting factor W2.

3. The two weighted inputs are summed with a bias to produce the value z.

4. The output, A3, is produced by the activation function, g, accepting the summed and biased value z. This output now goes to the next layer or is used as an output.

Considering the details of data movement through the neural network

When you understand the passage from two neurons to one, you can understand the entire feed-forward process, even when more layers and neurons are involved. For more explanation, here are the seven steps used to produce a prediction in a neural network made of four layers (refer to Figure 2-4):

1. The first layer (notice the superscript 1 on a) loads the value of each feature in a different unit:

   $$a^{(1)} = X$$

2. The weights of the connections bridging the input layer with the second layer are multiplied by the values of the units in the first layer. A matrix multiplication weights and sums the inputs for the second layer together.

   $$z^{(2)} = W^{(1)}a^{(1)}$$

3. The algorithm adds a bias constant to layer two before running the activation function. The activation function transforms the second layer inputs. The resulting values are ready to pass to the connections.

   $$a^{(2)} = g(z^{(2)} + bias^{(2)})$$

4. The third layer connections weight and sum the outputs of layer two.

   $$z^{(3)} = W^{(2)}a^{(2)}$$

5. The algorithm adds a bias constant to layer three before running the activation function. The activation function transforms the layer-three inputs.

   $$a^{(3)} = g(z^{(3)} + bias^{(3)})$$

6. The layer-three outputs are weighted and summed by the connections to the output layer.

   $$z^{(4)} = W^{(3)}a^{(3)}$$

7. Finally, the algorithm adds a bias constant to layer four before running the activation function. The output units receive their inputs and transform the input using the activation function. After this final transformation, the output units are ready to release the resulting predictions of the neural network.

   $$a^{(4)} = g(z^{(4)} + bias^{(4)})$$

The activation function plays the role of a signal filter, helping to select the relevant signals and avoid the weak and noisy ones (because it discards values below a certain threshold). Activation functions also provide nonlinearity to the output because they enhance or damp the values passing through them in a nonproportional way.

REMEMBER

The weights of the connections provide a way to mix and compose the features in a new way, creating new features in a way not too different from a polynomial expansion. The activation renders nonlinear the resulting recombination of the features by the connections. Both of these neural network components enable the algorithm to learn complex target functions that represent the relationship between the input features and the target outcome.

Using backpropagation to adjust learning

From an architectural perspective, a neural network does a great job of mixing signals from examples and turning them into new features to achieve an approximation of complex nonlinear functions (functions that you can't represent as a straight line in the features' space). To create this capability, neural networks work as *universal approximators* (for more details, go to `https://www.techleer.com/articles/449-the-universal-approximation-theorem-for-neural-networks/`), which means that they can guess any target function. However, you have to consider that one aspect of this feature is the capacity to model complex functions (*representation capability*), and another aspect is the capability to learn from data effectively.

Learning occurs in a brain because of the formation and modification of synapses between neurons, based on stimuli received by trial-and-error experience. Neural networks provide a way to replicate this process as a mathematical formulation called *backpropagation*. The following sections tell you more about backpropagation.

Delving into backpropagation beginnings

Since its early appearance in the 1970s, the backpropagation algorithm has been given many fixes. Each neural network learning process improvement resulted in new applications and a renewed interest in the technique. In addition, the current deep learning revolution, a revival of neural networks, which were abandoned at the beginning of the 1990s, is the result of key advances in the way neural networks learn from their errors. As seen in other algorithms, the cost function activates the necessity to learn certain examples better (large errors correspond to high costs). When an example with a large error occurs, the cost function outputs a high value that is minimized by changing the parameters in the algorithm. The optimization algorithm determines the best action for reducing the high outputs from the cost function.

In linear regression, finding an update rule to apply to each parameter (the vector of beta coefficients) is straightforward. However, in a neural network, things are a bit more complicated. The architecture is variable and the parameter coefficients (the connections) relate to each other because the connections in a layer depend on how the connections in the previous layers recombined the inputs. The solution to this problem is the backpropagation algorithm. Backpropagation is a smart way to propagate the errors back into the network and make each connection adjust its weights accordingly. If you initially feed-forward propagated information to the network, it's time to go backward and give feedback on what went wrong in the forward phase.

REMEMBER

Backpropagation is how adjustments required by the optimization algorithm are propagated through the neural network. Distinguishing between optimization and backpropagation is important. In fact, all neural networks use backpropagation, but the "Relying on a smart optimizer" section, later in this chapter, discusses many different optimization algorithms.

Understanding how backpropagation works

Discovering how backpropagation works isn't complicated, even though demonstrating how it works using formulas and mathematics requires derivatives and the proving of some formulations, which is quite tricky and beyond the scope of this book. To get a sense of how backpropagation operates, start from the end of the network, just at the moment when an example has been processed and you have a prediction as an output. At this point, you can compare the prediction with the real result and, by subtracting the two values, get an offset, which is the error. Now that you know the mismatch of the results at the output layer, you can progress backward to distribute the error information to all the units in the network.

TIP

The cost function of a neural network for classification is based on cross-entropy (as seen in logistic regression):

```
Cost = y * log(h_w(X)) + (1 - y)*log(1 - h_w(X))
```

This is a formulation involving logarithms. It refers to the prediction produced by the neural network and expressed as $h_w(X)$ (which reads as the result of the network given connections W and X as input). To make things easier, when thinking of the cost, it helps to think of it as computing the offset between the expected results and the neural network output.

The first step in transmitting the error back into the network relies on backward multiplication. Because the values fed to the output layer are made of the contributions of all units, proportional to the weight of their connections, you can redistribute the error according to each contribution. For instance, the vector of errors of a layer n in the network, a vector indicated by the Greek letter delta (δ), is the result of the following formulation:

$$\delta^{(n)} = W^{(n)T} * \delta^{(n+1)}$$

This formula says that, starting from the final delta, you can continue redistributing delta going backward in the network and using the weights you used to push forward the value to partition the error to the different units. In this way, you can get the terminal error redistributed to each neural unit, and you can use it to recalculate a more appropriate weight for each network connection to minimize the error. To update the weights W of layer l, you just apply the following formula:

$$W^{(1)} = W^{(1)} + \eta * \delta^{(1)} * g'(z^{(1)}) * a^{(1)}$$

The formula may appear puzzling at first sight, but it is a summation, and you can discover how it works by looking at its elements. First, look at the function g'. It's the first derivative of the activation function g, evaluated by the input values z. In fact, this is the Gradient Descent method. Gradient Descent determines how to reduce the error measure by finding, among the possible combinations of values, the weights that most reduce the error.

The Greek letter eta (η), sometimes also called alpha (α) or epsilon (ε) depending on the textbook you consult, is the learning rate. As found in other algorithms, it reduces the effect of the update suggested by the Gradient Descent derivative. In fact, the direction provided may be only partially correct or just roughly correct. By taking multiple small steps in the descent, the algorithm can take a more precise direction toward the global minimum error, which is the target you want to achieve (that is, a neural network producing the least possible prediction error).

Setting the eta value

Different methods are available for setting the right eta value, because the optimization largely depends on it. One method sets the eta value starting high and reduces it during the optimization process. Another method variably increases or decreases eta based on the improvements obtained by the algorithm: Large improvements call a larger eta (because the descent is easy and straight); smaller improvements call a smaller eta so that the optimization will move slower, looking for the best opportunities to descend. Think of it as being on a tortuous path in the mountains: You slow down and try not to be struck or thrown off the road as you descend.

Most implementations offer an automatic setting of the correct eta. You need to note this setting's relevance when training a neural network because it's one of the important parameters to tweak to obtain better predictions, together with the layer architecture. Weight updates can happen in different ways with respect to the training set of examples:

>> **Online mode:** The weight update happens after every example traverses the network. In this way, the algorithm treats the learning examples as a stream from which to learn in real time. This mode is perfect when you have to learn *out of core*, that is, when the training set can't fit into RAM memory. However, this method is sensitive to outliers, so you have to keep your learning rate low. (Consequently, the algorithm is slow to converge to a solution.)

>> **Batch mode:** The weight update happens after processing all the examples in the training set. This technique makes optimization fast and less subject to having variance appear in the example stream. In batch mode, the backpropagation considers the summed gradients of all examples.

>> **Mini-batch (or stochastic) mode:** The weight update happens after the network has processed a subsample of randomly selected training set examples. This approach mixes the advantages of online mode (low memory usage) and batch mode (a rapid convergence) while introducing a random element (the subsampling) to avoid having the Gradient Descent stuck in a *local minima* (a drop in value that isn't the true minimum).

Understanding More about Neural Networks

You can find many discussions about neural network architectures online (such as the one at https://www.kdnuggets.com/2018/02/8-neural-network-architectures-machine-learning-researchers-need-learn.html). The problem, however, is that they all quickly become insanely complex, making normal people want to pull out their hair. Some unwritten law seems to say that math has to become instantly abstract and so complicated that no mere mortal can understand it, but anyone can understand a neural network. The material in the "Hitting Complexity with Neural Networks" section, earlier in this chapter, gives you a good start. Even though this earlier section does rely a little on math to get its point across, the math is relatively simple. The following sections help you use what you now know about neural networks to create an example using Python or R.

Getting an overview of the neural network process

What a neural network truly represents is a kind of filter. You pour data into the top, that data percolates through the various layers you create, and an output appears at the bottom. The things that differentiate neural networks are the same sorts of things you might look for in a filter. For example, the kind of algorithm you choose determines the kind of filtering the neural network will perform. You may want to filter the lead out of the water but leave the calcium and other beneficial minerals intact, which means choosing a kind of filter to do that.

However, filters can come with controls. For example, you might choose to filter particles of one size but let particles of another size pass. The use of weights and biases in a neural network are simply a kind of control. You adjust the control to fine-tune the filtering you receive. In this case, because you're using electrical signals modeled after those found in the brain, a signal is allowed to pass when it meets a particular condition — a threshold defined by an activation function. To keep things simple for now, though, just think about it as you would adjustments to any filter's basic operation.

You can monitor the activity of your filter. However, unless you want to stand there all day looking at it, you probably rely on some sort of automation to ensure that the filter's output remains constant. This is where an optimizer comes into play. By optimizing the output of the neural network, you see the results you need without constantly tuning it manually.

Finally, you want to allow a filter to work at a speed and capacity that allows it to perform its tasks correctly. Pouring water or some other substance through the filter too quickly would cause it to overflow. If you don't pour fast enough, the filter might clog or work erratically. Adjusting the learning rate of the optimizer of a neural network enables you to ensure that the neural network produces the output you want. It's like adjusting the pouring rate of a filter.

Neural networks can seem hard to understand. The fact that much of what they do is shrouded in mathematical complexity doesn't help matters. However, you don't have to be a rocket scientist to understand what neural networks are all about. All you really need to do is break them down into manageable pieces and use the right perspective to look at them.

Defining the basic architecture

A neural network relies on numerous computation units, the *neurons*, arranged into hierarchical layers. Each neuron accepts inputs from all its predecessors and provides outputs to its successors until the neural network as a whole satisfies a requirement. At this point, the network processing ends and you receive the output.

All these computations occur singularly in a neural network. The network passes over each of them using loops for loop iterations. You can also leverage the fact that most of these operations are plain multiplications, followed by addition, and take advantage of the matrix calculations shown in Book 2, Chapter 3.

The example in this section creates a network with an input layer (whose dimensions are defined by the input), a hidden layer with three neurons, and a single output layer that tells whether the input is part of a class (a binary 0/1 answer). This architecture implies creating two sets of weights represented by two matrices (when you're actually using matrices):

>> The first matrix uses a size determined by the number of inputs x 3, represents the weights that multiply the inputs, and sums them into three neurons.

>> The second matrix uses a size of 3 x 1, gathers all the outputs from the hidden layer, and makes that layer converge into the output.

Here's the required Python script (which may take a while to complete running, depending on the speed of your system):

```
import numpy as np
from sklearn.datasets import make_moons
from sklearn.model_selection import train_test_split
import matplotlib.pyplot as plt
%matplotlib inline

def init(inp, out):
    return np.random.randn(inp, out) / np.sqrt(inp)

def create_architecture(input_layer, first_layer,
                        output_layer, random_seed=0):
    np.random.seed(random_seed)
    layers = X.shape[1], 3 , 1
    arch = list(zip(layers[:-1], layers[1:]))
    weights = [init(inp, out) for inp, out in arch]
    return weights
```

The interesting point of this initialization is that it uses a sequence of matrices to automate the network calculations. How the code initializes them matters because you can't use numbers that are too small — there will be too little signal for the network to work. However, you must also avoid numbers that are too big because the calculations become too cumbersome to handle. Sometimes they fail, which causes the *exploding gradient problem* (wherein the neural network ceases to function because of the exploding values; see the article at https://machinelearningmastery.com/exploding-gradients-in-neural-networks/ for details) or, more often, causes *saturation of the neurons*, which means that you can't correctly train a network because all the neurons are always activated.

REMEMBER

Initializing your network using all zeros is always a bad idea because if all the neurons have the same value, they will react in the same way to the training input. No matter how many neurons the architecture contains, they operate as a single neuron.

The simpler solution is to start with initial random weights that are in the range required for the *activation functions*, which are the transformation functions that add flexibility to solving problems using the network. A possible simple solution is to set the weights to zero mean and one standard deviation, which in statistics is called the *standard normal distribution* and in the code appears as the np.random.radn command.

TIP

However, smarter weight initializations exist for more complex networks, such as those found in this article: https://towardsdatascience.com/weight-initialization-techniques-in-neural-networks-26c649eb3b78.

Moreover, because each neuron accepts the inputs of all previous neurons, the code rescales the random normal distributed weights using the square root of the number of inputs. Consequently, the neurons and their activation functions always compute the right size for everything to work smoothly.

Documenting the essential modules

The architecture is just one part of a neural network. You can imagine it as the structure of the network. Architecture explains how the network processes data and provides results. However, for any processing to happen, you also need to code the neural network's core functionalities.

The first building block of the network is the activation function. The "Considering the neuron" section, earlier in this chapter, details a few activation functions used in neural networks without explaining them in much detail. The example in this section provides code for the sigmoid function, one of the basic neural network activation functions. The sigmoid function is a step up from the *Heaviside step* function, which acts as a switch that activates at a certain threshold. A Heaviside step function outputs 1 for inputs above the threshold and 0 for inputs below it.

The sigmoid functions outputs 0 or 1, respectively, for small input values below zero or high values above zero. For input values in the range between −5 and +5, the function outputs values in the range 0–1, slowly increasing the output of released values until it reaches around 0.2 and then growing fast in a linear way until reaching 0.8. It then decreases again as the output rate approaches 1. Such behavior represents a logistic curve, which is useful for describing many natural phenomena, such as the growth of a population that starts growing slowly and then fully blossoms and develops until it slows down before hitting a resource limit (such as available living space or food).

In neural networks, the sigmoid function is particularly useful for modeling inputs that resemble probabilities, and it's *differentiable*, which is a mathematical aspect that helps reverse its effects and works out the best backpropagation phase:

```
def sigmoid(z):
    return 1/(1 + np.exp(-z))

def sigmoid_prime(s):
    return s * (1 -s)
```

After you have an activation function, you can create a *forward procedure*, which is a matrix multiplication between the input to each layer and the weights of the connection. After completing the multiplication, the code applies the activation function to the results to transform them in a nonlinear way. The following code embeds the sigmoid function into the network's feed-forward code. Of course, you can use any other activation function if desired:

```
def feed_forward(X, weights):
    a = X.copy()
    out = list()
    for W in weights:
        z = np.dot(a, W)
        a = sigmoid(z)
        out.append(a)
    return out
```

By applying the feed forward to the complete network, you finally arrive at a result in the output layer. Now you can compare the output against the real values you want the network to obtain. The accuracy function determines whether the neural network is performing predictions well by comparing the number of correct guesses to the total number of predictions provided:

```
def accuracy(true_label, predicted):
    correct_preds = np.ravel(predicted)==true_label
    return np.sum(correct_preds) / len(true_label)
```

The backpropagation function comes next because the network is working but all or some of the predictions are incorrect. Correcting predictions during training enables you to create a neural network that can take on new examples and provide good predictions. The training is incorporated into its connection weights as patterns present in data that can help predict the results correctly.

To perform backpropagation, you first compute the error at the end of each layer (this architecture has two). Using this error, you multiply it by the derivative of the activation function. The result provides you with a gradient, that is, the change in weights necessary to compute predictions more correctly. The code starts by comparing the output with the correct answers (l2_error), and then computes the gradients, which are the necessary weight corrections (l2_delta). The code then proceeds to multiply the gradients by the weights the code must correct. The operation distributes the error from the output layer to the intermediate one (l1_error). A new gradient computation (l1_delta) also provides the weight corrections to apply to the input layer, which completes the process for a network with an input layer, a hidden layer, and an output layer:

```
def backpropagation(l1, l2, weights, y):
    l2_error = y.reshape(-1, 1) - l2
    l2_delta = l2_error * sigmoid_prime(l2)
    l1_error = l2_delta.dot(weights[1].T)
    l1_delta = l1_error * sigmoid_prime(l1)
    return l2_error, l1_delta, l2_delta
```

REMEMBER

This is a Python code translation, in simplified form, of the formulas you find in the "Understanding how backpropagation works" section, earlier in this chapter. The cost function is the difference between the network's output and the correct answers. The example doesn't add biases during the feed-forward phase, which reduces the complexity of the backpropagation process and makes it easier to understand.

After backpropagation assigns each connection its part of the correction that should be applied over the entire network, you adjust the initial weights to represent an updated neural network. You do so by adding to the weights of each layer, the multiplication of the input to that layer, and the delta corrections for the layer as a whole. This is a Gradient Descent method step in which you approach the solution by taking repeated small steps in the right direction, so you may need to adjust the step size used to solve the problem. The alpha parameters help make changing the step size possible. Using a value of 1 won't affect the impact of the previous weight correction, but values smaller than 1 effectively reduce it:

```
def update_weights(X, l1, l1_delta, l2_delta, weights,
                   alpha=1.0):
    weights[1] = weights[1] + (alpha * l1.T.dot(l2_delta))
```

```
        weights[0] = weights[0] + (alpha * X.T.dot(l1_delta))
        return weights
```

A neural network is not complete if it can only learn from data, but not predict. The last predict function pushes new data using feed forward, reads the last output layer, and transforms its values to problem predictions. Because the sigmoid activation function is so adept at modeling probability, the code uses a value halfway between 0 and 1, that is, 0.5, as the threshold for having a positive or negative output. Such a binary output could help in classifying two classes or a single class against all the others if a dataset has three or more types of outcomes to classify.

```
def predict(X, weights):
    _, l2 = feed_forward(X, weights)
    preds = np.ravel((l2 > 0.5).astype(int))
    return preds
```

At this point, the example has all the parts that make a neural network work. You just need a problem that demonstrates how the neural network works.

Solving a simple problem

In this section, you test the neural network code you wrote by asking it to solve a simple, but not banal, data problem. The code uses the Scikit-learn package's make_moons function to create two interleaving circles of points shaped as two half moons. Separating these two circles requires an algorithm capable of defining a nonlinear separation function that generalizes to new cases of the same kind. A neural network, such as the one presented earlier in the chapter, can easily handle the challenge.

```
np.random.seed(0)

coord, cl = make_moons(300, noise=0.05)
X, Xt, y, yt = train_test_split(coord, cl,
                                test_size=0.30,
                                random_state=0)

plt.scatter(X[:,0], X[:,1], s=25, c=y, cmap=plt.cm.Set1)
plt.show()
```

The code first sets the random seed to produce the same result anytime you want to run the example. The next step is to produce 300 data examples and split them into a train and a test dataset. (The test dataset is 30 percent of the total.) The data consists of two variables representing the x and y coordinates of points on a Cartesian graph. Figure 2-6 shows the output of this process.

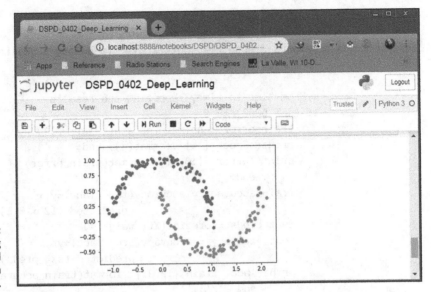

FIGURE 2-6:
Two interleaving
moon-shaped
clouds of data
points.

Because learning in a neural network happens in successive iterations (called *epochs*), after creating and initializing the sets of weights, the code loops 30,000 iterations of the two half moons data (each passage is an epoch). On each iteration, the script calls some of the previously prepared core neural network functions:

» Feed forward the data through the entire network.

» Backpropagate the error back into the network.

» Update the weights of each layer in the network, based on the backpropagated error.

» Compute the training and validation errors.

The following code uses comments to detail when each function operates:

```
weights = create_architecture(X, 3, 1)

for j in range(30000 + 1):

    # First, feed forward through the hidden layer
    l1, l2 = feed_forward(X, weights)

    # Then, error backpropagation from output to input
    l2_error, l1_delta, l2_delta = backpropagation(l1,
                                        l2, weights, y)
```

```
# Finally, updating the weights of the network
weights = update_weights(X, l1, l1_delta, l2_delta,
                         weights, alpha=0.05)

# From time to time, reporting the results
if (j % 5000) == 0:
    train_error = np.mean(np.abs(l2_error))
    print('Epoch {:5}'.format(j), end=' - ')
    print('error: {:0.4f}'.format(train_error),
          end= ' - ')
    train_accuracy = accuracy(true_label=y,
                              predicted=(l2 > 0.5))
    test_preds = predict(Xt, weights)
    test_accuracy = accuracy(true_label=yt,
                             predicted=test_preds)
    print('acc: train {:0.3f}'.format(train_accuracy),
          end= '/')
    print('test {:0.3f}'.format(test_accuracy))
```

Variable j counts the iterations. At each iteration, the code tries to divide j by 5,000 and check whether the division leaves a module. When the module is zero, the code infers that 5,000 epochs have passed since the previous check, and summarizing the neural network error is possible by examining its accuracy (how many times the prediction is correct with respect to the total number of predictions) on the training set and on the test set. The accuracy on the training set shows how well the neural network is fitting the data by adapting its parameters by the backpropagation process. The accuracy on the test set provides an idea of how well the solution generalized to new data and thus whether you can reuse it.

TIP

The test accuracy should matter the most because it shows the potential usability of the neural network with other data. The training accuracy just tells you how the network scores with the present data you are using. Here is an example of what you might see as output:

```
Epoch     0 - error: 0.5077 - acc: train 0.462/test 0.656
Epoch  5000 - error: 0.0991 - acc: train 0.952/test 0.944
Epoch 10000 - error: 0.0872 - acc: train 0.952/test 0.944
Epoch 15000 - error: 0.0809 - acc: train 0.957/test 0.956
Epoch 20000 - error: 0.0766 - acc: train 0.967/test 0.956
Epoch 25000 - error: 0.0797 - acc: train 0.962/test 0.967
Epoch 30000 - error: 0.0713 - acc: train 0.957/test 0.956
```

Looking Under the Hood of Neural Networks

After you know how neural networks basically work, you need a better understanding of what differentiates them. Beyond the different architectures, the choice of the activation functions, the optimizers and the neural network's learning rate can make the difference. Knowing basic operations isn't enough because you won't get the results you want. Looking under the hood helps you understand how you can tune your neural network solution to model specific problems. In addition, understanding the various algorithms used to create a neural network will help you obtain better results with less effort and in a shorter time. The following sections focus on three areas of neural network differentiation.

Choosing the right activation function

An activation function simply defines when a neuron fires. Consider it a sort of tipping point: Input of a certain value won't cause the neuron to fire because it's not enough, but just a little more input *can* cause the neuron to fire. A neuron is defined in a simple manner, as follows:

```
y = Σ (weight * input) + bias
```

The output, y, can be any value between + infinity and − infinity. The problem, then, is to decide on what value of y is the firing value, which is where an activation function comes into play. The activation function determines which value is high or low enough to reflect a decision point in the neural network for a particular neuron or group of neurons.

As with everything else in neural networks, you don't have just one activation function. You use the activation function that works best in a particular scenario. With this in mind, you can break the activation functions into these categories:

» **Step:** A step function (also called a binary function) relies on a specific threshold for making the decision about activating or not. Using a step function means that you know which specific value will cause an activation. However, step functions are limited in that they're either fully activated or fully deactivated — no shades of gray exist. Consequently, when attempting to determine which class is most likely correct based on a given input, a step function won't work.

>> **Linear:** A linear function ($A = cx$) provides a straight-line determination of activation based on input. Using a linear function helps you determine which output to activate based on which output is most correct (as expressed by weighting). However, linear functions work only as a single layer. If you were to stack multiple linear function layers, the output would be the same as using a single layer, which defeats the purpose of using neural networks. Consequently, a linear function may appear as a single layer, but never as multiple layers.

>> **Sigmoid:** A sigmoid function ($A = 1 / 1 + e^{-x}$), which produces a curve shaped like the letter C or S, is nonlinear. It begins by looking sort of like the step function, except that the values between two points actually exist on a curve, which means that you can stack sigmoid functions to perform classification with multiple outputs. The range of a sigmoid function is between 0 and 1, not – infinity to + infinity as with a linear function, so the activations are bound within a specific range. However, the sigmoid function suffers from a problem called *vanishing gradient,* which means that the function refuses to learn after a certain point because the propagated error shrinks to zero as it approaches faraway layers.

>> **TanH:** A tanh function ($A = (2 / 1 + e^{-2x}) - 1$) is actually a scaled sigmoid function. It has a range of –1 to 1, so again, it's a precise method for activating neurons. The big difference between sigmoid functions and tanh functions is that the tanh function gradient is stronger, which means that detecting small differences is easier, making classification more sensitive. Like the sigmoid function, tanh suffers from vanishing gradient issues.

>> **ReLU:** A ReLU function ($A(x) = max(0, x)$) provides an output in the range of 0 to infinity, so it's similar to the linear function except that it's also nonlinear, enabling you to stack ReLU functions. An advantage of ReLU is that it requires less processing power because fewer neurons fire. The lack of activity as the neuron approaches the 0 part of the line means that there are fewer potential outputs to look at. However, this advantage can also become a disadvantage when you have a problem called the dying ReLU. After a while, the neural network weights don't provide the desired effect any longer (the network simply stops learning) and the affected neurons die — meaning that they don't respond to any input.

Also, the ReLU has some variants that you should consider:

>> **ELU (Exponential Linear Unit):** Differs from ReLU when the inputs are negative. In this case, the outputs don't go to zero but instead slowly decrease to –1 exponentially.

» **PReLU (Parametric Rectified Linear Unit):** Differs from ReLU when the inputs are negative. In this case, the output is a linear function whose parameters are learned using the same technique as any other parameter of the network.

» **LeakyReLU:** Similar to PReLU but the parameter for the linear side is fixed.

Relying on a smart optimizer

An optimizer serves to ensure that your neural network performs fast and correctly models whatever problem you want to solve by modifying the neural network's biases and weights. It turns out that an algorithm performs this task, but you must choose the correct algorithm to obtain the results you expect. As with all neural network scenarios, you have a number of optional algorithm types from which to choose (see `https://keras.io/optimizers/`):

» Stochastic Gradient Descent (SGD)

» RMSProp

» AdaGrad

» AdaDelta

» AMSGrad

» Adam and its variants, Adamax and Nadam

An optimizer works by minimizing or maximizing the output of an objective function (also known as an error function) represented as E(x). This function is dependent on the model's internal learnable parameters used to calculate the target values (Y) from the predictors (X). Two internal learnable parameters are weights (W) and bias (b). The various algorithms have different methods of dealing with the objective function.

You can categorize the optimizer functions by the manner in which they deal with the derivative (dy/dx), which is the instantaneous change of y with respect to x. Here are the two levels of derivative handling:

» **First order:** These algorithms minimize or maximize the objective function using gradient values with respect to the parameters.

» **Second order:** These algorithms minimize or maximize the object function using the second-order derivative values with respect to the parameters. The second-order derivative can give a hint as to whether the first-order derivative is increasing or decreasing, which provides information about the curvature of the line.

You commonly use first-order optimization techniques, such as Gradient Descent, because they require fewer computations and tend to converge to a good solution relatively fast when working on large datasets.

Setting a working learning rate

Each optimizer has completely different parameters to tune. One constant is fixing the *learning rate*, which represents the rate at which the code updates the network's weights (such as the alpha parameter used in the example for this chapter). The learning rate can affect both the time the neural network takes to learn a good solution (the number of epochs) and the result. In fact, if the learning rate is too low, your network will take forever to learn. Setting the value too high causes instability when updating the weights, and the network won't ever converge to a good solution.

Choosing a learning rate that works is daunting because you can effectively try values in the range from 0.000001 to 100. The best value varies from optimizer to optimizer. The value you choose depends on what type of data you have. Theory can be of little help here; you have to test different combinations before finding the most suitable learning rate for training your neural network successfully.

REMEMBER

In spite of all the math surrounding neural networks, tuning them and having them work best is mostly a matter of empirical efforts in trying different combinations of architectures and parameters.

Explaining Deep Learning Differences with Other Forms of AI

Given the embarrassment of riches that pertain to AI as a whole, such as large amounts of data, new and powerful computational hardware available to everyone, and plenty of private and public investments, you may be skeptical about the technology behind *deep learning*, which consists of neural networks that have more neurons and hidden layers than in the past. Deep networks contrast with the simpler, shallower networks of the past, which featured one or two hidden layers at best. Many solutions that render the deep learning of today possible are not at all new, but deep learning uses them in new ways.

REMEMBER

Deep learning isn't simply a rebranding of an old technology, the perceptron (see the section "Understanding perceptron functionality," earlier in this chapter). Deep learning works better because of the sophistication it adds through the full use of powerful computers and the availability of better (not just more) data. Deep learning also implies a profound qualitative change in the capabilities offered by the technology along with new and astonishing applications. The presence of these capabilities modernizes old but good neural networks, transforming them into something new. The following sections describe just how deep learning achieves its task.

Adding more layers

You may wonder why deep learning has blossomed only now when the technology used as the foundation of deep learning existed long ago. Computers are more powerful today, and deep learning can access huge amounts of data. However, these answers point only to important problems with deep learning in the past, and lower computing power along with less data weren't the only insurmountable obstacles. Until recently, deep learning also suffered from a key technical problem that kept neural networks from having enough layers to perform truly complex tasks.

Because it can use many layers, deep learning can solve problems that are out of reach of machine learning, such as image recognition, machine translation, and speech recognition. When fitted with only a few layers, a neural network is a perfect *universal function approximator*, which is a system that can re-create any possible mathematical function. When fitted with many more layers, a neural network becomes capable of creating, inside its internal chain of matrix multiplications, a sophisticated system of representations to solve complex problems. To understand how a complex task like image recognition works, consider this process:

1. A deep learning system trained to recognize images (such as a network capable of distinguishing photos of dogs from those featuring cats) defines internal weights that have the capability to recognize a picture topic.

2. After detecting each single contour and corner in the image, the deep learning network assembles all such basic traits into composite characteristic features.

3. The network matches such features to an ideal representation that provides the answer.

In other words, a deep learning network can distinguish dogs from cats using its internal weights to define a representation of what, ideally, a dog and a cat should resemble. It then uses these internal weights to match any new image you provide it with.

REMEMBER

One of the earliest achievements of deep learning that made the public aware of its potentiality is the *cat neuron*. The Google Brain team, run at that time by Andrew Ng and Jeff Dean, put together 16,000 computers to calculate a deep learning network with more than a billion weights, thus enabling unsupervised learning from YouTube videos. The computer network could even determine by itself, without any human intervention, what a cat is, and Google scientists managed to dig out of the network a representation of how the network itself expected a cat should look (see the "Wired" article at https://www.wired.com/2012/06/google-x-neural-network/).

During the time that scientists couldn't stack more layers into a neural network because of the limits of computer hardware, the potential of the technology remained buried, and scientists ignored neural networks. The lack of success added to the profound skepticism that arose around the technology during the last AI winter (1987 to 1993). However, what really prevented scientists from creating something more sophisticated was the problem with vanishing gradients.

A *vanishing gradient* occurs when you try to transmit a signal through a neural network and the signal quickly fades to near zero values; it can't get through the activation functions. This happens because neural networks are chained multiplications. Each below-zero multiplication decreases the incoming values rapidly, and activation functions need large enough values to let the signal pass. The farther neuron layers are from the output, the higher the likelihood that they'll get locked out of updates because the signals are too small and the activation functions will stop them. Consequently, your network stops learning as a whole, or it learns at an incredibly slow pace.

Every attempt at putting together and testing complex networks ended in failure during the last AI winter because the backpropagation algorithm couldn't update the layers nearer the input, thus rendering any learning from complex data, even when such data was available at the time, almost impossible. Today, deep networks are possible thanks to the studies of scholars from the University of Toronto in Canada, such as Geoffrey Hinton (https://www.utoronto.ca/news/artificial-intelligence-u-t), who insisted on working on neural networks even when they seemed to most to be an old-fashioned machine learning approach.

Professor Hinton, a veteran of the field of neural networks (he contributed to defining the backpropagation algorithm), and his team in Toronto devised a few methods to circumvent the problem of vanishing gradients. He opened the field to rethinking new solutions that made neural networks a crucial tool in machine learning and AI again.

REMEMBER

Professor Hinton and his team are memorable also for being among the first to test GPU usage in order to accelerate the training of a deep neural network. In 2012, they won an open competition, organized by the pharmaceutical company Merck and by Kaggle (https://www.kaggle.com/, a website for data science competitions), using their most recent deep learning discoveries. This event brought great attention to the Hinton team's work. You can read all the details of the Hinton team's revolutionary achievement with neural network layers from this Geoffrey Hinton interview: http://blog.kaggle.com/2012/11/01/deep-learning-how-i-did-it-merck-1st-place-interview/.

Changing the activations

Geoffrey Hinton's team (see preceding section) was able to add more layers to a neural architecture because of two solutions that prevented trouble with backpropagation:

>> They prevented the exploding gradients problem by using smarter network initialization. An *exploding gradient* differs from a vanishing gradient in that it can make a network blow up (stop functioning because of extremely high values) as the exploding gradient becomes too large to handle.

TIP

Your network can explode unless you correctly initialize the network to prevent it from computing large weight numbers. Then you solve the problem of vanishing gradients by changing the network activations.

>> The team realized that passing a signal through various activation layers tended to damp the backpropagation signal until it became too faint to pass anymore after examining how a sigmoid activation worked. They used a new activation as the solution for this problem. The choice of which algorithm to use fell to an old activation type of ReLU. An ReLU activation stopped the received signal if it was below zero, assuring the nonlinearity characteristic of neural networks and letting the signal pass as it was if above zero. (Using this type of activation is an example of combining old but still good technology with current technology.) Figure 2-7 shows how this process works.

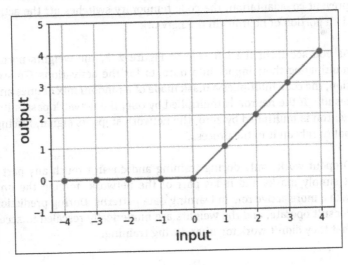

FIGURE 2-7:
How the ReLU
activation
function works
in receiving and
releasing signals.

The ReLU worked incredibly well and let the backpropagation signal arrive at the initial deep network layers. When the signal is positive, its derivative is 1. You can also find proof of the ReLU derivative in looking at Figure 2-7. Note that the rate of change is constant and equivalent to a unit when the input signal is positive (whereas when the signal is negative, the derivative is 0, thus preventing the signal from passing).

TIP

You can calculate the ReLU function using $f(x)=max(0,x)$. The use of this algorithm increased training speed a lot, allowing fast training of even deeper networks without incurring any dead neurons. A *dead neuron* is one that the network can't activate because the signals are too faint.

Adding regularization by dropout

The other introduction to deep learning made by Hinton's team (see preceding sections in this chapter) to complete the initial deep learning solution aimed at regularizing the network. A *regularized network* limits the network weights, which keeps the network from memorizing the input data and generalizing the witnessed data patterns.

Previous discussions in this chapter (see especially the "Adding more layers" section) note that certain neurons memorize specific information and force the other neurons to rely on this stronger neuron, causing the weak neurons to give up learning anything useful themselves (a situation called *co-adaptation*). To prevent co-adaptation, the code temporary switches off the activation of a random portion of neurons in the network.

As you see from the left side of Figure 2-8, the weights normally operate by multiplying their inputs into outputs for the activations. To switch off activation, the code multiplies a mask made of a random mix of ones and zeros with the results. If the neuron is multiplied by one, the network passes its signal. When a neuron is multiplied by zero, the network stops its signal, forcing other neurons not to rely on it in the process.

TECHNICAL
STUFF

Dropout works only during training and doesn't touch any part of the weights. It simply masks and hides part of the network, forcing the unmasked part to take a more active role in learning data patterns. During prediction time, dropout doesn't operate, and the weights are numerically rescaled to account for the fact that they didn't work together during training.

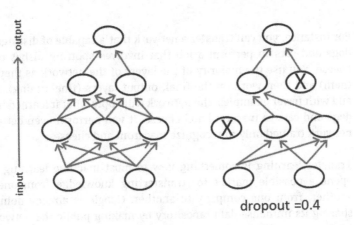

FIGURE 2-8:
Dropout temporarily rules out 40 percent of neurons from the training.

dropout =0.4

Using online learning

Neural networks are more flexible than other machine learning algorithms, and they can continue to train as they work on producing predictions and classifications. This capability comes from optimization algorithms that allow neural networks to learn, which can work repeatedly on small samples of examples (called *batch learning*) or even on single examples (called *online learning*). Deep learning networks can build their knowledge step by step and remain receptive to new information that may arrive (in a manner similar to a baby's mind, which is always open to new stimuli and to learning experiences).

For instance, a deep learning application on a social media website can train on cat images. As people post photos of cats, the application recognizes them and tags them with an appropriate label. When people start posting photos of dogs on the social network, the neural network doesn't need to restart training; it can continue by learning images of dogs as well. This capability is particularly useful for coping with the variability of Internet data. A deep learning network can be open to novelty and adapt its weights to deal with it.

Transferring learning

Flexibility is handy even when a network completes its training, but you must reuse it for purposes different from the initial learning. Networks that distinguish objects and correctly classify them require a long time and a lot of computational capacity to learn what to do. Extending a network's capability to new kinds of images that weren't part of the previous learning means transferring the knowledge to this new problem (*transfer learning*).

For instance, you can transfer a network that's capable of distinguishing between dogs and cats to perform a job that involves spotting dishes of macaroni and cheese. You use the majority of the layers of the network as they are (you freeze them) and then work on the final, output layers (fine-tuning). In a short time, and with fewer examples, the network will apply what it learned in distinguishing dogs and cats to macaroni and cheese. It will perform even better than a neural network trained only to recognize macaroni and cheese.

Transfer learning is something new to most machine learning algorithms and opens a possible market for transferring knowledge from one application to another, from one company to another. Google is already doing that, actually sharing its immense data repository by making public the networks that it built on it (as detailed in this post: https://techcrunch.com/2017/06/16/object-detection-api/). This is a step in democratizing deep learning by allowing everyone to access its potentiality.

Learning end to end

Finally, deep learning allows end-to-end learning, which means that it solves problems in an easier and more straightforward way than previous deep learning solutions. This flexibility might result in a greater impact when solving problems.

You may want to solve a difficult problem, such as having the AI recognize known faces or drive a car. When using the classical AI approach, you had to split the problem into more manageable subproblems to achieve an acceptable result in a feasible time. For instance, if you wanted to recognize faces in a photo, previous AI systems arranged the problem into parts, as follows:

1. Find the faces in the photo.

2. Crop the faces from the photo.

3. Process the cropped faces to have a pose similar to an ID card photo.

4. Feed the processed cropped faces as learning examples to a neural network for image recognition.

Today, you can feed the photo to a deep learning architecture, guide it to learn to find faces in the images, and then use the deep learning architecture to classify them. You can use the same approach for language translation, speech recognition, or even self-driving cars. In all cases, you simply pass the input to a deep learning system and obtain the wanted result.

Chapter **3**

Recognizing Images with CNNs

Humans are graphically (visually) oriented, but computers aren't. So, the task that humans most want performed by deep learning — recognizing items in images — is also one of the harder tasks to perform using a computer. The manner in which a computer deals with images is completely different from humans. When working with images, computers deal with the numeric values that make up individual pixels. The computer processes the numbers used to create an image much as it processes any other group of numbers. Consequently, this chapter deals with using a different kind of math to manipulate those pixel values so that a computer can output the desired result, despite having no concept whatsoever that it is even processing an image.

You have some methods of working with images that don't involve heavy-duty usage of deep learning techniques, but the output from these methods is also simple. However, these techniques make a good starting point for the discussions later in the chapter, so you see them in the first part of this chapter.

The real basis for more advanced image processing today is the Convolutional Neural Network (CNN). The next part of the chapter provides you with a basis for understand CNNs, which are actually specialized layers of a neural network.

The perceptron is discussed in the "Discovering the Incredible Perceptron" section of Book 4, Chapter 2. Of course, a CNN is much more sophisticated than just a bunch of perceptrons and the introduction to them in the second part of the book will help you understand the difference better.

The third part of the chapter helps you understand how CNNs get used in the real world to some extent. You won't see the full range of uses because that would take another book (possibly two). The examples in this chapter help you understand that CNNs are quite powerful because of how the computer uses them to work with images numerically. The final piece in the chapter shows how you can use CNNs to detect both edges and shapes in images, which is quite a feat because even humans can't always perform the task reliably.

REMEMBER

You don't have to type the source code for this chapter manually. In fact, using the downloadable source is a lot easier. The source code for this chapter appears in the DSPD_0403_CNN.ipynb source code file for Python and the DSPD_R_0403_CNN.ipynb source code file for R. See the Introduction for details on how to find these source files.

Beginning with Simple Image Recognition

Among the five senses, sight is certainly the most powerful in conveying knowledge and information derived from the world outside. Many people feel that the gift of sight helps children know about the different items and persons around them. In addition, humans receive and transmit knowledge across time by means of pictures, visual arts, and textual documents. The sections that follow help you understand how machine learning can help your computer interact with images using the two languages found in this book.

Considering the ramifications of sight

Because sight is so important and precious, it's invaluable for a machine learning algorithm because the graphic data obtained through sight sensors, such as cameras, opens the algorithm to new capabilities. Most information today is available in the following digital forms:

>> Text

>> Music

>> Photos

>> Videos

Being able to read visual information in a binary format doesn't help you to understand it and to use it properly. In recent years, one of the more important uses of vision in machine learning is to classify images for all sorts of reasons. Here are some examples to consider:

» A doctor could rely on a machine learning application to find the cancer in a scan of a patient.

» Image processing and detection also makes automation possible. Robots need to know which objects they should avoid and which objects they need to work with, yet without image classification, the task is impossible.

» Humans rely on image classification to perform tasks such as handwriting recognition and finding particular individuals in a crowd.

Here's a smattering of other vital tasks of image classification: assisting in forensic analysis; detecting pedestrians (an important feature to implement in cars and one that could save thousands of lives); and helping farmers determine where fields need the most water. Check out the state of the art in image classification at http://rodrigob.github.io/are_we_there_yet/build/.

Working with a set of images

At first sight, image files appear as unstructured data made up of a series of bits. The file doesn't separate the bits from each other in any way. You can't simply look into the file and see any image structure because none exists. As with other file formats, image files rely on the user to know how to interpret the data. For example, each pixel of a picture file could consist of three 32-bit fields. Knowing that each field is 32-bits is up to you. A header at the beginning of the file may provide clues about interpreting the file, but even so, it's up to you to know how to interact with the file using the right package or library. The following section discusses how to work directly with images.

Finding a library

You use Scikit-image for the Python examples presented in this section and those that follow. It's a Python package dedicated to processing images, picking them up from files, and handling them using NumPy arrays. By using Scikit-image, you can obtain all the skills needed to load and transform images for any machine learning algorithm. This package also helps you upload all the necessary images, resize or crop them, and flatten them into a vector of features in order to transform them for learning purposes.

DATA SCIENCE IMAGE PROCESSING IN R

Image processing can become a complex task, and trying to precisely mimic techniques across languages is difficult and sometimes impossible. You need a library for your language that does what you need it to using that language's native capabilities. When viewing the outputs for the various language examples in this section, you see essentially the same result, so any data scientist could use the associated output to perform analysis. The technique, however, differs some between languages, and you might not find a one-for-one correlation in lines of code. Consequently, the R examples are heavily commented to tell you when to expect a different approach and why the approach makes sense in that language.

The library used for R for this chapter (and any chapter that relies on image processing) is ImageMagick (`https://imagemagick.org/index.php`). You can read a review of it at `https://heartbeat.fritz.ai/image-manipulation-for-machine-learning-in-r-ff2b92069fef`. In some respects, ImageMagick is a little more comprehensive than its Scikit-image counterpart.

Scikit-image isn't the only package that can help you deal with images in Python. Other packages are available also, such as the following:

>> **scipy.ndimage** (`http://docs.scipy.org/doc/scipy/reference/ndimage.html`): Allows you to operate on multidimensional images

>> **Mahotas** (`http://mahotas.readthedocs.org/en/latest/`): A fast C++ based processing library

>> **OpenCV** (`https://opencv-python-tutroals.readthedocs.org/`): A powerful package that specializes in computer vision

>> **ITK** (`http://www.itk.org/`): Designed to work on 3D images for medical purposes

The example in this section shows how to work with a picture as an unstructured file. The example image is a public domain offering from `http://commons.wikimedia.org/wiki/Main_Page`. To work with images, you need to access the Scikit-image library (`http://scikit-image.org/`), which is an algorithm collection used for image processing. You can find a tutorial for this library at `http://scipy-lectures.github.io/packages/scikit-image/`. The first task is to display the image onscreen using the following code. (Be patient: The image is ready when the busy indicator disappears from the IPython Notebook tab.)

```
from skimage.io import imread
from skimage.transform import resize
from matplotlib import pyplot as plt
import matplotlib.cm as cm

%matplotlib inline

example_file = ("http://upload.wikimedia.org/" +
    "wikipedia/commons/6/69/GeraldHeaneyMagician.png")
image = imread(example_file, as_grey=False)
plt.imshow(image, cmap=cm.gray)
plt.show()
```

The code begins by importing a number of libraries. It then creates a string that points to the example file online and places it in `example_file`. This string is part of the `imread()` method call, along with `as_grey`, which is set to `True`. The `as_grey` argument tells Python to turn any color images into grayscale. Any images that are already in grayscale remain that way.

After you have an image loaded, you render it (make it ready to display onscreen). The `imshow()` function performs the rendering and uses a grayscale color map. The `show()` function actually displays `image` for you, as shown in Figure 3-1.

FIGURE 3-1:
The image appears onscreen after you render and show it.

Dealing with image issues

Sometimes images aren't perfect; they could present noise or other granularity. You must smooth the erroneous and unusable signals. Filters can help you achieve that smoothing without hiding or modifying important characteristics of the image, such as the edges. If you're looking for an image filter, you can clean up your images using the following:

» **Median filter:** Based on the idea that the true signal comes from a median of a neighborhood of pixels. A function disk provides the area used to apply the median, which creates a circular window on a neighborhood.

» **Total variation denoising:** Based on the idea that noise is variance, which this filter reduces.

» **Gaussian filter:** Uses a Gaussian function to define the pixels to smooth.

CHOOSING AN IMAGE

You need to exercise some caution in picture selection when performing filtering of the sort shown in this example. The picture chosen for this example works because it's already in grayscale format in the correct arrangement. If you use a color image, however, you need to convert it to grayscale by setting the as_grey=True argument in the call to image = imread(example_file, as_grey=False). The result would be a nearly usable image in grayscale for some types of filtering, but not all.

The problem with making this change is that the dtype (data type) of the output image changes from uint8 to float64 when you set as_grey=True. The filters.rank. median() method call expects a uint8 as input, so it displays a warning message. You could get rid of the warning message by making a simple call:

```
import warnings
warnings.filterwarnings("ignore")
```

but this isn't usually the best solution. Another option you might try is to set the image to the correct type by calling image.astype('uint8'). However, this change presents other problems. The best solution is to find a picture of the appropriate type or to convert the picture to the appropriate type outside the application as a preprocessing step, ensuring that the dtype stays at uint8 when you read it. You can test the dtype of an image by calling print(image.dtype).

The restoration.denoise_tv_chambolle() and filters.gaussian() method calls aren't so particular. Each of these methods will accept either uint8 or float64 without problem. So, the choice of filtering method becomes an issue as well.

The following code demonstrates the effect that every filter has on the final image:

```
from skimage import filters, restoration
from skimage.morphology import disk
median_filter = filters.rank.median(image, disk(1))
tv_filter = restoration.denoise_tv_chambolle(image,
                                            weight=0.1)
gaussian_filter = filters.gaussian(image, sigma=0.7)
```

To see the effect of the filtering, you must display the filtered images onscreen. The following code performs this task by using an enumeration to display the filter name as a string and the actual filtered image. Each image appears as a subplot of a main image:

```
fig = plt.figure()
for k,(t,F) in enumerate((('Median filter',median_filter),
                ('TV filter',tv_filter),
                ('Gaussian filter', gaussian_filter))):
    f=fig.add_subplot(1,3,k+1)
    plt.axis('off')
    f.set_title(t)
    plt.imshow(F, cmap=cm.gray)
plt.show()
```

Figure 3-2 shows the output of each of the filters. Notice that the TV filter entry shows the best filtering effects.

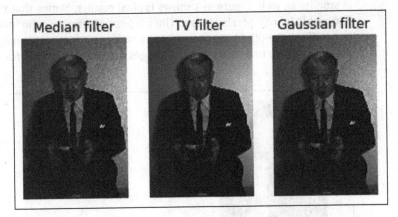

FIGURE 3-2:
Different filters
for different noise
cleaning.

TIP

If you aren't working in IPython (or you aren't using the magic command %matplotlib inline), just close the image when you've finished viewing it after filtering noise from the image. (The asterisk in the In [*]: entry in Notebook tells you that the code is still running and you can't move on to the next step.) The act of closing the image ends the code segment.

Manipulating the image

You now have an image in memory and you may want to find out more about it. When you run the following code, you discover the image type and size:

```
print("data type: %s, dtype: %s, shape: %s" %
      (type(image), image.dtype, image.shape))
```

The output from this call tells you that the image type is a numpy.ndarray, the dtype is uint8, and the image size is 1200 pixels by 800 pixels. The image is actually an array of pixels that you can manipulate in various ways. For example, if you want to crop the image, you can use the following code to manipulate the image array:

```
image2 = image[100:950,50:700]
plt.imshow(image2, cmap=cm.gray)
plt.show()
print("data type: %s, dtype: %s, shape: %s" %
      (type(image2), image2.dtype, image2.shape))
```

The numpy.ndarray in image2 is smaller than the one in image, so the output is smaller as well. Figure 3-3 shows typical results. Notice that the image is now 850 pixels by 650 pixels in size. The purpose of cropping the image is to make it a specific size. Both images must be the same size for you to analyze them. Cropping is one way to ensure that the images are the correct size for analysis.

FIGURE 3-3:
Cropping the image makes it smaller.

data type: <class 'numpy.ndarray'>, dtype: uint8, shape: (850, 650)

Another method that you can use to change the image size is to resize it. The following code resizes the image to a specific size for analysis:

```
image3 = resize(image2, (600, 460), mode='symmetric')
plt.imshow(image3, cmap=cm.gray)
print("data type: %s, dtype: %s, shape: %s" %
      (type(image3), image3.dtype, image3.shape))
```

The output from the `print()` function tells you that the image is now 600 pixels by 460 pixels in size. You can compare it to any image with the same dimensions.

After you have cleaned up all the images and made them the right size, you need to flatten them. A dataset row is always a single dimension, not two or more dimensions. The image is currently an array of 600 pixels by 460 pixels, so you can't make it part of a dataset. The following code flattens `image3`, so it becomes an array of 276,000 elements stored in `image_row`.

```
image_row = image3.flatten()
print("data type: %s, shape: %s" %
      (type(image_row), image_row.shape))
```

Notice that the type is still a `numpy.ndarray`. You can add this array to a dataset and then use the dataset for analysis purposes. The size is 276,000 elements, as anticipated.

Extracting visual features

Machine learning on images works because it can rely on features to compare pictures and associate an image with another one (because of similarity) or to a specific label (guessing, for instance, the represented objects). Humans can easily choose a car or a tree when we see one in a picture. Even if it's the first time that we see a certain kind of tree or car, we can correctly associate it with the right object (*labeling*) or compare it with similar objects in memory (*image recall*).

In the case of a car, having wheels, doors, a steering wheel, and so on are all elements that help you categorize a new example of a car among other cars. It happens because you see shapes and elements beyond the image itself; thus, no matter how unusual a tree or a car may be, if it owns certain characteristics, you can $ out what it is.

REMEMBER

An algorithm can infer elements (shapes, colors, particulars, relevant elements, and so on) directly from pixels only when you prepare data for it. Apart from special kinds of neural networks, called Convolutional Neural Networks, or CNNs (discussed later in this chapter), it's always necessary to prepare the right features when working with images. CNNs rank as the state of the art in image recognition because they can extract useful features from raw images by themselves.

Feature preparation from images is like playing with a jigsaw puzzle: You have to figure out any relevant particular, texture, or set of corners represented inside the image to recreate a picture from its details. All this information serves as the image features and makes up a precious element for any machine learning algorithm to complete its job.

CNNs filter information across multiple layers and train the parameters of their convolutions (which are kinds of image filters). In this way, they can filter out the features relevant to the images and the tasks they're trained to perform and exclude everything else. Other special layers, called *pooling layers,* help the neural net catch these features in the case of translation (they appear in unusual parts of the image) or rotation.

TIP

Applying deep learning requires special techniques and machines that are able to sustain the heavy computational workload. The Caffe library, developed by Yangqing Jia from the Berkeley Vision and Learning Center, allows building such neural networks but also leverages pretrained ones (http://caffe.berkeleyvision.org/model_zoo.html). A *pretrained neural network* is a CNN trained on a large number of varied images, thus it has learned how to filter out a large variety of features for classification purposes. The pretrained network lets you input your images and obtain a large number of values that correspond to a score on a certain kind of feature previously learned by the network as an output. The features may correspond to a certain shape or texture. What matters to your machine learning objectives is for the most revealing features for your purposes to be among those produced by the pretrained network. Therefore, you must choose the right features by making a selection using another neural network, an SVM, or a simple regression model.

When you can't use a CNN or pretrained library (because of memory or CPU constraints), OpenCV (https://opencv-python-tutroals.readthedocs.io/en/latest/py_tutorials/py_feature2d/py_table_of_contents_feature2d/py_table_of_contents_feature2d.html) or some Scikit-image functions can still help. For instance, to emphasize the borders of an image, you can apply a simple process using Scikit-image, as shown here:

```
from skimage import measure
contours = measure.find_contours(image, 0.55)
plt.imshow(image, cmap=cm.gray)
for n, contour in enumerate(contours):
    plt.plot(contour[:, 1], contour[:, 0], linewidth=2)
plt.axis('image')
plt.show()
```

You can read more about finding contours and other algorithms for feature extraction (histograms; corner and blob detection) in the tutorials at `https://scikit-image.org/docs/dev/auto_examples/`.

Recognizing faces using Eigenfaces

The capability to recognize a face in the crowd has become an essential tool for many professions. For example, both the military and law enforcement rely on it heavily. Of course, facial recognition has uses for security and other needs as well. This example looks at facial recognition in a more general sense. You may have wondered how social networks manage to tag images with the appropriate label or name. The following example demonstrates how to perform this task by creating the right features using eigenfaces.

Eigenfaces is an approach to facial recognition based on the overall appearance of a face, not on its particular details. By means of a technique that can intercept and reshape the variance present in the image, the reshaped information is treated like the DNA of a face, thus allowing the recovery of similar faces (because they have similar variances) in a host of facial images. It's a less effective technique than extracting features from the details of an image, yet it works, and you can implement it quickly on your computer. This approach demonstrates how machine learning can operate with raw pixels, but it's more effective when you change image data into another kind of data. You can learn more about eigenfaces at `https://towardsdatascience.com/eigenfaces-recovering-humans-from-ghosts-17606c328184` or by trying the tutorial that explores variance decompositions in Scikit-learn at `https://scikit-learn.org/stable/auto_examples/decomposition/plot_faces_decomposition.html`.

In this example, you use eigenfaces to associate images present in a training set with those in a test set, initially using some simple statistical measures:

```
import numpy as np
from sklearn.datasets import fetch_olivetti_faces
dataset = fetch_olivetti_faces(shuffle=True,
                               random_state=101)
train_faces = dataset.data[:350,:]
test_faces  = dataset.data[350:,:]
train_answers = dataset.target[:350]
test_answers = dataset.target[350:]
```

The example begins by using the Olivetti faces dataset, a public domain set of images readily available from Scikit-learn. The following code displays a description of the dataset that you can use to learn more about it:

```
print (dataset.DESCR)
```

For this experiment, the code divides the set of labeled images into a training and a test set. You need to pretend that you know the labels of the training set but don't know anything from the test set. As a result, you want to associate images from the test set to the most similar image from the training set.

The Olivetti dataset consists of 400 photos taken from 40 people (so it contains ten photos of each person). Even though the photos represent the same person, each photo has been taken at different times during the day, with different light and facial expressions or details (for example, with glasses and without). The images are 64 x 64 pixels, so unfolding all the pixels into features creates a dataset made of 400 cases and 4,096 variables. It seems like a high number of features, and actually, it is. Using PCA, as shown in the following code, you can reduce them to a smaller and more manageable number:

```
from sklearn.decomposition import PCA
n_components = 25
Rpca = PCA(svd_solver='randomized',
           n_components=n_components,
           whiten=True,
           random_state=101).fit(train_faces)
print ('Explained variance by %i components: %0.3f' %
       (n_components,
        np.sum(Rpca.explained_variance_ratio_)))
compressed_train_faces = Rpca.transform(train_faces)
compressed_test_faces  = Rpca.transform(test_faces)
```

The output from this code tells you about the explained variance of each selected component, based on the number of selected components, which is 25 in this case. If you had used the full set of components, the summed ratio would be 1.0 (or 100 percent).

```
Explained variance by 25 components: 0.794
```

DEPRECATION OF THE RandomizedPCA CLASS

At one point, sklearn.decomposition included a RandomizedPCA class. Later versions of sklearn.decomposition have deprecated this class. Consequently, if you see examples using the RandomizedPCA class, you must use the PCA class instead with the svd_solver='randomized' argument set. You can discover more about the PCA class at https://scikit-learn.org/stable/modules/generated/sklearn.decomposition.PCA.html.

The decomposition performed by PCA creates 25 new variables (n_components parameter) and whitening (whiten=True), removing some constant noise (created by textual and photo granularity) and irrelevant information from images in a different way from the filters just discussed. The resulting decomposition uses 25 components, which is about 80 percent of the information held in 4,096 features. The following code displays the effect of this processing:

```
import matplotlib.pyplot as plt
photo = 17 # This is the photo in the test set
print ('We are looking for face id=%i'
       % test_answers[photo])
plt.subplot(1, 2, 1)
plt.axis('off')
plt.title('Unknown face '+str(photo)+' in test set')
plt.imshow(test_faces[photo].reshape(64,64),
           cmap=plt.cm.gray, interpolation='nearest')
plt.show()
```

Figure 3-4 shows the chosen photo, subject number 34, from the test set.

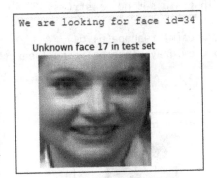

We are looking for face id=34

Unknown face 17 in test set

FIGURE 3-4:
The example application would like to find similar photos.

After the decomposition of the test set, the example takes the data relative only to photo 17 and subtracts it from the decomposition of the training set. Now the training set is made of differences with respect to the example photo. The code squares them (to remove negative values) and sums them by row, which results in a series of summed errors. The most similar photos are the ones with the least squared errors, that is, the ones whose differences are the least:

```
#Just the vector of value components of our photo
mask = compressed_test_faces[photo,]
squared_errors = np.sum(
    (compressed_train_faces - mask)**2,axis=1)
minimum_error_face = np.argmin(squared_errors)
```

```
most_resembling = list(np.where(squared_errors < 20)[0])
print ('Best resembling face in train test: %i' %
        train_answers[minimum_error_face])
```

After running this code, you find the following results:

```
Best resembling face in train test: 34
```

As it did before, the code can now display photo 17 using the following code. Photo 17 is the photo that best resembles images from the train set. Figure 3-5 shows typical output from this example.

```
import matplotlib.pyplot as plt
plt.subplot(2, 2, 1)
plt.axis('off')
plt.title('Unknown face '+str(photo)+' in test set')
plt.imshow(test_faces[photo].reshape(64,64),
        cmap=plt.cm.gray, interpolation='nearest')
for k,m in enumerate(most_resembling[:3]):
    plt.subplot(2, 2, 2+k)
    plt.title('Match in train set no. '+str(m))
    plt.axis('off')
    plt.imshow(train_faces[m].reshape(64,64),
            cmap=plt.cm.gray, interpolation='nearest')
plt.show()
```

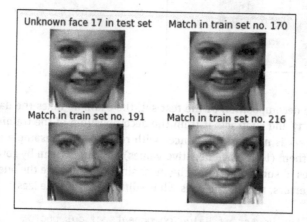

FIGURE 3-5:
The output shows the results that resemble the test image.

Even though the most similar photo is quite close to photo 17 (it's just scaled slightly differently), the other two photos are quite different. However, even though those photos don't match the text image as well, they really do show the same person as in photo 17.

Classifying images

This section adds to your knowledge of facial recognition, this time applying a learning algorithm to a complex set of images, called the `Labeled Faces in the Wild` dataset, which contains images of famous people collected over the Internet: `http://vis-www.cs.umass.edu/lfw/`. You must download the dataset from the Internet, using the Scikit-learn package in Python (see the `fetch_lfw_people` site at `https://scikit-learn.org/stable/modules/generated/sklearn.datasets.fetch_lfw_people.html` for details). The package mainly contains photos of well-known politicians.

```
import warnings
warnings.filterwarnings("ignore")
from sklearn.datasets import fetch_lfw_people
lfw_people = fetch_lfw_people(min_faces_per_person=60,
                              resize=0.4)
X = lfw_people.data
y = lfw_people.target
target_names = [lfw_people.target_names[a] for a in y]
n_samples, h, w = lfw_people.images.shape
from collections import Counter
for name, count in Counter(target_names).items():
    print ("%20s %i" % (name, count))
```

When you run this code, you see some downloading messages. These messages are quite normal, and you shouldn't worry about them. The downloading process can take a while because the dataset is relatively large. When the download process is complete, the example code outputs the name of each well-known politician, along with the number of associated pictures, as shown here:

```
         Colin Powell 236
        George W Bush 530
         Hugo Chavez 71
    Junichiro Koizumi 60
          Tony Blair 144
         Ariel Sharon 77
     Donald Rumsfeld 121
   Gerhard Schroeder 109
```

As an example of dataset variety, after dividing the examples into training and test sets, you can display a sample of pictures from both sets depicting Junichiro Koizumi, former Prime Minister of Japan from 2001 to 2006. Figure 3-6 shows the output of the following code:

```
from sklearn.cross_validation import \
    StratifiedShuffleSplit
```

```
train, test = list(StratifiedShuffleSplit(target_names,
        n_iter=1, test_size=0.1, random_state=101))[0]

plt.subplot(1, 4, 1)
plt.axis('off')
for k,m in enumerate(X[train][y[train]==6][:4]):
    plt.subplot(1, 4, 1+k)
    if k==0:
        plt.title('Train set')
    plt.axis('off')
    plt.imshow(m.reshape(50,37),
            cmap=plt.cm.gray, interpolation='nearest')
plt.show()

for k,m in enumerate(X[test][y[test]==6][:4]):
    plt.subplot(1, 4, 1+k)
    if k==0:
        plt.title('Test set')
    plt.axis('off')
    plt.imshow(m.reshape(50,37),
            cmap=plt.cm.gray, interpolation='nearest')
plt.show()
```

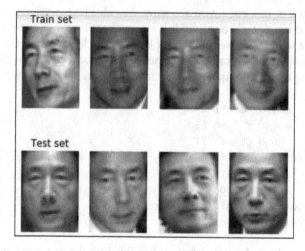

As you can see, the photos have quite a few variations, even among photos of the
same person, which makes the task challenging. The application must consider:

- » Expression

- » Pose

- » Light differences

- » Photo quality

For this reason, the example that follows applies the eigenfaces method described in the previous section, using different kinds of decompositions and reducing the initial large vector of pixel features (1850) to a simpler set of 150 features. The example uses PCA, the variance decomposition technique; Non-Negative Matrix Factorization (NMF), a technique for decomposing images into only positive features; and FastICA, an algorithm for Independent Component Analysis, which is an analysis that extracts signals from noise and other separated signals. (This algorithm is successful at handling problems like the cocktail party problem described at https://www.comsol.com/blogs/have-you-heard-about-the-cocktail-party-problem/.)

```
from sklearn import decomposition
n_components = 50
pca = decomposition.PCA(
    svd_solver='randomized',
    n_components=n_components,
    whiten=True).fit(X[train,:])
nmf = decomposition.NMF(n_components=n_components,
                        init='nndsvda',
                        tol=5e-3).fit(X[train,:])
fastica = decomposition.FastICA(n_components=n_components,
                                whiten=True).fit(X[train,:])
eigenfaces = pca.components_.reshape((n_components, h, w))
X_dec = np.column_stack((pca.transform(X[train,:]),
        nmf.transform(X[train,:]),
        fastica.transform(X[train,:])))
Xt_dec = np.column_stack((pca.transform(X[test,:]),
        nmf.transform(X[test,:]),
        fastica.transform(X[test,:])))
y_dec = y[train]
yt_dec = y[test]
```

After extracting and concatenating the image decompositions into a new training and test set of data examples, the code applies a grid search for the best combinations of parameters for a classification support vector machine (SVM) to perform a correct problem classification:

```
from sklearn.grid_search import GridSearchCV
from sklearn.svm import SVC
```

Recognizing Images with CNNs

```
param_grid = {'C': [0.1, 1.0, 10.0, 100.0, 1000.0],
              'gamma': [0.0001, 0.001, 0.01, 0.1], }
clf = GridSearchCV(SVC(kernel='rbf'), param_grid)
clf = clf.fit(X_dec, y_dec)
print ("Best parameters: %s" % clf.best_params_)
```

After the code runs, you see an output showing the best parameters to use, as shown here:

```
Best parameters: {'C': 10.0, 'gamma': 0.01}
```

After finding the best parameters, the following code checks for accuracy — that is, the percentage of correct answers in the test set. Obviously, using the preceding code doesn't pay if the accuracy produced by the SVM is too low; it would be too much like guessing.

```
from sklearn.metrics import accuracy_score
solution = clf.predict(Xt_dec)
print("Achieved accuracy: %0.3f"
      % accuracy_score(yt_dec, solution))
```

Fortunately, the example provides an estimate of about 0.84 (the measure may change when you run the code on your computer).

```
Achieved accuracy: 0.837
```

More interestingly, you can ask for a confusion matrix that shows the correct classes along the rows and the predictions in the columns. When a character in a row has counts in columns different from its row number, the code has mistakenly attributed one of the photos to someone else.

```
from sklearn.metrics import confusion_matrix
confusion = str(confusion_matrix(yt_dec, solution))
print (' '*26+ '  '.join(map(str,range(8))))
print (' '*26+ '-'*22)
for n, (label, row) in enumerate(
                  zip(lfw_people.target_names,
                      confusion.split('\n'))):
    print ('%s %18s > %s' % (n, label, row))
```

In this case, the example actually gets a perfect score for Junichiro Koizumi (notice that the output shows a 6 in row 6, column 6, and zeros in the remainder of the entries for that row). The code gets most confused about Gerhard Schroeder. Notice that the affected row shows 6 correct entries in column 4, but has a total of 5 incorrect entries in the other columns.

```
              0   1   2   3   4   5   6   7
              ─────────────────────────────────
0       Ariel Sharon >  [[ 7   0   0   0   1   0   0   0]
1       Colin Powell >   [ 0  22   0   2   0   0   0   0]
2    Donald Rumsfeld >   [ 0   0   8   2   1   0   0   1]
3      George W Bush >   [ 0   1   3  46   1   0   0   2]
4  Gerhard Schroeder >   [ 0   0   2   1   6   1   0   1]
5       Hugo Chavez >    [ 0   0   0   0   0   6   0   1]
6  Junichiro Koizumi >   [ 0   0   0   0   0   0   6   0]
7        Tony Blair >    [ 0   0   0   1   1   0   0  12]]
```

Understanding CNN Image Basics

Digital images are everywhere today because of the pervasive presence of digital cameras, webcams, and mobile phones with cameras. Because capturing images has become so easy, a new, huge stream of data is provided by images. Being able to process images opens the doors to new applications in fields such as robotics, autonomous driving, medicine, security, and surveillance.

Processing an image for use by a computer transforms it into data. Computers send images to a monitor as a data stream composed of pixels, so computer images are best represented as a matrix of pixels values, with each position in the matrix corresponding to a point in the image.

Modern computer images represent colors using a series of 32 bits (8 bits apiece for red, blue, green, and transparency — the alpha channel). You can use just 24 bits to create a true color image, however. The article at http://www.rit-mcsl.org/fairchild/WhyIsColor/Questions/4-5.html explains this process in more detail. Computer images represent color using three overlapping matrices, each one providing information relative to one of three colors: Red, Green, or Blue (also called RGB). Blending different amounts of these three colors enables you to represent any standard human-viewable color, but not those seen by people with extraordinary perception. (Most people can see a maximum of 1,000,000 colors, which is well within the color range of the 16,777,216 colors offered by 24-bit color. Tetrachromats can see 100,000,000 colors, so you couldn't use a computer to analyze what they see. The article at http://nymag.com/scienceofus/2015/02/what-like-see-a-hundred-million-colors.html tells you more about tetrachromats.)

Generally, an image is therefore manipulated by a computer as a three-dimensional matrix consisting of height, width, and the number of channels — which is three for an RGB image, but could be just one for a black-and-white image.

(Grayscale is a special sort of RGB image for which each of the three channels is the same number; see `https://introcomputing.org/image-6-grayscale.html` for a discussion of how conversions between color and grayscale occur.) With a grayscale image, a single matrix can suffice by having a single number represent the 256-grayscale colors, as demonstrated by the example in Figure 3-7. In that figure, each pixel of an image of a number is quantified by its matrix values.

255	255	170	34	102	238	255	255
255	255	34	0	85	0	170	255
255	204	0	221	255	68	119	255
255	187	51	255	255	119	119	255
255	170	119	255	255	102	119	255
255	187	68	255	238	51	136	255
255	221	17	170	85	51	255	255
255	255	153	34	85	255	255	255

FIGURE 3-7: Each pixel is read by the computer as a number in a matrix.

Given the fact that images are pixels (represented as numeric inputs), neural network practitioners initially achieved good results by connecting an image directly to a neural network. Each image pixel connected to an input node in the network. Then one or more following hidden layers completed the network, finally resulting in an output layer. The approach worked acceptably for small images and to solve small problems but eventually gave way to different approaches for solving image recognition. As an alternative, researchers used other machine learning algorithms or applied intensive feature creation to transform an image into newly processed data that could help algorithms recognize the image better. An example of image feature creation is the Histograms of Oriented Gradients (HOG), which is a computational way to detect patterns in an image and turn them into a numeric matrix. (You can explore how HOG works by viewing this tutorial from the Skimage package: `https://scikit-image.org/docs/dev/auto_examples/features_detection/plot_hog.html`.)

Neural network practitioners found image feature creation to be computationally intensive and often impractical. Connecting image pixels to neurons was difficult because it required computing an incredibly large number of parameters, and the network couldn't achieve translation invariance, which is the capability to decipher a represented object under different conditions of size, distortion, or position in the image, as shown in Figure 3-8.

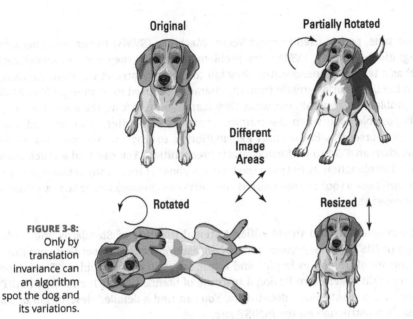

Original

Partially Rotated

Different Image Areas

Rotated

Resized

FIGURE 3-8:
Only by translation invariance can an algorithm spot the dog and its variations.

A neural network, which is made of dense layers, as described in the previous chapters in this minibook, can detect only images that are similar to those used for training — those that it has seen before — because it learns by spotting patterns at certain image locations. Also, a neural network can make many mistakes. Transforming an image before feeding it to the neural network can partially solve the problem by resizing, moving, cleaning the pixels, and creating special chunks of information for better network processing. This technique, called feature creation, requires expertise on the necessary image transformations, as well as many computations in terms of data analysis. Because of the intense level of custom work required, image recognition tasks are more the work of an artisan than a scientist. However, the amount of custom work has decreased over time as the base of libraries automating certain tasks has increased.

Moving to CNNs with Character Recognition

CNNs aren't a new idea. They appeared at the end of the 1980s as the solution for character recognition problems. Yann LeCun devised CNNs when he worked at AT&T Labs Research, together with other scientists such as Yoshua Bengio, Leon Bottou, and Patrick Haffner, on a network named LeNet5.

At one time, people used Support Vector Machines (SVMs) to perform character recognition. However, SVMs were problematic in that they need to model each pixel as a feature. Consequently, they fail to correctly predict the right character when the input varies greatly from the character set used for training. CNNs avoid this problem by generalizing what they learn, so predicting the correct character is possible even when the training character sets differ in some significant way. Of course, this is the short explanation as to why this section uses a CNN rather than an SVM to perform character recognition. You can find a much more detailed explanation at https://medium.com/analytics-vidhya/the-scuffle-between-two-algorithms-neural-network-vs-support-vector-machine-16abe0eb4181.

This example relies on the Modified National Institute of Standards and Technology (MNIST) (http://yann.lecun.com/exdb/mnist/) dataset that contains a training set of 60,000 examples and a test set of 10,000 examples. The dataset was originally taken from National Institute of Standards and Technology (NIST) (https://www.nist.gov/) documents. You can find a detailed description of the dataset's construction on the MNIST site.

Accessing the dataset

The first step is to obtain access to the MNIST dataset. The following code downloads the dataset and then displays a series of characters from it, as shown in Figure 3-9:

```
import matplotlib.pyplot as plt
%matplotlib inline
from keras.datasets import mnist

(X_train, y_train), (X_test, y_test) = mnist.load_data()

plt.plot()
plt.axis('off')
for k, m in enumerate(X_train[:4]):
    plt.subplot(1, 4, 1+k)
    plt.axis('off')
    plt.imshow(m, cmap=plt.cm.gray)

plt.show()
```

Reshaping the dataset

Each of the 60,000 images in X_train and the 10,000 images in X_test are 28 pixels by 28 pixels. In the "Manipulating the image" section, earlier in this chapter, you see how to flatten a single image using the numpy.ndarray.flatten (https://docs.scipy.org/doc/numpy-1.15.0/reference/generated/numpy.ndarray.flatten.html). This time, you rely on numpy.reshape (https://docs.scipy.org/doc/numpy/reference/generated/numpy.reshape.html) to perform the same task. To obtain the required output, you must supply the number of entries and the number of pixels, as shown here:

```
import numpy
from keras.utils import np_utils

numpy.random.seed(100)

pixels = X_train.shape[1] * X_train.shape[2]
train_entries = X_train.shape[0]
test_entries = X_test.shape[0]
X_train_row = X_train.reshape(train_entries, pixels)
X_test_row = X_test.reshape(test_entries, pixels)

print(X_train_row.shape)
print(X_test_row.shape)
```

The output of this part of the code is

```
(60000, 784)
(10000, 784)
```

Now that the individual entries are flattened rather than 2-D, you can normalize them. Normalization takes the 255 shades of gray and turns them into values between 0 and 1. However, the dtype of the X_train_row and X_test_row rows is currently unit8. What you really need is a float32, so this next step performs the required conversion as well:

```
# Change the data type
X_train_row = X_train_row.astype('float32')
X_test_row = X_test_row.astype('float32')
```

```
# Perform the normalization.
X_train_row = X_train_row / 255
X_test_row = X_test_row / 255
```

Encoding the categories

In the preceding sections, you're essentially asking the CNN to choose from ten different categories for each of the entries in X_train_row and X_test_row because the output can be from 0 through 9. This example uses a technique called one-hot encoding (https://hackernoon.com/what-is-one-hot-encoding-why-and-when-do-you-have-to-use-it-e3c6186d008f). When you start, the values in y_train and y_test range from 0 through 9. The problem with this approach is that the learning process will associate the value 9 as being a lot better than the value 0, even though it doesn't matter. So, this process converts a single scalar value, such as 7, into a binary vector. The following code shows how this works:

```
y_train_cat = np_utils.to_categorical(y_train)
y_test_cat = np_utils.to_categorical(y_test)
num_classes = y_test_cat.shape[1]
print(num_classes)
print(y_test[0])
print(y_test_cat[0])
```

When you run this code, you get this output:

```
10
7
[0. 0. 0. 0. 0. 0. 0. 1. 0. 0.]
```

The number of classes is still the same at 10. The original value of the first entry in y_test is 7. However, the encoding process turns it into the vector shown next, where the eighth value, which equates to 7 (when starting with 0), is set to 1 (or True). By encoding the entries this way, you preserve the label, 7, without giving the label any special weight.

Defining the model

In this section, you define a model to use to perform the analysis referred to in the preceding sections. A model starts with a framework of sorts and you then add layers to the model. Each layer performs a certain type of processing based on the attributes you set for it. After you create the model and define its layers, you then compile the model so that the application can use it, as shown here:

```
from keras.models import Sequential
from keras.layers import Dense
from keras.layers import Dropout

def baseline_model():
    # Specify which model to use.
    model = Sequential()

    # Add layers to the model.
    model.add(Dense(pixels, input_dim=pixels,
                    kernel_initializer='normal',
                    activation='relu'))
    model.add(Dense(num_classes,
                    kernel_initializer='normal',
                    activation='softmax'))

    # Compile the model
    model.compile(loss='categorical_crossentropy',
                  optimizer='adam', metrics=['accuracy'])
    return model
```

The Sequential model (explained at https://keras.io/models/sequential/ and https://keras.io/getting-started/sequential-model-guide/) provides the means to create a linear stack of layers. To add layers to this model, you simply call add(). The two layers used in this example are ReLU and softmax. Book 4, Chapters 2 and 3, respectively, give all the information you need to understand both of these layers and what they do. The final task is to compile the model so that you can use it to perform useful work.

Using the model

The final step in this process is to use the model to perform an analysis of the data. The following code actually creates a model using the definition from the previous section. It then fits this model to the data. When the training part of the process is complete, the code can evaluate the success or failure of the model in detecting the correct values for each handwritten character:

```
model = baseline_model()

model.fit(X_train_row, y_train_cat,
          validation_data=(X_test_row, y_test_cat),
          epochs=10, batch_size=200, verbose=2)
```

```
scores = model.evaluate(X_test_row, y_test_cat, verbose=0)
print("Baseline Error: %.2f%%" % (100-scores[1]*100))
```

The output tells you that the model works well but doesn't provide absolute reliability. The model has a 1.87 percent chance of choosing the wrong character, as shown here:

```
Train on 60000 samples, validate on 10000 samples
Epoch 1/10
 - 13s - loss: 0.2800 - acc: 0.9205 - val_loss: 0.1344
 - val_acc: 0.9623
Epoch 2/10
 - 13s - loss: 0.1116 - acc: 0.9681 - val_loss: 0.0916
 - val_acc: 0.9722
Epoch 3/10
 - 12s - loss: 0.0716 - acc: 0.9794 - val_loss: 0.0730
 - val_acc: 0.9775
Epoch 4/10
 - 12s - loss: 0.0501 - acc: 0.9854 - val_loss: 0.0677
 - val_acc: 0.9776
Epoch 5/10
 - 12s - loss: 0.0360 - acc: 0.9902 - val_loss: 0.0615
 - val_acc: 0.9812
Epoch 6/10
 - 12s - loss: 0.0264 - acc: 0.9929 - val_loss: 0.0643
 - val_acc: 0.9794
Epoch 7/10
 - 12s - loss: 0.0188 - acc: 0.9957 - val_loss: 0.0616
 - val_acc: 0.9802
Epoch 8/10
 - 12s - loss: 0.0144 - acc: 0.9967 - val_loss: 0.0609
 - val_acc: 0.9811
Epoch 9/10
 - 12s - loss: 0.0106 - acc: 0.9978 - val_loss: 0.0614
 - val_acc: 0.9820
Epoch 10/10
 - 13s - loss: 0.0087 - acc: 0.9980 - val_loss: 0.0587
 - val_acc: 0.9813
Baseline Error: 1.87%
```

Explaining How Convolutions Work

Convolutions easily solve the problem of translation invariance because they offer a different image-processing approach inside the neural network. The idea started from a biological point of view by observing what happens in the human visual cortex.

A 1962 experiment by Nobel Prize winners David Hunter Hubel and Torsten Wiesel demonstrated that only certain neurons activate in the brain when the eye sees certain patterns, such as horizontal, vertical, or diagonal edges. In addition, the two scientists found that the neurons organize vertically, in a hierarchy, suggesting that visual perception relies on the organized contribution of many single, specialized neurons. (You can find out more about this experiment by reading the article at `https://knowingneurons.com/2014/10/29/hubel-and-wiesel-the-neural-basis-of-visual-perception/`.) Convolutions simply take this idea and, by using mathematics, apply it to image processing in order to enhance the capabilities of a neural network to recognize different images accurately.

Understanding convolutions

To understand how convolutions work, you start from the input. The input is an image composed of one or more pixel layers, called channels, and the image uses values ranging from 0–255, with 0 meaning that the individual pixel is fully switched off and 255 meaning that the individual pixel is switched on. (Usually, the values are stored as integers to save memory.) As mentioned in the preceding section of this chapter, RGB images have individual channels for red, green, and blue colors. Mixing these channels generates the palette of colors as you see them on the screen.

A convolution works by operating on small image chunks across all image channels simultaneously. (Picture a slice of layer cake, with each piece showing all the layers). Image chunks are simply a moving image window: The convolution window can be a square or a rectangle, and it starts from the upper left of the image and moves from left to right and from top to bottom. The complete tour of the window over the image is called a *filter* and implies a complete transformation of the image. Also important to note is that when a new chunk is framed by the window, the window then shifts a certain number of pixels; the amount of the slide is called a *stride*. A stride of 1 means that the window is moving one pixel toward right or bottom; a stride of 2 implies a movement of two pixels; and so on.

Every time the convolution window moves to a new position, a filtering process occurs to create part of the filter described in the previous paragraph. In this process, the values in the convolution window are multiplied by the values in the kernel. (A *kernel* is a small matrix used for blurring, sharpening, embossing, edge detection, and more. You choose the kernel you need for the task in question. The article at http://setosa.io/ev/image-kernels/ tells you more about various kernel types.) The kernel is the same size as the convolution window. Multiplying each part of the image with the kernel creates a new value for each pixel, which in a sense is a new, processed feature of the image. The convolution outputs the pixel value and when the sliding window has completed its tour across the image, you have *filtered* the image. As a result of the convolution, you find a new image having the following characteristics:

>> If you use a single filtering process, the result is a transformed image of a single channel.

>> If you use multiple kernels, the new image has as many channels as the number of filters, each one containing specially processed new feature values. The number of filters is the *filter depth* of a convolution.

>> If you use a stride of 1, you get an image of the same dimensions as the original.

>> If you use strides of a size above 1, the resulting convoluted image is smaller than the original (a stride of size two implies halving the image size).

>> The resulting image may be smaller depending on the kernel size, because the kernel has to start and finish its tour on the image borders. When processing the image, a kernel will eat up its size minus one. For instance, a kernel of 3 x 3 pixels processing a 7-x-7 pixel image will eat up 2 pixels from the height and width of the image, and the result of the convolution will be an output of size 5 x 5 pixels. You have the option to pad the image with zeros at the border (meaning, in essence, to put a black border on the image) so that the convolution process won't reduce the final output size. This strategy is called *same padding*. If you just let the kernel reduce the size of your starting image, it's called *valid padding*.

Image processing has relied on the convolution process for a long time. Convolution filters can detect an edge or enhance certain characteristics of an image. Figure 3-10 provides an example of some convolutions transforming an image.

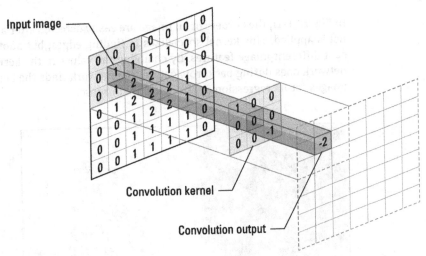

Input image

Convolution kernel

Convolution output

FIGURE 3-10:
A convolution
processes a
chunk of an
image by matrix
multiplication.

The problem with using convolutions is that they are human made and require effort to figure out. When using a neural network convolution instead, you just set:

» The number of filters (the number of kernels operating on an image that is its output channels)

» The kernel size (set just one side for a square; set width and height for a rectangle)

» The strides (usually 1- or 2-pixel steps)

» Whether you want the image black bordered (choose valid padding or same padding)

After determining the image–processing parameters, the optimization process determines the kernel values used to process the image in a way to allow the best classification of the final output layer. Each kernel matrix element is therefore a neural network neuron and modified during training using backpropagation for the best performance of the network itself.

Another interesting aspect of this process is that each kernel specializes in finding specific aspects of an image. For example, a kernel specialized in filtering features typical of cats can find a cat no matter where it is in an image and, if you use enough kernels, every possible variant of an image of a kind (resized, rotated, translated) is detected, rendering your neural network an efficient tool for image classification and recognition.

In Figure 3-11, the borders of an image are easily detected after a 3-x-3 pixel kernel is applied. This kernel specializes in finding edges, but another kernel could spot different image features. By changing the values in the kernel, as the neural network does during backpropagation, the network finds the best way to process images for its regression or classification purpose.

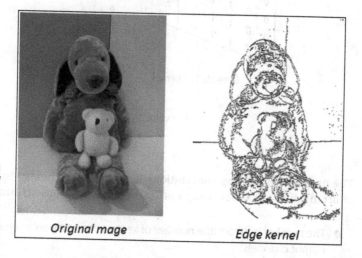

Original mage   *Edge kernel*

FIGURE 3-11:
The borders of an image are detected after applying a 3-x-3 pixel kernel.

TECHNICAL STUFF

The kernel is a matrix whose values are defined by the neural network optimization, multiplied by a small patch of the same size moving across the image, but it can be intended as a neural layer whose weights are shared across the different input neurons. You can see the patch as an immobile neural layer connected to the many parts of the image always using the same set of weights. It is exactly the same result.

Keras offers a convolutional layer, Conv2D, out of the box. This Keras layer can take both the input directly from the image (in a tuple, you have to set the input_shape the width, height, and number of channels of your image) or from another layer (such as another convolution). You can also set filters, kernel_size, strides, and padding, which are the basic parameters for any convolutional layers, as described earlier in the chapter.

TIP

When setting a Conv2D layer, you may also set many other parameters, which are actually a bit too technical and may not be necessary for your first experiments with CNNs. The only other parameters you may find useful now are activation, which can add an activation of your choice, and name, which sets a name for the layer.

Simplifying the use of pooling

Convolutional layers transform the original image using various kinds of filtering. Each layer finds specific patterns in the image (particular sets of shapes and colors that make the image recognizable). As this process continues, the complexity of the neural network grows because the number of parameters grows as the network gains more filters. To keep the complexity manageable, you need to speed the filtering and reduce the number of operations.

Pooling layers can simplify the output received from convolutional layers, thus reducing the number of successive operations performed and using fewer convolutional operations to perform filtering. Working in a fashion similar to convolutions (using a window size for the filter and a stride to slide it), pooling layers operate on patches of the input they receive and reduce a patch to a single number, thus effectively downsizing the data flowing through the neural network.

Figure 3-12 represents the operations done by a pooling layer. The pooling layer receives the filtered data, represented by the left 4-x-4 matrix, as input and operates on it using a window of size 2 pixels that moves by a stride of 2 pixels. As a result, the pooling layer produces the right output: a 2-x-2 matrix. The network applies the pooling operation on four patches represented by four different colored parts of the matrix. For each patch, the pooling layer computes the maximum value and saves it as an output.

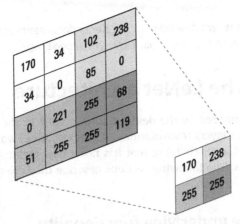

FIGURE 3-12:
A max pooling layer operating on chunks of a reduced image.

The current example relies on the max pooling layer because it uses the max transformation on its sliding window. You actually have access to four principal types of pooling layers:

» Max pooling

» Average pooling

» Global max pooling

» Global average pooling

In addition, these four pooling layer types have different versions, depending on the dimensionality of the input they can process:

» **1-D pooling:** Works on vectors. Thus, 1-D pooling is ideal for sequence data such as temporal data (data representing events following each other in time) or text (represented as sequences of letters or words). It takes the maximum or the average of contiguous parts of the sequence.

» **2-D pooling:** Fits spatial data that fits a matrix. You can use 2-D pooling for a grayscale image or each channel of an RBG image separately. It takes the maximum or the average of small patches (squares) of the data.

» **3-D pooling:** Fits spatial data represented as spatial-temporal data. You could use 3-D pooling for images taken across time. A typical example is to use magnetic resonance imaging (MRI) for a medical examination. Radiologists use an MRI to examine body tissues with magnetic fields and radio waves. (See the article from Stanford AI for healthcare to learn more about the contribution of deep learning: https://medium.com/stanford-ai-for-healthcare/dont-just-scan-this-deep-learning-techniques-for-mri-52610e9b7a85.) This kind of pooling takes the maximum or the average of small chunks (cubes) from the data.

You can find all these layers described in the Keras documentation, together with all their parameters, at https://keras.io/layers/pooling/.

Describing the LeNet architecture

You may have been amazed by the description of a CNN in the preceding section, and about how its layers (convolutions and max pooling) work, but you may be even more amazed at discovering that it's not a new technology; instead, it appeared in the 1990s. The following sections describe the LeNet architecture in more detail.

Considering the underlying functionality

The key person behind this innovation was Yann LeCun, who was working at AT&T Labs Research as head of the Image Processing Research Department. LeCun specialized in optical character recognition and computer vision. Yann LeCun is a French computer scientist who created CNNs with Léon Bottou, Yoshua Bengio, and Patrick Haffner. At present, he is the Chief AI Scientist at Facebook AI Research (FAIR) and a Silver Professor at New York University (mainly affiliated with the NYU Center for Data Science). His personal home page is at http://yann.lecun.com/.

In the late 1990s, AT&T implemented LeCun's LeNet5 to read ZIP codes for the United States Postal Service. The company also used LeNet5 for ATM check readers, which can automatically read the check amount. The system doesn't fail, as reported by LeCunn at https://pafnuty.wordpress.com/2009/06/13/yann-lecun/. However, the success of the LeNet passed almost unnoticed at the time because the AI sector was undergoing an *AI winter:* Both the public and investors were significantly less interested and attentive to improvements in neural technology than they are now.

REMEMBER

Part of the reason for an AI winter was that many researchers and investors lost faith in the idea that neural networks would revolutionize AI. Data of the time lacked the complexity for such a network to perform well. (ATMs and the USPS were notable exceptions because of the quantities of data they handled.) With a lack of data, convolutions only marginally outperform regular neural networks made of connected layers. In addition, many researchers achieved results comparable to LeNet5 using brand-new machine learning algorithms such as Support Vector Machines (SVMs) and Random Forests, which were algorithms based on mathematical principles different from those used for neural networks.

You can see the network in action at http://yann.lecun.com/exdb/lenet/ or in this video, in which a younger LeCun demonstrates an earlier version of the network: https://www.youtube.com/watch?v=FwFduRA_L6Q. At that time, having a machine able to decipher both typewritten and handwritten numbers was quite a feat.

As shown in Figure 3-13, the LeNet5 architecture consists of two sequences of convolutional and average pooling layers that perform image processing. The last layer of the sequence is then flattened; that is, each neuron in the resulting series of convoluted 2-D arrays is copied into a single line of neurons. At this point, two fully connected layers and a softmax classifier complete the network and provide the output in terms of probability. The LeNet5 network is really the basis of all the CNNs that follow. Re-creating the architecture using Keras, as you can do in the following sections, will explain it layer-by-layer and demonstrate how to build your own convolutional networks.

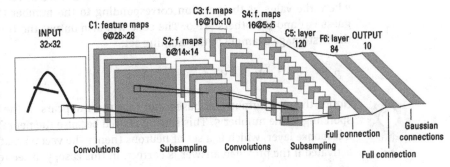

FIGURE 3-13:
The architecture of LeNet5, a neural network for handwritten digits recognition.

Building your own LeNet5 network

This network will be trained on a relevant amount of data (the digits dataset provided by Keras, consisting of more than 60,000 examples). You could therefore have an advantage if you run it on Colab, or on your local machine if you have a GPU available. After opening a new notebook, you start by importing the necessary packages and functions from Keras using the following code (note that some of this code is a repeat from the "Moving to CNNs with Character Recognition" section, earlier in this chapter):

```
import keras
import numpy as np
from keras.datasets import mnist
from keras.models import Sequential
from keras.layers import Conv2D, AveragePooling2D
from keras.layers import Dense, Flatten
from keras.losses import categorical_crossentropy
```

After importing the necessary tools, you need to collect the data:

```
(X_train, y_train), (X_test, y_test) = mnist.load_data()
```

The first time you execute this command, the `mnist` command will download all the data from the Internet, which could take a while. The downloaded data consists of single-channel 28-x-28-pixel images representing handwritten numbers from zero to nine. As a first step, you need to convert the response variable (y_train for the training phase and y_test for the test after the model is completed) into something that the neural network can understand and work on:

```
num_classes = len(np.unique(y_train))
print(y_train[0], end=' => ')
y_train = keras.utils.to_categorical(y_train, 10)
y_test = keras.utils.to_categorical(y_test, 10)
print(y_train[0])
```

This code snippet translates the response from numbers to vectors of numbers, where the value at the position corresponding to the number the network will guess is 1 and the others are 0. The code will also output the transformation for the first image example in the training set:

```
5 => [0. 0. 0. 0. 0. 1. 0. 0. 0. 0.]
```

Notice that the output is 0 based and that the 1 appears at the position corresponding to the number 5. This setting is used because the neural network needs a response layer, which is a set of neurons (hence the vector) that should become activated if the provided answer is correct. In this case, you see ten neurons, and in the training phase, the code activates the correct answer (the value at the correct position is set to 1) and turns the others off (their values are 0). In the test phase, the neural network uses its database of examples to turn the correct neuron on, or at least turn on more than the correct one. In the following code, the code prepares the training and test data:

```
X_train = X_train.astype(np.float32) / 255
X_test = X_test.astype(np.float32) / 255
img_rows, img_cols = X_train.shape[1:]
X_train = X_train.reshape(len(X_train),
                          img_rows, img_cols, 1)
X_test = X_test.reshape(len(X_test),
                        img_rows, img_cols, 1)
input_shape = (img_rows, img_cols, 1)
```

The pixel numbers, which range from 0 to 255, are transformed into a decimal value ranging from 0 to 1. The first two lines of code optimize the network to work properly with large numbers that could cause problems. The lines that follow reshape the images to have height, width, and channels.

The following line of code defines the LeNet5 architecture. You start by calling the `sequential` function that provides an empty model:

```
lenet = Sequential()
```

The first layer added is a convolutional layer, named C1:

```
lenet.add(Conv2D(6, kernel_size=(5, 5), activation='tanh',
          input_shape=input_shape, padding='same', name='C1'))
```

The convolution operates with a filter size of 6 (meaning that it will create six new channels made by convolutions) and a kernel size of 5 x 5 pixels.

TIP

The activation for all the layers of the network but the last one is *tanh* (Hyperbolic Tangent function), a nonlinear function that was state of the art for activation at the time Yann LeCun created LetNet5. The function is outdated today, but the example uses it to build a network that resembles the original LetNet5 architecture. To use such a network for your own projects, you should replace it with a modern ReLU (see https://www.kaggle.com/dansbecker/rectified-linear-units-relu-in-deep-learning for details). The example adds a pooling layer, named S2, which uses a 2-x-2-pixel kernel:

```
lenet.add(AveragePooling2D(
    pool_size=(2, 2), strides=(1, 1), padding='valid'))
```

At this point, the code proceeds with the sequence, always performed with a convolution and a pooling layer but this time using more filters:

```
lenet.add(Conv2D(16, kernel_size=(5, 5), strides=(1, 1),
                 activation='tanh', padding='valid'))
lenet.add(AveragePooling2D(
    pool_size=(2, 2), strides=(1, 1), padding='valid'))
```

The LeNet5 closes incrementally using a convolution with 120 filters. This convolution doesn't have a pooling layer but rather a flattening layer, which projects the neurons into the last convolution layer as a dense layer:

```
lenet.add(Conv2D(120, kernel_size=(5, 5),
                 activation='tanh', name='C5'))
lenet.add(Flatten())
```

The closing of the network is a sequence of two dense layers that process the convolution's outputs using the tanh and softmax activation. These two layers provide the final output layers where the neurons activate an output to signal the predicted answer. The softmax layer is actually the output layer, as specified by name='OUTPUT':

```
lenet.add(Dense(84, activation='tanh', name='FC6'))
lenet.add(Dense(10, activation='softmax', name='OUTPUT'))
```

REMEMBER

When the network is ready, you need Keras to compile it. (Behind all the Python code is some C language code.) Keras compiles it based on the SGD optimizer:

```
lenet.compile(loss=categorical_crossentropy,
              optimizer='SGD', metrics=['accuracy'])
lenet.summary()
```

The summary tells you about the structure of your model:

Layer (type)	Output Shape	Param #
C1 (Conv2D)	(None, 28, 28, 6)	156
average_pooling2d_1 (Average	(None, 27, 27, 6)	0
conv2d_1 (Conv2D)	(None, 23, 23, 16)	2416

```
average_pooling2d_2 (Average (None, 22, 22, 16)     0
_____
C5 (Conv2D)                  (None, 18, 18, 120)    48120
_____
flatten_1 (Flatten)          (None, 38880)          0
_____
FC6 (Dense)                  (None, 84)             3266004
_____
OUTPUT (Dense)               (None, 10)             850
=============================================================
Total params: 3,317,546
Trainable params: 3,317,546
Non-trainable params: 0
_____
```

At this point, you can run the network and wait for it to process the images:

```
batch_size = 64
epochs = 50
history = lenet.fit(X_train, y_train,
                    batch_size=batch_size,
                    epochs=epochs,
                    validation_data=(X_test,
                                     y_test))
```

Completing the run takes 50 epochs, with each epoch processing batches of 64 images at one time. (An *epoch* is the passing of the entire dataset through the neural network one time, and a *batch* is a part of the dataset, which means breaking the dataset into 64 chunks in this case.) With each epoch (lasting about eight seconds if you use Colab), you can monitor a progress bar telling you the time required to complete that epoch. You can also read the accuracy measures for both the training set (the optimistic estimate of the goodness of your model; see https://towardsdatascience.com/measuring-model-goodness-part-1-a24ed4d62f71 for details on what, precisely, *goodness* means) and the test set (the more realistic view). At the last epoch, you should read that a LeNet5 built in a few steps achieves an accuracy of 0.988, meaning that out every 100 handwritten numbers that it tries to recognize, the network should guess about 99 correctly. To see this number more clearly, you use the following code:

```
print("Best validation accuracy: {:0.3f}"
      .format(np.max(history.history['val_acc'])))
```

You can also create a plot of how the training process went using this code:

```
plt.plot(history.history['acc'])
plt.plot(history.history['val_acc'])
plt.ylabel('accuracy'); plt.xlabel('epochs')
plt.legend(['train', 'test'], loc='lower right')
plt.show()
```

Figure 3-14 shows typical output for the plotting process.

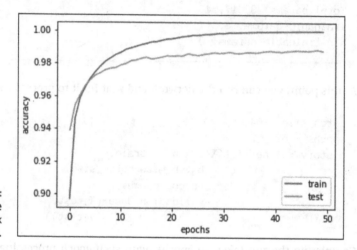

FIGURE 3-14:
A plot of the
LeNet5 network
training process.

Detecting Edges and Shapes from Images

Convolutions process images automatically and perform better than a densely connected layer because they learn image patterns at a local level and can retrace them in any other part of the image (a characteristic called *translation invariance*). On the other hand, traditional dense neural layers can determine the overall characteristics of an image in a rigid way without the benefit of translation invariance. The difference between convolutions and tradition layers is like that between learning a book by memorizing the text in meaningful chunks or memorizing it word by word. The student (or the convolutions) who learned chunk by chunk can better abstract the book content and is ready to apply that knowledge to similar cases. The student (or the dense layer) who learned it word by word struggles to extract something useful.

CNNs are not magic, nor are they a black box. You can understand them through image processing and leverage their functionality to extend their capabilities to new problems. This feature helps solve a series of computer vision problems that data scientists deemed too hard to crack using older strategies.

Visualizing convolutions

A CNN uses different layers to perform specific tasks in a hierarchical way. Yann LeCun (see the "Moving to CNNs with Character Recognition" section, earlier in this chapter) noticed how LeNet first processed edges and contours, and then motifs, and then categories, and finally objects. Recent studies further unveil how convolutions really work:

» **Initial layers:** Discover the image edges

» **Middle layers:** Detect complex shapes (created by edges)

» **Final layers:** Uncover distinctive image features that are characteristic of the image type that you want the network to classify (for instance, the nose of a dog or the ears of a cat)

This hierarchy of patterns discovered by convolutions also explains why deep convolutional networks perform better than shallow ones: The more stacked convolutions there are, the better the network can learn more and more complex and useful patterns for successful image recognition. Figure 3-15 provides an idea of how things work. The image of a dog is processed by convolutions, and the first layer grasps patterns. The second layer accepts these patterns and assembles them into a dog. If the patterns processed by the first layer seem too general to be of any use, the patterns unveiled by the second layer recreate more characteristic dog features that provide an advantage to the neural network in recognizing dogs.

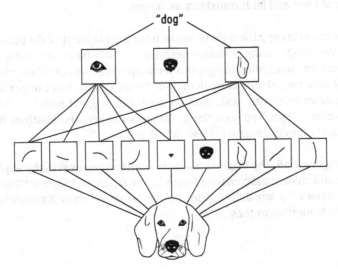

FIGURE 3-15: Processing a dog image using convolutions.

The difficulty in determining how a convolution works is in understanding how the kernel (matrix of numbers) creates the convolutions and how they work on image patches. When you have many convolutions working one after the other, determining the result through direct analysis is difficult. However, a technique designed for understanding such networks builds images that activate the most convolutions. When an image strongly activates a certain layer, you have an idea of what that layer perceives the most.

Analyzing convolutions helps you understand how things work, both to avoid bias in prediction and to devise new ways to process images. For instance, you may discover that your CNN is distinguishing dogs from cats by activating on the background of the image because the images you used for the training represents dogs outdoors and cats indoors.

A 2017 paper called "Feature Visualization," by Chris Olah, Alexander Mordvintsev, and Ludwig Schubert from the Google Research and Google Brain Team, explains this process in detail (https://distill.pub/2017/feature-visualization/). You can even inspect the images yourself by clicking and pointing at the layers of GoogleLeNet, a CNN built by Google at https://distill.pub/2017/feature-visualization/appendix/. The images from the Feature Visualization may remind you of *deepdream* images, if you had occasion to see some when they were a hit on the web (read the original deepdream paper and glance at some images at https://ai.googleblog.com/2015/06/inceptionism-going-deeper-into-neural.html). Feature Visualization is the same technique as deepdream, but instead of looking for images that activate a layer the most, you pick a convolutional layer and let it transform an image.

You can also copy the style of works from a great artist of the past, such as Picasso or Van Gogh, using a similar technique that's based on using convolutions to transform an existing image; this technique is a process called *artistic style transfer*. The resulting picture is modern, but the style isn't. You can get some interesting examples of artistic style transfer from the original paper "A Neural Algorithm of Artistic Style," by Leon Gatys, Alexander Ecker, and Matthias Bethge (found at https://arxiv.org/pdf/1508.06576.pdf).

In Figure 3-16, the original image is transformed in style by applying the drawing and color characteristics found in the Japanese Ukiyo-e "The Great Wave off Kanagawa," a woodblock print by the Japanese artist Katsushika Hokusai, who lived from 1760 to 1849.

FIGURE 3-16:
The content of an image is transformed by style transfer.

Original image   *Style image*   *Resulting image*

Unveiling successful architectures

In recent years, data scientists have achieved great progress thanks to deeper investigation into how CNNs work. Other methods have also added to the progress in understanding how CNNs work. Image competitions have played a major role by challenging researchers to improve their networks, which has made large quantities of images available.

The architecture update process started during the last AI winter. Fei-Fei Li, a computer science professor at the University of Illinois at Urbana Champaign (and now chief scientist at Google Cloud as well as professor at Stanford) decided to provide more real-world datasets to better test algorithms for neural networks. She started amassing an incredible number of images representing a large number of object classes. She and her team performed such a huge task by using Amazon's Mechanical Turk, a service that you use to ask people to do microtasks for you (such as classifying an image) for a small fee.

The resulting dataset, completed in 2009, was called ImageNet and initially contained 3.2 million labeled images (it now contains more than 10 million images) arranged into 5,247 hierarchically organized categories. If interested, you can explore the dataset at http://www.image-net.org/ or read the original paper at http://www.image-net.org/papers/imagenet_cvpr09.pdf.

ImageNet soon appeared at a 2010 competition in which neural networks, using convolutions (hence the revival and further development of the technology developed by Yann LeCun in the 1990s), proved their capability in correctly classifying images arranged into 1,000 classes. In seven years of competition (the challenge closed in 2017), the winning algorithms improved the accuracy of predicting images from 71.8 percent to 97.3 percent, which surpasses human capabilities.

(Humans make mistakes in classifying objects.) Here are some notable CNN architectures that were devised for the competition:

- » **AlexNet (2012):** Created by Alex Krizhevsky from the University of Toronto. It used CNNs with an 11-x-11-pixel filter, won the competition, and introduced the use of GPUs for training neural networks, together with the ReLU activation to control overfitting.

- » **VGGNet (2014):** This appeared in two versions, 16 and 19. It was created by the Visual Geometry Group at Oxford University and defined a new 3-x-3 standard in filter size for CNNs.

- » **ResNet (2015):** Created by Microsoft. This CNN not only extended the idea of different versions of the network (50, 101, 152) but also introduced *skip layers*, a way to connect deeper layers with shallower ones to prevent the vanishing gradient problem and allow much deeper networks that are more capable of recognizing patterns in images.

You can take advantage of all the innovations introduced by the ImageNet competition and even use each of the neural networks. This accessibility allows you to replicate the network performance seen in the competitions and successfully extend them to myriad other problems.

Discussing transfer learning

Networks that distinguish objects and correctly classify them require a lot of images, a long processing time, and vast computational capacity to learn what to do. Adapting a network's capability to new image types that weren't part of the initial training means transferring existing knowledge to the new problem. This process of adapting a network's capability is called *transfer learning*, and the network you are adapting is often referred to as a *pretrained* network. You can't apply transfer learning to other machine learning algorithms; only deep learning has the capability of transferring what it learned with one problem to another.

REMEMBER

Transfer learning is something new to most machine learning algorithms and opens a possible market for transferring knowledge from one application to another, and from one company to another. Google is already doing that; it is sharing its immense data repository by making public the networks it built on TF Hub (https://www.tensorflow.org/hub).

For instance, you can transfer a network that's capable of distinguishing between dogs and cats to perform a job that involves spotting dishes of macaroni and cheese. From a technical point of view, you achieve this task in different ways, depending on how similar the new image problem is to the previous one and how many new images you have for training. (A small image dataset amounts to a few thousand images, and sometimes even fewer.)

If your new image problem is similar to the old one, your network may know all the convolutions necessary (edge, shape, and high-level feature layers) to decipher similar images and classify them. In this case, you don't need to put too many images into training, add much computational power, or adapt your pretrained network too deeply. This type of transfer is the most common application of transfer learning, and you usually apply it by leveraging a network trained during the ImageNet competition (because those networks were trained on so many images that you probably have all the convolutions needed to transfer the knowledge to other tasks).

TIP

Say that the task you want to extend involves not only spotting dogs in images but also determining the dog's breed. You use the majority of the layers of an ImageNet network such as VGG16 as they are, without further adjustment. In transfer learning, you freeze the values of the pretrained coefficients of the convolutions so that they are not affected by any further training and the network won't overfit to the data you have, if it is too little. (You can see overfitting discussed in the "Checking the fit using R2" section of Book 3, Chapter 1.)

With the new images, you then train the output layers set on the new problem (a process known as fine-tuning). In a short time and with just a few examples, the network will apply what it learned in distinguishing dogs and cats to breeds of dogs. It will perform even better than a neural network trained only to recognize breeds of dogs because in fine-tuning, it is leveraging what the network has learned before from millions of images.

REMEMBER

A neural network identifies only objects that it has been trained to identify. Consequently, if you train a CNN to recognize major breeds of dogs such as a Labrador Retriever or a Husky, the CNN won't recognize mixes of those two breeds, such as a Labsky. Instead, the CNN will output the closest match based on the internal weights it develops during training.

If the task you have to transfer to the existing neural network is different from the task it was trained to do, which is spotting dishes of macaroni and cheese starting from a network used to identify dogs and cats, you have some options:

>> If you have little data, you can freeze the first and middle layers of the pretrained network and discard the final layers because they contain high-level features that probably aren't useful for your problem. Instead of the final

convolutions, you then add a response layer suitable to your problem. The fine-tuning will work out the best coefficients for the response layer, given the pretrained convolutional layers available.

>> If you have lots of data, you add the suitable response layer to the pretrained network, but you don't freeze the convolutional layers. You use the pretrained weights as a starting point and let the network fit your problem in the best way because you can train on lots of data.

The Keras package offers a few pretrained models that you can use for transfer learning. You can read about all the available models and their architectures at https://keras.io/applications/. The model descriptions also talk about some of the award-winning networks discussed in the "Delving into ImageNet and Coco" section of Book 5, Chapter 2: VGG16, VGG19, and ResNet50.

Chapter **4**

Processing Text and Other Sequences

N atural Language Processing (NLP) is all about taking text that humans can understand as words, even if those words don't form a sentence, and putting it in a form that computers can process in some manner to look for patterns. For example, the computer doesn't understand "Turn on the radio," but it can process that command into a specific pattern. Sometimes, the computer also reacts to the processed pattern to perform a task, such as turning on the radio. The processing and the action of performing the task are separate. In this chapter, you start with the basics needed to understand NLP and see how it can serve you in building better applications for language problems. For example, you discover some of the issues in processing even raw text and in storing some types of data using sparse matrices so that the data doesn't take so much space. You also discover how to score and classify text.

REMEMBER

You don't have to type the source code for this chapter manually. In fact, using the downloadable source is a lot easier. The source code for this chapter appears in the DSPD_0404_NLP.ipynb source code file for Python and the DSPD_R_0404_NLP. ipynb source code file for R. See the Introduction for details on how to find these source files.

Introducing Natural Language Processing

When thinking about language in data science, you need to consider it from two perspectives: human and computer. The human perspective defines what people expect of each other in the way of communication, as well as what people perceive that the computer is doing, even if it isn't doing it at all. The computer perspective considers how the computer gives the appearance of working with language. The following sections introduce both perspectives of language.

Defining the human perspective as it relates to data science

Text comes in a number of forms. Most of these forms are language based, even the name of items such as the parts of a product. When you call a piece of metal bent in a particular way a widget and use that name to order it from a company, the term *widget* is part of a language devised to make communication possible. However, just saying *widget* wouldn't convey enough meaning; you must place the term in a sentence or provide context by placing the name on an order form. Even though humans understand that a part name isn't a sentence, a computer doesn't understand the difference at all. In fact, a computer can't understand language; it only processes language for specific applications.

As human beings, understanding language is one our first achievements, and associating words to their meaning seems natural. It's also automatic to handle discourses that are ambiguous, unclear, or simply have a strong reference to the context of where we live or work (such as dialect, jargon, or terms that family or associates understand). In addition, humans can catch subtle references to feelings and sentiments in text, enabling people to understand polite speech that hides negative feelings and irony. Computers don't have these abilities but can rely on Natural Language Processing (NLP) — discussed in the next section.

Humans also resolve ambiguity by examining the text for hints about elements like place and time that express the details of the conversation (such as understanding what happened between John and Luca, or whether the conversion is about a computer when mentioning a mouse. Relying on additional information for understanding is part of the human experience. This sort of analysis is somewhat difficult for computers. Moreover, if the task requires critical contextual knowledge or demands that the listener resort to common sense and general expertise, the task for computers becomes daunting.

Considering the computer perspective as it relates to data science

Textual language elements include text-based numeric information and special symbols. It can also include certain kinds of encodings. A computer can perform math only on actual numbers (rather than on a category or text), and math is the only basis on which computers can process anything. The string 1 is different from the number 1 as far as the computer is concerned. A string 1 appears as the number 49 to the computer when using the ASCII encoding, while the numeric 1 is precisely that — a 1. Any text provided as input, regardless of whether a human considers it to be text, requires processing before the computer can perform math calculations (including comparisons) on it.

REMEMBER

A computer can't normally process language at all unless it's highly formal and precise, such as a programming language. Rigid syntax rules and grammar enable a computer to turn a program written by a developer in a computer language like Python into the machine language using a compiler or interpreter (special kinds of programs) that determines what tasks the computer will perform. The fact that most humans can barely read a program doesn't change the fact that a program is a kind of human language. The machine language that a computer processes is numbers consisting of opcodes (what to do) and operands (the data required to perform the task). You can see a listing of such numbers for Intel processors at http://www.mathemainzel.info/files/x86asmref.html. A human sees nothing but numbers; the computer sees a set of precise instructions telling it what to do and how to do it.

However, this chapter isn't about programming languages that are relatively easy to process because of the rigidity of their nature. Instead, it deals with human language of the sort used in conversation, both spoken and written. Human language is not at all similar to a computer's language because it

>> Lacks a precise structure

>> Is full of errors

>> Contains contradictions

>> Hides meaning in ambiguities

Yet human language works well for humans, with some effort on the part of the hearer, to serve human society and the progress of knowledge. Humans can overcome the deficiencies of the spoken or written word with relative ease; it's something that we do based on years of experience and a few errors in childhood. This kind of processing is outside the reach of a computer, however, even if it were to have a special compiler to help handle the task.

Since Alan Turing first devised the Turing Test in 1950, which aims at spotting an artificial intelligence based on how it communicates with humans (https://en.wikipedia.org/wiki/Turing_test), NLP experts have developed a series of techniques that define the state of the art in computer-human interaction by text. Simply put, NLP still has a lot of ground to cover in order to discover how to extract meaningful summaries from text effectively or how to complete missing information from text. Programming a computer to process human language is therefore a daunting task, which is only recently possible using the following:

>> Natural Language Processing (NLP)

>> Deep learning Recurrent Neural Networks (RNNs)

>> Word embeddings

TECHNICAL STUFF

Word embeddings is the name of the language-modeling and feature-learning technique in NLP that maps vocabulary to real number vectors using products like Word2vec, GloVe, and FastText. You also see it used in most recent state-of-the-art networks such as Google's open-sourced BERT that uses embeddings for words based on the context they appear in, allowing better performing NLP solutions.

A computer powered with NLP can successfully spot spam in your email, tag the part of a conversation that contains a verb or a noun, and spot an entity like the name of a person or a company (called *named entity recognition*; see https://medium.com/explore-artificial-intelligence/introduction-to-named-entity-recognition-eda8c97c2db1). All these achievements have found application in tasks such as spam filtering, predicting the stock market using news articles, and de-duplicating redundant information in data storage.

Things get more difficult for NLP when translating a text from another language and understanding whom or what the subject is in an ambiguous phrase. For example, consider the sentence, "John told Luca he shouldn't do that again." In this case, you can't really tell whether "he" refers John or Luca. Disambiguating words with many meanings, such as considering whether the word *mouse* in a phrase refers to an animal or a computer device, can prove difficult. Obviously, the difficulty in all these problems arises because of the context.

Understanding How Machines Read

Before a computer can do anything with text, it must be able to read the text in some manner. Book 3, Chapter 1 shows how you can prepare data to deal with categorical variables, such as a feature representing a color (for instance, representing whether an example relates to the colors red, green, or blue). Categorical data is a type of short text that you represent using binary variables, that is, variables coded using one or zero values according to whether a certain value is present in the categorical variable. Not surprisingly, you can represent complex text using the same logic.

Creating a corpus

Just as you transform a categorical color variable, having values such as red, green, and blue, into three binary variables, with each one representing one of the three colors, so you can transform a phrase like "The quick brown fox jumps over the lazy dog" using nine binary variables, one for each word that appears in the text.

When working with categories, "The" is distinct from "the" because of its initial capital letter. This is the bag-of-words (BoW) form of representation. In its simplest form, BoW shows whether a certain word is present in the text by flagging a specific feature in the dataset.

The input data is three phrases, text_1, text_2, and text_3, placed in a list, corpus. A *corpus* is a set of homogenous documents, put together for NLP analysis:

```
text_1 = 'The quick brown fox jumps over the lazy dog.'
text_2 = 'My dog is quick and can jump over fences.'
text_3 = 'Your dog is so lazy that it sleeps all the day.'
corpus = [text_1, text_2, text_3]
```

TIP

When you analyze text using a computer, you load the documents from disk or scrape them from the web and place each of them into a string variable. If you have multiple documents, you store them all in a list, called the corpus. When you have a single document, you can split it using chapters, paragraphs, or simply the end of each line. After splitting the document, place all its parts into a list and apply analysis as if the list were a corpus of documents.

Performing feature extraction

Now that you have a corpus, you use a class from the feature_extraction module in Scikit-learn, CountVectorizer, which easily transforms texts into BoW, like this:

```
from sklearn.feature_extraction import text
vectorizer = text.CountVectorizer(binary=True).fit(corpus)
vectorized_text = vectorizer.transform(corpus)
print(vectorized_text.todense())
```

The output is a list of lists, as shown here:

```
[[0 0 1 0 0 1 0 1 0 0 0 1 1 0 1 1 0 0 0 1 0]
 [0 1 0 1 0 1 1 0 1 0 1 0 0 1 1 1 0 0 0 0 0]
 [1 0 0 0 1 1 0 0 1 1 0 0 1 0 0 0 1 1 1 1 1]]
```

The CountVectorizer class learns the corpus content using the fit method and then turns it (using the transform method) into a list of lists. A list of lists is nothing more than a matrix in disguise, so what the class returns is actually a matrix made of three rows (the three documents, in the same order as the corpus) and 21 columns representing the content.

WARNING

When viewing the output of this part of the code, remember that the output is zero based. Consequently, the first entry in the list has a value of 0, not 1.

Understanding the BoW

The BoW representation turns words into the column features of a document matrix, and these features have a nonzero value when present in the processed text. For instance, consider the word *dog*. The following code shows its representation in the BoW:

```
print(vectorizer.vocabulary_)
```

The straightforward output appears here:

```
{'day': 4, 'jumps': 11, 'that': 18, 'the': 19, 'is': 8,
 'fences': 6, 'lazy': 12, 'and': 1, 'quick': 15, 'my': 13,
 'can': 3, 'it': 9, 'so': 17, 'all': 0, 'brown': 2,
 'dog': 5, 'jump': 10, 'over': 14, 'sleeps': 16,
 'your': 20, 'fox': 7}
```

Of course, if you have a larger vocabulary, you want it sorted. The following code will show a sorted version for you:

```
from collections import OrderedDict
ordered = OrderedDict(sorted(
    vectorizer.vocabulary_.items(),
    key=lambda x: x[1]))
print(dict(ordered))
```

The output now appears as

```
{'all': 0, 'and': 1, 'brown': 2, 'can': 3, 'day': 4,
 'dog': 5, 'fences': 6, 'fox': 7, 'is': 8, 'it': 9,
 'jump': 10, 'jumps': 11, 'lazy': 12, 'my': 13,
 'over': 14, 'quick': 15, 'sleeps': 16, 'so': 17,
 'that': 18, 'the': 19, 'your': 20}
```

Asking the `CountVectorizer` to print the vocabulary it learned from the sample text outputs a report that it associates *dog* with the number 5, which means that *dog* is the sixth element in the BoW representations. In fact, in the obtained BoW, the sixth element of each document list always has a value of 1 because *dog* is the only word present in all three documents.

REMEMBER

Storing documents in a document matrix form can be memory intensive because you must represent each document as a vector of the same length as the dictionary that created it. The dictionary in this example is quite limited, but when you use a larger corpus, you discover that a dictionary of the English language contains well over a million terms. The solution is to use sparse matrices. A *sparse matrix* is a way to store a matrix in your computer's memory without having zero values occupying memory space. You can read more about sparse matrices here: https://en.wikipedia.org/wiki/Sparse_matrix.

Processing and enhancing text

Marking whether a word is present in a text is a good start on machine reading, but sometimes it's not enough. The BoW model has its own limits. In a BoW, words lose their order relationship with each other; it's like putting stuff randomly into a bag. For instance, in the phrase *My dog is quick and can jump over fences*, you know that *quick* refers to *dog* because it is glued to it by *is*, a form of the verb *to be*. In a BoW, however, everything is mixed and some internal references are lost. Further processing can help prevent the reference losses. The following sections discuss how to process and enhance text.

Performing word counting

Instead of marking the presence or absence of an element of the phrase (technically called a *token*), you can instead count how many times it occurs, as shown in the following code:

```
text_4 = 'A black dog just passed by but my dog is brown.'
corpus.append(text_4)
vectorizer = text.CountVectorizer().fit(corpus)
vectorized_text = vectorizer.transform(corpus)
print(vectorized_text.todense()[-1])
```

When you run this code, you get the following output:

```
[[0 0 1 1 1 1 0 0 2 0 0 1 0 0 0 1 0 1 0 1 0 0 0 0 0 0 0]]
```

This code modifies the previous example by adding a new phrase with the word *dog* repeated two times. The code appends the new phrase to the corpus and retrains the vectorizer, but it omits the binary=True setting this time. The resulting vector for the last inserted document clearly shows a 2 value in the ninth position, thus the vectorizer counts the word *dog* twice.

Counting tokens helps make important words stand out. Yet, it's easy to repeat phrase elements, such as articles, that aren't important to the meaning of the expression. In the "Stemming and removing stop words" section, you discover how to exclude less important elements, but for the time being, the example underweights them using the Term Frequency-Inverse Document Frequency (TF-IDF) transformation.

Changing weights using TF-IDF

The TF-IDF transformation is a technique that, after counting how many times a token appears in a phrase, divides the value by the number of documents in which the token appears. Using this technique, the vectorizer deems a word less impor-tant, even if it appears many times in a text, when it also finds that word in other texts. In the example corpus, the word *dog* appears in every text. In a classification problem, you can't use the word to distinguish between texts because it appears everywhere in the corpus. The word *fox* appears in only one phrase, making it an important classification term.

You commonly apply a number of transformations when applying TF-IDF, with the most important transformation normalizing the text length. Clearly, a longer text has more chances to have more words that are distinctive when compared to a shorter text. For example, when the word *fox* appears in a short text, it appears relevant to the meaning of that expression because *fox* stands out among few other words. How-ever, having *fox* appear once in a long text might not seem to matter as much because it's a single word among many others. For this reason, the transformation divides the total tokens by the count of each token for each phrase. Treating a phrase like this turns token counting into a token percentage, so TF-IDF no longer considers how many times the word *fox* appears, but instead considers the percentage of times the word *fox* appears among all the tokens. The following example demonstrates how to complete the previous example using a combination of normalization and TF-IDF:

```
TfidF = text.TfidfTransformer(norm='l1')
tfidf = TfidF.fit_transform(vectorized_text)
```

```
phrase = 3 # choose a number from 0 to 3
total = 0
for word in vectorizer.vocabulary_:
    pos = vectorizer.vocabulary_[word]
    value = list(tfidf.toarray()[phrase])[pos]
    if value !=0:
        print ("%10s: %0.3f" % (word, value))
        total += value
print ('\nSummed values of a phrase: %0.1f' % total)
```

When you run this code, you see the following output:

```
     is: 0.077
     by: 0.121
  brown: 0.095
    dog: 0.126
   just: 0.121
     my: 0.095
  black: 0.121
 passed: 0.121
    but: 0.121

Summed values of a phrase: 1.0
```

Using this new TF-IDF model rescales the values of important words and makes the number of entries comparable between each text in the corpus.

Maintaining order using n-grams

Your text started out in a particular order and with various aids to make it readable. The current text ordering isn't useful to humans because the words appear in an order that makes analysis possible. To recover part of the ordering of the text before the BoW transformation, you add n-grams (https://en.wikipedia.org/wiki/N-gram). An *n-gram* is a continuous sequence of tokens in the text that you use as a single token in the BoW representation. For instance, in the phrase *The quick brown fox jumps over the lazy dog*, a *bi-gram* (pronounced "by gram") — that is, a sequence of two tokens — transforms *brown fox* and *lazy dog* into single tokens. A *tri-gram* may create a single token from *quick brown fox*.

An n-gram is a powerful tool, but it has a drawback because it doesn't know which combinations are important to the meaning of a phrase. N-grams create all the contiguous sequences of size N. The TF-IDF model can underweight the less useful n-grams, but only projects like Google's NGram viewer (you can read more about this viewer later in the chapter) can tell you which n-grams are useful in

NLP with any certainty. The following example uses `CountVectorizer` to model n-grams in the range of (2, 2), that is, bi-grams:

```
bigrams = text.CountVectorizer(ngram_range=(2,2))
ord_bigrams = OrderedDict(sorted(
    bigrams.fit(corpus).vocabulary_.items(),
    key=lambda x: x[1]))
print (dict(ord_bigrams))
```

Here is the output you see when running the example (in sorted order):

```
{'all the': 0, 'and can': 1, 'black dog': 2,
 'brown fox': 3, 'but my': 4, 'by but': 5,
 'can jump': 6, 'dog is': 7, 'dog just': 8,
 'fox jumps': 9, 'is brown': 10, 'is quick': 11,
 'is so': 12, 'it sleeps': 13, 'jump over': 14,
 'jumps over': 15, 'just passed': 16, 'lazy dog': 17,
 'lazy that': 18, 'my dog': 19, 'over fences': 20,
 'over the': 21, 'passed by': 22, 'quick and': 23,
 'quick brown': 24, 'sleeps all': 25, 'so lazy': 26,
 'that it': 27, 'the day': 28, 'the lazy': 29,
 'the quick': 30, 'your dog': 31}
```

If you don't care about order, you could simply print out the list of bi-grams, like this:

```
print (bigrams.fit(corpus).vocabulary_)
```

TIP

Setting different ranges lets you use both *unigrams* (single tokens) and n-grams in your NLP analysis. For instance, the setting `ngram_range=(1,3)` creates all tokens, all bi-grams, and all tri-grams. You usually never need more than tri-grams in an NLP analysis. Increasing the number of n-grams is slightly beneficial after trigrams and sometimes even just after bi-grams, depending on the corpus size and the NLP problem.

Stemming and removing stop words

Stemming is the process of reducing words to their stem (or root) word. This task isn't the same as understanding that some words come from Latin or other roots, but instead makes similar words equal to each other for the purpose of comparison or sharing. For example, the words *cats*, *catty*, and *catlike* all have the stem *cat*. The act of stemming helps you analyze sentences when tokenizing them because words having the same stem should have the same meaning (represented by a single feature).

GETTING THE NATURAL LANGUAGE TOOLKIT (NLTK)

This example requires the use of the Natural Language Toolkit (NLTK), which Anaconda doesn't install by default. The easy way to get this toolkit is to open the Anaconda prompt, ensure that you're in the (base) environment, and type this command:

```
conda install -c anaconda nltk
```

The conda command may appear to freeze because collecting the required information can take several minutes. Eventually, you see a message saying that conda is collecting the package metadata and you know that the installation is going as planned. Just be patient.

If you're working in an environment that doesn't match the book's environment, you must download and install NLTK using the instructions found at http://www.nltk.org/install.html for your platform. Make certain that you install the NLTK for whatever version of Python you're using for this book when you have multiple versions of Python installed on your system. After you install NLTK, you must also install the packages associated with it. The instructions at http://www.nltk.org/data.html tell you how to perform this task. (Install all the packages to ensure that you have everything.)

Creating stem words by removing suffixes to make tokenizing sentences easier isn't the only way to make the document matrix simpler. Languages include many glue words that don't mean much to a computer but have significant meaning to humans, such as *a, as, the, that,* and so on in English. They make the text flow and concatenate in a meaningful way. Yet, the BoW approach doesn't care much about how you arrange words in a text. Thus, removing such words is legitimate. These short, less useful words are called *stop words.*

REMEMBER

The act of stemming and removing stop words simplifies the text and reduces the number of textual elements so that only the essential elements remain. In addition, you keep just the terms that are nearest to the true sense of the phrase. By reducing the number of tokens, a computational algorithm can work faster and process the text more effectively when the corpus is large.

The following example demonstrates how to perform stemming and remove stop words from a sentence. It begins by training an algorithm to perform the required analysis using a test sentence. Afterward, the example checks a second sentence for words that appear in the first:

```
from sklearn.feature_extraction import text

import nltk
```

```
from nltk import word_tokenize
from nltk.stem.porter import PorterStemmer
nltk.download('punkt')

stemmer = PorterStemmer()

def stem_tokens(tokens, stemmer):
    stemmed = []
    for item in tokens:
        stemmed.append(stemmer.stem(item))
    return stemmed

def tokenize(text):
    tokens = word_tokenize(text)
    stems = stem_tokens(tokens, stemmer)
    return stems

vocab = ['Sam loves swimming so he swims all the time']
vect = text.CountVectorizer(tokenizer=tokenize,
                            stop_words='english')
vec = vect.fit(vocab)

sentence1 = vec.transform(['George loves swimming too!'])

print (vec.get_feature_names())
print (sentence1.toarray())
```

At the outset, the example creates a vocabulary using a test sentence and places it in the variable vocab. It then creates a CountVectorizer, vect, to hold a list of stemmed words, but it excludes the stop words. The stop_words parameter refers to a pickle file that contains the English stop words. The tokenizer parameter defines the function used to stem the words. The vocabulary is fitted into another CountVectorizer, vec, which is used to perform the actual transformation on a test sentence using the transform() function. (You can see other parameters for CountVectorizer() at

https://scikit-learn.org/stable/modules/generated/sklearn.feature_extraction.text.CountVectorizer.html.) Here's the output from this example (note that the data path information may differ on your system).

```
[nltk_data] Downloading package punkt to
[nltk_data]     C:\Users\Luca\AppData\Roaming\nltk_data...
 [nltk_data]   Unzipping tokenizers\punkt.zip.
['love', 'sam', 'swim', 'time']
[[1 0 1 0]]
```

The first output shows the stemmed words. Notice that the list contains only *swim*, not *swimming* or *swims*. All the stop words are missing as well. For example, you don't see the words *so, he, all,* or *the*.

The second output shows how many times each stemmed word appears in the test sentence. In this case, a *love* variant appears once and a *swim* variant appears once as well. The words *sam* and *time* don't appear in the second sentence, so those values are set to 0.

Scraping textual datasets from the web

Given NLP's capabilities, building complete language models is just a matter of gathering large text collections. Digging through large amounts of text enables machine learning algorithms using NLP to discover connections between words and derive useful concepts relative to specific contexts. For instance, when discussing a mouse in the form of a device or an animal, a machine learning algorithm powered by NLP text processing can derive the precise topic from other hints in the phrase. Humans decipher these hints by having lived, seen, talked about, or read about the topic of the conversation. The following sections discuss how computers interact with the web to develop better NLP capabilities.

Understanding web scraping

Computers also build information databases based on digital textual sources or inputs from sensors. As noted previously, computers don't see or hear as humans do, but only accept input in the form of data. The web offers access to millions of documents, most of them freely accessible without restrictions.

REMEMBER

Web scraping (the act of accessing text on websites and downloading it as a data source) allows machine learning algorithms to automatically feed NLP processes and build new capabilities in recognizing and classifying text. Developers have already done much to create NLP systems capable of processing textual

Processing Text and Other Sequences

information better by leveraging the richness of the web. The developer creatively directs the computer to process data in specific ways, and the computer then does the following:

>> Automates processing

>> Ensures that processing is done consistently

>> Presents new patterns that the developer must recognize as the result of processing

By using free text acquired from the web and other open text sources, such as dictionaries, scientists at Microsoft Research have developed various versions of MindNet, a semantic network that is a network of words connected by meaning. MindNet can find related words through the following:

>> Synonyms

>> Parts

>> Causes

>> Locations

>> Sources

For instance, when you ask for the word *car*, MindNet provides answers such as *vehicle* (a synonym) and then connects *vehicle* to *wheel* because it is a specific part of a car, thus providing knowledge directly derived from text even though nobody has specifically instructed MindNet about cars or how they're made. You can read more about MindNet at `https://research.microsoft.com/en-us/projects/mindnet/default.aspx`.

Google developed something similar based on its Google Books project, helping to build better language models for all Google's applications. A public API based on Google's work is the Ngram Viewer, which can explore how frequently certain combinations of tokens up to five-grams have appeared over time: `https://books.google.com/ngrams`.

The capability to retrieve information from the web allows even greater achievements. For example, you could build a dictionary of positive or negative words based on associated emoticons or emoji (`https://en.wikipedia.org/wiki/Emoji`).

Web scraping is a complex subject that could require an entire book to explain. This chapter offers an example of web scraping and an overview of what to expect.

Installing the Beautiful Soup package

You need to install the Beautiful Soup package when using Python to perform web scraping (http://www.crummy.com/software/BeautifulSoup/). This package should already be part of your Anaconda installation. To determine whether you have Beautiful Soup installed, enter the following command at the Anaconda Prompt:

```
conda search beautifulsoup4 --info
```

After you type this command at the Anaconda Prompt and press Enter, you see output like this when the package is installed:

```
beautifulsoup4 4.7.1 py37_1001
------------------------------
file name      : beautifulsoup4-4.7.1-py37_1001.tar.bz2
name           : beautifulsoup4
version        : 4.7.1
build          : py37_1001
build number   : 1001
size           : 140 KB
license        : MIT
subdir         : win-64
url            : https://conda.anaconda.org/conda-forge/...
-py37_1001.tar.bz2
md5            : 38cb1888a82d4a041fb5f7c087c66ff4
timestamp      : 2019-01-08 22:44:20 UTC
dependencies:
  - python >=3.7,<3.8.0a0
  - soupsieve
```

The precise presentation can vary by system, but this gives you a good idea of what to look for. When Beautiful Soup is missing, you can easily install it on your system by typing this command at the Anaconda Prompt and pressing Enter:

```
conda install -c anaconda beautifulsoup4
```

Beautiful Soup, created by Leonard Richardson, is an excellent tool for scraping data from HTML or XML files retrieved from the web, even if they are malformed or written in a nonstandard way. The package name refers to the fact that HTML documents are made of tags, and when they are a mess, many developers idiomatically call the document a *tag soup*. Thanks to Beautiful Soup, you can easily navigate in a page to locate the objects that matter and extract them as text, tables, or links.

Using Beautiful Soup in your code

This example demonstrates how to download a table from a Wikipedia page containing all the major U.S. cities. Wikipedia (https://www.wikipedia.org/) is a free-access and free-content Internet encyclopedia, enjoyed by millions of users every day, all around the world. Because its knowledge is free, open, and, most important, well structured, it's a precious resource for learning from the web.

```
from bs4 import BeautifulSoup
import pandas as pd
try:
    import urllib2 # Python 2.7.x
except:
    import urllib.request as urllib2 # Python 3.x

wiki = "https://en.wikipedia.org/wiki/\
List_of_United_States_cities_by_population"
header = {'User-Agent': 'Mozilla/5.0'}
query = urllib2.Request(wiki, headers=header)
page = urllib2.urlopen(query)
soup = BeautifulSoup(page, "lxml")
```

After you upload the Beautiful Soup package, the code defines a header (stating that you are a human user using a browser) and a target page. The target page is a document containing a list of major U.S. cities: https://en.wikipedia.org/wiki/List_of_United_States_cities_by_population. The list also contains information about the population and surface of the city.

```
table = soup.find("table",
    { "class" : "wikitable sortable" })
final_table = list()
for row in table.findAll('tr'):
    cells = row.findAll("td")
    if len(cells) >=6:
        v1 = cells[1].find(text=True)
        v2 = cells[2].find(text=True)
        v3 = cells[3].find(text=True)
        v4 = cells[4].find(text=True)
        v5 = cells[6].findAll(text=True)
        final_table.append([v1, v2, v3, v4, v5])
cols = ['City','State','Population_2017','Census_2010'
        ,'Land_Area_km2']
df = pd.DataFrame(final_table, columns=cols)

print(df[['City', 'Population_2017']])
```

WIKIPEDIA CAVEATS

Most publishers and many college instructors view Wikipedia as being a dubious source of information. Anyone can edit the entries it contains, and sometimes people do so in ways that slant the information politically or socially, or simply reflects a lack of knowledge (see https://www.foxbusiness.com/features/just-how-accurate-is-wikipedia). These issues can mean that the information you receive may not reflect reality. However, many studies show that the community effort behind creating Wikipedia (see https://www.livescience.com/32950-how-accurate-is-wikipedia.html, https://www.cnet.com/news/study-wikipedia-as-accurate-as-britannica/, and https://www.zmescience.com/science/study-wikipedia-25092014/) does tend to mitigate this issue partially.

No matter which side of the Wikipedia as an information source divide you fall on, you need to exercise some level of care in taking Wikipedia entries at face value, just as you would any Internet content. Just because someone tells you that something is so doesn't make it true (no matter what form that information source might take). You need to cross-reference the information and verify the facts before accepting any Internet information source as factual, even Wikipedia. This said, the authors have verified every Wikipedia source used in the book as much as possible to ensure that you receive accurate information.

Wikipedia also has its own rules and terms of service, which you may read at https://meta.wikimedia.org/wiki/Bot_policy#Unacceptable_usage. The terms of service forbid the use of bots for automated tasks, such as modifying the website (corrections and automatic posting), and bulk downloads (downloading massive amounts of data). Wikipedia is a great source for NLP analysis because you can download all its English articles at https://dumps.wikimedia.org/enwiki/. Other languages are also available for download. Just consult https://dumps.wikimedia.org/ for further information.

After downloading the page into the variable named soup, you can use the find() and findAll() methods to look for a table (the <tr> and <td> tags). The cells variable contains a number of cell entries, each of which can contain text. The code looks inside each cell for textual information (v1 through v5) that it stores in a list (final_table). It then turns the list into a pandas DataFrame for further processing later. For example, you can use the DataFrame, df, to turn strings into numbers. Simply printing df outputs the resulting table. Here is an example of what you see from the print() call, which selects only two of the available columns:

```
        City Population_2017
0  New York City    8,622,698
```

```
1          Los Angeles     3,999,759
2              Chicago     2,716,450
3              Houston     2,312,717
4              Phoenix     1,626,078
5         Philadelphia     1,580,863
...
308         Tuscaloosa       100,287
309         San Angelo       100,119
310          Vacaville       100,032

[311 rows x 2 columns]
```

Handling problems with raw text

Even though raw text wouldn't seem to present a problem in parsing because it doesn't contain any special formatting, you do have to consider how the text is stored and whether it contains special words within it. Some character sets don't quite match up, and converting between them can be difficult even when you don't think a problem should occur. Languages also use special character sets, and it can be hard to get anything but garbage when you try to transition the text to a form you can use within Python. The multiple forms of encoding on web pages can present interpretation problems that you need to consider as you work through the text. The following sections take a very brief look at some of the issues you'll encounter when working with supposedly raw text.

Dealing with encoding

The way the text is encoded can differ because of different operating systems, languages, and geographical areas. Be prepared to find a host of different encodings as you recover data from the web. Human language is complex, and the original ASCII coding, comprising just unaccented English letters, can't represent all the different alphabets. That's why so many encodings appeared with special characters. For example, a character can use either seven or eight bits for encoding purposes. The use of special characters can differ as well. In short, the interpretation of bits used to create characters differs from encoding to encoding. You can see a host of encodings at http://www.i18nguy.com/unicode/codepages.html. Fortunately, Python supports a huge number of encodings, as shown at https://docs.python.org/3/library/codecs.html#standard-encodings.

REMEMBER

Sometimes you need to work with encodings other than the default encoding set within the Python environment. When working with Python 3.x, you rely on Universal Transformation Format 8-bit (UTF-8) as the encoding used to read and write files by default. To check the default encoding, you use this code:

```
import sys
sys.getdefaultencoding()
```

In previous versions of Python, you had to go through all sorts of weird machinations to read other file formats. The discussions at https://stackoverflow.com/questions/2276200/changing-default-encoding-of-python and https://anonbadger.wordpress.com/2015/06/16/why-sys-setdefaultencoding-will-break-code/ will give you some idea of how bad things got. The point is that these old systems are no longer in place because you have easier options to use now. To encode and decode between the default Python UTF-8 and other encodings, you use the encode() and decode() methods, as shown here:

```
utf8_string = "Hello there!"
utf7_string = utf8_string.encode('utf7')
print(utf7_string, type(utf7_string))


utf7_string = "This is a new string!".encode("utf7")
utf8_string = utf7_string.decode('utf8')
print(utf8_string, type(utf8_string))
```

The output from this example code tells you something about Python:

```
b'Hello there!' <class 'bytes'>
This is a new string! <class 'str'>
```

REMEMBER

When a string uses an encoding other than UTF-8, Python stores it as a series of bytes. You can still see the string as output, but you may not be able to read every character if Python can't read it correctly. You must also encode and decode the strings as necessary to ensure that the strings remain readable. For example, if you encode the first string as UTF-32 instead, what you see for output is

```
b'\xff\xfe\x00\x00H\x00\x00\x00e\x00\x00\x001\x00\x00\x001
\x00\x00\x00o\x00\x00\x00\x00\x00\x00t\x00\x00\x00h\x00
\x00\x00e\x00\x00\x00r\x00\x00\x00e\x00\x00\x00!\x00\x00
\x00'
```

If you look carefully, you can still see the individual characters, such as H as \x00H (along with some padding). The biggest problem with Python and encoding is that Python will encode and decode text using whatever encoding you specify, which means that you might end up with garbage. The data is there; you just can't read it. One way to overcome this issue is to try to determine the encoding based on locale, like this:

```
import locale
locale.getpreferredencoding()
```

Unfortunately, knowing the locale doesn't always help or solve problems. For example, when you run this code on a Windows system, you discover that Windows relies on cp1252, where cp stands for code page. Oddly enough, problems occur when transitioning cp1252 to UTF-8, as discussed at https:// stackoverflow.com/questions/26324622/what-characters-do-not-directly-map-from-cp1252-to-utf-8. The most important issue, though, is for you to know what sort of encoding the text uses before you try to process it in Python.

Considering Unicode

Languages include all sorts of accented characters, and the Unicode character set also has a wealth of special characters. To work with certain characters, you must rely on Unicode encoding, as described at https://docs.python.org/3/howto/unicode.html. The problem is that you must know which kind of encoding to use. Consider the following code:

```
uString1 = "This is a winking face: \N{WINKING FACE}"
print(uString1)

uString2 = "This is a winking face: \U0001F609"
print(uString2)

uString3 = "This is not a winking face: \u1F609"
print(uString3)
```

REMEMBER

This is the three kinds of encoding that Python supports. The first two encodings, name and 32-bit, produce the desired output of a winking face. Of course, you have to know that the character is named WINKING FACE to use the first encoding, and you have to know the actual number of the character to use the second encoding, but the encoding is possible and works without problem. The 16-bit encoding won't work in this case because the character number is too high. So, you must choose the correct encoding to get the desired result. Python outputs a spade symbol and the number 9 in the third case.

A problem can occur when you try to encode and decode strings with Unicode characters. For example, the following code produces less than stellar results:

```
utf7_string = uString1.encode('utf7')
print(utf7_string)

uString4 = utf7_string.decode('utf8')
print(uString4)
```

You might think that the string will become impossible to read when you encode it as UTF-7 but that decoding it should fix the problem. Unfortunately, the results are something different:

```
b'This is a winking face: +2D3eCQ-'
This is a winking face: +2D3eCQ-
```

The encoding and decoding processes produce unusable results. The problem can become worse when you try to encode uString1 or uString2 as ASCII. In this case, Python actually raises an example. However, you have a perfectly usable alternative in this case, as shown in the following code:

```
utf7_string = uString1.encode('ascii', 'namereplace')
print(utf7_string)

uString4 = utf7_string.decode('utf8', 'replace')
print(uString4)
```

The output still doesn't quite recover the original content, but at least you know what the original content was:

```
b'This is a winking face: \\N{WINKING FACE}'
This is a winking face: \N{WINKING FACE}
```

In the end, you need to exercise care when processing raw text because raw text really isn't all that easy to process. It contains all sorts of extra bits of information that your application may not know how to handle.

Storing processed text data in sparse matrices

Feature extraction, as described in the "Performing feature extraction" section of the chapter, can produce relatively large matrices full of mostly zeros that would take considerable space to store. Compressing these matrices for storage would make sense because otherwise you'll spend considerable resources using them. Of course, you have to eventually expand the sparse matrices as well, so you need to know how to go both directions. The following sections discuss the use of sparse matrices.

Creating a sparse matrix

Fortunately, Python makes creating a sparse matrix easy. All you need is the scipy.sparse package, described at https://docs.scipy.org/doc/scipy/reference/sparse.html, which offers a number of sparse matrix conversions. The conversion you choose depends on how you want to see the sparse matrix afterward. This example relies on a row-based sparse matrix using the following code:

```
from scipy.sparse import csr_matrix
```

Processing Text and Other Sequences

```
full_matrix = vectorized_text.todense()
print(full_matrix)

sparse_matrix = csr_matrix(full_matrix)
print(sparse_matrix)
```

In this case, you see both the expansion and the compression of the data. The vectorized_text variable actually contains a sparse matrix to begin with, but using todense() forms it into the matrix shown here, which is the decompressed (non-sparse) version:

```
[[0 0 0 1 0 0 0 0 1 0 1 0 0 0 1 0 1 0 1 0 1 0 0 0 2 0]
 [0 1 0 0 0 0 1 0 1 1 0 1 0 1 0 0 0 1 1 0 1 0 0 0 0 0]
 [1 0 0 0 0 0 0 1 1 0 0 1 1 0 0 0 1 0 0 0 0 1 1 1 1 1]
 [0 0 1 1 1 1 0 0 2 0 0 1 0 0 0 1 0 1 0 1 0 0 0 0 0 0]]
```

To create a sparse matrix, you use one of the sparse matrix classes. This example uses the Compressed Sparse Row (CSR) matrix. The output looks like this (with the actual output appearing in a single column):

Coordinate	Number of Entries	Coordinate	Number of Entries
(0, 3)	1	(0, 8)	1
(0, 10)	1	(0, 14)	1
(0, 16)	1	(0, 18)	1
(0, 20)	1	(0, 24)	2
(1, 1)	1	(1, 6)	1
(1, 8)	1	(1, 9)	1
(1, 11)	1	(1, 13)	1
(1, 17)	1	(1, 18)	1
(1, 20)	1	(2, 0)	1
(2, 7)	1	(2, 8)	1
(2, 11)	1	(2, 12)	1
(2, 16)	1	(2, 21)	1
(2, 22)	1	(2, 23)	1
(2, 24)	1	(2, 25)	1
(3, 2)	1	(3, 3)	1
(3, 4)	1	(3, 5)	1

Coordinate	Number of Entries	Coordinate	Number of Entries
(3, 8)	2	(3, 11)	1
(3, 15)	1	(3, 17)	1
(3, 19)	1		

As shown in the table, each entry in the full matrix becomes a set of coordinates and the value at the coordinate. Remember that the coordinates are zero-based, so entry (0, 3) is actually the fourth entry in the first row of the original matrix, which had a value of 1, as shown in the table.

Using the MovieLens sparse matrix

The MovieLens site (https://movielens.org/) is all about helping you find a movie you might like. After all, with millions of movies out there, finding something new and interesting could take time that you don't want to spend. The setup works by asking you to input ratings for movies that you already know about. The MovieLens site then makes recommendations for you based on your ratings. In short, your ratings teach an algorithm what to look for, and then the site applies this algorithm to the entire dataset.

You can obtain the MovieLens dataset directly at https://grouplens.org/datasets/movielens/, but the following code obtains the file for you automatically. (Note that the url is on multiple lines using a line continuation character, \ or backslash, and that the second line must appear outdented as shown, or you can place the entire URL on a single line.)

```
import urllib.request
import os.path
from zipfile import ZipFile

filename = "ml-20m.zip"
if not os.path.exists("ml-20m.zip"):
    url = "https://files.grouplens.org/datasets/\
movielens/ml-20m.zip"
    urllib.request.urlretrieve(url, filename)

archive = ZipFile(filename)
archive.extractall()
```

The first part of the code retrieves the MovieLens datasets from its online location using urllib.request. You must assign it a local filename, which is simply the same name used online in this case. Because MovieLens actually contains a number of datasets, the files appear as .csv (Comma Separated Value) files in a .zip archive. You must extract these files using the extractall() method of the ZipFile package, which creates a subdirectory in your code directory named ml-20m. This subfolder contains the six datasets and a README.txt file.

The interesting thing about this site is that you can download all or part of the dataset based on how you want to interact with it. You can find downloads in the following sizes:

>> 100,000 ratings from 1,000 users on 1,700 movies

>> 1 million ratings from 6,000 users on 4,000 movies

>> 10 million ratings and 100,000 tag applications applied to 10,000 movies by 72,000 users

>> 20 million ratings and 465,000 tag applications applied to 27,000 movies by 138,000 users

>> MovieLens's latest dataset in small or full sizes (At this writing, the full size contained 21,000,000 ratings and 470,000 tag applications applied to 27,000 movies by 230,000 users; its size will increase in time.)

This dataset presents you with an opportunity to work with user-generated data using both supervised and unsupervised techniques. The large datasets present special challenges that only big data can provide. However, this example starts a little more simply by reading the data into the application and then seeing what it contains. The first step is to read in the ratings information, as shown here:

```
ratings = pd.read_csv("ml-20m/ratings.csv")
print(ratings.shape)
print(ratings.head())
```

Reading the data may take a few moments on your system. After it has been read, you can see the output shown here:

```
(20000263, 4)
   userId  movieId  rating  timestamp
0       1        2     3.5  1112486027
1       1       29     3.5  1112484676
2       1       32     3.5  1112484819
3       1       47     3.5  1112484727
4       1       50     3.5  1112484580
```

The column names are important because you use them later to create larger datasets on which you can perform various kinds of analysis. This example uses only two of the datasets, the second of which is the movie names. The following code shows how to import this second dataset:

```
names = pd.read_csv("ml-20m/movies.csv")
print(names.shape)
print(names.head())
```

The output of this code appears like this:

```
(27278, 3)
    movieId                                 title  \
0         1                      Toy Story (1995)
1         2                        Jumanji (1995)
2         3               Grumpier Old Men (1995)
3         4              Waiting to Exhale (1995)
4         5    Father of the Bride Part II (1995)


                                         genres
0    Adventure|Animation|Children|Comedy|Fantasy
1                     Adventure|Children|Fantasy
2                                 Comedy|Romance
3                           Comedy|Drama|Romance
4                                         Comedy
```

Note that both datasets have a movieId column. You can use this column to create a larger dataset using the following code:

```
movie_data = pd.merge(names, ratings, on="movieId")
print(movie_data.shape)
print(movie_data.head())
```

The dataset shape will change, of course, but because movieId is repeated, the output has only one copy, producing six, rather than seven, columns, as shown here:

```
(20000263, 6)
    movieId           title                    genres  \

1         1    Toy Story (1995)   Adventure|Animation|Child...
2         1    Toy Story (1995)   Adventure|Animation|Child...
3         1    Toy Story (1995)   Adventure|Animation|Child...
4         1    Toy Story (1995)   Adventure|Animation|Child...

    userId  rating   timestamp
```

```
0        3      4.0    944919407
1        6      5.0    858275452
2        8      4.0    833981871
3       10      4.0    943497887
4       11      4.5   1230858821
```

At this point, you can perform various kinds of analysis. For example, you might want to know the average rating of each movie. The following code sorts the movies by name and then finds the mean of the ratings for each movie:

```
print(movie_data.groupby('title')['rating'].mean()
.sort_values().head())
```

The code first groups the entries and then finds the mean of the entries by `title`. It then sorts the entries based on the `rating` and outputs the first five entries, as shown here:

```
title
Magic Christmas Tree, The (1964)             0.5
Vampir (Cuadecuc, vampir) (1971)             0.5
Prisoner of Zenda, The (1979)                0.5
Late Great Planet Earth, The (1979)          0.5
Last Warrior, The (Last Patrol, The) (2000)  0.5
Name: rating, dtype: float64
```

Sparse matrices enable you to provide a great deal of text in a raw text form for analysis. The .csv files used for this example qualify as a sort of raw text form in that they aren't processed in any manner other than to organize them. Often, organized raw text will require a great deal of manipulation before you can get anything useful out of it. Consider that MovieLens has four other .csv files that this example hasn't even touched and, even with these two datasets, you can combine the various pieces of information in many other ways.

Understanding Semantics Using Word Embeddings

Most of this chapter involves accessing textual data, forming it in the right way, determining what the words actually say, and performing statistical analysis while storing the information efficiently. All these techniques play into modern NLP approaches. However, you also need to consider the role that AI can play, most especially the neural networks used for deep learning.

Neural networks are incredibly fast at processing data and finding the right weights to achieve the best predictions, and so are all the deep learning layers you find discussed today, from Convolutional Neural Networks (CNNs) to Recurrent Neural Networks (RNNs). These neural networks have effectiveness limits based on the data they have to process, such as normalizing data to allow a neural network to work properly or forcing its range of input values between 0 to +1 or −1 to +1 to reduce trouble when updating network weights.

REMEMBER

Normalization is done internally to the network by using activation functions like tanh, which squeezes values to appear in the range from −1 to +1 (https://tex. stackexchange.com/questions/176101/plotting-the-graph-of-hyperbolic-tangent), or by using specialized layers like BatchNormalization (https://keras.io/layers/normalization/), which apply a statistical transformation on values transferred from one layer to another.

Another kind of problematic data that a neural network finds difficult to handle is sparse data. You have sparse data when your data mostly consists of zero values, which is exactly what happens when you process textual data using frequency or binary encoding, even if you don't use TF-IDF. When working with sparse data, not only will the neural network have difficulties finding a good solution (as technically explained in these Quora answers at https://www.quora.com/Why-are-deep-neural-networks-so-bad-with-sparse-data), but you'll also need to have a huge number of weights for the input layer because sparse matrices are usually quite wide (they have many columns).

Sparse data problems motivated the use of *word embeddings,* which is a way to transform a sparse matrix into a dense one. Word embeddings can reduce the number of columns in the matrix from hundreds of thousands to a few hundred. Also, they allow no zero values inside the matrix. The word embedding process isn't done randomly but is devised so that words get similar values when they have the same meaning or are found within the same topics. In other words, it's a complex mapping; each embedding column is a specialty map (or a scale, if you prefer) and the similar or related words gather near each other.

TIP

Word embeddings aren't the only advanced technique that you can use to make deep learning solutions shine with unstructured text, but they are the technique that recent research advancements are developing and enhancing the most. Recently, a series of pretrained networks appeared that make it even easier to model language problems because they take into account not just the word you want to embed but also the words around it. Using these pretrained networks allows a more precise modelling of words with multiple meanings depending on their context. For instance, one of the most promising is the Google Bidirectional Encoder Representations from Transformers (BERT). Here's a link to the Google AI blog post describing the technique: https://ai.googleblog.com/2018/11/open-sourcing-bert-state-of-art-pre.html.

Processing Text and
Other Sequences

As another example, you can have an embedding that transforms the name of different foods into columns of numeric values, which is a matrix of embedded words. On that matrix, the words that show fruits can have a similar score on a particular column. On the same column, vegetables can get different values, but not too far from those of fruit. Finally, the names of meat dishes can be far away in value from fruits and vegetables. An embedding performs this work by converting words into values in a matrix. The values are similar when the words are synonymous or refer to a similar concept. (This is called *semantic similarity*, with *semantic* referring to the meaning of words.)

REMEMBER

Because the same semantic meaning can occur across languages, you can use carefully built embeddings to help you translate from one language to another: A word in one language will have the same embedded scores as the same word in another language. Researchers at Facebook AI Research (FAIR) lab have found a way to synchronize different embeddings and leverage them to provide multilingual applications based on deep learning (go to `https://code.fb.com/ml-applications/under-the-hood-multilingual-embeddings/` for details).

An important aspect to keep in mind when working with word embeddings is that they are a product of data and thus reflect the content of the data used to create them. Because word embeddings require large amounts of text examples for proper generation, the content of texts fed into the embeddings during the training is often retrieved automatically from the web and not fully scrutinized. The use of unverified input may lead to word embeddings biases. For instance, you may be surprised to discover that the word embeddings create improper associations between words. You need to be aware of such a risk and test your application carefully because the consequence is adding the same unfair biases to the deep learning applications you create.

For now, the most popular word embeddings commonly used for deep learning applications are

» **Word2vec:** Created by a team of researchers led by Tomáš Mikolov at Google (you can read the original paper about this patented method here: `https://arxiv.org/pdf/1301.3781.pdf`). It relies on two shallow neural network layers that attempt to learn to predict a word by knowing the words that precede and follow it. Word2vec comes in two versions: one based on something like a bag-of-words model (called continuous bag-of-words, or CBoW), which is less sensitive to word order; and another based on n-grams (called continuous skip-gram), which is more sensitive to the order. Word2vec learns to predict a word given its context using *distributional hypothesis,* which means that similar words appear in similar contexts of words. By learning what words should appear in different contexts, Word2vec internalizes the contexts. Both versions are suitable for most applications, but the skip-gram version is actually better at representing infrequent words.

>> **GloVe (Global Vectors):** Developed as an open source project at Stanford University (https://nlp.stanford.edu/projects/glove/), the GloVe approach is similar to statistical linguist methods. It takes word-word co-occurrence statistics from a corpus and reduces the resulting sparse matrix to a dense one using *matrix factorization,* which is an algebraic method widely used in multivariate statistics.

>> **fastText:** Created by Facebook's AI Research (FAIR) lab, fastText (https://fasttext.cc/) is a word embedding, available in multiple languages that works with word subsequences instead of single words. It breaks a word down into many chunks of letters and embeds them. This technique has interesting implications because fastText offers a better representation of rare words (which are often composed of subsequences that aren't rare) and determines how to project misspelled words. The capability to handle misspellings and errors allows an effective use of the embedding with text coming from social networks, emails, and other sources people don't usually use a spell checker with.

EXPLAINING WHY (KING – MAN) + WOMAN = QUEEN

Word embeddings translate a word into a series of numbers representing its position in the embedding itself. This series of numbers is the *word vector*. It's usually made up of about 300 vectors (the number of vectors Google used in its model trained on the Google news dataset), and neural networks use it to process textual information better and more effectively. In fact, words with similar meaning or that are used in similar contexts have similar word vectors; therefore, neural networks can easily spot words with similar meaning. In addition, neural networks can work with analogies by manipulating vectors, which means that you can obtain amazing results, such as

- king – man + woman = queen

- paris – france + poland = warsaw

It may seem like magic but it's simple mathematics. You can see how things work by looking at the following figure, which represents two Word2vec vectors.

Each vector in Word2vec represents a different semantic; it could be food type, quality of a person, nationality, or gender. There are many semantics and they aren't predefined; the embedding training created them automatically based on the presented examples. The figure shows two vectors from Word2vec: one representing the quality of a person, another representing the gender of a person. The first vector defines roles, starting with king and queen with higher scores, passing through actor and actress, and finally ending

(continued)

(continued)

with man and woman having lower scores. If you add this vector to the gender vector, you see that the male and female variants separate by different scores on that vector. Now, when you subtract man and add woman to king, you are simply moving away from the coordinates of king and shifting along the gender vector until you reach the position of queen. This simple trick of coordinates, which doesn't imply any understanding of words by Word2vec, is possible because all the vectors of a word embedding are synchronized, representing the meaning of a language, and you can meaningfully shift from one coordinate to another as though you were shifting concepts in reasoning.

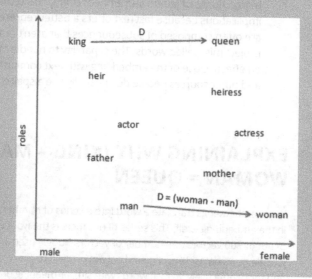

Using Scoring and Classification

The previous NLP discussions in this chapter show how a machine learning algorithm can read text (after scraping it from the web) using the BoW representation and how NLP can enhance its understanding of text using text length normalization, TF-IDF model, and n-grams. The following sections demonstrate how to put text processing into use by learning to solve two common problems in textual analysis: classification and sentiment analysis.

Performing classification tasks

When you classify texts, you assign a document to a class because of the topics it discusses. You can discover the topics in a document in different ways. The simplest approach is prompted by the idea that if a group of people talks or writes about a topic, the people tend to use words from a limited vocabulary because they refer or relate to the same topic. When you share some meaning or are part of the same group, you tend to use the same language. Consequently, if you have a collection of texts and don't know what topics the text references, you can reverse the previous reasoning; you can simply look for groups of words that tend to associate, so their newly formed group by dimensionality reduction may hint at the topics you'd like to know about. This is a typical unsupervised learning task.

This learning task is a perfect application for the Singular Value Decomposition (SVD) family of algorithms, because by reducing the number of columns, the features (which, in a document, are the words) will gather in dimensions, and you can discover the topics by checking high-scoring words. SVD and Principal Components Analysis (PCA) provide features to relate both positively and negatively to the newly created dimensions. So a resulting topic may be expressed by the presence of a word (high positive value) or by the absence of it (high negative value), making interpretation both tricky and counterintuitive for humans. The Scikit-learn package includes the Non-Negative Matrix Factorization (NMF) decomposition class, which allows an original feature to relate only positively with the resulting dimensions.

This example starts by loading the 20newsgroups dataset, a dataset collecting newsgroup postings scraped from the web, selecting only the posts regarding objects for sale and automatically removing headers, footers, and quotes. You may receive a warning message to the effect of WARNING:sklearn.datasets. twenty_newsgroups:Downloading dataset from ..., with the URL of the site used for the download when working with this code. The download will take a few moments because the dataset consumes 14MB.

```
import warnings
warnings.filterwarnings("ignore")
from sklearn.datasets import fetch_20newsgroups
dataset = fetch_20newsgroups(shuffle=True,
    categories = ['misc.forsale'],
      remove=('headers', 'footers', 'quotes'), random_state=101)
print ('Posts: %i' % len(dataset.data))
```

After the download is complete, you see the number of posts as output.

```
Posts: 585
```

The TfidVectorizer class is imported and set up to remove stop words (common words such as *the* or *and*) and keep only distinctive words, producing a matrix whose columns point to distinctive words:

```
from sklearn.feature_extraction.text import TfidfVectorizer
vectorizer = TfidfVectorizer(max_df=0.95,
          min_df=2, stop_words='english')
```

```
tfidf = vectorizer.fit_transform(dataset.data)
from sklearn.decomposition import NMF
n_topics = 5
nmf = NMF(n_components=n_topics, random_state=101).fit(tfidf)
```

REMEMBER

As noted earlier in the chapter, term frequency-inverse document frequency (TF-IDF) is a simple calculation based on the frequency of a word in a document. It is weighted by the rarity of the word among all the documents available. Weighting words is an effective way to rule out words that can't help you classify or identify the document when processing text. For example, you can eliminate common parts of speech or other common words.

As with other algorithms from the `sklearn.decomposition` module, the `n_components` parameter indicates the number of desired components. If you want to look for more topics, you use a higher number. As the required number of topics increases, the `reconstruction_err_` method reports lower error rates. It's up to you to decide when to stop, given the trade-off between more time spent on computations and more topics.

The last part of the script outputs the resulting five topics, as shown here:

```
feature_names = vectorizer.get_feature_names()
n_top_words = 15
for topic_idx, topic in enumerate(nmf.components_):
    print ("Topic #%d:" % (topic_idx+1),)
    print (" ".join([feature_names[i] for i in
                    topic.argsort()[:-n_top_words - 1:-1]]))
```

By reading the printed words, you can decide on the meaning of the extracted topics, thanks to product characteristics (for instance, the words *drive, hard, card,* and *floppy* refer to computers) or the exact product (for instance, *comics, car, stereo, games*):

```
Topic #1:
drive hard card floppy monitor meg ram disk motherboard
 vga scsi brand color internal modem
Topic #2:
00 50 dos 20 10 15 cover 1st new 25 price man 40 shipping
 comics
Topic #3:
condition excellent offer asking best car old sale good
 new miles 10 000 tape cd
Topic #4:
email looking games game mail interested send like thanks
```

```
 price package list sale want know
Topic #5:
shipping vcr stereo works obo included amp plus great
 volume vhs unc mathes gibbs radley
```

You can explore the resulting model by looking into the attribute `components_` from the trained `NMF` model. It consists of a NumPy `ndarray` holding positive values for words connected to the topic. By using the `argsort` method, you can get the indexes of the top associations, whose high values indicate that they are the most representative words.

```
print (nmf.components_[0,:].argsort()[:-n_top_words-1:-1])
```

Here are the indexes of the top words for topic 0:

```
[1337 1749  889 1572 2342 2263 2803 1290 2353 3615 3017  806
  1022 1938
  2334]
```

Decoding the words' indexes creates readable strings by calling them from the array derived from the `get_feature_names` method applied to the `TfidfVectorizer` that was previously fitted.

```
print (vectorizer.get_feature_names()[1337])
```

For example, here is the human-readable form of index 1337:

```
drive
```

Analyzing reviews from e-commerce

Sentiment is difficult to catch because humans use the same words to express even opposite sentiments. The expression you convey is a matter of how you construct your thoughts in a phrase, not simply the words used. Even though dictionaries of positive and negative words do exist and are helpful, they aren't decisive because word context matters. You can use these dictionaries as a way to enrich textual features, but you have to rely more on machine learning if you want to achieve good results.

TIP

Seeing how positive and negative word dictionaries work is a good idea. The AFINN-111 dictionary contains 2,477 positive and negative words and phrases (http://www2.imm.dtu.dk/pubdb/views/publication_details.php?id=6010). Another good choice is the larger opinion lexicon by Hu and Liu that appears at https://www.cs.uic.edu/~liub/FBS/sentiment-analysis.html#lexicon. Both dictionaries contain English words.

Using labeled examples that associate phrases to sentiments can create more effective predictors. In this example, you create a machine learning model based on a dataset containing reviews from Amazon, Yelp, and IMDb that you can find at the UCI, the machine learning repository, `https://archive.ics.uci.edu/ml/datasets/Sentiment+Labelled+Sentences`.

This dataset was created for the paper "From Group to Individual Labels Using Deep Features," by Kotzias and others, for KDD 2015. The dataset contains 3,000 labeled reviews equally divided from the three sources, and the data has a simple structure. Some text is separated by a tab from a binary sentiment label, where 1 is a positive sentiment and 0 a negative one. You can download the dataset and place it in your Python working directory using the following commands:

```python
import urllib.request as urllib2
import requests, io, os, zipfile

UCI_url = 'https://archive.ics.uci.edu/ml/\
machine-learning-databases/00331/sentiment%20\
labelled%20sentences.zip'

response = requests.get(UCI_url)
compressed_file = io.BytesIO(response.content)
z = zipfile.ZipFile(compressed_file)
print ('Extracting in %s' % os.getcwd())
for name in z.namelist():
    filename = name.split('/')[-1]
    nameOK = ('MACOSX' not in name and '.DS' not in name)
    if filename and nameOK:
            newfile = os.path.join(os.getcwd(),
                            os.path.basename(filename))
            with open(newfile, 'wb') as f:
                f.write(z.read(name))
            print ('\tunzipping %s' % newfile)
```

TIP

In case the previous script doesn't work, you can download the data (in ZIP format) directly from `https://archive.ics.uci.edu/ml/machine-learning-databases/00331/` and expand it using your favorite unzipper. You'll find the `imdb_labelled.txt` file inside the newly created `sentiment labelled sentences` directory. After downloading the files, you can upload the IMDb file to a pandas DataFrame by using the `read_csv` function:

```python
import numpy as np
import pandas as pd
dataset = 'imdb_labelled.txt'
```

```
data = pd.read_csv(dataset, header=None, sep=r"\t",
                   engine='python')
data.columns = ['review','sentiment']
```

Exploring the textual data is quite interesting. You'll find all short phrases such as "Wasted two hours" or "It was so cool." Some are clearly ambiguous for a computer, such as "Waste your money on this game." Even though waste has a negative meaning, the imperative makes the phrase sound positive. A machine learning algorithm can learn to decipher ambiguous phrases like these only after seeing many variants. The next step is to build the model by splitting the data into training and test sets:

```
from sklearn.cross_validation import train_test_split
corpus, test_corpus, y, yt = train_test_split(
    data.ix[:,0], data.ix[:,1],
    test_size=0.25, random_state=101)
```

After splitting the data, the code transforms the text using most of the NLP techniques described in this chapter: token counts, unigrams and bi-grams, stop words removal, text length normalization, and TF–IDF transformation.

```
from sklearn.feature_extraction import text
vectorizer = text.CountVectorizer(ngram_range=(1,2),
                   stop_words='english').fit(corpus)
TfidF = text.TfidfTransformer()
X = TfidF.fit_transform(vectorizer.transform(corpus))
Xt = TfidF.transform(vectorizer.transform(test_corpus))
```

After the text for both the training and test sets is ready, the algorithm can learn sentiment using a linear support vector machine. This kind of support vector machine supports L2 regularization, so the code must search for the best C parameter using the grid search approach:

```
from sklearn.svm import LinearSVC
from sklearn.grid_search import GridSearchCV
param_grid = {'C': [0.01, 0.1, 1.0, 10.0, 100.0]}
clf = GridSearchCV(LinearSVC(loss='hinge',
                   random_state=101), param_grid)
clf = clf.fit(X, y)
print ("Best parameters: %s" % clf.best_params_)
```

The output shows the best hyperparameter to use:

```
Best parameters: {'C': 1.0}
```

Now that the code has determined the best hyperparameter for the problem, you can test performance on the test set using the *accuracy measure*, the percentage of correct times that the code can guess the correct sentiment:

```
from sklearn.metrics import accuracy_score
solution = clf.predict(Xt)
print("Achieved accuracy: %0.3f" %
      accuracy_score(yt, solution))
```

The results indicate accuracy of higher than 80 percent, but determining which phrases tricked the algorithm into making a wrong prediction is interesting.

```
Achieved accuracy: 0.816
```

You can print the misclassified texts and consider what the learning algorithm is missing in terms of learning from text:

```
print(test_corpus[yt!=solution])
```

That's quite a bit of text (and you're not seeing all of it in the book):

```
601     There is simply no excuse for something this p...
32      This is the kind of money that is wasted prope...
887     At any rate this film stinks, its not funny, a...
668     Speaking of the music, it is unbearably predic...
408          It really created a unique feeling though.
413          The camera really likes her in this movie.
138     I saw "Mirrormask" last night and it was an un...
132     This was a poor remake of "My Best Friends Wed...
291                            Rating: 1 out of 10.
904     I'm so sorry but I really can't recommend it t...
410     A world better than 95% of the garbage in the ...
55      But I recommend waiting for their future effor...
826     The film deserves strong kudos for taking this...
100          I don't think you will be disappointed.
352                                   It is shameful.
171     This movie now joins Revenge of the Boogeyman ...
814     You share General Loewenhielm's exquisite joy ...
218     It's this pandering to the audience that sabot...
168     Still, I do like this movie for it's empowerme...
479                         Of course, the acting is blah.
31                      Waste your money on this game.
805     The only place good for this film is in the ga...
127     My only problem is I thought the actor playing...
```

```
613                                    Go watch it!
764                      This movie is also revealing.
107     I love Lane, but I've never seen her in a movi...
674     Tom Wilkinson broke my heart at the end... and...
30      There are massive levels, massive unlockable c...
667                                     It is not good.
823     I struggle to find anything bad to say about i...
739        What on earth is Irons doing in this film?
185                              Highly unrecommended.
621     A mature, subtle script that suggests and occa...
462     Considering the relations off screen between T...
595     Easily, none other cartoon made me laugh in a ...
8                                    A bit predictable.
446     I like Armand Assante & my cable company's sum...
449     I won't say any more - I don't like spoilers, ...
715     Im big fan of RPG games too, but this movie, i...
241     This would not even be good as a made for TV f...
471     At no point in the proceedings does it look re...
481     And, FINALLY, after all that, we get to an end...
104                             Too politically correct.
522     Rating: 0/10 (Grade: Z) Note: The Show Is So B...
174             This film has no redeeming features.
491     This movie creates its own universe, and is fa...
Name: review, dtype: object
```

5

Performing Data-Related Tasks

Contents at a Glance

Chapter 1

Making Recommendations

O ne of the oldest and most common sales techniques is to recommend something to a customer based on what you know about the customer's needs and wants. If people buy one product, they might buy another associated product if given a good reason to do so. They may not even have thought about the need for the second product until the salesperson recommends it, yet they really do need it to use the primary product. For this reason alone, most people actually like to get recommendations. Given that web pages now serve as a salesperson in many cases, recommender systems are a necessary part of any serious sales effort on the web. This chapter helps you better understand the significance of the recommender revolution in all sorts of venues.

Recommender systems serve all sorts of other needs. For example, you might see an interesting movie title, read the synopsis, and still not know whether you're likely to find it a good movie. Watching the trailer might prove equally fruitless. Only after you see the reviews provided by others do you feel that you have enough information to make a good decision. In this chapter, you also find methods for obtaining and using rating data.

Gathering, organizing, and ranking such information is hard, though, and information overflow is the bane of the Internet. A recommender system can perform all the required work for you in the background, making the work of getting to a decision a lot easier. You may not even realize that search engines are actually huge recommender systems. The Google search engine, for instance, can provide personalized search results based on your previous search history.

Recommender systems do more than just make recommendations. After reading images and texts, machine learning algorithms can also read a person's personality, preferences, and needs, and act accordingly. This chapter helps you understand how all these activities take place by exploring techniques such as singular value decomposition (SVD).

REMEMBER

You don't have to type the source code for this chapter manually. In fact, using the downloadable source is a lot easier. The source code for this chapter appears in the `DSPD_0501_Recommender.ipynb` source code file for Python and the `DSPD_R_0501_Recommender.ipynb` source code file for R. See the Introduction for details on how to find these source files.

Realizing the Recommendation Revolution

A recommender system can suggest items or actions of interest to a user, after having learned the user's preferences over time. The technology, which is based on data and machine learning techniques (both supervised and unsupervised), has appeared on the Internet for about two decades. Today you can find recommender systems almost everywhere, and they're likely to play an even larger role in the future under the guise of personal assistants, such as Siri (developed by Apple), Amazon Alexa, Google Home, or some other artificial-intelligence–based digital assistant. The drivers for users and companies to adopt recommender systems are different but complementary:

>> **Users:** Have a strong motivation to reduce the complexity of the modern world (regardless of whether the issue is finding the right product or a place to eat) and avoid information overload.

>> **Companies:** Need recommender to systems provide a practical way to communicate in a personalized way with their customers and successfully push sales.

REMEMBER

Recommender systems actually started as a means to handle information overload. The Xerox Palo Alto Research Center built the first recommender in 1992. Named Tapestry (see the story at `https://medium.com/the-graph/how-recommender-systems-make-their-suggestions-da6658029b76`), it handled the increasing number of emails received by center researchers. The idea of collaborative filtering was born by learning from users and leveraging similarities in preferences. The GroupLens project (`https://grouplens.org/`) soon extended recommender systems to news selection and movie recommendations (the MovieLens project, `https://movielens.org/`, whose data you initially work with in the "Using the MovieLens sparse matrix" section of Book 4, Chapter 4).

When giant players in the e-commerce sector, such as Amazon, started adopting recommender systems, the idea went mainstream and spread widely in e-commerce. Netflix did the rest by promoting recommenders as a business tool and sponsoring a competition to improve its recommender system (see `https://www.netflixprize.com/` and `https://www.thrillist.com/entertainment/nation/the-netflix-prize` for details) that involved various teams for quite a long time. The result is an innovative recommender technology that uses SVD and Restricted Boltzmann Machines (a kind of unsupervised neural network).

However, recommender systems aren't limited to promoting products. Since 2002, a new kind of Internet service has made its appearance: social networks such as Friendster, Myspace, Facebook, and LinkedIn. These services promote exchanges between users and share information such as posts, pictures, and videos. In addition, these services help create links between people with similar interests. Search engines, such as Google, amassed user response information to offer more personalized services and understand how to match user's desires when responding to users' queries better (`https://moz.com/learn/seo/google-rankbrain`).

Recommender systems have become so pervasive in guiding people's daily life that experts now worry about the impact on our ability to make independent decisions and perceive the world in freedom. A recommender system can blind people to other options — other opportunities — in a condition called *filter bubble*. By limiting choices, a recommender system can also have negative impacts, such as reducing innovation. You can read about this concern in the articles at `https://dorukkilitcioglu.com/2018/10/09/recommender-filter-serendipity.html` and `https://www.technologyreview.com/s/522111/how-to-burst-the-filter-bubble-that-protects-us-from-opposing-views/`. One detailed study of the effect, entitled "Exploring the Filter Bubble: The Effect of Using Recommender Systems on Content Diversity," appears on ACM at `https://dl.acm.org/citation.cfm?id=2568012`. The history of recommender systems is one of machines striving to learn about our minds and hearts, to make our lives easier, and to promote the business of their creators.

Downloading Rating Data

Getting good rating data can be hard. Later in this chapter, you use the MovieLens dataset to see how SVD can help you in creating movie recommendations. (MovieLens is a sparse matrix dataset that you can see demonstrated in Book 4, Chapter 4.) However, you have other databases at your disposal. The following sections tell you more about the MovieLens dataset and describe the data logs contained in MSWeb — both of which work quite well when experimenting with recommender systems.

Navigating through anonymous web data

One of the more interesting datasets that you can use to learn about preferences is the MSWeb dataset (https://archive.ics.uci.edu/ml/datasets/Anonymous+Microsoft+Web+Data). It consists of a week's worth of anonymously recorded data from the Microsoft website with these characteristics:

» **Number of instances:** 37,711

- **Training:** 32,711

- **Test:** 5,000

» **Number of attributes:** 294

» **Number of users:** 32,710

» **Number of Vroots:** 285

In this case (unlike the MovieLens dataset), the recorded information is about a behavior, not a judgment, thus values are expressed in a binary form. You can download the MSWeb dataset from https://github.com/amirkrifa/ms-web-dataset/raw/master/anonymous-msweb.data, get information about its structure, and explore how its values are distributed. The following code shows how to obtain the data using Python:

```
import urllib.request
import os.path

filename = "anonymous-msweb.data"
if not os.path.exists("anonymous-msweb.data"):
    url = "https://github.com/amirkrifa/ms-web-dataset/\
raw/master/anonymous-msweb.data"
    urllib.request.urlretrieve(url, filename)
```

REMEMBER

The technique for obtaining the file is similar to that used for the MovieLens dataset. In fact, this is a kind of CSV file, but you won't use Pandas to work with it because it has a complex dataset structure. The sections that follow describe how to work with this dataset in Python. R actually makes the process of working with the MSWeb dataset considerably easier because you can download the MSWeb dataset from the R recommenderlab library. If you want to see Python techniques in addition to those in this chapter for working with the MSWeb dataset, check out the site at https://github.com/amirkrifa/ms-web-dataset.

Parsing the data file

The data file contains complex data to track user behavior, and you may encounter this sort of data when performing data science tasks. It looks complicated at first, but if you break the data file down carefully, you can eventually tease out the file details. If you were to open this data file (it's text, so you can look if desired), you would find that it contains three kinds of records:

» **A:** Attributes of the particular page. Each attribute is a different page, so you could use the word page (or pages for multiples) in place of attributes, but the example uses attributes for clarity.

» **C:** Users who are looking at the pages.

» **V:** Vroots for each of the pages. A *Vroot* is a series of grouped website pages. Together they constitute an area of the website. The binary values show whether someone has visited a certain area. (You just see a flag; you don't see how many times the user has actually visited that website area.)

Each record appears on a separate line. Consequently, you build one dictionary for each of the record types to separate one from the other, as shown here:

```python
import codecs
import collections

# Open the file.
file = codecs.open(filename, 'r')

# Setup for attributes.
attribute = collections.namedtuple(
    'page', ['id', 'description', 'url'])
attributes = {}

# Setup for users
current_user_id = None
current_user_ids = []
user_visits = {}

# Setup for Vroots
page_visits = {}

# Process the data one line at a time and place
# each record in the appropriate storage unit.
for line in file:
    chunks = line.split(',')
```

```
        entry_type = chunks[0]

        if entry_type == 'A':
            type, id, ignored, description, url = chunks
            attributes[int(id)] = attribute(
                id=int(id), description=description, url=url)

        if entry_type == 'C':
            if not current_user_id == None:
                user_visits[current_user_id] = set(
                    current_user_ids)
                current_user_ids = []
            current_user_id = int(chunks[2])

        if entry_type == 'V':
            page_id = int(chunks[1])
            current_user_ids.append(page_id)
            page_visits.setdefault(page_id, [])
            page_visits[page_id].append(current_user_id)

# Display the totals
print('Total Number of Attributes: ',
      len(attributes.keys()))
print('Total Number of Users: ', len(user_visits.keys()))
print('Total Number of VRoots: ', len(page_visits.keys()))
```

The code begins by setting up variables to hold information for each of the record types. It then reads the file one line at a time and determines the record type. Each record requires a different kind of process. For example, an attribute contains a page number, description, and URL. User records contain the user ID and a list of pages that the user has visited. The Vroot entries associate pages with users. At the end of the process, you can see the number of each kind of record in the dataset.

```
Total Number of Attributes:  294
Total Number of Users:  32710
Total Number of VRoots:  285
```

The idea is that a user's visit to a certain area indicates a specific interest. For instance, when a user visits pages to learn about productivity software along with visits to a page containing terms and prices, this behavior indicates an interest in acquiring the productivity software soon. Useful recommendations can be based on such inferences about a user's desire to buy certain versions of the productivity software or bundles of different software and services.

Viewing the attributes

It's important to remember that the focus is on pages and users viewing them, so it pays to know a little something about the pages. After you parse the dataset, the following code will display the page information for you:

```
for k, v in attributes.items():
    print("{:4} {:30.30} {:12}".format(
        v.id, v.description, v.url))
```

When you run this code, you see all 294 attributes (pages). Here is a partial listing:

```
1287 "International AutoRoute"    "/autoroute"
1288 "library"                    "/library"
1289 "Master Chef Product Infor..." "/masterchef"
1297 "Central America"            "/centroam"
1215 "For Developers Only Info"   "/developer"
1279 "Multimedia Golf"            "/msgolf"
1239 "Microsoft Consulting"       "/msconsult"
```

Obtaining statistics

In addition to viewing the data, you can also perform analysis on it by various means, such as statistics. Here are some statistics you can try with the users:

```
nbr_visits = list(map(len, user_visits.values()))
average_visits = sum(nbr_visits) / len(nbr_visits)
one_visit = sum(x == 1 for x in nbr_visits)

print("Number of user visits: ", sum(nbr_visits))
print("Average number of visits: ", average_visits)
print("Users with just one visit: ", one_visit)
```

When you run this code, you see some interesting information about the users who visited the various pages:

```
Number of user visits:  98653
Average number of visits:  3.0159889941913787
Users with just one visit:  9994
```

Encountering the limits of rating data

For recommender systems to work well, they need to know about you as well as other people, both like you and different from you. Acquiring rating data allows a recommender system to learn from the experiences of multiple customers. Rating data could derive from a judgment (such as rating a product using stars or numbers) or a fact (a binary 1/0 that simply states that you bought the product, saw a movie, or stopped browsing at a certain web page).

REMEMBER

No matter the data source or type, rating data is always about behaviors. To rate a movie, you have to decide to see it, watch it, and then rate it based on your experience of seeing the movie. Actual recommender systems learn from rating data in different ways:

>> **Collaborative filtering:** Matches raters based on movie or product similarities used in the past. You can get recommendations based on items liked by people similar to you or on items similar to those you like.

>> **Content-based filtering:** Goes beyond the fact that you watched a movie. It examines the features relative to you and the movie to determine whether a match exists based on the larger categories that the features represent. For instance, if you are a female who likes action movies, the recommender will look for suggestions that include the intersection of these two categories.

>> **Knowledge based recommendations:** Based on metadata, such as preferences expressed by users and product descriptions. It relies on machine learning and is effective when you do not have enough behavioral data to determine user or product characteristics. This is called a *cold start* and represents one of the most difficult recommender tasks because you don't have access to either collaborative filtering or content-based filtering.

The example that appears in the sections that follow performs collaborative filtering. It locates the movies that are the most similar to *Young Frankenstein*.

Considering collaborative filtering

When using collaborative filtering, you need to calculate similarity. See Chapter 14 of *Machine Learning For Dummies*, by John Paul Mueller and Luca Massaron (Wiley), for a discussion of the use of similarity measures. Another good place to look is at `http://dataaspirant.com/2015/04/11/five-most-popular-similarity-measures-implementation-in-python/`. Apart from Euclidean, Manhattan, and Chebyshev distances, the remainder of this section discusses cosine similarity. *Cosine similarity* measures the angular cosine distance between two vectors, which may seem like a difficult concept to grasp but is just a way to measure angles in data spaces.

The idea behind the cosine distance is to use the angle created by the two points connected to the space origin (the point where all dimensions are zero) instead. If the points are near, the angle is narrow, no matter how many dimensions are there. If they are far away, the angle is quite large. Cosine similarity implements the cosine distance as a percentage and is quite effective in telling whether a user is similar to another or whether a film can be associated to another because the same users favor it.

Obtaining the data

The code in this section assumes that you have access to the MovieLens database using the code from the "Using the MovieLens sparse matrix" section of Book 4, Chapter 4. Assuming that you're working with a new notebook, however, you need to read the data into the notebook and merge the two datasets used for this example, as shown here:

```
import pandas as pd

ratings = pd.read_csv("ml-20m/ratings.csv")
movies = pd.read_csv("ml-20m/movies.csv")

movie_data = pd.merge(ratings, movies, on="movieId")
print(movie_data.head())
```

After you perform the merge, you see a new dataset, movie_data, which contains the combination of ratings and movies, as shown here:

```
   userId  movieId  rating   timestamp            title  \
0       1        2     3.5  1112486027  Jumanji (1995)
1       5        2     3.0   851527569  Jumanji (1995)
2      13        2     3.0   849082742  Jumanji (1995)
3      29        2     3.0   835562174  Jumanji (1995)
4      34        2     3.0   846509384  Jumanji (1995)

                        genres
0  Adventure|Children|Fantasy
1  Adventure|Children|Fantasy
2  Adventure|Children|Fantasy
3  Adventure|Children|Fantasy
4  Adventure|Children|Fantasy
```

All these entries are for *Jumanji* because head() shows only the first five entries in the movie_data dataset, and *Jumanji* obviously has at least five ratings. You can use the new dataset to obtain a simple statistic for the movies; however, the mean of the ratings for each movie is shown here:

```
print(movie_data.groupby('title')['rating'].mean().head())
```

This code looks rather complicated, but it isn't. Calling groupby('title') creates a grouping of the various movies by title. You can then access the ['rating'] column of that grouping to obtain a mean(). The output shows the first five entries, as shown here (note that groupby() automatically sorts the entries for you):

```
title
"Great Performances" Cats (1998)                    2.748387
#chicagoGirl: The Social Network Takes on a...       3.666667
$ (Dollars) (1971)                                  2.833333
$5 a Day (2008)                                     2.871795
$9.99 (2008)                                        3.009091
Name: rating, dtype: float64
```

The rating column doesn't have a title, but you see it listed on the last line as the column used to create the mean, which is of type float64.

Massaging the data

The current MovieLens dataset is huge and cumbersome. When working with an online product, such as Google Colab (see Book 1, Chapter 3 for details), the dataset might very well work in its current form. When working with a desktop system, you need to massage the data to ensure that you actually can get the desired results. In fact, massaging the data is an essential part of performing data science tasks because you may not actually have good data. This section looks at ways that you might want to massage the MovieLens dataset to ensure good results.

WARNING

Desktop setups can be particularly picky when you're working with huge data. One of the issues you can encounter when working with these datasets is memory. When performing certain tasks, such as creating the pivot table for this example, you might see ValueError: negative dimensions are not allowed as an output. What this really means is that your system ran out of memory. You have a number of options for countering this problem, some of the most important of which appear in this section.

You can reduce the memory requirements for working with the data by removing items that you don't really want in the analysis anyway. For this analysis, you have three extra columns: movieId, timestamp, and genres. In addition, a person would need to think enough of a movie to give it at least three out of five stars. Consequently, you can also get rid of the lesser value reviews using the following code:

```
reduced_movie = movie_data.loc[
    movie_data['rating'] >= 3.0]
reduced_movie = reduced_movie.drop(
    columns=['movieId','timestamp', 'genres'])
```

```
print(reduced_movie.head())
print()
print("Original Shape: {0}, New Shape: {1}".format(
    movie_data.shape, reduced_movie.shape))
```

The reduction in size doesn't actually affect the better movies. Instead, you just lose lesser movies that would have unfavorably affected the results. The size of the reduced_movie dataset is significantly smaller than the original movie_data dataset, as shown here:

```
   userId  rating        title
0       1     3.5  Jumanji (1995)
1       5     3.0  Jumanji (1995)
2      13     3.0  Jumanji (1995)
3      29     3.0  Jumanji (1995)
4      34     3.0  Jumanji (1995)

Original Shape: (20000263, 6), New Shape: (16486759, 3)
```

The number of reviews also reflects the popularity of a movie. When a movie has few reviews, it might reflect a *cult following* — a group of devotees who don't reflect the opinion of the public at large. You can remove movies with only a few reviews using the following code:

```
reduced_movie = reduced_movie[
    reduced_movie.groupby('title')['rating'].transform(
        'size') > 3000]

print(reduced_movie.groupby('title')[
    'rating'].count().sort_values().head())
print()
print("New shape: ", reduced_movie.shape)
```

The call to transform() selects only movies that have a certain number of reviews — more than 3,000 of them in this case. You can use transform() in a huge number of ways based solely on the function you provide as input, which is the built-in size function in this case. Here is the result of this particular bit of trimming:

```
title
Eastern Promises (2007)                            3001
Triplets of Belleville, The (Les triplettes de Bel...  3003
Bad Santa (2003)                                   3006
Mexican, The (2001)                                3010
```

```
1984 (Nineteen Eighty-Four) (1984)                    3010
Name: rating, dtype: int64

New shape:  (12083404, 3)
```

The way you shape your data will affect the output of any analysis you perform. You may not get the desired results the first time, so you may end up spending a lot of time trying different shaping methods. The point is to keep trying to shape the data in various ways until you obtain a good result.

A final way to save memory for analysis purposes is to clean up your variables, which can consume a lot of memory. This example uses the following code for this purpose:

```
ratings = None
movies = None
movie_data = None
```

Performing collaborative filtering

Making recommendations depends on finding the right kind of information on which to make a comparison. Of course, this is where the art of data science comes into play. If making a recommendation only involved performing analysis on data in a particular manner using a specific algorithm, anyone could do it. The art is in choosing the correct data to analyze. In this section, you use a combination of the user ID and the ratings assigned by those users to a particular movie as the means to perform collaborative filtering. In other words, you're making an assumption that people who have similar tastes in movies will rate those movies at a particular level.

After you've shaped your data, you can use it to create a pivot table. The pivot table will compare user IDs with the reviews that the user has created for particular movies. Here is the code used to create the pivot table:

```
user_rating = pd.pivot_table(
    reduced_movie,
    index='userId',
    columns='title',
    values='rating')

print(user_rating.head())
```

The results might look a little odd because the pivot table will be a sparse matrix like the sample shown here:

```
title    Young Frankenstein  Young Guns  Zodiac  \
userId
1                      4.0         NaN     NaN
2                      NaN         NaN     NaN
3                      5.0         NaN     NaN
4                      NaN         NaN     NaN
5                      NaN         NaN     NaN
```

In this case, you see that *Young Frankenstein* is the only movie that was rated by users 1 through 5. The point is that the rows contain individual user reviews and the columns are the names of movies they reviewed.

The next step in the process is to obtain a listing of reviews for the target movie, which is *Young Frankenstein*. The following code creates a list of reviewers:

```
YF_ratings = user_rating['Young Frankenstein (1974)']
print(YF_ratings.sort_values(ascending=False).head())
```

The output of this part of the code shows that *Jumanji* isn't the most popular movie around, but it'll work for the example:

```
userId
60898     5.0
52548     5.0
101177    5.0
101198    5.0
28648     5.0
Name: Young Frankenstein (1974), dtype: float64
```

Now that you have sample data to use, you can correlate it with the pivot table as a whole. The following code outputs the movies that most closely match *Jumanji* in appeal by the users who liked *Jumanji*:

```
print(user_rating.corrwith(
    YF_ratings).sort_values(
    ascending=False).head())
```

The output shows that you can derive some interesting results using collaborative filtering techniques:

```
title
Young Frankenstein (1974)                1.000000
Blazing Saddles (1974)                   0.421143
Monty Python and the Holy Grail (1975)   0.300413
```

```
Producers, The (1968)          0.297317
Magnificent Seven, The (1960)  0.291847
dtype: float64
```

Even though the correlation results seem a little low (with 1.000000 being the most desirable), the names of the movies selected make sense. For example, like *Young Frankenstein*, *Blazing Saddles* is a Mel Brooks movie, and *Monty Python and the Holy Grail* is a comedy.

Leveraging SVD

A property of SVD is to compress the original data at such a level and in such a smart way that, in certain situations, the technique can actually create new meaningful and useful features, not just compressed variables. The following sections help you understand what role SVD plays in recommender systems.

Considering the origins of SVD

SVD is a method from linear algebra that can decompose an initial matrix into the multiplication of three derived matrices. The three derived matrices contain the same information as the initial matrix, but in a way that expresses any redundant information (expressed by statistical variance) only once. The benefit of the new variable set is that the variables have an orderly arrangement according to the initial variance portion contained in the original matrix.

SVD builds the new features using a weighted summation of the initial features. It places features with the most variance leftmost in the new matrix, whereas features with the least or no variance appear on the right side. As a result, no correlation exists between the features. (Correlation between features is an indicator of information redundancy, as explained in the previous paragraph.) Here's the formulation of SVD:

```
A = U * D * Vᵀ
```

For compression purposes, you need to know only about matrices U and D, but examining the role of each resulting matrix helps you understand the values better, starting with the origin. A is a matrix n*p, where n is the number of examples and p is the number of variables. As an example, consider a matrix containing the purchase history of n customers, who bought something in the p range of available products. The matrix values are populated with quantities that customers purchased. As another example, imagine a matrix in which rows are individuals, columns are movies, and the content of the matrix is a movie rating (which is exactly what the MovieLens dataset contains).

After the SVD computation completes, you obtain the U, S, and V matrices. U is a matrix of dimensions n by k, where k is p, exactly the same dimensions of the original matrix. It contains the information about the original rows on a reconstructed set of columns. Therefore, if the first row on the original matrix is a vector of items that Mr. Smith bought, the first row of the reconstructed U matrix will still represent Mr. Smith, but the vector will have different values. The new U matrix values are a weighted combination of the values in the original columns.

Of course, you might wonder how the algorithm creates these combinations. The combinations are devised to concentrate the most variance possible on the first column. The algorithm then concentrates most of the residual variance in the second column, with the constraint that the second column is uncorrelated with the first one, thereby distributing the decreasing residual variance to each column in succession. By concentrating the variance in specific columns, the original features that were correlated are summed into the same columns of the new U matrix, thus cancelling any previous redundancy present. As a result, the new columns in U don't have any correlation between themselves, and SVD distributes all the original information in unique, nonredundant features. Moreover, given that correlations may indicate causality (but correlation isn't causation; it can simply hint at it — a necessary but not sufficient condition), cumulating the same variance creates a rough estimate of the variance's root cause.

V is the same as the U matrix, except that its shape is p*k and it expresses the original features with new cases as a combination of the original examples. This means that you'll find new examples composed of customers with the same buying habits. For instance, SVD compresses people buying certain products into a single case that you can interpret as a homogeneous group or as an archetypal customer.

In such reconstruction, D, a diagonal matrix (only the diagonal has values) contains information about the amount of variance computed and stored in each new feature in the U and V matrices. By cumulating the values along the matrix and making a ratio with the sum of all the diagonal values, you can see that the variance is concentrated on the first leftmost features, while the rightmost are almost zero or an insignificant value. Therefore, an original matrix with 100 features can be decomposed and have an S matrix whose first 10 newly reconstructed features represent more than 90 percent of the original variance.

SVD has many optimizing variants with slightly different objectives. The core functions of these algorithms are similar to SVD. Principal component analysis (PCA) focuses on common variance. It's the most popular algorithm and is used in machine learning preprocessing applications.

TIP

A great SVD property is that the technique can create new meaningful and useful features, not just compressed variables, as a by-product of compression in certain situations. In this sense, you can consider SVD a feature-creation technique.

Understanding the SVD connection

If your data contains hints and clues about a hidden cause or motif, an SVD can put them together and offer you proper answers and insights. That is especially true when your data consists of interesting pieces of information like the ones in the following list:

>> **Text in documents hints at ideas and meaningful categories:** Just as you can make up your mind about discussion topics by reading blogs and newsgroups, so can SVD help you deduce a meaningful classification of groups of documents or the specific topics being written about in each of them.

>> **Reviews of specific movies or books hint at your personal preferences and larger product categories:** If you say on a rating site that you loved the original *Star Trek* series collection, the algorithm can easily determine what you like in terms of other films, consumer products, or even personality types.

An example of a method based on SVD is latent semantic indexing (LSI), which has been successfully used to associate documents and words based on the idea that words, though different, tend to have the same meaning when placed in similar contexts. This type of analysis suggests not only synonymous words but also higher grouping concepts. For example, an LSI analysis on some sample sports news may group baseball teams of the major league based solely on the co-occurrence of team names in similar articles, without any previous knowledge of what a baseball team or the major league are.

Other interesting applications for data reduction are systems for generating recommendations about the things you may like to buy or know more about. You likely have quite a few occasions to see recommenders in action. On most e-commerce websites, after logging in, visiting some product pages, and rating or putting a product into your electronic basket, you see other buying opportunities based on other customers' previous experiences. (As mentioned previously, this method is called *collaborative filtering*.) SVD can implement collaborative filtering in a more robust way, relying not just on information from single products but also on the wider information about a product in a set. For example, collaborative filtering can determine not only that you liked the film *Raiders of the Lost Arc* but also that you generally like all action and adventure movies.

You can implement collaborative recommendations based on simple means or frequencies calculated on other customers' sets of purchased items or on ratings using SVD. This approach helps you reliably generate recommendations even in the case of products that the vendor seldom sells or that are quite new to users.

Chapter **2**

Performing Complex Classifications

D eep neural network solutions have been highly successful in the image-recognition field. The great part of this technology's success, especially in AI applications, comes from three key characteristics: the availability of suitable data to train and test image networks; the application of deep neural networks to different problems thanks to transfer learning; and increasing sophistication of the technology, which allows it to answer complex questions about image content.

In this chapter, you delve into the topic of object classification and detection challenges to discover their contribution to the foundation of the present deep learning renaissance. Competitions, such as those based on the ImageNet dataset, provide the right data to train reusable networks for different purposes (thanks to transfer learning, as discussed in Book 4, Chapter 3). Competitions serve another purpose as well, which is to push researchers to find new and smarter solutions for increasing the a neural network's capability to understand images.

The chapter closes with an example of how to use an image dataset. Using the dataset, you build your own CNN for recognizing traffic signs using image augmentation and weighting for balancing the frequency of different classes in the examples.

REMEMBER

You don't have to type the source code for this chapter manually. In fact, using the downloadable source is a lot easier. The source code for this chapter appears in the DSPD_0502_Classification.ipynb source code file for Python and the DSPD_R_0502_Classification.ipynb source code file for R. See the Introduction for details on how to find these source files.

Using Image Classification Challenges

The CNN layers for image recognition were first conceived by Yann LeCun and a team of researchers. AT&T actually implemented LeNet5 (the neural network for hand-written numbers described in Book 4, Chapter 3) into ATM check readers. However, the invention didn't prevent another AI winter, starting in the 1990s, with many researchers and investors losing faith again that computers could achieve any progress toward having a meaningful conversation with humans, translating from different languages, understanding images, and reasoning in the manner of human beings.

Actually, expert systems had already undermined public confidence. *Expert systems* are a set of automatic rules set by humans to allow computers to perform certain operations. Nevertheless, the new AI winter prevented neural networks from being developed in favor of different kinds of machine learning algorithms. At the time, computers lacked computational power and had certain limits, such as the vanishing gradient problem. (Book 4, Chapter 2 discusses the vanishing gradient and other limitations that prevented deep neural architectures.) The data also lacked complexity at the time, and consequently a complex and revolutionary CNN like LeNet5, which already worked with the technology and limitations of the time, had little opportunity to show its true power.

Only a handful of researchers, such as Geoffrey Hinton, Yann LeCun, Jürgen Schmidhuber, and Yoshua Bengio, kept developing neural network technologies striving to get a breakthrough that would have ended the AI winter. Meanwhile, 2006 saw an effort by Fei-Fei Li, a computer science professor at the University of Illinois Urbana-Champaign (now an associate professor at Stanford, as well as the director of the Stanford Artificial Intelligence Lab and the Stanford Vision Lab) to provide more real-world datasets to better test algorithms. She started amassing an incredible number of images, representing a large number of object classes. You can read about this effort in the "Unveiling successful architectures" section of Book 4, Chapter 3. The proposed classes range through different types of objects, both natural (for instance, 120 dog breeds) and human made (such as means of transportation). You can explore them all at http://image-net.org/challenges/LSVRC/2014/browse-synsets. By using this huge image dataset for training, researchers noticed that their algorithms started working better (nothing like ImageNet existed at that time) and then they started testing new ideas and improving neural network architectures.

OBTAINING A HUMAN PERSPECTIVE IN IMAGE CLASSIFICATION

Convolutional Neural Networks (CNNs) have seen considerable use in image recognition, and you can find CNNs discussed in Book 4, Chapter 3. However, it's possible to extend CNNs using other technologies, such as those described in this chapter. Local response normalization and inception modules are technological solutions that are too complex to discuss in this book, but you should be aware that they're revolutionary. All were introduced by neural networks that won the ImageNet competition: AlexNet (in 2012); GoogLeNet (in 2014); and ResNet (in 2015). You can read more about this technology at https://towardsdatascience.com/difference-between-local-response-normalization-and-batch-normalization-272308c034ac and https://prateekvjoshi.com/2016/04/05/what-is-local-response-normalization-in-convolutional-neural-networks/.

Delving into ImageNet and Coco

The impact and importance of the ImageNet competition (also known as ImageNet Large Scale Visual Recognition Challenge (ILSVRC; http://image-net.org/challenges/LSVRC/) on the development of deep learning solutions for image recognition can be summarized in three key points:

» **Helping establish a deep neural network renaissance:** The AlexNet CNN architecture (developed by Alex Krizhevsky, Ilya Sutskever, and Geoffrey Hinton) won the 2012 ILSVRC challenge by a large margin over other solutions.

» **Pushing various teams of researchers to develop more sophisticated solutions:** ILSVRC advanced the performance of CNNs. VGG16, VGG19, ResNet50, Inception V3, Xception, and NASNet are all neural networks tested on ImageNet images that you can find in the Keras package (https://keras.io/applications/). Each architecture represents an improvement over the previous architectures and introduces key deep learning innovations.

» **Making transfer learning possible:** The ImageNet competition helped make available the set of weights that made them work. The 1.2 million ImageNet training images, distributed over 1,000 separate classes, helped create convolutional networks whose upper layers can actually generalize to problems other than ImageNet.

Recently, a few researchers started suspecting that the more recent neural architectures are overfitting the ImageNet dataset. After all, the same test set has been used for many years to select the best networks, as researchers Benjamin Recht, Rebecca Roelofs, Ludwig Schmidt, and Vaishaal Shankar speculate at https://arxiv.org/pdf/1806.00451.pdf.

Other researchers from the Google Brain team (Simon Kornblith, Jonathon Shlens, and Quoc V. Le) have discovered a correlation between the accuracy obtained on ImageNet and the performance obtained by transfer learning of the same network on other datasets. They published their findings in the paper "Do Better ImageNet Models Transfer Better?" (https://arxiv.org/pdf/1805.08974.pdf). Interestingly, they also pointed out that if a network is overtuned on ImageNet, it could experience problems generalizing. It is therefore a good practice to test transfer learning based on the most recent and best performing network found on ImageNet, but not to stop there. You may find that some less performing networks are actually better for your problem.

Other objections about using ImageNet is that common pictures in everyday scenes contain more objects and that these objects may not be clearly visible when partially obstructed by other objects or because they mix with the background. If you want to use an ImageNet pretrained network in an everyday context, such as when creating an application or a robot, the performance may disappoint you. Consequently, since the ImageNet competition stopped (organizers claimed that improving performance by continuing to work on the dataset wouldn't be possible), researchers have increasingly focused on using alternative public datasets to challenge one's own CNNs and improve the state of the art in image recognition. Here are the alternatives so far:

>> **PASCAL VOC (Visual Object Classes)** http://host.robots.ox.ac.uk/pascal/VOC/: Developed by the University of Oxford, this dataset sets a neural network training standard for labeling multiple objects in the same picture, the PASCAL VOC xml standard. The competition associated with this dataset was halted in 2012.

>> **SUN** https://groups.csail.mit.edu/vision/SUN/: Created by the Massachusetts Institute of technology (MIT), this dataset provides benchmarks to help you determine your CNN performance. No competition is associated with it.

>> **MS COCO** http://cocodataset.org/: Prepared by Microsoft Corporation, this dataset offers a series of active competitions.

In particular, the Microsoft Common Objects in the Context dataset (hence the name MS COCO) offers fewer training images for your model than you find in ImageNet, but each image contains multiple objects. In addition, all objects appear in realistic positions (not staged) and settings (often in the open air and in public settings such as roads and streets). To distinguish the objects, the dataset provides both contours in pixel coordinates and labeling in the PASCAL VOC XML standard, having each object defined not just by a class but also by its coordinates in the images (a picture rectangle that shows where to find it). This rectangle is called a *bounding box*, defined in a simple way using four pixels, in contrast to the many pixels necessary for defining an object by its contours.

REMEMBER

The ImageNet dataset has recently started offering, in at least one million images, multiple objects to detect as well as their bounding boxes.

Learning the magic of data augmentation

Even if you have access to large amounts of data for your deep learning model, such as the ImageNet and MS COCO datasets, that may be not enough because of the multitude of parameters found in most complex neural architectures. In fact, even if you use techniques such as dropout (as explained in the "Adding regularization by dropout" section of Book 4, Chapter 2), overfitting is still possible. *Overfitting* occurs when the network memorizes the input data and learns no generally useful data patterns. Apart from dropout, other techniques that could help a network fight overfitting are LASSO, Ridge, and ElasticNet. However, nothing is as effective for enhancing your neural network's predictive capabilities as adding more examples to your training schedule.

REMEMBER

Originally, LASSO, Ridge, and ElasticNet were ways to constrain the weights of a linear regression model, which is a statistical algorithm for computing regression estimates. In a neural network, they work in a similar way by forcing the total sum of the weights in a network to be the lowest possible without harming the correctness of predictions. LASSO strives to put many weights down to zero, thus achieving a selection of the best weights. By contrast, Ridge instead tends to dampen all the weights, avoiding higher weights that can generate overfitting. Finally, ElasticNet is a mix of the LASSO and Ridge approaches, amounting to a trade-off between the selection and dampening strategies.

Image augmentation provides a solution to the problem of a lack of examples to feed a neural network to artificially create new images from existing ones. *Image augmentation* consists of different image-processing operations that are carried out separately or conjointly to produce an image different from the initial one. The result helps the neural network learn its recognition task better.

For instance, if you have training images that are too bright or too blurry, image processing modifies the existing images into darker and sharper versions. These new versions exemplify the characteristics that the neural network must focus on, rather than provide examples that focus on image quality. In addition, turning, cutting, or bending the image, as shown in Figure 2-1, could help because, again, they force the network to learn useful image features, no matter how the object appears.

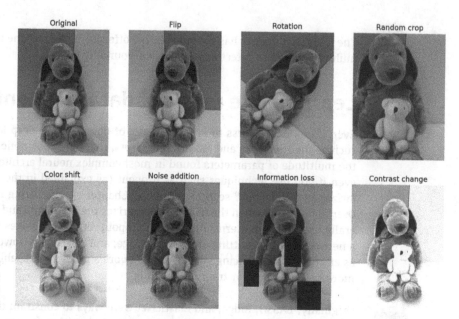

FIGURE 2-1:
Some common image augmentations.

The most common image augmentation procedures, as shown in Figure 2-1, are

- » **Flip:** Flipping your image on its axis tests the algorithm's capability to find it regardless of perspective. The overall sense of your image should hold even when flipped. Some algorithms can't find objects when upside down or even mirrored, especially if the original contains words or other specific signs.

- » **Rotation:** Rotating your image allows algorithm testing at certain angles, simulating different perspectives or imprecisely calibrated visuals.

- » **Random crop:** Cropping your image forces the algorithm to focus on an image component. Cutting an area and expanding it to the same size of a standard image enables you to test for recognition of partially hidden image features.

- » **Color shift:** Changing the nuances of image colors generalizes your example because the colors can change or be recorded differently in the real world.

- » **Noise addition:** Adding random noise tests the algorithm's capability to detect an object even when object quality is less than perfect.

- » **Information loss:** Randomly removing parts of an image simulates visual obstruction. It also helps the neural network rely on general image features, not on particulars (which could be randomly eliminated).

- » **Contrast change:** Changing the luminosity makes the neural network less sensitive to the light conditions (for instance, to daylight or artificial light).

Preparing the image data

The example begins by configuring the model, setting the optimizer, preprocessing the images, and creating the convolutions, the pooling, and the dense layers, as shown in the following code. (See Book 1, Chapter 5 for how to work with TensorFlow and Keras.)

```
import numpy as np
import zipfile
import pprint

from skimage.transform import resize
from skimage.io import imread

import matplotlib.pyplot as plt
%matplotlib inline

import warnings
warnings.filterwarnings("ignore")
```

Here are the Keras-specific imports needed for this example:

```
from keras.models import Sequential
from keras.optimizers import Adam
from keras.preprocessing.image import ImageDataGenerator
from keras.utils import to_categorical
from keras.layers import Conv2D, MaxPooling2D
from keras.layers import (Flatten, Dense, Dropout)
```

TIP

The dataset comprises more than 50,000 images, and the associated neural network can achieve a near-human level of accuracy in recognizing traffic signs. Such an application will require a large amount of computer calculations, and running this code locally could take a long time on your computer, depending on the kind of computer you have. Likewise, Colab can take longer depending on the resources that Google makes available to you, including whether you actually have access to a GPU, as mentioned in Book 1, Chapter 3. Timing this initial application on your setup will help you know whether your local machine or Colab is the fastest environment in which to run larger datasets. However, the best environment is the one that produces the most consistent and reliable results. You may not have a solid Internet connection to use, making Colab a poorer choice.

At this point, the example retrieves the GTSRB dataset from its location on the Internet (the INI Benchmark website, at the Ruhr-Universität Bochum specified previously). The following code snippet downloads it to the same directory as the Python code. Note that the download process can take a little time to complete, so now might be a good time to refill your teacup.

```
import urllib.request
import os.path
if not os.path.exists("GTSRB_Final_Training_Images.zip"):
    url = "https://sid.erda.dk/public/archives/\
    daaeac0d7ce1152aea9b61d9f1e19370/\
    GTSRB_Final_Training_Images.zip"
    filename = "./GTSRB_Final_Training_Images.zip"
    urllib.request.urlretrieve(url, filename)
```

After retrieving the dataset as a `.zip` file from the Internet, the code sets an image size. (All images are resized to square images, so the size represents the sides in pixels.) The code also sets the portion of data to keep for testing purposes, which means excluding certain images from training to have a more reliable measure of how the neural network works.

```
IMG_SIZE = 32
TEST_SIZE = 0.2
```

A loop through the files stored in the downloaded `.zip` file retrieves individual images, resizes them, stores the class labels, and appends the images to two separate lists: one for the training and one for testing purposes. The sorting uses a hash function, which translates the image name into a number and, based on that number, decides where to append the image:

```
X, Xt, y, yt = list(), list(), list(), list()

archive = zipfile.ZipFile(
        'GTSRB_Final_Training_Images.zip', 'r')
file_paths = [file for file in archive.namelist()
              if '.ppm' in file]

for filename in file_paths:
    img = imread(archive.open(filename))
    img = resize(img,
                output_shape=(IMG_SIZE, IMG_SIZE),
                mode='reflect')
    img_class = int(filename.split('/')[-2])

    if (hash(filename) % 1000) / 1000 > TEST_SIZE:
        X.append(img)
        y.append(img_class)
    else:
        Xt.append(img)
        yt.append(img_class)
archive.close()
```

After the job is completed, the code reports the consistency of the train and test examples:

```
test_ratio = len(Xt) / len(file_paths)
print("Train size:{} test size:{} ({:0.3f})".format(
    len(X),
    len(Xt),
    test_ratio))
```

The train size is more than 30,000 images, and the test almost is 8,000 (20 percent of the total):

```
Train size:31344 test size:7865 (0.201)
```

Your results may vary a little from those shown. For example, another run of the example produced a train size of 31,415 and a test size of 7,794. Neural networks can learn multiclass problems better when the classes are numerically similar or they tend to concentrate their attention on learning just the more populated classes. The following code checks the distribution of classes:

```
classes, dist = np.unique(y+yt, return_counts=True)
NUM_CLASSES = len(classes)
print ("No classes:{}".format(NUM_CLASSES))

plt.bar(classes, dist, align='center', alpha=0.5)
plt.show()
```

Figure 2-3 shows that the classes aren't balanced. Some traffic signs appear more frequently than others do (for instance, while driving, stop signs are encountered more frequently than a deer crossing sign).

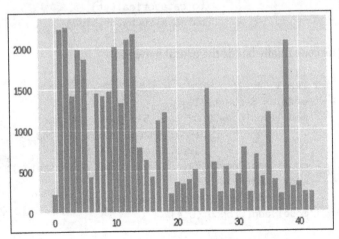

FIGURE 2-3: Distribution of classes.

As a solution, the code computes a *weight*, which is a ratio based on frequencies of classes that the neural network uses to increase the signal it receives from rarer examples and to dump the more frequent ones:

```
class_weight = {c:dist[c]/np.sum(dist) for c in classes}
```

Running a classification task

After setting the weights, the code defines the image generator, the part of the code that retrieves the images in batches (samples of a predefined size) for training and validation, normalizes their values, and applies augmentation to fight overfitting by slightly shifting and rotating them. Notice that the following code applies augmentation only on the training image generator, not the validation generator, because it's necessary to test the original images only.

```
batch_size = 256
tgen=ImageDataGenerator(rescale=1./255,
                        rotation_range=5,
                        width_shift_range=0.10,
                        height_shift_range=0.10)

train_gen = tgen.flow(np.array(X),
                      to_categorical(y),
                      batch_size=batch_size)
```

Here is the code for the validation generator:

```
vgen=ImageDataGenerator(rescale=1./255)

val_gen = vgen.flow(np.array(Xt),
                    to_categorical(yt),
                    batch_size=batch_size)
```

The code finally builds the neural network:

```
def small_cnn():
    model = Sequential()
    model.add(Conv2D(32, (5, 5), padding='same',
                     input_shape=(IMG_SIZE, IMG_SIZE, 3),
                     activation='relu'))
    model.add(Conv2D(64, (5, 5), activation='relu'))
    model.add(Flatten())
    model.add(Dense(768, activation='relu'))
    model.add(Dropout(0.4))
```

```
        model.add(Dense(NUM_CLASSES, activation='softmax'))
        return model


model = small_cnn()
model.compile(loss='categorical_crossentropy',
              optimizer=Adam(),
              metrics=['accuracy'])
```

The neural network consists of two convolutions, one with 32 channels, the other with 64, both working with a kernel of size (5,5). The convolutions are followed by a dense layer of 768 nodes. Dropout (dropping 40 percent of the nodes) regularizes this last layer, and softmax activates it (thus the sum of the output probabilities of all classes will sum to 100 percent).

On the optimization side, the loss to minimize is the categorical cross-entropy. The code measures success on *accuracy*, which is the percentage of correct answers provided by the algorithm. (The traffic sign class with the highest predicted probability is the answer.)

```
history = model.fit_generator(
    train_gen,
    steps_per_epoch=len(X) // batch_size,
    validation_data=val_gen,
    validation_steps=len(Xt) // batch_size,
    class_weight=class_weight,
    epochs=100,
    verbose=2)
```

Using the `fit_generator` on the model, the batches of images start being randomly extracted, normalized, and augmented for the training phase. After pulling out all the training images, the code sees an *epoch* (a training iteration using a full pass on the dataset) and computes a validation score on the validation images. After reading 100 epochs, the training and the model are completed.

TIP

If you don't use any augmentation, you can train your model in just about 30 epochs and reach a performance of your model that is almost comparable to a driver's skill in recognizing the different kinds of traffic signs (which is about 98.8 percent accuracy). The more aggressive the augmentation you use, the more epochs necessary for the model to reach its top potential, although accuracy performances will be higher, too. Here is the code that outputs the validation accuracy:

```
print("Best validation accuracy: {:0.3f}"
      .format(np.max(history.history['val_acc'])))
```

CONSIDERING THE COST OF REALISTIC OUTPUT

As mentioned a few times in this book already, deep learning training can take a considerable amount of time to complete. Whenever you see a fit function in the code, such as `model.fit_generator`, you're likely asking the system to perform training. The example code will always strive to provide you with realistic output — that is, what a scientist in the real world would consider acceptable.

Unfortunately, realistic output may cost you too much in the way of time. Not everyone has access to the latest high-technology system, and not everyone will get a GPU on Colab. The example in this chapter consumes a great deal of time to train in some cases. For example, testing the code on Colab took a little over 16 hours to complete when Colab didn't provide a GPU. The same example might run in as little as an hour if Colab does provide a GPU. (Book 1, Chapter 3 tells you more about the GPU issue.) Likewise, using a CPU-only system, a 16-core Xeon system required 4 hours and 23 minutes to complete training, but an Intel i7 processor with 8 cores took a little over 9 hours to do the same thing.

One way around this issue is to change the number of epochs used to train your model. The epochs=100 setting used for the example in this chapter provides an output accuracy of a little over 99 percent. However, if time is a factor, you may want to use a lower epochs setting when running this example to reduce the time you wait for the example to complete.

Another alternative for avoiding the problem is using GPU support on your local machine. However, to use this alternative, you must have a display adapter with the right kind of chip. Because the setup is complex and you're not likely to have the right GPU, this book takes the CPU-only route. However, you can certainly install the correct support by using Book 1, Chapter 3 as a starting point and then adding CUDA support. The article at https://towardsdatascience.com/tensorflow-gpu-installation-made-easy-use-conda-instead-of-pip-52e5249374bc provides additional details.

At this point, the code plots a graph depicting how the training and validation accuracy behaved during training:

```
plt.plot(history.history['acc'])
plt.plot(history.history['val_acc'])
plt.ylabel('accuracy'); plt.xlabel('epochs')
plt.legend(['train', 'test'], loc='lower right')
plt.show()
```

The code will report to you the best validation accuracy recorded and plot the accuracy curves achieved on training and validation data during the increasing epochs of learning, as shown in Figure 2-4. Notice how the training and validation accuracies are nearly similar at the end of training, although the validation is always better than the training. That's easily explained because the validation images are actually "easier" to guess than the training images because no augmentation is applied to them.

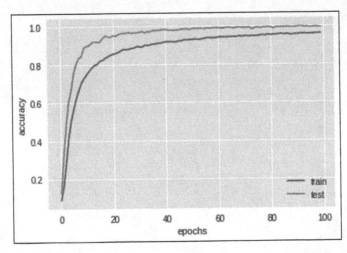

FIGURE 2-4:
Training and validation errors compared.

Given that the code can initialize the neural network in different ways, you may see different best results at the end of the training optimization. However, by the end of the 100 epochs set in the code, the validation accuracy should exceed 99 percent. (Sample runs achieved up to 99.5 percent on Colab.)

REMEMBER

A difference exists between the performance you obtain on the train data (which is often less) and on your validation subset, because train data is more complex and variable than validation data, given the image augmentations that the code sets up.

TECHNICAL STUFF

You should consider this result to be quite an excellent one based on the state-of-the-art benchmarks that you can read about in the paper called "HALOI, Mrinal. Traffic sign classification using deep inception-based convolutional networks" (https://arxiv.org/pdf/1511.02992.pdf). The paper hints at what can be easily achieved in terms of image recognition on limited problems using clean data and readily available tools such as TensorFlow and Keras.

Chapter **3**

Identifying Objects

Deep learning solutions for image recognition have become so impressive in their human-level performance that you see them used in developing or already marketed applications, such as self-driving cars and video-surveillance appliances. The video-surveillance appliances already perform tasks, such as automatic satellite image monitoring, facial detection, and people localization and counting. Yet you can't imagine a complex application when your network labels an image with only a single prediction. Even a simple dog or cat detector may not prove useful when the photos you analyze contain multiple dogs and cats. The real world is messy and complex. You can't expect, except in limited and controlled cases, laboratory-style images that consist of single, clearly depicted objects.

The need to handle complex images paved the way for variants of Convolutional Neural Networks (CNNs). Such variants offer sophistication that's still being developed and refined, such as multiple-object detection and localization. Multiple-object detection can deal with many different objects at a time. Localization can tell you where they are in the picture, and segmentation can find their exact contours. These new capabilities require complex neural architectures and image processing more advanced than the basic CNNs discussed in previous chapters. This chapter illustrates the fundamentals of how these solutions work, names key approaches and architectures, and, finally, tests one of the best performing object detection implementations.

The chapter closes by unveiling an expected weakness in an otherwise unbelievable technology. Someone could maliciously trick CNNs to report misleading detections or ignore seen objects using appropriate image-manipulation techniques. This puzzling discovery opens a new research front that shows that deep learning performance must also consider security for private and public use.

REMEMBER

You don't have to type the source code for this chapter manually. In fact, using the downloadable source is a lot easier. The source code for this chapter appears in the DSPD_0503_Object_ID.ipynb source code file for Python and DSPD_R_0503_Object_ID.ipynb source code file for R. See the Introduction for details on how to find these source files.

Distinguishing Classification Tasks

CNNs are the building blocks of deep learning–based image recognition, yet they answer only a basic classification need: Given a picture, can the CNN associate its content with a specific image class learned through previous examples? The following sections discuss the issues concerning this seemingly simple task. Humans can perform it with ease, but computers find the task difficult at best.

Understanding the problem

When you train a deep neural network to recognize dogs and cats, you can feed it a photo and obtain output that tells you whether the photo contains a dog or cat. If the last network layer is a softmax layer, the network outputs the probability of the photo containing a dog or a cat (the two classes you trained it to recognize) and the output sums to 100 percent. When the last layer is a sigmoid-activated layer, you obtain scores that you can interpret as probabilities of content belonging to each class, independently. The scores won't necessarily sum to 100 percent. In both cases, the classification may fail when the following occurs:

» **The main object isn't what you trained the network to recognize.** You may present the example neural network with a photo of a raccoon. In this case, the network will output an incorrect answer of dog or cat.

» **The main object is partially obstructed.** Your cat is playing hide and seek in the photo you show the network, and the network can't spot the cat because a piece of furniture partially hides it.

» **The photo contains many different objects to detect.** The image may include animals other than cats and dogs. In this case, the output from the network will suggest a single class rather than include all the objects.

Figure 3-1 shows image 47780 (http://cocodataset.org/#explore?id=47780) taken from the MS Coco dataset (released as part of the open source Creative Commons Attribution 4.0 License). The series of three outputs shows how a CNN detects, localizes, and segments the objects appearing in the image (a kitten and a dog standing on a field of grass). A plain CNN can't reproduce the examples in Figure 3-1 because its architecture will treat the entire image as being of a certain class. To overcome this limitation, researchers extend the basic CNN's capabilities to make them capable of the following:

Multiple detection   Localization by bounding boxes   Semantic Segmentation

>> **Detection:** Determining when an object is present in an image. Detection is different from classification because it involves just a portion of the image, implying that the network can detect multiple objects of the same and of different types. The capability to spot objects in partial images is called *instance spotting*.

>> **Localization:** Defining exactly where a detected object appears in an image. You can have different types of localizations. Depending on granularity, they distinguish the part of the image that contains the detected object.

>> **Segmentation:** Classification of objects at the pixel level. Segmentation takes localization to the extreme. This kind of neural model assigns each pixel of the image to a class or even an entity. For instance, the network marks all the pixels in a picture relative to dogs and distinguishes each one using a different label (called *instance segmentation*).

Performing localization

Localization is perhaps the easiest extension that you can get from a regular CNN. It requires that you train a regressor model alongside your deep learning classification model. A *regressor* is a model that guesses numbers. Defining object location in an image is possible using corner pixel coordinates, which means that you can train a neural network to output key measures that make it easy to determine where the classified object appears in the picture using a bounding box. Usually a bounding box uses the x and y coordinates of the lower-left corner, together with the width and the height of the area that encloses the object.

Classifying multiple objects

The classification of multiple objects begins by classifying those objects individually. A CNN performs these tasks on each object:

>> **Detect:** Predict an object's class.

>> **Localize:** Provide the object's coordinates.

You still use a CNN to classify multiple objects in an image, but this means working with each object present in the picture individually using one of two old image-processing solutions:

>> **Sliding window:** Analyzes only a portion (called a *region of interest*) of the image at a time. When the region of interest is small enough, it likely contains only a single object. The small region of interest allows the CNN to correctly classify the object. This technique is called *sliding window* because the software uses an image window to limit visibility to a particular area (the way a window in a home does) and slowly moves this window around the image. The technique is effective but could detect the same image multiple times, or you may find that some objects go undetected based on the window size that you decide to use to analyze the images.

>> **Image pyramids:** Solves the problem of using a window of fixed size because it generates increasingly smaller resolutions of the image. Therefore, you can apply a small sliding window. In this way, you transform the objects in the image, and one of the reductions may fit exactly into the sliding window used.

These techniques are computationally intensive. To apply them, you have to resize the image multiple times and then split it into chunks. You then process each chunk using your classification CNN. The number of operations for these activities is so large that rendering the output in real time is impossible.

The sliding window and image pyramid have inspired deep learning researchers to discover a couple of conceptually similar approaches that are less computationally intensive. The first approach is *one-stage detection*. It works by dividing the images into grids, and the neural network makes a prediction for every grid cell, predicting the class of the object inside. The prediction is quite rough, depending on the grid resolution (the higher the resolution, the more complex and slower the deep learning network). One-stage detection is very fast, having almost the same speed as a simple CNN for classification. The results have to be processed to gather the cells representing the same object together, and that may lead to further inaccuracies. Neural architectures based on this approach are Single-Shot Detector (SSD), You Only Look Once (YOLO), and RetinaNet. One-stage detectors are very fast, but not so precise.

The second approach is *two-stage detection*. This approach uses a second neural network to refine the predictions of the first one. The first stage is the proposal network, which outputs its predictions on a grid. The second stage fine-tunes these proposals and outputs a final detection and localization of the objects. Region Convolutional Neural Network (R-CNN), Fast R-CNN, and Faster R-CNN are all two-stage detection models that are much slower than their one-stage equivalents, but more precise in their predictions. You can read a more in-depth version of the technology behind R-CNN, Fast R-CNN, and Faster R-CNN at https://towardsdatascience.com/r-cnn-fast-r-cnn-faster-r-cnn-yolo-object-detection-algorithms-36d53571365e.

Annotating multiple objects in images

To train deep learning models to detect multiple objects, you need to provide more information than in simple classification. For each object, you provide both a classification and coordinates within the image using the annotation process, which contrasts with the labeling used in simple image classification.

Labeling images in a dataset is a daunting task even in simple classification. Given a picture, the network must provide a correct classification for the training and test phases. In labeling, the network decides on the right label for each picture, and not every part of the network will perceive the depicted image in the same way. The people who created the ImageNet dataset used the classification provided by multiple users from the Amazon Mechanical Turk crowdsourcing platform. (ImageNet used the Amazon service so much that in 2012, it turned out to be Amazon's most important academic customer.)

In a similar way, you rely on the work of multiple people when annotating an image using bounding boxes. Annotation requires that you not only label each object in a picture but also determine the best box with which to enclose each object. These two tasks make the annotation even more complex than labeling and more prone to producing erroneous results. Performing annotation correctly requires the work of more people who can provide a consensus on the accuracy of the annotation.

Identifying Objects

TIP

Some open source software can help in annotation for image detection (as well as for image segmentation, discussed in the following section). These tools are particularly effective:

» **LabelImg** (`https://github.com/tzutalin/labelImg`): Created by TzuTa Lin using Python, it relies on the Qt graphical interface (`https://doc.qt.io/qt-5.9/qtgui-index.html`). You can find a tutorial for this tool at `https://www.youtube.com/watch?v=p0nR2YsCY_U`).

» **LabelMe** (`https://github.com/wkentaro/labelme`): A powerful tool for image segmentation that provides an online service. The advantage of this tool is that you can use more than just squares to build a box to enclose each object, which makes it more time consuming to use but also more accurate.

» **FastAnnotationTool** (`https://github.com/christopher5106/FastAnnotationTool`): Based on the OpenCV computer vision library (`https://developer.nvidia.com/opencv`). This package isn't maintained as well as the others in the list but is still viable.

Segmenting images

Semantic segmentation predicts a class for each pixel in the image, which is a different perspective from either labeling or annotation. Some people also call this task *dense prediction* because it makes a prediction for every pixel in an image. The task doesn't specifically distinguish different objects in the prediction. For instance, a semantic segmentation can show all the pixels that are of the class cat, but it won't provide any information about what the cat (or cats) is doing in the picture. You can easily get all the objects in a segmented image by *postprocessing*, because after performing the prediction, you can get the object pixel areas and distinguish between different instances of them, if multiple separated areas exist under the same class prediction.

Different deep learning architectures can achieve image segmentation. Fully Convolutional Networks (FCNs) and U-Nets (`https://arxiv.org/abs/1505.04597`) are among the most effective. FCNs are built for the first part (called the *encoder*), which is the same as CNNs. After the initial series of convolutional layers, FCNs end with another series of CNNs that operate in a reverse fashion as the encoder (making them a *decoder*). The decoder is constructed to re-create the original input image size and output as pixels the classification of each pixel in the image. In such a fashion, the FCN achieves the semantic segmentation of the image. FCNs are too computationally intensive for most real-time applications. In addition, they require large training sets to learn their tasks well; otherwise, their segmentation results are often coarse.

REMEMBER

Finding the encoder part of the FCN pretrained on ImageNet, which accelerates training and improves learning performance, is common.

U-Nets are an evolution of FCN devised by Olaf Ronneberger, Philipp Fischer, and Thomas Brox in 2015 for medical purposes (see `https://lmb.informatik.uni-freiburg.de/people/ronneber/U-Net/`). U-Nets present advantages compared to FCNs. The encoding (also called *contraction*) and the decoding parts (also referred to as *expansion*) are perfectly symmetric. In addition, U-Nets use shortcut connections between the encoder and the decoder layers. These shortcuts allow the details of objects to pass easily from the encoding to the decoding parts of the U-Net, and the resulting segmentation is precise and fine-grained.

TIP

Building a segmentation model from scratch can be a daunting task, but you don't need to do that. You can use some pretrained U-Net architectures and immediately start using this kind of neural network by leveraging the segmentation *model zoo* (a term used to describe the collection of pretrained models offered by many frameworks; see `https://modelzoo.co/` for details) offered by segmentation models, a package offered by Pavel Yakubovskiy. You can find installation instructions, the source code, and plenty of usage examples at `https://github.com/qubvel/segmentation_models`. The commands from the package seamlessly integrate with Keras.

Perceiving Objects in Their Surroundings

As automation takes a larger role in all aspects of human existence, the need for automation to perceive objects becomes greater. Robots need to see obstacles, self-driving cars need to see pedestrians, and even medical systems need to see patients. The computer that controls the automation can't understand what an object is or how it functions; instead, it uses camera input in the form of digital images to identify objects and then interact with those objects in predefined ways. The following sections discuss how automation uses this form of perception (which differs from human perception) through 2-D camera imagery to perform tasks.

Considering vision needs in self-driving cars

Integrating vision capabilities into the sensing system of a self-driving car could enhance how safely it drives. A segmentation algorithm could help the car distinguish lanes from sidewalks, as well as from other obstacles the car should notice. The car could even feature a complete end-to-end system, such as NVidia's, that controls steering, acceleration, and braking in a reactive manner based on its

Identifying Objects

visual inputs. (You can learn more about the NVidia self-driving car efforts at https://www.nvidia.com/en-us/self-driving-cars/.) A visual system could spot certain objects on the road relevant to driving, such as traffic signs and traffic lights. It could visually track the trajectories of other cars. In all cases, a deep learning network could provide the solution.

REMEMBER

No concept of emotion exists for a computer, so a computer performs an analysis and then follows rules to perform tasks such as steering. A computer can't drive confidently because confidence is an expression of an emotional state brought on by success. A successful computer only performs its tasks with greater precision. The lack of emotion also means that computers don't experience an adrenaline rush prior to an accident, making the capability to act faster than normal a reality. A computer can make decisions at the one speed at which analysis allows it to make decisions. In short, no matter how well you program a computer to mimic human processes, the computer will still perform differently from a human and react to environmental issues in different ways.

The "Distinguishing Classification Tasks" section, at the start of this chapter, discusses how object detection improves upon single-object classification offered by CNNs. This section also clarifies the architectures and current models of the two main approaches: one-stage detection (or one-shot detection) and two-stage detection (also known as region proposal). This section tells how a one-stage detection system works and provides help for an autonomous vehicle. You need to consider these issues in light of how computers differ from humans when driving a car, but you can apply the principles to any form of automation where a computer takes over a task from a human.

Programming such a detection system from scratch would be a daunting task, one requiring an entire book of its own. Fortunately, you can employ open source projects on GitHub such as Keras-RetinaNet (https://github.com/fizyr/keras-retinanet). The next section of the chapter provides additional details on how using RetinaNet works.

TIP

Isaac Newton stated, "If I have seen further, it is by standing on the shoulders of Giants." Likewise, you can achieve more in deep learning when you make use of existing neural architectures and pretrained networks. For instance, you can find many models on GitHub (www.github.com) such as the TensorFlow model zoo (https://github.com/tensorflow/models).

Discovering how RetinaNet works

The RetinaNet is a sophisticated and interesting object-detection model that strives to be as fast as other one-stage detection models while also achieving the accuracy of bounding box predictions of two-stage detection systems like

Faster R-CNN (the top-performing model). Thanks to its architecture, RetinaNet achieves its goals, using techniques similar to the U-Net architecture discussed for semantic segmentation. RetinaNet is part of a group of models called Feature Pyramid Networks (FPN).

RetinaNet owes its performance to its authors, Tsung-Yi Lin, Priya Goyal, Ross Girshick, Kaiming He, and Piotr Dollár, who noted that one-stage detection models don't always detect objects precisely because they are affected by the overwhelming presence of distracting elements in the images used for training. Their paper, "Focal Loss for Dense Object Detection" (https://arxiv.org/pdf/1708.02002.pdf), provides details of the techniques RetinaNet uses. The problem is that the images present few objects of interest to detect. In fact, one-stage detection networks are trained to guess the class of each cell in an image divided by a fixed grid, where the majority of cells are empty of objects of interest.

REMEMBER

In semantic segmentation, the targets of the classification are single pixels. In one-stage detection, the targets are sets of contiguous pixels, performing a task similar to semantic segmentation but at a different granularity level.

Here's what happens when you have such a predominance of null examples in images and are using a training approach that examines all available cells as examples. The network will be more likely to predict that nothing is in a processed image cell than to provide a correctly predicted class. Neural networks always take the most efficient route to learn, and in this case, predicting the background is easier than anything else. In this situation, which goes under the name of *unbalanced learning*, many objects are undetected by the neural network using a single-shot object detection approach.

In machine learning, when you want to predict two numerically different classes (one is the majority class and the other is the minority class), you have an unbalanced classification problem. Most algorithms don't perform properly when the classes are unbalanced because they tend to prefer the majority class. A few solutions are available for this problem:

>> **Sampling:** Selecting some examples and discarding others.

>> **Downsample:** Reducing the effect of the majority class by choosing to use only a part of it, which balances the majority and minority predictions. In many cases, this is the easiest approach.

>> **Upsample:** Increasing the effect of the minority class by replicating its examples many times until the minority class has the same number of examples as the majority class.

The creators of RetinaNet take a different route, as they note in their paper "Focal Loss for Dense Object Detection" mentioned earlier in this section. They discount the majority class examples that are easier to classify and concentrate on the cells that are difficult to classify. The result is that the network cost function focuses more on adapting its weights to recognize background objects. This is the *focal loss* solution and represents a smart way to make one-stage detection perform more correctly, yet speedily, which is a real-time application requirement, such as for obstacle or object detection in self-driving cars, or processing large quantities of images in video surveillance.

Using the Keras-RetinaNet code

Released under the open source Apache License 2.0, Keras-RetinaNet is a project sponsored by the Dutch robotic company Fitz and made possible by many contributors (the top contributors are Hans Gaiser and Maarten de Vries). It's an implementation of the RetinaNet neural network written in Python using Keras (https://github.com/fizyr/keras-retinanet/). You find Keras-RetinaNet used successfully by many projects — the most notable and impressive of which is the winning model for the NATO Innovation Challenge, a competition whose task was to detect cars in aerial images. (You can read the narrative from the winning team in this blog post: https://medium.com/data-from-the-trenches/object-detection-with-deep-learning-on-aerial-imagery-2465078db8a9.)

Object detection network code is too complex to explain in a few pages, plus you can use an existing network to set up deep learning solutions, so this section demonstrates how to download and use Keras-RetinaNet on your computer. Before you try this process, ensure that you have configured your computer as described in Book 1, Chapter 5, and consider the trade-offs involved in using various execution options described in the "Considering the cost of realistic output" sidebar in Book 5, Chapter 2.

Obtaining Keras-RetinaNet

As a first step, you upload the necessary packages and start downloading the zipped version of the GitHub repository. This example uses the 0.5.0 version of Keras-RetinaNet, which was the most recent version available at the time of writing.

```
import os
import zipfile
import urllib.request
import warnings
warnings.filterwarnings("ignore")
url = "https://github.com/fizyr/\
keras-retinanet/archive/0.5.0.zip"
urllib.request.urlretrieve(url, './'+url.split('/')[-1])
```

After downloading the zipped code, the example code automatically extracts it using these commands:

```
zip_ref = zipfile.ZipFile('./0.5.0.zip', 'r')
for name in zip_ref.namelist():
  zip_ref.extract(name, './')
zip_ref.close()
```

The execution creates a new directory called keras-retinanet-0.5.0, which contains the code for setting up the neural network. The code then executes the compilation and installation of the package using the pip command:

```
os.chdir('./keras-retinanet-0.5.0')
!python setup.py build_ext --inplace
!pip install .
```

As the setup process proceeds, you see a long series of messages as output. The task can also require a little time to complete. Both the messages and the installation time are normal. The best thing you can do is get a cup of coffee and wait.

Obtaining pretrained weights

All the commands in the previous section retrieved the code that builds the network architecture. The example now needs the pretrained weights and relies on weights trained on the MS Coco dataset using the ResNet50 CNN, the neural network that Microsoft used to win the 2015 ImageNet competition.

```
os.chdir('../')
url = "https://github.com/fizyr/keras-retinanet/\
releases/download/0.5.0/resnet50_coco_best_v2.1.0.h5"
urllib.request.urlretrieve(url, './'+url.split('/')[-1])
```

Downloading all the weights takes a while, so now would be a good time to catch up on your reading (assuming you don't need more coffee).

Initializing the RetinaNet model

After you have completed the downloads, the example is ready to import all the necessary commands and to initialize the RetinaNet model using the pretrained weights retrieved from the Internet. This step also sets a dictionary to convert the numeric network results into understandable classes. The selection of classes is useful for the detector on a self-driving car or any other solution that has to understand images taken from a road or an intersection.

```
import os
import numpy as np
from collections import defaultdict
import keras
from keras_retinanet import models
from keras_retinanet.utils.image import (read_image_bgr,
        preprocess_image, resize_image)
from keras_retinanet.utils.visualization import (draw_box,
        draw_caption)
from keras_retinanet.utils.colors import label_color
import matplotlib.pyplot as plt
%matplotlib inline

model_path = os.path.join('.',
        'resnet50_coco_best_v2.1.0.h5')

model = models.load_model(model_path,
        backbone_name='resnet50')

labels_to_names = defaultdict(lambda: 'object',
        {0: 'person', 1: 'bicycle', 2: 'car',
         3: 'motorcycle', 4: 'airplane', 5: 'bus',
         6: 'train', 7: 'truck', 8: 'boat',
         9: 'traffic light', 10: 'fire hydrant',
         11: 'stop sign', 12: 'parking meter',
         25: 'umbrella'})
```

Downloading the test image

To make the example useful, you need a sample image to test the RetinaNet model. The example relies on a free image from Wikimedia representing an intersection with people expecting to cross the road, some stopped vehicles, traffic lights, and traffic signs.

```
url = "https://upload.wikimedia.org/wikipedia/commons/\
thumb/f/f8/Woman_with_blue_parasol_at_intersection.png/\
640px-Woman_with_blue_parasol_at_intersection.png"
urllib.request.urlretrieve(url, './'+url.split('/')[-1])
```

Testing the neural network

Now that the download process and initialization are complete, it's time to test the neural network. In the code snippet that follows this explanation, the code reads the image from disk and then switches the blue with red image channels (because the image is uploaded in BGR format, but RetinaNet works with RGB images). Finally, the code preprocesses and resizes the image. All these steps complete using the provided functions and require no special settings.

The model will output the detected bounding boxes, the level of confidence (a probability score that the network truly detected something), and a code label that will convert into text using the previously defined dictionary of labels. The loop filters the boxes printed on the image by the example. The code uses a confidence threshold of 0.5, implying that the example will keep any detection whose confidence is at least at 50 percent. Using a lower confidence threshold results in more detections, especially of those objects that appear small in the image, but also increases wrong detections (for instance, some shadows may start being detected as objects).

TIP

Depending on your objectives using RetinaNet, you may decide that using a lower confidence threshold is fine. You'll notice that as you lower the confidence, the proportion of the resulting exact guesses (those with nearly 100 percent confidence) will diminish. Such a proportion is called the *precision* of the detection, and by deciding what precision you can tolerate, you can set the best confidence for your purposes.

```python
image = read_image_bgr(
    '640px-Woman_with_blue_parasol_at_intersection.png')
draw = image.copy()
draw[:,:,0], draw[:,:,2] = image[:,:,2], image[:,:,0]

image = preprocess_image(image)
image, scale = resize_image(image)

boxes, scores, labels = model.predict_on_batch(
    np.expand_dims(image, axis=0))
boxes /= scale

for box, score, label in zip(
    boxes[0], scores[0], labels[0]):

    if score > 0.5:
        color = label_color(label)
        b = box.astype(int)
        draw_box(draw, b, color=color)
        caption = "{} {:.3f}".format(
            labels_to_names[label], score)
        draw_caption(draw, b, caption.upper())
plt.figure(figsize=(12, 6))
plt.axis('off')
plt.imshow(draw)
plt.show()
```

The first time you run the code may take a while, but after some computations, you should obtain the output reproduced in Figure 3-2.

FIGURE 3-2:
Object detection resulting from Keras-RetinaNet.

The network can successfully detect various objects, some extremely small (such as a person in the background), some partially shown (such as the nose of a car on the right of the image). Each detected object is delimited by its bounding box, which creates a large range of possible applications.

For instance, you could use the network to detect that an umbrella — or some object — is being used by a person. When processing the results, you can relate the fact that two bounding boxes are overlapping, with one being an umbrella and the other one being a person, and that the first box is positioned on top of the second in order to infer that a person is holding an umbrella. This is called *visual relationship detection*. In the same way, by the overall setting of detected objects and their relative positions, you can train a second deep learning network to infer an overall description of the scene.

Overcoming Adversarial Attacks on Deep Learning Applications

As deep learning finds many applications in self-driving cars, such as detecting and interpreting traffic signs and lights; detecting the road and its lanes; detecting crossing pedestrians and other vehicles; controlling the car by steering and braking in an end-to-end approach to automatic driving; and so on, questions may arise about the safety of a self-driving car. Driving isn't the only common activity that's undergoing a revolution because of deep learning applications.

Recently introduced applications that are accessible by the public include facial recognition for security access. (You can read about this use in ATMs in China at `https://www.telegraph.co.uk/news/worldnews/asia/china/11643314/China-unveils-worlds-first-facial-recognition-ATM.html`.) Another example of a deep learning application is in speech recognition used for Voice Controllable Systems (VCSs), as provided by a plethora of companies such as Apple, Amazon, Microsoft, and Google in a wide variety of applications that include Siri, Alexa, and Google Home.

Some of these deep learning applications may cause economic damage or even be life threatening when they fail to provide the correct answer. Therefore, you may be surprised to discover that hackers can intentionally trick deep neural networks and guide them into failing predictions by using particular techniques called adversarial examples.

An *adversarial example* is a handcrafted piece of data that is processed by a neural network as training or test inputs. A hacker modifies the data to force the algorithm to fail in its task. Each adversarial example bears modifications that are indeed slight, subtle, and deliberately made imperceptible to humans. The modifications, although ineffective on humans, are still quite effective in reducing the effectiveness and usefulness of a neural network. Often, such malicious examples aim at leading a neural network to fail in a predictable way to create some illegal advantage for the hacker. Here are just a few malicious uses of adversarial examples (the list is far from exhaustive):

>> Misleading a self-driving car into an accident

>> Obtaining money from an insurance fraud by having fake claim photos trusted as true ones by automatic systems

>> Tricking a facial recognition system to recognize the wrong face and grant access to money in a bank account or personal data on a mobile device

Tricking pixels

First made known by the paper "Intriguing Properties of Neural Networks" (go to `https://arxiv.org/pdf/1312.6199.pdf`), adversarial examples have attracted much attention in recent years, and successful (and shocking) discoveries in the field have led many researchers to devise faster and more effective ways of creating such examples than the original paper pointed out.

DISCOVERING THAT A MUFFIN IS NOT A CHIHUAHUA

Sometimes deep learning image classification fails to provide the right answer because the target image is inherently ambiguous or rendered to puzzle observers. For instance, some images are so misleading that they can even mystify a human examiner for a while, such as the Internet memes Chihuahua vs Muffin (see https://imgur.com/QWQiBYU) or Labradoodle vs Fried Chicken (see https://imgur.com/5EnWOJU). A neural network can misunderstand confusing images if its architecture isn't adequate to the task and its training hasn't been exhaustive in terms of seen examples. The AI technology columnist Mariya Yao has compared different computer vision APIs at https://medium.freecodecamp.org/chihuahua-or-muffin-my-search-for-the-best-computer-vision-api-cbda4d6b425d) and found that even full-fledged vision products can be tricked by ambiguous pictures.

Recently, other studies have challenged deep neural networks by proposing unexpected perspectives of known objects. In the paper called "Strike (with) a Pose: Neural Networks Are Easily Fooled by Strange Poses of Familiar Objects" at https://arxiv.org/pdf/1811.11553.pdf, researchers found that simple ambiguity can trick state-of-the-art image classifiers and object detectors trained on large-scale image datasets.

Often, objects are learned by neural networks from pictures taken in *canonical poses* (which means in common and usual situations). When faced with an object in an unusual pose or outside its usual environment, some neural networks can't categorize the resulting object. For instance, you expect a school bus to be running on the road, but if you rotate and twist it in the air and then land it in the middle of the road, a neural network can easily see it as a garbage truck, a punching bag, or even a snowplow. You may argue that the misclassification occurs because of learning bias (teaching a neural network using only images in canonical poses). Yet that implies that at present, you shouldn't rely such technology under all circumstances, especially, as the authors of the paper point out, in self-driving car applications because objects may suddenly appear on the road in new poses or circumstances.

REMEMBER

Adversarial examples are still confined to deep learning research laboratories. For this reason, you find many scientific papers quoted in these paragraphs when referring to various kinds of examples. However, you should never discount adversarial examples as being some kind of academic diversion because their potential for damage is high.

At the foundations of all these approaches the idea that mixing some numeric information, called a perturbation, with the image can lead a neural network to behave differently from expectations, although in a controlled way. When you create an adversarial example, you add some specially devised noise (which appear to be random numbers when you view them) to an existing image, and that's enough to trick most CNNs (because often the same trick works with different architectures when trained by the same data). Generally, you can discover such perturbations by having access to the model (its architecture and weights). You then exploit its backpropagation algorithm to systematically discover the best set of numeric information to add to an image so that you can mutate one predicted class into another one.

TIP

You can create the perturbation effect by changing a single pixel in an image. Researchers have obtained perfectly working adversarial examples using this approach, as discovered by researchers Jiawei Su, Danilo Vasconcellos Vargas, and Kouichi Sakurai from Kyushu University and described in their paper "One Pixel Attack for Fooling Deep Neural Networks" (https://arxiv.org/pdf/1710.08864.pdf).

Hacking with stickers and other artifacts

Most adversarial examples are laboratory experiments on vision robustness, and those examples can demonstrate all their capabilities because they are produced by directly modifying data inputs and tested images during the training phase. However, many applications based on deep learning operate in the real world, and the use of laboratory techniques doesn't prevent malicious attacks. Such attacks don't need access to the underlying neural model to be effective. Some examples may take the form of a sticker or an inaudible sound that the neural network doesn't know how to handle.

A paper called "Adversarial Examples in the Physical World" by Alexey Kurakin, Ian J. Goodfellow, and Samy Bengio (found at https://arxiv.org/pdf/1607.02533.pdf) demonstrates that various attacks are also possible in a nonlaboratory setting. All you need is to print the adversarial examples and show them to the camera feeding the neural network (for instance, by using the camera in a mobile phone). This approach demonstrates that the efficacy of an adversarial example is not strictly due to the numerical input fed into a neural network. It's the ensemble of shapes, colors, and contrast present in the image that achieves the trick, and you don't need any direct access to the neural model to find out what ensemble works best. You can see how a network could mistake the image of a washing machine for a safe or a loudspeaker directly from this video made by the authors, who tricked the TensorFlow camera demo, an application for mobile devices that performs on-the-fly image classification: https://www.youtube.com/watch?v=zQ_uMenoBCk.

Other researchers from Carnegie Mellon University have found a way to trick face detection into believing a person is a celebrity by fabricating eyeglass frames that can affect how a deep neural network recognizes instances. As automated security systems become widespread, the ability to trick the system by using simple add-ons like eyeglasses could turn into a serious security threat. A paper called "Accessorize to a Crime: Real and Stealthy Attacks on State-of-the-Art Face Recognition" (https://www.cs.cmu.edu/~sbhagava/papers/face-rec-ccs16.pdf) describes how accessories could allow both dodging personal recognition and impersonation.

Finally, another disturbing real-world use of an adversarial example appears in the paper "Robust Physical-World Attacks on Deep Learning Visual Classification" (https://arxiv.org/pdf/1707.08945.pdf). Plain black-and-white stickers placed on a stop sign can affect how a self-driving car understands the signal, causing it to see the stop sign as another road indication. When you use more colorful (but also more noticeable) stickers, such as the ones described in the paper "Adversarial Patch" (https://arxiv.org/pdf/1712.09665.pdf), you can guide the predictions of a neural network in a particular direction by having it ignore anything but the sticker and its misleading information. As explained in the paper, a neural network could predict a banana to be anything else just by placing a proper deceitful sticker nearby.

At this point, you may wonder whether any defense against adversarial examples is possible, or if sooner or later they will destroy the public confidence in deep learning applications, especially in the self-driving car field. By intensely studying how to mislead a neural network, researchers are also finding how to protect it against any misuse. First, neural networks can approximate any function. If the neural networks are complex enough, they can also determine by themselves how to rule out adversarial examples when taught by other examples. Second, novel techniques such as constraining the values in a neural network or reducing the neural network size after training it (a technique called *distillation*, used previously to make a network viable on devices with little memory) have been successfully tested against many different kinds of adversarial attacks.

Chapter **4**

Analyzing Music and Video

Y ou can find considerable discussions online about whether computers can be creative by employing deep learning. The dialogue goes to the very essence of what it means to be creative. Philosophers and others have discussed the topic endlessly throughout human history without arriving at a conclusion as to what, precisely, creativity means. Consequently, a single chapter in a book written in just a few months won't solve the problem for you.

However, to provide a basis for the discussions in this chapter, this book defines *creativity* as the ability to define new ideas, patterns, relationships, and so on. The emphasis is on *new*: the originality, progressiveness, and imagination that humans provide. It doesn't include copying someone else's style and calling it one's own. Of course, this definition will almost certainly raise the ire of some while garnering the accepting nods of others, but to make the discussion work at all, you need a definition. Mind you, this definition doesn't exclude creativity by nonhumans. For example, some people can make a case for creative apes (see http://www.bbc.com/future/story/20140723-are-we-the-only-creative-species for more details).

Creativity and computers can definitely come together in a fascinating collaboration. As you know, computers rely on math to do everything, and their association with art and music is no exception. A computer can transfer existing art or music patterns to a neural network and use the result to generate something that looks new but actually relies on the existing pattern. Generative Adversarial Networks (GANs) are the best available technology for this task of transferring patterns to neural networks today, but you can count on other technologies appearing in the future.

Computers don't perform the tasks involved in outputting art on their own; they rely on a human to provide the means to accomplish such tasks. For example, a human designs the algorithm that the computer uses to perform the statistical analysis of the patterns. Moreover, a human decides which artistic style to mimic, and a human defines what sort of output might prove aesthetically pleasing. In short, the computer ends up being a tool in the hands of an exceptionally smart human to automate the process of creating what could be deemed as new, but really isn't.

As part of the process of defining how some can see a computer as creative, the chapter also defines how computers mimic an established style. You can see for yourself that deep learning relies on math to perform a task generally not associated with math at all. An artist or musician doesn't rely on calculations to create something new, but could rely on calculations to see how others performed their task. When an artist or musician employs math to study another style, the process is called learning, not creating. Of course, this entire minibook (part of a larger discussion on data science programming) is about how deep learning performs learning tasks, and even that process differs greatly from how humans learn.

Learning to Imitate Art and Life

You have likely seen interesting visions of AI art, such as those mentioned in the article at https://news.artnet.com/art-world/ai-art-comes-to-market-is-it-worth-the-hype-1352011. The art undeniably has aesthetic appeal. In fact, the article mentions that Christie's, one of the most famous auction houses in the world, originally expected to sell the piece of art for $7,000 to $10,000 but actually it sold for $432,000, according to the *Guardian* (https://www.theguardian.com/artanddesign/shortcuts/2018/oct/26/call-that-art-can-a-computer-be-a-painter) and the *New York Times* (https://www.nytimes.com/2018/10/25/arts/design/ai-art-sold-christies.html). So not only is this type of art appealing, it can also generate a lot of money. However, in every unbiased story you read, the question remains as to whether the AI art actually is art at all. The following sections help you understand that computer generation doesn't correlate to creativity; instead, it translates to amazing algorithms employing the latest in statistics.

Transferring an artistic style

One of the differentiators of art is the artistic style. Even when someone takes a photograph and displays it as art (https://www.wallartprints.com.au/blog/artistic-photography/), the method in which the photograph is taken, processed, and optionally touched up all define a particular style. In many cases, depending on the skill of the artist, you can't even tell that you're looking at a photograph because of its artistic elements (https://www.pinterest.com/lorimcneeartist/artistic-photography/?lp=true).

Some artists become so famous for their particular style that others take time to study it in depth to improve their own technique. For example, Vincent van Gogh's unique style is often mimicked (https://www.artble.com/artists/vincent_van_gogh/more_information/style_and_technique). Van Gogh's style — his use of colors, methods, media, subject matter, and a wealth of other considerations — requires intense study for humans to replicate. Humans improvise, so the adjective suffix *esque* often appears as a descriptor of a person's style. A critic might say that a particular artist uses a van Goghesque methodology.

REMEMBER

To create art, the computer relies on a particular artistic style to modify the appearance of a source picture. In contrast to a human, a computer can perfectly replicate a particular style given enough consistent examples. Of course, you could create a sort of mixed style by using examples from various periods in the artist's life. The point is that the computer isn't creating a new style, nor is it improvising. The source image isn't new, either. You see a perfectly copied style and a perfectly copied source image when working with a computer, and you transfer the style to the source image to create something that looks a little like both.

The process used to transfer the style to the source picture and produce an output is complex and generates a lot of discussion. For example, considering where source code ends and elements such as training begin is important. The article at https://www.theverge.com/2018/10/23/18013190/ai-art-portrait-auction-christies-belamy-obvious-robbie-barrat-gans discusses one such situation that involves the use of existing code but different training from the original implementation, which has people wondering over issues such as attribution when art is generated by computer. Mind you, all the discussion focuses on the humans who create the code and perform the training of the computer; the computer itself doesn't figure in to the discussion because the computer is simply crunching numbers.

Reducing the problem to statistics

Computers can't actually see anything, so analyzing images doesn't occur in the same manner as humans use; you must solve the problem in another way. Someone takes a digital image of a real-world object or creates a fanciful drawing like the one in Figure 4-1, and each pixel in that image appears as tuples of numbers representing the red, blue, and green values of each pixel, as shown in Figure 4-2. These numbers, in turn, are what the computer interacts with using an algorithm. The computer doesn't understand that the numbers form a tuple; that's a human convention. All it knows is that the algorithm defines the operations that must take place on the series of numbers. In short, the art becomes a matter of manipulating numbers using a variety of methods, including statistics.

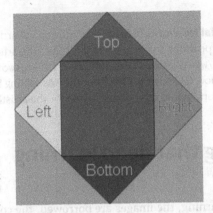

FIGURE 4-1:
A human might see a fanciful drawing.

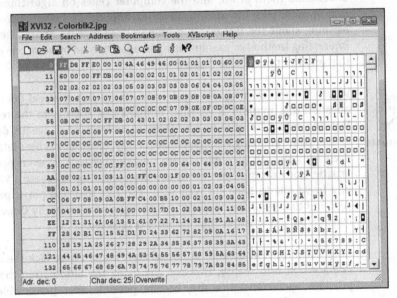

FIGURE 4-2:
The computer sees a series of numbers.

REMEMBER

Deep learning relies on a number of algorithms to manipulate the pixels in a source drawing in a variety of ways to reflect the particular style you want to use. In fact, you can find a dizzying array of such algorithms because everyone appears to have a different idea of how to force a computer to create particular kinds of art. The point is that all these methods rely on algorithms that act on a series of numbers to perform the task; the computer never takes brush in hand to actually create something new. Two methods appear to drive the current strategies, though:

>> **Convolutional Neural Networks (CNNs):** See Book 4, Chapter 3 for an overview; also see the "Defining a new piece based on a single artist" section, later in this chapter, for the artistic perspective.

>> **Generative Adversarial Networks (GANs):** The "Moving toward GANs" section of this chapter provides an overview of this topic. The article at https://skymind.ai/wiki/generative-adversarial-network-gan is also helpful in seeing how GANs work. Check out the "Visualizing how neural networks dream" section, later in this chapter, again for the artistic perspective.

Understanding that deep learning doesn't create

For art created by deep learning, the images are borrowed, the computer doesn't understand them at all, and the computer relies on algorithms to perform the task of modifying the images. Deep learning doesn't even choose the method of learning about the images — a human does that. In short, deep learning is an interesting method of manipulating images created by someone else using a style that another person also created.

REMEMBER

Whether deep learning can create something isn't the real question to ask. The question that matters is whether humans can appreciate the result of the deep learning output. Despite its incapacity to understand or create, deep learning can deliver some amazing results. Consequently, creativity is best left to humans, but deep learning can give everyone an expressive tool — even people who aren't artistic. For example, you could use deep learning to create a van Gogh version of a loved one to hang on your wall. The fact that you participated in the process and that you have something that looks professionally drawn is the point to consider — not whether the computer is creative.

Deep learning is also about automation. A human may lack the ability to translate a vision into reality. However, by using the automation that deep learning provides, such translation may become possible, even predictable. Humans have always relied on tools to overcome deficiencies, and deep learning is just another in a very long line of tools. In addition, the automation that deep learning provides also makes repetition possible, supplying consistent and predictable output from even less skilled humans.

Mimicking an Artist

Deep learning helps you mimic a particular artist. You can mimic any artist you want because the computer doesn't understand anything about style or drawing. The deep learning algorithm will faithfully reproduce a style based on the inputs you provide (even if you can't reproduce the style on your own). Consequently, mimicking is a flexible way to produce a particular output, as described in the following sections.

Defining a new piece based on a single artist

Convolutional Neural Networks (CNNs) appear in a number of uses for deep learning applications. For example, they're used for self-driving cars and facial recognition systems. Book 4, Chapter 3 provides some additional examples of how CNNs do their job, but the point is that a CNN can perform recognition tasks well given enough training.

Interestingly, CNNs work particularly well in recognizing art style. So you can combine two pieces of art into a single piece. However, those two pieces supply two different kinds of input for the CNN:

>> **Content:** The image that defines the desired output. For example, if you provide a content image of a cat, the output will look like a cat. It won't be the same cat you started with, but the content defines the desired output with regard to what a human will see.

>> **Style:** The image that defines the desired modification. For example, if you provide an example of a van Gogh painting, the output will reflect that style.

TIP

In general, you see CNNs that rely on a single content image and a single style image. Using just the two images like this lets you see how content and style work together to produce a particular output. The example at https://medium.com/ mlreview/making-ai-art-with-style-transfer-using-keras-8bb5fa44b216 provides a method for combining two images in this manner.

Of course, you need to decide how to combine the images. In fact, this is where the statistics of deep learning come into play. To perform this task, you use a *neural style transfer*, as outlined in the paper "A Neural Algorithm of Artistic Style," by Leon A. Gatys, Alexander S. Ecker, and Matthias Bethge (https:// arxiv.org/pdf/1508.06576.pdf or https://www.robots.ox.ac.uk/~vgg/rg/ papers/1508.06576v2.pdf).

The algorithm works with these kinds of images: a *content image*, which depicts the object you want to represent; a *style image*, which provides the art style you want to mimic; and an *input image*, which is the image to transform. The input image is usually a random image or the same image as the content image. Transferring the style implies preserving the content (that is, if you start with a photo of a dog, the result will still depict a dog). However, the transformed input image is nearer to the style image in presentation. The algorithm you use will define two loss measures:

>> **Content loss:** Determines the amount of the original image that the CNN uses to provide output. A greater loss here means that the output will better reflect the style you provide. However, you can reach a point at which the loss is so great that you can no longer see the content.

>> **Style loss:** Determines the manner in which the style is applied to the content. A higher level of loss means that the content retains more of its original style. The style loss must be low enough for you to end up with a new piece of art that reflects the desired style.

Having just two images doesn't allow for extensive training, so you use a pre-trained deep learning network, such as VGG-19 (the 2014 winner of the ImageNet challenge created by the Visual Geometry Group, VGG, at Oxford University). The pretrained deep learning network already knows how to process an image into image features of different complexity. The algorithm for neural style transfer picks the CNN of a VGG-19, excluding the final, fully connected layers. In this way, you have the network that acts as a processing filter for images. When you send in an image, VGG-19 transforms it into a neural network representation, which could be completely different from the original. However, when you use only the top layers of the network as image filters, the network transforms the resulting image but doesn't completely change it.

Taking advantage of such transformative neural network properties, the neural transfer style doesn't use all the convolutions in the VGG-19. Instead, it monitors them using the two loss measures to assure that, in spite of the transformations applied to the image, the network maintains the content and applies the style. In this way, when you pass the input image through VGG-19 several times, its weights adjust to accomplish the double task of content preservation and style learning. After a few iterations, which actually require a lot of computations and weight updates, the network transforms your input image into the anticipated image and art style.

TIP

You often see the output of a CNN referred to as a *pastiche*. It's a fancy word that generally means an artistic piece composed of elements borrowed from motifs or techniques of other artists. Given the nature of deep learning art, the term is appropriate.

Combining styles to create new art

If you really want to get fancy, you can create a pastiche based on multiple style images. For example, you could train the CNN using multiple Monet works so that the pastiche looks more like a Monet piece in general. Of course, you could just as easily combine the styles of multiple impressionist painters to create what appears to be a unique piece of art that reflects the impressionist style in general. The actual method for performing this task varies, but the article at https://ai.googleblog.com/2016/10/supercharging-style-transfer.html offers ideas for accomplishing the task.

Visualizing how neural networks dream

Using a CNN is essentially a manual process with regard to choosing the loss functions. The success or failure of a CNN depends on the human setting the various values. A GAN takes a different approach. It relies on two interactive deep networks to automatically adjust the values to provide better output. You can see these two deep networks having these names:

» **Generator:** Creates an image based on the inputs you provide. The image needs to retain the original content, but with the appropriate level of style to produce a pastiche that is hard to distinguish from an original.

» **Discriminator:** Determines whether the generator output is real enough to pass as an original. If not, the discriminator provides feedback telling the generator what is wrong with the pastiche.

To make this setup work, you actually train two models: one for the generator and another for the discriminator. The two act in concert, with the generator creating new samples and the discriminator telling the generator what is wrong with each sample. The process goes back and forth between generator and discriminator until the pastiche achieves a specific level of perfection. In the "Moving toward GANs" section, later in this chapter, you can find an even more detailed explanation about how GANs work.

TIP

This approach is advantageous because it provides a greater level of automation and a higher probability of good results than using a CNN. The disadvantage is that this approach also requires considerable time to implement, and the processing requirements are much greater. Consequently, using the CNN approach is often better to achieve a result that's good enough. You can see an example of the GAN approach at https://towardsdatascience.com/gan-by-example-using-keras-on-tensorflow-backend-1a6d515a60d0.

Using a network to compose music

This chapter focuses mainly on visual art because you can easily judge the subtle changes that occur to it. However, the same techniques also work with music. You can use CNNs and GANs to create music based on a specific style. Computers can't see visual art, nor can they hear music. The musical tones become numbers that the computer manipulates just as it manipulates the numbers associated with pixels. The computer doesn't see any difference at all.

However, deep learning does detect a difference. Yes, you use the same algorithms for music as for visual art, but the settings you use are different, and the training is unique as well. In addition, some sources say that training for music is a lot harder than for art (see `https://motherboard.vice.com/en_us/article/qvq54v/why-is-ai-generated-music-still-so-bad` for details). Of course, part of the difficulty stems from the differences among the humans listening to the music. As a group, humans seem to have a hard time defining aesthetically pleasing music, and even people who like a particular style or particular artists rarely like everything those artists produce.

In some respects, the tools used to compose music using AI are more formalized and mature than those used for visual art. This doesn't mean that the music composition tools always produce great results, but it does mean that you can easily buy a package to perform music composition tasks. Here are the two most popular offerings today:

>> **Amper:** `https://www.ampermusic.com/`

>> **Jukedeck:** `https://www.jukedeck.com/`

REMEMBER

AI music composition is different from visual art generation because the music tools have been around for a longer time, according to the article at `https://www.theverge.com/2018/8/31/17777008/artificial-intelligence-taryn-southern-amper-music`. The late songwriter and performer David Bowie used an older application called Verbasizer (`https://motherboard.vice.com/en_us/article/xygxpn/the-verbasizer-was-david-bowies-1995-lyric-writing-mac-app`) in 1995 to aid in his work. The key idea here is that this tool aided in, rather than produced, work. The human being is the creative talent; the AI serves as a creative tool to produce better music. Consequently, music takes on a collaborative feel, rather than giving the AI center stage.

Other creative avenues

One of the more interesting demonstrations of the fact that computers can't create is in writing. The article at `https://medium.com/deep-writing/how-to-write-with-artificial-intelligence-45747ed073c` describes a deep learning network used to generate text based on a particular writing style. Although the technique is interesting, the text that the computer generates is nonsense. The computer can't generate new text based on a given style because the computer doesn't actually understand anything.

The article at `https://www.grammarly.com/blog/transforming-writing-style-with-ai/` provides a more promising avenue of interaction between human and AI. In this case, a human writes the text and the computer analyzes the style to generate something more appropriate to a given situation. The problem is that the computer still doesn't understand the text. Consequently, the results will require cleanup by a human to ensure reliable results.

WARNING

To realize just how severe the problem can become when using an AI in certain creative fields, consider the problems that occurred when the *New York Times* decided to favor technology over humans (see the article at `https://www.chronicle.com/blogs/linguafranca/2018/06/14/new-york-times-gets-rid-of-copy-editors-mistakes-ensue/`). Without copy editors to verify the text, the resulting paper contains more errors. Of course, you've likely seen this problem when a spell checker or a grammar checker fixes your perfectly acceptable prose in a manner that makes it incorrect. Relying on technology to the exclusion of human aid seems like a less than useful solution to the problem of creating truly inspiring text.

Eventually, most humans will augment their creativity using various AI-driven tools. In fact, we're probably there now. This book benefits from the use of a spelling and grammar checker, along with various other aids. However, the writer is still human, and the book would never make it into print without an entire staff of humans to check the accuracy and readability of the text. When you think of deep learning and its effect on creativity, think augmentation, not replacement.

Moving toward GANs

In 2014, at the Département d'informatique et de recherche opérationnelle at Montréal University, Ian Goodfellow and other researchers (among whom is Yoshua Bengio, one of Canada's most noted scientists working on artificial neural networks and deep learning) published the first paper on GANs. You can read the work at `https://arxiv.org/pdf/1406.2661v1.pdf` or `https://papers.nips.cc/paper/5423-generative-adversarial-nets.pdf`. In the following months, the paper attracted attention and was deemed innovative for its proposed mix of deep learning and game theory. The idea became widespread because of its accessibility in terms of neural network architecture: You can train a working GAN using a standard computer. (The technique works better if you can invest a lot of computational power.)

Contrary to other deep learning neural networks that classify images or sequences, the specialty of GANs is their capability to generate new data by deriving inspiration from training data. This capability becomes particularly impressive when dealing with image data, because well-trained GANs can generate new pieces of art that people sell at auctions (such as the artwork sold at Christie's for nearly half a million dollars, mentioned earlier in this chapter). This feat is even more incredible because previous results obtained using other mathematical and statistical techniques were far from credible or usable.

Finding the key in the competition

The GAN name contains the term *adversarial* because the key idea behind GANs is the competition between two networks, which play as adversaries against each other. Ian Goodfellow, the principal author of the original paper on GANs, used a simple metaphor to describe how everything works. Goodfellow described the process as an endless challenge between a forger and a detective: The forger has to create a fake piece of art by copying some real art masterpiece, so he starts painting something. After the forger completes the fake painting, a detective examines it and decides whether the forger created a real piece of art or simply a fake. If the detective sees a fake, the forger receives notice that something is wrong with the work (but not where the fault lies). When the forger shows that the art is real despite the negative feedback of the detective, the detective receives notice of the mistake and changes the detection technique to avoid failure during the next attempt. As the forger continues attempts to fool the detective, both the forger and the detective grow in expertise in their respective duties. Given time, the art produced by the forger becomes extremely high in quality and is almost undistinguishable from the real thing except by someone with an expert eye.

Figure 4-3 illustrates the story of GANs as a simple schema, in which inputs and neural architectures interact together in closed loop of reciprocal feedbacks. The generator network plays the part of the forger, and a discriminator network plays the detective. GANs use the term *discriminator* because of the similarity in purpose to electronic circuits that accept or reject signals based on their characteristics. The discriminator in a GAN accepts (wrongly) or refuses (correctly) the work created by the generator. The interesting aspect of this architecture is that the generator never sees a single training example. Only the discriminator accesses such data in its training. The generator receives random inputs (noise) to provide a random starting point each time, which forces it to produce a different result.

The generator may seem take all the glory (after all, it generates the data product). However, the real powerhouse of the architecture is the discriminator. The discriminator computes errors that are backpropagated to its own network to learn how best to distinguish between real and fake data. The errors also propagate to the generator, which optimizes itself to cause the discriminator to fail during the next round.

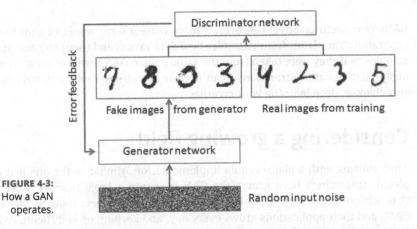

FIGURE 4-3:
How a GAN
operates.

THE PROBLEM WITH FAKE DATA

Just as a GAN can generate impressive art, so it can generate fake people. Look at
https://www.thispersondoesnotexist.com/ to see a person who doesn't exist.
Unless you know where to look, the pictures are really quite convincing. However, little
details give them away for now:

- The backgrounds look muddy or lack that real feel in some manner.

- Those who have watched the movie *The Matrix* will be familiar with the episodic
glitches that appear in some images.

- The foreground pixel texture may not be quite right. For example, you might see
moiré patterns (https://photographylife.com/what-is-moire) where they
aren't expected.

However, recognizing these sorts of issues requires a human. In addition, the various
problems will eventually go away when GANs improve. GANs can fake more than just
pictures. You could create a completely fake human identity in an incredibly short time
with little effort. GANs could have all the right records in all the right places. The technology exists today to create fake human identities that could possibly appear in places
where rooting them out would be extremely inconvenient. For example, imagine the
effect of flooding an airport with fake terrorist identities immediately before a real terrorist attack. The authorities could be confused about who is a real terrorist and who is
a fake one just long enough for the attack to succeed. This is the sort of problem that
you need to be aware of — not killer robots.

GANs may seem creative. However, a more correct term would be that they are generative: They learn from examples how data varies, and they can generate new samples as if they were taken from the same data. A GAN learns to mimic a previously existing data distribution; it can't create something new. As stated earlier in this chapter, deep learning isn't creative.

Considering a growing field

After starting with a plain-vanilla implementation, similar to the one just completed, researchers have grown the GAN idea into a large number of variants that achieve tasks more complex than simply creating new images. The list of GANs and their applications grows every day, and keeping up is difficult. Avinash Hindupur has built a "GAN Zoo" by tracking all the variants, a task that's becoming more difficult daily. (You can see the most recent updates at https://github.com/hindupuravinash/the-gan-zoo.) Zheng Liu favors a historical approach instead, and you can see the GAN timeline he maintains at https://github.com/dongb5/GAN-timeline. No matter how you approach GANs, seeing how each new idea sprouts from previous ones is a useful exercise.

Inventing realistic pictures of celebrities

The chief application of GANs is to create images. The first GAN network that evolved from the original paper by Goodfellow and others is the DCGAN, which was based on convolutional layers.

DCGAN greatly improved the generative capabilities of the original GANs, and they soon impressed everyone when they created fake images of faces by taking examples from photos of celebrities. Of course, not all the DCGAN-created faces were realistic, but the effort was just the starting point of a rush to create more realistic images. EBGAN-PT, BEGAN, and Progressive GAN are all improvements that achieve a higher degree of realism. You can read the NVidia paper prepared on Progressive GANs to gain a more precise idea of the quality reached by such state-of-the-art techniques: https://research.nvidia.com/publication/2017-10_Progressive-Growing-of.

Another great enhancement to GANs is the conditional GAN (CGAN). Although having a network produce realistic images of all kinds is interesting, it's of little use when you can't control the type of output you receive in some way. CGANs manipulate the input and the network to suggest to the GAN what it should produce. Now, for instance, you have networks that produce images of faces of persons who don't exist, based on your preferences of how hair, eyes, and other details appear, as shown by this demonstrative video by NVidia: https://www.youtube.com/watch?v=kSLJria0umA.

Enhancing details and image translation

Producing images of higher quality and possibly controlling the output generated has opened the way to more applications. This chapter doesn't have room to discuss them all, but the following list offers an overview of what you can find:

» **Cycle GAN:** Applied to neural transfer style. For example, you can turn a horse into a zebra or a Monet painting into one that appears to come from van Gogh. By exploring the project at https://github.com/junyanz/CycleGAN, you can see how it works and consider the kind of transformations it can apply to images.

» **Super Resolution GAN (SRGAN):** Transforms images by making blurred, low-resolution images into clear, high-resolution ones. The application of this technique to photography and cinema is interesting because it improves low-quality images at nearly no cost. You can find the paper describing the technique and results here: https://arxiv.org/pdf/1609.04802.pdf.

» **Pose Guided Person Image Generation:** Controls the pose of the person depicted in the created image. The paper at https://arxiv.org/pdf/1705.09368.pdf describes practical uses in the fashion industry to generate more poses of a model, but you might be surprised to know that the same approach can create videos of one person dancing exactly the same as another one: https://www.youtube.com/watch?v=PCBTZh41Ris.

» **Pix2Pix:** Translates sketches and maps into real images and vice versa. You can use this application to transform architectural sketches into a picture of a real building or to convert a satellite photo into a drawn map. The paper at https://arxiv.org/pdf/1611.07004.pdf discusses more of the possibilities offered by the Pix2Pix network.

» **Image repairing:** Repairs or modifies an existing image by determining what's missing, cancelled, or obscured: https://github.com/pathak22/context-encoder.

» **Face Aging:** Determines how a face will age. You can read about it at https://arxiv.org/pdf/1702.01983.pdf.

» **Midi Net:** Creates music in your favorite style, as described at https://arxiv.org/pdf/1703.10847.pdf.

Chapter **5**

Considering Other Task Types

ook 4, Chapter 4 introduces you to the topic of Natural Language Processing (NLP), where you consider how a computer can process text despite not understanding it. The chapter points out that programming a computer to process human language is a daunting task, which is only recently possible using Natural Language Processing (NLP), deep learning Recurrent Neural Networks (RNNs), and word embeddings. This chapter takes you further by looking more closely at tokenization, the bag-of-words approach to analysis, and sentiment analysis. These approaches rely on building a model using Keras and employing deep learning techniques.

REMEMBER

You don't have to type the source code for this chapter manually. In fact, using the downloadable source is a lot easier. The source code for this chapter appears in the DSPD_0505_Other_Tasks.ipynb source code file for Python and the DSPD_R_0505_Other_Tasks.ipynb source code file for R. See the Introduction for details on how to find these source files.

Processing Language in Texts

Even though Book 4, Chapter 4 shows how to turn text (no matter what source you use) into data that a computer can analyze, it never really gets into the issue of language, which is a lot more than simply text. Language includes nuanced terms and hidden meanings that express more than the text would say on its own. Obviously, a computer can't understand things like sentiment, but you can make it appear that it does to a degree by performing certain types of deep learning analysis, which is where the following sections lead you. Of course, no matter how much analysis you perform, a computer can't ever discover the true meaning of sentences said with differing vocal inflections or possessing hidden meanings known only to the people engaging in the conversation.

Considering the processing methodologies

As a simplification, you can view language as a sequence of words made of letters (as well as punctuation marks, symbols, emoticons, and so on). Deep learning processes language best by using layers of RNNs, such as Long Short-Term Memory (LSTM) or Gated Recurrent Units (GRU). (Chapter 11 of *Deep Learning For Dummies*, by John Paul Mueller and Luca Massaron [Wiley], explains the use of LTSM and GRU.) However, knowing to use RNNs doesn't tell you how to use sequences as inputs; you need to determine the kind of sequences. In fact, deep learning networks accept only numeric input values. Computers encode letter sequences that you understand into numbers according to a protocol, such as Unicode Transformation Format-8 bit (UTF-8). UTF-8 is the most widely used encoding. (You can read the primer about encodings at `https://www.alexreisner.com/code/character-encoding`.)

REMEMBER

Deep learning can also process textual data using Convolutional Neural Networks (CNNs) instead of RNNs by representing sequences as matrices (similar to image processing). Keras supports CNN layers, such as the `Conv1D` (`https://keras.io/layers/convolutional/`), which can operate on ordered features in time — that is, sequences of words or other signals. The 1D convolution output is usually followed by a `MaxPooling1D` layer that summarizes the outputs. CNNs applied to sequences find a limit in their insensitivity to the global order of the sequence. (They tend to spot local patterns.) For this reason, they're best used in sequence processing in combination with RNNs, not as their replacement.

Natural Language Processing (NLP) consists of a series of procedures that improve the processing of words and phrases for statistical analysis, machine learning algorithms, and deep learning. NLP owes its roots to computational linguistics that powered AI rule-based systems, such as expert systems, which made decisions based on a computer translation of human knowledge, experience, and way of thinking. NLP digested textual information, which is unstructured, into more structured data so that expert systems could easily manipulate and evaluate it.

Deep learning has taken the upper hand today, and expert systems are limited to specific applications in which interpretability and control of decision processes are paramount (for instance, in medical applications and driving-behavior decision systems in some self-driving cars). Yet, the NLP pipeline is still quite relevant for many deep learning applications.

Defining understanding as tokenization

In an NLP pipeline, the first step is to obtain raw text. Usually you store it in memory or access it from disk. When the data is too large to fit in memory, you maintain a pointer to it on disk (such as the directory name and the filename). In the following example, you use three documents (represented by string variables) stored in a list (in computational linguistics, the document container is the *corpus*):

```
import numpy as np

texts = ["My dog gets along with cats",
         "That cat is vicious",
         "My dog is happy when it is lunch"]
```

After obtaining the text, you process it. As you process each phrase, you extract the relevant features from the text (you usually create a *bag-of-words* matrix) and pass everything to a learning model, such as a deep learning algorithm. During text processing, you can use different transformations to manipulate the text (with tokenization being the only mandatory transformation):

>> **Tokenization (mandatory):** Split a sentence into individual words.

>> **Cleaning:** Remove nontextual elements such as punctuation and numbers.

>> **Lemmatization:** Transform a word into its dictionary form (the lemma). It's an alternative to stemming, but it's more complex because you don't use an algorithm. Instead, you use a dictionary to convert every word into its lemma.

>> **N-grams:** Associate every word with a certain number (the *n* in n-gram), of following words and treat them as a unique set. Usually, *bi-grams* (a series of two adjacent elements or tokens) and *tri-grams* (a series of three adjacent elements or tokens) work the best for analysis purposes.

>> **Normalization:** Remove capitalization.

>> **Pos-tagging:** Tag every word in a phrase with its grammatical role in the sentence (such as tagging a word as a verb or as a noun). You can read more about Parts of Speech (POS) tagging at https://medium.com/analytics-vidhya/pos-tagging-using-conditional-random-fields-92077e5eaa31.

>> **Stemming:** Reduce a word to its stem (which is the word form before adding inflectional affixes, as you can read here: https://www.thoughtco.com/stem-word-forms-1692141). An algorithm, called a stemmer, can do this based on a series of rules.

>> **Stop word removal:** Remove common, uninformative words that don't add meaning to the sentence, such as the articles *the* and *a*. Removing negations such as *not* could be detrimental if you want to guess the sentiment.

To achieve these transformations, you may need a specialized Python package such as NLTK (http://www.nltk.org/api/nltk.html) or Scikit-learn (see the tutorial at https://scikit-learn.org/stable/tutorial/text_analytics/working_with_text_data.html). When working with deep learning and a large number of examples, you need only basic transformations: normalization, cleaning, and tokenization. The deep learning layers can determine what information to extract and process. When working with few examples, you do need to provide as much NLP processing as possible to help the deep learning network determine what to do in spite of the little guidance provided by the few examples.

TIP

Keras offers a function, keras.preprocessing.text.Tokenizer, that normalizes (using the lower parameter set to True), cleans (the filters parameter contains a string of the characters to remove, usually these: '!"#$%&()*+,-./:;<=>?@[\]^_`{|}~ '), and tokenizes.

Putting all the documents into a bag

After processing the text, you have to extract the relevant features, which means transforming the remaining text into numeric information for the neural network to process. This is commonly done using the bag-of-words approach, which is obtained by frequency encoding or binary encoding the text. This process equates to transforming each word into a matrix column as wide as the number of words you need to represent. The following example shows how to achieve this process and what it implies.

Obtaining the vocabulary size

The example uses the texts list instantiated earlier in the chapter. As a first step, you prepare a basic normalization and tokenization using a few Python commands to determine the word vocabulary size for processing:

```
unique_words = set(word.lower() for phrase in texts for
                   word in phrase.split(" "))
print(f"There are {len(unique_words)} unique words")
```

When you run this code using the texts list defined in the previous section, you see this output:

```
There are 14 unique words
```

Processing the text

You now proceed to load the Tokenizer function from Keras and set it to process the text by providing the expected vocabulary size:

```
from keras.preprocessing.text import Tokenizer
vocabulary_size = len(unique_words) + 1
tokenizer = Tokenizer(num_words=vocabulary_size)
```

TIP

Using a vocabulary_size that's too small may exclude important words from the learning process. One that's too large may uselessly consume computer memory. You need to provide Tokenizer with a correct estimate of the number of distinct words contained in the list of texts. You also always add 1 to the vocabulary_size to provide an extra word for the start of a phrase (a term that helps the deep learning network). At this point, Tokenizer maps the words present in the texts to indexes, which are numeric values representing the words in text:

```
tokenizer.fit_on_texts(texts)
print(tokenizer.index_word)
```

The resulting indexes are as follows:

```
{1: 'is', 2: 'my', 3: 'dog', 4: 'gets', 5: 'along',
 6: 'with', 7: 'cats', 8: 'that', 9: 'cat', 10: 'vicious',
 11: 'happy', 12: 'when', 13: 'it', 14: 'lunch'}
```

The indexes represent the column number that houses the word information:

```
print(tokenizer.texts_to_matrix(texts))
```

Here's the resulting matrix:

```
[[0. 0. 1. 1. 1. 1. 1. 1. 0. 0. 0. 0. 0. 0. 0.]
 [0. 1. 0. 0. 0. 0. 0. 0. 1. 1. 1. 0. 0. 0. 0.]
 [0. 1. 1. 1. 0. 0. 0. 0. 0. 0. 0. 1. 1. 1. 1.]]
```

The matrix consists of 15 columns (14 words plus the start of phrase pointer) and three rows, representing the three processed texts. This is the text matrix to process using a shallow neural network (RNNs require a different format, as discussed later), which is always sized as vocabulary_size by the number of texts.

The numbers inside the matrix represent the number of times a word appears in the phrase. This isn't the only representation possible, though. Here are the others:

>> **Frequency encoding:** Counts the number of word appearances in the phrase.

>> **One-hot-encoding or binary encoding:** Notes the presence of a word in a phrase, no matter how many times it appears.

>> **Term Frequency-Inverse Document Frequency (TF-IDF) score:** Encodes a measure relative to how many times a word appears in a document relative to the overall number of words in the matrix. (Words with higher scores are more distinctive; words with lower scores are less informative.)

Using the TF-IDF transformation instead

You can use the TF-IDF transformation from Keras directly. The Tokenizer offers a method, texts_to_matrix, that by default encodes your text and transforms it into a matrix in which the columns are your words, the rows are your texts, and the values are the word frequency within a text. If you apply the transformation by specifying mode='tfidf', the transformation uses TF-IDF instead of word frequencies to fill the matrix values:

```
print(np.round(tokenizer.texts_to_matrix(texts,
                               mode='tfidf'), 1))
```

The new output matrix looks like this:

```
[[0.  0.  0.7 0.7 0.9 0.9 0.9 0.9 0.  0.  0.  0.  0.
  0. ]
 [0.  0.7 0.  0.  0.  0.  0.  0.  0.9 0.9 0.9 0.  0.
  0. ]
 [0.  1.2 0.7 0.7 0.  0.  0.  0.  0.  0.  0.  0.9 0.9 0.9
  0.9]]
```

Note that by using a matrix representation, no matter whether you use binary, frequency, or the more sophisticated TF-IDF, you have lost any sense of word ordering that exists in the phrase. During processing, the words scatter in different columns, and the neural network can't guess the word order in a phrase.

This lack of order is why you call it a bag-of-words approach. The bag-of-words approach is used in many machine learning algorithms, often with results ranging from good to fair, and you can apply it to a neural network using dense architecture layers. Transformations of words encoded into n_grams (discussed in the previous paragraph as an NLP processing transformation) provide some more information, but again, you can't relate the words.

Retaining order using RNNs

RNNs keep track of sequences, so they still use one-hot-encoding, but they don't encode the entire phrase; rather, they individually encode each token (which could be a word, a character, or even a bunch of characters). For this reason, they expect a sequence of indexes representing the phrase:

```
sequences = tokenizer.texts_to_sequences(texts)
print(sequences)
```

The output sequences look like this:

```
[[2, 3, 4, 5, 6, 7], [8, 9, 1, 10], [2, 3, 1, 11, 12, 13,
 1, 14]]
```

TIP

By matching the indexes found in the "Processing the text" section, earlier in this chapter, to the numbers in these lists, you can re-create the original sentences. For example, 2 is the 2: 'my' in the index, which is the first word in "My dog gets along with cats", the first entry in texts.

As each phrase passes to a neural network input as a sequence of index numbers, the number is turned into a one-hot encoded vector. You can use this code to see how the encoding works:

```
from keras.utils import to_categorical
print(to_categorical(sequences[0]))
```

The one-hot encoded vectors are then fed into the RNN's layers one at a time, making them easy to learn. For instance, here's the transformation of the first phrase in the matrix:

```
[[0. 0. 1. 0. 0. 0. 0. 0. 0. 0. 0. 0. 0. 0. 0.]
 [0. 0. 0. 1. 0. 0. 0. 0. 0. 0. 0. 0. 0. 0. 0.]
 [0. 0. 0. 0. 1. 0. 0. 0. 0. 0. 0. 0. 0. 0. 0.]
 [0. 0. 0. 0. 0. 1. 0. 0. 0. 0. 0. 0. 0. 0. 0.]
 [0. 0. 0. 0. 0. 0. 1. 0. 0. 0. 0. 0. 0. 0. 0.]
 [0. 0. 0. 0. 0. 0. 0. 1. 0. 0. 0. 0. 0. 0. 0.]]
```

In this representation, you get a distinct matrix for each piece of text. Each matrix represents the individual texts as distinct words using columns, but now the rows represent the word appearance order. (The first row is the first word, the second row is the second word, and so on.)

Using AI for sentiment analysis

Sentiment analysis computationally derives from a written text using the writer's attitude (whether positive, negative, or neutral), toward the text topic. This kind of analysis proves useful for people working in marketing and communication because it helps them understand what customers and consumers think of a product or service and thus act appropriately (for instance, by trying to recover unsatisfied customers or deciding to use a different sales strategy). Everyone performs sentiment analysis. For example, when reading text, people naturally try to determine the sentiment that moved the person who wrote it. However, when the number of texts to read and understand is too huge and the text constantly accumulates, as in social media and customer emails, automating the task is important.

The example in the following sections show a test run of RNNs using Keras and TensorFlow that builds a sentiment analysis algorithm capable of classifying the attitudes expressed in a film review. The data is a sample of the IMDb dataset that contains 50,000 reviews (split in half between train and test sets) of movies accompanied by a label expressing the sentiment of the review (0=negative, 1=positive). IMDb (https://www.imdb.com/) is a large online database containing information about films, TV series, and video games. Originally maintained by a fan base, it's now run by an Amazon subsidiary. On IMDb, people find the information they need about their favorite show as well as post their comments or write a review for other visitors to read.

Getting the IMDb data

Keras offers a downloadable wrapper for IMDb data. You prepare, shuffle, and arrange this data into a train and a test set. This dataset appears among other useful datasets at https://keras.io/datasets/. In particular, the IMDb textual data offered by Keras is cleansed of punctuation, normalized into lowercase, and transformed into numeric values. Each word is coded into a number representing its ranking in frequency. The most frequent words have low numbers; the less frequent words have higher numbers.

As a starting point, the code imports the imdb function from Keras and uses it to retrieve the data from the Internet (about a 17.5MB download). The parameters that the example uses encompass just the top 10,000 words, and Keras should shuffle the data using a specific random seed. (Knowing the seed enables you to reproduce the shuffle as needed.) The function returns two train and test sets, both made of text sequences and the sentiment outcome.

```
from keras.datasets import imdb

top_words = 10000
((x_train, y_train),
 (x_test, y_test)) = imdb.load_data(num_words=top_words,
                                     seed=21)
```

After the previous code completes, you can check the number of examples using the following code:

```
print("Training examples: %i" % len(x_train))
print("Test examples: %i" % len(x_test))
```

The following output shows that the examples are split evenly between training and testing:

```
Training examples: 25000
Test examples: 25000
```

This dataset is a relatively small one for a language problem; clearly the dataset is mainly for demonstration purposes. In addition, the code determines whether the dataset is balanced, which means it has an almost equal number of positive and negative sentiment examples.

```
import numpy as np
print(np.unique(y_train, return_counts=True))
```

Here's the output you should see:

```
(array([0, 1], dtype=int64), array([12500, 12500],
  dtype=int64))
```

The result, array([12500, 12500]), confirms that the dataset is split evenly between positive and negative outcomes. Such a balance between the response classes is exclusively because of the demonstrative nature of the dataset. In the real world, you seldom find balanced datasets.

Creating the review dictionaries

Now that you have a dataset to use, it's time to create some Python dictionaries that can convert between the code used in the dataset and the real words. In fact, the dataset used in this example is preprocessed and provides sequences of numbers representing the words, not the words themselves. (LSTM and GRU algorithms that you find in Keras expect sequences of numbers as numbers.)

```python
word_to_id = {w:i+3 for w,i in
  imdb.get_word_index().items()}
id_to_word = {0:'<PAD>', 1:'<START>', 2:'<UNK>'}
id_to_word.update({i+3:w for w,i in
  imdb.get_word_index().items()})

def convert_to_text(sequence):
    return ' '.join(
        [id_to_word[s] for s in sequence if s>=3])

print(convert_to_text(x_train[8]))
```

Here's the output from this part of the example:

```
this movie was like a bad train wreck as horrible as it
was you still had to continue to watch my boyfriend and i
rented it and wasted two hours of our day now don't get
me wrong the acting is good just the movie as a whole
just both of us there wasn't anything positive or good
about this scenario after this movie i had to go rent
something else that was a little lighter jennifer is as
usual a very dramatic actress her character seems manic
and not all there hannah though over played she does a
wonderful job playing out the situation she is in more
than once i found myself yelling at the tv telling her to
fight back or to get violent all in all very violent
movie not for the faint of heart
```

The previous code snippet defines two conversion dictionaries (from words to numeric codes and vice versa) and a function that translates the dataset examples into readable text. As an example, the code prints the ninth example: "this movie was like a bad train wreck as horrible as it was . . .". From this excerpt, you can easily anticipate that the sentiment for this movie isn't positive. Words such as *bad*, *wreck*, and *horrible* convey a strong negative feeling, and that makes guessing the correct sentiment easy.

TIP

In this example, you receive the numeric sequences and turn them back into words, but the opposite is common. Usually, you get phrases made up of words and turn them into sequences of integers to feed to a layer of RNNs. Keras offers a specialized function, Tokenizer (see https://keras.io/preprocessing/text/#tokenizer), which can do that for you. It uses the methods fit_on_text, to learn how to map words to integers from training data, and `texts_to_matrix`, to transform text into a sequence.

However, in other reviews, you may not find revealing words like *bad*, *wreck*, and *horrible*. The feeling is expressed in a more subtle or indirect way, and understanding the sentiment early in the text may not be possible because revealing phrases and words may appear much later in the discourse. For this reason, you also need to decide how much of the review you want to analyze. Conventionally, you take an initial part of the text, a *phrase*, and use it as representative of the entire review. Sometimes you just need a few initial words — for instance, the first 50 words — to get the sense; sometimes you need more. Especially long texts don't reveal their orientation early. It's therefore up to you to understand the type of text you're working with and decide how many words to analyze using deep learning. This example considers only the first 200 words, which should suffice.

Performing input padding

You may have noticed that the code starts encoding words beginning with the number 3, thus leaving codes from 0 to 2. Lower numbers are used for special tags, such as signaling the start of the phrase, filling empty spaces to have the sequence fixed at a certain length, and marking the words that are excluded because they're not frequent enough. This example picks up only the most frequent 10,000 words. Using tags to point out start, end, and notable situations is a trick that works with RNNs, especially for machine translation.

```
from keras.preprocessing.sequence import pad_sequences

max_pad = 200
x_train = pad_sequences(x_train,
                        maxlen=max_pad)

x_test = pad_sequences(x_test,
                       maxlen=max_pad)

print(x_train[0])
```

As output, you see the following list (shortened to fit in the book):

```
[  88     4 3310   406 6762     2     4   427 2140 1656...
   2   494    46  1954 4712   198    51    13   683 1193...
  89     4   114   495 7303   197     4  1168 1656    61...
  21    13   839    90  145     8   113    34  8253    27...
   6  8870 3310    88 8222    92     2     8  5388     5...
   2   449   168     6  404     2   112   207  1075     4...
```

```
 406 1522    13   124   903    97    90     2    21     2...
   2    2    93    61   492     2   305     7     2     4...
5679   83    27   117  2687  5419    29   941  1889    90...
 793    4  1526    84    37    28    34    96     7    49...
  56   23    61  2301  1111     9     4   255     8   937...
 159   29  1131    13  2134  3872    81    41    32    14...
 576 1301     5  5348  3134   255   335   170     8     2...
  29    9     2     2  3310   415    11  5215    89  1047...
 106   14    20   126]
```

By using the pad_sequences function from Keras with max_pad set to 200, the code takes the first two hundred words of each review. In case the review contains fewer than two hundred words, as many zero values as necessary precede the sequence to reach the required number of sequence elements. Cutting the sequences to a certain length and filling the voids with zero values is called *input padding*, an important processing activity when using RNNs like deep learning algorithms.

Designing an architecture

To perform an analysis of the reviews, you need to create a model that includes the needed algorithms. The resulting model is the architecture of your analysis engine. This example uses the following architecture:

```
from keras.models import Sequential
from keras.layers import Bidirectional, Dense, Dropout
from keras.layers import GlobalMaxPool1D, LSTM
from keras.layers.embeddings import Embedding

embedding_vector_length = 32
model = Sequential()
model.add(Embedding(top_words,
                    embedding_vector_length,
                    input_length=max_pad))

model.add(Bidirectional(LSTM(64, return_sequences=True)))
model.add(GlobalMaxPool1D())
model.add(Dense(16, activation="relu"))
model.add(Dense(1, activation="sigmoid"))

model.compile(loss='binary_crossentropy',
              optimizer='adam',
              metrics=['accuracy'])

print(model.summary())
```

The previous code snippet defines the shape of the deep learning model, where it uses a few specialized layers for natural language processing from Keras. The example also has required a summary of the model (model.summary() command) to determine what is happening with architecture by using different neural layers. Here's the summary of the model in this case:

```
_____
Layer (type)                    Output Shape            Param #
====================================================================
embedding_1 (Embedding)         (None, 200, 32)         320000
_____
bidirectional_1 (Bidirection    (None, 200, 128)        49664
_____
global_max_pooling1d_1 (Glob    (None, 128)             0
_____
dense_1 (Dense)                 (None, 16)              2064
_____
dense_2 (Dense)                 (None, 1)               17
====================================================================
Total params: 371,745
Trainable params: 371,745
Non-trainable params: 0
_____
None
```

You have the Embedding layer, which transforms the numeric sequences into a dense word embedding. A dense word embedding is easier for the layer of RNNs to learn, as discussed in the "Understanding Semantics Using Word Embeddings" section of Book 4, Chapter 4. Keras provides an Embedding layer, which, apart from having to be the first layer of the network, can accomplish two tasks:

>> Applying pretrained word embedding (such as Word2vec or GloVe) to the sequence input. You just need to pass the matrix containing the embedding to its parameter weights.

>> Creating a word embedding from scratch, based on the inputs it receives.

In this second case, Embedding needs to know:

>> input_dim: The size of the vocabulary expected from data

>> output_dim: The size of the embedding space that will be produced (the so-called dimensions)

>> input_length: The sequence size to expect

After you determine the parameters, Embedding will find better weights to transform the sequences into a dense matrix during training. The dense matrix size is given by the length of sequences and the dimensionality of the embedding.

REMEMBER

If you use The Embedding layer provided by Keras, you have to remember that the function provides only a weight matrix of the size of the vocabulary by the dimension of the desired embedding. It maps the words to the columns of the matrix and then tunes the matrix weights to the provided examples. This solution, although practical for nonstandard language problems, is not analogous to the word embeddings discussed previously, which are trained in a different way and on millions of examples.

The example uses Bidirectional wrapping — an LSTM layer of 64 cells. Bidirectional transforms a normal LSTM layer by doubling it: On the first side, it applies the normal sequence of inputs you provide; on the second, it passes the reverse of the sequence. You use this approach because sometimes you use words in a different order, and building a bidirectional layer will catch any word pattern, no matter the order. The Keras implementation is straightforward; you apply it as a function on the layer you want to render bidirectionally.

The bidirectional LSTM is set to return sequences (return_sequences=True); that is, for each cell, it returns the result provided after seeing each element of the sequence. The results, for each sequence, is an output matrix of 200 x 128, where 200 is the number of sequence elements and 128 is the number of LSTM cells used in the layer. This technique prevents the RNN from taking the last result of each LSTM cell. Hints about the sentiment of the text could actually appear anywhere in the embedded words sequence.

In short, it's important not to take the last result of each cell, but rather the best result of it. The code therefore relies on the following layer, GlobalMaxPool1D, to check each sequence of results provided by each LSTM cell and retain only the maximum result. That should ensure that the example picks the strongest signal from each LSTM cell, which is hopefully specialized by its training to pick some meaningful signals.

After the neural signals are filtered, the example has a layer of 128 outputs, one for each LSTM cell. The code reduces and mixes the signals using a successive dense layer of 16 neurons with ReLU activation (thus making only positive signals pass through; see the "Choosing the right activation function" section of Book 4, Chapter 2 for details). The architecture ends with a final node using sigmoid activation, which will squeeze the results into the 0–1 range and make them look like probabilities.

Training and testing the network

Having defined the architecture, you can now train the network. Three epochs (passing the data three times through the network to have it learn the patterns) will suffice. The code uses batches of 256 reviews each time, which allows the network to see enough variety of words and sentiments each time before updating its weights using backpropagation. Finally, the code focuses on the results provided by the validation data (which isn't part of the training data). Getting a good result from the validation data means that the neural net is processing the input correctly. The code reports on validation data just after each epoch finishes.

```
history = model.fit(x_train, y_train,
                    validation_data=(x_test, y_test),
                    epochs=3, batch_size=256)
```

Getting the results takes a while, but if you are using a GPU, it will complete in the time you take to drink a cup of coffee. At this point, you can evaluate the results, again using the validation data. (The results shouldn't have any surprises or differences from what the code reported during training.)

```
loss, metric = model.evaluate(x_test, y_test, verbose=0)
print("Test accuracy: %0.3f" % metric)
```

The final accuracy, which is the percentage of correct answers from the deep neural network, will be a value of around 85–86 percent. The result will change slightly each time you run the experiment because of randomization when building your neural network. That's perfectly normal given the small size of the data you are working with. If you start with the right lucky weights, the learning will be easier in such a short training session.

In the end, your network is a sentiment analyzer that can guess the sentiment expressed in a movie review correctly about 85 percent of the time. Using even more training data and more sophisticated neural architectures, you can get results that are even more impressive. In marketing, a similar tool is used to automate many processes that require reading text and taking action. Again, you could couple a network like this with a neural network that listens to a voice and turns it into text. (This is another application of RNNs, which now power Alexa, Siri, Google Voice, and many other personal assistants.) The transition allows the application to understand the sentiment even in vocal expressions, such as a phone call from a customer.

Processing Time Series

It's possible to use RNNs for time series predictions. Unlike regression analysis, a time series prediction adds the complexity of a sequence to the prediction. Simply predicting a value overall is not enough; you must now predict that value based on where it fits in a sequence. For example, you may want to predict the sales for a store in a given month based on previous data for that month. Merely viewing the sales as a whole is not enough because stores commonly go through sales cycles such that 100 sales in January might be quite good, while 100 sales in July is abysmal. However, you also can't just use the sales for that month because the store will experience an overall sales trend that appears as sales increases or decreases in all the months as a whole.

Defining sequences of events

To better understand how a time series works, it pays to look at a dataset that includes a time series. The example in this and the sections that follow relies on the Airline Passengers Prediction dataset, found at https://raw.githubusercontent. com/jbrownlee/Datasets/master/airline-passengers.csv. The following code downloads the dataset when you don't already have it installed on your system:

```
import urllib.request
import os.path

filename = "airline-passengers.csv"
if not os.path.exists(filename):
    url = "https://raw.githubusercontent.com/\
jbrownlee/Datasets/master/airline-passengers.csv"
    urllib.request.urlretrieve(url, filename)
```

After you have a copy of the dataset, you can display the pertinent data as a plot so that you can see how the data varies over time using the following code:

```
%matplotlib inline

import pandas
import matplotlib.pyplot as plt

apDataset = pandas.read_csv('airline-passengers.csv',
                            usecols=[1])
plt.plot(apDataset)
plt.show()
```

Figure 5-1 shows how the data varies. Notice that the number of passengers varies over time, steadily increasing. However, the data also has a cycle that you must account for when working with it.

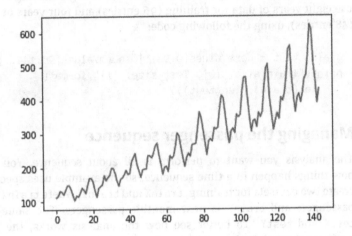

FIGURE 5-1:
Working with
cyclic data that
varies over time.

Performing a prediction using LSTM

As mentioned in the "Considering the processing methodologies" section, early in this chapter, LSTM is one of the processing methodologies you have at your disposal when performing certain tasks. You can use it to perform predictions on time-series data using RNNs. The following sections show how to perform predictions on the Airline Passengers Prediction dataset using LSTM.

Creating training and testing datasets

The first step is to obtain the values from the dataset you just imported, using this code:

```
values = apDataset.values.astype('float32')
```

LSTM is sensitive to the range of data you provide. This next step normalizes the data so that it falls in the range between 0 and 1.

```
from sklearn.preprocessing import MinMaxScaler

scaler = MinMaxScaler(feature_range=(0, 1))
normValues = scaler.fit_transform(values)
```

If you were to print normValues, you'd find that the values range between 0 and 1 as expected. As you can see from the graph in Figure 5-1, the dataset contains 144 entries, constituting 12 years of data. You need to split the normalized dataset into training and testing datasets. To provide enough training data, you want to use eight years of data for training (96 entries) and four years of data for testing (48 entries), using the following code:

```
train, test = normValues[0:96,:], normValues[96:144,:]
print("Train size: {0}, Test size: {1}".format(
    len(train), len(test)))
```

Managing the passenger sequence

The analysis you want to perform is all about sequence. You want to know how things happen in a time sequence, so the example uses special functions to create two datasets for training, trainX and trainY, where trainX is this month's passengers and trainY is next month's passengers. The same holds true for testX and testY. To better see how the analysis works, the following code performs the task in the original (before normalization) dataset first:

```
import numpy as np

np.random.seed(5)

def create_dataset(dataset):
        dataX, dataY = [], []
        for i in range(len(dataset)-2):
                a = dataset[i:(i+1), 0]
                dataX.append(a)
                dataY.append(dataset[i + 1, 0])
        return np.array(dataX), np.array(dataY)

valuesX, valuesY = create_dataset(values)

for a, b in zip(valuesX, valuesY):
    print("{0}    {1}".format(a, b))
```

The output (shortened for the book) shows how the next month, b, is always one ahead of this month, a:

```
[112.]    118.0
[118.]    132.0
[132.]    129.0
[129.]    121.0
[121.]    135.0
```

Of course, you now need to do the same thing to the normalized values, using this code:

```
trainX, trainY = create_dataset(train)
testX, testY = create_dataset(test)
```

Each row in the `trainX` and `testX` datasets are currently one-month samples. Within that sample is a feature — the number of passengers in a normalized form. So, a value like [0.01544401] is a sample feature configuration. To perform the analysis, what you really need is a sample, a step within that sample, and then a feature. The following code reshapes the `trainX` and `testX` datasets so that they appear as [[0.01544401]]:

```
trainX = np.reshape(trainX, (trainX.shape[0],
                        1, trainX.shape[1]))
testX = np.reshape(testX, (testX.shape[0], 1,
                        testX.shape[1]))
```

Defining the passenger analysis model

After all the required preparation is complete, you can finally create a model to perform the desired analysis. The following code specifies the elements in the model and then compiles it. It then fits the data to the model.

```
from keras.models import Sequential
from keras.layers import Dense
from keras.layers import LSTM
from sklearn.metrics import mean_squared_error

model = Sequential()
model.add(LSTM(4, input_shape=(1, look_back)))
model.add(Dense(1))
model.compile(loss='mean_squared_error', optimizer='adam')
model.fit(trainX, trainY, epochs=50, batch_size=1,
        verbose=2)
```

You could use additional epochs, but if you view the output, you see that the model stabilizes by epoch 25, so using 50 epochs is a little overkill.

Making a prediction

It's time to use the model to make a prediction. The following code makes a prediction using the training and testing models:

```
trainPredict = model.predict(trainX)
testPredict = model.predict(testX)
```

Because of the method used to perform the prediction, it's essential to invert the data so that you see the results in the original form of thousands of passengers per month:

```
trainPredict = scaler.inverse_transform(trainPredict)
trainY = scaler.inverse_transform([trainY])
testPredict = scaler.inverse_transform(testPredict)
testY = scaler.inverse_transform([testY])
```

Finally, you can calculate the root-mean-square-error (RMSE) of the predictions. This score shows the goodness of the model:

```
import math

trainScore = math.sqrt(mean_squared_error(
    trainY[0], trainPredict[:,0]))
print('Train Score: %.2f RMSE' % (trainScore))
testScore = math.sqrt(mean_squared_error(
    testY[0], testPredict[:,0]))
print('Test Score: %.2f RMSE' % (testScore))
```

Here's the output you can expect:

```
Train Score: 23.19 RMSE
Test Score: 49.74 RMSE
```

Chapter 6

Developing Impressive Charts and Plots

Many people think that data science is all about data manipulation and analysis; a few add data cleaning and selection into the mix. The idea of being able to see patterns in data that no one else can see is intoxicating — akin to going on a treasure hunt and finding something fabulous. Of course, if you've ever watched treasure hunters, you know that they don't keep their discoveries to themselves. They blast the radio and television waves with their finds, they show up in bookstores, their adventures appear in blogs, and they most definitely talk about them on Facebook and Twitter. After all, what's the use in finding something amazing and then keeping it to yourself? That's what this chapter is about: telling others about your data science finds. Most people react more strongly to visual experiences than to text, though, so this chapter talks about graphical communication methods. The goal is to make you look impressive when you present the most dazzling data find ever using a bit of pizzazz.

REMEMBER

You don't need to be a graphic designer to use graphs, charts, and plots in your notebooks (don't worry if you don't know the difference now; you'll discover the difference between these forms of presentation early in the chapter). In fact, if you follow a simple process of following where your data leads, you'll likely end up with something usable without a lot of effort. The first part of this chapter discusses how to create a basic presentation without a lot of augmentation so that you can see whether your selection will actually work.

The second section of this chapter discusses various kinds of augmentation you perform to make your presentation eye grabbing and informative. You use graphs, charts, and plots to communicate specific ideas to people who don't necessarily know (or care) about data science. The graphic nature of the presentation gives up some precision in favor of communicating more clearly.

Some types of graphs, charts, and plots see more use in data science because they communicate big data, statistics, and various kinds of analysis so well. You see some of these presentations in earlier chapters in the book, and you can be sure of seeing more of them later. The third section of the chapter describes these special data science perspectives in more detail so that you know, for example, why a scatterplot often works better for presenting data than a line chart.

The final section of the chapter discusses the presentation of data abstractions used in data science in graphical form. For example, a hierarchy is hard to visualize, even for an experienced data scientist, in some cases. Using the correct directed or undirected graph can make a huge difference in understanding the data you want to analyze.

REMEMBER

You don't have to type the source code for this chapter manually. In fact, using the downloadable source is a lot easier. The source code for this chapter appears in the `DSPD_0506_Graphics.ipynb` source code file for Python and the `DSPD_R_0506_Graphics.ipynb` source code file for R. See the Introduction for details on how to find these source files.

Starting a Graph, Chart, or Plot

Graphs, charts, and plots don't suddenly appear in your notebook out of nowhere; you must create them. The problem for many data scientists, who are used to looking at the big picture, is that the task can seem overwhelming. However, every task has a beginning, and by breaking the task down into small enough pieces, you can make it quite doable. The following sections discuss the starting point for any graph, chart, or plot that you need to present your data.

Understanding the differences between graphs, charts, and plots

The terms *graph*, *chart*, and *plot* are used relatively often in the chapter, and you might be confused by their use. The problem is that many people are confused, and this confusion leads to a lack of consensus on precisely what the terms mean.

However, before the chapter can proceed, you need to know how the book uses the terms *graph*, *chart*, and *plot*:

» **Graph:** Used to present data abstractions, such as the output of a mathematical formula or an algorithm, in a continuous form, such as a line graph. In addition, you see graphs used to present abstract data, such as the points in a hierarchy or the connections between nodes in a representation of a complex relationship. A graph is also used as the output for certain kinds of analysis, such as trying to compute the best route from one point to another based on time, distance, fuel use, or some other criterion.

» **Chart:** Presents data as discrete elements using specialized symbols, such as bars. A chart normally presents discrete real data, as opposed to data abstractions. There is usually some x/y element to the data presentation, such that each data element is compared according to some common constraint. For example, a chart might show the number of passengers who travel by air in a given month, with the chart presenting the number of passengers for each month over a given time frame as individual bars.

USING *PLOT*, *GRAPH*, OR *CHART* GENERICALLY

For many people, any graphic presentation of data, no matter the form, is a *plot*. The term is just a shorthand method of referring to a graphic presentation when speaking informally. Likewise, you find other people using *graph* or *chart* in the same manner. The use of a term generically often reflects a person's preference for a particular presentation — the presentation they use most often.

In many respects, this sort of informal use is inaccurate because the person hearing the term doesn't quite know what sort of graphic presentation to expect, yet people will continue to use these terms generically simply because precision isn't always necessary or even possible. For example, it's hard to know how to refer to a graphic presentation that includes both a line graph and a bar chart, which happens more often than you might think. Likewise, data scientists often show plots with lines graphs added to show a general trend or the results of an analysis against the plotted data.

When possible, try to use the correct term so that people will know what sort of graphic presentation to expect. However, even in this book, you'll find some generic uses of the term *plot* simply because it's more convenient and easier to read than listing multiple terms constantly. In addition, data science is more prone to using plots because of the interest in seeing data clusters and trends.

>> **Plot:** Presents data in a coordinate system in which both the x and y axis are continuous and two points can occupy the same place at the same time. Plots normally rely on dots or other symbols to display each data element within the coordinate system without any connectivity between each of the data elements. The grouping and clustering of plot points tends to present patterns to the viewer, rather than showing a specific average or other calculated value. Plots often add another dimension to a data display using color for each of the data categories or size for the data values.

Considering the graph, chart, and plot types

This book considers the use of MatPlotLib (https://matplotlib.org/) for drawing in Python because it's flexible and is found in many source code examples online. However, you can find a long list of graphic packages for Python online, including those found here: https://wiki.python.org/moin/UsefulModules#Plotting. Even if you restrict yourself to MatPlotLib, you still have access to a broad range of graph, chart, and plot types, as described here: https://matplotlib.org/3.1.0/tutorials/introductory/sample_plots.html.

When working with R, the best solution is to rely on built-in functionality for most needs, as described at https://www.statmethods.net/graphs/index.html. However, you also have specialized alternatives, such as ggplot2 (https://ggplot2.tidyverse.org/).

No matter which language you work in, the variety of graph, chart, and plot types can be overwhelming. However, if you limit yourself to these kinds of graphs, charts, and plots at the outset, you find that you can cover the majority of your needs without getting that second degree in graphic design:

>> **Line graph:** This is the standby for every sort of continuous data. The emphasis here is on continuous; you want to have an ongoing relationship between the various data elements. This is why this particular kind of graph works so well for the output of certain kinds of algorithms. You use this graph to smooth differences — that is, to see trends.

>> **Bar chart:** This is the standby for every sort of discrete data, where each value stands on its own. To see how sales increase over time, for example, you must choose a discrete time interval and chart the sales for the interval as a unit, rather than consider the sales from any other interval. You use this chart to amplify differences — to see specifically how things differ.

>> **Histogram:** This is a kind of bar chart that groups data within a range in a practice called binning. For example, you may want to see how many trees fall within specific height ranges, so you group the data elements by height and then display discrete heights on screen. In addition, you may want to have the trees that grow to 10 feet fall into one bin, those that grow to 20 feet fall into a second bin, those that grow to 30 feet into a third bin, and so on.

>> **Pie chart:** This is a special sort of chart for statistical analysis that considers parts of a whole. You often see it used for financial data, but it also has uses for other needs. Because this is a part of a whole chart, the values depicted are percentages, not actual values. (However, you can label each wedge with the specific value for that wedge.) As a result, this is a special kind of analysis chart.

>> **Scatter plot:** This is the standby for discrete data displayed using coordinates. Unlike other display types, this one shows actual data values when compared to some specific criteria. For example, you might use this kind of plot to show the number and size of messages generated by individual users on a particular day. The x-axis might show the number of messages, while the y-axis shows the message size.

Defining the plot

Most libraries use a type of line graph for quick or simple displays. You create two variables to hold the x and y coordinates and then plot them, as shown in the following code:

```
%matplotlib inline

import matplotlib.pyplot as plt

x = [1, 2, 3, 4, 5, 6]
y = [2, 8, 4, 3, 2, 5]
plt.plot(x, y)
plt.show()
```

In this particular case, you see the line graph shown in Figure 6-1. There aren't any labels to tell you about the line graph, but you can see the layout of the data. In some cases, this is really all you need to get your point across when the viewer can also see the code.

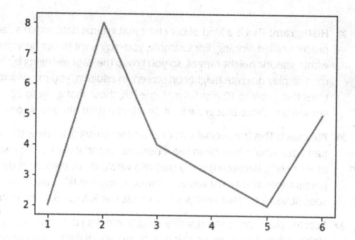

FIGURE 6-1:
The output of a
plain line graph.

Drawing multiple lines

Sometimes a single plot will contain multiple datasets. You can to compare the two datasets, so you use a single line for each to make comparison easy. In this case, you plot each of the lines separately, but in the same graph, as shown here:

```
x = [1, 2, 3, 4, 5, 6]
y1 = [2, 8, 4, 3, 2, 5]
y2 = [1, 3, 9, 2, 4, 6]

plt.plot(x, y1)
plt.plot(x, y2)
plt.show()
```

Even using the default settings, you see the two lines in different colors or using unique symbols for each of the data points. The lines help you keep the two plots apart, as shown in Figure 6-2.

Drawing multiple plots

You might need to show multiple kinds of subplots as part of the same plot (or figure). Perhaps direct comparison isn't possible, or you may simply want to use different plot types. The following code shows how to draw multiple subplots in the same plot.

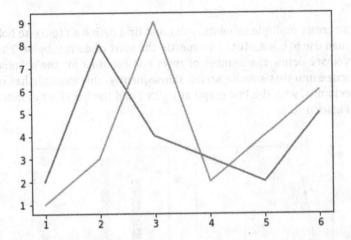

FIGURE 6-2:
The output of
multiple datasets
in a single line
graph.

```
import numpy as np

width = .5
spots = np.arange(len(y1))
x1 = 1 + spots - width / 2
x2 = 1 + spots + width / 2

figure = plt.figure(1)

plt.subplot(1,2,1)
plt.plot(x, y1)
plt.plot(x, y2)

plt.subplot(1,2,2)
plt.bar(x1, y1, width)
plt.bar(x2, y2, width)
plt.show()
```

This presentation requires a little more explanation. In order to display the bar chart elements side by side, you need to define a new x-axis that provides one set of values for the first set of bars and a second, offset, x-axis that provides a second set of values for the second set of bars. The rather odd-looking code calculates these values. If you were to print x1 and x2 out, you'd see these values:

```
[0.75 1.75 2.75 3.75 4.75 5.75]
[1.25 2.25 3.25 4.25 5.25 6.25]
```

To create multiple subplots, you must first define a `figure` to hold each plot. You then use `plt.subplot()` to specify the start of each subplot. The three numbers you see define the number of rows and columns for the subplot, along with an index into that subplot series. Consequently, this example has one row and two columns, with the line graph at index 1 and the bar chart at index 2, as shown in Figure 6-3.

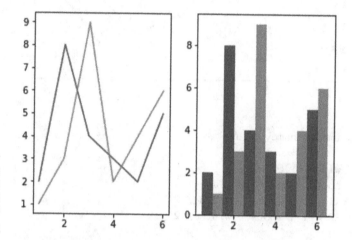

FIGURE 6-3:
The output of multiple presentations in a single figure.

Saving your work

Sometimes you want to save just the output of an analysis as a plot to disk. Perhaps you want to put it in a report other than the kind you can create with Notebook.

To save your work, you must have access to a `figure`. The previous section saves figure number 1 to the variable `figure` using `figure = plt.figure(1)`. Without this variable, you can't save the plot to disk. The actual act of saving the figure requires just one line of code, as shown here:

```
figure.savefig('MyFig.png', dpi=300)
```

The filename extension defines the format of the saved figure. You can also specify the format separately. Defining the `dpi` value is important because the default setting is `None`, which can cause some issues when you try to import the figure into certain graphics applications.

Setting the Axis, Ticks, and Grids

Even though a plot will never be quite as accurate for obtaining measurements as actual text, you can still make it possible to perform rough measurement using an axis, ticks, and grids. As with many other aspects of graphic presentations, these three terms can mean different things to different people. Here is how the book uses them:

>> **Axis:** The line used to differentiate data planes within the graphic presentation. The x-axis, which is horizontal, and the y-axis, which is vertical, are the two most common. A three-dimensional graphic presentation will have a z-axis. The axis controls formatting such as the minimum and maximum values, scaling (with linear and logarithmic being common), labeling, and so on.

>> **Ticks:** The placement of markers along the axis to show data measurements. The ticks represent values that the viewer can see and use to determine the value of a data point at a specific place along the line. You can control tick labeling, color, and size, among other things.

>> **Grids:** The addition of lines across the graphic presentation as a whole that usually extend the ticks to make measurement easier. A grid can make data measurements easier but can also obscure some data points, so using a grid carefully is essential. The data grid can include variations in color, thickness, and other formatting elements.

REMEMBER

Even though axes is the plural of axis, some graphics libraries make a significant difference between axes and axis. For example, in MatPlotLib, the Axes object contains most of the figure elements, and you use it to set the coordinate system. The Axes object contains Axis, Tick, Line2D, Text, Polygon, and other graphic elements used to define a graphic presentation, so you need to exercise care when using axes as the plural of axis.

Getting the axis

When working with R, you need to perform all the tasks required to create a graphic within a single cell. However, you have the same access to graphing functionality as you do with Python. The example source for the R example in this section shows you some additional details.

When working with Python, you may notice that after you call plt.show() when using the %matplotlib inline magic, you can't get the plot to display again without essentially rebuilding it. The article at https://matplotlib.org/users/artists.html describes the technical details that explain why this inability to display the graphic output again occurs. However, you can present changes to a graph as part of a Notebook by using another technique. It starts by using the `%matplotlib notebook` magic and `figure.canvas.draw()` instead, as shown here:

```
%matplotlib notebook

figure = plt.figure(1)

ax1 = figure.add_subplot(1,2,1)
ax1.plot(x, y1)
ax1.plot(x, y2)

figure.canvas.draw()
```

The output differs from the previous outputs in this chapter, as shown in Figure 6-4. This form of output presents you with considerable leeway in sizing, printing, and interacting with the figure in other ways. You also see just one image, rather than multiple images, for each step of the modification process.

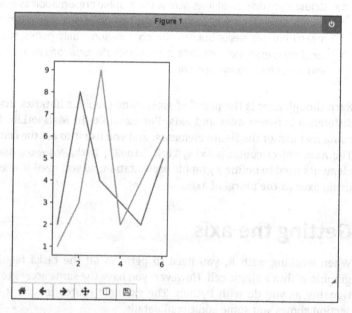

FIGURE 6-4:
Allowing multiple
revisions to a
single output
graphic.

This same figure remains in place as you make changes. For example, if you want to change the color used for the graph, you access the `patch` attribute and set the desired color, as shown here:

```
ax1.patch.set_facecolor('yellow')
figure.canvas.draw()
```

When you run this code, you see the background of the original figure change, rather than see a new figure created. The point is that the changes can occur over multiple cells, making this approach more flexible in some respects, even if you can't see an actual progression using multiple figures. You can even add new graphics by using the following code:

```
width = .5
spots = np.arange(len(y1))
x1 = 1 + spots - width / 2
x2 = 1 + spots + width / 2


ax2 = figure.add_subplot(1,2,2)
ax2.bar(x1, y1, width)
ax2.bar(x2, y2, width)
figure.canvas.draw()
```

You can also make additions to existing graphics. The following code adds titles to the existing graphics. You can see the output in Figure 6-5.

```
ax1.set_title("Line Graph")
ax2.set_title("Bar Chart")
figure.canvas.draw()
```

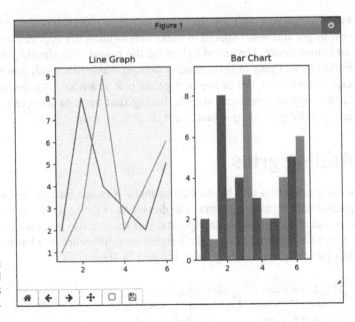

FIGURE 6-5:
The original figure changes as needed.

Formatting the ticks

The ticks you use to draw your chart help define how easily someone can use the data. It may seem at first that providing small tick increments and precise measures would provide better information, but sometimes doing so just makes the plot look cramped and hard to read. In addition, when working with ticks, you often find that the labeling is critical in making the data understandable. The following code takes the line shown in Figure 6-2 and augments the ticks to make them easier to see:

```
figure2 = plt.figure(2)

ax3 = figure2.add_subplot(1,1,1)
ax3.plot(x, y1)
ax3.plot(x, y2)

plt.xticks(np.arange(start=1, stop=7),
            ('A', 'B', 'C', 'D', 'E', 'F'))
plt.yticks(np.arange(start=1, stop=10, step=2))
plt.tick_params('both', color='red', length=10,
                labelcolor='darkgreen', labelsize='large')

figure2.canvas.draw()
```

Even though you can't see the colors in Figure 6-6, you can see that the ticks are now larger and wider spaced to make determining the approximate values of each data point easier. The use of letters for the x-axis ticks simply points out that you could use any sort of textual label desired. Notice that you don't work with the axis variable, ax3, but rather change the plot as a whole. To see more tick manipulation pyplot functions, see the listing that appears at https://matplotlib.org/3.1.0/api/_as_gen/matplotlib.pyplot.html.

Adding grids

Adding grids to a plot is one way to make it easier for the viewer to make more precise data value judgments. The downside of using them, however, is that they can also obscure precise data points. You want to use grids with caution, and the correct configuration can make a significant difference in what the reviewer sees. The following code adds grids to the plot in Figure 6-6:

```
plt.grid(axis='x', linestyle='-.',
         color='lightgray', linewidth=1)
plt.grid(axis='y', linestyle='--',
         color='blue', linewidth=2)
```

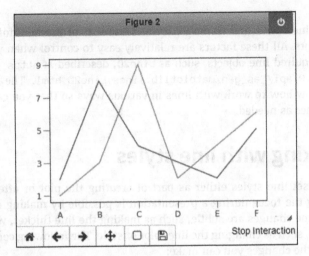

FIGURE 6-6:
Modifying the
plot ticks.

You can choose to create various grid presentations to meet the needs of your
audience using separate calls, as shown here. Figure 6-7 doesn't show the colors,
but you can see the effect of the settings quite well. If you don't provide an `axis`
argument, the grid settings apply to both axes.

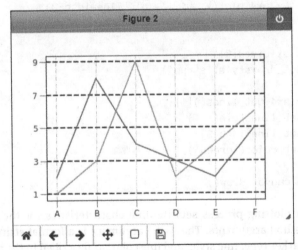

FIGURE 6-7:
Adding grid lines
to make data
easier to read.

Defining the Line Appearance

The formatting of lines in your graphics can make a big difference in visibil-
ity, ease of understanding, and focus (heavier lines tend to focus the viewers'
attention). So far, the various graphics have used solid lines to present relationships between data points as needed. In addition, the examples have used the

default line colors and haven't provided any sort of markers for the individual data points. All these factors are relatively easy to control when you have access to the required line objects, such as Line2D, described at https://matplotlib.org/3.1.0/api/_as_gen/matplotlib.lines.Line2D.html. The following sections show how to work with lines in various ways so that you can change their appearance as needed.

Working with line styles

You can set line styles either as part of creating the plot or afterward. In fact, changing the focus during a presentation is possible by making changes to line style. Some changes are subtle, such as making the line thicker, while others are dramatic, such as changing the line color or style. The following code presents just a few of the changes you can make:

```
import matplotlib.lines as lines

figure3 = plt.figure(3)

ax4 = figure3.add_subplot(1,1,1)
ax4Lines = ax4.plot(x, y1, '-.b', linewidth=2)
ax4.plot(x, y2)

line1 = ax4Lines[0]
line1.set_drawstyle('steps')

line2 = ax4.get_lines()[1]
line2.set_linestyle(':')
line2.set_linewidth(3)
line2.set_color('green')

figure3.canvas.draw()
```

The initial plotting process sets the line characteristics for the first line using plot() method arguments. The '-.b' argument is a format string that can contain the marker type, line style, and line color, as described in the plot() methods notes at https://matplotlib.org/3.1.0/api/_as_gen/matplotlib.pyplot.plot.html#matplotlib.pyplot.plot.

Notice that you can obtain the list of lines in a plot using one of two methods:

TIP

>> Saving the plot output

>> Using the get_lines() method on the plot

Instead of the `'default'` draw style, the first line now uses the `'steps'` draw style, which can make seeing data transitions significantly easier. This example obtains the parameters for the second line in the subplot using the `get_lines()` method. It sets the three properties for the line that the code set as part of the plot for the first line. Figure 6-8 shows how these changes appear in the output.

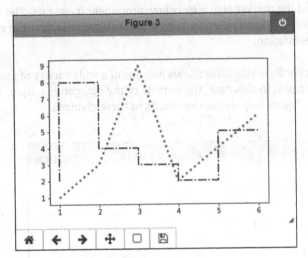

FIGURE 6-8: Making changes to a line as part of the plot or separately.

Adding markers

Markers, like grid lines, can serve to emphasize data. In this case, you emphasize individual data points and sometimes data transitions as well. Like grid lines, the size of the marker can affect the viewer's ability to see precisely where the data point lies, reducing accuracy in the process. Consequently, you must always consider the trade-offs of using certain marker configurations on a plot; that is, you need to consider whether the goal is to emphasize a data point or to make it possible for a viewer to see the data more accurately. The following code adds markers to the plot shown previously in Figure 6-8.

```
line1.set_marker('s')
line1.set_markerfacecolor('red')
line1.set_markersize(10)


line2.set_marker('8')
line2.set_markerfacecolor('yellow')
line2.set_markeredgecolor('purple')
line2.set_markersize(6)
```

The kind of marker you choose can affect how easily someone can see the marker and how much it interferes with the data points. In this example, the square used for line1 is definitely more intrusive than the octagon used for line2. MatPlotLib supports a number of different markers that you can see at https://matplotlib.org/3.1.0/api/markers_api.html#module-matplotlib.markers.

REMEMBER

The size of the marker also affects how prominent it appears. The various markers have different default sizes, so you definitely want to look at the size when creating a presentation.

The line2 configuration also shows just one of a wide variety of special effects that you can create. In this case, the outside of the octagon is purple, while the inside is yellow. Figure 6-9 shows the results of these changes.

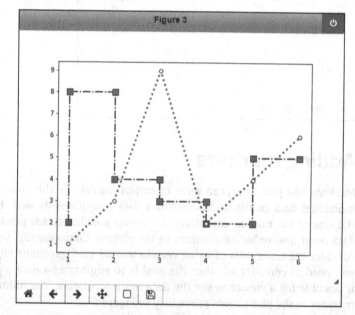

FIGURE 6-9:
Adding markers
to emphasize
the data points.

Using Labels, Annotations, and Legends

A graphic might not tell the story of the data by itself, especially when the graphic is complex or reflects complex data. However, you might not be around to explain the meaning behind the graphic — perhaps you're sending a report to another office. Consequently, you rely on various methods of adding explanations to a graphic so that others can better understand precisely what you mean. The three common approaches to adding explanations appear in the following list:

» **Labels:** The addition of explanatory text to a particular element, such as the line or bar in a graphic. You can also label individual data points.

» **Annotation:** The addition of explanatory text in a free-form manner that reflects on one or more graphic elements as a whole, rather than on specific graphic elements.

» **Legend:** A method of identifying the data elements within a graphic that are normally associated with related data elements, such as all the elements for a particular month of sales.

Some crossover occurs between explanatory methods depending on the language and associated library you use. For example, whether a title is actually a kind of label or a kind of annotation depends on the person you're talking with. The following sections describe how to use various kinds of explanatory text with your graphics, using the definitions found in the previous list.

Adding labels

Labels enable you to point out specific features of a graphic. In this example, the labels specify the minimum and maximum values for each of the lines. Of course, the text can say anything you want, and you have full formatting capabilities for the text, as shown in the following code:

```
figure4 = plt.figure(4, figsize=(7.7, 7.0))
ax5 = figure4.add_subplot(1,1,1)
ax5.plot(x, y1, color='red')
ax5.plot(x, y2, color='blue')

plt.text(2.2, 7.5, 'Line 1\nMax', color='red')
plt.text(1.2, 2.2, 'Line 1\nMin 1', color='red')
plt.text(5.2, 1.6, 'Line 1\nMin 2', color='red',
        bbox=dict(facecolor='yellow'))
plt.text(3.2, 8.5, 'Line 2\nMax', color='blue')
plt.text(1.4, 1.0, 'Line 2\nMin', color='blue')
figure4.canvas.draw()
```

This example begins by creating a new figure, but with a specific size, rather than using the default as usual. The size used will accommodate the various kinds of explanation added to this example. It's important to remember that figures are configurable when creating reports. You can see all the figure arguments at `https://matplotlib.org/3.1.0/api/_as_gen/matplotlib.pyplot.figure.html`.

One way to create labels, besides using titles and other direct graphic features, is to use the text() function. You specify where to place the text and the text you want to see. The display text can use escape characters, such as \n for a new-line. You have access to the same escape characters as those you use in Python. All the text() calls in this example use the color argument to associate the text with a particular line. The second minimum value for line one also uses the bbox (bounding box) argument, which has its own list of arguments as defined for the Rectangle at https://matplotlib.org/3.1.0/api/_as_gen/matplotlib. patches.Rectangle.html#matplotlib.patches.Rectangle. You can find other text() function features described at https://matplotlib.org/3.1.0/api/_as_gen/matplotlib.pyplot.text.html. Figure 6-10 shows how the labeling looks.

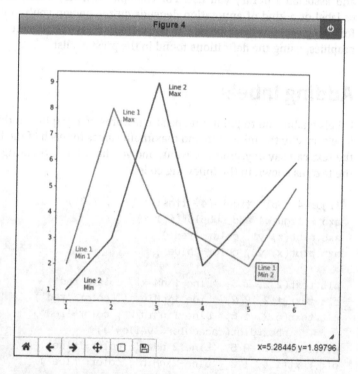

FIGURE 6-10: Labels identify specific graphic elements.

Annotating the chart

At first, some kinds of annotation might look like labeling in disguise. However, annotation takes a somewhat different course in that you use it to point some-thing out. So, for example, annotation can have an arrow, whereas labeling can't, as described at https://matplotlib.org/3.1.0/api/_as_gen/matplotlib.pyplot. annotate.html. The following code adds annotation to the example shown in Figure 6-10.

```
ax5.annotate('This is some\nannotation.', xy=(2.8, 8.0),
             xytext=(1.0, 8.5), color='green',
             weight='bold', fontsize=14,
             arrowprops=dict(facecolor='black'))
```

As with labels, you can use all the standard escape characters with the annotation text. The xy argument is the starting point for the annotation. It's where the head of the arrow will go should you choose to include one. The xytext argument defaults to the same value as xy, but you need to provide this value when using an arrow or the arrow will simply appear on top of the annotation.

The remaining arguments define formatting. You can define the color, weight, and fontsize of the annotation text using the same approach that you do with labels. The arrowprops argument is a dict containing arguments that define the arrow appearance. Most of the bbox arguments work with an arrow, along with the special arrowprop arguments, such as the kind of arrow to draw. Figure 6-11 shows the example with the annotation added.

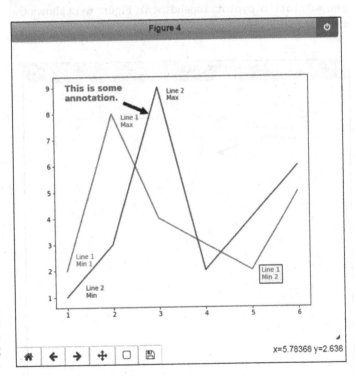

FIGURE 6-11:
Annotation
provides the
means of pointing
something out.

Creating a legend

A legend is a box that appears within the graphic identifying grouped data elements, such as the data points used for a line graph or the bars used for a chart. Legends are important because they enable you to differentiate between the grouped elements. The legend depends on the `label` argument for each of the plots. Given that the example doesn't define this argument during the initial setup, the code begins by adding the labels before displaying the legend in the following code:

```
lines1 = ax5.get_lines()[0]
lines1.set_label('Line 1')
lines2 = ax5.get_lines()[1]
lines2.set_label('Line 2')
plt.legend()
```

As with any other sort of explanatory text, `legend()` provides a wealth of formatting features, as described at `https://matplotlib.org/3.1.0/api/_as_gen/matplotlib.pyplot.legend.html`. Figure 6-12 shows the final form of this example.

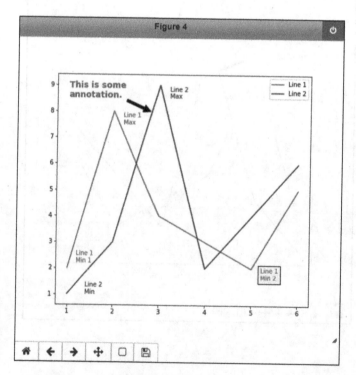

FIGURE 6-12: Legends identify the individual grouped data elements.

Creating Scatterplots

You see scatterplots used a lot in data science because they help people see patterns in seemingly random data. The data points may not form a line or work well as bars because they're simply coordinates that express something other than precise values, such as the number of sales during December. In fact, you may not know what the data represents until you actually do see the pattern.

REMEMBER

Unfortunately, humans can still miss the patterns all those dots in the screen. No matter how hard a person looks, there just doesn't seem to be anything there worthy of consideration. That's where certain kinds of augmentation come into play. You can use color, shapes, size, and other methods to emphasize particular data points so that the pattern does become more obvious. The following sections consider some of the augmentations you can perform on a scatterplot to see the patterns.

Depicting groups

Seeing groups in data is critical for data science. Entire books of algorithms exist to find ways to see where groups lie in the data — to make sense of where the data belongs. Without the ability to see groups, it's often difficult to make any sort of determination of what the data means. Consider the data presented by the following code:

```
%matplotlib inline

x1 = [2.3, 1.1, 1.5, 2.1, 1.3, 2.2, 1.0]
x2 = [2.6, 3.3, 3.1, 3.5, 3.9, 4.0, 4.1]
y1 = [2.4, 1.0, 2.1, 3.2, 4.3, 2.1, 2.0]
y2 = [2.5, 3.3, 1.9, 3.7, 3.2, 1.4, 4.5]
```

This data is excessively simple, so you could probably see patterns without doing any analysis at all. However, real datasets aren't nearly so easy. The following code plots these data points in a generic manner that might match some of the plots you've worked with:

```
plt.scatter([x1, x2], [y1, y2])
plt.show()
```

The output shown in Figure 6-13 doesn't tell you anything about the data. All you really see is a random bunch of dots.

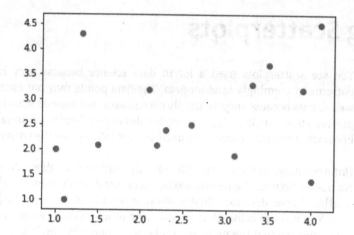

FIGURE 6-13:
Some plots really don't say anything at all.

However, when you plot the same data in a different way, using the following code, you get a completely different result:

```
s1 = [20*3**n for n in y1]
s2 = [20*3**n for n in y2]

plt.scatter(x1, y1, s=s1, c='red', marker="*")
plt.scatter(x2, y2, s=s2, c='blue', marker="^")
plt.show()
```

In this case, the code differentiates the two groups within the data using different plots that have different colors and markers. In addition, the size of the dots used within the plot reflect the output of a particular algorithm, which is straightforward in this case. The output of the algorithm depends on the y-axis position of the dot. Figure 6-14 shows the output, which is infinitely easier to interpret. Now you can see the differences between each group.

Showing correlations

Most of this book deals with showing where separations occur between data points in a dataset. Book 3 starts with simple techniques, Book 4 moves on to more advanced methods, and Book 5 uses AI to separate data elements in a smart manner. The analysis of data generally results in data categorization or the prediction of probabilities. A correlation looks at data relationships. The correlation value falls between −1 and 1 where:

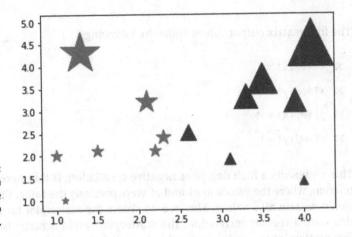

FIGURE 6-14:
Differentiation
makes the
plots easier to
interpret.

>> **Magnitude:** Defines the strength of correlation. Values that are closer to –1 or 1 specify a stronger correlation.

>> **Sign:** A positive value defines a positive (or regular) correlation, where a minus value defines an inverse correlation.

To see how correlations can work, consider this example:

```
x1 = [1.0, 1.5, 2.0, 2.5, 3.0, 3.5, 4.0]
y1 = [4.0, 3.5, 3.0, 2.5, 2.0, 1.5, 1.0]

z1 = np.corrcoef(x1, y1)
print(z1)

s1 = [(20*(n-p))**2 for n,p in zip(x1,y1)]
plt.scatter(x1, y1, s=s1)
plt.show()
```

In this case, x1 increases as y1 decreases, so there is a negative correlation. The output from z1 demonstrates this fact:

```
[[ 1. -1.]
 [-1.  1.]]
```

The four matrix output values show the following:

- » x1 with x1 = 1
- » x1 with y1 = -1
- » y1 with x1 = -1
- » y1 with y1 = 1

This represents a high degree of negative correlation. If this were a positive correlation, where the values in x1 and y1 were precisely the same, the output matrix would contain all 1 values. Figure 6-15 shows the scatterplot for this example. If this were a regular correlation, the scatterplot would actually be blank because this scatterplot shows increasing levels of difference and there would be no differences if x1 and y1 contain the same values.

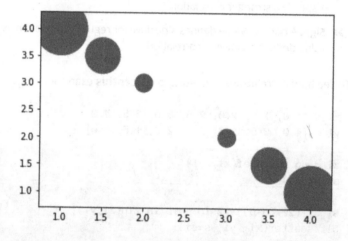

FIGURE 6-15:
A scatterplot showing a high degree of negative correlation.

Here's another example:

```
x2 = [2.0, 2.5, 3.0, 3.5, 4.0, 4.0, 4.0]
y2 = [1.0, 1.5, 2.0, 2.5, 3.0, 3.5, 4.0]

z2 = np.corrcoef(x2, y2)
print(z2)

s2 = [(20*(n-p))**2 for n,p in zip(x2,y2)]
plt.scatter(x2, y2, s=s2)
plt.show()
```

In this case, the correlation is positive. As x2 increases, so does y2. However, the correlation isn't perfect because x2 is a value of 1 above y2 until it plateaus and y2 catches up. The output of this example is

```
[[1.          0.95346259]
 [0.95346259 1.          ]]
```

REMEMBER

The correlation is still high, but not as high as the previous example. Figure 6-16 shows the scatterplot of this example. Notice that the angle of the data is in the opposite direction from the example in Figure 6-15 — one is negative (upper left to lower right), while the other is positive (lower left to upper right).

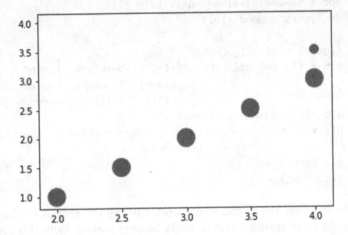

FIGURE 6-16:
A scatterplot showing a high degree of positive correlation.

Plotting Time Series

Working with time is an essential part of many analyses. You need to know what happened at a particular time or over a length of time. Reviewing the number of sales in January this year as contrasted to those last year is a common occurrence. The "Processing Time Series" section of Book 5, Chapter 5 discusses how you can use time-related data to perform predictions. In short, many business situations require you to consider how time affects past, present, and future business needs.

REMEMBER

The following sections don't do anything too fancy with time with regard to the data. What they focus on is how you can present time-related data so that it makes the most sense to your viewer. Note that these examples rely on the airline-passengers.csv file originally downloaded in the "Defining sequences of events" section of Book 5, Chapter 5.

Representing time on axes

You have multiple options for presenting time on axes. The easiest method to use with most of the data out there is the plot() shown here:

```
import pandas

apDataset = pandas.read_csv('airline-passengers.csv',
                            usecols=[1])
xAxis = pandas.read_csv('airline-passengers.csv',
                        usecols=[0])
years = []
for x in xAxis.values.tolist()[::12]:
    years.append(x[0])

figure5 = plt.figure(5)
ax6 = figure5.add_subplot(111, xlabel="Year/Month",
                               ylabel="Number of Passengers",
                               title="Airline Passengers")
ax6.plot(apDataset.values)
plt.xticks(np.arange(start=1, stop=len(xAxis), step=12),
           years, rotation=90)
plt.grid()
plt.show()
```

The ticks for the x-axis won't work with all the entries in place. The labeling would be so crowded that it would become useless. With this idea in mind, the example converts the NumPy DataFrame into a simple list containing just the entries needed for labeling. Even with the conversion, you must rotate the labels 90 degrees using the rotation argument of xticks() to make them fit. Compare the output in Figure 6-17 with the similar graphic in Figure 5-1 of Book 5, Chapter 5.

Another method of performing this task is to use plot_date() instead. In this case, you must convert the date strings in the data to actual dates. This approach can require less time and effort than using a standard plot(), as shown here:

```
from datetime import datetime
yearsAsDate = []
for x in xAxis.values.tolist():
    yearsAsDate.append(datetime.strptime(x[0], '%Y-%m'))

figure6 = plt.figure(6)
ax7 = figure6.add_subplot(111, xlabel="Year",
```

```
                                    ylabel="Number of Passengers",
                                    title="Airline Passengers")
ax7.plot_date(yearsAsDate, apDataset, fmt='-')
plt.grid()
plt.show()
```

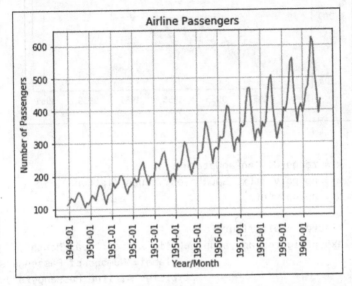

FIGURE 6-17:
Using a general
plot to display
date-oriented
data.

Notice that you must provide the correct string format to strptime(), which is just the four-digit year and the month in this case. The function assumes a day value of 1 to create a complete date. For example, even though the date might appear as 1950-02 in the `airline-passengers.csv` file, the actual date will appear as 01-02-1950 after the conversion. Figure 6-18 shows the output of this example.

Plotting trends over time

In looking at the graphics in Figures 6-17 and 6-18, you can discern that the trend is to generally see more passengers flying to their destination each year. You can't be more specific than to say that there are more, however. To be able to give more information, you need to perform a relatively simple analysis, one that defines how many more passengers, on average, that you can expect to see, as shown in the following example.

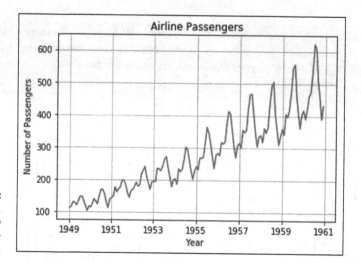

FIGURE 6-18:
Using `plot_date()` to display date-oriented data.

```
x = range(0, len(apDataset.values))
z = np.polyfit(x, apDataset.values.flatten(), 1)
p = np.poly1d(z)

figure5 = plt.figure(5)
ax6 = figure5.add_subplot(111, xlabel="Year/Month",
                          ylabel="Number of Passengers",
                          title="Airline Passengers")
ax6.plot(x, apDataset.values)
zeroPoint = min(apDataset.values)
ax6.plot(apDataset.values-zeroPoint,
         p(apDataset.values-zeroPoint), 'm-')

plt.xticks(np.arange(start=1, stop=len(xAxis), step=12),
           years, rotation=90)
plt.ylim(0,max(apDataset.values))
plt.xlim(0,len(apDataset.values))
plt.grid()
plt.show()
```

The code begins by computing the line that defines the data trend. This line goes straight across the graphic to show the actual direction of change. It requires these three steps:

1. Define the number of steps to use in presenting the line, which must equal the number of data values used for the computation.

2. Perform a least squares linear regression calculation using NumPy `polyfit()` (https://docs.scipy.org/doc/numpy/reference/generated/numpy.polyfit.html) to determine the line that will best fit the data points. You can discover more about linear regression in Book 3, Chapter 1. The least squares calculation also appears at https://www.technologynetworks.com/informatics/articles/calculating-a-least-squares-regression-line-equation-example-explanation-310265.

3. Use the coefficient calculation results from Step 2 to define a one-dimensional polynomial class (essentially a model for a line) using `poly1d()` (https://docs.scipy.org/doc/numpy/reference/generated/numpy.poly1d.html).

After the calculation is finished, the plotting begins. This example uses the `plot()` technique shown previously in Figure 6-17 to show the original data. Over the original data, you see a line representing the trend. This line is the result of the model created earlier. Figure 6-19 shows the results of this example. Notice how the trend line goes directly through the middle of the data points.

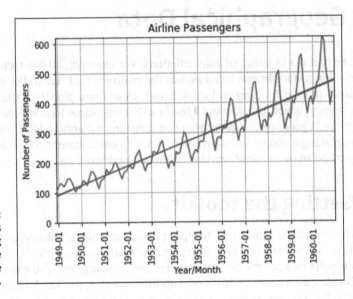

FIGURE 6-19: The results of calculating a trend line for the airline passenger data.

Plotting Geographical Data

The real world is full of contradictions. For example, all the factors might favor placing a store in one location, but the reality is that due to the geography of an area, another location will work better. Unless you plot the various locations on a map, you won't realize until too late that the prime location really isn't all that prime. A geographical plot helps you move from planning locations based on data to making a choice based on the real-world environment. The following sections provide an overview of working with geographical data.

Getting the toolkit

You can find a number of mapping packages online, but one of the more common is Basemap (https://matplotlib.org/basemap/). This mapping package supports most of the projections used for mapping, and you can provide detailed drawing instructions with it. To run this example, you need the Basemap package installed on your system. To begin, open the Anaconda Prompt on your system and type the following command:

```
conda search basemap --info
```

If the package is installed, you see information about it like this:

```
basemap 1.2.0 py37hd3253e1_3
--------------------------------
file name    : basemap-1.2.0-py37hd3253e1_3.tar.bz2
name         : basemap
version      : 1.2.0
build        : py37hd3253e1_3
build number: 3
size         : 15.2 MB
license      : MIT
subdir       : win-64
url          : https://conda.anaconda.org/conda-forge/...
3253e1_3.tar.bz2
md5          : 857574e2b82e6ce057c18eabe4cbdba0
timestamp    : 2019-05-26 18:25:46 UTC
dependencies:
  - geos >=3.7.1,<3.7.2.0a0
  - matplotlib-base >=1.0.0
  - numpy >=1.14.6,<2.0a0
  - pyproj >=1.9.3,<2
  - pyshp >=1.2.0
  - python >=3.7,<3.8.0a0
  - six
  - vc >=14,<15.0a0
```

WARNING

Notice that this example uses version 1.2.0; using a different version may produce different results or may not work at all with the example code. Otherwise, you need to type the following command to install it:

```
conda install -c anaconda basemap
```

The conda utility will require some time to set things up. In fact, it may very well look stuck, but eventually it will solve the new environment requirements. After it resolves the environment requirements, conda will ask permission to perform the installation, which will take significantly less time than the original setup.

Drawing the map

Working with geographical data begins with the map. You need the right sort of map to present the data or seeing how the data fits the map might be difficult. The following sections discuss a number of map types and presentations, but they don't even start to describe what sorts of things you can do. Experimentation is your best bet in finding precisely what you need.

Starting simply

You can see a number of Basemap projections at `https://matplotlib.org/basemap/users/mapsetup.html`. Here is an example of an orthographic projection:

```python
from mpl_toolkits.basemap import Basemap

map = Basemap(projection='ortho',
              lat_0=41.8781,lon_0=-87.6298,
              resolution='l')

map.drawcoastlines(linewidth=0.25)
map.drawcountries(linewidth=0.25)
map.fillcontinents(color='green',lake_color='lightblue')
map.drawmapboundary(fill_color='lightblue')
map.drawmeridians(np.arange(0,360,30))
map.drawparallels(np.arange(-90,90,30))

plt.show()
```

The process for creating a map generally follows four or five steps:

1. Import the required packages, including Basemap.

2. Define the kind of projection you want to use, along with the project's parameters (see `https://matplotlib.org/basemap/api/basemap_api.html` for details). The parameters normally require these arguments as a minimum:
   - Projection name
   - Latitude and longitude of the map center
   - Resolution of the coastal boundaries, with l, low resolution, being the fastest to draw

3. Specify the map particulars, such as the thickness of the various lines, whether the map displays country boundaries, and the presence of meridians and parallels. You also define the colors used for various map elements.

4. (Optional) Add points of interest to the map. The points of interest need not be cities or structures; you can also draw things like wind flow patterns. The documentation at `https://matplotlib.org/basemap/users/examples.html` tells more about the large number of items you can add to your map.

5. Specify plotting details and plot the map.

The number of permutations for Basemap are nearly endless. Figure 6-20 shows the orthographic projection defined by the example code.

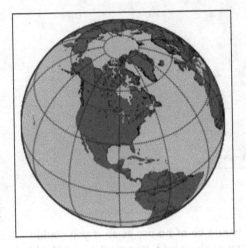

FIGURE 6-20:
An orthographic
projection of
the world.

Creating a real-world look

Don't get the idea that the maps are only of the colored sort found for presentations. You also have access to realistically colored maps using the bluemarble() and shadedrelief() functions (among others). Here is an example of the shadedrelief() form that includes the terminator between night and day for 6/24/19 at 12:00 noon UTC (the required support is already imported):

```
map = Basemap(projection='ortho',
              lat_0=41.8781,lon_0=-87.6298,
              resolution='l')

map.shadedrelief()
date = datetime(2019, 6, 24, 12, 0, 0)
map.nightshade(date)

plt.show()
```

The output shown in Figure 6-21 looks reasonably like the real world. The bluemarble() output is even more realistic. It's the form that you might see in a NASA photograph. Note that you may get a warning message when using this particular form, but you can safely ignore it.

FIGURE 6-21:
Your maps can look quite realistic.

Zooming in

Of course, the maps would be of no use at all if you couldn't zoom in and show a much smaller portion of the world. You need to use the kind of projection that allows zooming to perform this task. This example relies on a Stereographic Projection:

```
map = Basemap(projection='stere',
              lat_0=41.8781,lon_0=-87.6298,
              height=400000, width=400000,
              resolution='l')

map.drawcoastlines(linewidth=0.25)
map.drawstates(linewidth=0.25)
map.drawrivers(color='lightblue')
map.fillcontinents(color='green',lake_color='blue')
map.drawmapboundary(fill_color='lightblue')

plt.show()
```

REMEMBER

Notice that you must include some type of limit on the map size when using the Stereographic Projection. This example uses `height` and `width` in meters. You can also define the four corners of the bounding box using the upper right and lower left of the longitude and latitude: `llcrnrlon`, `llcrnrlat`, `urcrnrlon`, and `urcrnrlat`.

The location on this map is of North America, so you have some additional kinds of map items you can include. For example, you can draw lines between the states and add rivers. Some of these features aren't available in other world locations. Figure 6-22 shows how this map appears when drawn.

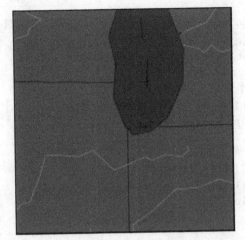

FIGURE 6-22:
Some projections
allow for a
close look.

Plotting the data

Plotting data precisely as you want it can be a little tricky but doesn't have to be hard if you follow a few rules. The most important rule is that, even though the documentation at `https://matplotlib.org/basemap/users/examples.html` shows all kinds of fancy ways of presenting information, using an approach that you already know usually works better. The second rule is that you need to modify your well-known techniques to fit the map. The rules for working with graphics are just a little different when working with `Basemap`.

You probably noticed that `Basemap` doesn't provide any sort of means for adding cities to your map. To perform this task, you begin by obtaining the latitude and longitude for each of the cities you want to add. If the longitude appears as so many degrees west, you must add a minus sign to the measurement. Making the measures as accurate as possible is important, especially when working on street-level maps.

When you have the latitude and longitude, you can ask the map to provide x and y coordinates so that you can interact with that location on the map. The following code shows how to use standard pyplot functions to add locations for Milwaukee and Chicago to the map you see in Figure 6-22.

```
map = Basemap(projection='stere',
              lat_0=41.8781,lon_0=-87.6298,
              height=400000, width=400000,
              resolution='l')

map.drawcoastlines(linewidth=0.25)
map.drawstates(linewidth=0.25)
```

```
map.drawrivers(color='lightblue')
map.fillcontinents(color='green',lake_color='blue')
map.drawmapboundary(fill_color='lightblue')

x1, y1 = map(-87.6298, 41.8781)
plt.annotate('Chicago', xy=(x1+5000, y1+5000),
             color='white')
plt.plot(x1, y1, '*', markersize=12, color='orange')

x2, y2 = map(-87.9065, 43.0389)
plt.annotate('Milwaukee', xy=(x2+5000, y2+5000),
             color='white')
plt.plot(x2, y2, 'o', markersize=6, color='yellow')
plt.show()
```

The basic map construction is the same as in the previous example. All this example adds are markers and text for the two cities. The call to the map object you create with longitude and latitude produces coordinates you can use for that location on the map.

You need to add offsets for the text or it appears directly on top of the marker, making the marker hard to see. You can make the markers different types, colors, and sizes to indicate preferences, just as you would any other sort of graphic. Figure 6-23 shows the results of this example.

FIGURE 6-23:
Adding locations or other information to the map.

Visualizing Graphs

Imagine data points that are connected to other data points, such as how one web page is connected to another web page through hyperlinks. Each of these data points is a *node*. The nodes connect to each other using *links*. Not every node links to every other node, so the node connections become important. By analyzing the nodes and their links, you can perform all sorts of interesting tasks in data science, such as define the best way to get from work to your home using streets and highways. The following sections describe how graphs work and how to perform basic tasks with them.

Understanding the adjacency matrix

An *adjacency matrix* represents the connections between nodes of a graph. When a connection exists between one node and another, the matrix indicates it as a value greater than 0. The precise representation of connections in the matrix depends on whether the graph is directed (where the direction of the connection matters) or undirected.

A problem with many online examples is that the authors keep them simple for explanation purposes. However, real-world graphs are often immense, and they defy easy analysis simply through visualization. Just think about the number of nodes that even a small city would have when considering street intersections (with the links being the streets themselves). Many other graphs are far larger, and simply looking at them will never reveal any interesting patterns. Data scientists call the problem in presenting any complex graph using an adjacency matrix a *hairball*.

One key to analyzing adjacency matrices is to sort them in specific ways. For example, you might choose to sort the data according to properties other than the actual connections. A graph of street connections might include the date the street was last paved with the data, enabling you to look for patterns to direct someone to a location based on the streets that are in the best repair. In short, making the graph data useful becomes a matter of manipulating the organization of that data in specific ways.

Using NetworkX basics

Working with graphs could become difficult if you had to write all the code from scratch. Fortunately, the NetworkX package for Python makes it easy to create, manipulate, and study the structure, dynamics, and functions of complex networks (or graphs). Even though this book covers only graphs, you can use the package to work with *digraphs* (or directed graphs, where each of the edges between nodes have a specific direction; see http://mathworld.wolfram.com/DirectedGraph.html as an example) and *multigraphs* (a kind of graph in which two nodes can have multiple connections; see http://mathworld.wolfram.com/Multigraph.html as an example) as well.

The main emphasis of NetworkX is to avoid the whole issue of hairballs. The use of simple calls hides much of the complexity of working with graphs and adjacency matrices from view. The following example shows how to create a basic adjacency matrix from one of the NetworkX-supplied graphs:

```
import networkx as nx


G = nx.cycle_graph(10)
A = nx.adjacency_matrix(G)


print(A.todense())
```

The example begins by importing the required package. It then creates a graph using the cycle_graph() template. The graph contains ten nodes. Calling adjacency_matrix() creates the adjacency matrix from the graph. The final step is to print the output as a matrix, as shown here:

```
[[0 1 0 0 0 0 0 0 0 1]
 [1 0 1 0 0 0 0 0 0 0]
 [0 1 0 1 0 0 0 0 0 0]
 [0 0 1 0 1 0 0 0 0 0]
 [0 0 0 1 0 1 0 0 0 0]
 [0 0 0 0 1 0 1 0 0 0]
 [0 0 0 0 0 1 0 1 0 0]
 [0 0 0 0 0 0 1 0 1 0]
 [0 0 0 0 0 0 0 1 0 1]
 [1 0 0 0 0 0 0 0 1 0]]
```

TIP

You don't have to build your own graph from scratch for testing purposes. The NetworkX site documents a number of standard graph types that you can use, all of which are available within Notebook. The list appears at https://networkx.github.io/documentation/latest/reference/generators.html.

It's interesting to see how the graph looks after you generate it. The following code displays the graph for you. Figure 6-24 shows the result of the plot.

```
nx.draw_networkx(G)
plt.show()
```

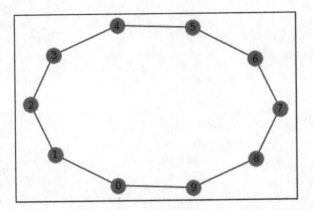

FIGURE 6-24:
Plotting the
original graph.

The plot shows that you can add an edge between nodes 1 and 5. Here's the code needed to perform this task using the add_edge() function. Figure 6-25 shows the result.

```
G.add_edge(1,5)
nx.draw_networkx(G)
plt.show()
```

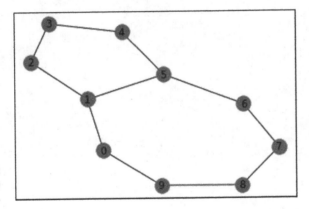

FIGURE 6-25:
Plotting the
graph addition.

6

Diagnosing and Fixing Errors

Contents at a Glance

Chapter **1**

Locating Errors in Your Data

Your data likely contains errors, which seems like a sweeping statement when you consider that only you really understand your data. However, most data available today contains various kinds of errors that can derail your analysis. If you don't catch these errors, you may make a prediction that has no chance whatsoever of being accurate — even if your algorithms and logic are both bulletproof. The problem is in figuring out where the errors lie because they can be quite difficult to see. Consequently, this chapter begins by helping you understand the types of data errors so that you have a better chance of finding them.

The source of your data often determines the kind of errors you find, how deep you have to go into the code to locate them, and how difficult they are to find. Consider the simple act of scraping data from a website online. Even if the data is in the right form, doesn't have any missing elements, and appears reasonably correct, you have no way of knowing that the data is accurate unless you research it yourself. Of course, if you take all the time required to perform in depth research, you may as well generate the data yourself to ensure accuracy.

One means of ensuring that the data is less error prone is to perform various kinds of automated data validation. The validation process can tell you a lot about the data and even indicate, to some degree, the data accuracy. The process isn't perfect, but anything you can do to reduce errors will make your analysis more accurate.

After validating your data, you can use various methods of trimming the data to include only those elements you can be sure will contain accurate information. The act of trimming the data, and performing other sorts of data maintenance, will greatly improve the results you receive from your analysis. Many data scientists spend a majority of their time performing the process outlined in this chapter. The act of ensuring that data is as accurate as possible consumes considerable time, but it's a necessary part of any data analysis.

REMEMBER

You don't have to type the source code for this chapter manually. In fact, using the downloadable source is a lot easier. The source code for this chapter appears in the DSPD_0601_Data_Errors.ipynb source code file for Python and the DSPD_R_0601_Data_Errors.ipynb source code file for R. See the Introduction for details on how to find these source files.

Considering the Types of Data Errors

For many people, *error* equates to *wrong*. However, in many cases, data is correct, yet also erroneous. You can consider data errant when it meets any of these criteria:

>> Incorrect

>> Missing

>> Wrong type

>> Malformatted (perhaps using an outdated standard)

>> Wrong format for the task

>> Incomplete

>> Imprecise

>> Misaligned (shifted in position within a field)

>> Outdated

>> Consists of opinion rather than fact

>> Misclassified

In fact, this list could extend further, but it presents the kinds of things you should consider when looking for data errors. Trying to find just these types of data errors would be difficult, to say the least, but you can also classify data errors in another way:

>> Automatic code detection, such as missingness

>> Deterrence through form design, such as incompleteness

>> External cleaning, such as misalignment

>> Time stamping and other currency techniques, such as outdated data

Classifying the data error types by the techniques used to avoid or fix them is also helpful when considering how to manage your database. Part of your initial assessment of a data source must include a thorough examination of the kinds of data errors that the data contains, along with measures you can use to fix these errors well enough to perform analysis text.

Locating Errors in Your Data

IT'S ALL IN THE PREPARATION

This minibook may seem to spend a lot of time massaging data and little time in actually analyzing it. However, the majority of a data scientist's time is actually spent preparing data because the data is seldom in any order to actually perform analysis. To prepare data for use, a data scientist must:

- Get the data
- Aggregate the data
- Create data subsets
- Clean the data
- Develop a single dataset by merging various datasets together

Fortunately, you don't need to die of boredom while wading your way through these various tasks. Using Python and the various libraries it provides makes the task a lot simpler, faster, and more efficient, which is the point of spending all the time on seemingly mundane topics in these early chapters. The better you know how to use Python to speed your way through these repetitive tasks, the sooner you begin having fun performing various sorts of analysis on the data.

WARNING

After spending hours fixing a data source, it's always easy to think that the data is now somehow clean and pure. The problem is that it isn't clean or pure because many measures of correctness are subjective and biased toward a specific need. You must always assume that your data contains some number of errant entries, even when those entries might normally be considered correct, because they aren't correct for your particular need.

Obtaining the Required Data

Having plentiful data available isn't enough to perform analysis tasks successfully. Presently, an algorithm can't extract information directly from raw data. You can't simply tell an algorithm to analyze data from a number of unrelated sites and expect anything but gibberish as a result — assuming that the analysis even completes. Most algorithms rely on external collection and manipulation prior to analysis. When an algorithm collects useful information, it may not represent the right information. The following sections help you understand how to collect, manipulate, and automate data collection from an overview perspective.

Considering the data sources

The data you use comes from a number of sources. The most common data source is from information entered by humans at some point. Even when a system collects shopping-site data automatically, humans initially enter the information. A human clicks various items, adds them to a shopping cart, specifies characteristics (such as size) and quantity, and then checks out. Later, after the sale, the human gives the shopping experience, product, and delivery method a rating and makes comments. In short, every shopping experience becomes a data collection exercise as well.

WARNING

Consider that most data sources are incomplete or provide a biased perspective. For example, the shopping-site data may include purchases, but not returns or failed deliveries. As a consequence, the view the algorithm receives of sales is both incomplete and biased because it doesn't reflect the reality of the actual sales.

Many data sources today rely on input gathered from human sources. Humans also provide manual input. You call or go into an office somewhere to make an appointment with a professional. A receptionist then gathers information from you that's needed for the appointment. This manually collected data eventually ends up in a dataset somewhere for analysis purposes. When the receptionist makes a mistake, the mistake also appears in the dataset.

Data is also collected from sensors, and these sensors can take almost any form. For example, many organizations base physical data collection, such as the number of people viewing an object in a window, on cellphone detection. Facial recognition software could potentially detect repeat customers.

Sensors can create datasets from almost anything; however, their recordings are not always completely reliable. Depending on the application, you need a certain amount of data adjustment and cleaning. The weather service relies on datasets created by sensors that monitor environmental conditions such as rain, temperature, humidity, cloud cover, and so on. Robotic monitoring systems help correct small flaws in robotic operation by constantly analyzing data collected by monitoring sensors. A sensor, combined with a small AI application, could tell you when your dinner is cooked to perfection tonight. The sensor collects data, but the AI application uses rules to help define when the food is properly cooked.

Obtaining reliable data

The word *reliable* seems so easy to define, yet so hard to implement. Something is reliable when the results it produces are both expected and consistent. A reliable data source produces mundane data that contains no surprises; no one is shocked in the least by the outcome. Depending on your perspective, it could actually be a good thing that most people aren't yawning and then falling asleep when reviewing data. The surprises make the data worth analyzing and reviewing. Consequently, data has an aspect of duality. People want reliable, mundane, fully anticipated data that simply confirms what they already know, but the unexpected is what makes collecting the data useful in the first place.

Still, you don't want data that is so far out of the ordinary that it becomes almost frightening to review. You need to maintain balance when obtaining data. The data must fit within certain limits (as described in the "Manicuring the Data" section, later in this chapter). It must also meet specific criteria as to truth value (as described in the "Considering the Five Mistruths in Data" section of Chapter 2 of this minibook). The data must also come at expected intervals, and all the fields of the incoming data record must be complete.

REMEMBER

To some extent, data security also affects data reliability. Data consistency comes in several forms. When the data arrives, you can ensure that it falls within expected ranges and appears in a particular form. However, after you store the data, the reliability can decrease unless you ensure that the data remains in the expected form. An entity fiddling with the data affects reliability, making the data suspect and potentially unusable for analysis later. Ensuring data reliability means that after the data arrives, no one tampers with it to make it fit within an expected domain (making it mundane as a result).

Making human input more reliable

Humans make mistakes — it's part of being human. In fact, expecting that humans won't make mistakes is unreasonable. Yet, many application designs assume that humans somehow won't make mistakes of any sort. The design expects that everyone will simply follow the rules. Unfortunately, the vast majority of users are guaranteed to not even read the rules because most humans are also lazy or too pressed for time when it comes to doing things that don't really help them directly.

Consider the entry of a state into a form. If you provide just a text field, some users might input the entire state name, such as Kansas. Of course, some users will make a typo or capitalization error and come up with Kansus or kANSAS. People and organizations have various approaches to performing the task of entering a state name that makes these sorts of errors more prevalent:

>> Someone in the publishing industry might use the Associated Press (AP) style guide and input Kan.

>> Someone who is older and used to the Government Printing Office (GPO) guidelines might input Kans.

>> The U.S. Post Office (USPS) uses KS.

>> The U.S. Coast Guard uses KA.

>> The International Standards Organization (ISO) form goes with US-KS.

Mind you, this is just a state entry, which is reasonably straightforward — or so you thought before reading this section. Clearly, because the state isn't going to change names anytime soon, you could simply provide a drop-down list box on the form for choosing the state in the required format, thereby eliminating differences in abbreviation use, typos, and capitalization errors in one fell swoop.

REMEMBER

Drop-down list boxes work well for an amazing array of data inputs, and using them ensures that human input into those fields becomes extremely reliable because the human has no choice but to use one of the default entries. Of course, the human can always choose the incorrect entry, which is where double-checks come into play. Some newer applications compare the ZIP code to the city and state entries to see whether they match. When they don't match, the user is asked again to provide the correct input. This double-check verges on being annoying (see the "More annoying than useful input aids" sidebar for details), but the user is unlikely to see it very often, so it shouldn't become too annoying.

MORE ANNOYING THAN USEFUL
INPUT AIDS

Input validation is almost more of an art than a science because using rote rules seldom produces a useful and pleasurable input experience. Using a drop-down list for states works as long as the list is complete and the person is where you expect them to be. However, if you have an international customer who has an address outside the country for which you wrote the application, you suddenly find that the bulletproof input field almost makes it impossible for the user to complete the form. The input field has gone from being useful and convenient to being frustrating and annoying because of a limit on the kind of correct data the user can enter.

Input fields can also control the form of input, to an extent. The problem is that what the developer thinks is helpful really isn't helpful at all. You have probably encountered shopping sites that disallow dashes between the numbers of a credit card or require a telephone number to appear in a specific form. The form beeps unhelpfully in many cases until you discover just what format the developer wants. In some cases, the customer will finally give up and go anywhere else that has a better form and the desired product. A helpful input is one that accepts the odd formatting that the user may want to provide and automatically reformats the data as needed. When the user enters (555)123-4567, the form might automatically reformat it as 1-555-123-4567. The user is happy, the database is less error prone, and the developer gets to go home for the weekend.

A user may also not want to share certain personal details, such as age, gender, or sexual orientation. If your form requires such entries, the user might go somewhere else rather than provide the personal information. In fact, given the manner in which society has progressed, assuming anything about a person based on predefined biases will almost certainly cause problems for the business. For example, some people don't identify as either male or female, so assuming that they do is a bad choice.

Forms that require more information than the user is willing to provide are also unhelpful. A user may be willing to provide a numeric evaluation of a product, but may not want to provide a written comment. Many forms require both, which means that a survey or other means of obtaining information goes unanswered. A form should have a default non-answer value.

The ultimate of unhelpful aids, however, is the input field that simply assumes that the user knows what to fill in. Address fields are especially bad in this area. All you might see is a series of inputs that look sort of like a mailing label on an envelope, which

(continued)

(continued)

assumes that the user is aware of that particular label format. It also assumes that the user can see the form, although a user with special visual needs may use a screen reader that will have no idea of what to do with the form. Every input should have an associated label that's short, yet expresses precisely what information to provide. It should also have a help screen to provide more details and examples of what information to provide. The error message associated with the input should also say precisely what is wrong with the input, rather than make the user guess.

Even with cross-checks and static entries, humans still have plenty of room for making mistakes. For example, entering numbers can be problematic. When a user needs to enter 2.00, you might see 2, or 2.0, 2., or any of a variety of other entries. Fortunately, parsing the entry and reformatting it will fix the problem, and you can perform this task automatically, without the user's aid.

Unfortunately, reformatting won't correct an errant numeric input. You can partially mitigate such errors by including range checks. Consider, for example, how to process a customer's return of some purchased merchandise. A customer can't buy −5 bars of soap. The legitimate way to show the customer returning the bars of soap is to process a return, not a sale. However, the user might have simply made an error, and you can provide a message stating the proper input range for the value.

Using automated data collection

Some people think that automated data collection solves all the human input issues associated with datasets. In fact, automated data collection does provide a number of benefits:

>> Better consistency

>> Improved reliability

>> Lower probability of missing data

>> Enhanced accuracy

>> Reduced variance for things like timed inputs

Unfortunately, to say that automated data collection solves every issue is simply incorrect. Automated data collection still relies on sensors, applications, and computer hardware designed by humans that provide access only to the data that humans decide to allow. Because of the limits that humans place on the characteristics of automated data collection, the outcome often provides less helpful information than hoped for by the designers. Consequently, automated data collection is in a constant state of flux as designers try to solve the input issues.

Automated data collection also suffers from both software and hardware errors present in any computing system, but with a higher potential for *soft issues* (which arise when the system is apparently working but isn't providing the desired result) than other kinds of computer-based setups. When the system works, the reliability of the input far exceeds human abilities. However, when soft issues occur, the system often fails to recognize that a problem exists, as a human might, and therefore the dataset could end up containing more mediocre or even bad data.

Validating Your Data

When it comes to data, no one really knows what a large database contains. Yes, everyone has seen bits and pieces of it, but when you consider the size of some databases, viewing it all would be physically impossible. Because you don't know what's in there, you can't be sure that your analysis will actually work as desired and provide valid results. In short, you must validate your data before you use it to ensure that the data is at least close to what you expect it to be. This means performing tasks such as removing duplicate records before you use the data for any sort of analysis (duplicates would unfairly weight the results).

REMEMBER

However, you do need to consider what validation actually does for you. It doesn't tell you that the data is correct or that there won't be values outside the expected range. In fact, later chapters help you understand the techniques for handling these sorts of issues. What validation does is ensure that you can perform an analysis of the data and reasonably expect that analysis to succeed. Later, you need to perform additional massaging of the data to obtain the sort of results that you need in order to perform the task you set out to perform in the first place.

Figuring out what's in your data

Figuring out what your data contains is important because checking data by hand is sometimes simply impossible because of the number of observations and variables. In addition, hand verifying the content is time consuming, error prone, and, most important, really boring. Finding duplicates is important because you end up

>> Spending more computational time to process duplicates, which slows your algorithms down.

>> Obtaining false results because duplicates implicitly overweight the results. Because some entries appear more than once, the algorithm considers these entries more important.

As a data scientist, you want your data to enthrall you, so it's time to get it to talk to you — not figuratively, of course, but through the wonders of pandas, as shown in the following example:

```
from lxml import objectify
import pandas as pd

xml = objectify.parse(open('XMLData2.xml'))
root = xml.getroot()
df = pd.DataFrame(columns=('Number', 'String', 'Boolean'))

for i in range(0,4):
    obj = root.getchildren()[i].getchildren()
    row = dict(zip(['Number', 'String', 'Boolean'],
                   [obj[0].text, obj[1].text,
                    obj[2].text]))
    row_s = pd.Series(row)
    row_s.name = i
    df = df.append(row_s)

search = pd.DataFrame.duplicated(df)
print(df)
print()
print(search[search == True])
```

This example shows how to find duplicate rows. It relies on a modified version of the XMLData.xml file found in Book 2, Chapter 4, XMLData2.xml, which contains a simple repeated row in it. A real data file contains thousands (or more) of records and possibly hundreds of repeats, but this simple example does the job. The example begins by reading the data file into memory using the same technique as that explored in the "Working with a simple XML file" section of Book 2, Chapter 4. It then places the data into a DataFrame.

At this point, your data is corrupted because it contains a duplicate row. However, you can get rid of the duplicated row by searching for it. The first task is to create a search object containing a list of duplicated rows by calling pd.DataFrame.duplicated(). The duplicated rows contain a True next to their row number.

Of course, now you have an unordered list of rows that are and aren't duplicated. The easiest way to determine which rows are duplicated is to create an index in which you use search == True as the expression. Following is the output you see from this example. Notice that row 3 is duplicated in the DataFrame output and that row 3 is also called out in the search results:

```
   Number  String Boolean
0       1   First    True
1       2  Second   False
2       3   Third    True
3       3   Third    True


3    True
dtype: bool
```

Removing duplicates

To get a clean dataset, you want to remove the duplicates from it. Fortunately, you don't have to write any weird code to get the job done; pandas does it for you, as shown in the following example:

```
from lxml import objectify
import pandas as pd

xml = objectify.parse(open('XMLData2.xml'))
root = xml.getroot()
df = pd.DataFrame(columns=('Number', 'String', 'Boolean'))
for i in range(0,4):
    obj = root.getchildren()[i].getchildren()
    row = dict(zip(['Number', 'String', 'Boolean'],
                   [obj[0].text, obj[1].text,
                    obj[2].text]))
    row_s = pd.Series(row)
    row_s.name = i
    df = df.append(row_s)

print(df.drop_duplicates())
```

As with the previous example, you begin by creating a DataFrame that contains the duplicate record. To remove the errant record, all you need to do is call drop_duplicates(). Here's the result you get:

```
   Number  String Boolean
0       1   First    True
1       2  Second   False
2       3   Third    True
```

Creating a data map and a data plan

You need to know about your dataset — that is, how it looks statically. A *data map* is an overview of the dataset. You use it to spot potential problems in your data, such as

» Redundant variables

» Possible errors

» Missing values

» Variable transformations

Checking for these problems goes into a *data plan*, which is a list of tasks you have to perform to ensure the integrity of your data. The following example shows a data map, A, with two datasets, B and C:

```
import pandas as pd
pd.set_option('display.width', 55)

df = pd.DataFrame({'A': [0,0,0,0,0,1,1],
                   'B': [1,2,3,5,4,2,5],
                   'C': [5,3,4,1,1,2,3]})

a_group_desc = df.groupby('A').describe()
print(a_group_desc)
```

In this case, the data map uses 0s for the first series and 1s for the second series. The `groupby()` function places the datasets, B and C, into groups. To determine whether the data map is viable, you obtain statistics using `describe()`. What you end up with is a dataset B, series 0 and 1, and dataset C, series 0 and 1, as shown in the following output:

```
        B                                                      \
   count mean        std  min   25%  50%   75%  max
A
0    5.0  3.0  1.581139  1.0  2.00  3.0  4.00  5.0
1    2.0  3.5  2.121320  2.0  2.75  3.5  4.25  5.0


        C
   count mean        std  min   25%  50%   75%  max
A
0    5.0  2.8  1.788854  1.0  1.00  3.0  4.00  5.0
1    2.0  2.5  0.707107  2.0  2.25  2.5  2.75  3.0
```

These statistics tell you about the two dataset series. The breakup of the two datasets using specific cases is the *data plan*. As you can see, the statistics tell you that this data plan may not be viable because some statistics are relatively far apart.

TIP

The default output from describe() shows the data unstacked. Unfortunately, the unstacked data can print with an unfortunate break, making it very hard to read. To keep this break from happening, you set the width you want to use for the data by calling pd.set_option('display.width', 55). You can set a number of pandas options this way by using the information found at https://pandas.pydata.org/pandas-docs/stable/generated/pandas.set_option.html.

Although the unstacked data is relatively easy to read and compare, you may prefer a more compact presentation. In this case, you can stack the data using the following code:

```
stacked = a_group_desc.stack()
print(stacked)
```

Using stack() creates a new presentation. Here's the output shown in a compact form:

```
              B          C
A
0 count  5.000000   5.000000
  mean   3.000000   2.800000
  std    1.581139   1.788854
  min    1.000000   1.000000
  25%    2.000000   1.000000
  50%    3.000000   3.000000
  75%    4.000000   4.000000
  max    5.000000   5.000000
1 count  2.000000   2.000000
  mean   3.500000   2.500000
  std    2.121320   0.707107
  min    2.000000   2.000000
  25%    2.750000   2.250000
  50%    3.500000   2.500000
  75%    4.250000   2.750000
  max    5.000000   3.000000
```

Of course, you may not want all the data that describe() provides. Perhaps you really just want to see the number of items in each series and their mean. Here's how you reduce the size of the information output:

```
print(a_group_desc.loc[:,(slice(None),['count','mean']),])
```

Using `loc` lets you obtain specific columns. Here's the final output from the example showing just the information you absolutely need to make a decision:

```
       B         C
   count mean count mean
A
0   5.0  3.0   5.0  2.8
1   2.0  3.5   2.0  2.5
```

Manicuring the Data

Some people use the term *manipulation* when speaking about data, giving the impression that the data is somehow changed in an unscrupulous or devious manner. Perhaps a better term would be *manicuring,* which makes the data well shaped and lovely. No matter what term you use, however, raw data seldom meets the requirements for processing and analysis. To get something out of the data, you must manicure it to meet specific needs. The following sections discuss data manicuring needs.

Dealing with missing data

To answer a given question correctly, you must have all the facts. You can guess the answer to a question without all the facts, but then the answer is just as likely to be wrong as correct. Often, someone who makes a decision, essentially answering a question, without all the facts is said to jump to a conclusion. The following sections discuss the issue of missing data and what to do about it.

Understanding how missing data affects a dataset

When analyzing data, you have probably jumped to more conclusions than you think because of missing data. A *data record,* which is one entry in a *dataset* (which in turn is all the data), consists of *fields* that contain facts used to answer a question. Each field contains a single kind of data that addresses a single fact. If that field is empty, you don't have the data you need to answer the question using that particular data record.

REMEMBER

As part of the process of dealing with missing data, you must know that the data is missing. Identifying that your dataset is missing information can actually be quite hard because it requires you to look at the data at a low level — something that most people aren't prepared to do and is time consuming even if you do have the required skills. Often, your first clue that data is missing is the preposterous answers that your questions get from the algorithm and associated dataset. When the algorithm is the right one to use, the dataset must be at fault.

A problem can occur when the data collection process doesn't include all the data needed to answer a particular question. Sometimes you're better off to actually drop a fact rather than use a considerably damaged fact.

Less damaged fields can have data missing in one of two ways. Randomly missing data is often the result of human or sensor error. It occurs when data records throughout the dataset have missing entries. Sometimes a simple glitch causes the damage. Sequentially missing data occurs during some type of generalized failure. An entire segment of the data records in the dataset lack the required information, which means that the resulting analysis can become quite skewed.

Fixing randomly missing data is easiest. You can use a simple median or average value as a replacement. No, the dataset isn't completely accurate, but it will likely work well enough to obtain a reasonable answer. In some cases, data scientists used a special algorithm to compute the missing value, which can make the dataset more accurate at the expense of computational time.

Sequentially missing data is significantly harder, if not impossible, to fix because you lack any surrounding data on which to base any sort of guess. If you can find the cause of the missing data, you can sometimes reconstruct it. However, when reconstruction becomes impossible, you can choose to ignore the field. Unfortunately, some answers will require that field, which means that you might need to ignore that particular sequence of data records — potentially causing incorrect output.

Finding the missing data

TIP

As a first step, count the number of missing cases in each variable. When a variable has too many missing cases, you may need to drop it from the training and test dataset. A good rule of thumb is to drop a variable if more than 90 percent of its instances are missing.

Some learning algorithms do not know how to deal with missing values and report errors in both training and test phases, whereas other models treat them as zero values, causing an underestimation of the predicted value or probability (it's just as if part of the formula isn't working properly). Consequently, you need to replace all the missing values in your data matrix with some suitable value for your analysis to succeed.

Many reasons exist for missing data, but the essential point is whether the data is missing randomly or in a specific order. Random missing data is ideal because you can guess its value using a simple average, a median, or another algorithm without too many concerns. Some cases contain a strong bias toward certain kinds of examples. For instance, think of the case of studying the income of a population. Wealthy people (for taxation reasons, presumably) tend to hide their true income by reporting to you that they don't know. Poor people, on the other hand, may say that they don't want to report their income for fear of negative judgement. If you miss information from certain strata of the population, repairing the missing data can be difficult and misleading because you may think that such cases are just like the others. Instead, they are quite different. Therefore, you can't simply use average values to replace the missing values — you must use complex approaches and tune them carefully. Moreover, identifying cases that aren't missing data at random is difficult because it requires a closer inspection of how missing values are associated with other variables in the dataset.

REMEMBER

When data is missing at random, you can easily repair the empty values because you obtain hints to their true value from other variables. When data isn't missing at random, you can't get good hints from other available information unless you understand the data association with the missing case. Therefore, if you have to figure out missing income in your data, and it is missing because the person is wealthy, you can't replace the missing value with a simple average because you'll replace it with a medium income. Instead, you should use an average of the income of wealthy people as a replacement.

TIP

When data isn't missing at random, the fact that the value is missing is informative because it helps track down the missing group. You can leave the chore of looking for the reason that it's missing to your algorithm by building a new binary feature that reports when the value of a variable is missing. Consequently, the algorithm will determine the best value to use as a replacement by itself.

Encoding missingness

You have a few possible strategies to handle missing data effectively. Your strategy may change if you have to handle missing values in *quantitative* (values expressed as numbers) or qualitative features. *Qualitative* features, although also expressed by numbers, are in reality referring to concepts, so their values are somewhat arbitrary and you cannot meaningfully compute an average or perform other computations on them.

TIP

When working with qualitative features, your value guessing should always produce integer numbers, based on the numbers used as codes. Common strategies for missing data handling are as follows:

>> **Replace missing values with a computed constant such as the mean or the median value.** If your feature is a category, you must provide a specific value because the numbering is arbitrary, and using mean or median doesn't make sense. Use this strategy when the missing values are random.

>> **Replace missing values with a value outside the normal value range of the feature.** For instance, if the feature is positive, replace missing values with negative values. This approach works fine with decision tree–based algorithms and qualitative variables.

>> **Replace missing values with 0, which works well with regression models and standardized variables.** This approach is also applicable to qualitative variables when they contain binary values.

>> **Interpolate the missing values when they are part of a series of values tied to time.** This approach works only for quantitative values. For instance, if your feature is daily sales, you could use a moving average of the last seven days or pick the value at the same time the previous week.

>> **Impute their value using the information from other predictor features (but never use the response variable).** Particularly in R, specialized libraries like missForest (https://cran.r-project.org/web/packages/missForest/index.html), MICE (https://cran.r-project.org/web/packages/mice/index.html), and Amelia II (https://gking.harvard.edu/amelia) can do everything for you. Scikit-learn recently introduced an experimental missing values imputer (which you can find at https://scikit-learn.org/stable/modules/generated/sklearn.impute.IterativeImputer.html) that allows imputing data in Python using Multivariate Imputation by Chained Equations (MICE), missForest, or even Amelia methodologies.

TIP

Another good practice is to create a new binary feature for each variable whose values you repaired. The binary variable will track variations due to replacement or imputing with a positive value, and your machine learning algorithm can figure out when it must make additional adjustments to the values you actually used.

Inputting missing data

In Python, notification of missing values is made possible using the ndarray data structure from the NumPy package. Python marks missing values with a special value that appears printed on the screen as NaN (Not a Number). The DataFrame data structure from the pandas package offers methods for both replacing missing values and dropping variables.

The following Python example demonstrates how to perform replacement tasks. It begins by creating a dataset of 5 observations and 3 features, named "A," "B," "C":

```
import pandas as pd
import numpy as np
data = pd.DataFrame([[1,2,np.nan],[np.nan,2,np.nan],
                     [3,np.nan,np.nan],[np.nan,3,8],
                     [5,3,np.nan]],columns=['A','B','C'])
```

```
print(data,'\n') # prints the data
# counts NaN values for each feature
print(data.isnull().sum(axis=0))
```

Notice the use of np.nan to mark missing values in the code. When you run this example, you see the following output:

```
    A    B    C
0   1    2  NaN
1 NaN    2  NaN
2   3  NaN  NaN
3 NaN    3    8
4   5    3  NaN

A    2
B    1
C    4
dtype: int64
```

Because feature C has just one value, you can drop it from the dataset. The code then replaces the missing values in feature B with a medium value and interpolates the value in feature A because it displays a progressive order:

```
# Drops definitely C from the dataset
data.drop('C', axis=1, inplace=True)
# Creates a placeholder for B's missing values
data['missing_B'] = data['B'].isnull().astype(int)
# Fills missings in B using B's average
data['B'].fillna(data['B'].mean(), inplace=True)
# Interpolates A
data['A'].interpolate(method='linear', inplace=True)
print(data)
```

Here is the output you see when you run the code:

```
   A    B  missing_B
0  1  2.0          0
1  2  2.0          0
2  3  2.5          1
3  4  3.0          0
4  5  3.0          0
```

The printed output is the final dataset. Be sure to note that the mean of B isn't an integer value, so the code converted all B values to floating numbers. This approach makes sense if B is numeric. If it were a category, and the numbering were marking a class, the code should have filled the feature using the command `data['B'].fillna(data['B'].mode().iloc[0], inplace=True)`, which uses the mode, that is, the first most frequent value in the series.

As shown in the example, sometimes you can't do much with examples that have a lot of missing values in their features. In such cases:

>> When the example is for training, remove it from the set (a procedure called *listwise deletion*) so that the incomplete cases won't affect learning.

>> When the example is part of your test, you shouldn't remove it, but rather use it to evaluate how well your algorithm handles such situations.

Considering data misalignments

Data might exist for each of the data records in a dataset, but it might not align with other data in other datasets you own. For example, the numeric data in a field in one dataset might be a floating-point type (with decimal point), but an integer type in another dataset. Before you can combine the two datasets, the fields must contain the same type of data.

All sorts of other kinds of misalignment can occur. For example, date fields are notorious for being formatted in various ways. To compare dates, the data formats must be the same. However, dates are also insidious in their propensity for looking the same but not being the same. For example, dates in one dataset might use Greenwich Mean Time (GMT) as a basis, while the dates in another dataset might use some other time zone. Before you can compare the times, you must align them to the same time zone. It can become even weirder when dates in one dataset come from a location that uses Daylight Saving Time (DST), but dates from another location don't.

Even when the data types and format are the same, other data misalignments can occur. For example, the fields in one dataset may not match the fields in the other dataset. In some cases, these differences are easy to correct. One dataset may treat first and last name as a single field, while another dataset might use separate fields for first and last name. The answer is to change all datasets to use a single field or to change them all to use separate fields for first and last name. Unfortunately, many misalignments in data content are harder to figure out. In fact, it's entirely possible that you might not be able to figure them out at all. However, before you give up, consider these potential solutions to the problem:

>> Calculate the missing data from other data that you can access.

>> Locate the missing data in another dataset.

>> Combine datasets to create a whole that provides consistent fields.

>> Collect additional data from various sources to fill in the missing data.

>> Redefine your question so that you no longer need the missing data.

Separating out useful data

Some organizations are of the opinion that they can never have too much data, but an excess of data becomes as much of a problem as not enough. To solve problems efficiently, an algorithm-based task, such as AI, requires just enough data. Defining the question that you want to answer concisely and clearly helps, as does using the correct algorithm (or algorithm ensemble). Of course, the major problems with having too much data are that finding the solution (after wading through all that extra data) takes longer, and sometimes you get confusing results because you can't see the forest for the trees.

WARNING

As part of creating the dataset you need for analysis, you make a copy of the original data rather than modify it. Always keep the original, raw data pure so that you can use it for other analyses later. In addition, creating the right data output for analysis can require a number of tries because you may find that the output doesn't meet your needs. The point is to create a dataset that contains only the data needed for analysis, but keep in mind that the data may need specific kinds of pruning to ensure the desired output.

Dealing with Dates in Your Data

Dates can present problems in data. For one thing, dates are stored as numeric values. However, the precise value of the number depends on the representation for the particular platform and could even depend on the users' preferences. For example, Excel users can choose to start dates in 1900 or 1904 (https://support.microsoft.com/en-us/help/214330/differences-between-the-1900-and-the-1904-date-system-in-excel). The numeric encoding for each is different, so the same date can have two numeric values depending on the starting date.

In addition to problems of representation, you also need to consider how to work with time values. Creating a time value format that represents a value that the user can understand is hard. For example, you might need to use Greenwich Mean Time (GMT) in some situations but a local time zone in others. Transforming between various times is also problematic, such as differentiating between 12-hour time and 24-hour time. With these kinds of time differences in mind, the following sections provide you with details on dealing with time issues.

Formatting date and time values

Obtaining the correct date and time representation can make performing analysis a lot easier. For example, you often have to change the representation to obtain a correct sorting of values. Python provides two common methods of formatting date and time. The first technique is to call str(), which simply turns a datetime value into a string without any formatting. The strftime() function requires more work because you must define how you want the datetime value to appear after conversion. When using strftime(), you must provide a string containing special directives that define the formatting. You can find a listing of these directives at http://strftime.org/.

Now that you have some idea of how time and date conversions work, it's time to see an example. The following example creates a datetime object and then converts it into a string using two different approaches:

```
import datetime as dt

now = dt.datetime.now()

print(str(now))
print(now.strftime('%a, %d %B %Y'))
```

In this case, you can see that using str() is the easiest approach. However, as shown by the following output, it may not provide the output you need. Using strftime() is infinitely more flexible:

```
2018-09-21 11:39:49.698891
Fri, 21 September 2018
```

Using the right time transformation

Time zones and differences in local time can cause all sorts of problems when you're performing analysis. In addition, some types of calculations simply require a time shift in order to get the right results. No matter what the reason, you may need to transform one time into another time at some point. The following examples show some techniques you can employ to perform the task:

```
import datetime as dt

now = dt.datetime.now()
timevalue = now + dt.timedelta(hours=2)

print(now.strftime('%H:%M:%S'))
print(timevalue.strftime('%H:%M:%S'))
print(timevalue - now)
```

The `timedelta()` function makes the time transformation straightforward. You can use any of these parameter names with `timedelta()` to change a time and date value:

» days

» seconds

» microseconds

» milliseconds

» minutes

» hours

» weeks

You can also manipulate time by performing addition or subtraction on time values. You can even subtract two time values to determine the difference between them. Here's the output from this example:

```
11:42:22
13:42:22
2:00:00
```

Note that `now` is the local time, `timevalue` is two time zones different from this one, and there is a two-hour difference between the two times. You can perform all sorts of transformations using these techniques to ensure that your analysis always shows precisely the time-oriented values you need.

Chapter **2**

Considering Outrageous Outcomes

I f you work with data long enough, you eventually start to gain an appreciation for when the output of an analysis looks right. It may not be the output you expected, but when you start thinking about it, the output is consistent with the data — it makes sense. Unfortunately, the output you receive might not always make sense, and that's when the output becomes outrageous. You start seeing results like the sun coming out at midnight and the anticipated income from a new store being well into the negative numbers. Of course, recognizing outrageous isn't always so easy, so the first part of this chapter begins with defining *outrageous*.

An *outlier* is data that lies outside the expected range. It's an indicator that something may be wrong with your data or the method used to analyze it. Outliers can skew the results of an analysis or they can indicate that your original assumptions are incorrect. In some cases, it can simply mean that not everything or everyone fits within the little box you'd like to put them in — an outlier can simply be a serendipitous event. The next section of the chapter looks at outliers and helps you understand what they can mean.

The last parts of the chapter discuss two kinds of statistical analysis: univariate and multivariate. In both cases, you look for patterns in the data to tell you something about that data. The univariate approach uses just one variable, while the multivariate approach uses two or more variables. Some texts include a bivariate approach, which specifically uses two variables, but you won't find this approach in this book. The goals of performing statistical analysis include understanding the relationship of a variable with the underlying data, understanding the relationships between multiple variables, and simplifying data.

REMEMBER

You don't have to type the source code for this chapter manually. In fact, using the downloadable source is a lot easier. The source code for this chapter appears in the `DSPD_0602_Outliers.ipynb` source code file for Python and the `DSPD_R_0602_Outliers.ipynb` source code file for R. See the Introduction for details on how to find these source files.

Deciding What Outrageous Means

An *outrageous result* is one that doesn't make sense and is at least marginally provable as incorrect. You can have a result that doesn't match your initial assumptions. Such analysis results occur all of the time. These unexpected results are unanticipated, but they aren't outrageous. However, a time comes when the result of an analysis simply doesn't make sense for one of these reasons:

>> The result is physically impossible.

>> The analysis never focuses in on a single provable result.

>> Different data produce widely varying results.

>> Variables that must correlate in some manner never do.

>> Analysis results never seem to match real-world outcomes.

REMEMBER

An important aspect of understanding the term *outrageous* is to keep an open mind. Data scientists and mathematicians continue to create and refine algorithms because the world is complex and humanity doesn't truly understand it. The universe is even more complex and the questions that humanity hasn't answered in even the smallest way would likely fill several libraries.

In addition, sometimes a result runs counter to common wisdom. If you perform an analysis that assumes that everyone in every country in the world reacts the same to a specific food ingredient, you're likely to find that this assumption is incorrect. For example, most Americans would quickly suffer from high blood pressure from drinking butter tea (https://www.yowangdu.com/tibetan-food/butter-tea.html and https://www.organicfacts.net/health-benefits/animal-product/butter-tea.html), yet this tea is a staple of places like Nepal, where people actually have a lower incidence of high blood pressure than in America.

Oddly enough, you can find papers on all sorts of things that run counter to common wisdom online and on reputable sites, such as the National Center for Biotechnology Information (NCBI) component of the National Institutes of Health (NIH) (https://www.ncbi.nlm.nih.gov/pmc/articles/PMC3880218/). When you determine the result of an analysis before you actually perform the analysis, you likely find that your conclusions are skewed and that it's the conclusion, not the result, that is outrageous.

Considering the Five Mistruths in Data

Humans are used to seeing data for what it is in many cases: an opinion. In fact, in some cases, people skew data to the point where it becomes useless, a *mistruth*. A computer can't tell the difference between truthful and untruthful data; all it sees is data. One of the issues that make it hard, if not impossible, to perform analysis accurately is that humans can work with mistruths and computers can't. The best you can hope to achieve is to see the errant data as outliers and then filter it out, but that technique doesn't necessarily solve the problem because a human would still use the data and attempt to determine a truth based on the mistruths that are there.

WARNING

A common thought about creating less contaminated datasets is that instead of allowing humans to enter the data, collecting the data through sensors or other means should be possible. Unfortunately, sensors and other mechanical input methodologies reflect the goals of their human inventors and the limits of what the particular technology is able to detect. Consequently, even machine-derived or sensor-derived data is also subject to generating mistruths that are quite difficult for an algorithm used for a task such as AI to detect and overcome.

The following sections use a car accident as the main example to illustrate five types of mistruths that can appear in data. The concepts that the accident is trying to portray may not always appear in data, and they may appear in different ways than discussed. The fact remains that you normally need to deal with these sorts of things when viewing data.

Commission

Mistruths of commission are those that reflect an outright attempt to substitute truthful information for untruthful information. For example, when filling out an accident report, someone could state that the sun momentarily blinded them, making it impossible to see someone they hit. In reality, perhaps the person was distracted by something else or wasn't actually thinking about driving (possibly considering a nice dinner instead). If no one can disprove this theory, the person might get by with a lesser charge. However, the data would also be contaminated. The effect is that an insurance company would now base premiums on errant data.

REMEMBER

Although mistruths of commission might seem to be completely avoidable, often they aren't. Humans tell "little white lies" to save others embarrassment or to deal with an issue with the least amount of personal effort. Sometimes a mistruth of commission is based on errant input or hearsay. In fact, the sources for errors of commission are so many that it really is hard to come up with a scenario where someone could avoid them entirely. All this said, mistruths of commission are one type of mistruth that someone can avoid more often than not.

Omission

Mistruths of omission occur when a person tells the truth in every stated fact but leaves out an important fact that would change the perception of an incident as a whole. Thinking again about the accident report, say that someone strikes a deer, causing significant damage to the car. The driver truthfully says:

>> The road was wet.

>> It was near twilight, so the light wasn't as good as it could be.

>> Slow response times delayed pressing on the brake.

>> The deer simply ran out from a thicket at the side of the road.

The conclusion would be that the incident is simply an accident. However, the person has left out an important fact by not mentioning an ongoing conversation through texting. If law enforcement knew about the texting, it would change the reason for the accident to inattentive driving. The driver might be fined and the insurance adjuster would use a different reason when entering the incident into the database. As with the mistruth of commission, the resulting errant data would change how the insurance company adjusts premiums.

REMEMBER

Completely avoiding mistruths of omission isn't possible. Yes, someone could purposely leave facts out of a report, but equally likely is that someone will simply forget to include all the facts. After all, most people are quite rattled after an accident, so they easily lose focus and report only those truths that left the most significant impression. Even if a person later remembers additional details and reports them, the database is unlikely to ever contain a full set of truths.

Perspective

Mistruths of perspective occur when multiple parties view an incident from multiple vantage points. For example, in considering an accident involving a struck pedestrian, the person driving the car, the person getting hit by the car, and a bystander who witnessed the event would all have different perspectives. An officer taking reports from each person would understandably get different facts from each one, even assuming that each person tells the truth as each knows it. In fact, experience shows that this is almost always the case, and what the officer submits as a report is the middle ground of what each of those involved states, augmented by personal experience. In other words, the report will be close to the truth, but not close enough for completely successful analysis.

When dealing with perspective, you need to consider vantage point. The driver of the car can see the dashboard and knows the car's condition at the time of the accident. This is information that the other two parties lack. Likewise, the person getting hit by the car has the best vantage point for seeing the driver's facial expression (intent). The bystander might be in the best position to see whether the driver made an attempt to stop and to assess issues such as whether the driver tried to swerve. Each party will have to make a report based on seen data without the benefit of hidden data.

WARNING

Perspective is perhaps the most dangerous of the mistruths because anyone who tries to derive the truth in this scenario will, at best, end up with an average of the various stories, which will never be fully correct. A human viewing the information can rely on intuition and instinct to potentially obtain a better approximation of the truth, but an algorithm will always use just the average, which means that the algorithm is always at a significant disadvantage. Unfortunately, avoiding mistruths of perspective is impossible because no matter how many witnesses you have to the event, the best you can hope to achieve is an approximation of the truth, not the actual truth. You also have another sort of mistruth of perspective to consider. Think about this scenario: You're a deaf person in 1927. Each week you go to the theater to view a silent film, and for an hour or more, you feel like everyone else. You can see the movie in just the same way as everyone else; differences don't exist. In October of that year, the deaf person sees a sign saying that the theater is upgrading to support a sound system so that it can display *talkies* — films with a sound track. The sign says that it's the best thing ever, and almost everyone seems to agree except for the deaf person, who is now made to feel like a second-class citizen, different from everyone else and even pretty much excluded from the theater. In the deaf person's eyes, that sign is a mistruth: Adding a sound system is the worst possible thing, not the best possible thing. What seems to be generally true isn't actually true for everyone. The idea of a general truth — one that is true for everyone — is a myth; it doesn't exist.

Bias

Mistruths of bias occur when someone is able to see (gather the required input) the truth but, because of personal concerns or beliefs, is unable to actually see (comprehend) it. For example, when thinking about an accident, a driver might

Considering Outrageous Outcomes

focus attention so completely on the middle of the road that the deer at the edge of the road becomes invisible. Consequently, the driver has no time to react when the deer suddenly decides to bolt out into the middle of the road in an effort to cross.

A problem with bias is that it can be incredibly hard to categorize. For example, a driver who fails to see the deer can have a genuine accident, meaning that the deer was hidden from view by shrubbery. However, the driver might also be guilty of inattentive driving because of incorrect focus. The driver might also experience a momentary distraction. In short, the fact that the driver didn't see the deer isn't the question; instead, it's a matter of *why* the driver didn't see the deer. In many cases, confirming the source of bias becomes important when creating an algorithm designed to avoid a bias source.

REMEMBER

Theoretically, avoiding mistruths of bias is always possible. In reality, however, all humans have biases of various types, and those biases will always result in mistruths that skew datasets. Just getting someone to actually look and then see something — to have it register in the person's brain — is a difficult task. Humans rely on filters to avoid information overload, and these filters are also a source of bias because they prevent people from actually seeing things.

Frame-of-reference

Of the five mistruths, frame of reference need not actually be the result of any sort of error, but one of understanding. A frame-of-reference mistruth occurs when one party describes something, such as an event like an accident, and because a second party lacks experience with the event, the details become muddled or completely misunderstood. Comedy routines abound that rely on frame-of-reference errors. One famous example is from Abbott and Costello, *Who's On First?*, as shown at https://www.youtube.com/watch?v=kTcRRaXV-fg. Getting one person to understand what a second person is saying can be impossible when the first person lacks experiential knowledge — the frame of reference.

Another frame-of-reference mistruth example occurs when one party can't possibly understand the other. For example, a sailor experiences a storm at sea. Perhaps it's a monsoon, but assume for a moment that the storm is substantial, perhaps even life threatening. Even with the use of videos, interviews, and a simulator, the experience of being at sea in a life-threatening storm would be impossible to convey to someone who hasn't experienced such a storm firsthand; such a person has no frame of reference for it.

REMEMBER

The best way to avoid frame-of-reference mistruths is to ensure that all parties involved can develop similar frames of reference. To accomplish this task, the various parties require similar experiential knowledge to ensure the accurate transfer of data from one person to another. However, when working with a dataset, which is necessarily recorded, static data, frame-of-reference errors will still occur when the prospective viewer lacks the required experiential knowledge.

An algorithm will always experience frame-of-reference issues because an algorithm necessarily lacks the ability to create an experience. A databank of acquired knowledge isn't quite the same thing. The databank would contain facts, but experience is based on not only facts but also conclusions that current technology is unable to duplicate.

Considering Detection of Outliers

As a general definition, *outliers* are data that differ significantly (they're distant) from other data in a sample. The reason they're distant is that one or more values are too high or too low when compared to the majority of the values. They could also display an almost unique combination of values. For instance, if you are analyzing records of students enlisted in a university, students who are too young or too old may catch your attention. Students studying unusual mixes of different subjects would also require scrutiny. The following sections discuss outliers as they pertain to data science.

Understanding outlier basics

Outliers skew your data distributions and affect all your basic *central tendency* (mean, median, or mode) statistics (see https://statistics.laerd.com/statistical-guides/measures-central-tendency-mean-mode-median.php for details). Means are pushed upward or downward, influencing all other descriptive measures. An outlier will always inflate variance and modify correlations, so you may obtain incorrect assumptions about your data and the relationships between variables.

This simple example can display the effect (on a small scale) of a single outlier with respect to more than 1,000 regular observations:

```
import matplotlib.pyplot as plt
plt.style.use('seaborn-whitegrid')
%matplotlib inline

import numpy as np
from scipy.stats.stats import pearsonr
np.random.seed(101)
normal = np.random.normal(loc=0.0, scale= 1.0, size=1000)
```

```
print('Mean: %0.3f Median: %0.3f Variance: %0.3f' %
                                    (np.mean(normal),
                                     np.median(normal),
                                     np.var(normal)))
```

Using the NumPy random generator, the example creates the variable named normal, which contains 1,000 observations derived from a standard normal distribution. Basic descriptive statistics (mean, median, variance) do not show anything unexpected. Here are the resulting mean, median, and variance:

```
Mean: 0.026 Median: 0.032 Variance: 1.109
```

Now you change a single value by inserting an outlying value:

```
outlying = normal.copy()
outlying[0] = 50.0
print('Mean: %0.3f Median: %0.3f Variance: %0.3f' %
                                    (np.mean(outlying),
                                     np.median(outlying),
                                     np.var(outlying)))

print('Pearson''s correlation: %0.3f p-value: %0.3f' %
                        pearsonr(normal,outlying))
```

You can call this new variable outlying and put an outlier into it (at index 0, you have a positive value of 50.0). Now you obtain more descriptive statistics:

```
Mean: 0.074 Median: 0.032 Variance: 3.597
Pearsons correlation coefficient: 0.619 p-value: 0.000
```

Now the statistics show that the mean has a value three times higher than before, and so does the variance. Only the median, which relies on position (it tells you the value occupying the middle position when all the observations are arranged in order), is not affected by the change.

More significantly, the correlation of the original variable and the outlying variable is quite far from being +1.0 (the correlation value of a variable with respect to itself is +1.0, see https://www.kellogg.northwestern.edu/faculty/weber/emp/_session_3/Correlation.htm for details), indicating that the measure of linear relationship between the two variables has been seriously damaged.

Finding more things that can go wrong

Outliers don't simply shift key measures in your explorative statistics; they also change the structure of the relationships between variables in your data. Outliers can affect algorithms in two ways:

>> Algorithms based on coefficients may take the wrong coefficient to minimize their inability to understand the outlying cases. Linear models are a clear example (they are sums of coefficients), but they are not the only ones. Outliers can also influence tree-based learners such as Adaboost (see https://towardsdatascience.com/basic-ensemble-learning-random-forest-adaboost-gradient-boosting-step-by-step-explained-95d49d1e2725 for additional information) or Gradient Boosting Machines (see https://machinelearningmastery.com/gentle-introduction-gradient-boosting-algorithm-machine-learning/ for additional information). Book 4, Chapter 1 provides you with an overview of Adaboost.

>> Because algorithms learn from data samples, outliers may induce the algorithm to overweight the likelihood of extremely low or high values given a certain variable configuration.

Both situations limit the capacity of a learning algorithm to generalize well to new data. In other words, they make your learning process overfit to the present dataset.

A few remedies exist for outliers, some of which require that you modify your present data and others that you choose a suitable error function for your algorithm. (Some algorithms offer you the possibility of choosing a different error function as a parameter when setting up the learning procedure.)

REMEMBER

Most algorithms used for tasks such as machine learning can accept different error functions. The error function is important because it helps the algorithm learn by understanding errors and enforcing adjustments in the learning process. However, some error functions are extremely sensitive to outliers, while others are quite resistant to them. For instance, a squared error measure tends to emphasize outliers because errors deriving from examples with large values are squared, thus becoming even more prominent.

Understanding anomalies and novel data

Because outliers occur as mistakes or anomalies in extremely rare cases, detecting an outlier is never an easy job; it is, however, an important one for obtaining effective results from your data science project. In certain fields, detecting anomalies is itself the purpose of data science: fraud detection in insurance and banking, fault detection in manufacturing, system monitoring in health and other critical applications, and event detection in security systems and for early warning.

An important distinction is when you look for existing outliers in data, or when you check for any new data containing anomalies with respect to existing cases. Maybe you spent a lot of time cleaning your data or you developed a machine learning application based on available data, so it would be critical to figure out whether the new data is similar to the old data and whether the algorithms will continue working well in classification or prediction.

In such cases, data scientists instead talk of novelty detection, because they need to know how well the new data resembles the old. Being exceptionally new is considered an anomaly: Novelty may conceal a significant event or may risk preventing an algorithm from working properly because tasks such as machine learning rely heavily on learning from past examples, and the algorithm may not generalize to completely novel cases. When working with new data, you should retrain the algorithm.

Experience teaches that the world is rarely stable. Sometimes novelties do naturally appear because the world is so mutable. Consequently, your data changes over time in unexpected ways, in both target and predictor variables. This phenomenon is called *concept drift*. The term *concept* refers to your target and *drift* to the source data used to perform a prediction that moves in a slow but uncontrollable way, like a boat drifting because of strong tides. When considering a data science model, you distinguish between different concept drift and novelty situations:

>> **Physical:** Face or voice recognition systems, or even climate models, never really change. Don't expect novelties, but check for outliers that result from data problems, such as erroneous measurements.

>> **Political and economic:** These models sometimes change, especially in the long run. You have to keep an eye out for long-term effects that start slowly and then propagate and consolidate, rendering your models ineffective.

>> **Social behavior:** Social networks and the language you use every day change over time. Expect novelties to appear, and take precautionary steps; otherwise, your model will suddenly deteriorate and turn unusable.

>> **Search engine data, banking, and e-commerce fraud schemes:** These models change quite often. You need to exercise extra care in checking for the appearance of novelties, telling you to train a new model to maintain accuracy.

>> **Cyber security threats and advertising trends:** These models change continuously. Spotting novelties is the norm, and reusing the same models over a long time is a hazard.

Examining a Simple Univariate Method

When looking for outliers, a good way to start, no matter how many variables you have in your data, is to look at every single variable by itself, using both graphical and statistical inspection. This is the univariate approach, which allows you to spot an outlier given an incongruous value on a variable. The following sections discuss this approach in more detail.

Using the pandas package

The pandas package can make spotting outliers quite easy thanks to

>> A straightforward describe method that informs you on mean, variance, quartiles, and extremes of your numeric values for each variable

>> A system of automatic boxplot visualizations

Using both techniques in tandem makes it easy to know when you have outliers and where to look for them. The diabetes dataset, from the Scikit-learn datasets module, is a good example to start with.

```
from sklearn.datasets import load_diabetes
diabetes = load_diabetes()
X,y = diabetes.data, diabetes.target
```

After these commands, all the data is contained in the X variable, a NumPy ndarray. The example then transforms it into a pandas DataFrame and asks for some descriptive statistics (see the output in Figure 2-1):

```
import pandas as pd
pd.options.display.float_format = '{:.2f}'.format
df = pd.DataFrame(X)
df.describe()
```

	0	1	2	3	4	5	6	7	8	9
count	442.00	442.00	442.00	442.00	442.00	442.00	442.00	442.00	442.00	442.00
mean	-0.00	0.00	-0.00	0.00	-0.00	0.00	-0.00	0.00	-0.00	-0.00
std	0.05	0.05	0.05	0.05	0.05	0.05	0.05	0.05	0.05	0.05
min	-0.11	-0.04	-0.09	-0.11	-0.13	-0.12	-0.10	-0.08	-0.13	-0.14
25%	-0.04	-0.04	-0.03	-0.04	-0.03	-0.03	-0.04	-0.04	-0.03	-0.03
50%	0.01	-0.04	-0.01	-0.01	-0.00	-0.00	-0.01	-0.00	-0.00	-0.00
75%	0.04	0.05	0.03	0.04	0.03	0.03	0.03	0.03	0.03	0.03
max	0.11	0.05	0.17	0.13	0.15	0.20	0.18	0.19	0.13	0.14

FIGURE 2-1: Descriptive statistics for a DataFrame.

You can spot the problematic variables by looking at the extremities of the distribution (the maximum value of a variable). For example, you must consider whether the minimum and maximum values lie respectively far from the 25th and 75th percentile. As shown in the output, many variables have suspiciously large maximum values. A boxplot analysis will clarify the situation. The following command creates the boxplot of all variables shown in Figure 2-2.

```
fig, axes = plt.subplots(nrows=1, ncols=1,
                         figsize=(10, 5))
df.boxplot(ax=axes);
```

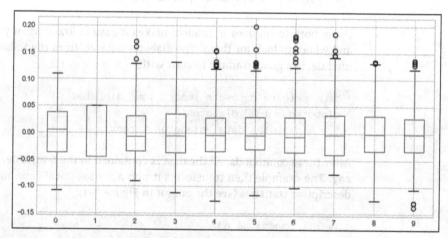

FIGURE 2-2: Boxplots.

Boxplots generated from pandas DataFrame will have whiskers set to plus or minus 1.5 IQR (*interquartile range* or the distance between the lower and upper quartile) with respect to the upper and lower side of the box (the upper and lower quartiles). This boxplot style is called the Tukey boxplot (from the name of statistician John Tukey, who created and promoted it among statisticians together with other explanatory data techniques) and it allows a visualization of the presence of cases outside the whiskers. (All points outside these whiskers are deemed outliers.)

Leveraging the Gaussian distribution

Another effective check for outliers in your data is accomplished by leveraging the normal distribution. Even if your data isn't normally distributed, standardizing it will allow you to assume certain probabilities of finding anomalous values. For instance, 99.7% of values found in a standardized normal distribution should be inside the range of +3 and −3 standard deviations from the mean, as shown in the following code.

```
from sklearn.preprocessing import StandardScaler
Xs = StandardScaler().fit_transform(X)
# .any(1) method will avoid duplicating
df[(np.abs(Xs)>3).any(1)]
```

In Figure 2-3, you see the results depicting the rows in the dataset featuring some possibly outlying values.

	0	1	2	3	4	5	6	7	8	9
58	0.04	-0.04	-0.06	0.04	0.01	-0.06	0.18	-0.08	-0.00	-0.05
123	0.01	0.05	0.03	-0.00	0.15	0.20	-0.06	0.19	0.02	0.07
216	0.01	0.05	0.04	0.05	0.05	0.07	-0.07	0.15	0.05	0.05
230	-0.04	0.05	0.07	-0.06	0.15	0.16	0.00	0.07	0.05	0.07
256	-0.05	-0.04	0.16	-0.05	-0.03	-0.02	-0.05	0.03	0.03	0.01
260	0.04	-0.04	-0.01	-0.06	0.01	-0.03	0.15	-0.08	-0.08	-0.02
261	0.05	-0.04	-0.04	0.10	0.04	-0.03	0.18	-0.08	-0.01	0.02
269	0.01	-0.04	-0.03	-0.03	0.04	-0.01	0.16	-0.08	-0.01	-0.04
322	0.02	0.05	0.06	0.06	0.02	-0.04	-0.09	0.16	0.13	0.08
336	-0.02	-0.04	0.09	-0.04	0.09	0.09	-0.06	0.15	0.08	0.05
367	-0.01	0.05	0.17	0.01	0.03	0.03	-0.02	0.03	0.03	0.03
441	-0.05	-0.04	-0.07	-0.08	0.08	0.03	0.17	-0.04	-0.00	0.00

FIGURE 2-3: Reporting possibly outlying examples.

The Scikit-learn module provides an easy way to standardize your data and to record all the transformations for later use on different datasets. This means that all your data, no matter whether it's for machine learning training or for performance test purposes, is standardized in the same way.

TIP

The 68-95-99.7 rule says that in a standardized normal distribution, 68 percent of values are within one standard deviation, 95 percent are within two standard deviations, and 99.7 percent are within three. When working with skewed data, the 68-95-99.7 rule may not hold true, and in such an occurrence, you may need some more conservative estimate, such as Chebyshev's inequality. *Chebyshev's inequality* relies on a formula that says that for k standard deviations around the mean, no more cases than a percentage of $1/k^2$ should be over the mean. Therefore, at seven standard deviations around the mean, your probability of finding a legitimate value is at most 2 percent, no matter what the distribution is. (Two percent is a low probability; your case could be deemed almost certainly an outlier.)

TIP

Chebyshev's inequality is conservative. A high probability of being an outlier corresponds to seven or more standard deviations away from the mean. Use it when it may be costly to deem a value an outlier when it isn't. For all other applications, the 68-95-99.7 rule will suffice.

Making assumptions and checking out

Having found some possible univariate outliers, you now have to decide how to deal with them. If you completely distrust the outlying cases, under the assumption that they were unfortunate errors or mistakes, you can just delete them. (In Python, you can just deselect them using fancy indexing.)

TIP

Modifying the values in your data or deciding to exclude certain values is a decision to make after you understand why you have some outliers in your data. You can rule out unusual values or cases for which you presume that some error in measurement has occurred, in recording or previous handling of the data. If instead you realize that the outlying case is a legitimate, though rare, one, the best approach would be to underweight it (when the learning algorithms uses weight for the observations) or to increase the size of your data sample.

In this case, after deciding to keep the data and standardizing it, you could just cap the outlying values by using a simple multiplier of the standard deviation:

```
Xs_capped = Xs.copy()
o_idx = np.where(np.abs(Xs)>3)
Xs_capped[o_idx] = np.sign(Xs[o_idx]) * 3
```

In the proposed code, the sign function from NumPy recovers the sign of the outlying observation (+1 or −1), which is then multiplied by the value of 3 and assigned to the respective data point recovered by a Boolean indexing of the standardized array.

This approach does have a limitation. Because the standard deviation is used both for high and low values, it implies symmetry in your data distribution, an assumption often unverified in real data. As an alternative, you can use a bit more sophisticated approach called winsorizing. When using *winsorizing*, the values deemed outliers are clipped to the value of specific percentiles that act as value limits (usually the 5th percentile for the lower bound and the 95th for the upper):

```
from scipy.stats.mstats import winsorize
Xs_winsorized = winsorize(Xs, limits=(0.05, 0.95))
```

In this way, you create a different hurdle value for larger and smaller values, taking into account any asymmetry in the data distribution. Whatever you choose to use for capping (by standard deviation or by winsorizing), your data is now ready for further processing and analysis.

Finally, an alternative, automatic solution is to let Scikit-learn automatically transform your data and clip outliers by using the RobustScaler, a scaler based on the IQR (as in the boxplot previously discussed in this chapter; refer to Figure 2-2):

```
from sklearn.preprocessing import RobustScaler
Xs_rescaled = RobustScaler().fit_transform(Xs)
```

Developing a Multivariate Approach

Working on single variables allows you to spot a large number of outlying observations. However, outliers do not necessarily display values too far from the norm. Sometimes outliers are made of unusual combinations of values in more variables. They are rare, but influential, combinations that can especially trick machine learning algorithms.

In such cases, the precise inspection of every single variable won't suffice to rule out anomalous cases from your dataset. Only a few selected techniques, taking in consideration more variables at a time, will manage to reveal problems in your data.

The presented techniques approach the problem from different points of view:

>> Dimensionality reduction

>> Density clustering

>> Nonlinear distribution modeling

Using these techniques allows you to compare their results, taking notice of the recurring signals on particular cases — sometimes already located by the univariate exploration, sometimes as yet unknown.

Using principle component analysis

Principal component analysis can completely restructure the data, removing redundancies and ordering newly obtained components according to the amount of the original variance that they express. This type of analysis offers a synthetic and complete view over data distribution, making multivariate outliers particularly evident.

The first two components, being the most informative in term of variance, can depict the general distribution of the data if visualized. The output provides a good hint at possible evident outliers.

The last two components, being the most residual, depict all the information that could not be otherwise fitted by the PCA method. They can also provide a suggestion about possible but less evident outliers.

```
from sklearn.decomposition import PCA
from sklearn.preprocessing import scale
from pandas.plotting import scatter_matrix
pca = PCA()
Xc = pca.fit_transform(scale(X))

first_2 = sum(pca.explained_variance_ratio_[:2]*100)
last_2 = sum(pca.explained_variance_ratio_[-2:]*100)

print('variance by the components 1&2: %0.1f%%' % first_2)
print('variance by the last components: %0.1f%%' % last_2)

df = pd.DataFrame(Xc, columns=['comp_' + str(j)
                               for j in range(10)])
fig, axes = plt.subplots(nrows=1, ncols=2,
                         figsize=(15, 5))
first_two = df.plot.scatter(x='comp_0', y='comp_1',
                            s=50, grid=True, c='Azure',
                            edgecolors='DarkBlue',
                            ax=axes[0])
```

```
last_two  = df.plot.scatter(x='comp_8', y='comp_9',
                            s=50, grid=True, c='Azure',
                            edgecolors='DarkBlue',
                            ax=axes[1])


plt.show()
```

Figure 2-4 shows two scatterplots of the first and last components. The output also reports the variance explained by the first two components (half of the informative content of the dataset) of the PCA and by the last two ones:

```
variance by the components 1&2: 55.2%
variance by the last components: 0.9%
```

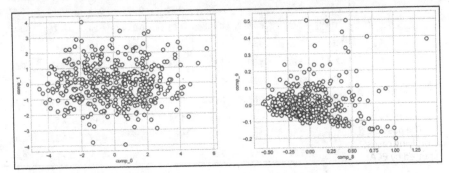

FIGURE 2-4:
The first two
and last two
components
from the PCA.

Pay particular attention to the data points along the axis (where the x axis defines the independent variable and the y axis defines the dependent variable). You can see a possible threshold to use for separating regular data from suspect data.

Using the two last components, you can locate a few points to investigate using the threshold of –0.3 for the tenth component and of –1.0 for the ninth. All cases below these values are possible outliers (see Figure 2-5).

```
outlying = (Xc[:,-1] > 0.3) | (Xc[:,-2] > 1.0)
df[outlying]
```

Using cluster analysis

Outliers are isolated points in the space of variables, and DBScan is a clustering algorithm that links dense data parts together and marks the too-sparse parts. DBScan is therefore an ideal tool for an automated exploration of your data for possible outliers to verify. Here is an example of how you can use DBScan for outlier detection:

```
from sklearn.cluster import DBSCAN
DB = DBSCAN(eps=2.5, min_samples=25)
DB.fit(Xc)

from collections import Counter
print(Counter(DB.labels_))
df[DB.labels_==-1]
```

	comp_0	comp_1	comp_2	comp_3	comp_4	comp_5	comp_6	comp_7	comp_8	comp_9
23	3.77	-1.76	1.09	0.72	-0.64	1.90	0.56	1.09	0.44	0.50
58	-2.65	2.23	2.79	-0.63	0.26	-0.13	1.44	0.67	1.01	-0.21
110	-2.04	-0.76	0.74	-1.93	-0.07	0.24	-1.75	-0.41	0.47	0.31
169	2.35	0.15	-0.13	1.19	-0.64	0.64	2.65	-0.31	0.22	0.50
254	3.82	-1.03	1.06	0.44	0.27	0.86	0.97	0.66	0.43	0.33
322	4.52	-2.24	-0.14	0.85	-0.47	0.73	1.28	0.34	1.39	0.38
323	3.87	-0.69	0.26	-0.58	-0.97	0.76	1.79	0.36	0.69	0.40
353	0.98	1.61	-1.16	1.14	-0.36	1.46	2.53	0.90	-0.02	0.50
371	2.11	-0.28	0.64	-0.65	-0.36	-0.26	2.22	1.09	0.07	0.35
394	2.24	-1.13	0.51	1.54	-1.30	-0.12	2.28	-0.10	0.40	0.43

FIGURE 2-5: The possible outlying cases spotted by PCA.

However, DBSCAN requires two parameters, eps and min_samples. These two parameters require multiple tries to locate the right values, which makes using the parameters a little tricky.

Start with a low value of min_samples and try growing the values of eps from 0.1 upward. After every trial with modified parameters, check the situation by counting the number of observations in the class by comparing the attribute labels_, with the value –1, and stop when the number of outliers seems reasonable for a visual inspection.

TIP

There will always be points on the fringe of the dense parts' distribution, so it's hard to provide you with a threshold for the number of cases that might be classified in the –1 class. Normally, outliers should not be more than 5 percent of cases, so use this indication as a generic rule of thumb.

The output from the previous example will report to you how many examples are in the –1 group, which the algorithm considers not part of the main cluster, and the list of the cases that are part of it.

TIP

It is less automated, but you can also use the K-means clustering algorithm for outlier detection. You first run a cluster analysis with a reasonable enough number of clusters. (You can try different solutions if you're not sure.) Then you look for clusters featuring just a few examples (or maybe a single one); they are probably outliers because they appear as small, distinct clusters that are separate from the large clusters that contain the majority of examples.

Automating outliers detection with Isolation Forests

Random Forests and Extremely Randomized Trees are powerful machine learning techniques. They work by dividing your dataset into smaller sets based on certain variable values to make it easier to predict the classification or regression on each smaller subset (a *divide et impera* solution).

IsolationForest is an algorithm that takes advantage of the fact that an outlier is easier to separate from majority cases based on differences between its values or combination of values. The algorithm keeps track of how long it takes to separate a case from the others and get it into its own subset. The less effort it takes to separate it, the more likely the case is an outlier. As a measure of such effort, IsolationForest produces a distance measurement (the shorter the distance, the more likely the case that it's an outlier).

TIP

When your machine learning algorithms are in production, a trained Isolation-Forest can act as a sanity check because many algorithms can't cope with outlying and novel examples.

To set IsolationForest to catch outliers, all you have to decide is the level of contamination, which is the percentage of cases considered outliers based on the distance measurement. You decide such a percentage based on your experience and expectation of data quality. Executing the following script will create a working IsolationForest:

```
from sklearn.ensemble import IsolationForest
auto_detection = IsolationForest(max_samples=50,
                                 contamination=0.05,
                                 random_state=0)
auto_detection.fit(Xc)
evaluation = auto_detection.predict(Xc)
df[evaluation==-1]
```

Considering Outrageous Outcomes

The output reports the list of the cases suspected of being outliers. In addition, the algorithm is trained to recognize normal dataset examples. When you provide new cases to the dataset and you evaluate them using the trained `IsolationForest`, you can immediately spot whether something is wrong with your new data.

REMEMBER

`IsolationForest` is a computationally intensive algorithm. Performing an analysis on a large dataset takes a long time and a lot of memory.

Chapter **3**

Dealing with Model Overfitting and Underfitting

A model is the description of the data points in the form of an algorithm (often represented by a mathematical function). Book 3 discusses various kinds of modeling associated with particular data point patterns. For example, data points that form a straight line rely on linear regression. The purpose of creating a model is to either predict the location of future data points or to categorize data based on where it falls within the model. However, a model is only as good as the underlying algorithm. An algorithm that follows the original data points too closely *overfits* the curve to the data. An algorithm that doesn't follow the original data points well enough *underfits* the curve to the data. Of course, overfitting and underfitting are both problems, which is why you need this chapter. Unless a model runs true to the data, anything you use the model for is suspect.

After you know why overfitting and underfitting occur, you need to consider the sources of these two problems. In some cases, the problem is definitely related to the data itself, but often the problem is in the manner that the data is collected and manicured for use. Poor assumptions about the data can also cause problems.

One of the most important concerns with overfitting and underfitting pertains to the *features* you select — that is, one or more columns in the data table containing the data. Each of the rows is a *case* (or sometimes called an item, event, or instance). Analysis involves viewing the features for each case and using them to construct the model. When you choose the wrong features, the model won't work. The last part of this chapter discusses working with features.

REMEMBER

You don't have to type the source code for this chapter manually. In fact, using the downloadable source is a lot easier. The source code for this chapter appears in the `DSPD_0603_Fitting.ipynb` source code file for Python and the `DSPD_R_0603_Fitting.ipynb` source code file for R. See the Introduction for details on how to find these source files.

Understanding the Causes

It's an oversimplification to state that overfitting and underfitting are issues surrounding the construction of a model based on the data. Something must cause the problem to occur. In fact, more than one problem can occur with the modeling of data, making the solution to overfitting and underfitting more complex than you might think. The following sections discuss common causes of overfitting and underfitting so that you can better understand how to locate the causes of these problems in your own models.

Considering the problem

Fitting a model implies learning from data a representation of the rules that generated the data in the first place. From a mathematical perspective, fitting a model is analogous to guessing an unknown function of the kind you faced in high school, such as y=4x^2+2x, just by observing its y results. Therefore, under the hood, you expect that data analysis algorithms generate mathematical formulations by determining how reality works based on the examples provided.

REMEMBER

Demonstrating whether such formulations are real is beyond the scope of data science. What is most important is that they work by producing exact predictions. For example, even though you can describe much of the physical world using mathematical functions, you often can't describe social and economic dynamics this way, but people try guessing them anyway.

To summarize, as a data scientist, you should always strive to approximate the real, unknown functions underlying the problems you face by using the best information available. The result of your work is evaluated based on your capacity to predict specific outcomes (the target outcome) given certain premises (the data) thanks to a useful range of algorithms (the machine learning algorithms).

Earlier in the book, you see something akin to a real function or law when the book presents a linear regression, which has its own formulation. The linear formula y=Bx + a, which mathematically represents a line on a plane, can often approximate training data well, even if the data is not representing a line or something similar to a line. As with linear regression, all other algorithms used for tasks such as machine learning have an internal formulation (and some, such as neural networks, even require you to define their formulation from scratch). The linear regression's formulation is one of the simplest ones; formulations from other learning algorithms can appear quite complex. You don't need to know exactly how they work. You do need to have an idea of how complex they are, whether they represent a line or a curve, and whether they can sense outliers or noisy data. When planning to learn from data, you should address these problematic aspects based on the formulation you intend to use:

1. Whether the learning algorithm is the best one to approximate the unknown function that you imagine is behind the data you use. In order to make such a decision, you must consider the learning algorithm's formulation performance on the data at hand and compare it with other, alternative formulations from other algorithms.

2. Whether the specific formulation of the learning algorithm is too simple, with respect to the hidden function, to make an estimate (this is called a *bias* problem).

3. Whether the specific formulation of the learning algorithm is too complex, with respect to the hidden function you need to guess (leading to the *variance* problem).

REMEMBER

Not all algorithms are suitable for every data problem. If you don't have enough data or the data is full of erroneous information, some formulations may have too much difficulty figuring out the real function.

Looking at underfitting

As previously mentioned, underfitting means that the model you create doesn't actually follow the data points very well, so any prediction or categorization is suspect. Of course, using visualization to see how this process works is helpful. The first step is to generate some data using this code:

```
import numpy as np
import matplotlib.pyplot as plt
%matplotlib inline
```

```
np.random.seed(51)

x = np.array(range(1, 50))
vary = (np.random.random(len(x))) / 5
y = np.sin(x * np.pi / 50.) + vary
```

What this code normally generates is a curve based on sine. Without `vary`, the output would be a nearly perfect sinewave, in fact. Adding `vary` means that the data will look more like the real world with little variations in the data points. Setting the `np.random.seed()` value ensures that the random values provided by `vary` remain the same for each test.

You can simulate underfitting by using a linear regression, as discussed in Book 3, Chapter 1. For this example, the degree of polynomial fitting provided by `polyfit()` as described at `https://docs.scipy.org/doc/numpy/reference/generated/numpy.polyfit.html` becomes important. A linear regression uses a single degree of polynomial fitting, as shown in the following code:

```
plt.scatter(x, y)

z = np.polyfit(x, y, 1)
p = np.poly1d(z)
print(p)

plt.plot(x, p(x), 'g-')
plt.legend(['Model', 'Data'])
plt.show()
```

Figure 3-1 shows the output of this example. Notice that the line charges straight through the data, so any analysis would be accurate only where the model happens to cross the data, which is only two points in the range.

Examination of `p` shows that the model does indeed use only one degree of fitting:

```
0.0005854 x + 0.7309
```

When your model isn't complex enough, it won't fit your data properly, and you end up with inaccuracy rather than something useful.

Looking at overfitting

Overfitting means that the model fits the data too closely, so the model is unlikely to work with any new data you provide. The data developed in the previous section can also work to demonstrate overfitting. In fact, all you really need to do is add degrees of polynomial fitting, as shown in the following code:

```
plt.scatter(x, y)

z = np.polyfit(x, y, 18)
p = np.poly1d(z)
print(p)

plt.plot(x, p(x), 'g-')
plt.legend(['Model', 'Data'])
plt.show()
```

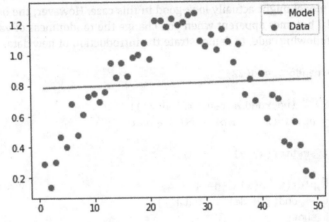

FIGURE 3-1:
Underfitting is the result of using a model that isn't complex enough.

In this case, you use 18 degrees of polynomial fitting. Printing p demonstrates this fact:

```
        18              17             16             15             14
1.44e-22 x-6.054e-20 x+1.17e-17 x-1.379e-15 x+1.109e-13 x
            13             12             11             10
 - 6.465e-12 x+2.826e-10 x-9.461e-09 x+2.458e-07 x
         9              8              7              6              5
 - 4.99e-06 x+7.923e-05 x-0.0009799 x+0.00935 x-0.06763 x
         4        3        2
 + 0.3602 x-1.346 x+3.247 x-4.253 x+2.339
```

The graphic output of the example differs considerably, too. Figure 3-2 shows the results of overfitting against the data for which the model is created.

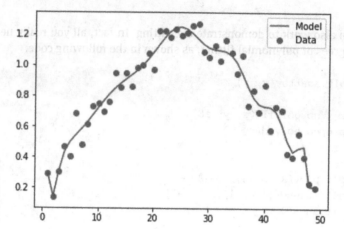

FIGURE 3-2:
Overfitting causes
the model to
follow the data
too closely.

WARNING

The model might actually look good in this case. However, the brittleness of this model becomes apparent when you change the randomness of vary, as shown in the following code, to demonstrate the introduction of new data.

```
np.random.seed(22)

vary = (np.random.random(len(x))) / 3
y = np.sin(x * np.pi / 50.) + vary

plt.scatter(x, y)

plt.plot(x, p(x), 'g-')
plt.legend(['Model', 'Data'])
plt.show()
```

The new output, shown in Figure 3-3, introduces all sorts of possible prediction errors. The problem with overfitting becomes evident in this case.

Plotting learning curves for insights

This chapter contains a number of examples of using algorithms and plots to see where problems may lie in data. Of course, nothing is guaranteed to work all the time, so you need to apply the correct algorithm to gain the insights you need. The examples in the previous sections demonstrate that you also need to experiment with the configuration of the algorithm — that is, experiment with how it performs its work. The following code shows what happens when you tune the degrees of polynomial fitting:

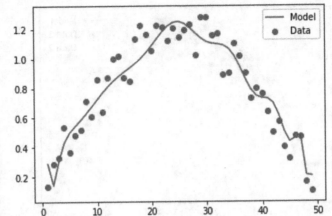

FIGURE 3-3:
Applying the
model to slightly
different data
shows the
problem with
overfitting in
more detail.

```
np.random.seed(51)

x = np.array(range(1, 50))
vary = (np.random.random(len(x))) / 3
y = np.sin(x * np.pi / 50.) + vary
plt.scatter(x, y)

z = np.polyfit(x, y, 2)
p = np.poly1d(z)
plt.plot(x, p(x), 'g-')

np.random.seed(22)
vary = (np.random.random(len(x))) / 3
y = np.sin(x * np.pi / 50.) + vary
plt.scatter(x, y)

plt.legend(['Model', 'Data 1', 'Data 2'])
plt.show()
```

REMEMBER

The output shown in Figure 3-4 demonstrates that the model runs through the middle of both datasets with enough accuracy for you to perform predictions with some level of accuracy. However, the more important point is that this example also demonstrates the need to experiment with the algorithms at your disposal and the arguments they provide to create a useful model.

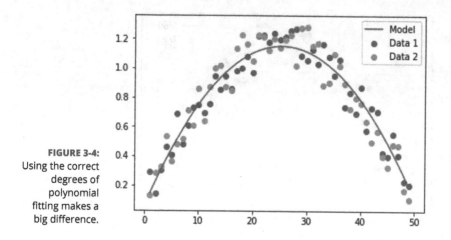

FIGURE 3-4:
Using the correct
degrees of
polynomial
fitting makes a
big difference.

Determining the Sources of Overfitting and Underfitting

Merely knowing the causes of overfitting and underfitting isn't sufficient because the causes have a source that you must deal with in order to obtain the desired algorithmic output. For example, when you experience bias or variance, you need to look at the formulation of your model. The following sections help you understand the sources of overfitting and underfitting better.

NO SILVER BULLET IN ANALYSIS

You can see thousands of message threads on various forums online where someone is looking to solve a particular data problem precisely and completely. However, in reviewing the material in this book, you often encounter terms like *confidence level* (how well an algorithm can predict an outcome) that would seem to say that you can only partly achieve your goal of perfection. This chapter considers the matter of overfitting and underfitting, but it comes with a caveat: You can't really achieve perfection in this area because the data will change over time and the methods used to model data aren't perfect. What you really end up with is a solution that works within a particular margin of error, not perfection. Driving yourself crazy trying to find perfection will only frustrate you and keep your project from completing on time. So, part of the hidden fix for the issues surrounding data analysis is deciding when the solution works well enough to meet your needs.

Understanding bias and variance

If your chosen learning algorithm can't learn properly from data and is not performing well, the cause is bias or variance in its estimates.

>> **Bias:** Given the simplicity of a formulation, your algorithm tends to overestimate or underestimate the real rules behind the data and is systematically wrong in certain situations. Simple algorithms have high bias; having few internal parameters, they tend to represent only simple formulations well.

>> **Variance:** Given the complexity of a formulation, your algorithm tends to learn too much information from the data and detects rules that don't exist, which causes its predictions to be erratic when faced with new data. You can think of variance as a problem connected to memorization. Complex algorithms can memorize data features thanks to the algorithm's high number of internal parameters. However, memorization doesn't imply any understanding about the rules.

Bias and variance depend on the complexity of the formulation at the core of the learning algorithm with respect to the complexity of the formulation that is presumed to have generated the data you are observing. However, when you consider a specific problem using the available data rules, you're better off having high bias or variance when

>> **You have few observations:** Simpler algorithms perform better, no matter what the unknown function is. Complex algorithms tend to learn too much from data, causing inaccurate estimates.

>> **You have many observations:** Complex algorithms always reduce variance. The reduction occurs because even complex algorithms can't learn all that much from data, so they learn just the rules, not any erratic noise.

>> **You have many variables:** Provided that you also have many observations, simpler algorithms tend to find a way to approximate even complex hidden functions.

Having insufficient data

If you only have one data point, predicting the next data point is impossible (unless you're incredibly lucky). When you have two data points, predictions work only when the next data point happens to be in a straight line with the other two. Breaking the problem down this way makes it obvious that more data is better. Each additional data point you add can increase the accuracy of the prediction because you provide more data that the algorithm uses to learn.

Insufficient data tends to make your model underfit. The effect of insufficient data is that the model you create is inaccurate because it hasn't learned enough about the data. Without enough data points, you can't use something like least squares to create a model that accurately reflects the trend of the data. (Book 3, Chapter 1 describes how linear regression uses the least squares method.)

Being fooled by data leakage

Data leakage is defined as the creation of unexpected additional information in your data (most especially training data, when you split your dataset into training and testing sets), allowing a model or machine learning algorithm to make unrealistically good predictions. Normally, this additional data isn't available to the model in the real world, so introducing it into the training process causes the learning process to fail; the model learns incorrectly. Here are some common causes of data leakage:

» **Preprocessing:** The data is preprocessed in such a manner that it becomes skewed in an unrealistic way. For example, if you apply transformations to your training set, but also include the test set as part of the transformation, data will leak from the test set to the training set. Any transformations you apply should appear as part of the training set alone.

» **Duplicates:** The existence of the same data point, even from different observations, in both the training set and the test set could cause the model to fixate on that data point. Removing duplicates so that the training set and test set contain unique data points is essential.

» **Temporal information:** Data is especially prone to leakage when it relies on time because the variation of data over time tends to follow patterns that may not reflect reality in general. The best way to avoid this problem is to ensure that the training set and the test set contain a mix of data points across the entire time frame used for data collection.

Guessing the Right Features

Ensuring that you have the right *features*, which means the properties used to perform an analysis, is essential. The features determine what the algorithm considers when performing its analysis. Without the right information, the algorithm can't perform its task. The following sections discuss how to obtain and use the right features in your analysis.

Selecting variables like a pro

Selecting the right variables can improve the learning process by reducing the amount of noise (useless information) that can influence the learner's estimates. Variable selection, therefore, can effectively reduce the variance of predictions. In order to involve just the useful variables in training and leave out the redundant ones, you can use these techniques:

>> **Univariate approach:** Select the variables most related to the target outcome.

>> **Greedy or backward approach:** Keep only the variables that you can remove from the learning process without damaging its performance.

This example relies on the Boston dataset. The following code imports the dataset so that it's available for use:

```
from sklearn.datasets import load_boston
from sklearn.preprocessing import import scale
from sklearn.metrics import mean_squared_error

boston = load_boston()
X = scale(boston.data)
y = boston.target
```

Selecting by univariate measures

If you decide to select a variable by its level of association with its target, the class `SelectPercentile` provides an automatic procedure for keeping only a certain percentage of the best, associated features. The available metrics for association are

>> `f_regression`: Used only for numeric targets and based on linear regression performance

>> `f_classif`: Used only for categorical targets and based on the Analysis of Variance (ANOVA) statistical test

>> `chi2`: Performs the chi-square statistic for categorical targets, which is less sensitive to the nonlinear relationship between the predictive variable and its target

TIP

When evaluating candidates for a classification problem, `f_classif` and `chi2` tend to provide the same set of top variables. It's still a good practice to test the selections from both the association metrics.

Apart from applying a direct selection of the top percentile associations, Select-Percentile can also rank the best variables to make it easier to decide at what percentile to exclude a feature from participating in the learning process. The class SelectKBest is analogous in its functionality, but it selects the top k variables, where k is a number, not a percentile.

```
from sklearn.feature_selection import SelectPercentile
from sklearn.feature_selection import f_regression
Selector_f = SelectPercentile(f_regression, percentile=25)
Selector_f.fit(X, y)
for n,s in zip(boston.feature_names,Selector_f.scores_):
    print('F-score: %3.2f\t for feature %s ' % (s,n))
```

After a few iterations, the code prints the following results (your precise scores may differ from those shown):

```
F-score: 88.15      for feature CRIM
F-score: 75.26      for feature ZN
F-score: 153.95     for feature INDUS
F-score: 15.97      for feature CHAS
F-score: 112.59     for feature NOX
F-score: 471.85     for feature RM
F-score: 83.48      for feature AGE
F-score: 33.58      for feature DIS
F-score: 85.91      for feature RAD
F-score: 141.76     for feature TAX
F-score: 175.11     for feature PTRATIO
F-score: 63.05      for feature B
F-score: 601.62     for feature LSTAT
```

Using the level of association output (higher values signal more association of a feature with the target variable) helps you to choose the most important variables for your model, but you should watch out for these possible problems:

» Some variables with high association could also be highly correlated, introducing duplicated information, which acts as noise in the learning process.

» Some variables may be penalized, especially binary ones (variables indicating a status or characteristic using the value 1 when it is present, 0 when it is not). For example, notice that the output shows the binary variable CHAS as the least associated with the target variable (but you know from previous examples that it's influential during the cross-validation phase).

TIP

The univariate selection process can give you a real advantage when you have a huge number of variables to select from and all other methods turn computationally infeasible. The best procedure is to reduce the value of `SelectPercentile` by half or more of the available variables, reduce the number of variables to a manageable number, and consequently allow the use of a more sophisticated and more precise method, such as a greedy selection.

Using a greedy search

When using a univariate selection, you have to decide for yourself how many variables to keep: Greedy selection automatically reduces the number of features involved in a learning model on the basis of their effective contribution to the performance measured by the error measure.

The Boston dataset contains more than 500 observations and 13 features. The target is a price measure, so you decide to use linear regression to perform your analysis and to optimize the result using the mean squared error. The objective is to ensure that a linear regression is a good model for analyzing the Boston dataset and to quantify how good the analysis result is using the mean squared error (which lets you compare it with alternative models).

```
from sklearn.linear_model import LinearRegression
regression = LinearRegression()
regression.fit(X,y)
print('Mean squared error: %.2f' % mean_squared_error(
    y_true=y, y_pred=regression.predict(X)))
```

The output from this code is

```
Mean squared error: 21.89
```

The RFECV class, after fitting the data, can do the following:

>> Give information about the number of useful features

>> Point these features out to you

>> Automatically transform the X data into a reduced variable set

as shown in the following example:

```
from sklearn.feature_selection import RFECV
selector = RFECV(estimator=regression,
                 cv=10,
                 scoring='neg_mean_squared_error')
```

```
selector.fit(X, y)
print("Optimal number of features : %d"
      % selector.n_features_)
```

The example outputs an optimal number of features for the problem:

```
Optimal number of features: 6
```

Obtaining an index to the optimum variable set is possible by calling the attribute `support_` from the RFECV class after you fit it:

```
print(boston.feature_names[selector.support_])
```

The command will print the list containing the features:

```
['CHAS' 'NOX' 'RM' 'DIS' 'PTRATIO' 'LSTAT']
```

Notice that CHAS is now included among the most predictive features, which contrasts with the result from the univariate search in the previous section. The RFECV method can detect whether a variable is important, no matter whether it is binary, categorical, or numeric, because it directly evaluates the role played by the feature in the prediction.

REMEMBER

The RFECV method is certainly more efficient, when compared to the univariate approach, because it considers highly correlated features and is tuned to optimize the evaluation measure (which usually is not Chi-square or F-score). Being a greedy process, it's somehow computationally demanding and may only approximate the best set of predictors.

TIP

As RFECV learns the best set of variables from data, the selection may overfit, which is what happens with all other machine learning algorithms. Trying RFECV on different samples of the training data can confirm the best variables to use.

Using nonlinear transformations

Linear models, such as linear and logistic regression, are actually linear combinations that sum your features (weighted by learned coefficients) and provide a simple but effective model. In most situations, they offer a good approximation of the complex reality they represent. Even though they're characterized by a high bias, using a large number of observations can improve their coefficients and make them more competitive when compared to complex algorithms.

However, they can perform better when solving certain problems if you pre-analyze the data using the Exploratory Data Analysis (EDA) approach. After performing the analysis, you can transform and enrich the existing features by:

» Linearizing the relationships between features and the target variable using transformations that increase their correlation and make their point cloud in the scatterplot more similar to a line (see https://whatis.techtarget.com/definition/point-cloud for details on how point clouds work).

» Making variables interact by multiplying them so that you can better represent their conjoint behavior.

» Expanding the existing variables using the polynomial expansion in order to represent relationships more realistically (such as ideal point curves, when there is a peak in the variable representing a maximum, akin to a parabola).

Doing variable transformations

An example is the best way to explain the kind of transformations you can successfully apply to data to improve a linear model. The example in this section, and the "Regularizing linear models" section that follows, relies on the Boston dataset. The problem relies on regression, and the data originally has ten variables to explain the different housing prices in Boston during the 1970s. The dataset also has implicit ordering. Fortunately, order doesn't influence most algorithms because they learn the data as a whole. When an algorithm learns in a progressive manner, ordering can interfere with effective model building. By using seed (to fix a preordinated sequence of random numbers) and shuffle from the random package (to shuffle the index), you can reindex the dataset.

```
import random
from random import shuffle

random.seed(0) # Creates a replicable shuffling
new_index = list(range(boston.data.shape[0]))
shuffle(new_index) # shuffling the index
X, y = boston.data[new_index], boston.target[new_index]
print(X.shape, y.shape, boston.feature_names)
```

In the code, random.seed(0) creates a replicable shuffling operation, and shuffle(new_index) creates the new shuffled index used to reorder the data. After that, the code prints the X and y shapes as well as the list of dataset variable names:

```
(506, 13) (506,) ['CRIM' 'ZN' 'INDUS' 'CHAS' 'NOX' 'RM'
 'AGE' 'DIS' 'RAD' 'TAX' 'PTRATIO'  'B' 'LSTAT']
```

TIP

You can find out more detail about the meaning of the variables present in the Boston dataset by issuing the following command: `print(boston.DESCR)`. You see the output of this command in the downloadable source code.

Converting the array of predictors and the target variable into a pandas DataFrame helps support the series of explorations and operations on data. Moreover, although Scikit-learn requires an ndarray as input, it will also accept DataFrame objects:

```
import pandas as pd
df = pd.DataFrame(X,columns=boston.feature_names)
df['target'] = y
```

The best way to spot possible transformations is by graphical exploration, and using a scatterplot can tell you a lot about two variables. You need to make the relationship between the predictors and the target outcome as linear as possible, so you should try various combinations, such as the following:

```
ax = df.plot(kind='scatter', x='LSTAT', y='target', c='b')
```

In Figure 3-5, you see a representation of the resulting scatterplot. Notice that you can approximate the cloud of points by using a curved line rather than a straight line. In particular, when LSTAT is around 5, the target seems to vary between values of 20 to 50. As LSTAT increases, the target decreases to 10, reducing the variation.

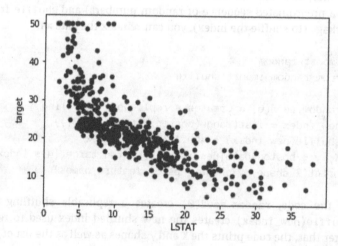

FIGURE 3-5:
Nonlinear
relationship
between variable
LSTAT and
target prices.

Logarithmic transformation can help in such conditions. However, your values, such as percentages, should range from zero to one, as demonstrated in this example. In other cases, other useful transformations for your x variable could include x**2, x**3, 1/x, 1/x**2, 1/x**3, and sqrt(x). The key is to try them and test the result. As for testing, you can use the following script as an example:

```
single_variable = df['LSTAT'].values.reshape(-1, 1)
F, pval = f_regression(single_variable, y)
print('F score for the original feature %.1f' % F)
F, pval = f_regression(np.log(single_variable),y)
print('F score for the transformed feature %.1f' % F)
```

The code prints the F score, a measure to evaluate how a feature is predictive in a machine learning problem, both the original and the transformed feature. The score for the transformed feature is a great improvement over the untransformed one.

```
F score for the original feature 601.6
F score for the transformed feature 1000.2
```

The F score is useful for variable selection. You can also use it to assess the usefulness of a transformation because both f_regression and f_classif are themselves based on linear models, and are therefore sensitive to every effective transformation used to make variable relationships more linear.

Creating interactions between variables

In a linear combination, the model reacts to how a variable changes in an independent way with respect to changes in the other variables. In statistics, this kind of model is a *main effects* model.

REMEMBER

The Naïve Bayes classifier makes a similar assumption for probabilities; also, it works well with complex text problems.

Even though machine learning works by using approximations, and a set of independent variables can make your predictions work well in most situations, sometimes you may miss an important part of the picture. You can easily catch this problem by depicting the variation in your target associated with the conjoint variation of two or more variables in two simple and straightforward ways:

>> **Existing domain knowledge of the problem:** For instance, in the car market, having a noisy engine is a nuisance in a family car but considered a plus for sports cars. (Car aficionados want to hear that you have an ultra-cool and expensive car.) By knowing a consumer preference, you can model a noise

level variable and a car-type variable together to obtain exact predictions using a predictive analytic model that guesses the car's value based on its features.

>> **Testing combinations of different variables:** By performing group tests, you can see the effect that certain variables have on your target variable. Therefore, even without knowing about noisy engines and sports cars, you could have caught a different average of preference level when analyzing your dataset split by type of cars and noise level.

The following example shows how to test and detect interactions in the Boston dataset. The first task is to load a few helper classes, as shown here:

```
from sklearn.model_selection import cross_val_score, KFold
regression = LinearRegression(normalize=True)
crossvalidation = KFold(n_splits=10, shuffle=True,
                        random_state=1)
```

The code reinitializes the pandas DataFrame using only the predictor variables. A for loop matches the different predictors and creates a new variable containing each interaction. The mathematical formulation of an interaction is simply a multiplication.

```
df = pd.DataFrame(X,columns=boston.feature_names)
baseline = np.mean(cross_val_score(regression, df, y,
                                   scoring='r2',
                                   cv=crossvalidation))
interactions = list()
for var_A in boston.feature_names:
    for var_B in boston.feature_names:
        if var_A > var_B:
            df['interaction'] = df[var_A] * df[var_B]
            cv = cross_val_score(regression, df, y,
                                 scoring='r2',
                                 cv=crossvalidation)
            score = round(np.mean(cv), 3)
            if score > baseline:
                interactions.append((var_A, var_B, score))
print('Baseline R2: %.3f' % baseline)
print('Top 10 interactions: %s' % sorted(interactions,
                                 key=lambda x :x[2],
                                 reverse=True)[:10])
```

The code starts by printing the baseline R² score for the regression; then it reports the top ten interactions whose addition to the mode increases the score:

```
Baseline R2: 0.716
Top 10 interactions: [('RM', 'LSTAT', 0.79), ('TAX', 'RM',
  0.782), ('RM', 'RAD', 0.778), ('RM', 'PTRATIO', 0.766),
  ('RM', 'INDUS', 0.76), ('RM', 'NOX', 0.747), ('RM',
  'AGE', 0.742), ('RM', 'B', 0.738), ('RM', 'DIS', 0.736),
  ('ZN', 'RM', 0.73)]
```

The code tests the specific addition of each interaction to the model using a 10 folds cross-validation. The code records the change in the R² measure into a stack (a simple list) that an application can order and explore later.

The baseline score is 0.699, so a reported improvement of the stack of interactions to 0.782 looks quite impressive. It's important to know how this improvement is made possible. The two variables involved are RM (the average number of rooms) and LSTAT (the percentage of lower-status population). A plot will disclose the case about these two variables:

```
colors = ['b' if v > np.mean(y) else 'r' for v in y]
scatter = df.plot(kind='scatter', x='RM', y='LSTAT',
                  c=colors)
```

The scatterplot in Figure 3-6 clarifies the improvement. In a portion of houses at the center of the plot, you need to know both LSTAT and RM to correctly separate the high-value houses from the low-value houses; therefore, an interaction is indispensable in this case.

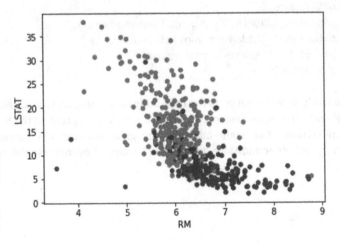

FIGURE 3-6: Combined variables LSTAT and RM help to separate high from low prices.

Adding interactions and transformed variables leads to an extended linear regression model, a polynomial regression. Data scientists rely on testing and experimenting to validate an approach to solving a problem, so the following code slightly modifies the previous code to redefine the set of predictors using interactions and quadratic terms by squaring the variables:

```
polyX = pd.DataFrame(X,columns=boston.feature_names)
cv = cross_val_score(regression, polyX, y,
                        scoring='neg_mean_squared_error',
                        cv=crossvalidation)
baseline = np.mean(cv)
improvements = [baseline]
for var_A in boston.feature_names:
    polyX[var_A+'^2'] = polyX[var_A]**2
    cv = cross_val_score(regression, polyX, y,
                        scoring='neg_mean_squared_error',
                        cv=crossvalidation)
    improvements.append(np.mean(cv))
    for var_B in boston.feature_names:
        if var_A > var_B:
            poly_var = var_A + '*' + var_B
            polyX[poly_var] = polyX[var_A] * polyX[var_B]
            cv = cross_val_score(regression, polyX, y,
                        scoring='neg_mean_squared_error',
                        cv=crossvalidation)
            improvements.append(np.mean(cv))
```

This bit of code plots the results for you:

```
plt.figure()
plt.plot(range(0,92),np.abs(improvements),'-')
plt.xlabel('Added polynomial features')
plt.ylabel('Mean squared error')
plt.show()
```

To track improvements as the code adds new, complex terms, the example places values in the improvements list. Figure 3-7 shows a graph of the results. The graph demonstrates that some additions are great because they decrease the squared error, and other additions are terrible because they increase the error instead.

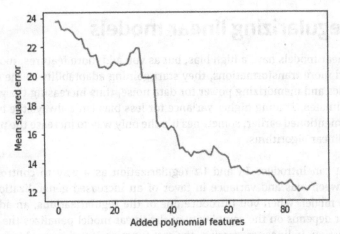

FIGURE 3-7:
Adding
polynomial
features
increases the
predictive
power.

Of course, instead of unconditionally adding all the generated variables, you could perform an ongoing test before deciding to add a quadratic term or an interaction, checking by cross-validation to see whether each addition is really useful for your predictive purposes. This example is a good foundation for checking other ways of controlling the existing complexity of your datasets or the complexity that you have to induce with transformation and feature creation in the course of data-exploration efforts. Before moving on, you check both the shape of the actual dataset and its cross-validated mean squared error:

```
print('New shape of X:', np.shape(polyX))
crossvalidation = KFold(n_splits=10, shuffle=True,
                        random_state=1)
cv = cross_val_score(regression, polyX, y,
                     scoring='neg_mean_squared_error',
                     cv=crossvalidation)
print('Mean squared error: %.3f' % abs(np.mean(cv)))
```

Even though the mean squared error is good, the ratio between 506 observations and 104 features isn't all that good because the number of observations may not be enough for a correct estimate of the coefficients.

```
New shape of X: (506, 104)
Mean squared error: 12.514
```

TIP

As a rule of thumb, divide the number of observations by the number of coefficients. The code should have at least 10 to 20 observations for every coefficient you want to estimate in linear models. However, experience shows that having at least 30 of them is better.

Regularizing linear models

Linear models have a high bias, but as you add more features, more interactions, and more transformations, they start gaining adaptability to the data characteristics and memorizing power for data noise, thus increasing the variance of their estimates. Trading higher variance for less bias isn't always the best choice, but, as mentioned earlier, sometimes it's the only way to increase the predictive power of linear algorithms.

You can introduce L1 and L2 regularization as a way to control the trade-off between bias and variance in favor of an increased generalization capability of the model. When you introduce one of the regularizations, an additive function that depends on the complexity of the linear model penalizes the optimized cost function. In linear regression, the cost function is the squared error of the predictions, and the cost function is penalized using a summation of the coefficients of the predictor variables.

If the model is complex but the predictive gain is little, the penalization forces the optimization procedure to remove the useless variables, or to reduce their impact on the estimate. The regularization also acts on highly correlated features — attenuating or excluding their contribution, thus stabilizing the results and reducing the consequent variance of the estimates:

>> **L1 (also called Lasso):** Shrinks some coefficients to zero, making your coefficients sparse. It performs variable selection.

>> **L2 (also called Ridge):** Reduces the coefficients of the most problematic features, making them smaller, but seldom equal to zero. All coefficients keep participating in the estimate, but many become small and irrelevant.

REMEMBER

You can control the strength of the regularization using a hyperparameter, usually a coefficient itself, often called `alpha`. When alpha approaches 1.0, you have stronger regularization and a greater reduction of the coefficients. In some cases, the coefficients are reduced to zero. Don't confuse `alpha` with `C`, a parameter used by `LogisticRegression` and by support vector machines, because `C` is `1/alpha`, so it can be greater than 1. Smaller `C` numbers actually correspond to more regularization, exactly the opposite of `alpha`.

TIP

Regularization works because it is the sum of the coefficients of the predictor variables; therefore they need to be on the same scale or the regularization may find it difficult to converge, and variables with larger absolute coefficient values will greatly influence it, generating an infective regularization. It's good practice to standardize the predictor values or bind them to a common min-max, such as the [-1,+1] range. The following sections demonstrate various methods of using both L1 and L2 regularization to achieve various effects.

Relying on Ridge regression (L2)

The first example uses the L2 type regularization, reducing the strength of the coefficients. The Ridge class implements L2 for linear regression. Its usage is simple; it presents just the parameter alpha to fix. Ridge also has another parameter, normalize, that automatically normalizes the inputted predictors to zero mean and unit variance.

```
from sklearn.model_selection import GridSearchCV
from sklearn.linear_model import Ridge
ridge = Ridge(normalize=True)
search_grid = {'alpha':np.logspace(-5,2,8)}
search = GridSearchCV(estimator=ridge,
                      param_grid=search_grid,
                      scoring='neg_mean_squared_error',
                      refit=True, cv=10, iid=False)
search.fit(polyX,y)
print('Best parameters: %s' % search.best_params_)
score = abs(search.best_score_)
print('CV MSE of best parameters: %.3f' % score)
```

After searching for the best alpha parameter, the resulting best model is

```
Best parameters: {'alpha': 0.001}
CV MSE of best parameters: 11.630
```

TIP

A good search space for the alpha value is in the range np.logspace(-5,2,8). Of course, if the resulting optimum value is on one of the extremities of the tested range, you need to enlarge the range and retest.

REMEMBER

The polyX and y variables used for the examples in this section and the sections that follow are created as part of the example in the "Creating interactions between variables" section, earlier in this chapter. If you haven't worked through that section, the examples in this section will fail to work properly.

Using the Lasso (L1)

The second example uses the L1 regularization, the Lasso class, whose principal characteristic is to reduce the effect of less useful coefficients down toward zero. This action enforces sparsity in the coefficients, with just a few having values above zero. The class uses the same parameters of the Ridge class that are demonstrated in the previous section.

```
from sklearn.linear_model import Lasso
lasso = Lasso(normalize=True,tol=0.05, selection='random')
```

Dealing with Model
Overfitting and Underfitting

```
search_grid = {'alpha':np.logspace(-2,3,8)}
search = GridSearchCV(estimator=lasso,
                      param_grid=search_grid,
                      scoring='neg_mean_squared_error',
                      refit=True, cv=10, iid=False)
search.fit(polyX,y)
print('Best parameters: %s' % search.best_params_)
score = abs(search.best_score_)
print('CV MSE of best parameters: %.3f' % score)
```

In setting the `Lasso`, the code uses a less sensitive algorithm (`tol=0.05`) and a random approach for its optimization (`selection='random'`). The resulting mean squared error obtained is higher than it is using the L2 regularization:

```
Best parameters: {'alpha': 0.01}
CV MSE of best parameters: 20.406
```

Leveraging regularization

Because you can indent the sparse coefficients resulting from a L1 regression as a feature selection procedure, you can effectively use the `Lasso` class for selecting the most important variables. By tuning the alpha parameter, you can select a greater or lesser number of variables. In this case, the code sets the `alpha` parameter to 0.01, obtaining a much simplified solution as a result:

```
lasso = Lasso(normalize=True, alpha=0.01)
lasso.fit(polyX,y)
print(polyX.columns[np.abs(lasso.coef_)>0.0001].values)
```

The simplified solution is made of a handful of interactions:

```
['CRIM*CHAS' 'ZN*CRIM' 'ZN*CHAS' 'INDUS*DIS' 'CHAS*B'
 'NOX^2' 'NOX*DIS' 'RM^2' 'RM*CRIM' 'RM*NOX' 'RM*PTRATIO'
 'RM*B' 'RM*LSTAT' 'RAD*B' 'TAX*DIS' 'PTRATIO*NOX'
 'LSTAT^2']
```

TIP

You can apply L1-based variable selection automatically to both regression and classification using the `RandomizedLasso` and `RandomizedLogisticRegression` classes. Both classes create a series of randomized L1 regularized models. The code keeps track of the resulting coefficients. At the end of the process, the application keeps any coefficients that the class didn't reduce to zero because they're considered important. You can train the two classes using the `fit` method, but they don't have a predict method; instead, they have just a transform method that effectively reduces your dataset, as is true of most classes in the sklearn.preprocessing module.

Combining L1 & L2: Elasticnet

L2 regularization reduces the impact of correlated features, whereas L1 regularization tends to select them. A good strategy is to mix them using a weighted sum by using the ElasticNet class. You control both L1 and L2 effects by using the same alpha parameter, but you can decide the L1 effect's share by using the l1_ratio parameter. Clearly, if l1_ratio is 0, you have a Ridge regression; on the other hand, when l1_ratio is 1, you have a Lasso.

```
from sklearn.linear_model import ElasticNet
elastic = ElasticNet(normalize=True, selection='random')
search_grid = {'alpha':np.logspace(-4,3,8),
               'l1_ratio': [0.10 ,0.25, 0.5, 0.75]}
search = GridSearchCV(estimator=elastic,
                      param_grid=search_grid,
                      scoring='neg_mean_squared_error',
                      refit=True, cv=10, iid=False)
search.fit(polyX,y)
print('Best parameters: %s' % search.best_params_)
score = abs(search.best_score_)
print('CV MSE of best parameters: %.3f' % score)
```

After a while, you get a result that's quite comparable to L1's:

```
Best parameters: {'alpha': 0.0001, 'l1_ratio': 0.75}
CV MSE of best parameters: 12.581
```

Chapter 4

Obtaining the Correct Output Presentation

Throughout this book, you discover methods for obtaining, cleaning, and analyzing data using a wide variety of techniques. Oddly enough, data scientists spend most of their time cleaning the data (see https://www.analyticsindiamag.com/6-tasks-data-scientists-spend-the-most-time-doing/ for details). The next most common task is simply obtaining the data. Yet, all this effort doesn't amount to anything if no one can understand the results. Other data scientists are likely to understand, but you must work with people who don't have six degrees in math, two in computer science, and another in logic. Consequently, simply generating output that depicts the results of your efforts isn't enough; you must generate output that speaks to the viewer, which is the first consideration in this chapter.

In some respects, you become a detective when it comes to output, because what you really need is a profile of the people who will look at the output you create. If you don't understand the needs of the people who view your analysis, you won't ever create useful output for them. The problem is that people differ widely around the world with regard to what they expect given their occupation, environment, and cultural norms, among many other factors. So, no boxed solution exists to address the problem of how to present your output in a manner that others will understand. You must prepare a profile, which is the purpose of the second part of this chapter.

Just like everyone else, data scientists get stuck in a rut. If you view examples online, you find that most of them use scatterplots, followed by line graphs. In some cases, you find rare examples of histograms or boxplots, depending on the skill of the data scientist. Fortunately, you have many other options at your disposal, and the third section of this chapter explores only a few of them.

Oddly enough, in a world filled with emoji and many other assorted graphic presentations, the data analyses provided in most of the examples you see online are devoid of any sort of decoration. Most of them are outright bland to the point of making you somnolent. The last section of this chapter addresses the use of external data, such as graphics, to add a bit of pizzazz to your presentation.

REMEMBER

You don't have to type the source code for this chapter manually. In fact, using the downloadable source is a lot easier. The source code for this chapter appears in the DSPD_0604_Presentation.ipynb source code file for Python and the DSPD_R_0604_Presentation.ipynb source code file for R. See the Introduction for details on how to find these source files.

Considering the Meaning of Correct

The term *correct* is a loaded one. In fact, most terms are loaded because each could mean something different to every person reading this text. What is correct to one person can be incorrect to another based on a wealth of qualifiers, such as:

>> Bias

>> Experience

>> Environment

>> Personal knowledge

>> Technological changes

>> World events

In fact, it wouldn't take long to compile a long enough list of qualifiers to make any discussion of correctness meaningless. However, at some point you must decide that a particular output presentation is correct. The next section of this chapter discusses what the presentation must contain to be correct. However, the presentation alone doesn't determine correctness overall.

REMEMBER

A good starting point for ensuring that the output of your analysis contains the fewest possible mistruths is to use the material from the "Considering the Five Mistruths in Data" section of Chapter 2 of this minibook. The fact that your output is believable will make it more correct as well. However, the essential characteristic of data you have vetted and manicured for the highest level of truthfulness is that you also believe in that data, which in turn makes you, as a person, more believable.

The fit and finish of your output also matters. Ensuring that you use the correct kind of graphic output is essential because some types of graphic output can actually obscure the point you want to make, thereby making it less correct. Adding various kinds of graphics and other external data is important because it helps you draw a parallel between the abstract data in your presentation and the physical world.

The issue of correctness is also personal. Always remember that the correctness you perceive may appear as incorrectness to someone else, so getting a second, third, or fourth opinion is helpful, too. Of course, presentation by committee leads to the muddying of your presentation, also making it less correct. The clarity of the vision of an individual augmented by insights provided by a small number of others generally results in a presentation that is correct from a number of perspectives, but remains focused.

Determining a Presentation Type

The presentation of your analysis output is how it appears to others. Of course, how they see it depends on their point of view. If you ask any number of people to look at a painting of nearly anything in nearly any style, each person will likely see something slightly different. The painting doesn't change; the perspective of the person does. Consequently, the presentation of the output of an analysis matters and is one of the determining factors in conveying information to others in an unambiguous manner.

Considering the audience

One of the most difficult and confounding aspects of creating a presentation is frame of reference. Your audience has

>> Had certain experiences

>> Obtained a particular level of education

>> Engaged in a particular set of jobs

>> A need for specific kinds of information

The inability for various groups to communicate stems from the lack of a frame of reference between them. Part of your task is to try to see things from the perspective of your audience, which may feel uncomfortable but is a requirement if you want to communicate your ideas and the results of your analysis.

TIP

Avoid using stereotypes to define your audience. Even seasoned presenters fall flat when sizing up an audience incorrectly. One audience may have certain characteristics in common with other audiences, but each audience is unique in one or more ways. It's important to consider these differences whether your method of presentation is in person, through writing, or by various means online.

Defining a depth of detail

As a data scientist, you may find that you like to see all the details. In fact, you might be downright exuberant about details and find them fascinating. Not every audience wants details, however. You may have encountered a manager who felt that a presentation was mired in unnecessary detail. All the manager needed was an overview. The manager hired others to deal with the details, but needed just an overview to get the big picture as part of running a large business. If your audience doesn't not need detailed information, that fact affects everything from the amount of data you provide to the kind of graphics you choose.

Another issue to consider is that when an audience does need detail, the details may reflect specific needs. The audience might not need to know about the raw data but may instead need only to look at specific areas of the manicured data you provide. In fact, you may find that you have to research particular areas to provide more detail than needed to perform your analysis. A particular presentation may require that you provide historical information with the data. You don't need the historical information to perform the analysis, but your audience needs it to make sense of the data.

TIP

When considering the depth of detail for a presentation, look at other successful reports, videos, or oral presentations for the same group. You know when a source is successful because people talk about it, and you see it cited in still other reports. Look for the buzz factor when thinking about depth of detail because anyone can get friends to provide positive reviews, but no one can generate buzz as an act of will.

Ensuring that the data is consistent with audience needs

The attention span of your audience is likely short. In fact, according to the info-graphic at `https://www.digitalinformationworld.com/2018/09/the-human-attention-span-infographic.html`, humans now have a shorter attention span than goldfish. Consequently, you may have as little as nine seconds before your audience assumes a blank expression and enters its own little world, which does-n't include you or your data. To keep your audience from becoming comatose, you need to provide data that the audience wants and needs:

» **Wants:** Has a strong desire to obtain, even when the data isn't needed, usually because the information has become popular. People's wants change so fast that you may get dizzy tracking them.

» **Needs:** Required to perform tasks or to discover something new related to an occupation or activity. The audience may not recognize a need, especially when a need isn't popular. You know when you've been successful because the audience will suddenly experience that lightbulb moment when the need becomes clear. Needs tend to change slowly.

TIP

You likely used an immense database to perform your analysis, and if you pres-ent all of it, your audience will go from comatose to somnolent to fully asleep. By drawing up a list of wants and needs for this particular audience, you can whittle the data down to a manageable size. The important thing is to focus on just a few of these wants and needs based on what you know about your audience. Remem-ber that you need to grab the audience's undivided attention in only nine seconds.

Understanding timeliness

The timeliness of your data depends on the sort of information you present and the focus of your audience. When performing a medical analysis for a disease with a long history, you might use data that's 10, 15, or even 20 years old, espe-cially when the presentation is for medical researchers (versus family practitio-ners) who are looking for trends. Your data may span hundreds or thousands of years when talking with historians. However, if your analysis is for graphics designers who specialize in website design, having data any more than a year old may be ruinous. Deciding on how old is too old is an essential part of creating your presentation.

Choosing the Right Graph

The kind of graph you choose determines how people view the associated data, so choosing the right graph from the outset is important. For example, if you want to show how various data elements contribute toward a whole, you really need to use a pie chart. On the other hand, when you want people to form opinions on how data elements compare, you use a bar chart. The idea is to choose a graph that naturally leads people to draw the conclusion that you need them to draw about the data that you've carefully massaged from various data sources. The following sections describe the various graph types and offer basic examples of how to use them.

Telling a story with your graphs

You use the graphics you create to tell a story pictorially. The goal isn't to display data; you can use a table to do that. Instead, the goal is to see the data in a particular way that doesn't lend itself easily to either tables or text.

REMEMBER

The difference between presenting data and telling a story is important because many people don't relate well to abstract information. You can show them the data, explore it in detail, and consider every possible approach to demonstrating that the data contains useful patterns, yet your audience still won't understand. As an example from this book, Chapter 3 of this minibook shows how underfitting appears in Figure 3-1. The graphic nature of the example shows in concrete terms what underfitting is all about and in a way that words really can't adequately describe.

When working with graphics, think about the story you want to tell using those graphics. A graph can have characters involved with it. You can show chases and escapes, deal a death blow to a nefarious villain, and show how the good person wins. If you can't see the story in your graphic, neither will your audience.

Showing parts of a whole with pie charts

Pie charts focus on showing parts of a whole. The entire pie represents 100 percent. The question is how much of that percentage each value occupies. The following example shows how to create a pie chart with many of the special features in place:

```
import matplotlib.pyplot as plt
%matplotlib inline
```

```
values = [5, 8, 9, 10, 4, 7]
colors = ['b', 'g', 'r', 'c', 'm', 'y']
labels = ['A', 'B', 'C', 'D', 'E', 'F']
explode = (0, 0.2, 0, 0, 0, 0)

plt.pie(values, colors=colors, labels=labels,
        explode=explode, autopct='%1.1f%%',
        counterclock=False, shadow=True)
plt.title('Values')

plt.show()
```

The essential part of a pie chart is the values. You could create a basic pie chart using just the values as input.

The colors parameter lets you choose custom colors for each pie wedge. You use the labels parameter to identify each wedge. In many cases, you need to make one wedge stand out from the others, so you add the explode parameter with a list of explode values. A value of 0 keeps the wedge in place; any other value moves the wedge out from the center of the pie.

Each pie wedge can show various kinds of information. This example shows the percentage occupied by each wedge with the autopct parameter. You must provide a format string to format the percentages.

TIP

Some parameters affect how the pie chart is drawn. Use the counterclock parameter to determine the direction of the wedges. The shadow parameter determines whether the pie appears with a shadow beneath it (for a 3-D effect). You can find other parameters at https://matplotlib.org/api/pyplot_api.html.

In most cases, you also want to give your pie chart a title so that others know what it represents. You do this using the title() function. Figure 4-1 shows the output from this example.

Creating comparisons with bar charts

Bar charts make comparing values easy. The wide bars and segregated measurements emphasize the differences between values, rather than the flow of one value to another, as a line graph would do. Fortunately, you have all sorts of methods at your disposal for emphasizing specific values and performing other tricks. The following example shows just some of the things you can do with a vertical bar chart:

```
import matplotlib.pyplot as plt
%matplotlib inline

values = [5, 8, 9, 10, 4, 7]
widths = [0.7, 0.8, 0.7, 0.7, 0.7, 0.7]
colors = ['b', 'r', 'b', 'b', 'b', 'b']
plt.bar(range(0, 6), values, width=widths,
        color=colors, align='center')

plt.show()
```

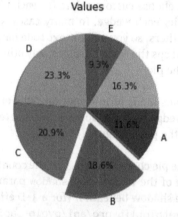

To create even a basic bar chart, you must provide a series of x coordinates and the heights of the bars. The example uses the range() function to create the x coordinates, and values contains the heights.

Of course, you may want more than a basic bar chart, and MatPlotLib provides a number of ways to get the job done. In this case, the example uses the width parameter to control the width of each bar, emphasizing the second bar by making it slightly larger. The larger width would show up even in a black-and-white printout. The example also uses the color parameter to change the color of the target bar to red. (The rest are blue.)

As with other chart types, the bar chart provides some special features that you can use to make your presentation stand out. The example uses the align parameter to center the data on the x coordinate. (The standard position is to the left.)

You can also use other parameters, such as hatch, to enhance the visual appearance of your bar chart. Figure 4-2 shows the output of this example.

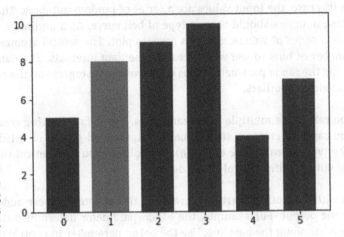

FIGURE 4-2:
Bar charts make
performing
comparisons
easier.

TIP

This chapter helps you get started using MatPlotLib to create a variety of chart and graph types. Of course, more examples are better, so you can also find some more advanced examples on the MatPlotLib site at `https://matplotlib.org/1.2.1/` `examples/index.html`. Some of the examples, such as those that demonstrate animation techniques, become quite advanced, but with practice you can use any of them to improve your own charts and graphs.

Showing distributions using histograms

Histograms categorize data by breaking it into *bins*, where each bin contains a subset of the data range. A histogram then displays the number of items in each bin so that you can see the distribution of data and the progression of data from bin to bin. In most cases, you see a curve of some type, such as a bell curve. The following example shows how to create a histogram with randomized data:

```
import numpy as np
import matplotlib.pyplot as plt
%matplotlib inline

x = 20 * np.random.randn(10000)

plt.hist(x, 25, range=(-50, 50), histtype='stepfilled',
         align='mid', color='g', label='Test Data')
plt.legend()
```

```
plt.title('Step Filled Histogram')
plt.show()
```

In this case, the input values are a series of random numbers. The distribution of these numbers should show a type of bell curve. As a minimum, you must provide a series of values, x in this case, to plot. The second argument contains the number of bins to use when creating the data intervals. The default value is 10. Using the range parameter helps you focus the histogram on the relevant data and exclude any outliers.

You can create multiple histogram types. The default setting creates a bar chart. You can also create a stacked bar chart, stepped graph, or filled stepped graph (the type shown in the example). In addition, you can control the orientation of the output, with vertical as the default.

As with most other charts and graphs in this chapter, you can add special features to the output. For example, the align parameter determines the alignment of each bar along the baseline. Use the color parameter to control the colors of the bars. The label parameter doesn't actually appear unless you also create a legend (as shown in this example). Figure 4-3 shows typical output from this example.

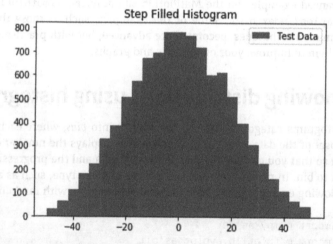

FIGURE 4-3: Histograms let you see distributions of numbers.

REMEMBER

Random data varies call by call. Every time you run the example, you see slightly different results because the random-generation process differs.

Depicting groups using boxplots

Boxplots provide a means of depicting groups of numbers through their *quartiles* (three points dividing a group into four equal parts). A boxplot may also have lines, called *whiskers*, indicating data outside the upper and lower quartiles. The spacing shown within a boxplot helps indicate the skew and dispersion of the data. The following example shows how to create a boxplot with randomized data:

```python
import numpy as np
import matplotlib.pyplot as plt
%matplotlib inline

spread = 100 * np.random.rand(100)
center = np.ones(50) * 50
flier_high = 100 * np.random.rand(10) + 100
flier_low = -100 * np.random.rand(10)
data = np.concatenate((spread, center,
                       flier_high, flier_low))

plt.boxplot(data, sym='gx', widths=.75, notch=True)
plt.show()
```

To create a usable dataset, you need to combine several different number-generation techniques, as shown at the beginning of the example. Here's how these techniques work:

>> spread: Contains a set of random numbers between 0 and 100

>> center: Provides 50 values directly in the center of the range of 50

>> flier_high: Simulates outliers between 100 and 200

>> flier_low: Simulates outliers between 0 and –100

The code combines all these values into a single dataset using concatenate(). Being randomly generated with specific characteristics (such as a large number of points in the middle), the output will show specific characteristics but will work fine for the example.

The call to boxplot() requires only data as input. All other parameters have default settings. In this case, the code sets the presentation of outliers to green Xs by setting the sym parameter. You use widths to modify the size of the box (made extra large in this case to make the box easier to see). Finally, you can create a square box or a box with a notch using the notch parameter (which normally defaults to False). Figure 4-4 shows typical output from this example.

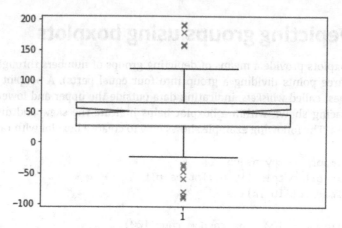

The box shows the three data points as the box, with the red line in the middle being the median. The two black horizontal lines connected to the box by whiskers show the upper and lower limits (for four quartiles). The outliers appear above and below the upper and lower limit lines as green Xs.

Defining a data flow using line graphs

One of the most commonly used graphs in this book is the line graph, which shows trends in data. You see not only the data points but also the flow between the data points. Using a line graph helps you to see the predictive nature of data science by drawing a line showing the missing data between the existing data points. What you receive is a continuous view of the data — at least, if the data is perfect. (See Chapter 3 of this minibook for a discussion of overfitting and underfitting of data.) The following example shows how to create a line graph with multiple lines:

```python
import matplotlib.pyplot as plt
%matplotlib inline


x = range(0, 6)
y1 = [5, 8, 9, 10, 4, 7]
y2 = [2, 3, 0, 11, 5, 6]


plt.plot(x, y1, 'o--g', markersize=4, linewidth=1)
plt.plot(x, y2, 'h-.b', markersize=10,
         markeredgecolor='red',
         markerfacecolor='purple', markevery=2,
         dash_capstyle='round', linewidth=3)
plt.legend(['Old', 'New'])


plt.show()
```

This line graph uses a few features that you don't actually see in the book. The first line is standard, but with the addition of a specific marker size and line width. The second line includes all sorts of addition features that emphasize the New option over the Old option. The point of this example is that you don't have to stick with any particular set of rules. If you want your audience to pay particular attention to something, emphasize it. Figure 4-5 shows the output from this example.

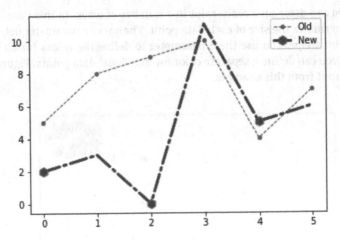

FIGURE 4-5: Use line graphs to show trends.

Seeing data patterns using scatterplots

Scatterplots show clusters of data rather than trends (as with line graphs) or discrete values (as with bar charts). The purpose of a scatterplot is to help you see data patterns. The following example shows how to create a scatterplot using randomized data:

```
import numpy as np
import matplotlib.pyplot as plt
%matplotlib inline

x1 = 5 * np.random.rand(40)
x2 = 5 * np.random.rand(40) + 25
x3 = 25 * np.random.rand(20)
x = np.concatenate((x1, x2, x3))

y1 = 5 * np.random.rand(40)
y2 = 5 * np.random.rand(40) + 25
y3 = 25 * np.random.rand(20)
y = np.concatenate((y1, y2, y3))
```

```
plt.scatter(x, y, s=[100], marker='^', c='m')
plt.show()
```

The example begins by generating random x and y coordinates. For each x coordinate, you must have a corresponding y coordinate. Creating a scatterplot is possible using just the x and y coordinates.

You can dress up a scatterplot in a number of ways. In this case, the s parameter determines the size of each data point. The marker parameter determines the data point shape. You use the c parameter to define the colors for all the data points, or you can define a separate color for individual data points. Figure 4-6 shows the output from this example.

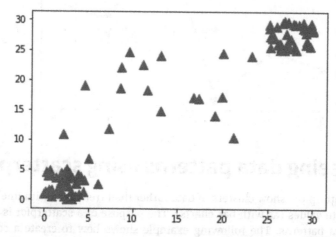

FIGURE 4-6:
Use scatterplots to show groups of data points and their associated patterns.

REMEMBER

You actually see a large number of scatterplots in this book because they appear quite commonly in data science output. Book 5, Chapter 6 shows how to create some advanced scatterplot presentations that you find helpful with complex data. The point is that you shouldn't rely too much on scatterplots and line graphs. Other kinds of presentations may help your viewer focus on the data in ways that you hadn't originally envisioned.

Working with External Data

Pictures say a lot of things that words can't (or at least they do it with far less effort). Notebook is both a coding platform and a presentation platform. You may be surprised at just what you can do with it. The following sections provide a brief overview of some of the more interesting features.

Embedding plots and other images

At some point, you might have spotted a notebook with multimedia or graphics embedded into it and wondered why you didn't see the same effects in your own files. In fact, all the graphics examples in the book appear as part of the code. Fortunately, you can perform some more magic by using the %matplotlib magic function. The possible values for this function are: 'gtk', 'gtk3', 'inline', 'nbagg', 'osx', 'qt', 'qt4', 'qt5', 'tk', and 'wx', each of which defines a different *plotting backend* (the code used to actually render the plot) for presenting information onscreen.

When you run %matplotlib inline, any plots you create appear as part of the document. That's how Figure 4-1, earlier in this chapter, shows the plot it creates immediately below the affected code.

Loading examples from online sites

Because some examples you see online can be hard to understand unless you have them loaded on your own system, you should also keep the %load magic function in mind. All you need is the URL of an example you want to see on your system. For example, try %load https://matplotlib.org/_downloads/pyplot_text.py. When you click Run Cell, Notebook loads the example directly in the cell and comments the %load call out, as shown in Figure 4-7. (The actual code is much longer than that shown in the figure.) You can then run the example and see the output from it on your own system.

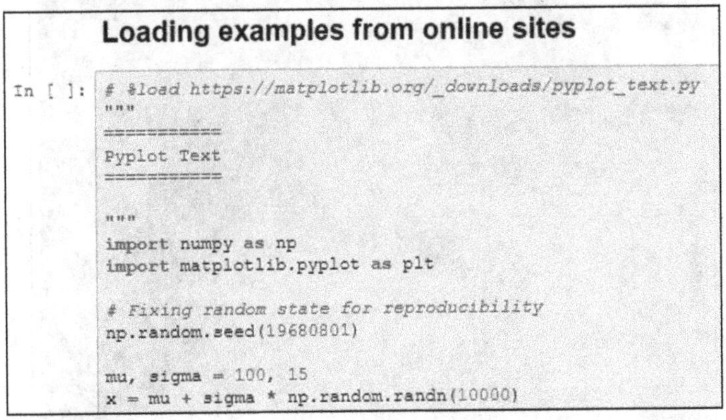

FIGURE 4-7:
Load external code as needed to provide specific information for your presentation.

```
Loading examples from online sites

In [ ]:  # %load https://matplotlib.org/_downloads/pyplot_text.py
         """
         ============
         Pyplot Text
         ============

         """
         import numpy as np
         import matplotlib.pyplot as plt

         # Fixing random state for reproducibility
         np.random.seed(19680801)

         mu, sigma = 100, 15
         x = mu + sigma * np.random.randn(10000)
```

Obtaining online graphics and multimedia

A lot of the functionality required to perform special multimedia and graphics processing appears within IPython.display. By importing a required class, you can perform tasks such as embedding images into your notebook. Here's an example of embedding one of the pictures from the author's blog into the notebook for this chapter:

```
from IPython.display import Image, display
Embed = Image(
'http://blog.johnmuellerbooks.com/' +
'wp-content/uploads/2015/04/Layer-Hens.jpg',
    width=600, height=450,
    metadata={'Animal': 'Chicks'})
print('A picture of: ' + Embed.metadata['Animal'])
display(Embed)
```

The code begins by importing the required class, Image, and then using features from it to first define what to embed and then actually embed the image. Notice that you can attach metadata to the image and display it later. The output you see from this example appears in Figure 4-8.

A picture of: Chicks

FIGURE 4-8:
Embedding
images can dress
up your notebook
presentation.

704   BOOK 6 Diagnosing and Fixing Errors

If you expect an image to change over time, you might want to create a link to it instead of embedding it. You must refresh a link because the content in the notebook is only a reference rather than the actual image. However, as the image changes, you see the change in your notebook as well. To accomplish this task, you use SoftLinked = Image(url='http://blog.johnmuellerbooks.com/wp-content/uploads/2015/04/Layer-Hens.jpg') instead of Embed.

When working with embedded images on a regular basis, you might want to set the form in which the images are embedded. For example, you may prefer to embed them as PDFs. To perform this task, you use code similar to this:

```
from IPython.display import set_matplotlib_formats
set_matplotlib_formats('pdf', 'svg')
```

You have access to a wide number of formats when working with a notebook. The commonly supported formats are 'png', 'retina', 'jpeg', 'svg', and 'pdf'.

The IPython display system is nothing short of amazing, and this section hasn't even begun to tap the surface for you. For example, you can import a YouTube video and place it directly into your notebook as part of your presentation if you want. You can see quite a few more of the display features demonstrated at http://nbviewer. jupyter.org/github/ipython/ipython/blob/1.x/examples/notebooks/ Part%205%20-%20Rich%20Display%20System.ipynb.

Chapter **5**

Developing Consistent Strategies

Some people view data merely as a disorganized collection of unkempt information from various sources. Throughout this book, you have seen strategies for organizing and manicuring data prior to performing analysis on it. All these strategies see use in business today because data scientists spend an inconceivable amount of time just obtaining, organizing, and manicuring data. Unfortunately, the output of these efforts is often lacking in usefulness because the data simply won't be tamed. The problem is one of consistency in obtaining, organizing, and manicuring the data. If consistency is absent, it's reasonable to assume that the output of an analysis will be suspect. The purpose of this chapter is to define methods of making the act of interacting with raw data more consistent so that the outcome of an analysis is more predictable and, therefore more reliable.

Standardizing Data Collection Techniques

The data you use comes from a number of sources. The most common data source is from information entered by humans at some point. Even when a system collects shopping-site data automatically, humans initially enter the information.

A human clicks various items, adds them to a shopping cart, specifies characteristics (such as size) and quantity, and then checks out. Later, after the sale, the human gives the shopping experience, product, and delivery method a rating and makes comments. In short, every shopping experience becomes a data-collection exercise as well.

REMEMBER

You can't sit by each shopper's side and provide instructions on how to enter data consistently. Consequently, the data you receive is inconsistent and nearly unusable at times. By reviewing forms of successful online stores, however, you can see how to provide a virtual self to assist the shopper in making consistent entries. The forms you provide for entering information have a great deal to do with the data you obtain. When a form contains fewer handwritten entries and more check boxes, it tends to provide a better experience for the customer and a more consistent data source for you.

Many data sources today rely on input gathered from human sources. Humans also provide manual input. You call or go into an office somewhere to make an appointment with a professional. A receptionist then gathers information from you that's needed for the appointment. This manually collected data eventually ends up in a dataset somewhere for analysis purposes.

By providing training on proper data entry techniques, you can improve the consistency of input that the receptionist provides. In addition, you're unlikely to have just one receptionist providing input, so training can also help the entire group of receptionists provide consistent input despite individual differences in perspective. Some forms of regulated data entry of this sort have become so complex today that the people doing it actually require a formal education, such as medical data entry personnel (see the course at https://study.com/articles/Medical_Data_Entry_Training_Programs_and_Courses.html). The point is that the industry, as a whole, is generally moving toward trained data entry people, so your organization should make use of this trend to improve the consistency of the data you receive.

Data is also collected from sensors, and these sensors can take almost any form. For example, many organizations base physical data collection, such as the number of people viewing an object in a window, on cellphone detection. Facial recognition software could potentially detect repeat customers.

However, sensors can create datasets from almost anything. The weather service relies on datasets created by sensors that monitor environmental conditions such as rain, temperature, humidity, cloud cover, and so on. Robotic monitoring systems help correct small flaws in robotic operation by constantly analyzing data collected by monitoring sensors. A sensor, combined with a small AI application, could tell you when your dinner is cooked to perfection tonight. The sensor collects data, but the AI application uses rules to help define when the food is properly cooked.

TIP

Of the forms of data collection, the data provided by sensors is the easiest to make consistent. However, sensor data is often inconsistent because vendors keep adding functionality as a means of differentiation. The solution to this problem is better data standards so that vendors must adhere to certain specifics when creating data. Standards efforts are ongoing, but it pays to ensure that the sensors you use to collect data all rely on the same standards to ensure that you obtain consistent input.

Using Reliable Sources

The word *reliable* seems so easy to define, yet so hard to implement. Something is reliable when the results it produces are both expected and consistent. A reliable data source produces mundane data that contains no surprises; no one is shocked in the least by the outcome. On the other hand, depending on your perspective, it could actually be a good thing that most people aren't yawning and then falling asleep when reviewing data. That's because the surprises make the data worth analyzing and reviewing. Consequently, data has an aspect of duality. You want reliable, mundane, fully anticipated data that simply confirms what you already know, but the unexpected is what makes collecting the data useful in the first place.

You can also define reliability by the number of failure points contained in any measured resource. More failure points automatically mean lower reliability if you have two data sources of equal reliability. Given that general data analysis, AI, machine learning, and deep learning all require huge amounts of information, the methodology used automatically reduces the reliability of such data because you have more failure points to consider. Consequently, you must have data from highly reliable sources of the correct type.

Scientists began fighting against impressive amounts of data for years before anyone coined the term *big data*. At that point, the Internet didn't produce the vast sums for data that it does today. Remember that big data is not just simply a fad created by software and hardware vendors but has a basis in many of the following fields:

>> **Astronomy:** Consider the data received from spacecraft on a mission (such as *Voyager* or *Galileo*) and all the data received from radio telescopes, which are specialized antennas used to receive radio waves from astronomical bodies. A common example is the Search for Extraterrestrial Intelligence (SETI) project (https://www.seti.org/), which looks for extraterrestrial signals by

observing radio frequencies arriving from space. The amount of data received and the computer power used to analyze a portion of the sky for a single hour is impressive (http://www.setileague.org/askdr/howmuch.htm). If aliens are out there, it's very hard to spot them. (The movie *Contact,* which you can read about at https://www.amazon.com/exec/obidos/ASIN/B002GHHHKQ/datacservip0f-20/, explores what could happen should humans actually intercept a signal.)

» **Meteorology:** Think about trying to predict weather for the near term given the large number of required measures, such as temperature, atmospheric pressure, humidity, winds, and precipitation at different times, locations, and altitudes. Weather forecasting is really one of the first problems in big data, and quite a relevant one. According to Weather Analytics, a company that provides climate data, more than 33 percent of the Worldwide Gross Domestic Product (GDP) is determined by how weather conditions affect agriculture, fishing, tourism, and transportation, just to name a few. Dating back to the 1950s, the first supercomputers of the time were used to crunch as much as data as possible because, in meteorology, the more data, the more accurate the forecast. That's the reason everyone is amassing more storage and processing capacity, as you can read in this story regarding the Korean Meteorological Association (https://www.wired.com/insights/2013/02/how-big-data-can-boost-weather-forecasting/) for weather forecasting and studying climate change.

» **Physics:** Consider the large amounts of data produced by experiments using particle accelerators in an attempt to determine the structure of matter, space, and time. For example, the Large Hadron Collider (https://home.cern/topics/large-hadron-collider), the largest particle accelerator ever created, produces 15PB (petabytes) of data every year as a result of particle collisions (https://home.cern/science/computing).

» **Genomics:** Sequencing a single DNA strand, which means determining the precise order of the many combinations of the four bases — adenine, guanine, cytosine, and thymine — that constitute the structure of the associated molecule, requires quite a lot of data. For instance, a single chromosome, a structure containing the DNA in the cell, may require from 50MB to 300MB. A human being normally has 46 chromosomes, and the DNA data for just one person consumes an entire DVD. Just imagine the massive storage required to document the DNA data of a large number of people or to sequence other life forms on earth (https://www.wired.com/2013/10/big-data-biology/).

» **Oceanography:** Gathers data from the many sensors placed in the oceans to measure statistics, such as temperature and currents, using hydrophones and other sensors. This data even includes sounds for acoustic monitoring for scientific purposes (discovering characteristics about fish, whales, and plankton) and military defense purposes (finding sneaky submarines from other countries). You can have a sneak peek at this old surveillance problem, which is turning more complex and digital, by reading this article: `https://www.theatlantic.com/technology/archive/2014/08/listening-in-the-navy-is-tracking-ocean-sounds-collected-by-scientists/378630/`.

» **Satellites:** Recording images from the entire globe and sending them back to earth to monitor the Earth's surface and its atmosphere isn't a new business (TIROS 1, the first satellite to send back images and data, dates back to 1960). Over the years, however, the world has launched more than 1,400 active satellites that provide earth observation. The amount of data arriving on earth is astonishing and serves both military (surveillance) and civilian purposes, such as tracking economic development, monitoring agriculture, and monitoring changes and risks. A single European Space Agency's satellite, Sentinel 1A, generates 5PB of data during two years of operation, as you can read from `https://spaceflightnow.com/2016/04/28/europes-sentinel-satellites-generating-huge-big-data-archive/`).

All these data sources have one thing in common: Someone collects and stores the data as static information (once collected, the data doesn't change). This means that if errors are found, correcting them with an overall increase in reliability is possible. The next section of this chapter discusses dynamic data, which isn't nearly so easy to make reliable.

REMEMBER

What you need to take away from this section is that you likely deal with immense amounts of data from various sources that could have any number of errors. Finding these errors in such huge quantities is nearly impossible. Using the most reliable sources that you can will increase the overall quality of the original data, reducing the effect of individual data failure points. In other words, sources that provide consistent data are more valuable than sources that don't.

Verifying Dynamic Data Sources

Dynamic data provides you with timely sources of information to use for analysis. The trade-off is trying to manage all that data. When data flows in huge amounts, storing it all may be difficult or even impossible. In fact, storing it all might not even be useful. Here are some figures of just some of what you can expect to happen within a single minute on the Internet:

» 150 million emails sent

» 350,000 new tweets sent on Twitter

>> 2.4 million queries requested on Google

>> 700,000 people logged in to their account on Facebook

The following sections consider the effects of such huge amounts of dynamic data used for analysis purposes. Because dynamic data constantly changes, it presents significant management issues that you don't encounter with static data.

Considering the problem

Dynamic data likely makes up more of the data you use for various forms of analysis today. When working with dynamic data, you often don't provide long-term storage because doing so would prove impossible and the data has a definite shelf life. In addition, the related data sources continue to churn out new data at an incredible rate. Consider the problems associated with trying to store data from these sources:

>> As reported by the National Security Agency (NSA), the amount of information flowing through the Internet every day from all over the world amounted to 1,826PB of data in 2013, and 1.6 percent of it consisted of emails and telephone calls. To assure national security, the NSA must verify the content of at least 0.025 percent of all emails and phone calls (looking for key words that could signal something like a terrorist plot). That still amounts to 25PB per year, which equates to 37,500 CD-ROMs every year of data stored and analyzed (and that's growing). You can read the full story at https://www.business-standard.com/article/news-ani/nsa-claims-analysts-look-at-only-0-00004-of-world-s-internet-traffic-for-surveillance-113081100.

>> The Internet of Things (IoT) is a reality. You may have heard the term many times in the past, but now the growth of items connected to the Internet is exploding. The idea is to put sensors and transmitters on everything and use the data to both better control what happens in the world and to make objects smarter. Transmitting devices are getting tinier, cheaper, and less power demanding; some are already so small that they can be put everywhere. (Just look at the ant-sized radio developed by Stanford engineers at https://news.stanford.edu/news/2014/september/ant-radio-arbabian-090914.html.) Experts estimate that by 2020, there will be six times as many connected things on earth as there are people, but many research companies and think tanks are already revisiting those figures.

Given such volumes of data, accumulating the data all day for incremental analysis might not seem efficient. In the past, a vendor would collect the information and store it in a data warehouse for batch analysis. However, useful data queries tend to ask about the most recent data in the stream, and data becomes less useful when it ages. (In some sectors, like financial, a day can be a lot of time.) In fact, many marketing firms analyze data on a constant basis to determine the effectiveness of marketing campaigns. Data collected just a few minutes ago might see use in tweaking a campaign to make it more effective (see the article at `https://www.sas.com/en_us/insights/articles/marketing/do-marketers-need-real-time-analytics.html` for details).

Moreover, you can expect even more data to arrive tomorrow (the amount of data increases daily) and that makes it difficult, if not impossible, to pull data from repositories as you push new data in. Pulling old data from repositories as fresh data pours in is akin to the punishment of Sisyphus. Sisyphus, as a Greek myth narrative, received a terrible punishment from the god Zeus: being forced to eternally roll an immense boulder up on the top of a hill, only to watch it roll back down each time (see `http://www.mythweb.com/encyc/entries/sisyphus.html` for additional details).

Sometimes, rendering things even more impossible to handle, data can arrive so fast and in such large quantities that writing it to disk is impossible: New information arrives faster than the time required to write it to the hard disk. This is a problem typical of particle experiments with particle accelerators such as the Large Hadron Collider, requiring scientists to decide what data to keep (`https://home.cern/science/computing/processing-what-record`). Of course, you may queue data for some time, but not for too long, because the queue will quickly grow and become impossible to maintain. For instance, if kept in memory, queue data will soon lead to an out-of-memory error.

REMEMBER

Because new data flows may render older processing techniques used on static data obsolete, and procrastination is not a solution, people have devised multiple strategies to deal instantaneously with massive and changeable data amounts. People use three ways to deal with large amounts of data:

>> **Stored:** Some data is stored because it may help answer unclear questions later. This method relies on techniques to store it immediately and analyze it later very fast, no matter how massive it is.

>> **Summarized:** Some data is summarized because keeping it all as it is makes no sense; only the important data is kept.

>> **Consumed:** The remaining data is consumed because its usage is predetermined. Algorithms can instantly read, digest, and turn the data into information. After that, the system forgets the data forever.

TIP

When talking of massive data arriving into a computer system, you will often hear it compared to water: streaming data, data streams, data fire hose. You discover how working with a data stream is like consuming tap water: Opening the tap lets you store the water in cups or drinking bottles, or you can use it for cooking, scrubbing food, cleaning plates, or washing hands. In any case, most or all of the water is gone, yet it proves very useful and indeed vital.

Analyzing streams with the right recipe

Streaming data needs streaming algorithms, and the key thing to know about streaming algorithms is that, apart from a few measures that it can compute exactly, a streaming algorithm necessarily provides approximate results. The algorithm output is almost correct, not quite guessing the correct answer, but close to it.

When dealing with streams, you clearly have to concentrate only on the measures of interest and leave out many details. You could be interested in a statistical measurement, such as mean, minimum, or maximum. Moreover, you could want to count elements in the stream or distinguish old from new information. There are many algorithms to use, depending on the problem, yet the recipes always use the same ingredients. The trick of cooking the perfect stream is to use one or all of these algorithmic tools as ingredients:

» **Sampling:** Reduce your stream to a more manageable data size; represent the entire stream or the most recent observations using a shifting data window.

» **Hashing:** Reduce infinite stream variety to a limited set of simple integer numbers.

» **Sketching:** Create a short summary of the measure you need, removing the less useful details. This approach lets you leverage a simple working storage, which can be your computer's main memory or its hard disk.

Another characteristic to keep in mind about algorithms operating on streams is their simplicity and low computational complexity. Data streams can be quite fast. Algorithms that require too many calculations can miss essential data, which means that the data is gone forever. When you view the situation in this light, you can appreciate how hash functions prove useful because they're prompt in transforming inputs into something easier to handle and search for both operations. You can also appreciate the sketching and sampling techniques, which bring about the idea of *lossy compression* that enables you to represent something complex by using a simpler form. You lose some detail but save a great deal of computer time and storage.

Sampling means drawing a limited set of examples from your stream and treating them as if they represented the entire stream. It is a well-known tool in statistics through which you can make inferences on a larger context (technically called the universe or the population) by using a small part of it.

Looking for New Data Collection Trends

Because data is so valuable and users are sometimes adverse to giving it up, vendors constantly find new ways to collect data. One such method comes down to spying. Microsoft, for example, was recently accused (yet again) of spying on Windows 10 users even when the user doesn't want to share the data (see `https://www.extremetech.com/computing/282263-microsoft-windows-10-data-collection` for details). Lest you think that Microsoft is solely interested in your computing concerns, think again. The data it admits to collecting (and there is likely more) is pretty amazing (see `https://www.theverge.com/2017/4/5/15188636/microsoft-windows-10-data-collection-documents-privacy-concerns` for details).

Microsoft's data gathering doesn't stop with your Windows 10 actions; it also collects data with Cortana, the personal assistant (see `https://www.computerworld.com/article/3106863/cortana-the-spy-in-windows-10.html`). Mind you, Alexa is accused of doing the same thing (`https://www.washingtonpost.com/news/powerpost/paloma/the-technology-202/2019/05/06/the-technology-202-alexa-are-you-spying-on-me-here-s-why-smart-speakers-raise-serious-privacy-concerns/5ccf46a9a7a0a46cfe152c3c/`). Google, likewise, does the same thing (see `https://www.consumerwatchdog.org/privacy-technology/how-google-and-amazon-are-spying-you`). So, one of the trends the vendors are using is spying, and it doesn't stop with Microsoft, nor does it stop with the obvious spying sources.

It might actually be possible to write an entire book on the ways in which people are spying on you, but that would make for a very paranoid book, and there are other new data collection trends to consider. You may have noticed that you get more email from everyone about the services or products you were provided. Everyone wants you to provide free information about your experiences in one of these forms:

>> **Close-ended surveys:** A close-ended survey is one in which the questions have specific answers that you check mark. The advantage is greater consistency of feedback. The disadvantage is that you can't learn anything beyond the predefined answers.

>> **Open-ended surveys:** An open-ended survey is one in which the questions rely on text boxes in which the user enters data manually. In some cases, this form of survey enables you to find new information, but at the cost of consistency, reliability, and cleanliness of the data.

>> **One-on-one interviews:** Someone calls you or approaches you at a place like the mall and talks to you. When the interviewer is well trained, you obtain consistent data and can also discover new information. However, the quality of this information comes at the cost of paying someone to obtain it.

>> **Focus group:** Three or more people meet with an interviewer to discuss a topic (including products). Because the interviewer acts as a moderator, the consistency, reliability, and cleanliness of the data remain high and the costs are lower. However, now the data suffers contamination from the interaction between members of the focus group.

>> **Direct observation:** No conversation occurs in this case; someone monitors the interactions of another party with a product or service and records the responses using a script. However, because you now rely on a third party to interpret someone else's actions, you have a problem with contamination in the form of bias. In addition, if the subject of the observation is aware of being monitored, the interactions likely won't reflect reality.

REMEMBER

These are just a few of the methods that are seeing greater use in data collection today. They're just the tip of the iceberg. The concepts you should take away from this section is that no perfect means for collecting some types of data exists and that all data collection methods require some sort of participative event.

Weeding Old Data

Contrary to fine wine, data doesn't age well and you need to think about methods of keeping it fresh. The problem is most apparent when working with static data. You collect data from a source like a robotic mission to Mars, and then use it to make decisions about future missions. The problem is determining when that data is too old. At some point, the data becomes useless because it no longer reflects state-of-the-art technology.

The problem with old data is monumental because you can't really create a rule that says the data is actually useless. You may not be able to use data for a current analysis for a line of business decision, but the same data may have historical value. In addition, old data often provides examples for use in creating models that reflect special, uncommon events. Consequently, the rule that states that you really don't need something until after you throw it out comes into play. Of course, you could always archive the data in some unused location for all eternity, but that's not really practical, either.

REMEMBER

When thinking about old data, you must consider a number of factors that determine whether the data isn't useful any longer. These factors include (but aren't limited to):

>> Technology to which the data refers

>> Environment in which the data is collected

>> Attitudes of society as a whole

>> Use of data within an analysis

>> Cost of storing the data versus value gained

>> Legal or other requirements

>> Data format with regard to analysis techniques

Considering the Need for Randomness

Oddly enough, creating a consistent analysis often means training your algorithm using randomized data so that it doesn't learn a specific pattern. Randomization relies on the capability by your computer to generate random numbers, which means creating the number without a plan. Therefore, a random number is unpredictable, and as you generate subsequent random numbers, they shouldn't relate to each other.

REMEMBER

However, randomness is hard to achieve. Even when you throw dice, the result can't be completely unexpected because of the way you hold the dice, the way you throw them, and the fact that the dice aren't perfectly shaped. Computers aren't good at creating random numbers, either. They generate randomness by using algorithms or pseudorandom tables (which work by using a *seed* value as a starting point, a number equivalent to an index) because a computer can't create a truly random number. Computers are deterministic machines; everything inside them responds to a well-defined response pattern, which means that it imitates randomness in some way.

Considering why randomization is needed

Even if a computer can't create true randomness, streams of pseudorandom numbers (numbers that appear as random but that are somehow predetermined) can still make the difference in many computer science problems. Any algorithm that employs randomness in its logic can appear as a randomized algorithm, no matter whether randomness determines its results, improves performance, or mitigates the risk of failing by providing a solution in certain cases.

Usually you find randomness employed in selecting input data, the start point of the optimization, or the number and kind of operations to apply to the data. When randomness is a core part of the algorithm logic and not just an aid to its performance, the expected running time of the algorithm and even its results may become uncertain and subject to randomness, too; for instance, an algorithm may provide different, though equally good, results during each run. It's therefore useful to distinguish between kinds of randomized solutions, each one named after iconic gambling locations:

» **Las Vegas:** These algorithms are notable for using random inputs or resources to provide the correct problem answer every time. Obtaining a result may take an uncertain amount of time because of its random procedures. An example is the Quicksort algorithm.

» **Monte Carlo:** Because of their use of randomness, Monte Carlo algorithms may not provide a correct answer or even an answer at all, although these outcomes seldom happen. Because the result is uncertain, a maximum number of trials in their running time may bind them. Monte Carlo algorithms demonstrate that algorithms do not necessarily always successfully solve the problems they are supposed to. An example is the Solovay–Strassen primality test.

» **Atlantic City:** These algorithms provide a correct problem answer at least 75 percent of the time. Monte Carlo algorithms are always fast but not always correct, and Las Vegas algorithms are always correct but not always fast. People therefore think of Atlantic City algorithms as halfway between the two because they are usually both fast and correct. This class of algorithms was introduced in 1982 by J. Finn in an unpublished manuscript entitled *Comparison of Probabilistic Test for Primality*. Created for theoretical reasons to test for prime numbers, this class comprises hard-to-design solutions, thus very few of them exist today.

Understanding how probability works

Probability tells you the likelihood of an event, which you normally express as a number. In this book, and generally in the field of probabilistic studies, the probability of an event is measured in the range between 0 (no probability that an event will occur) and 1 (certainty that an event will occur). Intermediate values, such as 0.25 or 0.75, indicate that the event will happen with a certain frequency under conditions that should lead to that event (referred to as *trials*). Even if a numeric range from 0 to 1 doesn't seem intuitive at first, working with probability over time makes the reason for using such a range easier to understand. When an event occurs with probability 0.25, you know that out of 100 trials, the event will happen 0.25 * 100 = 25 times.

For instance, when the probability of your favorite sports team winning is 0.75, you can use the number to determine the chances of success when your team plays a game against another team. You can even get more specific information, such as the probability of winning a certain tournament (your team has a 0.65 probability of winning a match in this tournament) or conditioned by another event (when you aren't playing on your home court, the probability of winning for your team decreases to 0.60).

Probabilities can tell you a lot about an event, and they're helpful for algorithms, too. In a randomized algorithmic approach, you may wonder when to stop an algorithm because it should have reached a solution. It's good to know how long to look for a solution before giving up. Probabilities can help you determine how many iterations you may need.

REMEMBER

You commonly hear about probabilities as percentages in sports and economics, telling you that an event occurs a certain number of times after 100 trials. It's exactly the same probability no matter whether you express it as 0.25 or 25 percent. That's just a matter of conventions. In gambling, you even hear about odds, which is another way of expressing probability, where you compare the likelihood of an event (for example, having a certain horse win the race) against not having the event happen at all. In this case, you express 0.25 as 25 against 75 or in any other way resulting in the same ratio.

You can multiply a probability for a number of trials and get an estimated number of occurrences of the event, but by doing the inverse, you can empirically estimate a probability. Perform a certain number of trials, observe each of them, and count the number of times an event occurs. The ratio between the number of occurrences and the number of trials is your probability estimate. For instance, the probability 0.25 is the probability of picking a certain suit when choosing a card randomly from a deck of cards. French playing cards (the most widely used type of deck, which also appears in America and Britain) provide a classic example for explaining probabilities. (The Italians, Germans, and Swiss, for example, use decks with different suits, which you can read about at http://healthy. uwaterloo.ca/museum/VirtualExhibits/Playing%20Cards/decks/index. html.) The deck contains 52 cards equally distributed into four suits: clubs and spades, which are black, and diamonds and hearts, which are red. If you want to determine the probability of picking an ace, you must consider that, by picking cards from a deck, you will observe four aces, which affects the probability of picking an ace (rather than a specific ace, such as the ace of hearts). Your trials at picking the cards are 52 (the number of cards); therefore the answer in terms of probability is 4/52 = 0.077.

TIP

You can get a more reliable estimate of an empirical probability by using a larger number of trials. When using a few trials, you may not get a correct estimate of the event probability because of the influence of chance. As the number of trials grows, event observations will get nearer to the true probability of the event itself. The principle there is a generating process behind events. To understand how the generating process works, you need many trials. Using trials in such a way is also known as *sampling* from a probabilistic distribution.

Index

charts
  annotating, 596–597
  bar, 582, 695–697
  defined, 581
  pie, 583, 694–695
cheat sheet, 5
Chebyshev distance, 345, 500
Chebyshev inequality, 656
Chen, Tianqi, 371
Chihuahua vs Muffin (Internet meme), 540
Christie's, 544
classification, 294
Classification and Regression Training (CARET), 90
classification tasks. *See also* convolutional neural
    networks (CNNs)
  annotating multiple objects in images, 529–530
  classification of multiple objects, 528–529
  image pyramids, 528
  image segmentation, 530–531
  localization, 527–528
  one-stage detection, 528
  sliding window, 528
  two-stage detection, 529
  understanding problem, 526–527
Cleveland, William S., 10
close-ended surveys, 715
cluster analysis, 659–661
CNNs. *See* convolutional neural networks (CNNs)
co-adaptation, 406
Codd, Edgar Frank, 224
code repository
  Python, 64–69
  R, 75–76
coding styles, 23
coefficient vectors, 375, 377
coefficients, 274
Cognitive Toolkit (CNTK), 87
Colab, 502, 522
Colaboratory, 69–71, 517
cold start, 500
collaborative filtering. *See also* recommender systems
  defined, 500, 507
  history, 494
  performing, 504–506
color shift, image augmentation, 514
colorization, 16
colors, 15–16, 427–428

Columbia University, 10
columns, slicing, 188–189
comma-separated value (CSV) files
  about, 205
  flat-file formatting, 113
  header information, 208–209
  working with, 205–207
commission, 645–646
Common Object Request Broker Architecture (CORBA), 120
companion files, 5
Comparison of Probabilistic Test for Primality (Finn), 718
comparison tasks, 176
complex analysis, 42
composite key, 227
Comprehensive R Archive Network (CRAN), 24
Compressed Sparse Row (CSR) matrix, 474
Compute Unified Device Architecture (CUDA), 55
computer generated imagery (CGI), 546
computer perspective, 455–456
computerized axial tomography (CAT), 37
concat( ) method, 191
concatenation, 146, 189–190
concept drift, 652
conda utility, 72–73
conditional GANs, 556. *See also* generative adversarial
    networks (GANs)
confidence level, 670
connectionism, 375
constructs, 155
consumed data, 713
content
  defined, 549
  image, 549
  loss, 550
content-based filtering, 500–501
continuous text, 125
continuous value, 292
contraction, 531
contrast change, image augmentation, 514
control characters, 153
ConviD, 560
convolutional neural networks (CNNs)
  accessing datasets, 430
  AlexNet, 450
  architectures, 449–450
  Bayesian, 324
  character recognition, 429–434

O

P

packages
  about, 51
  datasets, 218–219
  defined, 82
  third-party code, 82–83
pandas, 84, 85, 113, 215, 233, 265, 653–654
paradigms
  declarative, 132, 136–137
  defined, 131
  imperative, 133, 135
  object-oriented, 136
  procedural, 136
parameter learning, 332
parametric rectified linear unit (PReLU), 401
Parinov, Alex, 515
parsers, 202
parsing
  data file, 497–498
  HTML files using Beautiful Soup, 88–89
  HTML files using rvest, 92
  XML files, 211–212
partial_fit( ) method, 285–286
Pascal, 136
PASCAL VOC (Visual Object Classes), 512
passing
  functions, 164–165
  by reference vs. by value, 140–142
pattern-matching
  analysis with, 155–156
  defined, 150
  in Python, 156–159
patterns
  abstract, 151
  in data, 150–152
  defined, 150
  matching, 150
  progression, 151
  transitional, 151
Pearl, Raymond, 291
perceptrons
  activation function, 376
  bias, 376
  coefficient vectors, 375, 377
  in ensembles, 369
  functionality, 375–376
  history of, 375

iterative learning, 376
  learning rate, 377
  nonseparability limit, 376–378
  numeric processing of input, 376
  summation of results, 376
  weights, 376
performance, 49
person poses, 16
perspective, 646–647
physics, 710
pickles, 465
pie charts, 583, 694–695
Pillow library, 251
Pix2Pix, 557
pixels
  data stream, 427
  in neural networks, 428
  tricking, 539–541
plot( ) method, 592, 604
plot_date( ) method, 604
plots
  defined, 582
  defining, 583
  multiple, 584–586
plotting backend, 703
point-of-sale (POS) systems, 32, 125, 203, 224
poly1d( ) output, 608
polyfit( ) function, 258, 261
polyid( ) function, 258–259
polynomial regression, 280
pooling layers, 418, 439–440
population growth, 290
ports, 230
pose guided person image generation, 557
PoseNet, 17
positional data files, 203–205
positron emission tomography (PET), 37
POS-tagging, 562
PostgreSQL, 230
postprocessing, 530
precision, 300
predictability, analysis performance, 49
predictions, using networked Bayes in, 328–331
predictors
  averaging, 372
  bagging with AdaBoost, 365–369
  defined, 272

presentation, 11

pretrained neural network, 418, 450

Price, Richard, 312

principal component analysis (PCA), 338–339, 420, 425, 483, 658–659

print( ) function, 218, 417

prior probability, 312

private data, 120–121

probabilistic graphical model (PGM), 324

probabilities
  binary response, 301–302
  defined, 312
  measurement of, 718–720
  prior, 312
  solving with logistic regression, 294
  transforming numeric estimates into, 302–304

problem domain, 76

procedural coding style, 23

procedural programming, 136

procedure, 140

processors, 53, 54

products, enticing people to buy, 13–14

programming
  declarative, 132, 136–137
  imperative, 133, 135
  object-oriented, 136
  procedural, 136
  role of, 12–13

programming languages
  choosing, 56–57
  comparing, 20
  criteria for choosing, 12–13
  impure, 134–135
  overview, 20–21
  pure, 134
  Python, 58–71
  R, 72–76

Progressive GAN, 556

pseudo-random sequence, 323

psychological testing, 37

public data, 117–119

public domain datasets
  downloading, 219–220
  opening and using archives, 220–221

pure functions, 137

pure language, 134

pure text, 124–125

purrr, 93

PyMC3, 318–319, 334

PyMongo, 249

PyTables, 84

Python
  AdaBoost and, 366
  choosing, 56
  code repository, 64–69
  dictionaries, 147–148, 163
  functional programming with, 137–138
  gradient boosting machines (GBMs), 370
  lists, 142–147
  modules, 82
  multiple programming paradigm support in, 135
  obtaining and using, 57
  online tutorials, 3
  overview, 20, 58
  packages, 58
  pattern matching in, 156–159
  pros and cons, 22–23
  recursion in, 161–162
  requirements, 58
  sets, 147–148
  strings, 148–149
  support for different coding styles, 23
  trees, 195–198
  using Azure Notebooks with, 71–72

Python for Data Science for Dummies (Mueller and Massaron), 69, 316

Python packages
  about, 82
  Beautiful Soup, 88–89
  Keras, 86–87
  matplotlib, 87–88
  NetworkX, 88
  NumPy, 85
  online resources, 84
  pandas, 85
  Scikit-learn, 85
  SciPy, 83–84
  TensorFlow, 87

Q

Quetelet, Adolphe, 290

Quora, 134, 479

R

R (programming language)
about, 57
AdaBoost, 366
code repository, 75–76
distributions, 24–25
gradient boosting machines (GBMs), 370
image processing in, 412
installing, 72–73
libraries, 82
online tutorials, 3
overview, 21
packages, 82
pros and cons, 23–25
SciPy functionality, 85
starting, 73–75
using Azure Notebooks with, 71–72
R libraries
Classification and Regression Training (CARET), 90
dplyr, 93
ggplot2, 91
igraph, 91–92
lubridate, 92–93
mlr, 90–91
purrr, 93
reticulate, 89–90
rvest, 92
R_env environment, 72–73
R^2, 273, 279
random crop, image augmentation, 514
random flips, image augmentation, 515
random forests, 661
Random Forests
about, 357
benefits, 360
example, 358–359
importance measures, 360–364
online resources, 357
steps in, 357
random rotation, image augmentation, 515
random shifts, image augmentation, 515
RandomForestClassifier, 357
RandomizedPCA class, 420
randomness, 717–720
raster graphics, 127
rating column, 502

rating data. *See also* recommender systems
anonymous web data, 496–499
collaborative filtering, 500–501
limits of, 499–506
massaging, 502–504
obtaining, 501–502
obtaining statistics, 499
parsing data file, 497–498
viewing attributes, 498
rational actions, 38
rational thinking, 37–38
Rattle, 25
raw data, 111–112
raw text, handling problems with, 470–473
rb( ) function, 167
re( ) function, 167
re library, 157
reactive machines, 38
read_csv( ) method, 202–203
read_csv function, 486
read_fwf( ) function, 205
read_sql( ) method, 230
read_sql_query( ) method, 230
read_sql_table( ) method, 230
reasoning, 34
recall, 300
Recht, Benjamin, 511
recommender systems
companies, 494
defined, 494
overview, 493–494
rating data, 495–506
singular value decomposition (SVD), 504–506
users, 494
reconstruction_err_ method, 484
rectified linear unit (ReLU), 381, 400–401, 405–406, 443
recurrent neural networks (RNNs), 456, 565–566
recursion
in functional programming, 138
lambda functions in, 163
vs. looping, 160–161
overview, 159
in Python, 161–162
task repetition, 159–160
using on lists, 162–163
recursive task, 163–164

T

tables
  combining data from multiple, 233–234
  defining use of, 225–226
tag soup, 467
tanh function, 400, 443
Tapestry, 494
tasks
  comparison, 176
  logical, 176
  recursive, 163–164
  repeating, 159–160
Taylor, Allen, 230
telerehabilitation, 17
tensor processing units (TPUs), 80
TensorFlow, 55, 80, 87, 516
tensors, 185–186
term frequency-inverse document frequency (TFIDF), 484
ternary tree, 244
tetrachromats, 427
text
  data, 119–120
  enhancing, 459–461
  flat files, 113
  predicting classifications, 315–318
  processing, 459–461
text-based freeform, 125
text-processing tasks, 314
TF Hub, 450
TF-IDF transformations, 460–461, 564–565
TfidfVectorizer, 484
Theano, 87
theory of mind, 39
Theory That Would Not Die, The (McGrayne), 309
third-party code, 82–83
3-D art, 17
3-D pooling, 440
Thucydides, 10
ticks
  defined, 586
  formatting, 590
time, formatting, 641
time series
  plotting, 603–608
  plotting trends over time, 605–607
  poly1d( ) output, 608
  time on axes, 603–604

time series predictions
  creating training and testing datasets, 575–576
  defining sequences of events, 574–575
  making prediction, 578
  passenger analysis model, 577–578
  passenger sequence management, 576–577
  using LSTM, 575–578
timedelta( ) function, 642
timevalue, 642
Tiobe, 57
TIOBE index, 134
Titan V, 55
T-node, 248
tokenization, 561–562
tokenizer parameter, 464
tokens, 459–460
traffic signs, reading
  accuracy, 521
  classification tasks, 520–523
  output cost, 522
  preparing image data, 517–520
train_test_split( ) function, 362
transfer learning, 407–408, 450–452, 511
transform( ) method, 194, 458, 503
transformations, variable
  effect of ordering, 275
  looking for, 276
  nonlinear, 677–679
  storing Boston database in DataFrame, 276
translation invariance, 446
transposition, 183
tree-based feature selection, 360
trees
  Adelson-Velsky and Landis, 244
  balanced, 198, 243
  binary search, 244–245
  building, 196–197
  heaps, 243
  nodes, 195–196
  overview, 195
  ternary, 244
  traversing, 197
  unbalanced, 198, 243
Trello, 118
trials, 719
T-tree, 248
Turing, Alan, 456

Turing Test, 456
tutorial kernel, 220
TV filter, 415
2-D pooling, 440
two-stage detection, 529, 531

U

Ubuntu, 63
UCI, 486
unbalanced learning, 533
unbalanced trees, 198, 243
underfitting
  bias and, 671
  causes of, 665–666
  data leakage, 672
  defined, 273
  greedy search, 675–676
  insufficient data, 671–672
  linear model regularization, 684–687
  nonlinear transformations, 676–683
  overview, 663–664
  selecting variables, 673–676
  sources of, 670–672
  univariate measures, 673–675
  variance and, 671
understanding, 34
undirected graph, 326
U-Nets, 530–531
Unicode, 471–472
Unicode Transformation Format 8-bit (UTF-8), 124,
    470–472, 560
unigrams, 462
unit, 379
univariate approach. *See also* multivariate approach
  assumptions, 656–657
  Gaussian distribution, 655–656
  pandas package, 653–654
  in variable selection, 673–675
universal approximators, 387
universal function approximator, 403
updates, 5
upsample, 533
use of data
  art and entertainment, 17
  creating new technologies, 14–15
  enticing people to buy products, 13–14

keeping people safer, 14–15
making life more interesting, 18
performing analysis for research, 16–17
user monitoring, 121–122

V

valid padding, 436
validation
  data map, 632–634
  data plan, 632–634
  figuring what data contains, 629–631
  input, 627–628
  removing duplicates, 631
value
  continuous, 292
  discrete, 292
  passing by, 140–142
value of color, 15
van Gogh, Vincent, 545
vanishing gradient, 400, 404
Vargas, Danilo Vasconcellos, 541
variables
  adding, 190–191
  categorical, 265–269
  combining, 257–264
  creating interactions between, 277–282
  defined, 255
  independent, 263–264
  interactions between, 679–683
  in larger datasets, 271–274
  selecting, 673–676
  testing combinations of, 278
  transformations, 274–277, 677–679
variance decomposition, 425, 671
vectAdd function, 187
vectorization, 186–187
vectors. *See also* matrices; scalars
  creating, 175–176
  creating organized data with, 174–178
  defined, 172
  defining, 175
  logical and comparison tasks on, 176–177
  multiplying, 177–178
  performing math on, 176
Verbasizer, 552

About the Authors

Luca Massaron is a data scientist and a marketing research director who specializes in multivariate statistical analysis, machine learning, and customer insight, with over a decade of experience in solving real-world problems and generating value for stakeholders by applying reasoning, statistics, data mining, and algorithms. From being a pioneer of web audience analysis in Italy to achieving the rank of top ten Kaggler on kaggle.com, he has always been passionate about everything regarding data and analysis and about demonstrating the potentiality of data-driven knowledge discovery to both experts and non experts. Favoring simplicity over unnecessary sophistication, he believes that a lot can be achieved in data science by understanding and practicing the essentials of it. Luca is also a Google Developer Expert (GDE) in machine learning.

John Mueller is a freelance author and technical editor. He has writing in his blood, having produced 114 books and more than 600 articles to date. The topics range from networking to artificial intelligence and from database management to heads-down programming. Some of his current books include discussions of data science, machine learning, and algorithms. His technical editing skills have helped more than 70 authors refine the content of their manuscripts. John has provided technical editing services to various magazines, performed various kinds of consulting, and writes certification exams. Be sure to read John's blog at http://blog.johnmuellerbooks.com/. You can reach John on the Internet at John@JohnMuellerBooks.com. John also has a website at http://www.johnmuellerbooks.com/. Be sure to follow John on Amazon at https://www.amazon.com/John-Mueller/.

Luca's Dedication

I would like to dedicate this book to my family, Yukiko and Amelia, to my parents, Renzo and Licia, and to Yukiko's family, Yoshiki, Takayo and Makiko.

John's Dedication

Over the years, a great many people have been kind to me and believed in my work. Otherwise, I wouldn't have made it to where I am now. This book is for them in thanks for all they have done.

Luca's Acknowledgments

My greatest thanks to my family, Yukiko and Amelia, for their support and loving patience. I also want to thank Simone Scardapane, an assistant professor at Sapienza University (Rome) and a fellow Google Developer Expert, who provided invaluable feedback during the writing of this book.

John's Acknowledgments

Thanks to my wife, Rebecca. Even though she is gone now, her spirit is in every book I write, in every word that appears on the page. She believed in me when no one else would.

Russ Mullen deserves thanks for his technical edit of this book. He greatly added to the accuracy and depth of the material you see here. Russ worked exceptionally hard helping with the research for this book by locating hard-to-find URLs and also offering a lot of suggestions. The code was also exceptionally difficult to check in this book and I feel he did an amazing job doing it.

Matt Wagner, my agent, deserves credit for helping me get the contract in the first place and taking care of all the details that most authors don't really consider. I always appreciate his assistance. It's good to know that someone wants to help.

A number of people read all or part of this book to help me refine the approach, test application code, verify the extensive text, and generally provide input that all readers wish they could have. These unpaid volunteers helped in ways too numerous to mention here. I especially appreciate the efforts of Eva Beattie, who provided general input, read the entire book, and selflessly devoted herself to this project.

Finally, I would like to thank Katie Mohr, Susan Christophersen, and the rest of the editorial and production staff.

Publisher's Acknowledgments

Associate Publisher: Katie Mohr

Project and Copy Editor: Susan Christophersen

Technical Editor: Russ Mullen

Proofreader: Debbye Butler

Editorial Assistant: Matthew Lowe

Production Editor: Magesh Elangovan

Cover Image: © enot-poloskun/Getty Images